Woodrow Wilson: *The Academic Years*

Woodrow Wilson

The Academic Years

Henry Wilkinson Bragdon

The Belknap Press of Harvard University Press

Cambridge, Massachusetts · 1967

For Helena

Preface

WOODROW WILSON once wrote of Abraham Lincoln that he could only be known by "a close and prolonged study of his life before he became President. The years of his Presidency were not years to form but rather years to test character." This dictum may fairly be applied to Wilson himself. When he was inaugurated President of the United States in 1913, he was fifty-six and had been in politics less than three years. During the entire preceding portion of his adult life, save for a brief attempt to practice law, he had been engaged in academic pursuits.

The principal purpose of this book is to investigate Wilson's academic career: first as a student, then as a teacher and writer, finally as a college president and educational innovator. The introductory chapter on Wilson's family background and youth is based for the most part on secondary sources, as is Chapter V, dealing with the period during which he practiced law. A principal source for the last chapter, describing his entrance into active politics, is Arthur S. Link's *Wilson: The Road to the White House.* For the rest, although secondary sources have not been ignored, this volume is the end result of twenty-eight years of search for and examination of original materials. Yet it still cannot be regarded as definitive: important new materials have recently been discovered that are not as yet accessible to me, and more will undoubtedly turn up in the future.

In dealing with Wilson as a political scientist, historian, and educator, I have attempted to place him in the context of his period. For instance, I have made a thorough search for contemporary reviews of his books. With regard to Wilson's place in political science, this study does not purport to be a full assessment but is limited to tracing in some detail his changing attitudes toward democracy in America, toward the American governmental system, and toward the role of the state in the economy. Finally, to a greater degree than has perhaps heretofore been suspected, Wilson's behavior and opinions were affected by particular situations. Pains have been taken to describe the successive academic environments in which he was placed and to show how he adapted to each. The individuals with whom he came most significantly into contact are portrayed in detail.

In the course of the investigations for this book I interviewed some 150 individuals who knew Wilson in one context or another, and I corresponded with about 100 more. Their reminiscences were especially useful in providing background. They have also been quoted frequently in the text—although with caution, since one cannot gather recollections from scores of septuagenarians without becoming aware of the fallibility of human memory. Many of those with whom I communicated furnished me directly with previously undiscovered contemporary evidence or gave me valuable leads.

I wish to extend thanks to members of the staffs of the following libraries where I have worked: Alderman Library, University of Virginia; Bryn Mawr College Library; Davis Library, Phillips Exeter Academy; Forbes Library, Northampton, Mass.; Harvard College Library; Johns Hopkins University Library; Pratt Institute, Baltimore Maryland; Syracuse Public Library; Syracuse University Library; Wesleyan University Library; and Yale University Library. Above all, I am beholden to the staffs of the two principal repositories of Wilsoniana: the Manuscript Division of the Library of Congress and the Princeton University Library. I am especially grateful to Katherine E. Brand, who after serving as secretary to Ray Stannard Baker while he was composing the eight volumes of his *Woodrow Wilson: Life and Letters,* became a guide and friend to those who studied the Woodrow Wilson and R. S. Baker Papers in the Manuscript Division. Thanks are also due to Frederick R. Goff, Chief of the Rare Books Division of the Library of Congress, for making arrangements for me to examine Wilson's personal library. On the staff of the Princeton University Library I must express special gratitude to G. Vinton Duffield, former Chief of Circulation; Lawrence Heyl, former Associate Librarian; Henry L. Savage, former Archivist; Alexander P. Clark, Curator of Manuscripts; Julie Hudson, Curator of Rare Books; and M. Halsey Thomas, Archivist.

The present work would never have been undertaken but for a sabbatical leave granted me by the Trustees of Brooks School in 1938-1939; the Brooks trustees later made special grants to help in the research. Again in 1959-1960 the Trustees of the Phillips Exeter Academy permitted me a sabbatical leave to further the work. For these favors I am profoundly grateful. So many people have aided me in my search for Wilsoniana that to attempt to name them all would make this preface impossibly long. At the risk of appearing invidious, I must mention the following, who were conspicuously useful: the late Professor Jacob N. Beam of Princeton University; Arthur S. Link, Editor of *The Papers of Woodrow Wilson*, and his associates, John Wells Davison, David W. Hirsch, and T. Vail Motter; John D. Davies, Editor of the *Princeton Alumni Weekly*; and E. S. Wells Kerr, formerly a colleague at Exeter.

I acknowledge with thanks permission received from the late Mrs. Woodrow Wilson to examine her husband's personal library; from Mrs. Eleanor Wilson McAdoo to quote from unpublished letters written by her mother to John Bates Clark; and from the Trustees of Princeton University to consult a variety of records, notably their minutes from 1875 until 1912.

During the long and lonely business of writing this volume I benefited greatly from the meticulous criticism and encouragement I received from Mrs. Maud Wilcox. I am scarcely less indebted to Mrs. Virginia La Plante for the severe yet sympathetic editing she gave the manuscript. A third invaluable editor was my wife, Helena, to whom the work is dedicated.

HWB

Exeter, New Hampshire
July 1967

Contents

Illustrations

Part One: Student

I

Family Background and Youth

1856–1875

It is all very well to talk of detachment of view, and of the effort to be national in spirit and purpose, but a boy never gets over his boyhood, and can never change those subtle influences which have become a part of him, that were bred in him when he was a child.

—Woodrow Wilson, 1909[1]

THE SOURCES on which to base an account of Woodrow Wilson's early years are meager. Missing is the wealth of contemporary material that makes it possible, for instance, to describe Theodore Roosevelt's boyhood with accuracy and richness of detail. The biographer must base much of his account upon recollections gathered from elderly cousins, in-laws, friends of the family, and servants after Wilson had become famous. Yet the childhood influences on Wilson were so unique, and explain so much of what came later, that they deserve to be assessed. The picture of his childhood may be fuzzy in detail, but certain major facts stand out.

Wilson's inheritance was Presbyterian and Scottish. His paternal grandparents were Scotch-Irish and migrated to America in their teens; his maternal grandparents, the Woodrows, came from the north of England but were born in Scotland. Both the Wilsons and the Woodrows abundantly revealed a typically Calvinistic blend of religious devotion and concern for worldly success. Wilson's father, his maternal grandfather, and a maternal uncle were all ministers. A collateral branch of the Woodrows had been ministers and scholars for centuries.

The paternal grandfather, James Wilson, came to America in 1807 at the age of twenty with no more capital than a knowledge of the

3

printer's trade. Five years later he was editor of a famous Jeffersonian newspaper, the *Philadelphia Aurora*. After moving west in 1815, he became a leading citizen of Steubenville, Ohio. He was proprietor of two newspapers, director of a bank and railroad, member of the Ohio legislature, judge (although without legal training), and a person of sufficient wealth to build a mansion. Four of his seven sons achieved eminence. Two were generals in the Union Army during the Civil War. Another was a successful newspaper editor, prominent in the Grange movement. Still another, Wilson's father, was a leader of the Southern Presbyterian Church.

Among the Woodrows, high practical ability was revealed by Wilson's uncle, James Woodrow, whom he was said to resemble and whom he much admired. James Woodrow was a minister and professor of theology, a scientist with a doctorate *summa cum laude* from Heidelberg, a successful editor, and proprietor of a profitable printing shop. When his support for the theory of evolution cost him his professorship in a theological seminary, he became a college president and bank director.[2]

It is thus apparent that when Thomas Woodrow Wilson came into the world in Staunton, Virginia, on December 28, 1856, he was surrounded by people who heeded the Biblical injunction to go forth into the earth and subdue it. They expected to enter a community and assume a position of leadership. They had a habit of success.

During Wilson's entire childhood he was cushioned from the world to an extraordinary degree. His family was so well off that even in the South during the Civil War and Reconstruction they never knew want. They lived comfortably in four different, capacious manses with servants' quarters, gardens, and stables. "Tommy," a rather frail, bespectacled boy, was the youngest child and only son until he was ten years old, when his brother Joseph, Jr., arrived. His playmates were for a time his two older sisters, Marion and Anne, and his cousin Isabella Bones. The latter retained a vivid recollection of her first encounter with him, "a delicate, silent child, shy amid a group of noisy cousins." Although he was bashful in a crowd and did not yet know his letters, he proposed and directed games that kept his playmates enthralled: "Tommy soon became our leader, never aggressive or noisy, but with quiet determination and firmness he suggested and carried out some historic event. There was no discussion, he led, we followed, without question as to his ability to put through the great adventure. A certain huge Euonymus bush in my Aunt's garden was a Medieval Castle, which must be taken from the Turks and the Christian maidens, imprisoned and hopeless, rescued at great risk and daring. Again we were led by Peter the Hermit to the rescue of the Holy Sepulchre. Always our play was for succor, never for revenge or ambition. Years afterward I realized that many of our games were scenes from the Talisman."[3]

Wilson's mother believed that children should not be confined in schoolrooms. Consequently, the boy did not learn to read until he was nine or ten years old and did not go to school until he was almost twelve. Since he was kept at home, he grew closer to his parents than do most children, and their influence on him was correspondingly great. His father's was the more obvious, his mother's perhaps the more profound.

The Reverend Joseph Ruggles Wilson was a commanding figure. To occupy a pulpit in a big congregation was to become automatically a leader in the community, but Dr. Wilson's influence extended farther. Although he had been in the South only ten years when the Civil War began, he was one of the leaders of the Southern Presbyterians when they broke with their Northern brethren in 1861. In fact, the meeting at which the Southern Presbyterians set up a separate organization was held at his church in Augusta, Georgia, and he was elected Stated Clerk, a position he held for thirty-four years. During Wilson's childhood and youth his father held pastorates in Staunton, Virginia (1855-1857), Augusta, Georgia (1857-1869), Columbia, South Carolina (1870-1874), and Wilmington, North Carolina (1874-1885). He later became Professor of Theology at Southwestern Presbyterian University, Clarksville, Tennessee. He was generously paid: while at Wilmington, he is reported to have received $4000 a year, which meant affluence at a time when eggs were fifteen cents a dozen and it cost four or five hundred dollars a year to send a boy to college. His wife inherited a legacy from a brother that also gave her some money of her own.[4]

According to a contemporary account, Dr. Wilson became known throughout the South as "a preacher of remarkable power, a scholar of wide learning, and an attractive personality." By the standards of his day and sect he was liberal. Although drawing the line at cards and dancing, he liked to play chess and billiards and enjoyed the English novelists. As the following passage from a letter to his son reveals, he preached a religion of forgiveness and love: "one of the principal uses of our wonderfully humane religion is to promote buoyancy of disposition, by freeing the souled from that which is alone worthy of the name *Burden:* the sense of sin. I trust that your good spirits, my dear boy, are due in great part to an easy conscience—to the smile of God."[5]

Dr. Wilson was not without faults. He occasionally suffered from

fits of depression, and he was not always charitable toward his parish-
ioners or fellow clergymen. He was a bit vain and given to talking too
much. But on balance he was an outgoing, public-spirited, and impressive man. Of above average height and powerfully built, he was strikingly handsome. He had a streak of gaiety, which he liked to at-
tribute to an Irish inheritance, and a sharp wit, marred by atrocious
punning. George McLean Harper, who knew him in later years, remembered him as a "distinguished and delightful old man. If there
were a play in which Jove appears, his appearance would have ideally
fitted him for the part—a Jove in a play by Euripides, with a touch of
humor."[6]

Father and son vastly enjoyed each other's company. Dr. Wilson
played a major part in his son's education. Himself a precisionist in
speech, he trained young Tommy in his image. Over and over Wilson
recalled in his later years the thorough and unremitting verbal training
he had received at home from "the best teacher he ever had." His father
insisted not merely upon correctness in speech but upon the *mot juste*.
If the boy fumbled a sentence, his father would ask, "What do you
mean by that?" When Tommy explained, he received the reply, "Well,
why don't you say so?" In his late teens Wilson began to assist his
father in editing the minutes and journals of the Southern Presbyterian
Church. Both during college and later he continually sought his father's
advice on literary and practical matters.[7]

From his father Wilson inherited what might be called his public
personality: his ease on the platform; his ability to amuse, instruct, and
dominate an audience. He inherited his father's gift of anecdote, even
something of his addiction to punning. To his father he owed the
notion that he had a streak of Irish blood relieving the dour Scottish
inheritance. He once told the Sons of Saint Patrick in New York City:
"I myself am happy that there runs in my veins a very considerable
strain of Irish blood . . . There is something delightful in me that every
now and then takes the strain off my Scotch conscience and affords me
periods of most enjoyable irresponsibility when I do not care whether
school keeps or not, whether anybody gets educated or not."[8]

Joseph Wilson's greatest gift was unstinted admiration for the boy's
capacities and a sustaining trust. Other fathers might have doubted
the potentialities of such a son. Young Wilson was an indifferent student in school, and his later education was broken by periods of ill
health. After college, unable to decide what to do, he first tried the
law, then graduate work in political science; he was therefore nearly
twenty-nine before earning his own living. Yet throughout, Dr. Wilson
supported his son financially and maintained the conviction that he had

a "gem-like" mind and was destined for great things. His unwavering support and affection carried young Wilson through discouragements that might otherwise have broken or intimidated him. In turn, Wilson never stopped speaking of his debt to his "life-long friend and companion." Josephus Daniels remembered that during the eight years he had served as Secretary of State in Wilson's cabinet, the President frequently referred to comments his father had made. Daniels gathered that Dr. Wilson was "a man of infinite zest, scholarship, and meticulous about correct English."[9]

Wilson's mother is more difficult to assess. Jessie Woodrow Wilson was as retiring and quiet as her husband was gregarious and loquacious. But if gentle in manner, in character she was at least as strong as Dr. Wilson. She had more pride of family and seems to have been more intensely religious. She was an accomplished musician. Surviving letters, written in a copperplate hand that she passed on to her son, are well composed. Although generous and affectionate in her family circle, she had as little as possible to do with the world outside, so that some of her neighbors thought her "stand-offish" and charged her with "English ways." She could be a passionate partisan, as when her brother James Woodrow was accused of heresy for defending the theory of evolution; his assailants, she wrote, were "ignorant and malicious men," and the attacks on him drove her to "impotent anger."[10]

Mrs. Wilson kept her son at her apron strings. He later remembered that he "clung to her" until he was "a great big fellow." He continued until her death to be an utterly devoted and dutiful son. A former butler in the Wilson household observed, "Outside Mr. Tommy was his father's boy. But inside he was his mother all over." The butler was only one of several, including Wilson himself, who thought the boy took after his mother in particular and the Woodrows in general. From her he seems to have inherited his intense love of secluded family life, his family pride, a tendency to partisanship, and a reserve that sometimes made normal human communication difficult and exhausting.[11]

Something of his childhood always remained with Wilson. In mature years he felt completely safe and off-guard only in the bosom of his family, but in that environment he could be full of play and fantasy. He got on well with children, who saw him as a natural ally. He retained a vivid memory of what it was like to be young, and what he had to give up when entering maturity. When he was just short of fifty, he wrote: "I suppose that nothing is more painful in the recollections of some of us than the efforts that were made to make us like grown-up people. The delightful follies that we had to eschew, the delicious nonsense that we had to disbelieve, the number of odious prudences that we had to learn, the knowledge that though the truth was less interesting than fiction, it was more important than fiction,—the fact that what people told you could not always be relied on, and that it must be tested by the most uninteresting tests."[12]

Raymond S. Fosdick has said of Woodrow Wilson, "With the exception of Gladstone, probably no other man in supreme power in the life of any nation was so profoundly imbued with the Christian faith." Religion was certainly the most pervasive influence in his inheritance. He was brought up in a home where daily prayer and Bible reading were taken as much for granted as were meals. Every Sunday from an early age he heard his father preach. Total immersion in a pious environment sometimes produces rebellion, but not so with young Wilson, perhaps because of his peculiarly close relationship with his father. During his seventeenth year he duly experienced formal conversion and was admitted to Dr. Wilson's church in Columbia. That this was no mere formality is suggested by an entry in one of his student notebooks, tucked in with Greek exercises and lecture notes: "May 3, 1874—I am now in my seventeenth year and it is sad, when looking over my past life to see how few of those seventeen years I have spent in the fear of God, and how much in the service of the Devil . . . *If God will give me the grace I will try to serve Him from this time on, and will endeavor to attain nearer and nearer to perfection.*"[13]

From the time of this conversion Wilson appears never to have been afflicted by doubt. He once confided to a diary, "I used to wonder vaguely why I did not have the same deep-reaching spiritual difficulties that I read of other young men having. I *saw* the intellectual difficulties, but I was not *troubled* by them; they seemed to have no connection with my faith in the essentials of the religion I had been taught." A clergyman who knew him both as an undergraduate and later noted, "Religion was so much an ingrained habit of Wilson's life that there was never any speculation in it." Wilson once remarked to Admiral Grayson, "So far as religion is concerned, argument is adjourned." Yet his faith was not of a dogmatic kind. He was neither a theologian nor a sectarian. When one of his daughters worried about "hell-fire," he told her that hell was no more than a frame of mind. He was tolerant of other faiths, including Roman Catholicism. "He seemed," wrote his long-time friend and colleague Winthrop Daniels, "to regard religious character very much as he did physical health, something all-important but naturally springing from the laws of right living and not over enhanced by theological discussion."[14]

Although Wilson's creed was not fundamentalist or bigoted, neither was it formless. He believed that each man was a rational, responsible, and moral agent of God. He must be guided by "a standard set for us in the heavens . . . the fixed and eternal standard by which we judge ourselves." Each man's conscience must dictate how he interpreted this standard and acted upon it. "In the war with human passions and the war with human wrong, every man must do battle for the forces of light against the forces of ignorance and sin . . . For a man who has lost the sense of struggle, life has ceased."[15]

Wilson's religious faith was a strong support throughout his life. In his battles for educational and political reform, as well as for a just and lasting peace among nations, he could feel that he was doing the Lord's work and that he was directed and aided by a Power greater than himself. Much of his effectiveness in government came from the fact that he appeared more prophet than politician. Once convinced that a course of action was right, however, he was inclined to confuse his purposes with divine will. Although this assumption saved him from self-doubt and indecision, it sometimes made him inflexible. A favorite phrase was, "God save us from compromise," for compromise often seemed a concession to the forces of evil. The opposition must be crushed. Wilson's later career was strewn with the wreckage of friendships that foundered on the rock of his insistence on the Biblical injunction, "He who is not with me is against me."

From this Calvinist background Wilson also concluded that men should be governed by a natural aristocracy, somehow divinely selected both to lead and to serve them. Nor did he doubt, given his family background of successful preachers, teachers, and men of affairs, that he might enter this elite.

Wilson was close to his British origins. His Wilson grandparents arrived in the United States only in 1807; the Woodrows, not until 1836. His mother spent the first nine years of her childhood in the north of England. No other President of the United States was closer in time to his immigrant ancestors except Andrew Jackson, born only two years after his parents had emigrated from Ireland. But Jackson's father died before he was born, his mother died when he was in his teens, and his early life was spent on the frontier. No one has ever suggested that Old Hickory felt any ties with his British background. Just the opposite was true of Wilson.

Although the Wilsons and Woodrows prospered in America, they did so on their own terms. Each family, especially the Woodrows, held fast to its Presbyterian faith and its imported cultural heritage. Young Tommy Wilson was brought up not merely to read his Bible and learn his

catechism but also to hear his mother sing Scottish ballads and lullabies
or his father tell Scottish anecdotes. He was intensely conscious and
proud of his inheritance. The "Covenant" of the League of Nations is
witness of his devotion to the stern Covenanter tradition of the Woodrows. In public speeches and writings he repeatedly paid tribute to
his paternal stock, "that adventurous, indomitable people, the Scots-
Irish."[16]

His affection for Britain was reinforced by the literature to which he
was exposed as a child. His father loved to read aloud to his children
and encouraged them to read for themselves. The poets to whom he
introduced them were Burns, Tennyson, and Wordsworth—not Long-
fellow and Whittier. The novelists, save Cooper, were also British. Dr.
Wilson was especially fond of Dickens. Young Wilson acquired his
tastes in reading as uncritically as he accepted his religious beliefs; his
favorite poets became Wordsworth and Tennyson, his favorite novelist,
Dickens.

When Wilson reached his late teens and began to read contemporary
magazines, his father again supplied him with British models. One was
the *Edinburgh Review*. Another, *The Nation,* was published in America, but its editor, E. L. Godkin, was a transplanted Scots-Irishman who
saw America through alien and critical eyes and never ceased to scold
American politicians for not aping the British Liberals.

Although Wilson had to learn some French and German for his professional studies, there is no evidence that he gained any appreciation
of their literature. In his letters and essays one can find myriad references to English and Scottish writers, but almost none to Hawthorne,
Emerson, or Thoreau. The British historians Macaulay and J. H. Green
appear far more frequently than Parkman, Motley, or Prescott. When in
later life Wilson made six vacation trips abroad, he invariably went to
England and Scotland. In fact, he had set foot on the Continent only
once before he attended the Versailles Conference in 1919.

This strong bias in favor of things British ran throughout Wilson's
public career. His reputation as a political scientist was first established
with proposals to adapt parliamentary practices to the American constitutional system. As President of Princeton, determined to raise the
standards of undergraduate scholarship, he sought inspiration in the
tutorial system and collegiate organization of Oxford and Cambridge.
His political ambitions, realized when he became Governor of New
Jersey and then President of the United States, had their origin in his
boyhood desire to emulate Gladstone, Cobden, and Bright.

Wilson had a special, if irrational, pride in being a Virginian. The
claim was tenuous, resting upon a year's residence in infancy plus

about ten months as a student at the University of Virginia. And yet, dreaming of the great line of Virginia statesmen, he wanted to identify himself with the Old Dominion.

Whether a Virginian or not, Wilson had every right to say that the South was "the region where I naturally belong," for it was his home until his late twenties. He often remarked that the South was the only part of the country where nothing had to be explained to him. He was a Southerner in his courtly manners, in his attitude toward women, and in the hospitality with which he received numberless in-laws and cousins into his home. He was curiously indifferent to the moral iniquity of slavery and accepted uncritically the post-Reconstruction arrangements to keep the Negro in his place.[17]

Wilson's earliest political recollection was of hearing his father say that Mr. Lincoln had been elected President and there was going to be a war. His father was enrolled as a chaplain in the Confederate Army, and his uncle James Woodrow served as a civilian in the medical corps. The actual fighting passed Wilson by, but the battles of Kenesaw Mountain and Atlanta were near enough to Augusta so that Dr. Wilson's church was turned into an emergency hospital, and Union prisoners were billeted in a grove of elms outside. It was remembered that young Wilson stood on the sidewalk, "his thin pale face turned anxiously toward the groups in the grove," and no one could say "which touched him most, the stern, defiant men in their blue uniforms—prisoners in a hostile land, closely guarded night and day and marching around the enclosure while no friendly faces cheered them, or the wounded boys in gray, borne groaning into the dim recesses of the great Church." The romantic adventures with his sisters and Isabella Bones were abandoned. Later in Columbia he saw the wanton destruction wrought by Sherman's troops. He never ceased to revere General Lee, of whom he once caught a glimpse, nor to feel pride in the courage of the Confederate soldiers who fought for the Lost Cause. Later as a historian he sometimes betrayed a pro-Southern and anti-New England bias.[18]

Yet Wilson's commitment to the South was not complete. At the age of nineteen he is reported to have said "that he thought it unfortunate to have a Decoration Day for the graves of the Southern dead, as it sustained a national bitterness." In a speech at the University of Virginia only fifteen years after the close of the war he rejoiced in the restoration of the Union. His first and best historical work, *Division and Reunion*, celebrated both in title and text the victory of the nation. Although he spent his first twenty-eight years in the South, he lived thereafter in the North. The fact that certain attitudes of the mature Wilson reflected his southern boyhood and that he sometimes assumed the mantle of a Southerner was evidence of a sentimental attachment rather than a bias profoundly conditioning his thinking.[19]

Wilson's secluded childhood, lack of systematic early education, and delicate health left scars. It is possible that the effort to overcome these inadequacies was a major element in determining the course of his life. His late entrance into school meant that he never quite adjusted to the normal world of boys. More than one biographer has remarked that this was a serious weakness in his education. He was apparently never in a fight, and when things did not go his way, he was likely to run home. Yet he somehow managed to become a leader. When a group of boys in Augusta formed a short-lived organization known as the "Lightfoot Club," they elected him president. The Lightfoots played baseball with other teams, indulged in secret rituals in the Wilsons' barn under a portrait of the Devil, and—prophetically—engaged in debate under a constitution written by Wilson.

It was unfortunate for Wilson that his family moved from Augusta to Columbia in 1870, when he was thirteen years old, and from Columbia to Wilmington four years later. Forced to re-establish himself twice, he seems to have acquired few intimates in his new homes. The first extant letter to him from his mother, written on the eve of the second move, refers to his feeling that he was not popular in Columbia and that he would make no friends in Wilmington. According to the recollection of a fellow student in Columbia, "He was not like the other boys. He had a way of going off by himself." In Wilmington he had only one close friend and struck people as "an old young man."[20]

However valuable his father's training in literature and language, Wilson was undoubtedly handicapped by his lack of early formal schooling. According to his daughter Margaret, he was never able to add figures easily and was unsure of the multiplication table. There is abundant testimony that he had a poor memory. When he did go to school, his work was below average. In later years he remembered that his uncle Woodrow lost patience and told him that if he had no ambition to be a scholar, he might at least wish to be a gentleman.

In his last year of school, when he was sixteen years old, Wilson began to do better academically. As a freshman at Davidson College, he came into his own in other ways. He was active in the Eumenean Literary Society, a debating club, and played second base on the freshman baseball team. A contemporary remembered him as "witty, genial, superior, but languid." That he appeared languid may have been no fault of his because he fell ill during this time. He abandoned formal schooling for a year and a half and thus was almost nineteen when he finally entered Princeton, again as a freshman, in 1875.[21]

Faced with a world to which he had difficulty adjusting, young Wilson took refuge in fantasy. In his early teens he imagined himself in various heroic roles suggested by the novels of Cooper, Marryat, and Scott. He dreamed of going to sea and hoped to enter Annapolis. He made sketches of ships and filled scrapbooks with wood engravings of them, clipped from current magazines. As Admiral Wilson of the United States Navy, he roamed the southern seas and fought battles with pirates, writing daily reports of his activities to an imaginary Secretary of the Navy. More often he imagined himself in high position in England—"Thomas W. Wilson, Duke of Eagleton, vice-admiral of the red," or "Lord Wilson, Fifth Duke of Eagleton," commanding the "Royal Lance Guards." These fantasies were elaborately worked out. Thus, each of the six ships composing a flotilla commanded by Admiral Wilson was described in detail as to its design, rigging, armament, and complement of officers and men. He issued formal written orders to his troops. Wilson continued to indulge in this kind of elaborate daydreaming until the eve of his departure for Princeton.[22]

Wilson never lost his childlike tendency to indulge in fantasy. He dreamed of becoming the American Burke, whose writings would exercise a "statesmanship of opinion." His most enduring book, *Congressional Government,* was an imitation of Bagehot's analysis of the British constitution. When he wrote a history of the United States, he entitled it *A History of the American People,* inviting comparison with John Richard Green's *History of the English People.* He revealed much of himself when describing such public figures as Cleveland, Lincoln, and Lee. The dream that most deeply affected his future was his ambition to become a statesman like Gladstone, who swayed men to high purpose through the power of eloquence. From the age of fifteen or sixteen, when he hung a picture of Gladstone over his desk, he consciously prepared himself for political leadership. His choice of hero reflected his British background, the sense of mission inherited from his Presbyterian forebears, and a belief in the power of public utterance acquired from his father. To equip himself for statesmanship, he began to read the great British political writers. He studied history and current affairs. He mastered shorthand, the better to record speeches and to annotate books. Driven by a strangely prophetic dream of future eminence, the boy who had been considered too lazy to do well in school started to take his education into his own hands.

In some ways Wilson's early years ran curiously parallel to those of his distant in-law and future political rival, Theodore Roosevelt. Both Wilson and Roosevelt came from the "best people" in their communities —families who expected to serve through leadership. Neither boy ever knew want. They were both rather frail and were brought up at home. Surrounded by affection and feminine companionship, they were very much at the center of their little worlds. Both boys adored their fathers, and both fathers took great pains with their sons' development.

At about the age of twelve or thirteen each child began to realize his inadequacy in dealing with boys his own age. Wilson recalled that he was "a laughed at 'Mamma's boy,'" and Roosevelt, that he was attacked by two bullies who easily, almost contemptuously, beat him up and broke his glasses. They apparently suffered shock at these confrontations and took refuge in fantasy and dreams of a great future. As Wilson dreamed of becoming an admiral and then a statesman, Roosevelt hoped to become a "man with the bark on," an Andrew Jackson or Davy Crockett. The fathers encouraged their sons. Dr. Wilson, training his son in speech and style, led him to believe that he had a great destiny. Mr. Roosevelt encouraged his son to overcome his physical handicaps by *making* his body.[23]

With a self-assurance that stemmed from established social position, early emotional security, and the support of understanding fathers, both Wilson and Roosevelt pursued their boyhood dreams into maturity. Wilson's political ambition was his great secret, revealed only to intimates, and temporarily abandoned for an academic career only because there seemed no other choice. Roosevelt's boxing lessons and summers in the woods were the prelude to the "strenuous life" that had its finest hour at San Juan Hill. The idea that a Harvard-trained dude could make a career in the rough-and-tumble of politics appeared ludicrous, and it seemed equally unlikely that such a plunge could be taken by a middle-aged professor with no practical experience in government. Yet such was the force of each man's personality and such the force of his vision that each somehow made men and events serve his purpose, and the dude and the professor became respectively the twenty-sixth and twenty-eighth Presidents of the United States.

Campus Leader

1875–1879

The most influential Seniors govern their own class and the University in all matters of opinion and of undergraduate activity. They are the leading citizens of the little community. They are self-elected. They lead because they have been found to be the men who can do things best, the men who have the most initiative and seem best to embody the spirit of the place and determine mooted questions of action.

—Woodrow Wilson, 1905[1]

IN SEPTEMBER 1875, Wilson entered the College of New Jersey, popularly known as "Princeton College." He was to be associated with Princeton for twenty-four of his next thirty-five years: from 1875 to 1879 as an undergraduate, from 1890 to 1902 as a professor of political science and jurisprudence, and from 1902 to 1910 as president. It was as a student at Princeton that he first revealed his gifts for leadership and began the serious study of politics. While a professor, he established a position near the forefront of American scholarship and became a brilliant academic and popular lecturer. As president of Princeton, he gained a national reputation as a creative and controversial educational reformer.

In the mid-1870's Princeton College was in some respects hardly distinguishable from scores of other small denominational colleges. Its nearly five hundred undergraduates and eight graduate fellows were taught by a faculty of twenty-seven. Eleven faculty members and fourteen of the twenty-five trustees were Presbyterian ministers. Although the college had no formal connection with the Princeton Theological Seminary, another Presbyterian institution, the public mind confused the two and tended to regard Princeton College as primarily a training ground for future preachers and missionaries.

Princeton was then in truth a country college. Its stone buildings,

dominated by Nassau Hall, stood bare in an almost treeless pastureland.
To the north, Nassau Street was a wide dirt road, dusty in summer
and ankle-deep in mud in winter, with a line of hitching posts in front
of the stores that faced the campus. South of the college buildings lay
a rectangle of whitewashed brick latrines, set below ground and known
variously as "South Campus," "the cloaca maxima," or "Egypt." These
had been built in desperation because no wooden outhouses were safe
from undergraduates seeking materials for bonfires. The only tie to the
outside world was a spur of the Pennsylvania Railroad, which poked
its way into one side of the campus. Certain winds carried odors of
open cesspools and sewers. Even in that less hygienic age the careless
sanitary arrangements and inadequate water supply in Princeton were
notorious and found frequent mention in the pages of undergraduate
periodicals and the minutes of the Board of Trustees.

In faculty, curriculum, and treatment of students the college was
more like a preparatory school than a university. Except for a few
men in the sciences, none of the faculty members was in the forefront
of his field. The holders of established chairs had often been chosen
more for piety and doctrinal soundness than for scholarship, and the
instructors or "tutors" were likely to be, in the words of the *Princetonian,* "indigent candidates for the Presbyterian ministry."[2]

The curriculum was largely that of an earlier age, with prescribed
Latin, Greek, mathematics, and religious instruction. To this foundation had recently been added a superstructure of philosophy, history,
French, psychology, and the physical sciences, with the result that
juniors and seniors divided their energies among as many as eight or
nine courses at once. The courses were inevitably thin. According to
an editorial in the *Nassau Literary Magazine,* "Our weekly glimpses
at certain fields of thought are as unsatisfactory as a five-minute stare
through a telescope." Required standards of performance, which were
not high, were weakened further by the too common practices of
"shanannigagging" (copying another man's paper) and "cracking a
crib" (procuring test papers in advance). The fact that cheating was
considered no serious violation of undergraduate morality was sympto-
matic of the general relationship of students and faculty. According to
Professor William B. Scott of the class of 1878, "they [Scott's class-
mates] brought to college the schoolboy habit of mind, especially in
the matter of distrust of their teachers, whom they regarded as in a
perpetual conspiracy to play some unseemingly trick on the students.
In consequence there was hostility toward the faculty which, happily,
has long since given way to a much better relationship."[3]

The college attempted to keep a strict surveillance of its students.

Undergraduates were forbidden to play cards, blow horns, make "bois-
terous noise," or leave town without permission. Above all, they must
not go to nearby Trenton, which President McCosh called a "graveyard
of purity." The various regulations were enforced by the tutors. In return for salaries as low as $700 the college authorities felt themselves
"entitled to all the time of each tutor." In addition to carrying heavy
teaching schedules, these unenviable young men were expected to take
attendance and monitor behavior in chapel, keep students quiet during
study hours, and "watch over . . . the morals of students in their rooms"
so that dormitories and boarding houses should not become "places
of drinking and licentiousness."[4]

Against this "half-boarding-school half-university discipline" the students often revolted. An account of Wilson's class published at graduation, is a saga of successful escapades. In addition to the traditional
amusements of stealing the clapper of the bell in Nassau Hall and
making a bonfire of the college boardwalks, members of '79 engaged in
all sorts of disorders whose primary purpose was discomfiture of the
faculty. They set off a bomb containing a pound of gunpower under
a tutor's door; threw firecrackers in lectures; cheered President McCosh
in chapel when he announced as a text, "I am a wandering sheep"; set
fire to the rug in Greek class; and held a "grand old horn spree" when
examinations were over, serenading every tutor.[5]

Added to the antifaculty disorder was an intense interclass rivalry,
which frequently erupted into violence. There was an annual "cane
spree," when freshmen carrying canes were attacked by sophomores
attempting to take them away. There were riots at the post office, when
one class would try to prevent another from getting its mail. Large
scurrilous posters called "rakes" appeared, in which classes addressed
each other in letters six inches high by such epithets as "Puerile Pukes
of Low Degree," "Fetid Particles of a Consumptive's Breath," and
"Lineal Descendants of Baalam's Ass." Hazing sometimes reached the
point of real persecution. In February 1878 an incident occurred that
was fully reported in the New York press and received the attention
of such widely differing periodicals as *The Police Gazette* and the
Presbyterian. A group of sophomores had carried hazing to such
lengths as shaving their victims' heads except for a topknot and drag-
ging a freshman, who could not swim, across the Raritan Canal with
a rope. The practices came into the open when a freshman wounded
a sophomore in the leg with a revolver.[6]

In spite of this disorder, there is abundant evidence that most of the
students came to Princeton with serious purpose. According to a poll
taken at graduation, over two-thirds of the members of '79 intended

to enter a profession. Furthermore, the religious tone of the college was not simply superimposed by the authorities. Twice a week each class held prayer meetings run by its own representatives. All but two members of '79 declared they were members of a church. In 1876 a great revival swept the college, primarily emanating from the students themselves. The undergraduate magazine noted that after the revival had gone on for four weeks there were over 115 conversions. President McCosh reported to the Trustees that during this period there were voluntary prayer meetings every night and sometimes also at noon and that every student was waited on by men of known piety. At Dr. McCosh's request, ministers came in from outside to fan the flame, including the famous revivalists Moody and Sankey.[7]

Undergraduate life at Princeton was undergoing significant change in the late 1870's. What Wilson later called the sideshows—extracurricular activities—were just beginning to rival the main tent. Intercollegiate athletics were getting underway. Princeton started to play a formal schedule of football games in 1876. In 1877 the faculty overruled President McCosh and allowed a Princeton baseball team to leave college for four days to play Harvard and Yale. Two years later the baseball team was playing a schedule of fourteen games. In 1876 appeared the first number of a yearbook, *The Princeton Bric-à-Brac*, started, the editors explained, because in the college catalogue "the interests of the undergraduates were not represented." In the spring of 1876 the faculty granted the petition of a group of undergraduates to found the *Princetonian*, a fortnightly newspaper. These developments in turn reflected the beginnings of a change in the kind of students going to Princeton. There was an increasing number of young men of means who went to enjoy "college life" rather than to prepare themselves for a profession.[8]

One reason Princeton was something other than a run-of-the-mill country college was the personality of James McCosh, who served as its President from 1868 to 1888. He was a Scottish divine who, before being called to Princeton at the age of fifty-seven, had been Professor of Philosophy at Queen's College, Belfast. He was a notable figure in the theological and epistemological battles of his day, who struck a line of his own in attempting to resolve the apparent conflict between Darwinism and revealed religion. He was a lucid and vigorous writer and a fair-minded controversialist. He was also a first-rate teacher.[9]

McCosh's influence on the College of New Jersey was profound. As Nicholas Murray Butler described it, the Scotsman shook up "the dry bones of an institution which had been little more than a country high school in New Jersey. Intense and narrow, restless and persistent, impatient and abounding in new suggestions and ideas, Doctor McCosh brought about in Princeton a virtual revolution."[10]

McCosh dreamed of creating a college that would rival the great universities of Europe. He attacked the problem of raising Princeton's standards from all sides. At the time of his inauguration, a part-time librarian opened the library to students only one hour a week. Under his influence the college hired a full-time man, erected a new building, and rapidly filled its empty shelves, even sending the librarian to Europe to make purchases. When McCosh stepped down in 1888, Princeton had the second largest college library in the country. Along with it came new laboratories, an engineering school, three dormitories, the first gymnasium in any American college, an astronomical observatory, and efforts to beautify as well as to enlarge the campus.

Over the protests of intensely conservative trustees McCosh tried to make the choice of faculty members depend more on scholarship than on piety. By the time he left office there was the nucleus of a genuine university faculty. He also introduced graduate fellowships and graduate degrees, so that during his presidency the College of New Jersey edged toward the new title it assumed in 1896—Princeton University.

McCosh had known rowdyism at the Scottish universities, but the disorder at Princeton, especially the hazing, appalled him. Supported by student opinion, McCosh managed to do away with violent hazing, but rioting and cheating continued, perhaps because he was not ready to grant undergraduates sufficient freedom and the right to police themselves. He also won a battle to abolish Greek letter fraternities, which existed sub rosa at Princeton in spite of college rules forbidding them. When McCosh came to this country, other college presidents told him that these societies were a divisive influence, that they tended to lower standards of scholarship, and that in some cases they encouraged dissipation—opinions which coincided with his own observations. In 1875, during Wilson's freshman year, matters came to a head when a faculty committee of investigation discovered the names of several fraternity members. They were summoned before the faculty, and eventually thirteen were suspended from college. A group of outraged alumni, including several trustees, called a meeting at Delmonico's Restaurant in New York, where they passed a formal resolution condemning the faculty action and demanding that it be overruled by the Board of Trustees. But McCosh was determined, even to the extent of being willing to resign if the fraternities were allowed to exist. The Trustees accepted the faculty action, the societies were permanently disbanded, and every student was obliged henceforth to take an oath that he would belong to no secret organization other than Princeton's two literary societies, Whig and Clio.[11]

McCosh kept in close touch with the undergraduates. He not only taught courses in religion, psychology, and philosophy but also maintained informal contacts. He organized library meetings where professors, graduate students, seniors, and juniors met to hear scholarly papers, followed by discussion in which everyone joined.

All reminiscences of McCosh agree with what Woodrow Wilson said of him: "he was a man whom you could laugh at every day, and yet never for a moment despise." His idiosyncrasies were many. He had quick, nervous gestures and a habit of stroking his head rapidly when he talked. He walked across the campus at a dog trot, head down, oblivious of his surroundings. The students mimicked his Scottish speech. He sometimes did ridiculous things, such as trying to catch a robin that had flown into his classroom while at the same time admonishing the class to stop laughing and warning them that levity was a sin.[12]

McCosh was handicapped by manners that were sometimes less than ingratiating and by a short temper. He was balked by trustees who were apt to be more interested in a prospective teacher's theology than in his competence, and more concerned that undergraduates be shielded from sin than that they be well taught. In devising a new curriculum, he felt obliged to retain so many required courses from an earlier era that instruction in new studies, such as science, modern languages, and history, was inevitably superficial. On top of these difficulties came a stroke of pure bad luck in the form of a typhoid fever epidemic in 1880, which scared away prospective students and seriously delayed the growth of the college.

Although McCosh failed fully to achieve his purposes, he left an enduring legacy. Under his inspiration Princeton reared a crop of first-rate scholars who were asked to join the faculty. McCosh called them "me bright young men," and they were his special pride. After he resigned, they became the core of the "young faculty" who carried on his ideals through the slack administration of President Patton. Woodrow Wilson had some claim to be included in this group. Even though he did not join the Princeton faculty until 1890, he came with McCosh's blessing.[13]

Certainly McCosh made a deep impression on Wilson. For the most part Wilson was rather an indifferent student at Princeton, but in McCosh's courses in psychology and the history of philosophy his grades were high—he once stood second in the class with a mark of 99.8. From these courses he undoubtedly gained something of McCosh's belief that the search for truth was a matter neither of purely empirical reasoning from data nor of merely a priori deduction, but a common sense combination of both observation and intuition, plus hard work, careful definition of terms, and clear exposition. In educational theory Wilson was patently McCosh's disciple. When he himself later became President of Princeton, every one of his major lines of policy—in regard to curriculum, recruitment of faculty, discipline, the social life of undergraduates, and the place of graduate studies in the university—followed lines laid down by his predecessor.[14]

When Princeton's most famous son entered college in September 1875, there was no room for him in the campus dormitories. After a few days with family friends, the Duffields, he found lodging with Mrs. Wright, who also provided meals for a group of undergraduates. His classmate Robert McCarter remembered him clearly:

In my freshman year I roomed at the boarding house of a Mrs. Wright. Adjoining my room was another with an outside private staircase to the two. I found occupying the other room a pimply-faced, hungry-looking young man named Tommy Wilson, who knew no one else in the class. I began then a friendship which lasted many years; I am sure I was Wilson's first friend at Princeton.

He was quiet and retiring and for a time had few, if any, other friends; we were, therefore, constantly in each other's room, he perhaps more in mine than I in his. We were very thick and used to spend hours—sometimes even all night—chinning together . . .

He was very full of the South and quite a Secessionist. One night we sat up until dawn talking about it, he taking the Southern side and getting quite bitter.

In his conversation his admiration for his father was evident. He was obviously devoted to him and frequently referred to him and to his opinions.

The college laws at the time were old-fashioned and inelastic. Among other innocent diversions they forbade card-playing. One night we decided to play a game of euchre. We shut the door, pulled down the shades, and, feeling free from intrusion, sat down to our play. Suddenly there was a knock on the door. It frightened us both out of our skins. I hastily shoved the cards under the table-cloth, and Wilson grabbed the first book he could lay his hands on, and pretended to be reading; what made the situation funnier was that the book was the Bible given me by my mother before I went to college . . .

Years afterward, after Wilson had entered public life, I met a Mrs. James C. Frick of Pittsburgh who, hearing I was from Princeton, asked me about him—wasn't he a terrible hypocrite? I asked how she got that idea. She told me the story I have just told you with the emphasis on pretending to read the Bible when he had really been playing cards. I had not infrequently told the story, as I am telling it to you, to show that Wilson was a simple, normal boy, if quieter and more thought-ful than most.[15]

Other classmates agree that Wilson was little known in his freshman year. In his studies he stood twenty-sixth among 114 freshmen ranked—a respectable record, but not brilliant. He won no distinctions in de-bating or writing. To some he seemed remote. The class historian later reported that Wilson no sooner arrived in Princeton than he rushed off to the library to take out Kant's *Critique of Pure Reason*. David C. Reid, who sat next to him in class for three terms, remem-bered him as "a tall striking figure, somewhat thin from recent illness," who seemed "to make no effort to enter into conversation, or at least with a very few. But this seemed to be due not to any false pride but solely because his mind was so absorbed in thought that it did not enter his mind to seek acquaintance with others." Edwin A. Alderman, who met Wilson when he was in Wilmington on vacation, had a similar recollection of "a tall slender youth of curious homeliness, detachment, and distinction."[16]

Little more was known about Wilson during his first years at Prince-ton until about 1963, when the editors of the Woodrow Wilson Papers arranged the transcription of a shorthand diary that Wilson had kept at this time. Entitled "My Journal," it contains fifty-five closely written pages and runs from June 3 to November, 1876—from the latter part, that is, of his freshman year until well on into his sophomore year. It opens as follows: "June 3rd: I now commence my diary which I have for some time contemplated. I am now 19 years old and am by the bless-ings of God in the enjoyment of excellent health. I have not employed the day to very much advantage having spent most of my time in loafing. My only reading today has been the life of Samuel Pepys pre-fixed to his diary in the edition of '69. I like Pepys am writing my diary in shorthand but here the resemblance between his diary and mine cease[s]."[17]

This first entry presages much that follows. It appears again and again that Wilson was worried about his health. If it was not possible for him to walk or play baseball, he exercised in the gymnasium be-cause his well-being, he was sure, depended on it. Often he ended a day's entry, "Thank God for health and strength." He also frequently lamented wasting time that should have been devoted to his studies, in part by allowing himself to be drawn off to more congenial intellectual pursuits. During the half year covered by the diary the range, rigor, and systematic quality of his private reading was remarkable.

"My Journal" shows that by the end of his freshman year Wilson had entered actively into the life of the college. He and fellow members of his boarding house, who called themselves the Wright Bower, formed a baseball team, the "Bowery Boys," and played frequent games with similar organizations. Indeed, Wilson sometimes played baseball twice a day and once played every day for six days running. Failing that, unless the weather forced him into the gymnasium, he played catch or went on a walk, usually with a friend, around one of the "triangles" of country roads leading out from the village of Princeton and back. He followed with keen interest and intense partisanship the fortunes of the college baseball team. When class rowing races were held on the nearby Raritan Canal, he ran with the crews. At the end of freshman year he joined his classmates in a "spree" to celebrate the event with horn-blowing, firecrackers, and discharge of cannon. He cared intensely about the prowess of '79 in the annual "cane sprees." Once he bet two sodas on the outcome. Another time he rather unwillingly accepted the challenge of a freshman to a private cane spree. Wilson won the contest but noted that it was not greatly to his credit since his opponent was smaller.

On occasion Wilson revealed the cocksureness that one expects of a college sophomore. After attending an Episcopalian service in Princeton, he wrote that he thought it was "very stupid indeed . . . a ridiculous way of worshiping God, and one which must give very little pleasure to God." He remarked that an acquaintance in Wilmington was pleasant but not bright. "In fact," he went on, "I have come to the conclusion that very few people are bright." He dismissed *Romeo and Juliet* as "not scholarly" and one of Shakespeare's poorest pieces. At other times he was less brash. After an evening in Whig Hall, a debating society, he felt discouraged because men he thought to have no great ability did better than he. "I have come to the conclusion," he wrote, "that my friends have no doubt come to long ago and that is that my mind is a very ordinary one indeed. I am nothing as far as intellect goes. But I can plod and work."[18]

The diary shows that Wilson was already intensely interested in politics and that he took a dim view of the American political scene. On July 4, 1876, he wrote: "The One Hundredth Anniversary of American Independence. One hundred years ago America conquered England in an unequal struggle and this year she glories over it. How much happier she would be now if she had England's form of government instead of the miserable delusion of a republic. A republic too founded upon the notion of abstract liberty. I venture to say that this country will never celebrate another centennial as a republic. The English form of government is the only true one." Wilson was already an ardent Democrat: he thought that "the salvation of the country from frauds and the reviving of trade" depended on a Democratic victory in the Hayes-Tilden presidential election of 1876. When it was at first reported that Tilden had won, he attended a bonfire to celebrate the victory and went to bed "tired out with shouting and excitement." Later, when it turned out that the result was in doubt, he suffered almost intolerable suspense and was unable to settle down to anything for two days.[19]

During three months in the summer of 1876 Wilson was at home with his family in Wilmington. The picture "My Journal" gives of his relationship with his family is attractive. He showed in many ways that he was an affectionate brother and a dutiful, devoted son—whether by making a wooden sword for his much younger brother Joseph, Jr. ("Josie"), mending the back fence for his father, or working in his mother's garden and helping her lay a carpet. He often played a form of billiards with his father and worked with him on the accounts and minutes of the assembly of the Southern Presbyterian Church. He took over his father's correspondence when Dr. Wilson went off on a vacation. He also wrote half a dozen articles for the *North Carolina Presbyterian,* a journal that Dr. Wilson edited. When it came time to return to Princeton, he remarked how hard it was to part from his family and wrote in his diary, "How blessed I am in my home!"[20]

"My Journal" suddenly stopped in November 1877. Later in his undergraduate years Wilson made attempts to keep a diary, but entries are few. Fortunately for our ability to trace his doings, an almost equally rich source of information picks up just as the diary leaves off. This is a collection of several scores of letters to Wilson from his father and mother. Except for a single one in 1874, the file begins on November 15, 1876, just five days before the diary was abandoned. From then on, there is a letter from one parent or another about every week, sometimes more frequently, except when Wilson was at home. The letters show that he not only kept his parents informed of his doings but confided to them many of his intimate feelings. Thus, the very first letter, from his mother, strikingly reveals how strongly he felt about politics and how bitterly he resented the Republican attempt to "steal" the Hayes-Tilden election:

I have been thinking more than usual, even, about you the last few days. The fear that you may be provoked beyond endurance, during these anxious days by those Radical [Republican] companions of yours, has crept into my heart. I know your self-control or I would be miserable—but it is so hard to bear their ignorant thrusts quietly—and yet it is the only thing to be done—for one's own self respect's sake. I trust you have been sensible enough to disregard their insolence. Tommy dear

don't talk about knocking anybody down—no matter what they say—
or rather, don't *think* of doing such a thing. Such people are beneath
your notice. Besides they don't mean anything personal—strange as it may
seem.[21]

Many of Jessie Wilson's letters show her anxious concern about
Wilson's physical well-being. She advised him to be careful about his
diet, to spare his eyes, to keep his room dry by building a fire even on
warm spring days, and to remember to wear his warm underwear. She
sent him extra money for clothing or furnishings for his room and urged
that he let his parents know if he was in want of anything. In all matters she took his part. On one occasion Wilson thought he had been
unfairly graded. When the report reached his mother, she wrote, "It
[the midyear report] came to me while you were in Baltimore—and I
understood it to be miserably unjust. I knew that you had reason to expect a better report than usual. The only feeling I had was that of indignation at what I knew to be injustice—and sorrow for what I knew
would be your feeling in regard to it." Jessie Wilson's letters to her son
abundantly reveal that she was an oversolicitous, overprotective
mother.[22]

The letters from Dr. Wilson to his son show a close intimacy and mutual admiration. Wilson constantly sought his father's opinions, and
the advice he received in return was sensible, temperate, and designed
to build up the young man's confidence. Dr. Wilson repeatedly encouraged his son when he was despondent and urged him not to be
puffed up when he was successful. He often adjured the young man
to moderate ambition and desire for immediate reward and to work
honestly from day to day, having faith in the ultimate outcome.
Whereas the influence of his mother was designed to make Wilson
self-centered, his father urged him to get outside himself, as when he
concluded a passage on the subject of ambition: "In short, dearest boy,
do not allow yourself to dwell upon *yourself*—concentrate your thoughts
upon *thoughts* and *things* and *events*. Self-consciousness is a torment:
was mine at your age; has, often since then, been such. Go out from
your own personality."[23]

The letters from father to son reveal how many interests they shared.
Dr. Wilson wrote at length about the politics of the Southern Presbyterian Church, and his son told of college debates. In his sophomore
year Wilson asked his father for advice on how to prepare a formal
talk: should one memorize it or arrange one's thoughts under headings
and then speak extempore? Either method, wrote Dr. Wilson, would
produce successful results, but he preferred the latter because it was
more natural. Always to be avoided was a slipshod performance. Wil-

son followed this advice to the letter and continually put himself in situations where he had to think on his feet. Two years later his father wrote him: "I am greatly pleased to know that extemporaneous speaking is your forte. By all means cultivate the gift—or rather assemblage of gifts. It is the *diamond* among those accomplishments which ensure the future of a public man." On another occasion Dr. Wilson wrote his son, "true oratory, whether of the bar or the pulpit or the hustings, consists in the statement of connected thought . . . uttered with the energy and courage of conviction." So strongly did young Wilson agree with this sentiment that in college debates he flatly refused to argue against his convictions, and he invented a type of debating society in which no member was called upon to do so.[24]

Wilson often sent his more serious writings home for his father's perusal. The criticisms he received in return bear out his later recollection that he owed his father a great debt for insisting on accuracy in speech and writing. The following advice, which Dr. Wilson gave in relation to an essay on Carlyle that never saw print, was exactly tailored to his son's needs:

Like most young composers, you are apt to *generalize* too broadly—do not qualify with sufficient care. A *perfectly fair* statement of a case or a fact is extremely difficult, especially where we wish to *make a point*. Bold thinking is very desirable; but it loses its power so soon as it ceases to be without a show of *caution*: for it then, by becoming too sweeping, *thins*. I am very anxious to have you reach a high standard of cautious (not timid or doubting) thinking: that habit of thinking which has mental eyes for looking all around and all through a subject; and which indulges in no statements for the support of which there is not good proof.[25]

Only one of the letters that Wilson wrote home during his undergraduate years has been preserved. It is worth quoting here in full because it reveals his intense admiration for his father and a willingness to look at himself with humorous detachment. It was written while Dr. Wilson was attending the annual convocation of the Southern Presbyterian Church as clerk:

My dear father:

It is a great comfort to have easy means of communication with you while you are so far away; and although you are, no doubt, very busy, I know that a letter from me is never unwelcome and will be all the more acceptable to you while you are away from home. Please give the General Assembly my respects and tell it that it cannot do better than listen to and heed the advice of its Stated Clerk. The said Stated Clerk has a very inconvenient way of seeing right into the heart of any matter which comes under his observation. The son of the Stated Clerk is a queer fellow. He is entirely free from anything like his father's clear-sightedness and altogether his mind seems to be remarkably bright and empty. You could easily distinguish him in a crowd by his long nose, open mouth, and consequential manner. He is noted in college as a man who can make a remarkably good show with little or no material. But, after all, he is a good enough sort of fellow and what he lacks in solidity he makes up in good intentions and spasmodic endeavors. He has a few ideas of his own and very few are his own. He writes sometimes but his style lacks clearness and his choice of words is far from good. Ideas are scarce in his compositions and what few there are go limping about in a cloud of wordy expressions and under a heavy cloud of lost nouns and adjectives. Ideas are to his writings what oases are in the desert, except that his ideas are very seldom distinguishable from the waste which surrounds them. He attended a ball game between the Princeton and Yale base ball nines to-day on the Princeton grounds. He reports the game to have been an unusually beautiful one but that, much to his chagrin, Princeton was defeated by a score of six (6) to four (4). Last Saturday Princeton was defeated by Harvard by a score of seven (7) to five (5) and these two (2) defeats following close upon one another have thrown him into a state of despondency about Princeton viewed from an athletic point of view. From what I have seen of him he is apt to allow himself to sympathise almost too heartily with everything that is afloat and, consequently, subjects his nervous system to frequent severe and, sometimes, rather unnecessary strains. Examinations are again close upon him, I believe, and, as he does not stand remarkably high in his class, he seems to look forward to them with some degree of anxiety. But perhaps the anxious look I have of late observed upon his rather unexpressive countenance is caused by dislike of the large amount of studying before him. He seems in fine health and sends love in large quantities to his father, the Stated Clerk.

Your loving son Thomas[26]

One of Wilson's principal biographers relates that he arrived at college in his freshman year carrying "a ministerial-looking old black bag that belonged to his father" and that "he had no overcoat, so that as the term wore along into the Northern autumn he shivered painfully." This suggestion of a threadbare minister's son is at variance with the memory of a classmate, who recalled Wilson as "a well-dressed young man, who had been reared in a family of education and refinement, who was well-to-do and had none of the hard experience of poverty or financial care." All contemporary evidence is on the side of this latter recollection, for Wilson's father was well rewarded by the standards of the day, and his mother had modest independent means. Moreover, his parents were so generous to Wilson that he could afford to spend thirty dollars on an overcoat from a New York tailor or an equal amount for books to add to his personal library. The rent of $105 that he paid for the corner room in Witherspoon Hall into which he moved in his junior year was more than twice the prevailing rate for other dormitories. Late in his sophomore year he joined an eating club, the "Alliga-

Princeton, New Jersey
5/23/77

My dear father:

It is a great comfort to have easy means of communicating with you while you are so far away, and, although you are, no doubt, very busy, I know that a letter from me is never unwelcome and will be all the more acceptable to you while you are away from home. Please give the General Assembly my respects and tell it that it cannot do better than listen to and heed the advice of its Stated Clerk. The said Stated Clerk has a very inconvenient way of seeing right to the heart of any matter which comes under his observation. The son of the said Stated Clerk is a queer fellow. He is entirely free from anything like his father's clear-sightedness and altogether his mind seems to be remarkably bright and empty. You could easily distinguish him in a crowd by his long nose, open mouth, and consequential manner. He is noted in college as a man who can make a remarkably good show with little or no material. But, after all, he is a good enough sort of fellow and what he lacks in solidity he makes up in good intentions and spasmodic endeavors. He has a few queer ideas of his own and very few of them are his own. He writes sometimes but his style

First page of a letter written during Wilson's sophomore year at Princeton, revealing his intense admiration for and easy communication with his father.

tors," composed of well-to-do members of the class of '79. Although numbering only fourteen, the Alligators were affluent enough to hire a house of their own on Nassau Street, facing the college campus.[27]

The impression that Wilson gave to some of his classmates was of a person who found time to enjoy himself. One thought him "companionable, friendly, genial, generally popular in the class"; another considered him "friendly and cordial." He had a fund of amusing stories and enjoyed singing. He sometimes went to the theater in New York, and he one saw Booth act twice in a single day. He knew the airs from *Pinafore*. Although it may have shocked the pious, he took part in perhaps the first Princeton "dramatical performance," playing Marc Antony in "The Sanguinary Tragedy of Julius Sneezer," a skit written by two classmates and staged in the secrecy of Whig Hall.[28]

Wilson's most intimate friends were made in Witherspoon Hall, where he became the central figure in a group called the Witherspoon Gang. According to Robert Bridges, one of its number:

Many of us would meet in the various rooms, and I have often thought that perhaps the intervals of loafing were more permanent in their effect than the intervals of study. One of the crowd, Hiram Woods, who could read Latin better than the rest of us, would sit at his desk and, under our keen and often cutting remarks, make translations while we followed the text. On one occasion of this kind, when the reading was long, the deep voice of Webster was heard to say, "Tommy, let us lean back." Long years afterward, while many of the same group were waiting in the White House to go down to the dinner which Wilson gave to about sixty in the Class, there was a long delay and the President turned to the same man and said, "Dan'l, let us lean back." Over forty years had gone by since the original remark was made in 10 East Witherspoon.

Bridges wrote that Wilson especially enjoyed the "play of the mind." His diary and surviving letters from classmates bear this out. He liked to push people into discussion or carry on a dialogue by mail in order to examine a question that interested him. Many years later he said to an audience of college men: "I do not believe that men ever thoroughly know or enjoy each other until they lay their minds alongside each other and have tests of their quality; then you are tying in perfectly with your friend, when you have shared his thoughts, when you have discussed his ideals, when you have cried an echo to his purposes, when there begin to be wrought those links of steel which bind you to him for life, and every other spirit of comradeship is superficial."[29]

Only with a few intimates, however, could Wilson feel at ease. What he wrote in the memory book of a classmate, Frank Garmany, shows that something held him back from intimacy, even with men he liked;

it also shows how much he was imbued with the ideal of the southern gentleman:

Dear Frank,
   Although our friendship has not been as great as our common sympathies would have warranted, I have always looked upon you, as I hope you have looked upon me, as one upon whose friendship safe reliance may safely be put. I, perhaps, am colder and more reserved than most of those who are fortunate enough to have been born in our beloved South; but my affection is none the less real because less demonstrative. It shall always be my aim to claim and win and retain and, if possible, deserve the love and intimate communion of all who cultivate the courage, the chivalry, and high purpose which have hitherto been the birthrights and most cherished virtues of Southern Gentlemen; and among the number of these may I ever remember Frank Garmany.

Even with his closest friends Wilson had a hard time giving himself, as witness this passage from a letter to Charles Talcott: "When I am with anyone in whom I am especially and sincerely interested, the hardest subject for me to broach is just that which is nearest my heart. An unfortunate disposition indeed! I hope to overcome it in time!"[30]

   Wilson appears to have been thrown in with the wealthier young men whose invasion of Princeton was causing some alarm to pious alumni and trustees. That his closest campanions were drawn from the more worldly element is suggested by the fact that, although twenty-four members of the class of '79 entered the ministry—a proportion of one in five of those who graduated—not one of them came from the Alligators or the Witherspoon Gang. Yet it must be emphasized that the tradition of Princeton was democratic, the college small and intimate, and the class spirit intense, so that all undergraduates were in touch with men outside their own circle. Wilson had more than the ordinary opportunity for broad contact because he was extraordinarily active and successful in extracurricular organizations. Fellow students chose him for no less than four of the six or seven most important executive positions on the campus: Speaker of Whig Hall, Managing Editor of the *Princetonian,* Secretary of the Football Association, and President of the Base Ball Association (although he resigned the last office). Contemporary sources give a vivid picture of Wilson as a leader of men in the microcosm of the Princeton campus.

   It was as a member of the American Whig Society (known as Whig for short) that Wilson first came into prominence at Princeton. In many colleges and even some schools at this time there were rival literary and debating societies: in North Carolina there were Di and Phi; in Columbia, Philolexian and Peithologian; in the University of Virginia, Jefferson and George Washington; in the Phillips Exeter Academy, the Golden Branch and G. L. Soule. Perhaps nowhere were such organizations as important as at Princeton. Nearly ninety percent of the class of 1879 were enrolled either in Whig or its rival, the Cliosophic Society. Each had its own building and library. The college authorities were at pains to encourage the societies or "halls," as they were called; students were excused from prayer meeting on Friday evening, the night they met. Until 1877 the college diplomas of members of Whig and Clio were tied with the colors of their society rather than with those of the college. President McCosh frequently paid tribute to the literary societies; it was partly to prevent any lessening of their beneficial influence that he abolished the fraternities.[31]

In Wilson's time the halls were at the height of their power and influence. All questions were carefully put and argued according to strict parliamentary procedure. There were numerous standing committees, plus ad hoc committees to investigate such momentous questions as the design of new prize medals. Each committee duly reported to the society in writing. Fines were exacted for absence, nonperformance of duties, and disorder, the latter being on a graduated scale, from ten cents for "sitting on the window sill" to twelve dollars for "disturbance during initiation." Whig had an excellent library, from which Wilson in a single year borrowed thirty books. In the reading room there were current copies of a score of periodicals and many more newspapers.

The purpose of the American Whig Society was the self-improvement of its members. Offering practice in essay writing, oratory, debating, and parliamentary procedure, it was a fine training ground for future ministers, lawyers, editors, teachers, and members of professional societies. Every Friday afternoon there was a business meeting, and the same evening there were "literary exercises," set speeches, formal debates, and essay readings, starting at half past seven and lasting until eleven. The older members taught the younger, both by formal literary instruction and by example. Thus, Whig became an avenue of communication cutting across the rigid lines that elsewhere separated the members of rival classes.

A usual way to achieve prominence in Whig was through the many competitive debates and oratorical contests, in which members were sometimes rewarded with medals or monetary prizes. In these Wilson met with only modest success. He entered two oratorical contests, winning second prize as a sophomore for an oration entitled "The Ideal Statesman." In four competitive debates he was only once chosen best

speaker. Nor did he shine in the strictly literary exercises; in fact, he
regularly paid a twenty-five cent fine rather than submit essays for
judging.

Yet college mates who could sometimes recall little else about Wilson
remembered that he was one of the most prominent and respected
members of Whig Hall. He seems to have achieved this position by
his effectiveness in the informal discussions that followed assigned
speeches and in the business meetings. According to Robert McCarter:
"He did not appear to care particularly about honors. He took them if
they came, but he did not ardently seek them. As I remember it,
though, he was looked on as the leading man in Hall, as we called it.
He gave splendid addresses in extempore debate; he was a careful
speaker; he spoke without yelling. He prided himself upon his ability
to talk correctly and trained himself to think on his feet. Walking with
me, he would provoke a discussion, so that he might think out loud.
He excelled in debate rather than in set speeches."[32]

The carefully kept Whig records show that Wilson was intensely
active in other ways. The American Whig Society was a little republic.
Except for slight supervision by an alumni Senate, it ran its own affairs.
The activities of an elaborate slate of officers and standing committees
were subject to continuous scrutiny. Wilson threw himself into this
practical business. At one time he proposed that the hall purchase a
skull and crossbones, the same not to cost more than five dollars, and at
another time, that the alumni be solicited for an endowment of $10,000.
He served on the Book Committee, on the Committee for Hall Improvement (dealing with repair and upkeep of the building), on a
committee to amend the bylaws to allow expenditure of the sinking
fund for repairs, and on still another to thank an ex-governor of New
Jersey for his address to the hall at Commencement. Eventually he was
elected Second Comptroller, the beginning of a *cursus honorum* that
ultimately led him to the highest office of Speaker. One member of
Whig recalled that he was "a fine presiding officer—firm and decisive."[33]

One reason Wilson did not shine in the formal debates and oratorical
contests in Whig was that they fostered an ornate, pompous, vapid style
of declamation. In his memoirs George Santayana, who was at Harvard
shortly after Wilson was at Princeton, wrote about the training in public
speaking he had received in such a society: "It had nothing of that
political timeliness which characterizes young people's debates in
England. With us the subject matter was legendary, the language
learned by rote, stilted and inflated, the thought platitudinous. Apart
from the mere training in *elocution* (as indeed it was called) it was
practice in feigning, in working up verbal enthusiasm for any cause,

and seeming to prophesy any event. Very useful, no doubt, for future lawyers, politicians or clergymen—training for that reversible sophistry and propaganda that intoxicates the demagogue and misleads the people." Young Wilson had written in much the same vein more than sixty years before, in the pages of the *Princetonian:* "Until we eschew declamation and court oratory [defined earlier as skill in debate] we must expect to be ciphers in the world's struggles for principles and the advancement of causes. Oratory is persuasion, not the declamation of essays. The passion and force of oratory is spontaneous, not carefully elaborated."[34]

As Santayana remarked, in Britain quite a different style of oratory prevailed, inspired by the House of Commons, where the small size of the chamber made shouting ridiculous, where the speaker attempted to persuade other gentlemen rather than to impress the galleries or an invisible constituency, and where there was always the dramatic possibility that the decision of the House on a particular measure might cause the fall of the government. This parliamentary type of oratory served Wilson for a model. An article describing the speaking in the House of Commons in a bound volume of *The Gentlemen's Magazine* for 1874 "so fired his imagination that he remembered all his life the exact place at the head of the south stairs in the Chancellor Green Library where he read it."[35]

So anxious was Wilson to practice speaking before an imaginary House of Commons that he founded among his classmates a small society, known as the Liberal Debating Club, modeled on the British Parliament. The constitution, which Wilson wrote, stated that the society should discuss contemporary questions and that these questions should come before the club in the form of bills. Every bill was to go through three readings. The effective head of the society was a "Secretary of State," whose duty was "to form and express an opinion on every question which comes before the Club" and who was to "remain in or be removed from his office according as his views coincide with or differ from those of his fellow members." The society was planned so that each member would have a chance to speak on every bill. A member spoke not to impress judges or to make a good appearance but "to arrive at the truth, or to influence the opinions of his comrades." The constitution ruled that the society should not include more than eight members, although eventually nine were admitted.[36]

Since the members of the Liberal Debating Club were pledged to secrecy, the society was in technical violation of the college laws against fraternities. Adhering to the fundamental principles of "*Justice, Morality,* and *Friendship*." its members were to form a brotherhood to "assist and encourage each other in every possible way." Wilson hoped not merely to imitate Parliament but to create a guild of able men who, through discussion and mutual aid, might advance right principles. Associated with him were some of the most capable of his classmates. Of the nine members, six achieved a degree of eminence; of the other three, one died young, one was afflicted with inherited wealth, and the third deliberately sought a life of obscure service in a slum parish. Letters to Wilson from several of them show that they shared his political and literary interests. They also apparently shared his own belief that he might rise to political eminence. Thus, one of them wrote him at graduation: "I am certain that if every power I ever dreamed of possessing were increased a hundred fold I could never become a Bright but I am equally certain that if your talents are well directed your influence in America will not be less than Cobden's was in England."[37]

The Liberal Debating Club met on Saturday nights, usually for about an hour and a half. It debated contemporary political topics, both foreign and domestic. In spite of Wilson's opposition, the members decided to discuss literature as well. In addition to the extempore discussion, there were set speeches, which received formal criticism. The debates were apparently frank and lively. Robert McCarter remembered a discussion of the Civil War that went so much against the South that Wilson could not stand it and left the room. Once when the society voted down his proposition that terms of congressmen should be increased from two to six years, Wilson reported in his diary, "I was overcome by opinion rather than by argument from other members present. That my arguments were sound I am convinced as I have put considerable thought on the subject." But apparently he learned to take defeat with good grace; even on this occasion he reported that he had had "an unusually pleasant time." The society continued in vigorous existence from its founding in March 1877 until its members graduated two years later. Both the formation of the Liberal Debating Society and its ensuing prosperity are striking evidence of Wilson's ability to enlist others in matters that interested him.[38]

The position that brought Wilson into greatest prominence at college was his editorship of the *Princetonian*, then a fortnightly newspaper. He was first elected an editor toward the end of his sophomore year. When the regular Managing Editor temporarily withdrew in the autumn of 1877, Wilson was one of two chosen to fill his place. Finally, at a class meeting in February 1878 he was elected to the top position in his own right by the members of the class of '79. Editors of the *Princetonian*

Janet Woodrow Wilson and Joseph Ruggles Wilson. Although affectionate within the family, Wilson's mother was shy and reserved in public. His father, a Clerk of the Southern Presbyterian Church, was an effective preacher and skilled parliamentarian.

Campus of the College of New Jersey in 1879. The building on the right is the newly constructed Witherspoon Hall, the dormitory that some alumni criticized as over-luxurious. Wilson occupied a corner room.

The Alligator, a Princeton eating club composed of relatively affluent members of the class of 1879. Wilson, standing third from right, joined it during his sophomore year.

The board of editors of the *Princetonian*, 1878–1879. Seated at far left is Robert Mc-Carter, Wilson's first close friend at Princeton. Seated, far right, is Henry B. Fine, who succeeded Wilson as Managing Editor and later became his chief lieutenant during Wilson's presidency of Princeton. Charles Talcott, with whom Wilson formed a "solemn covenant" to elevate American political life, is standing, second from left.

and the *Nassau Literary Magazine* were chosen on a single class ballot, the successful candidates choosing which periodical they would serve. The tally sheet of the nine editors elected from '79 was as follows: Wilson, 96; Magie, 75; Bridges, 86; Wilder, 93; Godwin, 88; E. Davis, 54; Martin, 54; Talcott, 74; and McCarter, 56. The attendance at the meeting was 105, so it is apparent that Wilson was close to a unanimous choice.[39]

Wilson entered on his duties as head of the *Princetonian* in May 1878, and apparently he ran the show. According to a fellow editor: "He formulated policies; he was the chief. He would come around to me and say that he would like me to write on such and such. If he did not like what I wrote, it would not go in. The editors were not a cabinet and seldom if ever met as a group. He was boss and deserved to be. He ran a good paper. I can remember him now running around with a memo pad, taking shorthand notes; he worked hard." In addition to allocating assignments, Wilson wrote much of the *Princetonian* himself. His contributions included many of the news stories, especially accounts of football and baseball games; occasional book reviews; regular critical commentary on the student monthly, the *Nassau Literary Magazine;* and probably "The College World," a column devoted to summaries and quotations from the student publications of other colleges. He also wrote most of the editorials.[40]

In the lead editorial of the first number under his sole direction Wilson wrote that the purpose of the *Princetonian* was "to be an impartial record of College incident and a medium for a bold, frank, and manly expression of College opinion." Putting the second aim into immediate action, he went on in another editorial to denounce the faculty for a "tendency to overlegislation." In particular, he found it "insulting and contemptible" that students should be required to post an advance bond for payment of room rent. In later editions he took up the perennial theme of Princeton's bad water supply and primitive sewage and finally declared: "We had thought that all that would be necessary in order to bring about a thorough overhauling and cleansing of the three wells on the campus was to mention to the authorities the need for such action, trusting that their good sense would show them that they ought to act immediately. But it is always a mistake to trust their good sense, we have found." On another occasion his criticism of the college administration incidentally revealed his political bias:

We have come back from the summer's vacation, to find that the zeal of Civil Service Reform has spread to our College officers, and sundry reforms have been instituted which move us to wonder, although hardly to admiration. We are inclined to look upon these late reforms in our civil service, which are quite as spasmodically effected as those of Mr. Hayes, as in every way as ridiculous as his. The men servants who last year did good service in the entries of our various dormitories, dismissed, and we are left to have all our work done by a few superannuated Irish women, who are required to do an immense amount of work in so short a time that they necessarily do it in a careless, partial manner, which is worse than absolute neglect.[41]

Such criticism of college authorities is part of established ritual. Student editors are expected to denounce and deplore, to find or invent grievances. What is more significant is the ways in which Wilson's editorial pages varied from others. Comparison of Volume III of the *Princetonian,* under his direction, with Volume II, under the editorship of C. J. Williams '78, and Volume IV, under Henry B. Fine '80, reveals quite striking differences. In Volume II there was marked attention to the religious life of the campus, and the tone was appropriate for a college that could undergo several months of revival meetings. The authorities were criticized for giving too many tests on Monday, which tempted students into "polling" (cramming) on the Sabbath, and for encouraging gambling by choosing speakers for certain exercises by lot. Wilson, however, although the son and grandson of Presbyterian divines, seldom mentioned the religious side of the college, and never in a pious fashion. The only references to religion in the editorial pages of the twenty numbers of Volume III were a satire directed against Paley's *Natural Theology* as the intellectual treat of the junior year, a query whether too many Princeton scholarships were not granted to candidates for the ministry, a criticism of the Second Presbyterian Church for not opening its doors to the actress Mrs. Scott-Siddons, and a suggestion that college prayer meetings be reduced from four to two per week. In Volume IV the editorials dealt mostly with the academic side of Princeton, especially the sciences and mathematics, which reflected the interests of Fine, who later became a noted mathematician and Dean of Science at Princeton. Although Wilson was to make his first public reputation as a scholar and to become a college president, his editorials were little concerned with matters academic, except to criticize the instruction in public speaking and to advocate a professor of reading. Instead of the aspects of the college that faculty and trustees thought central—the spiritual and intellectual life—Wilson's editorials centered on the sideshows: the social life of undergraduates, their musical clubs, debates, class activities, and athletics. His requests for contributions from candidates for the editorial board made this clear: "Pointed comments on live College topics; poetry; short spicy stories, and well-told anecdotes; notices of events interesting to college men;

items of current news and current College jokes; information as to the whereabouts and employments of alumni; and brief, pungent criticisms of magazine articles and books whose subject matter is of immediate interest to place in our columns and entitle their writers to a consideration in the final choice of editors."[42]

This list sounds frivolous, but there was little frivolity in the way Wilson approached the two major themes of his editorials: better decorum in the college and better organization of extracurricular activities. In the *Princetonian* he repeatedly inveighed against the disorder on campus. A certain amount of "noisy disturbance" could be regarded, he admitted, as unavoidable outbursts of animal spirits. But disorderly conduct at public exercises and in the recitation room seemed "ungentlemanly and unworthy of men." He condemned the sophomore class for disturbing the juniors and seniors at examinations, and his own classmates for "disgraceful" actions in Professor Guyot's lectures. He criticized freshmen who wore too scanty shirts in the gymnasium. Snowballing he called an "unmitigated nuisance. . . Not a day passes but some one's cherished tyle, procured regardless of expense at Dunlap's or Terhune's, is crushed into a shapeless mass. [Undergraduates then wore derby hats.] We can be saved only by an awakening of public conscience or a general thaw."[43]

As befitted his Scottish ancestry, Wilson carried on through the *Princetonian* an unremitting campaign for financial solvency in undergraduate organizations. The first lines in his first number of the paper were: "All subscriptions to Vol. III. of the PRINCETONIAN, which opens with this number, must be paid in advance. No one will receive a copy of the paper, therefore, until he has paid his subscription." He continually urged students to lend financial support to the various athletic teams—football, baseball, crew, and track—and suggested means whereby they could raise funds. He appealed for contributions to pay for new uniforms for the football team. He proposed an entertainment —"we dare not suggest theatricals—to charm the dollars from the most tightly-buttoned pocket" for the benefit of the boat club. After all appeals for boat club funds had failed, he argued that rowing should be abandoned.[44]

Better financing was only one facet of his general crusade for greater efficiency in undergraduate societies. Starting with the first number of the *Princetonian*, Wilson urged that the choice of editors for the paper be transferred from class meetings to the editorial board itself, and that selection be based on actual contribution, not popularity or reputed ability to write. His intimate friend Robert Bridges, editor of the *Nassau Literary Magazine*, advocated a similar arrangement for his periodical. This proposal was denounced in strongly worded letters to the editor as "the rule of an oligarchy" and "entirely too underground to be satisfactory to the college." But Wilson and Bridges persisted. The *Princetonian* of October 10, 1879, announced that they would present their proposals at a college meeting called for the purpose of electing officers of the Baseball Association. The next issue duly reported that the college had voted by a large majority to accept schemes whereby the editorial boards would choose their successors, subject to veto by the college at large.[45]

Above all, the *Princetonian* harped on the theme that sports should be played to win and, to win, there must be better organization. On no other issue did the paper express itself so frequently or so forcibly. It devoted particular attention to the baseball team. If Princeton was to succeed on the diamond, Wilson kept reiterating, there must be thoroughly organized practice and careful coaching—instead of the players' trying to find out their own faults. There must be discipline; the nine should be "controlled entirely by the will of the Captain and President." Above all:

> *Everything* depends upon the character of the captain and the president. With a good captain and an efficient president success is no longer a matter of doubt . . . The old nine chooses the captain and the only duty of the College at large lies in the selection of the best president within their choice. It is not sufficient that he be well acquainted with the game. The majority of men in college are sufficiently familiar with the rules of the game to fill the office. The president must above all things else, be a man of unbiased judgment, energy, determination, intelligence, moral courage, *conscience*.[46]

This description of the perfect leader appeared in the *Princetonian* on September 26, 1878. On the same day Wilson had attended a baseball meeting called in the interest of electing C. C. Cuyler '79 to presidency of the baseball club. At Wilson's suggestion his friend Charles Talcott spoke effectively in favor of delaying the election until mid-October, the usual time. Others supported him, and the motion to postpone was carried by a large majority. After the meeting, according to Wilson's diary, he and Talcott "walked home . . . quite elated with our victory, for victory it was." A greater victory was to follow. Four weeks later this report appeared in the *Princetonian*: "A college meeting was called last Monday, after chapel, for the purpose of electing a president of the Base Ball Association, and to consider the method of electing the editors of the *Lit.* and *Princetonian*. Mr. T. W. Wilson '79 was elected to the presidency of the Base Ball Association." On another page of the same issue the paper solemnly wished success to the new officers of the baseball club and promised them its hearty support "in any course which may lead to success." Although Wilson shortly resigned from the presidency in order to devote more time to his personal studies of political theory, the incident suggests that he already knew a good deal about the art of politics.[47]

Still another area where Wilson exerted leadership and revealed organizing ability was football. He was Secretary of the Football Association at a time when American football was just beginning to assume importance, and his influence was such that he has been called "one of the founders of modern football." This claim may be exaggerated, but Wilson surely contributed to the success of an unbeaten Princeton team in the autumn of 1878.[48]

During Wilson's college years American football as we know it today developed. Before 1876 several Eastern colleges played a football somewhat similar to soccer, with twenty players on a side, in which the ball was advanced by kicking or striking with the fist. Then in 1876 Harvard and Yale decided to change to the British game of rugby football, and soon other colleges joined in adopting the rules of the British Rugby Union. Rugby was founded by that legendary schoolboy who "with fine disregard for the rules picked up the ball and ran with it." Its distinctive features were that a man could run with the ball until he was tackled and that he could pass the ball to others on his side. The game was more highly developed than the earlier form of American college football, demanding more practice and more team play.[49]

Somehow Wilson acquired a knowledge of the new game. Parke Davis claimed that he learned it from the students at the Staunton Military Institute, where it had been early imported from England. But since the Wilsons left Staunton when he was less than a year old, his only opportunity to watch rugby there would have been on his later visits to Staunton. It is also possible that in his intensive reading of British periodicals he happened upon articles on the tactics and strategy of the game.[50]

However he acquired it, Wilson had so much familiarity with rugby that he was elected one of the five directors of the Football Association, as well as its Secretary, for 1878-1879. He and the captain were the two chief officers of the organization. He not only took care of the practical business of finances and arranging games but had a part in coaching. Robert McCarter remembered him working out plays on the tablecloth in the Alligator Club with Earl Dodge, captain of the team. "He had," said McCarter, "clear-cut notions of how the game should be played and insisted on them."[51]

Here again, Wilson used the pages of the *Princetonian* as a rostrum to preach the gospel of success, and the price of success was discipline under leadership. Describing the 1878 team in the *Princetonian,* he wrote that its play inspired confidence but added: "The only thing worthy of serious reprehension in the playing of the team is the stubborn manner in which some of the men shut their ears to the command of the captain. Until they learn to obey they will never learn to play with effect."[52]

The Secretary of the Football Association had to raise money, which was no easy business because expenses were high by the standards of the day. The players had to be equipped with new uniforms, and traveling expenses had to be furnished for a team of fifteen. It cost $300 to hire a field at Hoboken for the game with Yale. Wilson not only appealed to the college for funds but raised the admission fee for football games to the unprecedented sum of fifty cents—a price he had to defend in the *Princetonian.* When the season ended, the Football Association had made such a profit that it later contributed $100 to help pay off the baseball deficit. This gift may be the first recorded example of the now universal practice of using football gate receipts to support other sports.[53]

The football team of 1878 proved to be one of Princeton's great teams. They won all six games, beating both Harvard and Yale and being scored on only once. At the close of the season the *Princetonian* claimed the football championship and attempted to explain Princeton's success. The team had been overmatched in weight and strength but had won because of constant practice, teamwork, and skill. "We played," wrote the *Princetonian's* football editor, perhaps with self-gratulation, "a much more scientific game than our opponents did."[54]

Wilson's active interest in football continued for many years. In 1889 he helped to coach a successful Wesleyan team. As a professor at Princeton, he was a member of the Graduate Advisory Committee on Athletics and regularly attended football practice as well as games, at which he was as much elated by victory or cast down by defeat as any undergraduate. Even as President of Princeton, he found time to attend practice two or three times a week and discussed the game intelligently with players and coaches. There can be no question that the game fascinated him. Throughout his life Wilson believed in struggle, and his major interest was human organization toward a clearly defined purpose. Of all sports, football apparently seemed to exemplify these qualities most clearly.

At the time of Wilson's election to the presidency of Princeton, a classmate, Albert Wylly, gave a reporter his remembrance of Wilson as an undergraduate: "I knew him well . . . He was a popular man among his classmates and the college at large. Straightforward, honest, earnest and fairminded, he was the admiration of all. His cool judgment was often appealed to in matters of importance among the students." Although contemporary records corroborate this judgment, there is also evidence to suggest that during Wilson's last year in college there was a mild reaction against him.[55]

About a fortnight after the college meeting that elected Wilson president of the Base Ball Association and accepted his scheme for choosing *Princetonian* editors, the class of 1879 held elections, both for permanent officers and for various positions at Commencement. There were twenty-four positions to be filled, yet Wilson was elected to none of them.

As some of the passages quoted from Wilson's pieces in the *Princetonian* show, he had a caustic pen and did not hesitate to use it. That he made enemies is apparent from the fact that on two or three occasions he was obliged to explain that he had not meant to cause offense.

At least two of his classmates wondered how it was that this quiet, unobtrusive person had gained such a position of influence and respect. Had he been playing a game—had it all been a preconceived scheme to gain a position on his own terms? One man argued that from the first Wilson chose his friends with an eye to preferment:

In our freshman year owing to a certain accident I sat next to him in College Chapel. When I entered college, I was a raw country lad under 16 years of age. I could then be of no use to him and according to my recollection he never spoke to me or recognized me in any way, although I daily sat next to him for several months . . . During his college course he was rather exclusive in his associations. He went mainly, first with those few who were interested in his specialty, and secondly with certain wealthy and rather sporting men whom we called the T.C. crowd and who were very influential in guiding the policy of the class and in certain more general college matters.[56]

Whether Wilson deliberately chose his friends to advance himself remains debatable; the available evidence suggests that it was simply a matter of propinquity and common interest. Yet there is no doubt that he belonged to the group most influential in class affairs. Of the twenty-four class officers, no less than fourteen were chosen from the nineteen men who belonged to the Witherspoon Gang, the Liberal Debating Club, or the Alligators. Resentment against this apparent domination of the class by a clique may have been directed against Wilson as perhaps the most prominent and most vocal.[57]

On at least one public appearance Wilson was ridiculed. The occasion was an exercise called "Chapel Stage"—a series of Saturday meetings in the college chapel, in the course of which each senior was required to make a speech. Wilson had been crusading against Chapel Stage in the pages of the *Princetonian,* to no avail. When it came his turn, the title of his address was "Richard Cobden—An Historical Lesson." His first words, "Richard Cobden needs no introduction to an intelligent audience," tickled the easy risibilities of his fellow students so that they laughed and cheered and clapped. Wilson's phrase became common currency, and at graduation he was mentioned as "Tommy Wilson, our model statesman . . . who . . . like Richard Cobden needs no introduction to an intelligent audience." In the pages of the *Princetonian* Wilson had set himself against rowdyism at public gatherings, and he could not have enjoyed being the victim of such behavior, especially since it occurred at an exercise he considered silly.[58]

As graduation approached, it became clear that a mediocre academic record and lack of recognition by his classmates would give Wilson a small part in the ceremonies. He and his friends could not conceal their disappointment. The highest position was Valedictorian, an honor awarded by the faculty. The Valedictorian of '79 was William F. Magie, later a professor of physics and dean at Princeton, who stood second in the class. One day Wilson's friend Robert Bridges met Magie and walked along with him, obviously morose about something. Finally he burst out, "Wilson ought to have had it." Wilson's disappointment reached the pages of the *Princetonian.* In the issue of February 13, 1879, he stated that of course the Valedictorian should be someone high in studies (there is a suggestion here of backing down from a previous position) but that the number of orations at graduation should be cut to ten—five to go to men receiving honors in their studies, and five to "men distinguished for writing or elocution." That Wilson felt he would certainly be included in the latter category is shown by a piece of self-revelation that appeared in the *Princetonian* two weeks later:

> It is common matter of everyday talk among the students themselves, that, under the forms and methods of education which obtain among American educational institutions, there is always found to be a set of men in each class which pursues the "classical" curriculum who stand below

the honor list and are yet among the brightest men of their class. They devote much of their time to outside reading; to study whose field lies without the course to the work of literary societies; or the acquirement of skill in writing, speaking, and debate. In order to pursue such a course they partially neglect some of the regular studies which are required of them, and thus, while winning and holding a creditable stand in their classes fail to carry off any College honors for scholarship. These men are not infrequently hard and conscientious workers. They are often men who are sure to do their life work well and bring honor upon their College. They are preparing themselves, amidst the varied requirements of a general classical course, for the special work that awaits them after graduation. And this work of theirs certainly deserves some recognition by the faculty.

This passage shows a naïve attitude toward the faculty, who are asked to recognize the futility of their own endeavors to educate their charges and to honor one who has deliberately not done his best at the tasks they set. It shows Wilson wanting to eat his cake and have it too: after neglecting his studies for larger ultimate returns, he wants to share in the traditional rewards reserved for those who have faithfully followed the prescribed course.[59]

The best-known story about Wilson's last months at Princeton concerns a competition in Whig Hall to determine which speakers should represent the society against its rival Clio in the Lynde Debate, which took place at Commencement. Winning the Lynde Debate was a matter of intense pride to members of the two societies, and the two men judged best speakers received prizes of $125 and $100. According to the story, which was based on Wilson's own recollection, after he had entered his name for the preliminary debate, he found that he had been chosen by lot to argue for a protective tariff for the United States rather than for free trade. Thereupon he withdrew, protesting, "No—never! First, last, and forever I'm a free trader. Nothing under Heaven will make me argue for a principle I do not believe."[60]

Wilson's biographers have moralized about this story. William Allen White took a critical view, arguing that "he never remotely realized the obligation to play out the game which was implied when he put the hand in the hat. The feeling of the society, left unprotected by his withdrawal, he did not understand. Nor did the desire of some other boy for a favorite side in the debate ever get to him." Ray Stannard Baker argued in defense:

By his decision not to enter the preliminaries, young Wilson probably lost a prize that he might, in the judgment of his fellows, easily have won; and he lost not only for himself but for the Hall.

Was he right? Though this was a mere college contest, yet it involved issues often raised at later times in his career. Which was the more important, a man's personal convictions—his intellectual integrity—or his obligations to his friends, the group? Is winning the important thing?

It may be said that this was only a kind of college game, and that he need not have been so squeamish; but to Wilson, with his high aspirations and his intense convictions, to argue for a cause in which he utterly disbelieved was intolerable.[61]

After so much has been written about this dramatic event, it is rather sad to report that Whig records cast doubt upon it. In the first place, Wilson was not "in the judgment of his fellows likely to win easily." He had not been particularly successful in debates against members of his own hall, let alone the best speakers from Clio. Second, the records show that the topic for debate was not "Free Trade vs. Tariff for Protection" but "*Resolved*: That it would be advantageous to the United States to abolish universal suffrage." The Whig historian, Jacob N. Beam, commented as follows:

It seems likely that if Wilson withdrew he must have withdrawn from the negative side, for after his withdrawal there was an uneven number of debaters (four arguing for the affirmative and three for the negative) . . . If he was the only one that withdrew it is obvious, therefore, that he withdrew from the negative side and if he withdrew as a matter of principle he must have been unwilling to defend universal suffrage, which may have meant that nine years after the passage of the Fifteenth Amendment he, a Southerner, could not defend Negro suffrage; or possibly, that he believed strongly in the restriction, in the English manner, of suffrage by property qualification.[62]

Recently discovered evidence entirely supports Beam's hypothesis. In March 1879 Wilson's father, apparently in response to a request for advice, wrote him: "Try for the 'Lynde Debate.' And you can try *best* by not having any anxiety as to whether you shall be chosen or not: for anxiety is partial paralysis." Apparently Wilson decided to compete but then had qualms because he did not find the subject of suffrage limitation interesting. Dr. Wilson was surprised because in his opinion it was of vital importance. "Either a limitation of suffrage," he wrote his son, "or anarchy in twenty-five years or sooner. I do not refer to Negroes any more than to the ignorant Northern voters." In this, as in other matters, Wilson wholly agreed with his father. In his journal he had called universal suffrage "the foundation of every evil in this country," and in an article, "Cabinet Government in the United States," he had just written of it as "a constant element of weakness," exposing us "to many dangers that we might otherwise escape." Why Wilson decided not to compete is revealed in a letter to him from Charles Talcott: "I am very sorry you were unfortunate in drawing: arguing against settled convictions, in my opinion, injures a man more than it benefits him." Thus, the recollection of Wilson's classmates, and of Wilson himself, about this incident were true in the essential fact: he refused to speak against his convictions. The substitution of the tariff for universal suffrage as the issue was natural, since he remained throughout his life a free trader, whereas his views on the suffrage changed.[63]

Wilson's withdrawal from the Lynde Debate trials, his failure to win class office, the ridicule he suffered when he spoke at Chapel Stage, and the pique displayed at his not gaining a place of prominence in the graduation exercises suggest that the sunset of his undergraduate career may have been somewhat clouded.

In mid-June 1879 Wilson's undergraduate years closed with three days of ceremonies. It was an age when audiences were far more patient than they are now. On one day alone—Class Day—there were three different gatherings, with six elaborate orations of various sorts, a reading from the class history, a poem, an ode, and eleven musical interludes. Wilson's only part in the proceedings was to deliver one of thirty "orations" given on another day, his topic being "Our Debt to England."

During the graduation ceremonies there was a much more unabashed expression of sentiment than is common today, and a more elaborate ritual. At the close of the Class Day ceremonies a wreath of rosebuds was torn apart, and each man took one. Some classmates kept those buds, gradually turning to dust, for the rest of their lives. After the ceremony they lingered long into the evening, singing and cheering. Shortly afterwards Wilson wrote his friend Charles Talcott: "Since Princeton I have not been in the brightest of moods. The parting after Commencement went harder than I had feared even. It most emphatically and literally *struck in.*"[65]

Wilson had reason to mourn the passing of his college years. His days had been full and happy, and he had achieved success. He had learned to deal with his fellows and had made at least a dozen friends of a lifetime. He had revealed a remarkable gift for promoting and organizing affairs. Although at the end they denied him class office, his classmates had called on him when they wanted something done effectively.

Wilson's personal success in the class of 1879 affected his future career. His was not only the largest class that had yet attended Princeton but also one with a peculiarly strong and continuing class feeling. Its members claimed that President McCosh said they were "the largest and finest class ever to attend me college." One of them admitted that they were "rather blatant" in insisting they were "the best class that

Princeton ever had," even to the extent of arousing resentment. A member of '78 wrote: " '79, Wilson's class, was peculiar. Overbearing, brushing everything and everybody else aside, they thought they were the only thing! They had their share of fine men. They had a group of wealthy men. But nothing must stand in their way!" A member of the class of 1880 had a similar recollection: "The class of '79 far outnumbered the class of '80 and exceeded it in wealth, social standing, and intellectual prowess. We put up a good fight against our competitors in foot-ball, rushes, and cane sprees. But otherwise, we were rather submerged, and we felt the depression of being second instead of first."[66]

The later influence of the class in Princeton affairs was in keeping with its size and spirit. With more than its share of men of great wealth, such as Cyrus McCormick, Cleveland Dodge, Cornelius C. Cuyler, and Edward Sheldon, it was one of the most generous classes in Princeton's history. On its tenth anniversary it hired Saint-Gaudens to do a statue of President McCosh; shortly after its twentieth it gave '79 Hall; on its thirtieth it gave the tigers that today flank the entrance to Nassau Hall; three years later, Cuyler Hall; and so forth. The class provided Princeton with six trustees, a number not exceeded by any other class until that of 1909. Certain of Wilson's classmates were instrumental in getting him back to Princeton as a professor; they put up funds to keep him in Princeton when other positions tempted him; they played a part in securing his election as President of Princeton; and after he left academic life, they contributed funds to advance him in politics.

On his part, Wilson's commitment to Princeton was profound. He corresponded with some of his classmates for the rest of his life and, as long as his affairs permitted, was a faithful attendant at class functions. He followed closely the fortunes of the teams. No sooner was he well launched on an academic career than he began to see what could be done to become a professor there, and once on the faculty, he passed up numerous opportunities to go elsewhere. When he was elected its President in 1902, his aim was to make Princeton the great university of which McCosh had dreamed.

The Study of Politics

His four years in college were years of wide and eager reading, but not years of systematic and disciplinary study. With singular, if not exemplary, self-confidence, he took his education into his own hands. He got at the heart of books through their spirit, it would seem, rather than through their grammar. He sought them out for what they could yield him in the way of thought rather than for what they could yield him in the way of exact scholarship. That this boy should have had such an appetite for the world's literature, old and new, need not surprise us. Other lads before and since have found big libraries all too small for them . . . They long for matter to expend themselves on: they will climb to any dizzy height from which an exciting prospect is promised: it is their joy by some means to see the world of men and affairs.

—Woodrow Wilson, on Edmund Burke, 1900[1]

THE ONLY aspect of Wilson's undergraduate career about which his father's letters to him frequently expressed anxiety was his relative neglect of the formal course of study at Princeton. He devoted so much time and energy to extracurricular activities and to his own reading that his academic record offered slight promise that he would later achieve fame as a scholar. In June of his freshman year he ranked near the bottom of the first quarter of his class. Thereafter he kept slipping, until at graduation he stood just below the top third: he was thirty-eighth of 105 men ranked.[2]

It has been suggested that one cause of Wilson's undistinguished college record was that he had been poorly prepared. "In general reading, in mental acumen, and in maturity," wrote Ray Stannard Baker, "he was far in advance of the ordinary student, but he was deficient in Greek roots and in mathematics." The records do not corroborate this statement. In point of fact Wilson ranked higher during the first two years, when he was obliged to study Greek, Latin, and mathematics—the subjects demanded for entrance—than he did later. In June of his freshman year he stood highest in these three subjects and lowest—strangely enough for the son of a minister—in Bible. He continued to study both Greek and Latin as electives after he was permitted to drop them at the end of his sophomore year. He sporadically kept up with Latin in later life and was a staunch defender of the value of a classical education.[3]

A detailed examination of Wilson's academic record—based on percentile rank, not on grades themselves—reveals that Wilson's gradual decline in class ranking did not mean a general slump in academic performance. On the contrary, in both junior and senior years he did very well in history, averaging in the first tenth in the class. He stood almost as high in various courses under the general heading of philosophy: during one semester he was third of the 120-odd students in Professor Atwater's course in logic, and second in President McCosh's course in psychology. If he had not been required to take science courses, he would have ranked higher during his upperclass years. Whether the subject was physics, chemistry, astronomy or anatomy, in science he was never above the middle of his class, and sometimes near the bottom.[4]

This record is consistent with Wilson's later career. To find history at the top is predictable, for Wilson, like others who have risen to political eminence—men as diverse as Napoleon and Harry Truman— found his schooling in the lessons of the past. His high standing in philosophy courses accords with his inveterate habit of generalizing. In later studies he was always seeking basic patterns, and a magnum opus that he projected but never finished was to have the title "The Philosophy of Politics." The strikingly low standing in science betrays other facets of his mind. The scientific method, insofar as it meant careful and meticulous accumulation of facts and caution in drawing conclusions, was never characteristic of Wilson's writings. His interests were wholly literary and political, and on at least one occasion—the Princeton Sesquicentennial Celebration in 1896—he expressed positive antipathy to both the influence and the methods of science.

Wilson had difficulty forcing himself to keep up from day to day in his college courses and in his diary he berated himself for wasted time. Like many of his classmates, he relied on cramming to get him through. This may have been an unfortunate result of the fact that his schooling started late and he never quite reconciled himself to performing set tasks, as witness this passage from his diary: "Studied review of Xenophon's Memorabilia for examinations all the afternoon and evening. Very stupid book. The book is not by any means stupid, but it is stupid

to read any book when you know that you are obliged to read it."
Wilson sometimes cut classes, and he had an antipathy to certain
teachers. In his diary he referred to one as "the jackass." He also
recorded an occasion when he deliberately defied authority. Called up
to recite in French class, he angered the professor by laughing. "He
reproved me so severely for so doing," Wilson wrote, "that I refused
to read any further, which made him still more provoked."[5]

The principal reason Wilson did not stand higher academically was
that his major energies were devoted to self-imposed tasks. When he
wrote the passage about Edmund Burke's college years that heads this
chapter, he came close to describing his own undergraduate career.
Although he gave less than his best to his courses, he worked unremit-
tingly and systematically when it came to acquiring a knowledge of
"the world of men and affairs" that would prepare him for political
leadership.

When describing the qualities of "the ideal statesman" in an address
delivered in Whig Hall during his sophomore year, Wilson argued that
no man had ever done anything worthy of note in the world except by
hard untiring work. He closed the speech with the words: "And let
me again remind you that it is only by working with an energy that
is almost superhuman and which looks to uninterested spectators like
insanity that we can accomplish anything worth the achievement. Work
is the keystone of the perfect life. Work and Trust in God."[6]

There is impressive evidence that Wilson tried to live up to this prescription for success. Throughout his time in college he read constantly,
both in term time and vacation. During the seven-month period when
he kept a daily record, he appears to have read Macaulay's entire
History of England, several of Macaulay's essays, a good deal of Pepys,
several plays of Shakespeare, Addison's Sir Roger de Coverley papers,
and a great deal else besides. At the same time he was working on an
Index Rerum, a commonplace book of quotations from readings, arranged alphabetically by topic. The first few headings suggest its
variety: "Addison's Essays," "Angels, battle of," "Aristotle (the Philosophy of)," "America, Burke on March 22, 1775," "Authors" [a list of
54 names, ancient and modern], "Bad Habits, How to break one's self
of", "Beauty," "British Empire," "Boccacio," and "Burke, Edmund."

Wilson's experience differed from what he wrote about Burke's
college years in that he did not find libraries "all too small" for him. To
be sure, he read Shakespeare and the English romantic poets and took
thirty volumes out of the Whig Hall library in a single year, but on
balance his reading was remarkable not so much for breadth as for
intensity. He later wrote his fiancée: "The man who reads everything

is like the man who eats everything: he can digest nothing; and the penalty for cramming one's mind with other men's thoughts is to have no thoughts of one's own. Only that which enables one to do his own thinking is of real value: which is my explanation of the fact that there are to be found in history so many great thinkers and great leaders who did little reading of books—if you reckon reading by volumes—but much reading of men and of their own times."[7]

In the same notebook in which he kept his journal Wilson noted year by year the principal books he had studied while in college. The catalog reveals a striking shift in emphasis from literature toward politics and history. Many of these books Wilson owned, since he had enough money to start building a personal library. Several of the volumes he acquired in college are now housed in the Library of Congress, and many are elaborately annotated with shorthand notes, commentary, and end-of-chapter summaries. Later Wilson urged Princeton students to make annotations, which, he said, "was like sharpening a weapon for use in the future: the rest of your life you would be surrounded by the carefully chosen and well-furnished arsenal of books."[8]

Wilson was also a close observer of the contemporary scene, as indicated by this rather smug comment on a *Nassau Literary Magazine* article entitled "Principles and Prospects of the Liberal Party in England": "For those who have not kept pace with the politics of modern England there is much of instruction and interest in this essay; for those who have carefully watched the progress of our kin beyond the sea it furnishes, of course, only an epitome of most familiar facts."[9]

Wilson's thorough, thoughtful study of selected books, plus constant reading of current magazines, bore fruit in his first published writings on history and political science. According to his own testimony, his later scholarly career simply "followed out the line of study which he planned when he was a student at Princeton." The direction in which he was heading is suggested by the titles of the major speeches and essays of his undergraduate years: "The Ideal Statesman" (Sophomore Oratorical Contest, American Whig Society, Jan. 30, 1877), "Thomas Carlyle" (oration, American Whig Society, Nov. 9, 1877), "Bismarck" (Junior Oratorical Contest, American Whig Society, Dec. 6, 1877), "Prince Bismarck" (essay, *Nassau Literary Magazine*, November 1878, signed "Atticus"), "William Earl Chatham" (prize essay, *Nassau Literary Magazine*, November 1878), "Our Debt to England" (Commencement oration, June 14, 1879), and "Cabinet Government in the United States" (essay, *International Review*, August 1879).[10]

Wilson's purpose in undertaking the study that lay behind these orations and essays appeared explictly in a "solemn covenant" made during his senior year with his classmate Charles Talcott, a fellow member of the Liberal Debating Club, who was later elected mayor of Utica, N.Y., and a member of Congress. According to Wilson, the two young men agreed "that we would school our powers and passions for the work of establishing the principles we held in common; that we would acquire knowledge that we might have power; and that we would drill ourselves in all the arts of persuasion, but especially in oratory . . . that we might have facility in leading others into our ways of thinking and enlisting them in our purposes."[11] Note that principles and political ambition are here inextricably combined. This was always a central element in Wilson's philosophy. Political aspiration must point toward the advancement of right principles rather than merely to office; political controversy must deal always with policies and never with personalities. The pages of the *Princetonian* during Wilson's editorship reveal these convictions, sometimes pushed to the point of absurdity, as when he appealed to "principle" in defending his criticism of an elocution teacher: "We were too severe in our strictures on a gentleman who has recently come among us as a private instructor in elocution. Our statements were overdrawn. We were attacking a principle and not a person,—the principle of unwisdom involved in getting any but the very highest talent at our command when instruction in any branch is desired." The same tactic appeared when he criticized the baseball team, referring in one issue to "the Base Ball doctrines which we have recently been upholding," and in another insisting, "Our quarrel is with principles, not with the men who represented them."[12]

If Wilson could feel so passionately about the organization of the baseball team that he elevated his opinions into "doctrines," it is obvious that he must have felt equally strongly about politics. What, then, were his political principles at this point in his life? Two issues on which the evidence is clear are sound money and the protective tariff. On both, his ideas came straight from the liberal economists. At Princeton he studied political economy under the Rev. Lyman H. Atwater, Professor of Logic and Moral and Political Science. Dr. Atwater believed almost as fervently in laissez-faire economics as in the Westminster Catechism. He considered it "the true science of human welfare," one in which "the ethical element is paramount," and one that laid down "principles which may not be disregarded." Although slow, solemn, and somewhat pompous in his swallowtail coat, Dr. Atwater was one of the most respected men on the faculty. He expressed himself clearly and wrote well. Wilson kept his notes on Atwater's lectures for many years.[13]

During the free-silver agitation that culminated in the Bland-Allison Act of 1878, Dr. Atwater presented at a college meeting "the many unanswerable arguments for the gold standard." "We most heartily thank him," wrote editor Wilson, "and must say there is now no excuse for any one among us entertaining such puerile theories upon finance as are now so shamefully present among the nation's representatives." Wilson remained so strongly devoted to sound money that in 1896 he supported the hopeless candidacy of the "Gold Democrat," John M. Palmer, rather than vote for Bryan and free silver.[14]

Repeatedly in later years Wilson revealed himself a free trader, and his first great legislative triumph as President was the Underwood-Simmons Act of 1913, which made the first general reduction in tariff schedules in over half a century. There is ample evidence that free trade was already part of his armory of political beliefs while he was at Princeton. He twice argued against protection in debates in Whig Hall and spoke in the college chapel in praise of that high priest of free trade, Richard Cobden.

As a public figure Woodrow Wilson was identified with democracy, but as a young man he did not include in his creed a faith either in democratic processes or in the wisdom of the popular will. His influence in undergraduate organizations, whether aimed at tighter discipline for the football and baseball teams, eliminating the selection of orators by vote of their classmates, or abolishing open elections of editors for the *Princetonian* and the *Nassau Literary Magazine,* was usually intended to reduce popular control in the interest of greater efficiency. During the debate over transferring the choice of editors from classmates to editorial boards those opposing the change attacked it as undemocratic. In answering these critics, Wilson indicated how tepid was his belief in democracy: "We would be loath to deny, in republican America, that democracy is a good thing; and yet an argument founded upon the democratic principle seems to us to be based on a pleasing sentiment rather than on reason."[15]

The first clause of the above quotation has the condescending tone that was characteristic of English travelers to America in the nineteenth century. Indeed, much that Wilson wrote as an undergraduate suggests the passionate Anglophile. In an ecstatic review of Green's *History of the English People* in the *Princetonian* he wrote: "It is a grateful thought that this History of the English People is a history of the American people as well; it is a high and solemn thought that we as a lusty strain of a noble race, are by our national history adding lustre or stain to so bright an escutcheon." We should build, he continued, on the principles of liberty perfected by nine centuries. His conclusion suggested that he had qualms about the American experiment: "How careful should we be that in this experiment of ours, in which sacred principles are stretched to their uttermost, the place of the Goddess of Liberty be not usurped by the Harlot. LICENSE."[16]

Wilson's intense admiration for all things British influenced his political creed. He did not need Dr. Atwater to tell him to be a free trader or a hard-money man because his identification with British liberalism made him accept these principles as axiomatic. In his attitude toward popular government he reflected his principal mentors, Edmund Burke and Walter Bagehot, both of whom distrusted pure democracy. Burke had defended the eighteenth-century British Parliament, rotten boroughs and all, and had been appalled by the French Revolution, even before the Terror. Bagehot, writing at a time when universal suffrage was in the offing, feared for England if the "numerous unwise" should ever cease to be "deferential." He hoped that the power of the ignorant multitude would be held in check by the "theatrical show" of court and aristocracy.

From his admiration of England Wilson gained the idea of a republic directed by a class of highly trained leaders, who would dedicate their lives to the public good. This was implicit in his "solemn covenant" with Charles Talcott and his organization of the Liberal Debating Club. It appears explicitly in an article he wrote for the *Princetonian* comparing English and American college education. At Oxford and Cambridge, he maintained, "the methods of education and instruction are such as promote individual development and encourage independent thought." They were "the great feeders for the two political parties. . . The young man who displays commanding talents is sure of an opening in public life." British youths therefore had a greater feeling than American ones that the future was in their hands. How could Princeton promote a situation in which "the educated young men of America" would become "as great a power in the state as are the educated young men of England?" In answer, Wilson presented ideas that would later be elaborated in two of his most famous speeches before his entrance into politics: "Princeton in the Nation's Service," 1896 and "Princeton for the Nation's Service," 1902.

Representing in her students, as she does, north, south, east and west, Princeton is eminently fitted to become a centre of political thought and a source from whence may flow influence to strengthen and purify our institutions. We are all too prone to think of national questions as of matters with which at present we have nothing to do, as of subjects which will properly come under our notice at some future time. If we do not grapple with these questions now, we will never do so, except at a disadvantage. If we are weak and careless thinkers now, we are but too apt always to remain such. *From early convictions spring mature power and well-advised action.* If we would all seek to study carefully each important question of national policy, and form an intelligent unprejudiced opinion thereon, future national policy would be materially affected by Princeton opinion.[17]

Wilson's early political principles are, on the whole, less well documented than his ideas about political leadership. He took principles for granted, as he did belief in the Calvinist God of his forefathers. He was endlessly preoccupied, however, with what made a stateman effective. His first published works of any importance were essays entitled "Prince Bismarck" and "William Earl Chatham," published in the *Nassau Literary Magazine* in November 1877 and October 1878. In both of these biographical sketches Wilson attempted to define what made the men great leaders. He found so many similar qualities that one can infer that he thought them universal attributes of successful statesman. First, a statesman must be bold. Of Bismarck he wrote, "with unmeasured energy and surprising power of concentration are combined the firmness, the quickness of resolve, and the ability for prompt action so necessary to leaders." He stated that Chatham was able to achieve so much, in a Parliament too nicely balanced between parties, only by "a few bold and rapid strokes." A statesman must be consumed by great purposes, acting for his country rather than himself. Bismarck's singleness of aim, "the extension and firm establishment of Prussian empire," concentrated his powers. Similarly, the warring elements in Chatham's complex character were "brought into harmony by the concentrating power of strong convictions." A further source of a leader's power is faith in himself. Bismarck foresaw Prussia's triumph partly because he "probably felt that in his own powers lay many bright possibilities." The elements of Chatham's power "lay almost entirely within himself." In neither essay is there any suggestion that a leader works *with* anyone: both Bismarck and Chatham—endowed with superior character, high purpose, and imperious will—simply dominated lesser men. "The British Parliament, the English nation, harkened with glad eagerness to the organ tones of Pitt's eloquence, and dared not disobey."[18]

These ideas were epitomized in two definitions of statesmanship in the essay on Chatham: "And certainly, if we conceive of statesmanship as being that resolute and vigorous advance towards the realization of high, definite, and consistent aims, which issues from the unreserved devotion of a strong intellect to the service of the state and to the multiform problems of high policy, Pitt's statesmanship was of a high order." And again: "His life drew rapidly toward its close; but he had done enough to set a seal to his fame—enough to mark *that* as the highest type of statesmanship which, with conscientious purity, by an undeviating course, with cool judgment and prompt determination, with a bright hope and a passionate patriotism, overpowering opposition, subordinating party to national interests, constantly and confidently seeks to build a great policy upon broad, deep, homogeneous principles."

In both essays Wilson so identified himself with his subjects that he condoned their faults. In the piece on Bismarck he described without condemnation the Chancellor's defiance of the Prussian Parliament, his use of war as an instrument of policy, and the rape of Alsace-Lorraine. He admitted that Bismarck's character was "not altogether free from the stain which intrigue invariably brings," that his firmness was "disfigured by harshness," and that he was unscrupulous in choice of means. Yet he found them hard to condemn:

> But our condemnation of Bismarck's occasional bad faith should be surrounded by many qualifications and explanations. We can never justify the wilful disregard of justice or the wilful breaking of faith. But in a man who is conscious of great powers, whose mind is teeming and overflowing with great political plans and dreaming of great national triumphs, and who, withal, is hampered on every side by almost every circumstance of his surroundings, we can at least understand an occasional breach of honor, and, in the presence of so many grand and peerless qualities and so many noble purposes, can perhaps forgive a want of integrity which so seldom exhibits itself. And even when uprightness is wanting in his purposes or in his choice of means, its place is filled by uncommon wisdom in action.

In spite of its pious gloss, this passage argues that the superior man of high purpose is not to be judged by ordinary morality. The idea that high purpose excuses faults of character is found again in the essay on "the great commoner," William Pitt, who became Earl Chatham. His "disfiguring arrogance and overbearing pride" were more easily forgiven than the egotism of "shrewd, fickle, brilliant, plausible Benjamin Disraeli" because Pitt devoted his life to higher ends: "In one respect Pitt resembled the now exalted Jew: he had an unhesitating, almost boundless confidence in himself, in the wisdom of his own aims. But Beaconsfield loves and has confidence in himself alone; Pitt loved and trusted the English people as well—for he was himself and Englishman."

Describing Pitt as "the first of parliamentary orators," Wilson wrote that his eloquence was characterized by "passion," which "is the pith of eloquence." But passion was not enough for "while it gives strength, it may be rugged and cumbersome . . . Imagination must be present to give it wings and graceful flight. And one of the most striking features of Pitt's mind was 'a poetic imaginativeness' which set his words fairly aglow with beauty." Even the most cursory reading of the essays on Bismarck and Chatham reveals that Wilson was attempting to develop such a style as he ascribed to Pitt. His effort was reflected in the occasional use of archaic or poetic terms, and in passages of purple prose, such as this:

A skillful sculptor might trace the lines of cunning policy and of secret scheming, the habitual air of authority upon the face of a Metternich, and would recognize the man himself in his effigy; he might chisel the marks of cruel purpose, of uncurbed and defiant ambition, of pitiless despotism upon the spare visage of a Richelieu, and we would wish for no better reminder of the man; he might preserve the deep-cut wrinkles that spoke of thought, the firmly-set mouth that indicated an inflexible determination, upon the open countenance of a Hampden; but the marble must have the warmth of life infused into it by the hand of God before it could resemble the dwelling of Chatham's high-wrought, passionate, many-sided nature.

In another passage Wilson played sedulous ape to Macaulay's use of balanced antithesis:

He was in everything enthusiastically earnest, and his age laughed at earnestness; he was vehement, and his age affected coldness and indifference; he was sternly virtuous, scorning corruption, and his age was sceptical of virtue, nursing corruption; he had eager, burning beliefs and was actuated by a warm love for principle, and his age delighted in doubtings and questionings, was guided by no principle save that of expediency; he was used constantly and confidently to appeal to the higher, brighter, purer instincts of human nature, and his age doubted the existence of any such instincts, nay, even argued from its own experience that all human nature was low and pulseless.

Such painful efforts to achieve a rhetorical, "literary" style were to bedevil Wilson's writing for many years, rendering such works as *George Washington* and *A History of the American People* almost unreadable today. It was fortunate that at the same time that he was developing a "style" he was also schooling himself in extempore speech, and that he had the discipline of the *Princetonian* to train him in a straightforward, less pretentious prose.

By far the most important example of Wilson's undergraduate writing was an article entitled "Cabinet Government in the United States," published in the *International Review* for August 1879. The editor of the magazine that gave him his first nationwide forum was Henry Cabot Lodge, who forty years later did his best to destroy Wilson politically. The article is a statement of ideas Wilson further developed in his first and best-known book, *Congressional Government*, and which he adapted to practical politics when Governor of New Jersey and President of the United States.[19]

An account of the genesis of the project is found in a draft of a letter Wilson wrote four years later to Professor William M. Sloane of Princeton:

> My reading in constitutional law and history had begun to widen about a year before I left Princeton and, though my college duties crowded system out of this extra course I had set myself, I had, before graduation, obtained, with Mr. Bagehot's aid, and by numerous more or less extended excursions into other writers of a like practical spirit, a pretty complete and accurate knowledge of the Eng. Constitution as it is. My appetite for the investigation was whetted by my admiration for certain Eng. statesmen and my desire to know more by the conditions of Parl.[iamentary] life; but, however whetted, it was made keener by partial satisfaction and finally demanded a comparative examination of our own constitution as it exists outside of the books and stripped of "the refinements of literary theory."

Presumably it was this "extra course" that led Wilson to resign his presidency of the Princeton baseball club: in November 1878 his mother wrote him, "Dear Tommy, if I were you, I would resign the Presidency of that Club—for the reasons you assign . . . You will be making a great mistake if you allow anything of the kind to stand in the way of doing your utmost in the direction of your future interests." In February he sent the completed article on cabinet government to his father, who returned it with high praise. Dr. Wilson thought the composition "neat, terse, manly, and sufficiently flowing," and advised his son not to tinker with it more. By April Lodge had accepted the article in a note that Dr. Wilson thought "very gratifying." [20]

In this first major article Wilson looks at the American political system and finds it bad. He opens with a gloomy picture:

> Our patriotism seems of late to have been exchanging its wonted tone of confident hope for one of desponding solicitude. Anxiety about the future of our institutions seems to be daily becoming stronger in the minds of thoughtful Americans. A feeling of uneasiness is undoubtedly prevalent, sometimes taking the shape of a fear that grave, perhaps radical, defects on our mode of government are militating against our liberty and posterity. A marked and alarming decline in statesmanship, a rule of levity and folly instead of wisdom and sober forethought in legislation, threaten to shake our trust not only in the men by whom our national policy is controlled, but also in the very principles upon which our government rests.

What is the principal cause of this unhappy situation? A growing minority, writes Wilson, agree with Dr. Woolsey, who argued that universal suffrage was at the root of the trouble. Theodore Dwight

Woolsey, a classicist and President of Yale, had published in 1877 a two-volume work entitled *Political Science, or The State Theoretically and Practically Considered,* which Wilson had purchased and annotated. In it Woolsey argued that universal suffrage was against "that maxim of English liberty, on which the American colonies insisted at the time of the revolution, that taxation and representation should go together." Furthermore, universal suffrage threatened property rights, liberty, and order, and failed to ensure government by the wisest men. In the opening paragraph of "Cabinet Government in the United States" Wilson repeats most of Woolsey's arguments and agrees that "universal suffrage is a constant element of weakness and exposes us to many dangers which we would otherwise escape." But those who have made it "the scapegoat of all our national grievances have made too superficial an analysis of the abuses about which they so loudly complain." [21]

The real cause of our troubles, writes Wilson, is "to be found in the absorption of all power by a legislature which is practically irresponsible for its acts," where power is fragmented among committees working almost in secret, with the result that Americans are in effect living under a despotism. The leaders of Congress are irresponsible because they do not operate in the full light of public opinion and open debate. Thus, the legislation they hatch in the dark is the product of "party trickery and legislative jobbery," or at best only "a limping compromise between the conflicting interests of the innumerable localities represented." The men attracted to this sordid business are "scheming, incompetent, political tradesmen whose aims and ambitions are merely personal."

As a cure for this situation Wilson proposes that cabinet members sit in Congress with the right to participate in debate and committee work. He assumes as a corollary that they would remain in office only so long as they commanded the support of Congress. If the legislation they proposed was voted down, they would be bound to resign, "and resignation upon defeat is the essence of responsible government." Eventually the country would realize that the President should select his cabinet directly from Congress itself, and then the United States would have full-fledged, responsible cabinet government.

Wilson admits that if Congress was controlled by the opposing party, the President would have to choose political opponents as advisers, but he answers that at present his cabinet may be composed "of political friends who are compelled to act in all matters of importance according to the dictation of Standing Committees which are ruled by the opposite party." In other words, the executive is already under the domination of a legislature that has absorbed all power. According to Wilson, the strongest man in the federal government, in peacetime at least, is the Speaker of the House, who is the chief political huckster, channeling legislation into the dark recesses of committee rooms and suppressing rather than directing open debate on public policy.

Wilson predicts several benefits from his proposals. First, "under the conditions of Cabinet government . . . full and free debates would serve to enlighten public opinion." No important measure would be passed until all its details had been "discussed and rediscussed, until all its essential, all its accidental features, and all its remotest tendencies had been dinned into the public ear, so that no man in the nation could have pretended ignorance of its meaning and object." Legislation under cabinet government would be based on coherent principles in the national interest instead of on secret bargaining between special interests. There would be strict party discipline because parties would stand or fall on the policies they openly espoused. Above all, American political life would attract a higher type: "broad-minded, masterful statesmen, whose sympathies and purposes are patriotic and national" and who "won the foremost places in their party by display of administrative talents, by evidence of high ability upon the floor of Congress in the stormy play of debate."

"Cabinet Government in the United States" offers clear evidence that, however Wilson might identify himself with the South, he was no devotee of either sectionalism or states' rights. He stresses national over local interests and scorns those who would sound "the alarm bell of *centralization*" against his proposal to provide more powerful executive leadership. He hopes that his proposals will bring into the federal government "worthy successors of Hamilton and Webster"—a choice of heroes that bears out his later statement to Albert Bushnell Hart, "Ever since I have had independent judgments of my own I have been a Federalist."[22]

As Wilson's letter to Professor Sloane shows, Wilson readily admitted a debt to Walter Bagehot's famous work *The English Constitution*, first published in 1867 and revised in 1872. It is nevertheless extraordinary to discover how complete was his dependence upon Bagehot at the time he wrote "Cabinet Government in the United States." In *The English Constitution* Bagehot attempted to describe the British government as it actually worked. According to his findings "the latent essence and effectual secret of the English Constitution" was fusion of the legislative and executive functions. This he contrasted to the erroneous "literary theory" of checks and balances and separation of powers. The peculiar virtues he found in the British system are exactly those that

Wilson wants to import through the introduction of "cabinet government"—namely, open debate informing and eliciting the opinion of the nation, careful scrutiny of legislation, party discipline based on coherent programs, and government by a trained and responsible elite.[23]

Bagehot repeatedly compared the "presidential" system of America unfavorably with the British parliamentary system. The Americans, he claimed, had no less genius for government than the English, and no less respect for law. The trouble was in their wretched Constitution, so badly framed that American politicians and constitutional lawyers were like "trustees carrying out a misdrawn will." Every one of his major criticisms of American practice is repeated by Wilson in "Cabinet Government in the United States." That Wilson saw the American Constitution through the eyes of Bagehot can be illustrated by parallel quotations, taken almost at random:

Walter Bagehot, *The English Constitution*	Woodrow Wilson, "Cabinet Government in the United States"
A ministerial government . . . is carried on in the face of day. Its life is in debate.	. . . *debate* is the essential function of a popular representative body.
The efficient secret of the English Constitution may be described as the close union, the nearly complete fusion, of the executive and legislative powers.	A complete separation of the executive and legislative is not in accord with the true spirit of those essentially English institutions of which our government is a characteristic offshoot.
The Presidential Government, by its nature, divides political life into two halves, an executive half and a legislative half; and, by so dividing it, makes neither half worth a man's having—worth his making a continuous career—worthy to absorb, as Cabinet government absorbs, his whole soul.	The President can seldom make himself recognized as a leader; he is merely the executor of the sovereign legislative will; his Cabinet officers are little more than chief clerks . . . The most ambitious Representative can rise no higher than the Chairmanship of the Ways and Means Committee or the Speakership of the House. The cardinal feature of Cabinet government, on the other hand, is responsible leadership . . . None but the ablest can become masters in this keen tournament in which arguments are the weapons, and the people the judges.[24]

One could continue these comparisons. Bagehot found the characteristic evil of American practice most apparent in legislation involving taxation and currency; so does Wilson. Bagehot ignored or minimized the great independent powers of the presidency; so does Wilson. Bagehot had no fear of concentration of power in a single body; nor does Wilson. The dependence on Bagehot extends even to style. Although Wilson's essays on Burke and Chatham were marred by over-elaborate verbiage in an effort to be "literary," in this essay the writing, imitative of Bagehot, is direct, relatively unadorned, and epigrammatic.[25]

Wilson's specific suggestion for a change in American practice—giving cabinet members seats in the legislature—was not found in the pages of Bagehot, but neither was it original. It had been one feature of the constitution of the Confederacy. Gamaliel Bradford in the pages of the *Nation,* a periodical that Wilson started reading as a boy, had advocated the idea of putting cabinet members on the floor of Congress as early as 1873, for the specific purpose of curing the abuses that Wilson later described in "Cabinet Government in the United States." In the actual description of the ills of Congress Wilson does little more than paraphrase Bradford's articles. Early in 1879 Senator Pendleton of Ohio had introduced a bill to give cabinet members seats in both houses with the privilege of debate and attendance at committee meetings.[26]

Wilson did not swallow and regurgitate other men's ideas without adding something of his own. Where he differed in emphasis from Bagehot and Bradford was in the importance he placed on the role of the parliamentary system in developing leadership and in attracting better men to public office. For Bagehot this was only one of several counts on which he preferred the British system; he was even a bit skeptical of *too much* ability in Parliament. The development of a better class of leaders was incidental to Bradford's arguments. But for Wilson it was central. "The most despotic of governments," he asserts, "under the control of wise statesmen is preferable to the freest ruled by demagogues." (This, incidentally, explains why he could stomach Bismarck.) Nearly a quarter of the text of "Cabinet Government in the United States" is devoted specifically to ways in which the adoption of the parliamentary system would elevate the caliber of American political leadership. As in the essay on Chatham, leadership is constantly tied to the enunciation of high principle. In dealing with the American party system, he states:

The two great national parties . . . are dying for want of unifying and vitalizing principle. Without leaders, they are also without policies, without aims. With leaders there must be followers, there must be parties. And with leaders whose leadership was earned in an open war of principle against principle, by the triumph of one opinion over all opposing opinions, parties must from the necessities of the case have definite policies. Platforms then must mean something. Broken promises then will end in broken power . . . Eight words contain the sum of the present degradation of our political parties: *No leaders, no principles; no principles, no parties.*

The main theme of Wilson's disquisition is that a parliamentary system in the United States would offer a career to men who combined dedication to the public service, knowledge of affairs, and skill in debate. Under such a system debate would be a channel to preferment: "To each member of the assembly every debate offers an opportunity for placing himself, by able argument, in a position to command a place in any future Cabinet that may be formed from the ranks of his own party; each speech goes to the building up (or the tearing down) of his own fortunes." Parties would be forced to enlist the ablest men: "And if party success in Congress—the ruling body of the nation—depends upon power in debate, skill and prescience in policy, successful defense of or attacks on ruling ministries, how ill can contending parties spare their men of ability from Congress!" Parliamentary government would of itself create an elite: "Drill in debate, by giving scope to talents, invites talents; raises up a race of men habituated to the methods of public business, skilled parliamentary chiefs. And, more than this, it creates a much-to-be-desired class who early make attendance upon public affairs the business of their lives, devoting to the service of their country all their better years."

Compare these passages with his early ambition to be a Gladstone, with his constant effort to acquire skill in extempore debate, with his intensive study of politics, with his leadership in undergraduate affairs, with his "solemn covenant" with Charles Talcott, and one conclusion becomes irresistible: that Wilson proposed such changes in the structure of the government of the United States as would provide an outlet for his special talents and a field where he might realize his high ambitions. He was in effect demanding that the entire American political system be radically altered so that he might realize his aspirations for public office and public service.[27]

During the summer after his graduation from Princeton Wilson occupied his time by writing an ambitious essay entitled "Self-Government in France." In September 1879 he sent it off to the *North American Review,* which refused it, as did others, so that the article never saw print until 1966, when it appeared in the first volume of *The Papers of Woodrow Wilson.* In some ways it is a more impressive performance than "Cabinet Government in the United States." Wilson had in effect been preparing to write the cabinet article for a number of years through his intensive study of British politics. Two years before he had proposed a similar scheme to the Liberal Debating Club. Thus, the article was the fruit of a long gestation, whereas the one on France appears to have been the fruit of ad hoc reading. Yet the later article is every bit as good as the first. It is based on solid reading, although entirely in sources written in English or in translation, and it is written in a straightforward style, unmarred by mannerisms or rhetorical effects. Perhaps the reason it failed to find a publisher was its extreme length: it is over 11,000 words long, half again as long as "Cabinet Government in the United States."[28]

In "Self-Government in France" Wilson attempts to assess the chances of survival of the Third Republic, then reaching the end of its first troubled decade. In the course of the analysis he reveals familiarity with both French history and the contemporary scene. As might be expected, he claims that the Englishman is a far superior political animal to the Frenchman. The Englishman "has grown old and therefore self-controlled in the exercise and defence of his liberties; while, on the other hand, all the weight of the past serves to drag the Frenchman down. He has been born and nurtured in servitude." Habits of thought and action have carried over from the old regime so that the political history of France since the Revolution "has been little more than a record of the alternation of centralized democracy with centralized monarchy, or imperialism—in all cases of a virtual despotism."

In dealing with the tradition of centralization in France, Wilson quotes the remark of a recent premier, Jules Simon, expressing opposition to the choice of the mayor of Paris by a local election: "An elected mayor at the head of a city of two millions of inhabitants could neither be subject to a King nor subordinate to a President." Wilson astutely remarks that if this is true, "France is not ripe for self-government; if it is not true, how can we hope to see France wisely and liberally ruled while her most enlightened statesmen are thus ignorant of the true principles and methods of true political liberty, thus blinded by the instincts of despotism."

Other elements that put the Third Republic into jeopardy are the nature of French society and the latent opposition of the Church. The bourgeoisie think only of private gain, and their first and only loyalty is to their families: they do not, like Englishmen or Americans, have "a constant eye for public business." The peasants are independent, thrifty, and pro-republican, but appallingly provincial and ignorant. The Church has lost hold of the minds of men but is still strong enough to head off schemes of universal education that are necessary to the formation of an enlightened citizenry. Wilson concludes that with all its handicaps the Third Republic has a chance of survival if the French people would learn that freedom depends on order: they must learn to "cherish the liberty of self-imposed obedience" rather than "license and violence."

"Self-Government in France" marked an important advance in Wilson's intellectual development. Hitherto his major orations and essays had concerned Anglo-American politics or political leadership—both topics in which his own personal ambitions were involved. Now for the first time he devoted full attention to an important political problem quite outside his usual frame of reference. He succeeded in reaching tenable conclusions and presenting them in such a fashion that even today his essay is highly readable—which cannot be said of much that he wrote both before and afterward. The study that went into the article later served Wilson well. The contrast between English and French politics was a recurrent theme in his writings, and the problem of how a nation without a tradition of self-government could achieve democracy was one to which he continued to address himself. This essay on France reveals how it was that Wilson was able to achieve eminence as a political scientist after he had abandoned hope of becoming a statesman.

IV

The Study of Law

1879–1881

The profession I chose was politics; the profession I entered was the law. I entered the one because I thought it would lead to the other. It was once the sure road; and Congress is still full of lawyers.

—Woodrow Wilson, 1883[1]

WHILE AN undergraduate at Princeton, Wilson had inscribed several calling cards: THOMAS WOODROW WILSON SENATOR FROM VIRGINIA. His daydream is not surprising. The Senate, after all, was still a debating body, where an individual orator could make an impact on the members, as well as on the country at large. And Wilson idealized the state where he had been born. He wished he could call himself a true Virginian, and he fully accepted the myth of the cultured, chivalrous, public-spirited, planter aristocracy as the closest American counterpart to the governing elite of Britain.[2]

It was thus with a dream of joining the long line of Virginia statesmen that Wilson entered the law school of the University of Virginia in October 1879. He saw the law as an avenue to politics, and the university as a means of identifying himself with the Old Dominion by something more than accident of birth. There were other practical considerations. Although his family was able to provide amply for his education, they could not support him indefinitely. Business never tempted him, nor—to his father's intense disappointment—was he drawn to the pulpit. The law represented an obvious means of livelihood as well as a stepping-stone to higher pursuits.

The University of Virginia had much to offer Wilson. Many of his fellow students were young men of high promise and serious purpose; several later achieved eminence. The atmosphere was more conducive to serious study than that at Princeton, and the instruction in law equaled any in the United States.

Even a casual visitor to the University of Virginia soon realizes that the spirit of Thomas Jefferson, its founder, broods over it. At the center is his architectural masterpiece, a complex of brick buildings arranged symmetrically around a rectangular greensward, the "lawn." The philosophy of the institution also embodies Jefferson's central principle—freedom. In Wilson's time the liberty enjoyed by the students was unique. Religious services, for instance, were entirely voluntary. There was even more freedom of choice in courses than at Harvard, which had recently made headlines by introducing the elective system. According to the university catalogue: "In establishing the University of Virginia, Mr. Jefferson for the first time in America, threw open the doors of the University in the true sense of the name . . . allowing students to select for themselves the departments to which they are led by their special tastes and proposed pursuits in life." In practice this meant that a student might enter at any level for which he thought himself prepared, that he might take three courses or seven, and that he might study liberal arts and medicine simultaneously, or attempt to cram two years of the study of law into one.[3]

The students at Virginia were neither kept under constant surveillance nor plagued by petty restrictions. Even existing parietal regulations, such as the prohibitions of guns and dogs, were so little enforced that a "man, if he chose, could have a whole battery of artillery in his room, and keep an entire pack of hounds, without being molested." The authorities simply expected students to behave like gentlemen and scholars. A remarkable manifestation of this trust was the honor system. There was no proctoring of examinations, no questioning a man's word that a piece of work was his own. Instead, the students pledged that they had neither given nor received assistance. Those accused of breaking their word were tried by a student court; if found guilty, they were usually forced to resign from the university. The honor system extended to any action involving the good name of the college, such as plagiarism in the college magazine.[4]

The success of the honor system was remarkable in the light of the fact that academic standards at Virginia were high and rigid, sometimes to the point of unreasonableness. The proportion of failures in a single course sometimes ran as high as eighty or ninety per cent. The result was that students worked hard. An article in the *Virginia University Magazine* for October 1880, entitled "We Study Too Much," warned that no one can enjoy the legitimate rewards of life "when his head is aching, or swimming with vertigo, or when he has become so dyspeptic that he can retain nothing on his stomach." After painting a horrifying picture of Virginia students ruining their health, the author suggested that no one need study more than ten hours a day. A reasonable program, allowing time for recreation, might go like this: "From seven to eight, dress and take breakfast; from eight to two, study; from two to half past three, dinner and conversation with friends; from half past three to five, English literature; from five to six, take exercise in the gymnasium or otherwise; from six to seven, supper and conversation; from seven to eleven, study; from eleven to seven, sleep."[5]

Of the 328 students in the university at the time of Wilson's matriculations, all but twelve came from the former slave states. There was little wealth in the post-bellum South; thus, most of these young men had limited financial resources. Although the authorities were worried by a few who showed a tendency to "silliness, extravagance, and dissipation," most students went to Virginia not to play but to better themselves, which contributed to the atmosphere of serious study.

The academic pressure discouraged extracurricular activities. Virginia students professed to scorn Harvard, Yale, and Princeton, where the undergraduates wasted their time in puerile amusements. Although there was a gymnasium, a boat club, and a fall track meet, organized baseball and football had not yet appeared, nor had regular competition of any sort with other colleges. There were no college songs or cheers. Two literary societies, named after Washington and Jefferson, were provided rooms by the college, but they were not so flourishing as Whig and Clio at Princeton. The Washington Society, in fact, was moribund. In addition to staging debates, "Wash" and "Jeff" published a monthly, the *Virginia University Magazine*, but there was no newspaper and no yearbook. The most active student organizations were sixteen fraternities, known as clubs, none of which owned a house or served meals. They met only once every week or two in rented rooms and held an occasional banquet.

At Virginia no social distinctions separated men in different years or different courses of study. Students of every sort, from sixteen-year-old matriculees in the academic department to twenty-five-year-olds in the medical and law schools, were on terms of complete equality. The younger men matured more rapidly than at colleges where they were hazed and forced to wear freshman caps. Nevertheless, a number of alumni feared that the lack of ritual and of identity with classmates inhibited the development of college spirit and of alumni loyalty.

Living conditions at the university were Spartan, and the food was poor. Yet this was true elsewhere in the post-bellum South. The great fact about the University of Virginia was that the intellectual fare was of superior quality, and the caliber of the faculty high.[6]

Although a Board of Visitors, responsible to the state legislature, exercised general control over the university, the faculty enjoyed a high degree of autonomy and were proud of their prerogatives. A chairman of the faculty, elected annually, presided at meetings but had no special powers. There was no president and no dean. Although the system was wasteful of time and resulted in inefficient administration, it was defended on the ground that "each professor, feeling that he is a constituent element of the governing body, with his proper share of influence in shaping its destiny and fortunes, is animated by a sense of duty, of responsibility, and of ambition, to devote his utmost powers of thought, care, and assiduous effort to augment its usefulness and prosperity."[7]

Faculty democracy was sacrificed to efficiency in 1904 when a president was appointed; later there appeared a full panoply of deans. According to Professor R. Heath Dabney, who had a lifetime connection with the university, this resulted in a decline both of academic standards and of respect for the faculty. There is no doubt that in Wilson's time the professors held the respect of the students. Disorders such as those that occurred at Princeton, even in President McCosh's classes, were unknown. There was a good deal of personal contact between students and teachers, fostered by Jefferson's design for the university, in which faculty apartments or "pavilions" were placed among the "ranges" of student rooms. When Woodrow Wilson was President of Princeton, his most cherished and controversial project was to divide the college into residential quadrangles where older and younger students would live together in close touch with members of the faculty. That this idea was partly inspired by his experience at Virginia is revealed by this passage from a speech in defense of his Quad Plan, delivered before the University Club of Chicago in 1908:

Why, I remember distinctly when I left Princeton and went to the University of Virginia, I went to a place by no means organized as I thought it ought to be organized, but so geometrically constituted that we were daily in contact with some of the most celebrated men in the faculty of the university. I shall never forget the influence upon me of merely passing every day of my life one of the most distinguished scholars in America and exchanging a few words with him and feeling that I was a campus comrade of his. Upon my intellectual maturity, merely to know that this man who [when he talked] upon certain topics, could hold the attention of the world was my daily comrade, gave me some conception of what a university was for, an idea I never got at Princeton.[8]

The hero in question was undoubtedly Professor John B. Minor, one of the two professors in law, who served the University of Virginia for half a century and drew pupils from all over the South. At the time of his death in 1895 his former students included the two Senators from

Virginia, two members of Cleveland's cabinet, and a justice of the Supreme Court. Minor's *Institutes of Common and Statute Law*, a 5,000-page work, went through several editions and was a vade mecum for the practicing lawyer. Wilson's carefully annotated set, now in the Library of Congress, was part of his personal library at the time of his death. In the opinion of John Bassett Moore, an authority on international law and a contemporary of Wilson's at Virginia, "Professor Minor was one of the greatest teachers that ever lived. He was a profound student of the common law, and he expounded it with unsurpassed clarity. He was also a man of most impressive appearance, and his students regarded him with profound respect as well as gratitude."[9]

An exacting taskmaster, Minor insisted that students should think about what they studied: "Thought is requisite as well as reading; for the purpose of thought, there must be time to *Digest*, as well as the *Industry* to acquire. One cannot expect to gorge himself with law as a Boa Constrictor does with masses of food, and then digest it afterwards; the process of assimilation must go on, if it is to proceed healthfully and beneficially at the same time with the reception of knowledge. So the athlete judges who wishes to train the physical man to the most vigorous development, and the intellectual athlete cannot do better than imitate the example." Minor demanded unremitting attention in class as well as industry outside it. He had no patience with parrot-like repetition of the textbook and insisted that the answers to his questions be both original and concise. In assessing written work, Minor was equally severe. "He calculated," wrote one of his students, "to a hair's breadth the answers to examination questions, but woe to the student that missed that hair's breadth, no class standing, no nothing could save him."[10]

Outside the classroom Minor was approachable and kindly. His office was always open to those needing advice or assistance, and out of his slender means he often helped poor students pay their bills. On Sundays he usually asked a crowd of young men, whether or not in the law school, to supper at his "pavilion" on the East Lawn, followed by the singing of familiar hymns. Young women helped to make these Sunday evenings "very pleasant social oases in a desert of work." Woodrow Wilson was one of those who enjoyed these oases.[11]

"Thos. Woodrow Wilson," as he signed himself, matriculated at Virginia on October 2, 1879, subscribing to a statement that he entered the institution with "a serious desire to reap the benefit of its instruction and with a determined resolution to conform to its laws." He took up rooms in Dawson's Row, a line of bleak brick dormitories, since torn

down, away from the center of the university. As at Princeton, he was
apparently better off than most students. Whereas some "messes" at the
University of Virginia charged only eleven dollars a week for food and
some boarding houses charged fifteen dollars, Wilson paid eighteen
dollars—the highest price anywhere—to board at a Mrs. Massie's.

At Princeton Wilson had relegated studies to a subordinate place,
but at Virginia he was forced to buckle down. Three months after his
arrival he complained to his Princeton classmate Charles Talcott:

> The Law is indeed a hard task-master. I am struggling hopefully but
> with not *over*-much courage, through its intricacies, and am swallowing
> the vast mass of its technicalities with as good a grace and as straight a
> face as an offended palate will allow. I have, of course, no idea of aban-
> doning this study because of a few unpleasant features . . . Still one
> may be permitted an occasional complaint, if for no other purpose than
> to relieve his feelings. To relieve my feelings, therefore, I wish now to
> record the confessions that I am most horribly bored by the noble study
> of Law sometimes, though in the main I am thoroughly satisfied with
> my choice of a profession . . . This excellent thing, the Law, gets as
> monotonous as that other immortal article of food, Hash, when served
> with such endless frequency.[12]

Prolonged exposure did not make the work palatable. In May 1880
he again wrote Talcott that the year was drawing to "a tedious close."
The work, he wrote, "has been unremitting, affording only the smallest
scraps of leisure, and the fewest opportunities for the perusal of anything but law, law, law." Wilson's dislike of his legal studies did not
extend to John B. Minor. "I cannot," he wrote, "sufficiently admire
Professor Minor's methods of instruction; and I try to appreciate my
advantages in spite of other things which are less admirable."[13]

Wilson's academic record at Virginia, as at Princeton, was no more
than satisfactory. In June 1880 he was reported to the faculty as one of
fifteen students who had incurred too many "delinquencies" (absences
from class), for which he was to be admonished by his professors. He
was not among the thirteen students who received "distinction" in the
first-year course in Constitutional and International Law or the twenty-
four honored for superior performance in Mercantile Law, Evidence,
and Equity, but was judged merely "proficient" in both. This was
nevertheless an achievement, for many of the seventy-nine students
who had matriculated in October had failed or withdrawn.[14]

Wilson at first complained to his parents that he found no congenial
companions, and he wrote his friends Charles Talcott and Robert
Bridges that there was no college life at Virginia to compare with the
life at Princeton; the university was "simply a place where men happen
to have congregated for study and nothing else." Yet other evidence

shows that Wilson made several warm friends and that the pattern of his life resembled his career at Princeton: in both institutions he achieved his principal eminence in extracurricular activities rather than in studies. The difference at Virginia was merely one of emphasis, because he had to put studies first in order to survive and there were fewer "sideshows" in which to perform. Another difference was that he entered Princeton as an unknown, but at Virginia he was noted from the first. Sixty years later his collegemates remembered his maturity and poise. "Although he was not much older than I . . . I looked up to him as an older brother," wrote one of them. According to another, "In appearance he was striking, tall, slim, quick in action, carried himself well. His face was not handsome, about as much so as Abraham Lincoln's, his expression was fine, illuminating as it changed with his thoughts." Still another reached a point of irritation because his roommate "so frequently and eloquently commended Wilson." Yet some men tempered their admiration with recollections that Wilson seemed aloof and self-centered. One wrote: "Coming from Princeton as a great graduate and winner of all prizes there, he seemed to appear as if he considered the University of Virginia below the standard of Princeton, and as a common, old-style place without much enjoyment. He associated with few students. I think he did not know one-half the members of the law class. At the end of a class lecture, he did not stand and talk with fellow classmen, but would hurry off to his room over on Dawson's Row."[15]

Wilson immediately achieved prominence in the college life. A fortnight after matriculation he joined the Jefferson debating society and five weeks later was chosen secretary. Meanwhile a university glee club had been formed—an octet, plus a leader—in which Wilson became first tenor. He also sang in the choir. In late November he was chosen to present the medals for the fall athletic games. There was popular demand that his speech be published in the *Virginia University Magazine*, but because he had not written it out, it could not be furnished. In December he presented the prizes after a gymnastic contest, and the magazine reported, "Mr. Wilson, in that happy manner so preeminently possessed by that gentleman, made a perfect little delivery speech."[16]

In October 1879 Wilson was initiated into Phi Kappa Psi, one of the two or three most sought-after fraternities. Later the members elected him secretary and chipped in three dollars apiece to send him to a fraternity convention in Washington. During his second year he was made head of the chapter. The eight or ten brothers in Phi Kappa Psi met formally once a week in a rented room above the post office and betweentimes were continually in each other's company. With them, as with the Witherspoon Gang at Princeton, Wilson was friendly and easygoing, revealing restraint only in his repugnance to dirty jokes or anything off-color. According to one brother, he was "dignified, courteous, cheerful, at times with his intimates playful, and loved a joke." Another wrote, "If Wilson was ever reserved or aloof in his attitude toward other students, he was never so in our company. With us he was a genial, witty, delightful friend and companion. For instance we frequently foregathered in the room of some one of us and sang the light songs of the day." [17]

Wilson's closest friend in Phi Kappa Psi was R. Heath Dabney, later a professor of English and a dean at the university. From their first meeting Dabney was fascinated by Wilson. They exercised together, playing catch or taking walks. Dabney found his new companion inspiring and bursting with ideas, but also "full of fun and tomfoolery." They had private jokes to which they often referred in a correspondence that continued throughout Wilson's life. Their pet names for each other were "illimitable idiot" and "thou very ass." For some reason Wilson was amused by the name of a college mate called Lippitt, and he would dance around Dabney, flitting his hands and saying "Lippitt-Lippitt-Lippitt." So "Lippitt-Lippitt-Lippitt" occasionally appeared in their later letters as a salutation or good-bye.[18]

A major purpose of the University Glee Club was to serenade girls. The college magazine described the club as "pouring out entrancing love songs of exquisite sweetness" below the windows of a professor's daughter who finally dropped them a bunch of flowers with a card of thanks. Wilson described such an occasion when the club was out until one o'clock, serenading girls in town and having "a very jolly, amusing time, listening to the tittering at the windows, and collecting in the dark the flowers that were thrown to us, with cards of thanks, &c., &c." With the Glee Club members, as with the brothers of Phi Kappa Psi, Wilson "would yield himself utterly to fun and frolic, like a boy out of school . . . He had an inexhaustible fund of anecdotes and was a very prince of story tellers, always suiting the action to the word. When in one of these moods, he was as good as a circus. I often thought what a wonderful actor he would have made. Having a wonderful mobile countenance, his facial expression was at times too ludicrous for description." [19]

Although affectionate and generous in admiration for his friends, Wilson was capable of violent dislikes. Witness this harsh judgment of a fellow student: "I was astounded, I must confess, at the result of the oratorical contest in the Wash. The materials must be poor indeed, if ———[name illegible] can be her best 'orator.' I remember the fellow well. That is, I remember his appearance—there was little else about him to strike one. He suggested to me a greasy, Junkshop Jew who had been partially washed and renovated and oiled that he might appear to his overwhelming disadvantage among decent people. The extravagantly long coat and the tilt of his hat were enough to fix upon him the stamp of vulgarity." [20]

During his first year at Virginia Wilson seems to have become seriously interested in girls. He "calicoed" several professors' daughters (that is, he called on them or took them out), and on one occasion he put on his dress suit and went to a Jefferson's birthday celebration with the purpose of being "hugely entertained" by seeking out the most vivacious girls. Unfortunately he did not dance, so that commencement was a time "of dancing and monotony." [21]

Only thirty miles away, across the Blue Ridge in Staunton, was the Augusta Female Seminary (once directed by Wilson's father), which at this time was attended by five of his cousins. The town was full of friends of his family, and he had visited there several times during earlier years. When he spent Christmas in Staunton at the end of his first fall term at Virginia, his host and uncle, James Bones, wrote to his mother about the event:

We had a quiet but very pleasant Christmas & our chief enjoyment was in having dear Tommie with us for a week. He captivated all our hearts most completely being such a manly, sensible, affectionate fellow. You certainly have great reason to be fond of your boy. His views of life are so just, his aims so high & his heart so full of affection & kindliness that he must succeed. We hope to see him frequently as he can easily run over Saturday afternoon & return by the early Monday train in time for his lecture. He has promised to come often. Hattie spent the week with us & she and Jessie & Tommy had nice times together.

Hattie was his first cousin Harriet Woodrow. A student at the Augusta Female Seminary, she was a high-spirited, pretty girl of nineteen, who won gold medals for excellence in the organ, the piano, and voice. Wilson fell in love with her. Since she was protected by the strict rules of the seminary, the romance did not develop far, but Wilson made such a parade of his affection that Hattie was embarrassed by it.[22]

The earlier noted "delinquencies" for which Wilson was admonished by the University of Virginia faculty were the result of his absenting himself from Charlottesville to pay court to Hattie Woodrow. In May 1880 Wilson's father complained about receiving a report from the university that Wilson had cut a quarter of his classes. Apparently he was then warned to improve his ways, but he cut more classes in order to pay a visit to Hattie in Staunton, which placed him in real difficulties, even in danger of expulsion.[23]

When Wilson reported his dereliction and his precarious situation to his parents, each of them reacted characteristically. His mother was distressed at the possibility of any disgrace visited upon her beloved boy. She was sure that the authorities would not be "so cruel as to take such extreme measures without previous warning." She urged him not to exasperate the authorities by showing resentment and at the same time to see Mr. Venable (a friend of Dr. Joseph Wilson on the Virginia faculty) and persuade him to use his influence.[24]

Dr. Wilson was apparently no less cast down than his wife, but he took a different line. He wrote his son that he had acted most imprudently; it seemed to him "that the faculty would be deserving of censure if they should overlook such a gross breach of discipline." Nevertheless, "come what will, *you possess our confidence*, because we well know your *character:* a blessed knowledge which you have confirmed in us by your straight-forward confessions of juvenile folly." In a second letter he again gave thanks that the son had neither concealed nor condoned his fault and continued, "Well, then, let us now dismiss the matter altogether. Be sure that you are not less dear to me, or less in my confidence as your father and friend, than you have always been." And so the incident was closed, and the culprit dismissed with a warning. It illustrates the close bond of understanding and trust that existed between Woodrow Wilson and his father.[25]

In one of his letters to Talcott, Wilson wrote that in spite of the law he found time for private reading. The library record, still extant, shows what books he took out. The list is largely what one would expect: Jebb's *Attic Orators*, Stubbs's *Constitutional History of England* (renewed), Shelley's poems (kept overtime), Newman's *Chats*, Lecky's *Eighteenth Century*, four volumes of the *Congressional Globe*, Goodrich's *British Eloquence*, a biography of Patrick Henry (renewed), and Parsons' *Contracts*. His uncle James Bones gave him a number of standard political works, including Chitty's *Blackstone*, John Stuart Mill's *Principles of Political Economy*, and *The Federalist*, which were more useful to him than the library books since he could annotate and summarize their contents in the margins. In signing out library books, incidentally, Wilson wrote his name in various ways: "T. W. Wilson," "Thos. W. Wilson," and "T. Woodrow Wilson." He was obviously groping toward a name with more impact than Tommy Wilson.[26]

He was an eager observer of the political scene, happy over the great Liberal victory in the British parliamentary election of 1880, pessimistic about American politics during the presidential campaign of the same year, in which the Republican candidate James A. Garfield was victorious over the Democrat Winfield Hancock. In two long letters to Charles Talcott he deplored the doings at the Republican convention, as well as the convention system itself; the corruption of "our English blood" by "the infusion of foreign elements"; the "degradation" of the Republican Party, "its only creed one of hatred for a section of their own country"; and the abasement of the Democratic Party that had abandoned its principles to ally itself "with every damnable heresy— with Greenbackers as with protectionists." In both letters Wilson expressed the conviction that great changes were to come.[27]

During this time Wilson completed an essay that went over much the same ground as the earlier "Cabinet Government in the United States." It was called "Congressional Government," the title that he later gave to his first book. Here again were detailed the vices of committee and caucus domination of Congress, the secret processes by which federal legislation was hatched, the irresponsibility of congressional leadership, the lack of debate, and the disastrous separation of executive and legislative powers. And here was presented the same panacea: the United States should adopt the English system whereby executive power centered in a cabinet drawn from the legislature. He concluded with a peroration that revealed, as did his letters to Talcott, his extreme distaste for contemporary American politics. To those who argued "let well enough alone" he replied:

Are a shameful Civil Service, rotten public morals, awkward administration, and clumsy, blind legislative tyranny "well enough"? Are finances which are the laughing stock of the world "well enough"? Is a high carnival of demagogy "well enough"? Are all these things well enough to let alone when a remedy is within easy reach? The spirit of the master-workmen of the Revolution has passed away, America has lost her breed of noble blood, the age of independence has gone and slavery has come, wisdom has departed from us and mocking folly reigns in her stead, if we thus sit idly, thus cowardly, by while our liberties are waning and our institutions are decaying. We will not so solve the problem.[28]

With Wilson it was not enough simply to study and to write. He must also find a forum where he could practice the art of debate. In Charlottesville the audience at hand was the Washington and Jefferson literary societies, which were supposed to represent the Federalist and states' rights traditions suggested by their names. With his Federalist leanings, Wilson might have been expected to join the Washington Society, but it had almost collapsed the previous year, not even electing officers. Therefore, he joined the Jefferson Society, in spite of its political complexion. It was not such a lively and prosperous little republic as Whig and Clio at Princeton. At its Saturday night meetings the attendance averaged no more than ten or fifteen. The debates were likely to be desultory, especially since the appointed speakers often failed to appear.[29]

Wilson, with his keen interest in public questions, his strongly held opinions, his eagerness to debate, and his fine previous training at Princeton, was a godsend to the Jefferson Society. He moved rapidly into prominence. He was admitted on October 18, 1879, and the very next week the society chose a topic certainly suggested by him: "Is the government of Great Britain better adapted to promote the welfare of society than that of the U.S.?" He was selected to defend the negative. Interestingly enough, when the question came up for discussion on November 15, he did not appear and paid a fifty-cent fine. This was the only time he was ever recorded absent. On November 22 he was appointed secretary and served for five sessions. During his term of office the records were kept in more careful detail than at any time in the previous four years, and his beautiful penmanship made the pages a pleasure to the eye. The minutes were invariably signed "T. Woodrow Wilson."

The Jefferson Society became a forum where Wilson tried out his theories of government. He further expressed his dislike of universal suffrage when, on February 6, 1880, he argued the affirmative on the question, "Would a restriction of the suffrage ameliorate our political condition?" One of the members, "a Jeffersonian Democrat of the Virginia School," remembered his surprise when on other occasions Wilson favored a constitutional amendment to give cabinet members nonvoting seats in the House of Representatives and proposed "that the U.S. Senate be abolished, and Congress then have only one body, the House of Representatives."[30]

On March 6, Wilson, chosen as the monthly orator, gave an address on John Bright. Such was the demand to hear him that the Jefferson Society voted to admit the public, including ladies. According to the college magazine many of "the calico" came with their escorts, and late-comers had to stand along the back or squat in the aisles. The minutes of the society reported, "Mr. Wilson inspired by the bright eyes and approving smiles of many fair visitants delivered his oration with an earnestness and vigor that drew down much well deserved applause." One of his Virginia friends wrote that he "never knew a man who more keenly relished applause" than Wilson.[31]

The text of the address on Bright was published as an article in the *Virginia University Magazine*. It hews closely to the lines laid down in Wilson's previous essays. Here is the same, sometimes painful effort to achieve a style. In this case the author is inspired by the rolling

It was then moved that the Faculty Committee to select final debaters and orators be elected now. Tabled.

Mr. Daniel moved the following amendment to the Constitution:

Resolved that Art. VIII. of the Constitution be amended by the addition of Sec. II.
"A Declaimer shall be elected at each regular meeting of the Society, to deliver his declamation two weeks thereafter. Seconded and Tabled.

A motion to adjourn was made, seconded, and lost.

The classes for debate were read; the Vice-President's report was heard, orators were offered; the second roll was called; and the House was adjourned.

R.S. Abbey Pres.t

T. Woodrow Wilson Sec'y.

Minutes kept by Wilson as Secretary of the Jefferson Society, a debating club at the University of Virginia. He was in process of dropping his first name.

periods of Edmund Burke. Here is the Burkean devotion to England as the exemplar of ordered liberty unmarred by license. Here again Wilson rings changes on the theme of his essays on Bismarck and Chatham: the great statesman must dedicate his life to great purposes. Principles come first—ahead of men, ahead of parties. And again he asks the reader to forget the flaws of his hero in admiration for the loftiness of his goals. The London *Times,* he writes, complained that Bright was bigoted and intolerant of the foes of liberalism. Wilson answers in words that foreshadow his later treatment of opponents as President of Princeton, Governor of New Jersey, and President of the United States:

> Tolerance is an admirable intellectual gift: but it is of little worth in politics. Politics is a war of *causes;* a joust of principles. Government is too serious a matter to admit of meaningless courtesies. In this grand contestation of warring principles he who doubts is a laggard and an impotent. Shall we condemn the statesman because in this intense strife, in which he fights, not for empty formulas or unpractical speculations, but for the triumphs of those principles which are in his eyes vitally essential to the welfare of the State in whose service he is spending and being spent—because in the very heat of this battle he does not stop to weigh out careful justice to his foe? He grants him all the privileges, he extends to him all the courtesies, of war.[32]

A reproach that many Southerners leveled against Bright was that he consistently defended the North in the Civil War. Wilson meets this charge head-on in a way calculated to shock his Virginia audience. In an eloquent passage he demonstrates that he was a nationalist before he was a Southerner:

> But I am conscious that there is one point at which Mr. Bright may seem to you to stand in need of defence. He was from the first a resolute opponent of the cause of the Southern Confederacy. Will you think I am undertaking an invidious task, if I endeavor to justify him in that opposition? I yield to no one precedence in love for the South. But because I love the South, I rejoice in the failure of the Confederacy. Suppose that secession had been accomplished? Conceive of this Union as divided into two separate and independent sovereignties! To the seaports of her northern neighbor the Southern Confederacy could have offered no equals; with her industries she could have supplied no parallel. The perpetuation of slavery would, beyond all question, have wrecked our agricultural and commercial interests, at the same time it supplied a fruitful source of irritation abroad and agitation within. We cannot conceal from ourselves the fact that slavery was enervating our Southern society and exhausting to Southern energies. We cannot conceal from ourselves the fact that the Northern union would have continued stronger than we, and always ready to use her commercial strength to compass our destruction. With this double certainty, then, of *weakness* and *danger,* our future would

have been more than dark—it would have been inevitably and overwhelmingly disastrous. Even the damnable cruelty and folly of reconstruction was to be preferred to helpless independence.

It took courage to say these things less than fifteen years after Appomattox, and only three years after the last federal troops were withdrawn from the South. Nor was this merely a random thought elicited by the occasion. The same ideas reappeared in his letters, speeches, and other writings and were to provide the theme of his first and best book on American history, *Division and Reunion*.

A month after the essay on Bright, the *Virginia University Magazine* published another piece, entitled "Mr. Gladstone: A Character Sketch," written under the pseudonym "Atticus," previously employed for Wilson's essay on Bismarck. The article purports to give the author's "few crude impressions" of the character and career of "the great member for Midlothian," and it bears marks of haste. It may have been solicited by an editor desperate for copy, especially since the college magazine was then an adjunct of the Jefferson Society. Part of the essay is merely a paraphrase of the article on parliamentary oratory in *The Gentlemen's Magazine* that had transfixed him at Princeton. The judgments of the oratorical abilities of Bright and Gladstone are based on this article, and Wilson employs the very metaphor used by the earlier author to describe Bright's voice, which "rings like a peal of bells." He even plagiarizes himself, repeating an apothegm that first appeared in his essay on Chatham: "Passion is the pith of eloquence."[33]

In the essay on Gladstone familiar themes, both large and petty, reappear. There are descriptions of the all-conquering power of oratory based on conviction and of politics as war. Wilson elaborates a notion touched on in his essay on Chatham—the statesman as a person gifted with poetical imagination. One of Gladstone's great qualities is "his keen poetical sensibility," defined as follows:

> By poetical sensibility I do not mean an imaginativeness which clothes all the common concerns of life with poetical forms or weds the mind to those things which are picturesque rather than to matters of practical business . . . I mean, rather, breadth of sympathy such as enables its possessor to take in the broader as well as the pettier concerns of life, with unconscious ease of apprehension and unfailing precision of judgment; to identify himself with interests far removed from the walks of his own life; to throw himself, as if by instinct, on that side of every public question which, in the face of present doubts, is in the long run to prove the side of wisdom and of clear-sighted policy, such a sympathy as makes a knowledge of men in him an *intuition* instead of an experience.

Repeatedly in future writings Wilson was to develop the theme that intuition may be a more trustworthy guide than cold reason, and that he who would know a nation must study it with the eye of a poet.

A most interesting portion of the essay on Gladstone is Wilson's defense of him against the charge of inconsistency. Wilson had all along been arguing that a man must stand by his principles and that only in such devotion is there strength, yet his hero had entered politics as a High Tory, changed his mind when in office, and eventually switched sides and sponsored legislation directly contrary to the principles of his youth. In dealing with Gladstone's apostasy, Wilson first gives the easy excuse that the great parliamentarian's earlier beliefs had been wrong, that he was simply converted by the true Liberal faith, like Saul on the road to Tarsus. But he goes on to assert that in any case a statesman's principles cannot be immutable, or he will find himself "irreconcilably at war with all the stronger tendencies, with all the healthier impulses of the day." "Few men," he writes, "stand in their old age where they stood in youth. The untested opinions of the early life do not always or often stand the trial of experience. In public life especially, so varied and varying are the conditions of government, their purposes must be trimmed to possibilities." Here, then, is a theory that not only permitted but encouraged Wilson to alter his own political opinions with changing times and circumstances.

One of the great events of the college year at Virginia in the seventies and eighties was the annual competitive debate of the Jefferson Society for two prizes, the Debater's Medal and the Orator's Medal. The former was considered the higher award, and the latter something of a consolation prize. In 1880 the question under debate was, "Is the Roman Catholic element in the United States a menace to American institutions?" Interest became so intense that the forum was moved from the Jefferson Society room to the larger hall of the Washington Society. The four contestants were Benjamin L. Abney, Junius H. Horner, William Cabell Bruce, and Woodrow Wilson. Abney and Horner were able speakers who later achieved prominence, the former as a lawyer, the latter as an Episcopalian bishop. Apparently, however, everyone expected the real contest to be between Bruce and Wilson.

When he matriculated in the law school in the same year as Wilson, William Cabell Bruce was already, at nineteen, a polished speaker and writer. He was well-born, hard-working, able, and ambitious. In an autobiographical fragment written in old age, he devoted twenty-two pages to describing his ancestry. His father, formerly a great plantation owner, had served in the Virginia Senate and raised his own artillery company for the Confederate cause. A maternal uncle had been Secretary of War in Jefferson Davis' cabinet. Going further back,

Bruce found he was related to at least forty owners of famous Virginia homesteads.[34]

Young Bruce's industry was prodigious, and his reading omnivorous. For the *Virginia University Magazine* he contributed articles on Hamlet, John Marshall, Edgar Allan Poe, and John Randolph, plus numerous jottings and observations about college life. He took out or renewed books fifty-seven times during the academic year 1879-1880, far more than any other student using the university library. During his first month in college his reading included Lamb, John Stuart Mill, Emerson, de Tocqueville, Shakespeare, Sir Thomas Browne, Hobbes, and Darwin.[35]

Bruce's nickname among his friends was "Senator," and he belonged to a fraternity, the "Eli Bananas," which attempted to monopolize college honors. In the Jefferson Society he was as prominent as Wilson. He was elected an editor of the magazine at the second meeting he attended, and soon after he was chosen orator for December. The minutes show him active and contentious in business meetings, constantly critical of rulings from the chair and actions of the officers. They support Heath Dabney's recollection that he was "acrimonious, opinionated, sometimes offensive" in debate. Dabney remembered Wilson to have once been so nettled by Bruce that he remarked, "the gentleman has yet to learn that personal abuse is not debate." Wilson must have described such an incident in a letter to his parents, for his mother replied, "We were much amused by your down-setting of Mr. Bruce— I think he must be a puppy."[36]

In the prize debate Bruce, arguing the affirmative, spoke first. He was tall and sparsely built, with a leonine head. He affected the fiery declamatory style of the period, moving forward, drawing back, making large studied gestures, raising his voice to hammer home his points. The report of his speech in the college magazine indicates that he piled argument on argument to great effect, closing with a denunciation of the Catholic Church as the enemy of freedom and progress. "The fires of Smithfield," he concluded, "have long been quenched and I can forgive the cruelties of honest intolerance; I can never forget or forgive the opposers of the advancement of human knowledge.[37]

Wilson's method of delivery was in dramatic contrast. One of his hearers characterized it as "the English style." He stood still, using no gestures except an occasional lift of the arm. His heavy-jawed but "wonderfully mobile" face came alight as he spoke, and its changing expression did service for gesture. He was so composed that when the oil lamp on the desk flared up and smoked, he paused briefly to blow it out and then proceeded without a break in the stream of his oratory.[38]

A summary of Wilson's speech in the *Virginia University Magazine* confirms the memory of Bruce and others that his argument was not quite clear. He made effective use of a standard debater's device, which is to concede your opponent's points but deny their importance. Wilson agreed with Bruce as to the pretensions and purposes of the Catholic Church but argued that it was nevertheless no real danger. His vital concession, however, came in the middle of the speech, where it broke the argument; it would have been more effective at the beginning. Wilson's essential thesis was that Anglo-Saxon institutions and traditions of freedom had always resisted the power of Rome and would continue to do so: "Our liberties are safe, until the memories and experiences of the past are blotted out and the *Mayflower* with its band of pilgrims forgotten; until our public-school system has fallen into decay and the nation into ignorance; until legislators have resigned their functions to ecclesiastics and their prerogatives to priests."[39]

At the conclusion of the debate it was clear that the choice lay between Bruce and Wilson, but the three faculty judges held up their decision for several days. This built up the tension as well as the latent ill-will between the rivals. The friends and followers of both men displayed a fervid partisanship, probably exacerbated by interfraternity rivalries. Finally the judges announced the selection of Bruce for the award as "best Debater," and Wilson for the lesser honor of "Orator." To salve the latter's feelings, they declared that they had a "very high appreciation" of his merits as a debater. Wilson's first reaction was to refuse the Orator's Medal. He was a debater, he said, not an orator. It must have been particularly galling to be defeated by a man over three years his junior, whose style of florid oratory he despised. That Bruce was an echt Virginian, while his own claim to being a Virginian was slender, probably did not help to reconcile him to the decision.

On the night the judges announced the awards, Samuel B. Woods, a fraternity brother, knowing that Wilson was disappointed and depressed, went over to his room and took him out for a walk. They talked the situation over, and finally Wilson admitted that he had been fairly beaten but added, in a tone of grim determination, "Bruce beat me on this, but I will beat him in life, for I'm a worker, he is not." Although this revealed that he had underestimated Bruce, it also showed his reaction to defeat: don't knuckle under—fight harder.[40]

Eventually Wilson was persuaded by his friends to accept the second prize. Possibly he restored his pride by scoring over Bruce in a later debate on the Monroe Doctrine. Apparently he considered his defeat in the prize debate an accident, for he soon wrote Charles Talcott, "Much to my surprise I've acquired the reputation of being the best debater and one of the best speakers in the University—because there are so few of either." Indeed, the whole experience with Bruce may have steeled his determination to achieve greatness. In any case he wrote to Talcott: "Those indistinct plans of which we used to talk grow on me daily, until a sort of calm confidence of great things to be accomplished has come over me which I am puzzled to analyze the nature of. I can't tell whether it is a mere figment of my own inordinate vanity, or a deep-rooted determination which it will be within my power to act up to."[41]

When the "Final Exercise" of the Jefferson Society was held in late June, Wilson gracefully accepted the Orator's Medal and gave a highly successful speech before an "immense crowd." The *Virginia University Magazine* reported, "The delivery of this medal to the Gladstone-like speaker of the University elicited one of the clearest, soundest, most logical, and thoroughly sensible addresses ever pronounced here at the University by a man so young."[42]

At the same meeting Bruce was awarded the gold medal for the best article in the college magazine on the basis of an essay entitled "John Randolph of Roanoke: A Sketch." Wilson had to be content with honorable mention and high praise from the judges for his pieces on Bright and Gladstone. A rereading of Bruce's and Wilson's essays shows that the decision was eminently fair. Bruce had a much firmer grasp of fact than Wilson, and a wider frame of literary and historical reference; he was a closer student of character; his writing had more terseness and wit. His essay portrays John Randolph as an utter eccentric, without discernible political or personal principles, and taunts Randolph's biographers for not telling the truth about him. It still reads well, which can only occasionally be said of Wilson's early writings.[43]

William Cabell Bruce went on to a distinguished career in Maryland politics, culminating in a term as United States Senator. He wrote a definitive life of John Randolph and won the Pulitzer Prize for a biography of Franklin. Yet he never ceased to exult in the fact that he had twice beaten Woodrow Wilson in fair combat; his biography in *Who's Who* for 1940-1941—when he was eighty years old—contains this passage: "While at University of Virginia, in competition with Woodrow Wilson and others, was awarded medal as debater of Jefferson Lit. Soc. and medal for best essay."

Wilson returned to law school for his second year early in October 1880 and moved into quarters in the "West Range," a low-lying brick dormitory that was part of Jefferson's original fabric. His friend Heath Dabney and several brothers in Phi Kappa Psi took rooms nearby, and they ate together at a round table in Mrs. Massie's boarding house. In a letter to his inamorata, Hattie Woodrow, he pictured himself as torn between his legal studies and other activities:

My fraternity has a large membership this year and I am trying to forget my loneliness by entering on its work with renewed vigor. The literary society has not yet reorganized, but that's a small matter to me this year, for I cannot hope to take as active a part in it this year as I did last. My law studies will, I am afraid, compel me to be a silent member most of the session—although there's no telling how soon I'll be tempted into making a speech. I'm going to be a systematic visitor of the young ladies this winter. This will be my last college year and next winter I will be obliged to go out into society. So this year I must put myself in training.[44]

Wilson, now head of Phi Kappa Psi, took his position seriously and went out of his way to befriend the younger members. One of them wrote him ten years later, "You may not recall now, as you must have recognized then, and as I am only too glad to acknowledge at all times, that your friendship, being that of an older and more experienced student, was directly beneficial and encouraging."[45]

Wilson did not stick to his intention to be a "silent member" of the Jefferson Society. Instead, he was unanimously elected president at its first meeting on October 9 and set about with vigor to meet his new responsibilities. His influence was immediately indicated by the way the society concentrated on political problems, some of them unquestionably suggested by him. Among the topics selected for debate during Wilson's presidency were these:

Should the features of ministerial responsibility be adopted in the Constitution of the U.S. Cabinet?
Is the bimetallic or unimetallic standard preferable?
Is Nihilism likely to attain its ends in overthrowing the existing Russian government?
Can U.S. Congress constitutionally control immigration?
Should the U.S. have a protective tariff? [Not surprisingly, Wilson was reported as speaking for the negative.]

Just as Wilson had at Princeton attempted to improve the efficiency of every organization he was connected with, so he now took the Jefferson Society in hand. No sooner was he elected president than he announced that he planned to revise the constitution. At the next meeting his *fidus Achates* Heath Dabney proposed the appointment of a committee on revision. The motion was tabled. A week later, on October 23, it was debated in private business, and Wilson vacated the chair to explain the urgent necessity for reform. A three-man committee was then elected, with the president as ex officio chairman. An interval of over a month elapsed, while presumably the committee deliberated. In the meantime, Wilson's term as president had expired, but he continued as chairman of the constitution committee. Its report was finally presented on December 4. Heath Dabney, coached by Wilson, immediately moved that the society go into committee of the whole for its consideration; his motion was duly passed. Several articles of the new constitution were adopted and one turned down. On December 17 the remaining articles were voted, but a new bylaw relating to a change in the method of awarding prize medals was rejected. The constitutional committee was then discharged with a formal vote of thanks for the way it had performed its duty. On January 15—by which time Wilson had left the university—the new constitution and bylaws were finally voted in.[46]

In this well-attested example of Wilson's leadership, every step was carefully planned, with scrupulous regard for procedure. He had, in fact, given the members a lesson in parliamentary practice; the use of the device of the committee of the whole, for instance, was his innovation. Throughout the episode he achieved his aims by counsel with others and by public persuasion. The members apparently were responsive: the attendance at meetings gradually climbed from a low of seven in mid-October to over twenty in late November and December.

The preamble of the new constitution of the Jefferson Society was a paraphrase of the preamble of the Constitution of the United States: "We, the members of the Jefferson Society of the University of Virginia, in order to form a more perfect organization, provide for our common improvement in the art of debate, promote general culture among ourselves and those around us, and drill ourselves in all those exercises which strengthen for the free duties of citizenship, do ordain and establish this Constitution for our government." The new constitution put major emphasis on realistic training in debate; a characteristically Wilsonian touch was a provision in the bylaws that the members should choose which side of a topic they wished to defend, so that no one should be forced to argue against his convictions. The rules of membership, election, and office-holding were changed in order to prevent fraternity politics from perverting the Jefferson Society. The election of president had become an open scandal. In the previous spring candidates backed by rival fraternities had herded in so many new members merely to get votes that the roster rose from 25 to over

130—in spite of a ten-dollar initiation fee. The actual choice of the president took place only after interfraternity logrolling and pledges of support in future elections. The new constitution contained provisions requiring that candidates for office have been active in debates and that only those who had been members for a certain time had the right to vote.[47]

The only nonpolitical debating topic in the Jefferson Society during Wilson's presidency was, "Ought the students to have gone down to resent the affront offered by the Circus-men?" This refers to an occasion when circus roustabouts roughed up a Virginia student, and a college meeting was called to organize a posse to wipe up the circus men. As the excitement reached its height, Wilson is reported to have stood on a chair, holding up his hand for silence. When he got the floor, he is supposed to have said, "I have listened with much attention to the plan you have outlined to ship the circus. I want to make a few remarks on how not to do it." Then he made "a powerful but quiet speech," and the students went quietly home to bed.[48]

Heath Dabney denied this story. He attended the mass meeting and doubted if Wilson was even there. According to Dabney, the man who calmed the students was William E. Echols, "a magnificent figure, a red-headed Texan, 6'3", a man of great courage, yet self-controlled." The student mob was at "fever heat" when Echols rose to say that if the students went, he would go with them, and stay with them. But they had better reflect that they were up against tough men, probably armed with pistols. "If we go down there," Echols said, "we can be sure of this: some of us will never come back—some of us—will—never—come—back. Now, if you're ready to face the risks, come on; I'll go with you." This calmed every one down.[49]

Therefore the dramatic account of Wilson and the circus men probably lies in the realm of myth. Yet myth may be as eloquent as fact in indicating the impression a man makes on his peers. It may be, too, that this incident was confused with another occasion when Wilson did make a mob see reason. According to the Reverend Edward Earle Bomar, a contemporary of Wilson's at Virginia, there was once a tumultuous gathering of students in the hall of the Washington Society to consider the punishment of a student whom the student government court had found guilty of violating the honor system. At this meeting Wilson, while agreeing that the man should be forced to leave the university, opposed those who wished to publish his name in the college magazine, and he carried the audience with him.[50]

The letters Wilson received from his father and mother during his time at Charlottesville contain expressions of concern about his health and the bad food that was endangering it. Toward the end of his first year his father suggested that if he could not make better boarding arrangements, he had better complete his law studies at home. During his second year he suffered severe dyspepsia and a skin infection, and both his parents begged him to come home. At first he refused; then he suddenly changed his mind and left the University of Virginia, without completing his studies and without a degree, in December 1880.[51]

Wilson's departure was so sudden that he left his books and his trunk behind him and did not say good-bye to all his friends. This lends color to the recollection of a fraternity brother, Joseph B. Blair, that his leaving was triggered by "a sharp exchange of words with that stern disciplinarian, John B. Minor." Blair also remembered Wilson's farewell: "On the day he left he came into my room with a suitcase in one hand and a German student lamp in the other. He gave me the lamp, saying it would be better for the eyes than the one I had."[52]

Although Wilson's stay at the University of Virginia was thus limited to a year and a term, it was an important chapter in his life. For one thing, he achieved greater identity with the Old Dominion. Although he honestly tried to refrain from calling himself a Virginian, others did it for him as his fame increased, so that in the end he found a place in the state's Valhalla alongside Washington, Jefferson, Madison, Marshall, and Lee.[53]

Wilson's legal studies were in some respects abortive: he never liked the details of law and abandoned its practice after a brief period. Yet the four terms of steady toil were of value for the discipline they imposed. At Virginia Wilson learned to study diligently, intelligently, and daily, whether he wanted to or not. The methodical and efficient work habits of his mature years stemmed partly from this training.

Although an altercation with John B. Minor may have occasioned his leaving the university, the misunderstanding could not have lasted long. Wilson later visited the Minors in Charlottesville, and he kept up a correspondence with this man whom he never ceased to regard with something like reverence. While in his first college post at Bryn Mawr, he wrote Minor that, as his work progressed, he was increasingly thankful for the instruction he had received at Virginia and for the firm grasp of English constitutional history that Minor had given him. Wilson's chosen field at Princeton was jurisprudence, and he dreamed of building at Princeton a great school of public law and legal philosophy. In all this he was certainly influenced by his Virginia teacher, for he often told his friend and brother-in-law, Stockton Axson, that Professor Minor did more to mold his views on the law than any other man.[54]

Wilson's connection with the University of Virginia proved enduring.

He professed himself a loyal alumnus, animated by feelings of deepest affection. Through two fraternity brothers on the faculty, Charles W. Kent and Heath Dabney, he kept up with university affairs, frequently asking for news, sometimes giving advice. Once he wrote Kent a strong letter against a proposal to allow women to attend, arguing that such a move would be "gratuitous folly" because "it would be fatal to the standards of delicacy as between men and women" that Southerners most valued. Another time he advised Dabney on the kind of man Virginia needed for its first president. Even during his last years when, broken in health, he retired to the house on S Street, he wrote a public letter protesting a proposal to move the university's medical school from Charlottesville to Richmond "as a very serious detriment to the University and also as a deplorable breach in the historical development of education in Virginia . . . If the thing were done, I should deplore it both as a wound to my pride as an alumnus of the University, and as distinctly contrary to my judgment as a student of education."[55]

Although critical of some aspects of Virginia student life, Wilson retained an admiration for others. While a professor at Princeton, he was the leader in a movement of students and faculty members to eliminate cheating and to introduce the Virginia honor system. His most radical proposals as President of Princeton—the Preceptorial System and the Quadrangle Plan—were influenced by his remembrances of the friendly relations between students and faculty and the mixing of older and younger students at the university.

During his four terms at Charlottesville Wilson made fast friends. Several of them so admired him that they were eager to see him attain high place. As early as 1890 he was being considered for a professorship at the university. In 1895 he was chosen to give the annual address before the Society of Alumni. In 1897 he delivered the principal address at a convocation of the Virginia Bar Association. The next year he was asked to become the first president of the university, an offer that he thought might be the highest honor of his lifetime but which he declined after a severe inner struggle. The Virginia authorities approached Wilson twice again before they would accept his refusal. In 1901 he was sounded out for the presidency of Washington and Lee. In every case men who had known Wilson at Virginia were promoters or intermediaries.[56]

When he at last entered politics, some of these men rallied round. Heath Dabney, who had statewide connections, helped to build a Wilson organization in Virginia in 1911 and 1912. Later he gave advice on Virginia patronage. Richard E. Byrd, a fraternity brother, and A. W. Patterson, a former member of the Glee Club, were founders of the Woodrow Wilson Club of Richmond in 1911. Partly through their efforts the Richmond City Council and the Virginia legislature asked Wilson to address two important gatherings at Richmond on February 1, 1912. In adjoining Maryland William Cabell Bruce was the most prominent of the original Wilson men. Bruce did all in his power "by pen, tongue, and purse" to advance the political fortunes of his former rival. Thus, Woodrow Wilson's experience at Virginia, like that at Princeton, revealed what an English scholar has termed "a striking fact in his life—his capacity for gathering around him men ready to support him and press him forward."[57]

V

Unhappy Interlude

1881–1883

Whoever thinks, as I thought, that he can practise law successfully and study history and politics at the same time is woefully mistaken.

—Woodrow Wilson, 1883[1]

THE COLLAPSE of Wilson's health in December 1880 was the prelude to nearly three years of frustration. The experience might have broken a young man less determined to succeed, less convinced that a great destiny awaited him. For well over a year he stayed with his family at the manse in Wilmington, N.C., tending his health and studying law. Then in the spring of 1882 he went to Atlanta, Georgia, to establish a legal practice, but this venture turned out to be so distasteful that Wilson abandoned it a year later and decided on an academic career instead.[2]

Although his family was genuinely glad to have him at hime, Wilson's return to Wilmington was not happy. His fears about his health were confirmed by a local doctor, who told him that he was in danger of becoming a chronic dyspeptic. His condition improved, and he was strong enough to ride his father's frisky little mare only a fortnight after the return from Charlottesville; for the rest of his life, however, his digestion was precarious. He had no friends of his own age in Wilmington, for the few young men he had known at an earlier period had gone away and the girls had married. He longed to return to Virginia and bombarded Heath Dabney with requests for news of the university. "Write me letters full of gossip about yourself," he pleaded, "and the boys and the Jeff., and everything else pertaining to our one-time walks and conversation."[3]

Wilson's mother was determined that he should not mope. As soon as his health improved, she arranged a musical evening at the manse where he joined in the performance and was introduced to a number of girls. At his mother's insistence he called on local belles, and he began to enjoy these stilted visits, if only because he talked and the girls listened. With the coming of spring there were church picnics, which he described as "promiscuous," meaning simply that all and sundry were invited.

The charms of the eligible young ladies of Wilmington were dimmed by the fact that Wilson was still in love with his cousin Harriet Woodrow. During the academic year 1880-1881 she attended a music school in Cincinnati, and Wilson wrote her long, self-conscious letters about his doings in Wilmington. In the summer of 1881 Wilson was invited to stay at Hattie's home in Chillicothe, Ohio, while serving as apprentice clerk in the law office of Henry Wilson Woodrow, their common uncle. According to his own account, given thirty years later, Henry Woodrow found that his nephew knew the law and could put a contract into the clearest language he ever saw, but he was a failure in dealing with clients.[4]

Meanwhile Wilson's courtship of Hattie came to a disastrous climax. One evening at a party he took her aside and made a formal proposal, which was promptly rejected on the ground that first cousins should not marry. Wilson argued the point, and Harriet finally told him that she was fond of him as a cousin but was really not in love with him. He was so distressed that he left the house immediately and spent a sleepless night at a hotel. From there he sent her a note written on a scrap of yellow paper, asking her to reconsider and save him from "the terror of despair." After a second refusal the next morning, he abruptly left Chillicothe. During the railroad journey back to Wilmington, which took four days, he wrote again, begging her at least to have herself photographed, at his expense, in profile, wearing a particular dress and sitting in a particular pose—and to give the picture to him alone. This request she granted, but nothing more. She insisted that the correspondence come to an end, and Wilson had no choice but to accept the fact that the romance was over. Later they resumed their friendship, but as cousins only.[5]

In spite of his uncertain health, his loneliness, and his ill-starred love affair, Wilson did not give up. He had learned the landmarks of the law so well at Virginia that he was able to continue his legal studies on his own. He set himself a rigid schedule of work and completed his preparation for the bar. As usual, he pursued other studies on the side. In the course of tutoring his younger brother in Latin, he reread Cicero's orations and with them Trollope's life of Cicero. He read and annotated a variety of books—literary, historical, and political. With a chart of suitable gestures in front of him, he practiced elocution daily; he had told Hattie Woodrow, "I intend to spare no trouble in gaining complete command of my voice in reading and speaking." He had used part of the fallow year between leaving Davidson and entering Princeton to teach himself shorthand; now he learned to type. His letters show that, as always, he was watching and judging the political scene: he gloated over the death of Disraeli and speculated on the results of the assassination of Garfield. His opinion of Decoration Day revealed his desire that Civil War hatreds should be forgotten: "Today, the 10th, is 'Decoration Day' with us—that is, it is the day on which the ladies of the *Ladies' Memorial Association* conduct the now empty ceremony of decorating the graves of the Confederate dead. It is a day of regrets for me; not of the same sort of regrets that are supposed to engage the thoughts of others, however. *My* regret is, that there should be any such ceremonious decoration of these graves. I think that anything that tends to revive or perpetuate the bitter memories of war is wicked folly."[6]

After more than a year of recuperation and study Wilson, at the age of twenty-five, was ready to start earning his living. Casting about for a place to practice law, he and his parents settled on Atlanta, Georgia. This seemed a logical decision. Atlanta had completely recovered from its partial destruction by Sherman in 1864. Served by five railroads, it was a prosperous center of trade, manufacturing, banking, and insurance. Between 1880 and 1890 its population almost doubled, rising from 37,000 to 67,000. Partly because of the International Cotton Exposition held there in 1881, partly through publicity given it by Charles W. Grady, editor of the Atlanta *Constitution,* the city was a symbol of the "New South."

Before going to Atlanta, Wilson agreed to form a partnership with Edward I. Renick, who had studied at the University of Virginia during Wilson's time, although the two men had then been strangers. Wilson reported in the triennial record of the Princeton class of '79 that the prospects for the firm of Renick and Wilson were "excellent." He wrote Charles Talcott that he was familiar with the South and "his mind might be expected to grow most freely in his native air." Furthermore, Atlanta was the capital of Georgia; this was important since Wilson hoped the law would be a stepping stone to politics.[7]

Renick & Wilson, Attorneys at Law, rented an upstairs office and hung out a shingle at 48 Marietta Street in downtown Atlanta in May 1882. The partners found rooms together in a big private home on Peachtree Street, in the best residential section of town. Since Wilson could not be admitted to the bar until September and lived on an allowance from his father, there was no great hurry about seeking clients. He studied the organization and practice of Georgia courts and filled over a hundred pages of a notebook with beautifully written notes under such headings as "Militia Districts," "Justices of the Peace," and "Garnishment." The partners proved to be kindred spirits. They were both fond of poetry and read the *Aeneid* together. They were both passionately interested in politics and political theory. Renick later went into the federal civil service, and he wrote articles on government for the *Nation* and the *Political Science Quarterly*. The two men kept in touch until Renick's untimely death in 1890.[8]

Wilson was admitted to the Georgia bar on October 19, 1882. The presiding judge at the examination remembered him as "a tall, dignified, bespectacled young man with blond hair." Professor John B. Minor's oral quizzes on knotty problems in law apparently stood him in good stead, for his answers to questions propounded in public session were said to have been "not short of brilliant." On March 12, 1883, he was also admitted to practice as "an Attorney and Counselor at Law, Solicitor in Chancery, and as Proctor and Advocate" in the federal courts.[9]

Even before his admission to the bar, it is apparent that Wilson had qualms about the active practice of law. In August 1882 his father wrote him that he was disturbed by his son's "law-distaste," although somewhat relieved by the candor with which he had admitted it and by his expressed determination to try to overcome it. Dr. Wilson urged his son to realize that all beginnings were hard, that he must not show the white feather before the battle was joined, and to ask for divine help. Other letters in the same vein followed.[10]

Renick and Wilson had neither the personal connections that would steer clients their way nor the inclination aggressively to seek for them. Wilson's principal legal business was connected with his mother's property. She granted him power of attorney, with control over certain securities and some 1800 acres of Nebraska farmland that she had inherited from an uncle. To get full control of the Nebraska lands, Wilson had to engage in extended negotiations with a rather slippery uncle by marriage. He was eventually successful—but only after he had given up the active practice of law—in getting full control of the lands and in selling them for what was apparently a good price. For the rest, he and Renick appear to have attracted too little business to make ends meet. At the age of twenty-six Wilson was still dependent on a monthly allowance from his father.[11]

In Atlanta, as at Princeton, Wilson dreamed of enlisting a group of high-minded men to enter politics. In a series of "Letters from a Southern Young Man to Southern Young Men," never published, he solemnly urged that young Southerners spend their evenings in the study of history and politics instead of frequenting bars or making calls. Their eventual renown and influence would more than compensate for their pains. Putting this adjuration into practice, Wilson started a branch of the Free Trade Club of New York, which met at the office of Renick and Wilson. Later the club reorganized at the "Georgia House of Commons," along the lines of the Liberal Debating Club at Princeton, and held fortnightly debates on public questions.[12]

But in politics as in law Wilson's stay in Atlanta was a disappointment. He found his fellow members of the bar little interested in either history, literature, or politics and wrote Robert Bridges of his disgust at the way they joined in a "universal drunk" at Christmas time. Active politics, as represented in the Georgia legislature, proved wholly distasteful to one who dreamed of leadership in an idealized House of Commons or a reformed United States Congress. He thought that state legislators were for the most part "a very low order of politicians," men of narrow views, and prisoners of local prejudice and selfish purpose. It shocked him that Georgia politicians solicited federal funds for education instead of raising funds by local taxation.[13]

Atlanta saw Wilson make a first brief appearance in the political arena. In 1882 Congress passed a bill to establish an "impartial" tariff commission, which after careful investigation was to submit new schedules of import duties and thus "take the tariff issue out of politics." But President Arthur, under pressure from the protectionists, made a farce of the proceeding by packing the body with representatives of the protected interests; the chairman was a former employee of the Wool Manufacturers Association. The members nevertheless solemnly went through the form of making a lengthy investigation and held hearings in many cities. In September 1882 they went to Atlanta. Accompanying them was Walter Hines Page, a young reporter who had been ridiculing the peripatetic commissioners in the pages of the *New York World*. Page was a friend of Renick's and thus met Wilson at the office on Marietta Street. He was so impressed by Wilson's knowledge of the tariff that he persuaded him to testify before the commission.

In a letter to Heath Dabney, Wilson described his encounter with the tariff commission. He had agreed to speak, he wrote, with only a night to prepare, not in any hope of changing the opinions of "this much ridiculed body of incompetencies" but to get his remarks in the public record. He found the commissioners seated behind a table in the breakfast room of the Kimball House; the rest of his audience were reporters, four or five friends, and a few local dignitaries. He was embarrassed, the told Dabney, by "the smallness of the audience" (when dealing with strangers Wilson preferred a crowd) and by "the ill-natured and sneering interruptions of the commissioners." He spoke, therefore, without sufficient self-possession. But he was compensated by the compliments of his friends, by favorable notice in the press, and by the remark of the local congressman that he "both knew what to say and how to say it."[14]

Examination of Wilson's testimony before the tariff commission shows that the praise was on the whole deserved. In spite of one misstatement of fact, he gave a trenchant summary of several standard arguments against the protective system, which he labeled both pernicious and corrupt. High tariffs were an unjustifiable tax on the community; they hurt farming and commerce; they discouraged enterprise; they fostered monopoly. They were not needed to protect infant industries, to provide for defense, to keep up wages, or to prevent unemployment. Wilson did not argue for completely free trade but only for a revenue tariff. It was the better part of wisdom, he said, for the federal government to derive its revenues from indirect taxation, leaving direct taxation entirely to the states. This, of course, was a highly conservative, strict-constructionist view of federal-state relations, and one that he later abandoned. He never changed his mind on the tariff, however. On no public issue was he more vehement or more consistent than in his opposition to protection. He enjoyed a belated revenge on the sneering commissioners in the Kimball House when, at his urging, Congress in 1913 passed the Underwood-Simmons tariff, the first major downward revision since before the Civil War.[15]

The most important aspect of the tariff commission incident proved to be the meeting with Walter Hines Page. Page, a Virginian and a former fellow in classics at Johns Hopkins, was, like Wilson, a lover of literature, an Anglophile, a liberal Democrat, and one who wanted the South to forget the Lost Cause and look ahead. He and Wilson kept in touch for the rest of their lives. In the 1890's Page, as editor first of the *Forum* and later of the *Atlantic Monthly*, solicited and published several of Wilson's best essays. Later, as editor of *World's Work*, he actively supported Wilson's candidacy for President of the United States. In 1913 he was rewarded by appointment as ambassador to the Court of St. James.

Bored with the law, Wilson envied Heath Dabney, who was studying for a Ph.D. at Heidelberg and Berlin. He found solace, however, in intellectual pursuits and managed to save his afternoons for writing and reading on his "old and loved topics, history and political science." On the eve of going to Atlanta he had written some articles on the South, which were submitted to the *New York Evening Post*; only one,

an article on industrial development in the New South, had been published. Now he returned to an earlier theme: the reformation of the
federal government through an adaptation of the British parliamentary
system. He wrote several articles around this topic—designed as chapters for a book—and sent them on to Bridges, who attempted to peddle
them to the *Nation*. They were returned with "Mr. Garrison's extremely
unfavorable opinion." Wilson condensed these articles into a single long
essay, which he eventually placed in the *Overland Monthly* for January
1884 under the title "Committee or Cabinet Government?"[16]

"Committee or Cabinet Government?" is an elaboration and revision
of the earlier essays, "Cabinet Government in the United States" and
"Congressional Government." In it Wilson again argues that the frag-
mentation of power and accountability among congressional committees results in shoddy leadership, piecemeal legislation, frustration
of the popular will, and corruption. He again sounds a note of alarm.
"None can doubt," he writes, "that we are fallen upon times of grave
crisis in our national affairs, and none can wonder that disgust for our
present system speaks from the lips of citizens respectable both for
numbers and for talents." The cure proposed is the same: imitate
Britain. The writing is more incisive and specific. In fact, there is a
description of the peculiar noisiness of the House of Representatives
that is a little masterpiece of acute and lively description.

In "Cabinet Government in the United States" Wilson argued that
the United States could achieve something very like the British parliamentary system by giving cabinet members the right to sit in Congress.
Here he promises the same end if the President will choose his cabinet
from among the leaders of the dominant party in Congress. This will
require an amendment to Article I, Section 6, of the Constitution, which
forbids members of the House and Senate to hold other federal office.
It is also advisable, Wilson argues, to increase the terms of office of
both the President and the House of Representatives to promote "that
sense of security without which there can be neither steadiness of
policy nor strength of statesmanship."

In his earlier essay Wilson was chiefly interested in the way parliamentary government offered scope for leadership; now he is more
concerned with the way it promotes the democratic process. He wants
informed public opinion in the Capitol, and public scrutiny of the dark
recesses of jobbery and corruption. His particular bête noire is the
caucus system, which at every level of government inhibits the popular
will by turning party nominations and legislative direction over to "a
narrow oligarchy of party managers." This is a significant change of
emphasis. Wilson had begun his novitiate as a prophet of democracy.

Wilson argues that the legislators at the head of executive departments will begin to "appreciate the complexity of the executive machinery." They will be "in a position to weigh the thousand minor
considerations which must sway the determination of administrative officers in the conduct of their official business, and will have every
means of ascertaining those necessities of the departments which it is
the province of legislation to supply." They would see the necessity of
civil service reform, since "their own mastery would depend upon the
efficiency of the administration, and efficiency of the administration
would depend upon the maintenance of true business principles." This
passage indicates that Wilson has begun to concern himself with administration as well as with legislation and matters of high policy. In
later years he made a thorough study of European administrative systems, gave courses in public administration at Johns Hopkins, and
attempted to find principles of administration that would make it possible to combine bureaucratic efficiency with popular control.

"Committee or Cabinet Government?" shows that by constant study,
reflection, and discussion Wilson had come closer to some of the realities of American politics than when he wrote "Cabinet Government in
the United States." Yet he also displays curious blind spots and mis-
conceptions. For one thing, he has little awareness of the latent powers
of the presidency. He therefore sees no difficulty in reducing the
President of the United States to a position like that of the President
of France under the Third Republic: an elective constitutional monarch,
indifferent to party and willing to choose his advisers and executive agents as others dictate. In Wilson's justification it must be remembered that he was writing in a period stretching roughly from the
impeachment of Andrew Johnson in 1868 to the inauguration of Grover
Cleveland in 1885, when the presidency was at a low ebb. Still, it
shows a cool indifference to the facts of history to write as though
Washington, Jefferson, Jackson, Polk, and Lincoln had never lived and
a Chester A. Arthur would always occupy the White House.

On occasion Wilson is guilty of grotesque exaggeration. He is so
obsessed with his proposals for reform of American government that
he warps facts to suit his purpose. He states, for instance, that the
House of Representatives is "omnipotent in all national affairs," like
the Commons in England and the Assembly in France, and that the
Senate (by inference) is subordinate, like the House of Lords or the
French Senate. This is simply not true. The House and Senate have
always been coordinate legislative bodies, and neither has ever gained
ascendancy over the other. Wilson also assumes that Congress exerts
a tyranny over the executive that it did not possess even during the

latter years of Andrew Johnson's administration, when congressional powers were at their zenith and those of the President were at their nadir. Meticulously and erroneously, he details the complete submission of every executive department to congressional committees: the Secretary of the Treasury to the Finance Committee of the Senate and the Ways and Means Committee of the House, the Secretary of War to the Committees on Military Affairs, and so forth. Blandly ignoring the independent powers of the executive in foreign affairs, he even writes, "the Secretary of State must in all things regard the will of the Foreign Affairs Committees of both Houses."

Wilson's scheme to substitute cabinet for committee government bristles with practical problems. How will it be possible to divest the President of his partisan role? What if the two houses of Congress are dominated by different parties? Is there to be a prime minister, and if so, how chosen? Wilson brushes such questions aside. Simply change a few words of the Constitution, and American politics will become suffused with wisdom and light.

After only a few months of active practice of the law, Attorney Wilson decided to throw in his hand. According to his own account, written not long afterward, he realized that he had been deluding himself:

> I left college with the intention of studying law and entering upon its practice; I will not say with the purpose of devoting myself to the law, because that would be more than the truth. My intention was to make my living in the practice of the law and my reputation by the pursuit of more congenial studies, into which I had been led before my graduation at Princeton:—and thereby hangs my tale. I did study law quite thoroughly, because under a competent and inspiring instructor—and I did set out upon the practice; but my license was scarcely passed under the seal before I saw the size of the mistake I was making. It had, of course, been only self-deception—more or less conscious, if I must confess all—that had enabled me to hope to succeed at the bar without the desire of making success there my chief success; and the more business I got— for I did get *some* during the year my shingle was out—the more uneasy I felt at my growing distaste for the practical duties of the profession and at my growing taste for studies in politics and administration.[17]

In April 1883 Wilson applied for a fellowship at Johns Hopkins University, and shortly thereafter his active career as a lawyer came to an end. In a long, rambling letter to Heath Dabney, written just before he left Atlanta, he discussed his present situation and future plans. He decided that he could never be happy unless he led an intellectual life, "and who can lead an intellectual life in ignorant Georgia?" He was inclined

Woodrow Wilson in 1882, when he was attempting unsuccessfully to establish a law practice in Atlanta, Georgia.

John B. Minor, Professor of Law at the University of Virginia, who failed to overcome Wilson's distaste for the study of law but earned his admiration as an educator.

R. Heath Dabney, with whom Wilson formed a lasting friendship at the University of Virginia. He became Professor of English there and once tried to persuade Wilson to become its first president.

Herbert Baxter Adams, who as Professor of History and head of the department of history, politics, and economics at Johns Hopkins trained a brilliant galaxy of scholars.

Richard T. Ely, who although ineffective as a lecturer at Johns Hopkins, influenced Wilson to make a serious study of American economic thought.

The Historical Seminary room at Johns Hopkins in the late 1880's. Its "high altar" was the red-covered table, where members gathered to read papers and argue. The Bluntschli Library is housed on shelves to the right. Seated, third from left, is Herbert B. Adams. At extreme left is Charles H. Haskins, one of Wilson's most successful students.

The Johns Hopkins Glee Club, 1884. The tall figure standing next to Wilson with his hand on a vase is his friend Albert Shaw, later editor of the *Review of Reviews*.

to think that anything more than a common school education was a handicap in North Georgia: "Here the chief end of man is to make money, and money cannot be made except by the most vulgar methods. The studious man is pronounced impractical and is suspected as a visionary." Wilson was of the opinion that the law itself was antagonistic to the intellectual life: "The philosophical *study* of the law—which must be a pleasure to any thoughtful man—is a very different thing from its scheming and haggling practice." He went on to explain his choice of a new profession:

You know my passion for original work, you know my love for composition, my keen desire to become a master of philosophic discourse, to become capable and apt in instructing as great a number of persons as possible. My plain necessity, then, is some profession which will afford me a moderate leisure; what better can I be, therefore, than a professor, a lecturer upon subjects whose study most delights me? Therefore it is that I have prayed to be made a fellow of Johns Hopkins, and therefore it is that I am determined if I fail of that appointment (as I probably shall, since it is not won but given) to go next winter anyhow to Baltimore to attend the University lectures and bury myself for a season in the grand libraries of that beautiful city.[18]

In his decision to go to Johns Hopkins, Wilson was consoled by the knowledge that two of his idols, Edmund Burke and Walter Bagehot, had found the practice of law intolerable. Both men, furthermore, had failed to achieve high office yet had instructed their own and later generations in the philosophy and practice of politics. Consciously following in their footsteps, Wilson abandoned the hope of becoming an American Gladstone and decided instead to become a "literary politician" who would serve his country by exercising a statesmanship of opinion. As he had foreseen, Wilson's application for a fellowship at Johns Hopkins was refused, but he was duly admitted to graduate studies in history and political science.

He set out for Baltimore in mid-September, 1883. On the way north there occurred one of the most fortunate events of his life: he became engaged to the woman he later married. The romance had begun the previous spring when Wilson went to Rome, Georgia, to do legal business for his mother. While there, he attended the First Presbyterian Church, where he saw a girl with "a bright, pretty face" and "splendid, mischievous, laughing eyes." On inquiry he discovered that she was Ellen Louise Axson, daughter of the Reverend Mr. Edward Axson, minister of the church. Meanwhile Ellen Axson had seen a tall, well-groomed young man, wearing a mustache and sideburns, passing by on the street. Asking, "Who is that fine-looking man?" she was told that it was Tommy Wilson, of whom she had often heard. He lost no time in arranging to meet "Ellie Lou" and soon overwhelmed her with attentions. They walked and drove together, went boating and picnicking. Wilson's courtship of Ellen Axson, like that of Hattie Woodrow, was as ardent as the proprieties of his upbringing permitted, and in this case it was welcomed. But there were difficulties. Mr. Axson was recently widowed and in precarious health. Ellen, as eldest daughter, not only kept house for him but acted as foster mother to two younger brothers and a baby sister. In the circumstances she claimed she did not feel free to marry. Then fate intervened. When Wilson stopped briefly at Asheville, North Carolina, on his way to Johns Hopkins, he happened to catch a glimpse of Ellen Axson, who was also just passing through. He bounded upstairs to the hotel porch where she was sitting and then and there declared his suit. Caught off guard, Ellen Axson accepted.[19]

As it turned out, Woodrow Wilson had found a partner to meet his needs. Utterly devoted, Ellen Axson steadied Wilson, rested him, gave him confidence, expanded his intellectual and aesthetic horizons, and reciprocated his ardor. They were in love until her death thirty years later.

The Historical Seminary at Johns Hopkins

1883–1885

What I have wished to emphasize is the *object* for which I came to the University: to get a special training in historical research and an insight into the most modern literary and political thoughts and methods, in order that my ambition to become an invigorating and enlightening power in the world of political thought and a master in some of the less serious branches of literary art may be the more easy of accomplishment.

—Woodrow Wilson, 1883[1]

IN THE mid-1880's graduate instruction in American universities was of recent development and could be obtained at so few institutions that a high proportion of young American scholars went to the great German universities. Most American colleges were still in a semisomnolent condition, so handicapped by sectarian bias that economics was likely to be taught by a clergyman as a branch of Moral Philosophy, and Philosophy itself by "a sort of plain-clothes chaplain employed . . . to see that science did not run away with the students' minds." The state of science in allegedly reputable institutions is suggested by the Princeton biology professor who as late as 1900 "believed on scientific grounds that Jonah had lived not in the belly of the whale but in its throat." At Harvard, where President Eliot had instituted a graduate school of arts and sciences in 1871-1872, the handful of advanced students enrolled in undergraduate courses as often as not and were given little training in research. Eliot himself later testified that not until after the founding of Johns Hopkins University in 1876 did the Harvard faculty seriously turn its attention to graduate instruction. "And what was true of Harvard," said Eliot, "was true of every other university in the land which aspired to create an advanced school of arts and sciences."[2]

Johns Hopkins University came into being as the result of a bequest of $7,000,000 by the wealthy Quaker merchant who gave the university its name. Its peculiar character was primarily determined by Daniel Coit Gilman, its first president, who insisted that it should provide "intellectual training of a higher sort than could be obtained at existing colleges and universities." This meant, according to Gilman, that its professors should be engaged in uninhibited search for truth. Dramatic —some thought scandalous—evidence of what he meant was given by the fact that there were no prayers at the opening ceremonies in 1876 and that the principal address was made by Thomas Huxley.[3]

Gilman considered it his primary task to recruit a faculty, mostly of younger men, from both sides of the Atlantic. He had remarkable success in finding productive scholars with communicable enthusiasm. He paid them well, and he turned them free, telling them that their job was "not so much to impart knowledge, as to whet the appetite, exhibit methods, develop powers, strengthen judgment, and invigorate the intellectual and moral forces."[4]

As Gilman put brains ahead of bricks, during the eighties the university was housed in a miscellaneous set of buildings sprawling haphazardly across three blocks in downtown Baltimore. There were no dormitories and no playing fields, although there was a gymnasium, but little was lacking to promote effective study. The libraries and laboratories were well equipped and up-to-date. In 1883, for instance, the university subscribed to no less than six hundred scholarly journals in various fields.

The growth of Johns Hopkins was slow, for Gilman was no more dazzled by numbers than by buildings. During Wilson's first year, 1883-1884, there were only 300 students, of whom 79 were undergraduates (called "matriculants"), 47 were special students seeking no degree, and 174 were in the graduate departments. The quality of the graduate students, judged by later eminence, was high, for Johns Hopkins attracted young scholars from all over the United States and even from abroad, partly by offering graduate fellowships with the then generous stipend of $500 a year plus remission of tuition.[5]

Johns Hopkins proved to be an almost instantaneous success. One of its first and foremost students, Josiah Royce, who received his Ph.D. in 1878 and later became professor of philosophy at Harvard, wrote of the early years: "The beginning of the Johns Hopkins University was a dawn wherein ''twas bliss to be alive.' Freedom and wise counsel one enjoyed together. The air was full of noteworthy work done by the older men of the place, and of hopes that one might find a way to get a little working-power one's self . . . One longed to be a doer of the word and not a hearer only, a creator of his own infinitesimal fraction of a product, bound in God's name to produce it when the time came."[6]

The practical results of this stimulation of creative scholarship are seen in the impressive array of publications that began to appear under the auspices of the university. They included *The American Journal of Mathematics* (1878), *The American Chemical Journal* (1879), *Studies from a Biological Laboratory* (1879), *The American Journal of Philology* (1880), and *Studies in Historical and Political Science* (1882). Johns Hopkins men were also active as promoters and officers of learned societies, such as the American Mathematical Society and the American Economic Association.

Gilman was vitally concerned with the social purposes of scholarship. He hoped that the ultimate result of higher studies would be "less misery among the poor, less ignorance in schools, less bigotry in the temple, less suffering in the hospital, less fraud in business, less folly in politics . . . more study of nature, more love of art, more lessons from history, more security in property, more health in cities, more virtue in the country, more wisdom in legislation, more intelligence, more happiness, more religion." He therefore gave special attention to the department of history, politics and economics, which in the mid-1880's attracted more students than any other. The head of this department was Herbert Baxter Adams, who had been called to the position when only twenty-six years of age.[7]

After graduating from Amherst at the head of his class, H. B. Adams studied for three years in Germany and gained a Ph.D. *summa cum laude* from Heidelberg. At Johns Hopkins his talents as a scholar were subordinated to his even greater gifts as a teacher and organizer. For two decades he did more than anyone else in the country to establish the study of history as a profession, and he helped to train a brilliant galaxy of scholars, including the economist Davis R. Dewey, the sociologist Edwin A. Ross, the historians H. C. Adams, J. Franklin Jameson, Charles H. Haskins, Frederick Jackson Turner, and Charles M. Andrews, plus a score of others of scarcely less eminence.

Adams never produced important scholarly work, nor was he a brilliant lecturer. But according to Woodrow Wilson, "his head was a veritable clearing house of ideas for historical study, and no one ever studied under him who did not get, in its most serviceable form, the modern ideals of work upon the sources." Trained as a political scientist and economist as well as historian, Adams agreed with Gilman that the way to prevent narrow specialization was to teach the social sciences together, especially with a view to what he regarded as "the greatest educational need of our time—*the application of historical and*

political science to American politics." Above all, Adams had an uncanny ability to inspire students to work on their own. "No teacher,"
said Charles M. Andrews, "ever more aroused the desire in his students
to be somebody, to do something."[8]

Seconding Adams at Johns Hopkins from 1879 to 1892 was the economist Richard T. Ely, also an Amherst graduate and a Heidelberg
Ph.D. A dull, uninspired lecturer, Ely was touchy, somewhat self-
centered, and rather disposed to use the talents of his students to promote his own purposes. But, like Adams, he was a seminal influence.
He was one of the first American economists to break away from ortho-
dox Manchester liberalism, and he so infected students with his own
liberal, inquiring, original point of view that they learned to do their
own thinking.[9]

A third member of the teaching staff was J. Franklin Jameson, later
to become one of America's foremost historians as editor of the *American Historical Review,* chief of the Bureau of Historical Research for
the Carnegie Institution, and chief of the Division of Manuscripts for
the Library of Congress. In the mid-eighties Jameson had yet to make
his mark; Adams kept him on at Johns Hopkins on a year-to-year basis
as a sort of man Friday performing a variety of duties.[10]

Adams and Ely taught a number of courses to both graduates and
undergraduates—perhaps too many, because they inevitably spread
themselves thin. Their most important teaching was performed not in
lecture halls but in the seminary room of the Bluntschli Library. The
library got its name when, in 1882, German-American citizens of Baltimore presented to Johns Hopkins the personal library of the famous
Swiss and German political scientist Johann Bluntschli, who had taught
both Adams and Ely at Heidelberg. A biology laboratory was made
over to house this collection, and Adams had the opportunity to design
a fascinating political laboratory. The books were placed in well-lighted
alcoves, with desks for the use of readers. There were separate but
adjoining rooms for maps, newspaper files, and statistical data, plus
offices for Adams and Ely. There were special arrangements for filing
pamphlets and back numbers of magazines. Six bulletin boards gave
up-to-date information on "International Politics," "American Politics,"
"Economic and Social Questions," "General History," "Ecclesiastical
Matters," and "Book Notices, Education, University Affairs." Along the
crowded walls and on top of the bookshelves were pictures and busts
of great statesmen, historians, and political scientists, ranging from
Cicero and Machiavelli to Bismarck and Bancroft, "giving to mere ag-
gregations of books the presence of personality." At one end of the

main room was a glass case in which were enshrined manuscripts and memorabilia of Bluntschli and Francis Lieber; at the other end in big letters was the dictum of the historian Edward A. Freeman, "History is past Politics and Politics present History." The center of everything, "the seminary altar," was a great red table, seating twenty-four, strewn with the latest journals and pamphlets. Here the Johns Hopkins Seminary of History and Politics met.[11]

Several American departments of history had in one way or another adapted the German seminary method, but none so successfully as Johns Hopkins, and its records still make exciting reading. The seminary usually met on Friday evenings for two hours, with Adams, Ely, and Jameson at one end of the table, the graduate students seated around it, and observers and undergraduates seated outside. Sometimes there were visiting speakers. During Wilson's first year these included Edward Channing (who spoke on local government, North and South), Josiah Royce (the development of government in California), Talcott Williams (Tammany Hall), Major J. W. Powell (Indian anthropology), and half a dozen others. At most meetings members reported on assigned contemporary magazines, and the instructors called attention to recent publications or new interpretations. Occasionally there was a debate. Above all, the seminary was a place where students presented their own work. "The main idea here," Adams told the members, "is that it is a place where students lecture, and is distinguished from class in that there the instructors lecture." At least half the time, therefore, the principal business of a seminary meeting was the presentation of a piece of original work by one of the graduate students, followed by free discussion and criticism. Adams could be severe with slipshod work, as when he interrupted one man and told him, "Take all that stuff and throw it in the wastebasket. Then start over." Generally, though, he rejected the methods of the German seminary as "brutal" and believed that "refined criticism" was better than "trampling." His students had the refreshing experience of being treated as colleagues and felt perfectly free to raise questions or to disagree with their instructors. Adams constantly played on the theme that research was a cooperative endeavor, and he promoted the idea that the members of his seminary were a band of brothers, motivated by individual ambition, to be sure, but also by ambition for the common cause of the advancement of knowledge. Under the varied stimuli of criticism, encouragement, and esprit de corps many a callow student underwent a remarkable ripening process and became an aspiring, assured research scholar and writer of history.[12]

Woodrow Wilson entered Johns Hopkins in September 1883, stating on his application blank that his purpose in coming was "to qualify myself for teaching the studies I wish to pursue, namely History and Political Science, as well as to fit myself for those studies of Constitutional history to which I have already bestowed some attention." He immediately enrolled in the historical seminary and was delighted with the arrangements for study, especially with the fact that each member was assigned a drawer in the great red table, where he could keep his papers. He rented a "cheery front room" which looked across at "the brave architecture" of the Peabody Institute, where he expected to do much of his reading. After consultation with his new chief, Professor Adams, he enrolled in the Advanced Political Economy course with Dr. Ely, English Constitutional History with Dr. Jameson, International Law and Sources of American Colonial History with Adams. He also learned that he must acquire "a sufficient knowledge of the modern languages to read at least French and German at sight"; his French was scanty, and he had never studied German.[13]

Wilson was soon overwhelmed with work. He wrote Ellen Axson that one of his companions suggested that lectures at Johns Hopkins were intended for "our recreation, as agreeable interruptions to our severer studies," and that graduate students were forced to study so many topics that they resembled "the unhappy spirits in Dante's Inferno who rose to the surface of the burning lake only to be thrust under again by the forked weapons of the guarding demons." Wilson soon rebelled against this regimen. "I like to read *much*," he wrote Ellen Axson, "but not *many things*—at least not many things *at once* . . . I can't 'cram': I must eat slowly and assimilate during periods of rest and diversion. My chief ground of complaint against my professors here is that they give a man infinitely more than he can digest. If I were not discreet enough to refuse many of the things set before me my mental digestion would be utterly ruined."[14]

One of H. B. Adams's hobbyhorses was the so-called "germ theory" of politics. According to this by-product of Darwinism, American political institutions were the result of a slow organic growth that began with the village organization the Angles and Saxons carried across from Germany in the fifth century. Over the centuries these "primordial cells of the body politic" developed into higher institutions. To understand the present, therefore, one must dig into the origins of government, especially local government, in England and America. In pursuit of this will-o'-the-wisp Adams set his students to a minute study of government in the thirteen colonies. Wilson was not the first to revolt against such work. His contemporary Davis R. Dewey complained that he was being sacrificed to Adam's ambition for his department, and Jameson wrote Albert Shaw that he could not pretend to "that consuming zeal in the study of the Anglo-Saxon origins of Policeman's Billies, the Historical Development of Pedler's Licenses and other points in the history of Institutions that I ought to have." Similarly Wilson wrote that he resented "digging into the dusty records of old settlements and colonial cities . . . and other rummaging work of a like dry kind, which seem very tiresome in comparison with the grand excursions among imperial policies which I had planned for myself."[15]

Less than a month after going to Baltimore, Wilson resolved to "have it out" with Adams and to ask if he might go his own way. Adams treated the request sympathetically and readily granted Wilson permission to abandon "institutional" work in order to pursue his own "constitutional" studies. Thus released, Wilson began preparation for his first major work, *Congressional Government.*[16]

Although grateful to Adams for the freedom he was allowed and appreciative of the facilities for study, Wilson was somewhat disappointed in Johns Hopkins, and not merely because he disliked the microscopic study of documents and the persistent digging for lumps of undigested facts. In a letter to Heath Dabney he insisted that neither the attainments of his teachers nor the methods of instruction were what he had a right to expect. Although Ely was "a hard-worker, a conscientious student, and chock full of the exact data of his subject," he was "moved only by outside impulse and . . . not fitted for the highest duties of a teacher." Adams was described as a "disciple of Machiavelli," intent on "the prosecution of schemes for his own advancement." Wilson was especially contemptuous of his teachers' "perfunctory lecturing" and lack of regard for style, both in writing and speaking. Ely in particular was a "dribbler," who could be infallibly relied upon to find the weakest form of expression.[17]

Whatever were Wilson's private opinions of his teachers, Adams and Ely realized at once that here was an unusual man promising a brilliant future. To Ely, Wilson's arrival at Johns Hopkins was "an ever memorable event." Adams soon came to regard Wilson as the ablest student he ever had—an opinion he never changed—although he did wonder whether "that young man from the South" was not "a little over-intense." "Is he solid?" Adams asked a friend of Wilson's. "Will he be able to see that there are more ways than one to Rome? Has he the temperament to endure strain?" [18]

Fellow students were drawn to Wilson at once. In January 1884, when he was called home for a time, he received a letter from one of his new friends, Charles H. Shinn, who wrote, "All the boys are anxiously awaiting your return . . . and everybody says, 'How can we survive a week without our dear Wilson?'" One of several students who ate with him at a boarding house run by two fresh-faced country girls, Jane and Hannah Ashton, recollected, "Mr. Wilson became the warm friend of every one . . . His friendly smile, his fine sense of humor and his wealth of good stories made him always and everywhere a welcome guest." A special intimate of Wilson's at Johns Hopkins was Albert Shaw, who nicknamed him "Colonel" because of his southern antecedents and bias. Although they disagreed on politics, Shaw became a longtime friend. In later years Wilson attempted to get him to Princeton as a member of the faculty. As editor of the *Review of Reviews*, Shaw lent Wilson support before the Democratic nominating convention of 1912 and in the ensuing presidential campaign.[19]

In spite of the academic pressures, Wilson again found time to become a leader in campus activities. As at Virginia, there was no social gulf between undergraduates and graduate students, so that it was easy for Wilson to join the undergraduate literary and forensic organization, the Matriculate Society. He became its Nestor, suggesting debate topics, giving instruction in oratory, and eventually rewriting the constitution and changing the name of the society. Wilson was also one of the founders of the Johns Hopkins Glee Club, which practiced every Monday night and occasionally gave a concert. He wrote Ellen Axson that a favorite number concerned the "hip-po-, hip-po-po-tamus, swimming the broad Euphrates and eating grass." He wrote doggerel verses for a song in which the glee club poked mild fun at the university:

> We get our learning served in bites
> Of German literature
> With now and then an Eng[lish] word
> Our ears to reassure
>
> Oh we don't care a wee bit oath
> For other colleges
> They don't know what flourish is
> They're mere apologies.[20]

Through family friends and Princeton classmates Wilson enjoyed some social life in Baltimore outside the university. This gave him opportunity to exhibit the love of nonsense that had characterized his relations with intimates at Virginia, as when he gave "grotesque addresses from chair seats," displayed "all variety of comic grimaces," simulated "sundry unnatural burlesque styles of voice and speech," and even danced the can-can. Perhaps because of his engagement to Ellen

Axson, he was no longer awkward in the company of young women; in fact, he impressed fellow students with his ability "to handle himself with the ladies." [21]

He had learned how to pay graceful compliments, also how to abstract the lady of his choice from the crush and to talk to her alone. At one Baltimore gathering a young man remarked to Wilson's friend Edith Gittings Reid, "Look at Woodrow Wilson . . . Now how does he manage that bed-side manner and make his dress clothes look like a preacher's? He's terribly clever but he's provincial." Mrs. Reid answered, "If he's provincial, he's making the provinces look bigger than the city; he is distinctly the personage in this room." Mrs. Reid remembered Wilson at this time as having "a remarkable face . . . strong and heavily marked, naively young but full of power. It must have been drawn, one might think, for the caricature of a Scotch covenanter and then transformed by an idealistic inner light that obliterated everything that might have been ugly." [22]

Nevertheless, his shyness in strange company and inability to give himself completely were still apparent. To one who saw him only casually he was "not a good mixer and seemed to have few friends." A fellow student who held him in high regard worried because Wilson's manner toward him seemed cold. Unlike other members of the warm-hearted band of young men in the historical seminary, Wilson was never seen to display affection, as by putting his arm around another man's shoulder. He told Mrs. Reid that one reason he would dread being in active politics was his dislike of easy familiarity. Asked how he would like having his back slapped, he replied, "I should just hate it; I should be most uncomfortable; I could not conceivably slap him back, and what a prig I should feel because I couldn't." [23]

Wilson reached perhaps his greatest fulfillment at Johns Hopkins on the platform. His constant training in debate and oratory now paid rich dividends. No one in the university, according to Professor Ely, could compete with him on his feet, except President Gilman. Augustus W. Long remembered Wilson speaking at meetings of the historical seminary: "Tall, slender, sinewy, wearing a drooping mustache a shade darker than his colorless hair, he spoke with an easy affability of manner and in a voice of peculiar charm . . . it was clear, penetrating and flexible; its modulations fell on the ear like the distant chime of bells." Wilson confessed to Ellen Axson, "I have a sense of power in dealing with men collectively which I do not feel always in dealing with them singly. In the former case the pride of reserve does not stand so much in my way as it does in the latter. One feels no sacrifice of pride necessary in courting the favour of an assembly of men such as he would have in seeking to please one man." Wilson admitted that there was intoxication in public speaking, too. He wrote Ellen Axson that it set his mind and all his faculties aglow, and probably this very excitement gave him an appearance of confidence and self-command that arrested attention. He felt a sort of transformation and found it hard to sleep afterwards.[24]

Richard T. Ely thought Wilson's speeches "always very convincing even if they were not absolutely sincere." He gave as one instance an occasion when he heard Wilson in a speech to a gathering at Towsonville, Maryland, refer to socialists as "long-haired and wild-eyed." Ely demurred; he had never seen a socialist who followed this description. Wilson's answer was, "If you say such things you make people believe you are a conservative and then you can go ahead and do progressive things."[25]

In the minutes of the historical seminary there are accounts of two debates in which Wilson played a leading part. The first was occasioned by a paper read at a meeting on January 18, 1884, by E. P. Allinson of Philadelphia on Hermann Von Holst's *Constitutional and Political History of the United States*. Wilson disapproved of Von Holst, who portrayed American history as a struggle of the forces of light, represented by nationalism and the North, against the southern "slavocracy" and "the extremist absurdity" of states' rights. In fact, one day Albert Shaw, who lived at the Ashtons', was entering Wilson's room when he heard a crash. "I found," said Shaw, "that Wilson had just thrown a big, heavy copy of a book by Von Holst across the room and had broken its back. Von Holst . . . wrote in an involved, heavy style and consistently took the pro-Northern side. Wilson detested him on both counts. I think he detested his lack of lucidity more than his constitutional and sectional position."[26]

At the seminary meeting Allinson praised Von Holst, "in spite of his lack of understanding of national and state rights in coexistence." Wilson was apparently the star of the "animated debate" that followed, for J. Franklin Jameson wrote in his diary, "Wilson showed the greatest logical skill in the discussion . . . and I greatly envied him."[27]

The second debate, on April 18, 1884, concerned federal aid to education, especially to increase schooling for Negroes. A bill to provide such aid had been introduced by Senator Blair of New Hampshire and had recently received senatorial approval. Herbert B. Adams was a strong supporter of federal subsidies to education. In opening the debate, he said that the Blair Bill had "won its way by sheer force of argument, from its first position of comparative contempt to its final passage," which "should be regarded as a strong point in favor of its wisdom and

expediency." Adams was followed by J. Burr Ramage, who supported
the bill on the ground that the North had a duty to aid Negro education
because the South was unable to do it alone, and because the very
safety of the South, threatened by "a black wave with a white foam,"
demanded it. Ramage was opposed by Albert Shaw, who presented
figures to show that the South was economically capable of supporting
adequate public education and that federal aid would work injustice
by "putting a premium upon the negligence and moral dereliction of
those states, that had not provided good schools." [28]

Wilson rose to second Shaw. The topic under discussion concerned
him deeply. He had been in the gallery when the Georgia legislature
refused to increase school appropriations and asked instead that their
Senators secure federal grants. He thought this action "a shameless
declaration on the part of a well-to-do community" of its abdication
of a manifest duty. Indeed, at this time he considered all federal subsidies an insidious form of federal encroachment on state power.[29]

Fifty-five years later John Dewey, who attended the historical seminary in 1884, had only one explicit recollection of Woodrow Wilson at
Johns Hopkins—his speech at this debate. According to Dewey, Wilson's "vigorous attack" on the Blair Bill was "quite logical" and marked
by "a good deal of eloquence. One hearing him could readily believe
he could go far in politics if he wished." The minutes record that Wilson "spoke at considerable length and with great clearness and force
against the Bill," confining himself mainly "to a strenuous argument
that the principle contained in this Bill was both *unconstitutional* and
politically inexpedient. The federal government should not in any way
interfere with, or become responsible for common school education.
Justice, Wisdom and the Constitution all agreed in leaving this matter
entirely to the respective states."[30]

John Dewey rose to answer Wilson, and the minutes suggest that he
did not win the audience. After he had retired, the debate was joined
so passionately by so many men that the members broke precedent by
voting to extend the meeting an hour. A week later some wanted to
continue the discussion but were overruled by Adams, who thought
"the subject had been sufficiently well ventilated." [31]

Once released by Adams from examining the minutiae of colonial
government, Wilson dreamed of producing a work that would survey
and illuminate the whole scene of American politics and thus exercise
the "statesmanship of opinion" that was his present ambition. In preparation, he so overtaxed his eyes that he spent a whole day with a dull
ache in his head and "throbbing orbs that refuse all use." He stayed in

Baltimore through the Christmas vacation in 1884 and went near none of his friends. He explained to Ellen Axson that as "an excessively proud and sensitive creature," he feared he might "interfere in some way with the freedom of their holiday arrangements. So to escape intolerable loneliness, I went in self-defense to my studies. As a natural consequence, I overdid the business." Ultimately he had to return to Wilmington in January 1884 to be nursed.[32]

Meanwhile he began to write the essays that together form his first book, *Congressional Government*. This was a more modest project than that which he described to Ellen Axson in October, but he was still covering a large canvas. He proposed to do for the American Constitution what Bagehot had done for the British: to portray "the living reality" as contrasted to "the paper description," to describe things as they were in 1884 rather than as the *Federalist* had said they ought to be in 1788.

By early April Wilson had completed two chapters and sent them off to Houghton Mifflin in Boston. Although they did not accept the book at once, they immediately asked to see the completed manuscript. On May 9 Wilson read the introductory chapter to the historical seminary, and it made a sensation. Franklin Jameson wrote in his diary, "At sem. we had about the ablest and maturest paper ever read there, the introduction to Wilson's series of papers on American government." Herbert B. Adams told the gathering that it was "better than anything else that has heretofore been done in the Seminary" and asked Wilson to read his second chapter at the next meeting. Adams showed his enthusiasm more tangibly by offering Wilson one of the two graduate fellowships in history for the next year.[33]

With this multiple encouragement, Wilson worked at his book all summer. He established the habit, which continued throughout his academic career, of doing his actual writing in the morning, right after breakfast. He found composition difficult and more exhausting than "any amount of reading," so that he kept at it for only two or three hours. His habit was to write a first draft either in shorthand or longhand—sometimes a combination of both—and then do the final draft on his Calligraph typewriter. Once a manuscript was completed, he made very few changes, and these were entirely in the direction of verbal felicity.

During that summer, after devoting the morning to writing and study, Wilson spent the early afternoon at his own and his father's correspondence. In the late afternoon he went for a drive (always by the same road) along the sea with his mother behind little Nellie, the mare. He generally spent the evenings reading aloud to his mother, while she sewed or embroidered.[34]

Progress sometimes seemed glacially slow, yet the book was all but completed when Wilson returned to Johns Hopkins in September 1884. He sent it off to Houghton Mifflin on October 7, hardly daring to hope that they would accept it, and fearing that it would shuttle in and out of editorial offices as had his earlier essay, "Committee or Cabinet Government?" As weeks went on and no word came, he wrote his fiancée that he was "very anxious" but had "suspended all definite expectations in the matter." Finally, on November 28, he sent her the good news not only that the manuscript had been accepted but that he had been offered such terms as he might only have expected if he were already well-known. "The success is of such proportions," he wrote, "as almost to take my breath away—it has distanced my biggest hopes." [35]

Congressional Government was published in January 1885. It was an immediate success. Hailed by Gamaliel Bradford in *The Nation* as "one of the most important books, dealing with political subjects, which have ever issued from the American press," it ran through three editions in a year and gave Wilson his first taste of fame.[36]

With this book behind him, Wilson was free to follow his own devices during his second year at Johns Hopkins. He formally enrolled in only three courses: the historical seminary, Professor Adams' History of Politics, and an "Educational Course" given in the Department of Psychology and Pedagogics, in which various members of the faculty, including President Gilman, lectured one hour a week on teaching.[37]

Successful, admired by teachers and students, relieved from financial dependence by the stipend of his fellowship, Wilson wrote Heath Dabney that he was "considerably better contented" with his courses than the year before, if only because he had learned "that everything of progress comes from one's private reading—not from lectures; that professors can give you always copious bibliographies or suggestion, but never learning." [38]

After consulting his father and Ellen Axson, Wilson decided not to be a candidate for a degree. He realized that he would be more "marketable" with "a Ph.D. label," but both "mental and physical health" would be "jeopardized by a forced march through fourteen thousand pages of dry reading." "I am quite sure," he wrote, "that I shall profit much more substantially from a line of reading of my own choosing." Friends protested the decision, but he was as sure he was right as if he had been guarding his lungs from consumption.[39]

In the second year at Johns Hopkins, as in the first, Wilson found time for extracurricular activities. In November 1884 he gave a talk on oratory before the college literary society and told the members that if they were to fit themselves to face larger audiences in the future, they must change their methods of debating. He thereupon persuaded them to reorganize as the Johns Hopkins House of Commons, with a constitution and bylaws written by him. The new society was modeled on the Liberal Debating Club of Wilson's Princeton years. A ministry, consisting of Prime Minister, Home Secretary, and Foreign Secretary, introduced bills for discussion, being compelled to take a stand on each. If unable to command the support of a majority of the members, they resigned, and another ministry took their place. There were provisions for such niceties of parliamentary procedure as putting bills through three readings and debating details of measures in committee of the whole.[40]

The Johns Hopkins House of Commons proved such a success that in May 1885 its members gave Wilson a handsome wedding present—two facing mantelpiece figures of cavaliers just drawing their swords—and expressed appreciation of "your efforts in our behalf, of your kind encouragement and advice, and of our esteem and regard for yourself." *The Debutante*, yearbook of the Johns Hopkins Class of 1889, declared that the foundation of the House of Commons marked "a new era in the history of debating societies in this country. It was a great and novel departure from older institutions of its purpose." By then its success had resulted in the founding of "Houses of Commons" in other institutions, including Bryn Mawr and the Columbia Law School. A "House of Commons" formed by citizens of Baltimore for the discussion of public questions was still in vigorous existence in 1941.[41]

Wilson continued to be a regular attendant at the historical seminary and to take a prominent part in its affairs. On October 17, 1884, he read before it still another chapter from *Congressional Government*—"The House of Representatives: Revenue and Supply"—prompted by H. B. Adams, who told him he wanted "to set a high standard of work for the new men." In the course of the year he reported on the *Revue de Droit International*, the *Bulletin de la Société de Législation Comparée*, and the *Journal des Économistes*, revealing that he could now read enough French for professional purposes. He also reviewed some American magazines and a paper on the appointing power in the United States by Miss Lucy Salmon, who was soon to be a student of his at Bryn Mawr.[42]

The seminary minutes report that on March 27, 1885, Wilson gave "the paper of the evening . . . a review of recent American political economists. He stated in brief the economic doctrines of Amasa Walker, Perry, Bowen, and Francis Walker, choosing the chief works of these writers as types of the recent works published in this country." The minutes go on to state that "remarks were made by Dr. Ely, justifying the method adopted by Mr. Wilson." Ely's praise was quite natural for the paper stemmed from a project he had persuaded Wilson to undertake. One day he had called Wilson and Davis R. Dewey, another graduate student, into his office to propose that the three of them produce a history of economic thought in America. Wilson took to the idea at once and soon completed his stint, but the venture proved still-born because Ely was unable to fulfill his share.[43]

Wilson's manuscript remained in Ely's hands, and a copy now reposes in the Library of Congress. Fifty-five typewritten pages long, it is a workmanlike account of the points of view of eight American economists: Henry L. Vethake, Francis Wayland, George Tucker, Francis Brown, Amasa Walker, Arthur Latham Perry, Francis Amasa Walker, and an anonymous "Southern Planter." The manuscript is refreshingly free of efforts to be "literary." As Ely remarked, "it is a careful, factual study and reflects little of Woodrow Wilson, the man." Perhaps its chief interest today is that in assessing the different economists, Wilson revealed something of his own economic views at the time.[44]

Wilson's early economic creed, derived from his reading of the *Nation* and from the lectures of Dr. Atwater at Princeton, was that of an old-fashioned Manchester liberal. There is reason to believe that sometime between Princeton and Johns Hopkins he began to abandon this attitude, if only because of his intense admiration for Walter Bagehot. Bagehot had come to doubt that the "laws" of political economy were of universal applicability and had attempted in his last important work, *Economic Studies,* to describe the British economy at it was, not as the "metaphysical" economists claimed it ought to be. At Johns Hopkins Wilson was subjected to new influences that assaulted the unthinking orthodoxy of his early years. In a course with Ely in 1883-1884 he was introduced to the German "historical" school of economists, who revolted against the almost purely deductive methods of Ricardo, Senior, James Mill, and Jevons. He read *The Wealth of Nations* entire and discovered that Adam Smith was far less dogmatic than the Manchester school who later turned laissez-faire economy into a fixed body of doctrine. He must have been exposed to socialism, for the seminary subscribed to no less than a dozen contemporary socialist periodicals. In any event, in reviewing the *Journal des Économistes* Wilson gave the gist of "three important articles on socialism," and his close friend Albert Shaw was interested in socialistic communities. Finally, there was Ely himself, who was one of the authors of a "Statement of Principles of the American Economic Association," published in 1885, which declared war on pure laissez faire. It opened with the declaration, "We regard the state as an agency whose positive assistance is one of the indispensable conditions of progress." Ely was seeking an alternative to ruthless competition—perhaps a development of the English cooperative movement, perhaps piecemeal socialism and social legislation.[45]

Although Wilson's account of American economists makes no explicit statement of his beliefs, it reveals that the new influences had penetrated. He is critical of purely deductive Ricardian economics. Thus, he finds somewhat ridiculous Francis Wayland's "constant tendency to call all seemingly established principles of the science laws of Divine Providence." In treating George Tucker, he maintains that too many American writers reflect too faithfully "the doctrines of the English writers and their French interpreters"; they describe "American scenery," but their thinking is alien. He has a good word to say for *Notes on Political Economy* by "a Southern Planter," even though the "beginning, body, and end of the notes is protection." "The author enunciates," writes Wilson, "with some force the principle that in economy, as in other practical affairs, the facts of history and the circumstances of each case, rather than *a priori* conclusions, should be the determining element in every discussion." In another passage Wilson inferentially praises "the open-eyed methods of Adam Smith dwelling much on actual economic conditions." Still elsewhere he comments favorably on "the German economists who first directed economic method into . . . historical channels." Most striking is his praise of Amasa Walker for his awareness that there is "an *art* of political economy . . . more or less governed by considerations of state policy."[46]

In sum, Wilson's treatment of American economists reveals that he had been shaken loose from Dr. Atwater, who had taught him that political economy was an a priori, pure science, deduced from obvious maxims that partook of divine law. He had been brought in touch with recent economic thought, on the Continent as well as in England and America, and had begun to suspect that there might be a legitimate place for state intervention in the economy.

No sooner had *Congressional Government* found a publisher than Wilson wrote Ellen Axson, "The acceptance of my book has of course given me the deepest satisfaction and has cleared away a whole storm of anxieties: it is an immense gain in every way. But it has sobered me a good deal too. The question is, What next? I must be prompt to follow up the advantage gained: and I must follow it up in the direction in which I have been preparing to do effectual political service. I feel as I suppose a general does who has gained a foothold in the enemy's country. I must push on: to linger would be fatal." In March and again in April 1885 he refused to undertake a history of North Carolina for Houghton Mifflin, partly because of lack of "special prerequisites" for the job, partly because of "something very like a break down in health" brought on by overwork, but also, he wrote them, because of a project on which he was already embarked and which would take him at least two years to complete. So far no record has been found describing what this proposed task was. Nothing of major importance issued from Wilson's pen during the next two years. His later books—*The State* and *Division and Reunion*—were suggested by publishers' representatives. It may well be that at this time he began preparations for "The Philosophy of Politics"—the work that was to have crowned his career but which never came to completion.[47]

It is almost certain, too, that Wilson was beginning a serious study of public administration. In February 1885 he confessed to Ellen Axson, in an extraordinary piece of prophetic self-revelation:

there is, and has long been, in my mind a 'lurking sense of disappointment and *loss,* as if I had missed from my life something upon which both my gifts and inclinations gave me a claim'; I do feel a very real regret that I have been shut out from my heart's first—primary—ambition and purpose, which was, to take an active, if possible a leading, part in public life, and strike out for myself, if I had the ability, a *statesman's* career. That is my heart's,—or, rather, my *mind's*—deepest secret . . . Had I had independent means of support, even of the most modest proportions, I should doubtless have sought an entrance into politics *anyhow,* and have tried to fight my way into predominant influence, even amidst the hurly-burly and helter-skelter of Congress. I have a strong instinct of leadership, an unmistakably oratorical temperament, and the keenest possible delight in affairs; and it has required very constant and stringent schooling to content me with the sober methods of the scholar and the man of letters. I have no patience for the tedious toil of what is known as 'research'; I have a passion for interpreting great thoughts to the world; I should be complete if I could inspire a great movement of opinion, if I could read the experiences of the past into the practical life of the men of to-day and so communicate the thought to the minds of the great mass of the people as to impel them to great political achievements. Burke was a *very* much greater man than Cobden or Bright; but the work of Cobden and Bright is much nearer to the measure of my powers, it seems to me, than the writings of imperishable thought upon the greatest problems in politics, which was Burke's mission. I think with you . . . that 'of all the world's workers those which take by far the highest rank are the writers of noble books.' If one could choose between the two careers, *with the assurance that he had the capacity for either,* it seems to me there would be no room for hesitation even. But my feeling has been that such literary talents as I have are *secondary* to my equipment for other things: that my power to write was meant to be a handmaiden to my power to speak and to organize action.[48]

Wilson may have thought that, as an alternative to elective office, from which he felt himself debarred by circumstance, he might find a way to an appointive position. A truly professional civil service had been a commonplace in France and Prussia for over a century, but in England it dated only from the reforms of Gladstone's Liberal ministry of 1868-1874. Wilson's essay "Committee or Cabinet Government?" revealed that even before going to Johns Hopkins he had begun to develop an interest in administration. With the election of Grover Cleveland to the presidency in November 1884, there appeared the prospect that high positions in the federal government might be taken away from the spoilsmen and opened to men of ability on a basis of merit. Henry Crew, one of Wilson's companions at the Ashtons' boarding house, had this recollection of a conversation with him during this period: "I asked him, what was then a very common question among students at Johns Hopkins, 'What are you driving at?' To which his instant reply was 'Administration!' At the moment, I took this to refer to the management of some academic department of history of economics: but I shortly discovered that he had in mind something quite different." [49]

There was probably no better place in America to study administration than Johns Hopkins. H. B. Adams was much interested in civil service reform and once proposed that Congress set up a tax-supported "civil academy" to train administrators, somewhat along the lines of West Point and Annapolis. Richard T. Ely had come back from Germany in 1880 with the idea that the problem of the age was "not one of legislation but fundamentally one of administration." He on occasion gave lectures, and once Wilson, as "scribe" of the historical seminary, wrote into the records an account of a short paper on administration read by Ely. According to Wilson, the speaker, "dwelt upon the importance of administrative study; upon the special necessity for it in this country, in view of the fact that our administration is the worst in the world; and upon the strange apathy which has hitherto reigned in the U.S. with regard to questions of this nature." Ely later wrote that when he talked of administration, he felt he had struck a spark in Wilson.[50]

Public administration as a formal academic discipline was mostly of German origin. In order to study the sources, Wilson was compelled to learn German. Efforts to teach himself the language may have been one of the reasons he worked himself so hard in the spring of 1885 that he came close to another breakdown in health. It is certain that he eventually did master the language sufficiently to become thoroughly conversant with the German literature on administration.

Wilson's time at Johns Hopkins coincided almost exactly with his engagement to Ellen Axson. His success at the university may in great part have stemmed from this fact. Surely it carried out the prediction of his mother, who wrote him just as he began his studies, "And now your heart is at rest you will be able to give yourself to the work before you with all your heart—and I have no fear for the result." [51]

During Wilson's first year at Johns Hopkins his fiancée studied at the Art Students League in New York City; during the second, she lived with her paternal grandfather in Savannah, Georgia. The fact that they were separated during most of this time is a fortunate one for the biographer. Wilson had to carry on his courtship by mail, and the scores of letters he wrote Ellen Axson at this time are full of incident, opinion, and self-revelation. [52]

Ellen Axson told her brother at the time of her engagement, "Woodrow is the greatest man in the world and the best," and she never wavered in that opinion. In return, Wilson dropped his guard. He wrote her, "you are the only person in the world—except the dear ones at home—with whom I do not *have* to act a part, to whom I do *not* have to deal out confidences cautiously; and you are the only person in the world—without *any* exception—to whom I can tell all that my heart contains." At another time he confessed to her, "I have an uncomfortable feeling that I am carrying a volcano about with me. My salvation is in being loved." His fiancée contributed to that salvation in many ways. She gave him self-confidence. "Until you loved me," he wrote, "I used to be tormented with 'uneasy questionings' about *everything* in my future; *now* I am uneasy about *nothing* in that future." She was receptive to everything on his mind—his ambitions, his tastes, his achievements and failures. The life of the intellectual, he told her, is inevitably solitary but, "Give him one friend who can understand him, who will not leave him, who will always be accessible by day and night—one friend, one kindly listener, just one, and the whole universe is changed. It is deaf and indifferent no longer, and whilst *she* listens, it seems as if all men and angels listened also, so perfectly his thought is mirrored in the light of her answering eyes." [53]

As a girl, Ellen Axson is reported to have always had a book before her as she dressed and to have memorized Wordsworth while skipping rope. Her knowledge of literature was deeper and her tastes more catholic than Woodrow Wilson's, which he realized. He facetiously suggested that since he must "work unceasingly on one or two rigid specialties," she might give "the best possible aid merely by doing for my proxy and my benefit (you see how selfish I am!) such reading as you delight most in doing . . . You can recite to me the plots and read to me the choice parts of the best novels of the day, and fill my prosy brain with the sweetest words of the poets; can, in short, keep my mind from dry rot by exposing it to an atmosphere of fact and entertainment and imaginative suggestion." [54]

Ellen Axson opened Wilson's eyes, apparently for the first time, to the visual arts and architecture. His letters to her from Baltimore show him going to galleries and somewhat doggedly attempting to enjoy painting. His tastes were utterly conventional. He liked pictures that told a story and was "disgusted" at an exhibit of Whistler's etchings: "As compared with these unsatisfactory dashes of helter-skelter lines and irresponsible patches of shade, recommend me to the staring *chromo* with its honest ugliness." [55]

In one area Ellen Axson's mind probed further than that of her fiancé. On occasion she was subject to doubt and sought to examine her religious beliefs. When she suggested her questionings to Wilson, he gave her the pat answers she had learned to expect from her ministerial father and grandfather. He accepted religious truth, and that was that; metaphysical discussions irritated him. When Ellen Axson worried about the death of her father, his answer was predictable: "Your father, however sad or tragic his death may have been, is happy now. His Saviour, we may be sure, did not desert his servant at the supreme moment; and it is a joy to think that he is now reunited to the sweet, noble mother who went before him." Yet her doubts would not down, and later in life she read Kant and Hegel to try to find the answers for herself.[56]

However great Ellen Axson's devotion, she did not surrender her judgment to Wilson's, and in many ways her judgment was steadier, less impulsive, than his. For instance, when he wanted to take a teaching position at the end of his first year at Johns Hopkins so that he could marry her, she insisted that he stay a second year to complete his training and finish his book.

Wilson had an eye for attractive women and was frank in telling Ellen Axson so. A particular Presbyterian church in Baltimore appealed to him, he told her, both because of "first rate preaching" and "plenty of pretty girls." Another time he described "a very jolly time" at a party at which he had engaged in "numerous frolics" with a young lady, once getting himself locked in the pantry with her as prisoner. Wilson had many close women friends throughout his thirty years with Ellen Axson, but there was never occasion for either concealment or embarrassment. Perhaps because he was brought up with sisters and girl cousins, Wilson needed extended female companionship; and since he was utterly devoted to Ellen Axson and she had complete trust in him, he could indulge this need without self-consciousness.[57]

In January 1885, Wilson received an appointment to the faculty of Bryn Mawr College, which was to open in September. The promised salary was $1500. Somehow he had saved $500 during his last year at Johns Hopkins, probably from royalties on *Congressional Government* plus some lecture fees. This was enough, he insisted, for him and Ellen Axson to marry and to enjoy a long honeymoon in "some quiet, unfashionable place." She agreed, and the two were married in Savannah on June 24, 1885, with his father and her grandfather performing the service. They spent most of the rest of the summer honeymooning in a cottage on a mountainside in Arden, North Carolina.[58]

During Woodrow Wilson's time at Johns Hopkins he made extraordinary advances in maturity, competence, self-confidence, and power. He had arrived at Baltimore in September 1883 an unknown. At twenty-seven he was still dependent on family bounty, and his parochial successes as a campus leader had to be balanced against his precarious health and false start at law. Scarcely two years later, he was on the high road to eminence. *Congressional Government* had earned him an immediate reputation as a political scientist, and publishers sought more from his pen. His appointment at Bryn Mawr revealed that he was regarded as a young man of the highest academic promise.

Wilson had gone to Baltimore a lonely provincial, whose contacts with other men engaged in political studies were limited. At Johns Hopkins he continued to pursue his own studies in his own way, but he gained immensely from the stimulus of the historical seminary. His fellow graduate students, several of them men of high ability, provided both stimulus and an audience. He met and enjoyed a number of the celebrities who went to the university as visiting lecturers, such as the philosopher Josiah Royce and the English literary critic Edmund Gosse. He made the acquaintance of James Bryce, who was already gathering materials for his famous work, *The American Commonwealth*. As critical students of American government, Wilson and Bryce had a common bond, and they kept in touch intermittently until one was President of the United States and the other, by then raised to the peerage, was British ambassador in Washington. Wilson found he was able to hold his own in such company. At the seminary he was surely "not least, but honored of them all" for his judgment, his knowledge of politics, and his ability as a speaker.[59]

What had Wilson gained from the university itself? Johns Hopkins surely did not mold him, as it did other young scholars, because he did not follow its prescriptions but, as at Princeton, took his education into his own hands. Yet if he had been completely on his own, he would not have acquired such familiarity with recent economic thought as he did under Richard T. Ely. Nor would his interest in public administration have developed so far without the encouragement and advice of Adams and Ely. Although he developed no taste for the "tedious toil of what is known as 'research,'" he learned research techniques. Although no linguist and without much interest in other cultures, he improved his French and learned enough German for his purposes. Finally, the books and periodicals in the Bluntschli Library were a godsend; through them he gained familiarity with the scholarly literature in his field. Thus, in a variety of ways, Johns Hopkins helped Wilson to change from a callow amateur to a professional political scientist in touch with the world of scholarship.

Wilson's attitude toward Johns Hopkins was ambivalent. He never displayed such loyalty toward the institution as he always felt toward Princeton and sometimes professed for Virginia. At Baltimore, however, he acquired a grasp of the university ideal that would have been difficult to gain at either Princeton or Virginia. At the end of his first year in the historical seminary Wilson wrote an article on American universities that was accepted by the *New York Evening Post,* in which he implicitly revealed his debt to Johns Hopkins by the statement: "A university of the highest order is a living loadstone, which draws men of power to itself from afar, and fills them with its own spirit of enthusiasm for knowledge, of absolute honesty in all research, of persistence in that study of books and men which is essential to all success." Yet Wilson never developed enthusiasm for the scientific method espoused at Johns Hopkins or overcame his scorn for the failure of the university to appreciate the higher literary values. Both his public and private writings of later years are studded with direct or implied criticism of the type of Germanic scholarship that Johns Hopkins represented.[60]

Whatever Wilson's opinion of Johns Hopkins, there can be no doubt of the continuing admiration he inspired there. Contemporaries, notably Albert Shaw and J. Franklin Jameson, kept in touch and later begged him to write for books and periodicals they edited. He received official recognition of esteem when in 1886 he was granted the Ph.D. by special dispensation, without regular examination, with *Congressional Government* being accepted as his thesis. In 1890 he served as president of the alumni association. In 1893 *Congressional Government* was awarded one of the first John Marshall prizes, established to recognize distinguished work published by members of the historical seminary. At the twenty-fifth anniversary celebration in 1901 Wilson made one of the principal addresses and was awarded an honorary degree.[61]

As Princeton brought Wilson back to the campus, first as professor and later as president, and the University of Virginia repeatedly tried to persuade him to guide its destinies, the same pattern reappeared at Johns Hopkins. Only a year after he had ended his studies there, H. B. Adams proposed that he be appointed to give lectures in American administration. In 1888 Wilson started to give a five-week course in administration and was reappointed annually for nine years. Adams also dreamed of making him head of a special school of administration at Johns Hopkins. President Gilman, fully sharing Adams's admiration, used to say that Woodrow Wilson was the only man who had a standing invitation to join his faculty. When Adams retired as head of the Department of Historical and Political Science in 1900, Wilson was Gilman's first choice for a successor.[62]

VII

Congressional Government

I want to contribute to our literature what no American has ever contributed, studies in the philosophy of our institutions, not the abstract and occult, but the practical and suggestive, philosophy which is at the core of our governmental methods; their use, their meaning, "the spirit that makes them workable." I want to divest them of the theory that obscures them and present their weakness and their strength without disguise, and with such skill and such plenitude of proof that it shall be seen that I have succeeded and that I have added something to the resources of knowledge upon which statecraft must depend.

—Woodrow Wilson, 1883[1]

WRITTEN and published during Woodrow Wilson's years at Johns Hopkins, *Congressional Government* has proved to be his most enduring book. Only one of the other works composed during his academic years is still in print, and none is still read widely. Only one is even readable—*Constitutional Government in the United States* (1908)—and it is in effect a gloss on *Congressional Government*. The rest include *The State* (1889), a textbook on government; *Division and Reunion* (1893), a short history of the United States from 1829 to 1889; *An Old Master* (1893) and *Mere Literature* (1896), two collections of essays; *George Washington* (1896), a short, saccharine biography; and *A History of the American People* (1902), a hastily written popular history of the United States. All except *Constitutional Government* are dated; not even the later eminence of their author is ever likely to bring them back from limbo.[2]

Why the enduring vitality of *Congressional Government*? It has serious blemishes in scholarship and style. Some of its confident judgments on the American political system were faulty at the time; many more have been contradicted by later history. Yet the book still has impact and is widely read. Most of Wilson's basic principles of political action are here enunciated—principles that he elaborated in later writings and lectures and eventually put into practice as President of the United States.

In this first book Wilson attempted no less a task than to do for the United States what Walter Bagehot had done for Britain in *The English Constitution*: to show how government actually worked, as opposed to the way it was supposed to; to explain "the living reality" that refuted the "literary theory." His debt to Bagehot was frankly expressed in a letter to Houghton Mifflin accompanying the manuscript of the first chapters: "As a constitutional study, the subject is, as you will perceive, a new one. Not that I have brought out any hitherto unseen facts; I have simply grouped facts which have not before stood together, and thus given them the setting of a new treatment. I have modeled my work chiefly on Mr. Bagehot's essays on the English Constitution, though I have been guided in some points of treatment by the method followed in some of the better volumes of MacMillan's admirable 'English Citizen Series.' "[3]

In his earlier articles, "Cabinet Government in the United States" and "Committee or Cabinet Government?" Wilson had already elaborated Bagehot's criticisms of the American government, and in this book he follows the same lines of attack. But *Congressional Government* is far better written and reveals far more grasp of the realities of American politics. Indeed, it is so far superior to anything he did before that it is hard to believe only twelve months had elapsed between the time he sent the amateurish "Committee or Cabinet Government?" to the *Overland Monthly* and his dispatch of the completed manuscript of *Congressional Government* to Houghton Mifflin. The multiple advantages of Johns Hopkins had apparently helped him to make the great leap forward.

At the time he was starting to write this book, Wilson confided in a letter to Ellen Axson what he hoped to achieve in the development of his style:

> I have imagined a style clear, bold, fresh, and facile; a style flexible but always strong, capable of light touches or of heavy blows; a style that could be driven at high speed—a brilliant, dashing, coursing speed —or constrained to the slow and stately progress of grave argument, as the case required; a style full of life, of colour and vivacity, of soul and energy, of inexhaustible power—of a thousand qualities of beauty and grace and strength that would make it immortal. Is it any wonder that I am disgusted with the stiff, dry, mechanical, monotonous sentences in which my meagre thoughts are compelled to masquerade, as in garments which are too mean even for *them!*[4]

Wilson was right on both counts: his style was improving, and he was still a long way from achieving his high ambitions. The writing in

Congressional Government is marked by a new movement and pace, as
well as by a kind of magisterial omniscience—to some degree borrowed
from Bagehot—which is sometimes so effective as to lull the reader into
suspension of critical judgment. There is a new trenchancy and wit, as
witness the following passages:

A President's usefulness is measured, not by efficiency, but by calendar
months. It is reckoned that if he be good at all he will be good for
four years. A Prime Minister must keep himself in favor with the majority, a President need only keep alive.

His [the Vice-President's] chief dignity, next to presiding over the
Senate, lies in the circumstance that he is awaiting the death or disability
of the President. And the chief embarrassment in discussing his office
is, that in explaining how little there is to be said about it one has
evidently said all there is to say.

. . . when the presidential candidate came to be chosen, it was recognized
that he should have as short a political record as possible, and that he
should wear a clean and irreproachable insignificance.

Sometimes there is bold and effective use of metaphor:

As a rule a bill committed is a bill doomed. When it goes from the
clerk's desk to the committee-room it crosses a parliamentary bridge of
sighs to dim dungeons of silence whence it will never return.

A decisive career which gives a man a well-understood place in public
estimation constitutes a positive disability for the presidency; because
candidacy must precede election, and the shoals of candidacy can be
passed only by a light boat which carries little freight and can be turned
readily about to suit the intricacies of the passage.[5]

At the same time there are passages in which Wilson's stylistic efforts
are almost grotesque. He sometimes goes in for tortured adjectives—
"that trenchant policy of reconstruction," "that puissant doctrine of implied powers," "the nimble progress of federal reconstruction"—and for
punning—"the reichstag of our cousin Germans." His search for bold
metaphor leads him into strange byways, for instance:

It is indispensable that, besides the House of Representatives which
runs on all fours with popular sentiment, we should have a body like the
Senate which may refuse to run with it at all when it seems to be wrong.

Money in its goings to and fro makes various mares go by the way,
so to speak.

The one [Hamilton] had inherited warm blood and a bold sagacity,
while in the other [Jefferson] a negative philosophy ran suitably through
cool veins.[6]

Often Wilson uses a great many words to say very little. When explaining why American legislators prefer indirect to direct taxes, he cannot simply say that taxpayers are less aware of the burden of the former than of the latter; he must elaborate the obvious in a passage of sustained banality:

> All direct taxes are heartily disliked by every one who has to pay them, and as heartily abused, except by those who have never owned an ounce or an inch of property, and have never seen a tax-bill. The heart of the ordinary citizen regards them with an inborn aversion. They are so straight-forward and peremptory in their demands. They soften their exactions with not a grain of consideration. The tax-collector, consequently is never esteemed a lovable man. His methods are too blunt, and his powers too obnoxious. He comes to us, with not a "please," but with a "must." His requisitions leave our pockets lighter and our hearts heavier. We cannot, for the life of us, help thinking, as we fold up his receipt and put it away, that government is much too expensive a luxury as nowadays conducted, and that that receipt is incontestable documentary proof of unendurable extortion. What we do not realize is, that life would be robbed of one of its chief satisfactions if this occasion for grumbling were to be taken away.[7]

The trouble with much of the writing is that it gets in the reader's way, serving neither to inform nor to enlighten but merely to give a sometimes irritating awareness of the presence of the author. Yet so much of *Congressional Government* has pace, confidence, persuasiveness, and even eloquence that one wishes Wilson had commandeered the services of a stern and competent editor.

As Wilson himself freely conceded in his letter to Houghton Mifflin, *Congressional Government* is not a work of original scholarship, at least in the sense in which that term is used in the academic world. There are only fifty-two citations. All of them are either obvious secondary sources, such as J. R. Green's *History of the English People* and articles in *The Nation* and *North American Review,* or readily available primary sources, such as Supreme Court decisions, the collected letters of John Adams, and the *Federalist* papers. There is no evidence of a first-hand study of Congress in action. Wilson later boasted that during the time he was writing *Congressional Government* he visited the Capital only once, even though Washington was only an hour by train from Baltimore.[8]

Nevertheless, the study shows that Wilson had gained a firm grasp of American constitutional history and practice. *Congressional Government* reveals no such ignorance and misunderstanding as marred the essay "Committee or Cabinet Government?" In fact, the book so abounds in illuminating generalizations that it has ever since been a gold mine for political scientists seeking striking quotations to brighten their pages or head their chapters.

His new knowledge and insight are apparent in the opening chapter, in which Wilson asks his readers to forsake blind worship of the Constitution and to look at the federal government as it is. According to the "literary theory," its distinguishing features are two: federalism—a balance of sovereignty between the states and the federal government— and checks and balances, whereby the executive, legislative, and judicial branches of government are nicely allocated overlapping powers so that no one can dominate the others. In a brief historical survey Wilson argues effectively that both these principles have been whittled away to the point of disappearance. The Civil War and Reconstruction completed an inexorable expansion of federal power so that now, instead of federalism, there is something that "smacks, rather, of federal omnipotence." At the same time Congress has so encroached on the Supreme Court and the executive branch that it has become the efficient center of federal power. In sum: "The balances of the Constitution are for the most part only ideal. For all practical purposes the national government is supreme over the state governments, and Congress predominant over its so-called coordinate branches."[9]

Wilson prophesies—and accurately—that within the near future the federal government will be forced to expand its power to deal with such matters as "the regulation of our vast systems of commerce and manufacture, the control of giant corporations, the restraint of monopolies, the perfection of fiscal arrangements, the facilitating of economic exchanges, and many other like national concerns." Both those who oppose such expansion of national power and those who accept it as inevitable would do well to assess the capacity of the federal government "both for the work it now does and for that which it may be called upon to do." In essence, the United States has developed "a government by the Standing Committees of Congress." Therefore, "as the House of Commons is the central object of examination in every study of the English Constitution, so should Congress be in every study of our own."[10]

Putting this adjuration into practice, Wilson devotes three of his six chapters and 185 of his 333 pages to an examination of Congress in action. He concentrates on the House of Representatives, which receives more than twice as much space as the Senate, and especially on the committee system. As in his two earlier essays on the federal government, he finds American legislative practices defective in comparison with those of Britain. The vices of the House are defined as follows (each balanced by a characteristic virtue of the cabinet system in the House of Commons):

1. Fractionalization of power among different committees leads to irresponsibility and the predominance of special interests over the general welfare.

2. Party discipline is lacking; parties therefore stand for no clear principles.

3. The secret processes of committee government prevent public scrutiny of the legislative process.

4. With no central control over finances and no real budget, "our fiscal policy has been without consistency or coherence, without progressive continuity," which has invited favor, corruption, and waste.

5. There is little real debate, with the result that the public remains unenlightened on public affairs.

6. Clear leadership is missing, since nothing attracts into politics men of ability, independence, and vision.[11]

Wilson's two earlier essays on the federal government had almost ignored the Senate, even to the extent of implying that it was a subordinate body like the House of Lords. He does not repeat this mistake in *Congressional Government*. He is now perfectly aware that the Senate has independent and coordinate powers. Yet he gives only one chapter and 49 pages to it, as compared with two chapters and 135 pages to the House. This is not as illogical as it might seem, for in his opinion the Senate is simply "a small, select, and leisurely House of Representatives."

Much of the chapter on the Senate is devoted to a disquisition on leadership in that body and in the federal government in general. Wilson argues that up to the end of the Civil War there were "three stages of national growth . . . each of them creative of a distinct class of political leaders":

In the period of erection there were great architects and master builders; in the period of constitutional interpretation there were, at a distance from the people, great political schoolmen who pondered and expounded the letter of the law, and, nearer the people, great constitutional advocates who cast the doctrines of the schoolmen into policy; and in the period of abolitionist agitation there were great masters of feeling and leaders of public purpose.[12]

Since the war, however, circumstances have no longer called forth leadership. The United States has been engaged in "that unexciting but none the less capitally important business of every-day development and judicious administration to which every nation in its middle age has to address itself with what sagacity, energy, and prudence it can command." What the country now needs is great administrators, but none appear because the affairs with which they must deal "are matters of a too quiet, business-like sort to enlist feeling or arouse enthusiasm."[13]

What is the remedy? Wilson suggests it by indirection when he remarks that there is no office in the American government set apart for the great party leaders, like the English cabinet—such a prize as would "stimulate men of strong talents to great and conspicuous public services." The powers of the Speaker of the House are "too cramped and covert"; those of the heads of standing committees too narrow; while the President must play the role of silent and inactive superintendent.[14]

Furthermore, the American political system has no place for great parliamentary orators such as Chatham, Burke, Peel, and Gladstone. Again Wilson returns to his familiar thesis that "orators should be the leaders of a self-governing people. Men may be clever and engaging speakers . . . but men can scarcely be orators without that force of character, that readiness of resource, that clearness of vision, that grasp of intellect, that courage of conviction, the earnestness of purpose, and that instinct and capacity for leadership which are the eight horses that draw the triumphal chariot of every leader and ruler of free men." One cannot resist the feeling that the writer saw himself in the chariot.[15]

One virtue of the Senate is that it has more freedom of debate than does the House, and sometimes the debates "are of a very high order of excellence." But, as in the House, too much legislation is hatched in committee, and too many Senators receive their early training as Representatives and are not schooled in the highest techniques of debate.[16]

The feature of the Senate in which Wilson finds most to commend is that, being "almost altogether removed from that temptation to servile obedience to the whims of popular constituencies to which the House is constantly subject," it can act as a brake on "hasty and impolitic movements of public opinion." In a passage showing how far he was as yet removed from any great faith in popular wisdom, he argues that the Senate "is valuable in our democracy in proportion as it is undemocratic." He even suggests that the six-year senatorial term is too short, and that the election of a third of the body every two years is a too frequent rotation in office, weakening the "legislative sinews" of the upper chamber.[17]

Wilson's conservatism is also revealed by his treatment of the charge that the upper house represents "aristocratic tendencies" because many senators are rich men. He disagrees with the notion that wealth is itself a class interest. In words reminiscent of the old defense of the unreformed Parliament as offering "virtual representation" to Englishmen denied the franchise and to towns denied the right to elect members of Parliament, Wilson argues:

> But even the rich Senators cannot be said to be representatives of a class, as if they were all opulent wool-growers or great landowners. Their wealth is in all sorts of stocks, in all sorts of machinery, in all sorts of buildings, in possessions of all the sorts possible in a land of bustling commerce and money-making industries. They have made their money in a hundred different ways, or have inherited it from their fathers who amassed it in enterprises too numerous to imagine; and they have it invested here, there, and everywhere, in this, that, and everything. Their wealth represents no class interests, but all the interests of the commercial world. It represents the majority of the nation, in a word.

If one were to ask a group of informed students of American history what President-to-be wrote the above passage, surely many more would guess McKinley, Taft or Calvin Coolidge than Woodrow Wilson.[18]

Congressional Government is critical of the two great executive powers of the Senate, ratification of treaties and of appointments. As to treaties, there is no real consultation between the President and Senate. Instead, the former "is made to approach that body as a servant conferring with his master, and of course deferring to that master." The President's "only power of compelling compliance on the part of the Senate lies in his initiative in negotiation, which affords him a chance to get the country into such scrapes, so pledged in the view of the world to certain courses of action, that the Senate hesitates to bring about the appearance of dishonor which would follow its refusal to ratify the rash promises or to support the indiscreet threats of the State Department." Here is the technique by which Wilson in 1919 attempted to force ratification of the Versailles Treaty.[19]

In appointments the executive is again subject to "irresponsible dictation" by the Senate. "The President may tire the Senate by dogged persistence, but he can never deal with it on a ground of real equality. He has no real presence in the Senate. His power does not extend beyond the most general suggestion. The Senate always has the last word." The only hope for improvement lies in the extension of civil service reform, which would put an end to political appointments.[20]

The fifth chapter of *Congressional Government* deals with the presidency. Although Wilson knows far more about the federal government and its history than when he wrote his earlier essays, he reaches the same conclusion: the executive department has become distinctly subordinate to Congress. The weakened power and prestige of the office are somewhat the result of faulty methods of choosing candidates for it. National conventions are irresponsible by their very nature: they are representative bodies that select candidates and then disband, and therefore they cannot be held accountable for the wisdom or unwisdom of their choice. Nor were the previous modes of nomination, by state legislatures or congressional caucus, any better. No method of selecting party leaders approaches, in fact, the British cabinet system. Wilson expresses approval, however, of the tendency to make state governorships a steppingstone to the presidency. "The governorship of a State is very like a smaller Presidency; or, rather, the Presidency is very like a big governorship. Training in the duties of one fits for the duties of the other." [21]

State governorships as a school for the presidency are especially to be commended because in Wilson's eyes the principal job of the President is administration. "The business of the President, occasionally great, is usually not above routine. Most of the time it is *mere* administration, mere obedience of directions from the masters of policy, the Standing Committees." Thus, "his duties call rather for training than for constructive genius. If there can be found in the official systems of the States a lower grade of service in which men can be advantageously drilled for Presidential functions, so much the better." By the same token the single four-year term is too short, because "administration is something that men must learn, not something to skill in which they were born . . . A President is dismissed almost as soon as he has learned the duties of his office." [22]

In describing the federal executive, Wilson finds the President not even master in his own house since the actual practice of administration is in the hands of his cabinet members, who in turn are under the dictation of the standing committees of Congress. This was an exaggerated view. In fact, the cabinet was, and nearly always has been, primarily responsible to the President. Here surely Wilson's vision appears to have been clouded by his preconceptions. It is as though he had been born and bred abroad and had not yet quite grasped that the American cabinet was wholly different from the British.

Wilson argued that whereas Congress was dominant in matters of legislation and appointments, it was helpless in the actual day-by-day conduct of government business. The resulting relationship between Congress and the executive departments "must be fatally demoralizing to both." Congress can exercise control over administrators only by disgracing them, either through investigation or impeachment. Investigation tends not merely to reveal but also to magnify and intensify scandals, while not necessarily resulting in the removal of inefficient officers. Impeachment is a weapon that can seldom be employed with justice because mere inefficiency is no high crime or misdemeanor. "A merchant would not think it fair, even if it were lawful, to shoot the clerk who could not learn the business." [23]

Thus, everything about the relations between the executive and Congress contributes to "hide-and-seek vagaries of authority." There is no clear responsibility anywhere. Yet "if there be one principle clearer than another, it is this: that in any business whether of government or of mere merchandising, *somebody must be trusted,* in order that when things go wrong it may be quite plain who should be punished. *Power and strict accountability for its use* are the essential constituents of good government." The great weakness of the federal system, then, is that "it parcels out power and confuses responsibility." Checks and balances "have proved mischievous just to the extent to which they have succeeded in establishing themselves as realities." If the fathers of the Constitution could view their work a century later, "they would be the first to admit that the only fruit of dividing power had been to make it irresponsible." [24]

The chapter on the executive department concludes with a historical survey of the development of the British cabinet, along with a description of the nonpolitical civil servant, chosen only on the criteria of ability and training. In England there is a clear distinction between policy-making and administration. In the United States, there is no such thing. The secretaries who head departments are both politicians and administrators, with the result that there is confusion of purpose and no one actually knows what goes on in the governmental process. [25]

There is little new in the sixth and concluding chapter of *Congressional Government.* Wilson's recently developed interest in administration shows up when he returns again to the relationship between Congress and the administrative officers. He suggests that Congress devotes too much time to the business of legislation and too little to "superintending all matters of government." He goes so far as to write, "The informing function of Congress should be preferred even to its legislative function." The argument is not only that "discussed and interrogated administration is the only pure and efficient administration," but also, "the only really self-governing people is that people which discusses and interrogates its administration." There is no suggestion how the functions of investigation and control are to be reformed. [26]

Wilson concludes by urging that the government of a country as vast as the United States, afflicted with all kinds of pressing problems, "be strong, prompt, wieldy, and efficient." Blind worship of the Constitution has prevented Americans from becoming aware of the defects of their system. Once they become aware, they will be quick to adopt "all thoroughly tested or well-considered expedients necessary to make self-government among us a straightforward thing of simple method, single, unstinted power, and clear responsibility."[27]

Just why Wilson held back from explicitly recommending adoption of cabinet government is not clear. Walter Lippmann hazarded the guess that in the summer of 1884, while writing *Congressional Government,* Wilson "began to undergo a fundamental change in his conception of the American system." Something caused him to begin to see the possibilities of the presidential office, which in turn made him realize that no such drastic remedy as the grafting of the British cabinet system on the American Constitution was necessary. That "something," hazards Lippmann, was "the rise of Grover Cleveland, the first public man in Wilson's own lifetime who aroused his interest in the office of President . . . In Cleveland . . . he discerned the possibility that the office of President might be restored to that 'first estate of dignity' from which it had 'fallen' since 'the early Presidents.' "[28]

This hypothesis is not convincing. It is true that Cleveland's career in the White House aroused Wilson's admiration and that as a result he began to revise his low opinion of the presidential office. But in 1884 Cleveland was only a candidate; Wilson had finished the manuscript and sent it off to the publishers before he even knew whether Cleveland would be elected. Furthermore, *Congressional Government* gives no evidence that the author had any inkling of the vast latent powers of the presidency.

The fact is that Wilson was just as intent as ever on persuading Americans to take over cabinet government. His constant reiteration of the superiority of British ways, and the consistency with which he found the American system defective just where the British system was strong, reveal this. But he thought it good tactics merely to display the vices of the American system alongside the virtues of the British and to trust his readers to transform the invidious comparison into the inexorable conclusion. In a letter to Heath Dabney he explained that he hoped *Congressional Government* might "stand as a permanent piece of constitutional criticism," but "its mission was to *stir* thought and to carry irresistible practical suggestion, and it was as such a missionary that it carried my hopes and ambitions with it." [29]

The first printing of *Congressional Government*—one thousand copies —reached the bookstores in January 1885. Wilson sent the first two copies to Ellen Axson and his father. When Dr. Wilson opened the book, he found that his son had dedicated it to him, "the patient guide of his youth, the gracious companion of his manhood, his best instructor and most lenient critic." Whereupon, admitted the old man, he broke down "and wept and sobbed in the stir of the glad pain." [30]

The book received immediate acclaim. The *Minneapolis Tribune* called it a "masterly book," and the *Philadelphia Evening Telegraph* asserted it was "an important contribution to current political literature." The *New York Examiner* recommended it to "every young man who takes an interest in politics," as did the *Yale Literary Magazine.* The *Atlantic Monthly* held the opinion: "Mr. Wilson is a keen observer, a fair-minded critic and so fresh and unhackneyed in his comments that any student of our history who once begins this interesting volume will read it to the end." [31]

Congressional Government received the ultimate accolade in a review by Gamaliel Bradford in *The Nation.* Woodrow Wilson was the first author, according to Bradford, to explain "the real working" of the United States government. "His book is evidently modeled on Mr. Bagehot's *English Constitution* and it will, though the praise is so high as to be almost extravagant, bear comparison with that estimable work." Bradford quarreled somewhat with Wilson's nomenclature and regretted he had not specifically recommended that cabinet members be granted seats in Congress, but on the whole the review was all that a young author might hope for. Bradford capped his praise of *Congressional Government* by journeying to Baltimore to spend most of a day with Wilson.[32]

Interest in *Congressional Government* was so widespread and immediate that the publishers issued two more printings of five hundred copies each before the year was out. Not all the attention, however, was favorable. The *New York Sun* and the *Independent* were critical. The *San Francisco Daily Evening Bulletin* castigated the work as "colored more or less by that condescending depreciation of American institutions, which in certain circles has become one of the intellectual fashions of the day." Wilson was so stung by "a sneering review . . . in a small local sheet of no circulation" that he walked the streets of Baltimore "to work off his bitterness." [33]

Interest in *Congressional Government* did not die down. Over a year after its publication, in March 1886, the *New England and Yale Review* published a long critique. Its author, Edward G. Bourne, pointed out that within a year *Congressional Government* had received "solid tokens of deserved success": it had run through several editions and earned its author "prompt election . . . to a College professorship." Yet its conclusions were outmoded and dangerous. It was not so much that Wilson was almost an "Anglomaniac" in his preference for the parliamentary system, but that "his views were reflections of thorough-going democratic ideas." Bourne, along with Sir Henry Maine, feared the rising tide of democracy. He could therefore find nothing to commend in the Bagehot-Wilson preference for government by an all-powerful executive dominating a disciplined party in control of an omnipotent legislature as against the checks and balances whereby the fathers of the American constitution deliberately impeded the legislative process. The checks that Bagehot had postulated—"a reverenced aristocracy" and "a stable throne"—were likely soon to be swept away. The Lords were already under heavy attack and a good deal of ridicule. Would the Crown be far behind? When Wilson wrote that the British government "is perfect in proportion that it is unmonarchical," did he mean "the more absolute the English democracy, the more perfect the government, provided there is a nominal monarch"? If so, where was protection from "headlong popular tyranny"? Bourne concluded by censuring Wilson's frequent lapses into "bad writing." He reprimanded him for "a journalistic smartness and flippancy ill suited to the dignity of his subject and distasteful to the reader," for an excess of "incongruous and tasteless" literary figures, and for his use of archaic forms such as "a-doing, a-making, and a-planning." [34]

Congressional Government came under even heavier fire in a lead article in the *Atlantic Monthly* for February 1886, entitled "Ministerial Responsibility and the Constitution." The author was Abbott Lawrence Lowell, then instructor in government at Harvard. Lowell made a frontal attack on the notion that the United States had anything to benefit from adoption of the parliamentary system. He admitted Wilson's contentions that cabinet government interested and instructed the people; that it led to intelligent, systematic legislation; and that it "let floods of light into every corner of administration." But he feared that the introduction of ministerial responsibility in the United States might make the popular will so powerful that the temporary whims of the majority would overwhelm minority interests.[35]

Woodrow Wilson immediately took up the gage in an article entitled "Responsible Government under the Constitution" in the *Atlantic Monthly* for April 1886. He revealed here the dialectical skill that had led to his election as president of debating societies at Princeton and Virginia. By a *reductio ad absurdum* he controverted Lowell's argument that cumbersome machinery is necessary to forestall a tyranny of the majority: if "any reform which would tend to give to national legislation that uniform, open, intelligent and responsible character which it now lacks would also tend to create that popular interest which would unhinge the Constitution," then "democracy is so delicate a form of government that it must break down if given too great facility or efficacy of operation." Wilson could not believe this; he had faith in the "conservative public opinion" in the United States, which in the last analysis was the only support of the Constitution itself. He contended that with "grave social and economic problems now putting themselves forward," the United States could not "afford to put up any longer with such legislation as we may happen upon . . . Instead of the present arrangements for compromise, piece-meal legislating, we must have coherent plans from recognized party leaders, and means for holding them to a faithful exercise of those plans in clear-cut acts of Congress." He still believed that some kind of "ministerial responsibility," such as that he had proposed in the *Overland Monthly,* was the only way "for resting recognized leadership in men chosen for their abilities by a natural selection of debate in a sovereign assembly of whose contests the whole country is witness.[36]

Note that Wilson, heretofore distrustful of democracy, has now become its defender. It may be that Mr. Lowell, abetted by Mr. Bourne, pushed him into this new role, but it marked an important milestone in the development of his mature political philosophy. It was a first great step from quasi-alien criticism of American politics to acceptance of democracy as a fact of American political life.

The debate in the *Atlantic* led to a cordial acquaintance. According to Mr. Lowell's recollection, "A few weeks later there appeared in my office a tall, lantern-jawed young man, just my age. He greeted me with the words: 'I'm Woodrow Wilson. I've come to heal a quarrel, not to make one.'" The two men liked each other at once, and Wilson made it a habit to call on Lowell whenever he went to Boston to lecture or to see his publishers. Lowell thought Wilson at this time "a very attractive figure." He had a presence and was "like Theodore Roosevelt in that one was immediately conscious that he was in a room, and he left a gap when he went out." Lowell never had much respect for Wilson as a scholar, however; he thought him a brilliant writer who "lacked a scientific mind" and saw everything "through the haze of his own preconceptions."[37]

Attacks on *Congressional Government* did not cease. In November 1889, Herbert B. Adams warned Wilson that he had better come to a forthcoming meeting of the American Historical Association in Washington, D. C., because "a Harvard man named Freeman Snow will deliver a paper on *Congressional Government* and take issue with you on several counts." Dr. Snow's paper was duly delivered and published in the collected papers of the A.H.A. He rang changes on the arguments of Sir Henry Maine, Bourne, and Lowell: cabinet government provided no safe check on the unrestrained will of the majority. The deference for their betters that supposedly kept the English *plebs* in order was a feudal survival that had no place in America. He saw grave danger in Wilson's willingness to wipe away constitutional safeguards against federal action in the questionable hope that with more unrestrained executive power the United States would develop abler political leadership.[38]

The next year Albert Bushnell Hart, the Harvard historian and Wilson's friend, entered the lists against him. Hart held that the cure for the "divided irresponsibility" and "wasteful system of conducting legislation" through committees was already in the making in the enlargement of the powers of the Speaker of the House. When the Speaker was able to appoint committees, control debate, lead the majority party, and steer the course of legislation through his position in the Rules Committee, he would be as much a force for coherent legislative programs as a prime minister. In 1893 there was still another attack. An article by Frederick V. Fisher entitled "Party Government," in the *Westminster Review,* assailed exactly what Wilson most admired about the British party system: its disciplined support of a legislative program. Fisher argued that there was less independent judgment among MP's than among Congressmen, and that to promote party discipline was to further "all that is vulgar and base" in American politics.[39]

Wilson's criticism of Congress had nettled at least one Senator. In June 1889, when Wilson was teaching at Wesleyan, Senator Joseph R. Harvey of Connecticut addressed the Wesleyan student body and warned them against the untruths to be found in *Congressional Government.* Condemning Wilson for his ignorance of American ways and his "English affection," the Senator expressed fear that he might undermine the patriotism of his students.[40]

Meanwhile Wilson had gained powerful support from a man he greatly admired. James Bryce in his recently published study of our politics, *The American Commonwealth,* had high praise for *Congressional Government,* "a lucid and interesting book" from which he "derived much help" in composing his chapters on "The Committees of Congress," "Congressional Legislation," and "Congressional Finance." In these chapters Bryce quoted Wilson four times and repeated almost verbatim his strictures on Congressional methods of legislating. When it came time to revise the work in 1891, Bryce called on Wilson for help.[41]

All this discussion stimulated study of the committee system. In 1893 at the Columbian Exposition in Chicago J. Franklin Jameson read a paper before the American Historical Association on the origins of standing committees, opening his remarks by saying, "Mr. Bryce and Mr. Woodrow Wilson have familiarized us all with the notion that the transaction of business through committees is one of the leading peculiarities of American legislative bodies . . . and indeed perhaps the most important of such peculiarities." Five years later Lauros G. McConachie published a detailed study of the origin and development of congressional committees. McConachie claimed to take a middle ground in the continuing controversy between advocates of the British and American systems of government, but he characterized Wilson as one of a group of "scathing, relentless faultfinders" of American practices, who "failed to suggest remedies, or to discover any process of self-correction in Congress itself" and simply offered "one stock model . . . the British parliamentary system." McConachie observed that Congress was in process of reforming the committee system through such means as enlarging committee membership and holding open hearings on bills. He thought that the system brought to the top able leaders—men of strong will and seasoned judgment, expert in particular fields of legistlation.[42]

This running controversy helped to keep *Congressional Government* alive, and its publishers issued small printings of the work almost annually. In 1900, at which time the work was translated into French, Wilson wrote a preface for the fifteenth printing. Rereading his "little volume . . . for the first time since its first appearance," he found that his description of the federal government was no longer accurate. Both in detail and in substance, patterns of power in the federal structure had changed. Forces of integration, especially the growing power of the Speaker and the Rules Committee, had created, "in germ at least, a recognized and sufficiently concentrated leadership within the House," although one to which "the taint of privacy attaches." Above all, the plunge into imperialism and international politics at the time of the Spanish-American War had exalted the power of the President to such a degree that Wilson foresaw that his book might soon become "hopelessly out of date." [43]

In 1907 Wilson gave a course of lectures at Columbia University and used the opportunity to make "a fresh analysis of the character and operation of constitutional government." By then—after Theodore Roosevelt had been in the White House for six years—he had come to believe that "the President is at liberty, both in law and in conscience, to be as big a man as he can." [44]

The question arises whether *Congressional Government* has in fact become "hopelessly out of date." Surely the vast expansion of presidential power in the twentieth century is a variance with the picture

Wilson painted of an officer without power over policy—a mere administrator. Wilson made the mistake of generalizing from the particular situation in the two decades after the Civil War, assuming that this period was a norm when in fact it proved an aberration. Modern critics have pointed to other shortcomings. According to Arthur Link, the ideas expressed in *Congressional Government* were not original and, "judged by modern critical standards, the book was not profound." It was "characterized by an amazing neglect or ignorance of economic factors in political life. It did not penetrate beneath the surface of political allegiances, nor did it lay bare the economic basis of allegiances and loyalties." Roland Young, in a "reconsideration" of the work in 1956, was equally severe. According to Professor Young, Wilson substituted rhetoric for facts, had little sense of the actual processes of legislation, and was guilty of fuzzy thinking generally. Although such criticisms have an element of unfairness, since they apply *ex post facto* standards to a book written when American political science, considered as a scholarly discipline, was in its infancy, they are essentially well founded. Why, then, does *Congressional Government* still attract so many readers that after it was reissued in 1956, as a paperback, it ran through four editions in eight years? [45]

Congressional Government is still pertinent because its essential contention is sound: the American government demands strong executive leadership. Furthermore, leadership in Congress still tends, as in Wilson's time, to be disorganized, diffuse, and irresponsible. Standing committees have proliferated to such a degree that there were in 1956 no less than 230 committees or subcommittees in the House and Senate, many of them with extraordinary power to impede legislation or to promote private interests. It is still a fact that the United States has no true budget because congressional control over finances is often, as Wilson described it in the 1880's, "without consistency or coherency, without progressive continuity." And whenever the White House is occupied by a President either unable or unwilling to use his powers to the utmost, the "morbid symptoms" described by Wilson reappear in full virulence. According to Walter Lippman, *Congressional Government* "was a good book to read during the Harding administration. It is a good book to have read at the end of the Truman and at the beginning of the Eisenhower administrations. It is one to be taken to heart by all who have seen the ravages of McCarthyism." For all its shortcomings, it lives on because it is still, as when it was written, an eloquent tract for the times, calling for a government that shall be honest, vigorous, and responsive to the general welfare—a government that above all shall attract the best men in the country to positions of leadership.[46]

Part Two: Teacher

VIII

Bryn Mawr

1885–1888

Lecturing to young women of the present generation on the history and principles of politics is about as appropriate and profitable as would be lecturing to stone masons on the evolution of fashion in dress.

—Woodrow Wilson, 1887[1]

IN 1878 a wealthy Quaker, Joseph Wright Taylor, died, leaving an estate of about $800,000 to establish a college or institution of learning, having for its object the advanced education of females," so that they might enjoy "all the advantages . . . which are freely offered to young men." For this purpose Mr. Taylor had purchased forty acres of gently sloping farmland in Bryn Mawr, Pennsylvania, a place reputedly free from endemic "low typhoid or malarial fever or dysentery or kindred epidemic diseases" and accessible to Philadelphia. The will named eleven members of the Society of Orthodox Friends as trustees. They were directed to see that Friends had preference for admission to the new college and that the officers and instructors "endeavor to instill into the minds and hearts of the students, the doctrine of the New Testament as accepted by Friends."[2]

The Bryn Mawr trustees acted with deliberation, so that it was not until September 1885 that the college began operation. By then they had put up two stone buildings in "bastard Gothic" style, Taylor and Merion Halls, to accommodate forty-odd students. They had provided housing for most of the faculty. As president, they had chosen James E. Rhoads, one of their own number. Of prime importance, they had decided that the new college should aim at the highest possible academic excellence. It was to be a "Joanna Hopkins."

The person who had most to do with determining the character of Bryn Mawr was neither President Rhoads nor any of the "weighty Friends" who composed the board of trustees but a young woman named Carey Thomas, who had already demonstrated extraordinary talents.

Carey Thomas was born in 1857 to the Quaker aristocracy; her father and an uncle, for example, served as trustees of both Johns Hopkins and Bryn Mawr. Two years of intense pain following severe burns suffered when she was seven years old had steeled her character. By the time she reached her teens she had dedicated her life to the proposition that women were equal to men. At the age of fourteen she wrote in her diary, "If ever I live and grow up my *one* aim and concentrated purpose *shall be* and *is* to show that women *can learn*, can reason, *can compete* with man in the grand fields of literature and science and conjecture that open before the nineteenth cntury, that a woman can be a woman and a *true* one without having all her time engrossed by dress and society." [3]

Putting this self-adjuration into practice, Carey Thomas pursued a brilliant academic career, in spite of parental and institutional opposition. After graduation from Cornell she fought her way into classes at Johns Hopkins and later into lectures at two German universities, although she was denied the right to take a degree. Finally she succeeded in taking her examination at the University of Zurich, in Switzerland, where she won a doctorate in Germanic philology and literature with the almost unheard-of distinction of *summa cum laude*. But her triumph over entrenched masculinity had not been achieved without personal cost. Handsome, high-spirited, and well dressed, she attracted men's attention but repelled their advances. During a long and active life she sought from the other sex not love, but justice. In dealing with her own sex she could charm, inspire, and lead, but she was often high-handed and arrogant.

When Carey Thomas, still in Europe, heard about plans for Bryn Mawr, she immediately saw her opportunity. "Of course I suppose it is impossible," she wrote her mother, "and that they would never give it to me, but I should love to have the presidency of Bryn Mawr. I believe that I could make it the best women's college there is." So manifest were her capabilities that the trustees seriously considered her candidacy, but they finally decided against it because of her youth, her possible rashness, and her questionable devotion to Quaker doctrine. In December 1883, however, they appointed her dean and professor of English. She was not yet twenty-seven years old.

Although second in command to President Rhoads, who in turn was answerable to the trustees, Carey Thomas was the principal architect of academic policy. Shortly after her appointment she visited other women's colleges—Smith, Vassar, Wellesley, Harvard Annex (later Radcliffe)—and a number of girls' schools. On her return, she persuaded the trustees to stiffen the entrance requirements so that they were as high as any in the country. She also heeded the advice of Professor Clement of Harvard: "In engaging professors do not take people who apply. The people you need are already busy. *Go out and look for them.*" At her prompting President Rhoads enlisted a young faculty of the highest caliber, offering as bait good salaries, freedom from extracurricular duties, and teaching loads light enough to provide time for active scholarship. In brief, Carey Thomas persuaded her elders to put scholarship before piety. Without her, Bryn Mawr might have become simply a respectable denominational college. Because of her, its academic standards were excelled by those of no other women's college.

Carey Thomas' influence was apparent in the selection of the nine full-time members of the academic faculty. All except one had doctorates; all except one had studied at European universities. The exception in both categories was Woodrow Wilson.

In November 1884 Herbert B. Adams had brought Wilson in touch with Dr. Rhoads and Miss Thomas. They were seeking a person to organize the history department, and it took them only a short time to offer Wilson the job. This was an accolade for a young man without a doctorate who had never taught a class. It revealed both the high regard in which he was held at Johns Hopkins and the personal impression he made on strangers. Dr. Rhoads quizzed Wilson on his religious beliefs and was glad to discover that the prospective member of his faculty believed that the hand of Providence could be seen in history and that he had a strong personal faith. Later Dr. Rhoads wrote Wilson, "From our conversation and from the testimony of others, I feel assured that the moral and religious lessons of History will in thy hands be used to fortify any wide and comprehensive yet well-defined faith in Christianity."[4]

Ellen Axson at first was dubious about Wilson's taking a position in a "female college," and he shared her doubts. There was also some haggling over status and salary. The Bryn Mawr authorities offered $1200 and the rank of Associate; Wilson held out for $2000 and the title of Associate Professor. At the urging of his father, he accepted the lower rank along with a raise in salary to $1500. He overcame his fiancée's objections by pointing out that the alternative to a women's college would probably be a coeducational institution. In January 1885 he signed a two-year contract in which he agreed to teach the students assigned to him, to organize the history department, to advise on curriculum, and to help build up the library. Wilson wrote Heath Dabney that the advantages of the position were "its situation in the most cultivated portion of the country" and the light schedule of teaching. The alternative would be "to teach this, that, and everything somewhere way off from all the great libraries and from the lively, stimulating centres of thought."[5]

Wilson arrived at Bryn Mawr with his bride of three months in September 1885. Three faculty cottages had been built in a row on the edge of the campus. The Wilsons were housed on an upper floor of the middle one, Yarrow, known as the "In-betweenery," and ate in a common dining room. It was Carey Thomas' notion that her teaching staff, "thankful to have the material framework of life ordered for them," would form a congenial academic community.[6]

At first the lack of privacy seems to have bothered Wilson little. He was absorbed in his work, and he was devoted to his new bride. Shortly after settling in at Bryn Mawr he informed Heath Dabney that he was happier than he had ever dared hope to be. "I was desperately in need of such a companion as Mrs. W.," he wrote. "I needed to be absorbed by somebody else and I am. My mind and heart expand under the new influences." He found his colleagues congenial and his students "interested and intelligent."[7]

Shortly after Ellen Axson Wilson reached Bryn Mawr, she was afflicted by illness attending her first pregnancy, and some months later she journeyed to the home of an aunt in Gainesville, Georgia, where she bore a daughter, Margaret, in April 1886. Thereafter she was preoccupied with the care of her family, especially after she produced a second child, Jessie, in August 1887. Thus, she did not have much to do with the Bryn Mawr community. "I think of her," wrote one student, "as a person of unusual appearance, rather striking and very sweet, of very refined and quiet manners, slightly aloof and retiring." Not merely poor health and her children kept Ellen Wilson aloof from the feminist society of Bryn Mawr; her southern upbringing also made her suspicious and fearful of "strong-minded women." It is not surprising to find another student reminiscing of the Wilsons, "I knew his wife slightly and thought her very dull and not good enough for him, but he seemed devoted to her."[8]

Though partaking little of social life in Bryn Mawr, Ellen Wilson shared more fully than most Victorian women in the rest of her husband's life. Her judgment about matters affecting his career continued to be better than his in many cases and was sometimes decisive, as it had been when she insisted that Wilson spend a second year at Johns Hopkins. During the first year at Bryn Mawr she joined Miss Thomas in urging him to reconsider his decision not to try for a Ph.D., and when it was awarded him, he wrote her, "I won the degree *for you.*

. . . my spur in the struggle of preparation I have just been through was to please *you,* and to make *you* more comfortable. In so far as the degree has a commercial value, it was earned for you; in so far as it has a sentimental value, it was won for you! If there's any triumph, it is *yours."* Ellen's help went even beyond advice: she learned enough German to help Wilson make a card file of German writings on politics. In May 1888, when congratulating a friend on his engagement, Woodrow Wilson looked back on nearly three years of marriage and found it good. "I speak from the card," he wrote, "when I say that you are about to do the very best thing a man—and especially a student, as it seems to me—could possibly do. No one is so sensitive, as a rule, as a student—and there's no cure for sensitivity like a wife's sympathy,—no strength like that to be gotten from her love and trust. Marriage has been the *making* of me both intellectually and morally."[9]

Wilson's colleagues at Bryn Mawr found him good company, although perhaps a little more formal than other members of the faculty —"a cheery, agreeable acquaintance," "a courteous kindly Southern gentleman." "Dr. Wilson," said one who shared meals with him, "was a charming table companion, full of a dry, pleasant humor." But behind his affable façade he was often lonely and bored. During his first month he wrote Walter Hines Page that he found no one more than mildly interested in the topics he most liked to discuss. He was also one for whom Miss Thomas' noble experiment of the faculty boarding house proved a failure. She had not comprehended "the common need for privacy and independence, for elbow room both spiritual and mental, though it was strongly within herself." Wilson complained of having "at every meal to hear nonsense rattle down from the empty pate to the clattering tongue of a fool or two." At the end of the academic year 1886-87 he moved to a small Baptist parsonage, just off the Bryn Mawr campus.[10]

This rented cottage on Gulph Road was the Wilsons' first true home. No sooner had they settled in than they began to share it with others. Mrs. Wilson asked a cousin, Mary Hoyt, to stay with them and attend the college. One of Ellen's brothers, Edward Axson, lived with them for a time, and another brother, Stockton Axson, made a long visit. Woodrow and Ellen Wilson were never rich, but they were better off than others in their families, so that it fell to them to provide for less fortunate brothers, sisters, and cousins. Continually for over twenty years they welcomed into their home one or more young relatives whom they helped through school and college.

Mary Hoyt had a vivid remembrance of life in the parsonage. Cousin Woodrow, she recalled, was no handyman, and Ellen tried to relieve him of every possible household responsibility, but he did necessary chores with good grace, and on one occasion he undertook to dismiss a temperamental cook. He was almost constantly at work during the day. His principal recreation was a walk in the afternoon, during which time he composed his lectures, jotting them down in shorthand first and later transcribing them on a typewriter. In the evenings he liked to sing college songs and hymns or to read aloud. "He had the tenderest heart in the world, and could never read aloud anything sad, because his voice would always break." On at least one occasion he was hard put to find money for the coal supply, and Ellen had to economize in various ways, such as making all the children's clothes. Yet they managed to have enough to live on and even to entertain. The home "was filled with so much kindness and courtesy, with so much devotion between Ellen and Cousin Woodrow that the air always seemed to have a kind of sparkle."[11]

During his years at Bryn Mawr Wilson worked hard on his teaching. He did not follow old grooves and allow textbooks to dictate the scope and character of his courses but struck out in new directions. For instance, he carried on the history of Greece and Rome concurrently, devoting alternate weeks to one and then to the other, so that the students might better see contrasts and likenesses. In the study of Greece he put emphasis on individuals and made the students prepare class reports on "the antecedents, lives, and work of the chief statesmen, dramatists, and orators." In Roman history the stress was on government, with textbook drill in constitutional development. In teaching the history of England and France, Wilson again carried the two along together, and he arranged the topics so that they cast light on contemporary questions. It was his purpose that students see the grand sweep of history. His lectures were designed "to group and explain facts separated from the narrative, and to keep the students mindful of the broad views of history to which the events in the lives of the individuals stand related."[12]

At the opening of each year Wilson delivered several lectures to orient students to historical study. His elaborate notes for the first of these, delivered in late September 1885, are in the Library of Congress. They are typed on large cards, with a few interlineations in ink. In these first academic lectures, as in his first political writings, he leaned heavily on Walter Bagehot. Three of the four lectures paraphrase *Physics and Politics,* a series of essays in which Bagehot attempted to trace the processes whereby the primitive, warlike, patriarchal society evolved into the highest type of polity—government by discussion. The fourth lecture ended with a homily on "the value of discussion," which perfectly expresses Wilson's oft-professed faith in government by debate:

There is a modern tendency to decry discussion, under the contemptuous name of "talk"; but talk which concerns itself with principles cannot be too much encouraged. (*1*) It means the substitution of reason for force, and thus of order for anarchy. It creates a disposition to hear both sides and to yield to the voice of the majority. (*2*) It offers prizes to intelligence by bringing all the faculties into active play. (*3*) It develops that type of intellect which is the highest of all—namely, the "speculative intellect"—by conditioning success on the better argument, on the use of the faculties. (*4*) Its detective processes discover the truth. (*5*) It begets tolerance, a very modern product. (*6*) It turns the old vigour of the race, which once went to produce eager, restless, oftentimes rash action, into channels of clear creative thought, and so produces that calmness without sluggishness and that deliberation without weakness, that "animated moderation" in action which the uncivilized man knows nothing of, but which is the perfect flower of social growth.[13]

It was Wilson's habit to "talk around" his topic for the greater part of the class period, during which time students were not allowed to take notes, and then he would dictate for fifteen or twenty minutes. He continued this method at Wesleyan and Princeton. The first part of the lecture was designed to open vistas; the dictated portion was concerned with "examinable" knowledge.

From the beginning Wilson was a polished and interesting lecturer. According to one of his former students:

He always entered the classroom smiling and animated and always in a good humour. I never saw him show the slightest irritability or impatience, and he was always amusing and witty . . . His lectures were fascinating and held me spellbound; each was an almost perfect little essay in itself, well rounded and with a distinct literary style. Never have I known a mind that could reason so profoundly and so clearly, with such breadth of vision. I can see now, however, that he was a little impatient of detail but that fundamental underlying laws and causes, whether of academic, political, or social problems, fascinated him and absorbed his best energies.

Another Bryn Mawr alumnus gave an equally rhapsodic account:

He was the most interesting and inspiring college lecturer that I ever heard. I followed his courses in American History and the Italian Renaissance, looking forward eagerly to each day's lecture. He charmed me by his vivid pictures of incidents and characters, by the smoothness of his periods and the clearness of his diction. His method was to give rapidly a description of the topic for the day with its lights and shades, its leading actors, its relation to former topics studied, its significance in relation to the whole subject. Then, after arousing our keenest interest, he proceeded more slowly to emphasize the main facts and conclusions, so clearly and closely connected, so logically developed that it was impossible to misunderstand or to forget the essential matter. Though serious in intent and solidly informing, every lesson was lighted up with touches of the most delightful humor.[14]

In addition to formal course instruction, Wilson gave informal talks on current affairs in the sitting room of one of the dormitories. These became so popular that they had to be moved to a larger room. A "House of Commons" also appeared at Bryn Mawr. Although there is no direct evidence, Wilson may well have been the founder, because the organization followed exactly the lines of the Liberal Debating Club at Princeton and the Johns Hopkins House of Commons.[15]

Most of the students liked Woodrow Wilson. They found him uniformly kind and courteous, if a little formal, and always desirous of giving help wherever possible. "I thought him," recollected one, "a Southern gentleman, good looking, and polite, and rather remote from the students, although certainly not harsh." Another wrote, "Most of the students thought him handsome. He was wearing a mustache and had courtly manners." She also found him "approachable if not intimate" and enjoyed playing tennis with him and E. B. Wilson, professor of biology; Wilson played a good game and, although serious, obviously enjoyed himself. One who took none of his courses recalled a "very pleasant personal friendliness."[16]

Yet Wilson was not wholly successful in teaching Bryn Mawr undergraduates. For one thing, he did not seem to welcome questions and preferred to carry on the main discussion himself. He lectured too much and expected very little from the students. There was not enough reading assigned, except for textbooks and a few class reports. Of course, the facilities for reading were limited, since the library was in its infancy, but Miss Thomas had arranged that three thousand dollars a year was available for accessions as the heads of departments might decide. Charles M. Andrews, who went to Bryn Mawr a year after Wilson had left, found that the library collection of works on history and politics was composed almost entirely of "heavy" books. Most of them were in Wilson's special field of jurisprudence and constitutional law, and many were in German. Few were books from which undergraduates could profit.[17]

The fundamental difficulty with Wilson's classes at Bryn Mawr was that many of the girls did not think he took them seriously. This was essentially true. He did not believe in higher education for women. His was the romantic southern attitude: women were to be cherished and loved as wives and mothers, but when they competed in the world of men, they lost their femininity. "He seemed to regard his students not as of a *lower* sort of intelligence, but as of a *different* sort from himself." They should be adored for their higher sensibilities, but the serious work of the mind was not their province. From his classes he expected docility, and then he complained when he got it. He even went to the extent of shaving his mustache so that, as he told the students, they would know when he was joking, and they resented the libel. Small wonder that he found less and less enjoyment in his classes and wrote his friend Bridges, "I find that teaching women relaxes my mental muscle."[18]

Partly to keep the professors from relaxing their mental muscle, Miss Thomas had insisted that there be a graduate fellow in every department. During each of his three years at Bryn Mawr Wilson had an advanced student in his charge. In no case was there a meeting of minds. With the graduates, indeed, he seems to have been markedly less successful than with the undergraduates.

The first fellowship was held by Jane Bancroft, who was just Wilson's age. For eight years she had been Dean of Women and Professor of French Languages at Northwestern University. When Miss Thomas consulted Wilson about Miss Bancroft's candidacy, he agreed that she was suitable because of her "very great industry and considerable culture." But he thought her claims to scholarship exaggerated. A paper of hers on the Parliament of Paris had not, as she claimed, been the subject of a whole evening's discussion at the Johns Hopkins seminary; it had merely been reported on by Dr. Jameson, who "spoke rather severely of one or two rather extraordinary errors." "In choosing such a subject," Wilson condescendingly added, "Miss Bancroft was guilty of the singular indiscretion of entering the lists with some of the greatest scholars of Europe over an exceedingly knotty question."[19]

Wilson and Jane Bancroft did not hit it off. All we know of his side of the story is that he continued to think her scholarship deficient. Miss Bancroft, in turn, found him "thoroughly versed in the political, and constitutional history of the United States, but not so well grounded in European history." She felt that he patronized her because she came from a western college and had received her Ph.D. from Syracuse University in absentia. The daughter of an abolitionist minister from Massachusetts, she "found it a new experience to meet a Southerner who had no special sympathy for Negroes as human beings." Only after Wilson became President of the United States did she manage to conceive much admiration for him and to become aware of his "large humanitarian ideas."[20]

The second historical fellow, Lucy Salmon, was older than Wilson. In the decade between her graduation from Michigan and her arrival at Bryn Mawr she had taught in both high school and normal school and gained an M.A. in history. A paper of hers on the appointing power of the President had been read before the American Historical Association and been favorably reviewed by Wilson himself before the Johns Hopkins seminary. On the eve of her departure for Bryn Mawr, Charles K. Adams, who had taught Miss Salmon at Michigan and had recently become President of Cornell, wrote her: "That Mr. Wilson will be able to help you much you must not anticipate. Indeed I should be very much surprised if you find that he knows nearly so much history as you do."[21]

Lucy Salmon was a young woman of a good deal of spirit, but she hid the fact from Wilson. Learning of the friction between him and Miss Bancroft, she decided "that the best way of getting on comfortably was to express no pronounced opinions, to be entirely passive and colorless, and to be a good listener." Throughout the year she and Wilson met three times weekly. Miss Salmon was supposed to report on her work, but she managed it so that he did most of the talking. Sometimes he lectured; for three dull weeks he read his lecture notes on Richard T. Ely's course in economic history at Johns Hopkins. Mostly he just talked informally, prodded by questions from his pupil, and then he revealed so much of himself that Miss Salmon thought she had never known any person so well—not because of any special skill on her part "but because of the transparency of his own thought, ambitions, and character." "He seemed," she wrote, "to have neither ability nor desire to conceal his thought from any one, or to adapt them to the presumable opinions of others. He often seemed to be 'thinking out loud' and he was apparently unconscious of the presence of others, except as they served as an audience to whom he could express his views."

According to Lucy Salmon's sometimes acid reminiscences, she was aware from the first that Wilson was unhappy at Bryn Mawr. It was obvious, she claimed, that he did not like teaching, as distinguished from lecturing. He lacked two important traits of the ideal teacher—"the capacity for vicariousness" and "the willingness to be forgot." Therefore his teaching, although conscientious, was done without enthusiasm. He was also "singularly ill adapted to teaching women." He simply assumed that women's minds were "somehow different" and never made any real effort to find out whether his assumptions were true. In this, as in other areas, he displayed an oddly incurious mind. He seemed interested only in what might be immediately useful to his purposes. At this time he was writing *The State* and had a number of other projects either under way or in contemplation, and he used Miss Salmon as a sounding board to try out his ideas. She heard many thoughts that went into later essays. She was impressed by his excessive interest in style—"it sometimes seemed to me that it played the same part in his conversation that the weather did with others. Lamb, Burke, Bagehot were his literary ideals and it seemed as if he were really more interested in their manner of expression than he was in the thoughts and ideals expressed."

The trait that most distinguished Woodrow Wilson from the many other young men Miss Salmon had known in a large family and at a co-educational university was one that did not appeal to her—his "extreme personal ambition." "He often said that if our system had been like that of England he would have gone into public life. In England a man entered Parliament and the road to the premiership was straight and open, but a man who entered Congress could never get beyond the chairmanship of a committee and there were nearly sixty committees in each house." In her opinion, "this thwarted ambition was the fundamental explanation of his deep-seated unhappiness."

Miss Salmon went on to Vassar, where she taught history with success for nearly forty years. She never again had personal contact with Woodrow Wilson, nor did she desire it. Unlike some others, she did not change her opinion of him when he achieved eminence. In an article written under a pen name for the *Nation* during the 1916 presidential campaign she expressed the opinion that Wilson was "inherently a self-centred man" who had always been "intensely interested in his own career."[22]

What the third graduate fellow thought of Woodrow Wilson is not known. But he expressed his opinion of her in a letter to his wife, and in its condescension and lack of charity it suggests why Wilson's teaching at Bryn Mawr was something less than successful:

I have just come from a long and exhausting interview with Miss ——, the New Fellow in History. I dread these first interviews, and am very glad this one is over with. Miss —— turns out to be a pleasant small person of a mind which it will be very hard, but I trust not impossible, to impress—a mind that has been pressed so often by other things at every point that it yields in a *habitual*, acquired way rather than in the way you wish . . . But she is amiable—"not wilful," she says—has some wholesome awe (quite diverting of course to me) of what is expected of her at Bryn Mawr, and can, I confidently expect, be dominated. But, dear me, what a strain and bore it is all year to be dominating . . . I'm *tired* of carrying female Fellows on my shoulders!

When I think of you, my little wife, I love this "College for Women," because *you* are a woman; but when I think only of myself, I hate the place very cordially.[23]

During his first year at Bryn Mawr, Wilson began to reconsider his earlier refusal to try for a Ph.D. at Johns Hopkins. In April 1886 he wrote to Herbert B. Adams that he had "all along coveted such recognition as a Ph.D. from the Hopkins would give." Explaining that he cut "a sorry figure in exams" and that he was so nervous he could not "pull in ordinary harness," he asked for and was granted a special dispensation. *Congressional Government* was accepted as a thesis; written examinations were waived. The only requirement was an oral examination, held in late May, and that hurdle he cleared easily.[24]

In the autumn of 1886 Adams urged Wilson to lecture on administration at Johns Hopkins, but Wilson refused on the ground that his studies were not far enough advanced. "I worked diligently all summer," he wrote, "and I am taking advantage of every scrap of leisure afforded by my duties here to push my special studies, which just now, unfortunately, cannot be made to come in in class; but I have not yet gone over, with even a full survey, the whole field; and the habit of my mind is such that until I see the *whole* subject I can't write on a part of it anything that I would like to put forth in public as *results*." A year later Adams tried again, and Wilson agreed to deliver twenty-five lectures on administration, starting in February 1888, for three successive years, dealing with a different aspect of the field each year. These lectures were such a great success that he was asked back annually to deliver them until 1898.[25]

A by-product of Wilson's preparation for the Johns Hopkins lectures was an essay entitled "The Study of Administration," published in the *Political Science Quarterly* for June 1887. Although Wilson professed to think it so slight as hardly to merit publication, this is one of the best things he ever wrote. According to one authority, it immediately became famous among specialists on administration and "has always been a mine of wisdom and of succinct statement." In it Wilson holds that the great failure of American democracy has been in the administrative field, and that the principal future tasks of government—especially the regulation of business enterprise, perhaps even outright socialization of public utilities—will demand greater administrative efficiency. The United States must learn to adapt the authoritarian bureaucratic methods of Prussia and France to the needs of a democratic, pluralistic society. It must be possible to achieve efficiency without sacrifice of liberty and popular control of officials: "if I see a monarchist dyed in the wool managing public business well," writes Wilson, "I can learn his business methods without changing one of my republican spots."[26]

The conclusion of the essay bears a hint of prophecy. It states that if the United States can solve the problem of combining local self-government with efficient and dedicated bureaucracy, "we shall again pilot the world," for there is "a tendency as yet dim, but always steadily impulsive and clearly destined to prevail," toward confederation, "first of parts of empires like the British, and finally of great states themselves . . . This is a tendency towards the American type—of governments joined with governments for the pursuit of common purposes, in honorary equality and honorable subordination."

During his Bryn Mawr years Wilson wrote in several different veins. He composed both a story and some occasional essays, using the nom de plume Edward Copplestone for fear the Bryn Mawr trustees would think him frivolous. These he sent to Robert Bridges, then an editor of *Scribner's Magazine*, but all were rejected. He wrote a protest against the Blair Bill, a scheme of federal aid to public schools to combat illiteracy, and had the satisfaction of seeing it published in the *New York Evening Post* as an unsigned editorial. At the insistence of his Johns Hopkins friend Albert Shaw he was one of eighteen who contributored to a small volume entitled *The National Revenues*. In it Wilson went over familiar ground in branding the American tariff system as "full of complexities and absurdities," designed to encourage extravagance. He argued that the way to achieve efficiency and economy was for Congress "to marry the two sides of its fiscal policy"—in other words, to appropriate money first, then find revenue exactly calculated to fill governmental needs.[27]

Attracted by the prospect of additional income, Wilson was also working on two textbooks. One of these was an American history for high schools; it was never published but undoubtedly served as apprentice work for his *A History of the American People*, published in 1902. The other was a college text in government, commissioned by D. C. Heath and published in 1889, entitled *The State*.

In later years Wilson was to enjoy constant demand as a speaker; popular lecturing became, in fact, a subsidiary career and a source of considerable income. But his first important public speech was an appalling failure. In March 1886 he spoke at a Princeton alumni dinner in New York, which he had been urged to do by his friend Robert Bridges, who hoped to see him appointed to a Princeton professorship. Wilson's talk on "The College and the Government" was unsuited to the occasion, being both too serious and too long. His audience became restive; some of them interrupted and others left the room. Chauncey Depew, the next speaker, poked mild fun at him. This was a hard defeat to take but, like Disraeli after his first disastrous appearance in the House of Commons, Wilson resolved that such an incident would never happen again. He would learn to charm and to dominate any audience he faced.[28]

Wilson was at the same time receiving tokens of increasing professional eminence. For instance, he could read Albert Shaw's characterization in *The National Revenues:* "Professor Woodrow Wilson, of Bryn Mawr College, is recognized as one of the keenest and most brilliant of all the writers who have undertaken the critical discussion of our constitutional machinery and administrative method." More significant evidence of a growing reputation were offers of a professorship in history at the University of Indiana and of the chancellorship at the Nashville, Tennessee, Normal School, the latter with a salary of $3000 plus a "beautiful home." In 1887 Wake Forest College in North Carolina granted him an LL.D., the first of many honorary degrees.[29]

But such successes could not satisfy Woodrow Wilson. Denied, as he thought, all chance at political leadership, he had other dreams no less lofty. He conceived the idea of writing a great, wide-ranging philosophical study of modern democracy. It was to be a work that would rank with Aristotle's *Politics* or Montesquieu's *Spirit of the Law*. In May 1886 he wrote to Horace Scudder of Houghton Mifflin, outlining the project and asking for an opinion as to its feasibility.[30]

Wilson's immediate purpose was to refute Sir Henry Maine's *Popular Government*. This book, published in 1885, reads almost as though its one purpose was to tear apart, root and branch, every argument in *Congressional Government*. Maine deplored just those characteristics of the British Constitution that Wilson held in inordinate esteem, and he praised the government of the United States for just those features that Wilson attacked. Behind Maine's attitude was fear of the rising tide of democracy. Popular government, whether in fifth-century Athens or nineteenth-century France, seemed to him generally to bring insecurity without progress. Democracy had proved successful in the United States, only because the Founding Fathers had written a constitution that curbed popular whim through a system of checks and balances. In contrast, the ancient restraints in Britain—the Crown and the House of Lords—were becoming more and more feeble in the face of the popularly elected House of Commons. In the Commons itself the cabinet—a small, self-appointed executive committee, controlling a supine majority of the members—could act much as it pleased.[31]

Whereas Wilson maintained that parliamentary government, through its schooling in debate, trained and rewarded the best leaders, Maine insisted that the rewards went to the "wire-pullers" who manipulated legislation and public opinion with a view to partisan advantage. And whereas Wilson asserted that disciplined parties were essential to effective government, Maine saw in the spirit of party merely "a survival of the primitive combativeness of mankind." As opposed to one of Wilson's principal criticisms of American government—its secrecy— Maine wrote:

After its first birth nothing can be more equable and nothing can be more plain to observation than the course of an American legislative measure. . . . An English Bill begins in petty rivulets or stagnant pools. Then it runs underground for most of its course, withdrawn from the eye by the secrecy of the Cabinet. Emerging into the House of Commons, it can no more escape from its embankments than the water of a canal; but once dismissed from that House, it overcomes all remaining obstacles with the rush of a cataract, and mixes with the trackless ocean of British institutions.

Maine saw grave dangers in the unrestrained omnipotence of the British cabinet. With the prospect of ever-widening suffrage and consequent pandering to the masses, he predicted a time when the electorate would resemble "a mutinous crew feasting on a ship's provisions, gorging themselves on the meat, and intoxicating themselves with the liquors, but refusing to navigate the vessel to port." How much more enviable was America, where "carefully devised precautionary formalities" protected property from "democratic impatience and Socialistic fantasy."[32]

As in his debate with A. Lawrence Lowell, Wilson's proposed defense of cabinet government pushed him toward acceptance of democracy. He wrote Scudder that he had already started to ponder and investigate "the nature, structure, ends, and functions of the modern democratic state." He hoped to treat "modern democratic tendencies from a much more truly historical point of view than he [Maine] has taken; keeping very close to the concrete examples of popular government by means of careful comparative constitutional study,—careful but not narrow; aiming to reckon with all the actual forces of thought and machinery in modern popular governments—especially our own, of course,—in as broad and philosophical a way as I could steadily command." Further essays would consider "political morality," "political progress," "political expediency," and "practical politics."[33]

Receiving encouragement from Scudder, Wilson wrote him again in July 1886. The second letter reveals the height of his ambition for the projected work:

I would trace the genesis and development of modern democratic institutions—which, so far, seem to me expressions of the adult age of the State, the organic people come to its self-possessed majority and no longer in need of the guardianship of king or aristocracy or priesthood . . . I would apply the now common inductive method to the study of demcratic government—to the study of the genesis and development of *our* democratic government in particular—; but I want to say more than that; I want that method to carry me farther than it carries most of those who employ it. Men study the material universe so; and stop short at the differentiated *forms* of matter and life. Aristotle studied politics so: but did not get farther than the outward differences of institutions:—did not then press on beyond logical distinctions to discover the spiritual oneness of government, the life that lives *within* it. The ideal thing to do, would be to penetrate to its *essential character* by way of a thorough knowledge of all its ouward manifestations of character.[34]

Wilson further detailed his prescription for writing a *novum organum* of modern democracy in an article entitled "Of the Study of Politics," published in the *New Princeton Review* for March 1887. The writer on politics, he averred, must concern himself with facts, not theory; he must deal less with statutes, legal precedents, and constitutions, and more with human conduct. The best writers on politics—men such as de Tocqueville, Bagehot, and Burke—were "not merely students, but *men of the world.*" As the great popular preacher reaches the heart of his audience not so much by knowledge of the Bible as "by showing himself a brother-man to his fellow-man," so the student of politics "must frequent the street, the countinghouse, the drawing-room, the club-house, the administration offices, the halls—yes, and the lobbies— of legislation. He must cross-examine the experience of government officials; he must hear the din of conventions, and see their intrigues; he must witness the scenes of election day." In brief, he must do all the things that Wilson did not do when he wrote *Congressional Government.*[35]

To write significantly about politics, therefore, Wilson felt that he must study more, see more, have more leisure. He wrote his friend Dabney about the possibility of going abroad. He thought especially of Berlin, where he could both acquire the facility in German necessary for his studies and observe the world while he was still young, with his "susceptibility to men and things . . . as yet unblunted."[36]

Encouraged by his former law partner Edward Renick, who held a minor post in the Treasury Department, Wilson also dreamed of getting an appointment in Washington. In an amazingly ingenuous letter he asked James B. Angell, president of the University of Michigan, for a recommendation to the position of Assistant Secretary of State. He had heard that Mr. Bayard, then Secretary, "likes scholarly men rather than politicians as assistants." Of course, a mere clerkship would have gotten him to Washington, but the salary would have been insufficient, he wrote, and the view of the processes of government from a clerk's desk would have been "too imperfect and limited to be of any real service to my thought. . . . "But I do want—and *need*—particularly, as it seems to me, at this juncture in my studies,—a seat on the inside of government —a seat high enough to command views of the system." The wild notion that he might be appointed without any practical experience or political influence reveals how far Wilson was from practical grasp of the realities of government. Also noteworthy is the frank, unself-conscious egoism of a young man who assumed that the desire to promote his personal studies was a sufficient recommendation for office.[37]

By the time Wilson wrote his letter to James B. Angell he was desperately anxious to leave Bryn Mawr. It was not merely that he found instructing women distasteful but that undergraduate teaching itself stood in the way of his ambitions. He confided his troubles to the pages of a diary:

I have devoted myself to a literary life; but I do not see how a literary life can be built on a foundation of undergraduate instruction. That instruction compels one to live with the commonplaces, the A.B.C., of every subject, to dwell upon these with an emphasis and an invention altogether disproportionate to their intrinsic weight and importance; it keeps one on dusty, century-traveled high roads of every subject, from which one gets no outlook except those that are catalogued and vulgarized in every guide-book. One gets weary plodding and yet grows habituated to it and finds all excursions aside more and more difficult. What is a fellow to do? How is he to earn bread and at the same time find leisure and (in the toils of such a routine) disposition of mind for thoughts entirely detached from and elevated high above the topics of his trade? [38]

Not only did Wilson fail to find stimulus in Bryn Mawr, but he came into conflict with Carey Thomas and thought himself ill used by the trustees. When he first accepted the position, he had tried to make sure that he would not serve under Miss Thomas but would be directly responsible to President Rhoads. In practice this was impossible because the real source of ideas and direction in the college was the aggressive young dean. It was with her that Wilson had to correspond about matters affecting his department. It was she who urged him to get the Ph.D. from Johns Hopkins. And it was she more than anyone else who gave Bryn Mawr a tone of aggressive feminism.

Just where and how Wilson and Carey Thomas first clashed is not known. Undergraduates heard rumors that the two had argued in faculty meeting and that Miss Thomas had tried to prevent Wilson from accepting the invitation to give a lecture course at Johns Hopkins. In any event, friction between the two strong-minded young persons was inevitable. They were by nature antipathetic, if only because of qualities in which they were alike, such as ambition, strength of will, and a sense of superiority. Furthermore, the dean considered Wilson's southern attitude toward women sentimental and degrading. Years later, when gathering ideas for a memoir of her life, she caustically jotted under his name a line from Tennyson, "Put thy sweet hand in mine and trust in me."[39]

Added to Miss Thomas' personal feelings about Wilson was the fact that she had little use for his field of study. She thought that history "neither gave nor demanded stiff enough intellectual discipline to be of value as a subject for college work, and was a subject to be read at will without previous guidance." Her opinion was at variance with that held by President Rhoads, but since so much of the actual policy of Bryn Mawr emanated from the dean rather than the president, it may have contributed to Wilson's sense of frustration. On his part, he had little use for the type of Germanic scholarship that Miss Thomas admired. The patient gathering and memorization of facts he regarded as "sheer, ignorant waste of energy . . . like eating for the sake of eating."[40]

During his second year at Bryn Mawr Wilson asked for an assistant. By then he was responsible for teaching no less than five courses, covering the entire span of European and American history. Although he apparently managed to keep his teaching hours down by such devices as giving courses in alternate years, the variety of subjects that he was expected to teach was at variance with the expressed policy of the college to "limit the time devoted by the instructors to their pedagogical duties so that they might have time for study and research." The Bryn Mawr trustees recognized the justice of Wilson's request in a three-year contract signed on March 14, 1887, in which it was agreed that he should have an assistant "as soon as practicable." Wilson regarded this as a promise; the trustees and President Rhoads meant to imply that the appointment should be dependent upon the financial situation of the college. The contract further stipulated that his rank was raised to Associate Professor and his salary to $2000. He was permitted to give twenty-five lectures at Johns Hopkins. Wilson on his part agreed to teach ten hours weekly, to supervise the instruction given by the assistant, and to direct the studies of a graduate fellow.[41]

Even before reading the contract, Wilson had received word that the "official plan" of the trustees was to provide him with a junior colleague, and on this assurance he had approached Heath Dabney in January 1887 about coming to Bryn Mawr at a stipend of $600. A month later the offer had been raised to $850, and Wilson hoped the trustees would not wait until June to make an appointment, since by then the field would be picked over. Apparently President Rhoads was in no hurry, because it was not until August that he interviewed a candidate. This person refused to teach ancient history, a course in which Wilson specially wanted relief, and ultimately no one was hired for the year 1887-1888.[42]

Wilson thought that the Bryn Mawr authorities had welched on their bargain. In December 1887 he wrote Robert Bridges that he felt free to accept any other position. In April 1888, even after an assistant was hired for the year 1888-1889, he went to President Rhoads and told him that he thought the contract was no longer binding. Rhoads, in turn, refused to accept Wilson's interpretation of the matter and told him he was expected to continue at Bryn Mawr for the next year with the same salary.[43]

Matters were close to an impasse when in mid-June 1888 Wilson was offered the Hedding Professorship of History and Political Economy at Wesleyan University in Middletown, Connecticut. He immediately accepted and informed President Rhoads of his decision. The latter was aghast, since the college was closed for the summer and he thought it impossible to get a substitute so late. He attempted to invoke the contract. Wilson said he regarded the agreement as terminable at his own discretion so long as he left Bryn Mawr time to find a successor, and in his judgment there was sufficient time. President Rhoads flatly disagreed. He thought Wilson "had formed his own interpretation of events and words." Nevertheless, he advised the Bryn Mawr trustees to release him since, if he stayed on, he would be "dissatisfied and exacting." But the trustees were disposed to fight the matter and hold him accountable for what they considered a serious breach of faith. He in turn went to a lawyer, who gave it as his opinion that the only possible action by the Bryn Mawr authorities was a suit for damages that they were sure to lose. Finally the trustees gave in and accepted Wilson's resignation.[44]

The manner of Wilson's departure from Bryn Mawr left scars. He did not admit that he had acted dishonorably in the slightest degree, and he smarted under the implication. At Bryn Mawr the incident might have been forgotten but for Carey Thomas, who let all and sundry know her opinion that the college had been badly treated. In a way Wilson had the last word, because Bryn Mawr quietly abandoned contracts that tied faculty members down for two or three years at a time and thereby limited their ability to better their position by accepting calls elsewhere.[45]

IX

Wesleyan

1888–1890

I have long been hungry for a class of men.
                              —Woodrow Wilson, 1888[1]

THERE was a marked periodicity in Woodrow Wilson's life. His withdrawal from Davidson College and the ensuing fallow time at home were followed by the happy undergraduate years at Princeton and the first year at Virginia. His ill-starred career at the bar was followed by his engagement to Ellen Axson and the successful years at Johns Hopkins. Now the frustrations of Bryn Mawr were superseded by manifold success during two years at Wesleyan University. He became an effective teacher of undergraduates and a leader in their affairs; he was equally successful with his graduate students at Johns Hopkins; he began to be in demand as a public lecturer; and he completed *The State,* his most solid book. No wonder he wrote his wife in March 1889 that "a distinct . . . *feeling of maturity,* or rather of maturing" had come over him—"always a slow fellow in mental development—long a child, longer a diffident youth, now at last, perhaps, becoming a self-confident (mayhap a self-assertive) man."[2]

The Hedding professorship held by Wilson at Wesleyan was an endowed chair established in 1847 by the New York Conference of the Methodist Episcopal Church. At various times its incumbent was called upon to teach moral science, belles-lettres, mental philosophy, and now political economy and history. Apparently the Wesleyan trustees appointed a man to the chair with caution: it had been empty for three years before Wilson occupied it, and it was unfilled for five years after he resigned. Wilson was not the trustees' first choice, two Johns Hopkins men having been approached before him. Albert Shaw "declined with thanks" and expressed surprise when Wilson took the place. J. Franklin Jameson was attracted by the salary of $2500 but thought it would be "poor fun teaching scrubby Methodist under-graduates"; he was happy to settle for a position at Brown that paid $500 less but offered "a fine vantage ground for work." But Wilson was so desperate to get out from under petticoat government at Bryn Mawr and back into a world of men that he jumped at the appointment.[3]

Since Wilson had been angling for a job at Princeton during his last two years at Bryn Mawr, Wesleyan was to him only a way station. Although he found it a pleasant place to work, as he wrote his friend Robert Bridges, "it is not a sufficiently *stimulating place*—largely because the class of students here is very inferior in point of preparatory culture—comes from a parentage, for the most part, of narrow circumstances and of correspondingly narrow thought. The New England men among them, besides, have an added New England narrowness in political study." Yet for a time Wilson was happy. He appreciated the "congenial masculine surroundings" and plunged into the life of the college.[4]

The most obvious attraction of Wesleyan University in the 1880's was its site. Set high above the thriving river port of Middletown, Connecticut, the college grounds looked over the winding reaches of the Connecticut River toward the east and commanded a prospect of distant hills to the west. Superficially, Wesleyan was indistinguishable from dozens of other small denominational colleges. Twenty-two of its fifty-four trustees were ministers, for it was a Methodist foundation; the charter specified that the majority of the faculty should be Methodists. The undergraduate body numbered 215, of whom 15 were girls. Wesleyan's claim to being a university rather than merely a college was only tenuously supported by the presence of five graduate students, candidates for the M.A. degree.[5]

Yet Wesleyan was not just another country college. In most ways it compared favorably with Princeton at the time Wilson was an undergraduate. The ratio of teachers to students at Princeton in 1875 was one to eighteen; at Wesleyan in 1888 it was one to eleven. The Princeton library in 1875 had about the same number of books as the Rich Library at Wesleyan in 1888, but it served a student body more than twice as large. Methods of instruction at Wesleyan were not merely superior to those Wilson had experienced at Princeton; they were advanced even by the standards of today. The instructors were trying to break out of the text-cum-recitation groove. They encouraged independent study, in both the library and the laboratories. Honors courses had been established for the abler students; candidates did collateral reading or independent experiments and were tested "by an examination oral or written, by a thesis or essay, by the exhibition of scientific specimens, preparations or processes, or by two or more of these methods combined."[6]

Above all, Wesleyan had a good faculty. In choosing professors, its trustees were less plagued than were Princeton's by narrow denominationalism. The professors were encouraged to pursue original studies and to give lectures outside the university. They had a large measure of autonomy. Wilson was pleased to find that his colleagues were "earnest and capable teachers and liberal men"; he often said later that there was "less dead wood on the Wesleyan faculty than any he had ever known." He was especially attracted to Caleb T. Winchester, professor of rhetoric and English literature, who became a warm friend. Winchester was an enthusiast of English literature, in particular the Romantic poets and Shakespeare. He edited the English classics with George Lyman Kittredge but published little else. His success was as a lyceum lecturer, giving lectures "as carefully worked over as a carved walnut shell." Wilson thought that he was "the greatest teacher he had ever known." That the high regard Wilson held for his Wesleyan colleagues was reciprocated is suggested by the fact that he was elected to the local chapter of Phi Beta Kappa in June 1889.[7]

Since the total income of the university from all sources was just over $50,000, the $2500 stipend of the Hedding professorship was generous. Supplemented by income from lecturing and writing, it allowed the Wilsons to live in comfort. They were fortunate in finding available for rent a roomy Greek revival house at 106 High Street, just a step from the college. On the crest of the college hill, with two stories in front and three in back, it commanded a view of the Connecticut River. There was plenty of room for the Wilsons, their two (soon three) girls, Ellen's two brothers, a procession of visiting relatives, and two Irish servant girls, Bridget and Annie.[8]

According to a contemporary account, Middletown possessed "the advantage of a central location between two large cities [Hartford and New Haven], the conveniences of a city, the out-of-door enjoyments of the country, and the social life of a wealthy, busy, and conservative community." The Wilsons enjoyed these advantages. They joined the First Congregational Church, whose minister, the Reverend A. W. Hazen, became an affectionate and lifelong friend. As Southerners, expecting New Englanders to be cold and grim, they were happily surprised to find themselves welcomed and made to feel at home. Wilson was soon elected to the Conversation Club, a small discussion group with members from both town and gown, and he was immediately called upon to speak at local gatherings. The countryside was almost at the door, and Wilson enjoyed bicycling through it; he also played tennis.[9]

A daughter, Eleanor, was born to the Wilsons on October 16, 1889. They so desperately wanted a boy that Ellen wept when she learned that she had produced a third girl. Eleanor, known as Nellie or Nennie, completed the immediate family. To the Wilsons, however, the concept of family had broad connotations. Ellen's young brother Edward moved with them from Bryn Mawr to Middletown, and soon the older brother Stockton joined the household. In 1889 Stockton, at the end of his rope financially, had been ready to leave the University of Georgia without a degree and enter the cotton business. Wilson, finding out that his brother-in-law's real ambition was to teach English literature, made Stockton "almost wild with enthusiasm" by inviting him to Middletown to study under the great Winchester. "Stock" entered the senior class at Wesleyan in 1889. After his graduation Wilson supported him in graduate study, and he became a successful professor of English literature, first at Princeton and later at Rice Institute. He and Woodrow soon achieved an absolute equality of friendship despite their ten-year difference in age. Axson thought that at this time Wilson was about the most considerate person he ever knew.[10]

As if a household of seven were not enough, the Wilsons entertained relatives and friends. Among the visitors was Wilson's father, who was asked to preach at Mr. Hazen's church. Letters from this period show that the relationship between father and son was as demonstratively affectionate as ever. "Never," wrote Dr. Wilson, "I think has father loved son as I love you." The son addressed himself with equal ardor to his "Precious Father." In one letter, interesting for what it reveals of himself, Wilson wrote:

As the Christmas season approaches I realize, as I have so often before, the pain there is in a season of holiday and rejoicing away from you. As you know, one of the chief things about which I feel most warranted in rejoicing is that I am your son. I realize the benefit of being your son more and more as my talents and experience grow; I recognize the strength growing in me as the nature of your strength; I become more and more conscious of that hereditary wealth I possess, that capital of principle, of literary force and skill, of capacity for first-hand thought; and I feel daily more and more bent toward creating in my children that combined respect and tender devotion for their father that you have given your children for you.[11]

Glimpses of the Wilson household can be caught in the diary and correspondence of J. Franklin Jameson. In November 1888, Jameson came for a visit and recorded in his diary that he and Wilson had "talked till midnight, and had a right good time of it, over Bryn Mawr, and his book *The State*, and northern colleges." Afterwards he wrote Wilson, "I don't know when I've had so pleasant a twenty-four hours as I spent at Middletown. I am greatly obliged to you for making so delightful an addition to the number of my friends as Mrs. Woodrow Wilson . . . Commend me to her, please; also to the two infants—the one with the oval face and the one with the spherical body. I wish you were all nearer." After another visit Jameson wrote, "I love to be the friend of a man especially of an able man of similar pursuits; but I also greatly love to be the friend of a family and it does me good."[12]

Wilson made an immediate hit with the Wesleyan undergraduates. The *Wesleyan Argus*, the student newspaper, praised his courses, re- tailed his witticisms, and expressed gratitude for his interest in student affairs. The local newspaper, the *Middletown Constitution*, reported, "When Prof. Wilson took charge of his department, he brought a new set of jokes, and they were so novel that they really won the admira- tion of his students." In 1890 *Olla Podrida*, the college yearbook, could find a good word to say for only one member of the Wesleyan faculty:

> Prof. W-l--n:
> "A merrier man
> Within the limit of becoming mirth
> I never spent an hour's talk withal."

As one former student more profoundly expressed it: although other members of the faculty were "first-rate scholars and fine teachers," none of them had quite Wilson's "air of academic aristocracy"; he "gave an impression of having arrived, of mastery."[13]

Wilson's courses consisted entirely of electives for juniors and seniors. He had two full-year courses. In one he continued the practice begun at Bryn Mawr of tracing English and French history coter- minously. The course ran from the early Middle Ages to the end of the Napoleonic era, and it apparently ranged wide, for the examinations included questions on Italian painting, sculpture, and literature, and on geography as well as on the more conventional political and ecclesiastical topics. The other full course dealt with comparative political institutions along the lines of his textbook *The State*. Wilson also taught a course in political economy and statistics for the first half- year and on the Constitution of the United States for the second. In the economics course his method was comparative and historical, be- cause political economy was "not a science of absolute truths, but of historical conditions and stages of development; of social conditions (from the economic point of view), their causes and cures." In the course on the Constitution he emphasized the practical working of government. In 1890 he added another course, American Institutional History, to be given in alternate years with the course in English and French history.[14]

Wilson's teaching load was not heavy, at least by the custom of the day. He taught nine periods a week for the first half-year, and alternately seven and eight periods a week for the second. But he set himself such high standards for academic lectures that much of his time was spent in class preparation. In an essay on Adam Smith entitled "An Old Master" he wrote, in words that show his own aspirations:

The success of his lectures was not always a triumph of natural gifts; it was, in great part, a triumph of sedulously cultivated art. With the true instinct of the orator and teacher, Adam Smith saw—what every one must see who speaks not for the patient ear of the closeted student only, but also to the often shallow ear of the pupil in the classroom, and to the always callous ear of the great world outside, which must be tickled in order to be made attentive—that clearness, force, and beauty of style are absolutely necessary to one who would draw men to his way of thinking; nay, to any one who would induce the great mass of mankind to give so much as passing heed to what he has to say. He knew that wit was of no avail, without wit's proper words; sagacity mean, without sagacity's measures of phrase. He bestowed the most painstaking care, therefore, not only upon what he was to say, but also upon the way he was to say it.[15]

No students of Wilson's got more out of him than those he taught at Wesleyan, nor remembered him more vividly. A half-century later, of the twenty-eight surviving members of his Wesleyan classes whom I approached for imformation, twenty-two responded. All but one person had specific memories of Wilson, and only two did not express strong admiration for him as a teacher.

Disorders in the classroom were as common at Wesleyan in the 1880's as at Princeton in the 1870's, but in Wilson's classes there was nearly perfect order. "The slightest inattention brought a gentle tapping of his pencil on the desk and a sharp look in the direction of the offender." He told the wife of a faculty member that "he always went to class feeling as if he were about to drive a team of wild horses. He never doubted his ability to control them, but he felt the same excitement. But no one else would have thought of anything but what he was saying while in his classes."[16]

Wilson usually stood while lecturing, although he sometimes sat behind a desk, spreading his hands, and leaning forward as he spoke. His students remembered a few mannerisms—how his nose twitched, how he occasionally pointed his forefinger for emphasis, the way a single lock of hair stood out in back. But mostly they remembered the clarity, charm, and elegance of his language, and his communicable enthusiasm. "He had a contagious interest—his eyes flashed." "I can see him now, with his hands forward, the tips of his fingers just touching the table, his face earnest and animated, many times illustrating an otherwise dry and tedious subject by his beautiful language and his apt way of putting things." "He . . . talked to us in the most informal, jolly way, yet with absolute clearness and sureness."[17]

Wilson's courses as Wesleyan were more thoroughly worked out than those he gave at Bryn Mawr. His students no longer complained that he did not give them enough outside reading. Rather the reverse. The *Wesleyan Argus* reported that when Wilson went off to Johns Hopkins for five weeks of lecturing in the winter of 1889, he assigned forty pages of reading per recitation during his absence, "with the promise of an examination at the end of the term." Students long remembered the close reading of *The Federalist* required in his course on the Constitution. Recently published works, such as John Fiske's *The Critical Period* and James Bryce's *The American Commonwealth*, enlivened the assignments. In the course on Political Economy the students wrote and publicly delivered papers on contemporary topics, such as "An Honest Dollar," "The Industrial Transition in China," "Socialism," and "The Growth of Cities." Perhaps one reason Wilson's former students at Wesleyan remembered more about him than did those at Bryn Mawr is that his lectures were tied to heavier assigned reading. In any case, many of the memories were graphic:

To this day I can repeat whole sentences from his lectures, something I cannot say of any other lecturer I ever had. For example:—"The secret of Queen Elizabeth's success was that she knew how to wait. She waited in one case five years, in another ten years, and in one case thirty, but she always won out and that too by peaceful means."

His lectures . . . were full of epigrams and witty expressions. For instance, he referred to one of the mad kings of England as follows: "When he came to years of discretion, he was found to have no discretion"; and again, "Business is business, which is just another way of saying that it is not Christianity."

From him I learned for the first time that there might be two sides to the War Between the States, that the South was civilized. I also got from him first the idea that all historical events were interlinked.

One idea in especial that I remember: that one should not follow one's country or party blindly—that is not true patriotism. Rather one should study it, know its strength and weakness, and strive in every way to make it better.[18]

Several of the Wesleyan alumni remembered with gratitude being entertained at his home on High Street. They recalled not only his conversation but Mrs. Wilson's charm and friendliness. The fact that Stockton Axson was in the college and living with them undoubtedly had something to do with these contacts, but apparently Wilson also invited in groups of students who were especially interested in history and politics. He brought out the baby girls for them to dandle and put them at their ease.[19]

During the Wesleyan years Wilson began to think about pedagogical problems. He wished that college-preparatory work could be made more lively. Boys should realize that Caesar was "a sure-enough man." If only "they could be given a fellow-feeling, an enthusiasm, or even a wonder for this versatile fellow-man of theirs, reading the Commentaries would never be forgotten . . . Maps help to give pictures of the fight: if the boys could be gotten to *play* at the campaigns it would be capital help: *anything* to dispel the notion that Caesar wrote grammatical exercises in hard words." In an article in the *Wesleyan University Bulletin* entitled "Preparatory Work in Roman History" Wilson wrote that the job of the secondary schools had been complicated by the fact there were really "two histories of Rome, the one traditional and improbable, the other that which has been produced by treating the traditional with the acids of criticism . . . The first is that which is told by Livy; the second, that proposed by Niebuhr, reduced to its coldest outlines by Ihne, expanded to new imaginative proportions by Mommsen." Wilson proposed that the schools go on teaching the traditional history, since it is an indispensable background for the study of literature and is "apparently made for schoolboys to believe." Reserve critical treatment for later. "Let the candidate for entrance into college be examined on the *story* of Rome, the candidate for graduation on her history."[20]

Even though Wilson was almost universally admired, the feeling of Wesleyan students toward him fell short of idolatry because they discovered he had a streak of stubbornness. On one occasion he apparently confused the grades of two men with the same last name and first initials, giving a high-ranking student a low grade on an examination, and a poor one a very high grade. When questioned about it, he flatly refused to "go back of the returns," and the affair caused "a considerable campus scandal." In class Wilson's students were made to feel that he did not like to be contradicted and that "he was distinctly not *open-minded* on any subject that he was interested in." He told one man who presumed to argue about a certain point: "Mr. Thompson, all the great constitutional questions have been settled." However charming he might be on the platform or free and easy socially, the Wesleyan undergraduates were somewhat in awe of Wilson. "He could," wrote one, "freeze you if you crossed him. That we all knew."[21]

Wilson's influence at Wesleyan went beyond the classroom and his home on High Street. As in his undergraduate days at Princeton, he became actively interested in the corporate life of the college. Foreshadowing his later campaign for the honor system at Princeton, Wilson set himself against cheating on examinations (called "skidding" at Wesleyan) and "urged that it be made a matter of college sentiment, that those who from principle were opposed to it should take it upon themselves to crush it out." Wilson had been at Wesleyan only four months when he again founded a debating society modeled on the English Parliament, similar to those he had established at Johns Hopkins and Bryn Mawr. The *Wesleyan Argus* reported:

> After consulting with the undergraduates throughout this college, and finding a favorable opinion he called a college meeting at 9 o'clock Saturday morning, Jan. 5th, and addressed those gathered as follows:
> In proposing to establish a Wesleyan House of Commons it is necessary to discuss the old style literary societies. They are uniformly of the same class and style; a galvanized movement simulating life, but not life. The effect of the ordinary debating society is unfortunate. To argue any case on one side, without the basis of a conviction of any sort, is mental suicide . . .
> The function of our new organization is the function of debate, which is the basis for the special art of oratory. Highest oratory is arrived at through the cultivation of the art of debate. To imitate the House of Representatives would be patriotic, but not interesting. The House of Representatives does not do its own debating, but refers most of its business to standing committees . . . So we shall imitate the British House of Commons, thereby introducing a dramatic element in that a body of ministers resign when defeated. The ministers will support the questions they believe in, and the natural party line will arise without any arbitrary divisions . . .

Wilson's remarks were applauded, and it was voted unanimously to inaugurate the new organization with a meeting a few days later to elect officers and adopt a Constitution and bylaws. In an editorial the *Argus* welcomed the new organization, not only because it promised to provide practice in debate but because it would help to overcome a "narrow, unhealthy, partisan spirit" bred by interfraternity rivalry and would provide "a center of corporate college interest."[22]

The Wesleyan House of Commons fared less well than that at Johns Hopkins. To Wilson's intense and publicly expressed annoyance, some members of the organization turned the proceedings into a farce by voting out the ministry on frivolous grounds. The college soon lost interest. Whereas at the first formal debate of the organization on January 15 no less than 137 members—nearly two-thirds of the undergraduates—were counted in a roll-call vote, by early March a debate on the annexation of Canada had to be adjourned because of no quorum. It was assumed that the mounting apathy was the result of Wilson's absence at Johns Hopkins and that on his return there would be a revival. But in May the *Argus* reported, "The pleasant spring evenings and the terrible grind for the approaching final examinations have proven too much for the House of Commons." Two successive meetings had been adjourned because of no quorum, the last attracting only six members.[23]

In 1889-90 the Wesleyan House of Commons was revived with a smaller membership, and it continued throughout the year, debating such matters as public aid to denominational schools, educational qualifications for voting, immigration restrictions, and the new rules of the House of Representatives. It did not, however, continue after Wilson went to Princeton in 1890.

As an English importation the House of Commons occasioned some distrust, and the members were ridiculed for imitating Wilson's pronunciation of "clerk" as "clark." There was even fear that the new professor was corrupting the young, as was indicated in June 1889 when Joseph R. Hawley, Republican Senator from Connecticut and a former abolitionist and Civil War hero, appeared on the Wesleyan campus and made a frontal attack on Wilson's views. Hawley ensured a large audience by letting his purpose be known in advance.

The *Middletown Constitution*, obviously sympathetic to the Senator, reported the event at length. It pointed out that *Congressional Government* had been widely read at Wesleyan, by both faculty and students, and that Wilson's antipathy to the way in which government was carried on in the House of Representatives was very well known. The report described the discomfiture of the members of the Wesleyan House of Commons as they listened "with trembling hearts and blanched faces" while Hawley "pointed out the errors of the book and showed clearly the supremacy of our form of government that has survived for more than a century in the face of the determined opposition of English Parliamentary rule . . . Their resentment knew no bounds when the speaker personally referred to the author and claimed that ignorance and English affectation alone formed the basis of his book." The audience also contained "patriotic admirers of our constitutional methods" who loudly applauded Senator Hawley's defense of American ways. Throughout the lecture Wilson sat in a front row and endured the attack with calmness. The next day he replied in his classes, claiming that the Senator had taken an unfair advantage. But, said the reporter for the *Constitution,* when "a pessimistic critic" had written a book and spread his doctrines all over the country and had "engrafted in the minds of the rising generation an opposition to our fundamental principles of government," it seemed only fair that he should be publicly rebutted.[24]

At Wesleyan Wilson revived his active interest in football. During his first year he did no coaching, even though it was known from the first that he had helped to coach the victorious Princeton team of 1879, but he attended practices and games, walking up and down the sidelines with a furled umbrella and exhibiting intense interest. One player, whose memory was otherwise trustworthy, remembered that Wilson gave a blackboard talk before the Princeton-Wesleyan game and that he put emphasis on speed in running off plays. The 1888 team had a poor season. It did not work together; there were too few substitutes; fraternity politics entered into the choice of the captain and possibly of the players. The *Wesleyan Argus* suggested that the college abandon the game.[25]

The season of 1889 opened disastrously with three humiliating defeats. At a college meeting called to deal with the situation Wilson and a graduate student, Seward V. Coffin (Wesleyan '89) were chosen directors of the football association and became a two-man advisory board. From that time on, Wesleyan fortunes improved. The team continued to lose to the big three (Harvard, Yale, and Princeton), but it won successive victories over Amherst, Rutgers, Williams, and Trinity, tied Lehigh, and finally on Thanksgiving Day won over a highly favored University of Pennsylvania team in New York City.

In a round-robin letter to fellow members of a Wesleyan senior society, "The Mystical Seven," Coffin explained how the advisory committee worked:

Prof. W., the Captain and your humble servant met before every important game and planned the plays. Now don't give this away, boys: because it will be just as well if other colleges don't know how we "work it."

Then we held meetings of the TEAM in Prof. Wilson's recitation room and made the plans on the blackboard. We planned, every time, a series of 5 or 6 plays to be used, without a signal, at the beginning of whichever half we had the kick-off. In the Williams game we planned to make a touchdown on the 5th play; Hall made one on the second. In the second Trinity and Lehigh games this planning helped the boys very much, I think, to say nothing of the great Thanksgiving Day victory.

Wilson attended practice, and sometimes he went with the team to a game out of town. But the captain directed the players on the field at all times. Although Wilson may have occasionally exhorted the team from the sidelines, his formal coaching was behind the scenes. Coffin implied that he was a secret weapon, which explains why he has received no mention in histories of Wesleyan football.[26]

Wilson's technical knowledge of football, valuable as it was, may have been less useful to the Wesleyan team than his influence in minimizing fraternity politics, promoting rigorous training, and rallying the college. He and Coffin coined a slogan, "The College first—the Fraternity afterward." At the close of the 1889 season the Wesleyan undergraduates formed a victory parade, during which they serenaded Wilson at his home. In response, Wilson made a speech, saying, "the victory was the victory not merely of one or two players, but the victory of the college. General interest, an awakened spirit, a determination to win, were the conditions that made men willing to disregard personal considerations and undergo severe training to make victory possible." These were the same virtues he had preached when managing the Princeton team ten years before.[27]

One of the strongest impressions gained from reading Wilson's correspondence during his years at Wesleyan is that he was under continuous pressure of work. During the years 1888, 1889, and 1890 he seems to have taken only one real vacation. In late August and early September 1889 he spent a week in New York, mostly with his friend Robert Bridges, during which time he went to several plays, traveled to Coney Island, saw his first professional baseball game, and visited publishers. Then at Bridges' insistence he took a steamer journey to Baltimore, where he dined with Princeton classmates, and continued by boat to Boston, whence he returned to Middletown. For the rest, his life was a steady round of reading, organizing courses, preparing public lectures, and writing. He worked either in the small, dark, book-lined study of his house on High Street or, during the summer months, in a deserted classroom.[28]

Wilson's principal achievement during his years at Middletown was to complete his textbook on government, *The State*. He worked at it continuously from early summer 1886 until the spring of 1889 and found it tedious. He had to gain enough command of German to go through hundreds of tomes and monographs; he told Charles H. McIlwain that he wore out a German dictionary while writing it. Ellen Wilson wrote out translations for her husband in intervals between housework and tending the children. Many sources were in French, which Wilson never quite mastered, although he had begun to study the language at Princeton. Even more difficult and distasteful than the chore of translation from alien languages was the character of the task. It was "a dull fact book," and Wilson had a positive aversion to facts as an end in themselves. He once wrote Ellen, "For my part I want to carry as little *information* in my head as possible—just as (to use some one else's illustration) I want to forget the figures in the column whose *sum* and *result* I have ascertained and went to keep. I must scan information, must question it closely as to every essential detail, in order that I may extract its meaning; but, the meaning once mastered, the information is lumber." To continue his metaphor, in writing *The State* Wilson probably felt that he was not building a mansion but simply arranging the boards in a lumberyard. What kept him going was not only that the book promised to bring in steady income but also that in the process of writing it he was, he hoped, preparing himself for a far greater work, "The Philosophy of Politics." As he approached the end of the task, he wrote Ellen: "What a job it has been! I am thoroughly tired of it and disgusted with it. I hope nothing with reference to it now except that it may some day be off my mind. Catch me undertaking another fact book! Hereafter I mean to be an *author*—never more a mere bookmaker. The discipline has been serviceable, but now that I am coming to the maturity of my powers I can't afford time for any more discipline of *that* kind."[29]

Although its author disparaged it as hack work, *The State: Elements of Historical and Practical Politics, A Sketch of Institutional History and Administration,* to give it its full title, had many merits. It was clear; it was informative; it made available in English for the first time much knowledge hitherto accessible only to advanced scholars. In the opinion of Arthur Link, "It was probably Wilson's greatest scholarly achievement." On only one other book, *Division and Reunion,* did Wilson expend such care and thoroughness. More than 150 "representative authorities" in German, French, and English were cited in chapter-end bibliographies. Portions of the manuscript were read by competent scholars. The book was also up to date, as indicated by the fact that it referred to events in British and French politics that had occurred only a few months before Wilson completed the manuscript.[30]

For the most part *The State* described institutions and events with little commentary. It nevertheless revealed a good deal of Wilson's political philosophy. He could not refrain from calling attention to the superiority of cabinet government in Britain, in comparison with France, "staggering under that most burdensome, that most intolerable of all forms of government, *government by mass meeting,*—by an inorganic popular assembly," or with the United States, where "our federal executive and legislature have been shut off from co-operation and mutual confidence to an extent to which no other modern system furnishes a parallel."[31]

The State dealt with contemporary governments only in northwestern Europe and the United States. Russia, the Orient, Spain, Italy, and Latin America were all deliberately excluded. In explaining why the work was so organized, Wilson revealed a simple Darwinian faith in the racial as well as political superiority of the West:

> In order to trace the lineage of the European and American governments which have constituted the order of social life for those stronger and nobler races which have made the most notable progress in civilization, it is essential to know the political history of the Greeks, the Latins, the Teutons, and the Celts principally, if not only, and the original political habits and ideas of the Aryan and Semitic races alone. The existing governments of Europe and America furnish the dominating types of today. To know other systems that are defeated or dead would aid only indirectly towards an understanding of those which are alive and triumphant, as the survived fittest.

Indeed, the grand design of *The State* was explicitly Darwinian. Wilson declared that his method was "that of historical evolution, in accordance with his [Darwin's] view that political development is accomplished by means of conservative adaptation through the transformation of old customs into new, through the modification of old means for the accomplishment of new ends." He saw a clear line of historical progress: "From the dim morning hours of history when the father was king and priest down to this modern time of history's high noon when nations stand forth full-grown and self-governed, the law of coherence and continuity in political development has suffered no serious breach . . . The evolutions of politics have been scarcely less orderly and coherent than those in the physical world."[32]

It would have been surprising had Wilson *not* come to a Darwinian explanation of political progress. In the book he revered, Walter Bagehot's *Physics and Politics,* he had read that only the races farthest along in the evolutionary process could achieve government by discussion. The same conclusions were presented in other works that he had read with care: Herbert Spencer's and Sir Henry Maine's books on the development of institutions, Edward A. Freeman's *Historical Essays,* Henry Cabot Lodge's *Short History of the English Colonies in America,* and many essays in the *Johns Hopkins University Studies in Historical and Social Sciences.*[33]

1. The Probable Original basis of govt. among Aryan races. The first forms of govt. Nature of the Evidence. Original relations of the State to territory.

2. Theories and traditions touching the Origin of the State. In what respects supported by the facts. The truth, in substance.

3. *The Stages· by* which the [shorthand]

4. [shorthand]

5. [shorthand]

6. The Solonian Const. [shorthand]

7. [shorthand] - Clisthenes

8. The Spartan [shorthand] - Lycurgus.

9. The Roman [shorthand]

10. [shorthand] jus gentium - jus civile /

11. Development [shorthand]

12. [shorthand]

13. The Feudal System; [shorthand]

14. [shorthand]

15. [shorthand]

16. How [shorthand]

17. [shorthand]

18. [shorthand]

19. [shorthand]

20. [shorthand]

Notes for an outline of a chapter in *The State,* Wilson's textbook on government. Whether Wilson used longhand or shorthand or, as here, combined the two, his writing was always meticulously neat and controlled.

The State dealt principally with political machinery, and economics seldom intruded. But in two final chapters Wilson addressed himself to the question: "What ought the functions of government to be?" and here he revealed that in his particular brand of social Darwinism he he did not follow Herbert Spencer and William Graham Sumner in defending unbridled free competition. On the contrary, he explicitly repudiated laissez faire. Government was not "a necessary evil" but "is no more evil than is society itself . . . If the name had not been restricted to a single, narrow, extreme, and radically mistaken class of thinkers, we ought all to regard ourselves as *socialists*, believers in the wholesomeness and beneficence of the body politic."[34]

Having declared himself a sort of socialist, Wilson stated further that, although the schemes of social reform put forward by those who had appropriated the name were mostly "mistaken enough to provoke the laughter of children," the Socialists were right in wanting to substitute cooperation and mutual helpfulness for "selfish, misguided individualism." In words that could as well have been written more than two decades later at the high noon of the progressive period, Wilson denounced the evils of unrestrained free enterprise: "The modern industrial organization has so distorted competition as to put it into the power of some to tyrannize over many, as to enable the rich and strong to combine against the poor and weak. It has given a woeful material meaning to that spiritual law that 'to him that hath shall be given, and from him that hath not shall be taken away even the little that he seemeth to have.' It has magnified that self-interest which is grasping selfishness and has thrust out love and compassion not only, but free competition in part, as well."[35]

It was not only proper but necessary, Wilson continued, for the state to intervene in the economy in order to equalize opportunity. To this end it may take over or regulate natural monopolies such as gas works, water systems, and railroads. It may restore competition destroyed by artificial monopolies. It may prohibit child labor, regulate the work of women, restrict the hours of men in certain trades, test the quality of goods, and improve working conditions in general. By acting in such ways, the government would be "making competition equal between those who would rightfully conduct enterprise and those who basely conduct it. It is in this way that society protects itself against permanent injury and deterioration, and secures healthy equality of opportunity for self-development."[36]

Although Wilson opposed outright socialism, intervention in morals or conscience, and merely "convenient" in contrast to "necessary" state action, he saw no fixed limit either in principle or in practice to state power. He insisted (the italics are his) that *"government does now whatever experience permits or the times demand."*[37]

Many of the ideas in the final chapters of *The State* were drawn from *The Philosophy of Wealth* by the economist John Bates Clark, first published in 1885. After Wilson had first read Clark's book, he wrote a warm letter to the author, saying that the book had fertilized his thought and cheered him by "its moderation and its Christianity." He was sure he would return to it again and again. It is evident that he did just that, because Wilson's definition of the proper functions of government in relation to the economy follows almost exactly the lines laid down in *The Philosophy of Wealth*. Clark had condemned much of what passed for legitimate business competition as "immoral," "a refinement of highway robbery." He explicitly repudiated laissez faire economics and welcomed positive state action to ameliorate working conditions. The actions he recommended were also advocated by Wilson—regulation of monopolies, social legislation, and oversight of business practices. Clark proposed to apply Christianity to the rules of the market place and sympathized with the generous purposes of socialism. Yet he too ruled out any immediate introduction of full-time socialism as impractical and dangerous. Thus, after Johns Hopkins had shaken Wilson loose from his safe moorings in the Manchester school of economics, John B. Clark apparently provided a new haven.[38]

The State proved a success. To be sure, a reviewer in the *Nation* found much to criticize: a number of inaccuracies, over-easy generalization and superficiality, the misuse of scientific vocabulary and concepts. He astutely remarked that it was too easy to mistake metaphors for demonstrations and to confuse facts with abstractions. But other reviewers were less perceptive and generally favorable. A short review in the *Atlantic Monthly* commended the author for the clarity of his writing, his scientific method, and his intuitive perception of underlying concepts. The *Overland Monthly* applauded his ability to clarify and condense historical development. A. B. Hart of Harvard, F. J. Turner of Wisconsin, J. W. Jenks of Indiana, and H. B. Adams of Johns Hopkins wrote Wilson that they were introducing it in their courses.[39]

The State came to be widely used in the United States and abroad—in universities as far apart as Cambridge and Bombay. It thus fulfilled its immediate purpose: the earning of royalties. Its sales were great enough, averaging well over a thousand copies a year, to justify a thorough rewriting and updating in 1898. In 1910 Charles H. McIlwain did a slight revision, especially of the chapter on Norway and Sweden. The book still had enough life to be translated into German and published in Berlin—the date has a certain irony—in 1913. The eminence of the author warranted a final revision in 1918. But with the decline of social Darwinism the historical sections became outmoded, and the rise of totalitarianism refuted its optimistic notion that there was inexorable progress toward constitutional democracy.[40]

In March 1889, Wilson reviewed James Bryce's *The American Commonwealth* for the *Political Science Quarterly*. That he was chosen to evaluate the most important work of its kind since the publication of de Tocqueville's *Democracy in America* is evidence of his high reputation in his chosen field. The result justified his selection, for the essay is admirably written; the criticism is acute, just, and sympathetic.[41]

Throughout the review Wilson displayed his own predilections. He obviously admired Bryce, partly for the simple reason that, like Dick Deadeye in *Pinafore*, he was an Englishman. "Perhaps no one," wrote Wilson, "can so readily understand our institutions as an English public man sufficiently read in our history and our constitutional law not to expect to find bishops in our Senate or prime ministers in the presidency." He found Bryce especially admirable when he agreed with him, as on the importance of comparative politics in studying institutions, or on the evils of separating the executive and legislative power, which results in "slipshod, haphazard, unskilled, and hasty legislation." Wilson praised Bryce for his detailed account of state governments; it was right that they should receive attention, for they were "laboratories" where English institutions were tested and from which laws of institutional growth could be learned. The states were also pioneering in economic and political reforms, perhaps ignorantly, even dangerously, but in directions that were necessary and instructive. Here again, as in the final chapters of *The State*, Wilson revealed that in his opinion the times called for positive government.

Wilson's principal criticism of *The American Commonwealth* was that it was somewhat pedestrian, both in style and matter. It informed the reader more than it instructed him. In other words, there was room at the top for Wilson's projected "Philosophy of Politics." Still to be accomplished was "the work of explaining democracy *by* America, in supplement of Mr. Bryce's admirable explanation of democracy *in* America":

Comparative politics must yet be made to yield an answer to the broad and all-important question: what is democracy that it should be possible, nay natural, to some nations, impossible as yet to others? Why has it been cordial and a tonic to little Switzerland and to big America, while it has been as yet only a quick intoxicant or a slow poison to France or Spain, a mere maddening draught to the South American States? Why has England approached democratic institutions by slow and steady stages of peaceful development, while so many other states have panted toward democracy by constant revolution? Why has democracy existed in America and Australia virtually from the first, while other states have utterly failed in every effort to establish it? Answers to such questions as these would serve to show the most truly significant thing now to be discovered concerning democracy: its place and office, namely, in the process of political development.

Wilson tentatively furnished an answer. Democracy was not a doctrine or a form of government but a stage in an organic development. "Its process is experience, its basis old wont, its meaning national organic untity and effectual life."

The lead article in the *Atlantic Monthly* for November 1889 was an essay by Wilson, "Character of Democracy in the United States," in which he expanded parts of the Bryce review. He insisted, at almost wearisome length, that democracy in the United States owed nothing to the French Enlightenment, everything to England; that it had been a "truly organic growth" with "nothing revolutionary in its movements." Now, however, it was being threatened by the flood of immigration from Europe. "Our own temperate blood," wrote Wilson, revealing his pseudo-Darwinian attitude toward race, "schooled to self-possession and to the measured conduct of self-government, is receiving a constant infusion and yearly experiencing a partial corruption of foreign blood." And with the immigrants came European habits and political philosophy—"a philosophy which has never been purged by the cold bath of practical politics."[42]

What was needed? Wilson's answer was predictable: leadership. Of all forms of government, democracy most needed leadership in order to escape disintegration. As often before, he argued that we must change our political machinery so as to "concentrate legislative leadership" and to give our democracy some of the elements that make men turn to monarchy—cohesion, loyalty to symbols and persons, concerted organization.

At first this essay seems to be an expression of conservatism: witness its repudiation of democratic theory, its fear of corruption of blood by "lesser breeds without the law," and its explicit admiration of monarchy. But Wilson's purpose was to promote change, not to avert it. To do so, he had to allay fears about democracy in this country which were hobbling American government. He derided English observers, such as Sir Henry Maine, who admired the restraints on quick action written into the Constitution. "We are asked to believe," Wilson wrote, "that we have succeeded because we have taken Sir Archibald Alison's advice, and have resisted the infection of revolution by staying quite still." But, continued Wilson, "progress is motion, government is action."

In his demand for a government that could act, as in his opinion that laissez faire was outmoded and that there must be positive state action to ameliorate the injustices of the industrial system, Woodrow Wilson revealed himself the future progressive. His message was deliberately shrouded in the language of conservatism because he was trying to persuade his readers that the changes he proposed were not radical but were merely part of a normal evolutionary process. He was applying what he had told Ely at Johns Hopkins: if you make people believe you are a conservative, "then you can go ahead and do progressive things."

In the nineteenth century the lecture platform was, much more than now, a means whereby authors and professors augmented their income. In 1889, for instance, Caleb Winchester made thirty appearances outside Wesleyan in four months, talking on such topics as Robert Burns, the English Lake Country, and Shakespeare's plays. During his years at Wesleyan Wilson began to supplement his income by public lecturing. In the year 1889 he made about a dozen public appearances in addition to his twenty-five lectures on administration at Johns Hopkins. Like Winchester, he developed a repertory of stock lectures that could be repeated or adapted for different audiences.[43]

On April 30, 1889, Wilson spoke in the North Church, Middletown, before a combined congregation representing the five Protestant churches of the city, on the hundredth anniversary of George Washington's inauguration as President of the United States. His manuscript has been preserved, and it enables one to see the practical economy of the public lecturer. Much of the speech was drawn from what he had already written; most of the rest was later to find its way into print. Wilson portrayed Washington less as a personality than as a manifestation "of such heroic stuff as God had for centuries been so graciously and so lavishly weaving into the character of our race."[44]

On July 20, Wilson delivered a carefully polished lecture on Bagehot, "A Literary Politician," before the Connecticut Valley Assembly, an adjunct of Chautauqua, which held an eight-day gathering of men, women, and children in Laurel Park, a former camp-meeting ground in Northampton, Massachusetts. The proceedings included temperance meetings, children's classes, prayers, choruses, fireworks, readings, and lectures on topics as varied as "The Ancient Egyptians" and "Lands of the Midnight Sun." The tent was reputed to hold a thousand people, but on the morning when Wilson spoke, the weather was so threatening that only a score arrived. They listened earnestly but, Wilson thought, unresponsively. Nevertheless, the newspapers played up his address in comparison with those given later in the day by two men of established reputation—George Makepeace Towle, an author, editor, and politician, and the Reverend Charles Pankhurst, minister of the Madison Avenue Presbyterian Church. Whether he won the audience or not, he obviously impressed the reporters.[45]

"A Literary Politician" became part of Wilson's repertoire of popular lectures. He presented it to "a select and cultured audience" at the Methodist church in Middletown on October 15, 1889, and delivered it on several later occasions, until it at last appeared as an article in the *Atlantic Monthly*, which was subsequently included in a book of essays. In December 1889 he gave a talk at the Hartford Y.M.C.A. entitled "Leaders of Men." This was delivered again as the commencement address at the University of Tennessee, Knoxville, on June 17, 1890, and at least three times thereafter.[46]

Wilson's career as a lyceum lecturer was both lucrative and successful. In his talks before earnest self-improvement groups he easily adapted to the mood of the audiences, who came for inspiration and uplift rather than for instruction. It is not certain that they remembered what he had said, but they knew he had said it beautifully and that they had been exposed to "culture." According to Winthrop Daniels, who heard Wilson about this time, "the effect produced was that of a finished literary essay such as some of the earlier and more scholarly lyceum demigods doubtless strove for."[47]

Quite different from the lyceum debates in both tone and substance were three addresses under the auspices of the Brown University Historical and Economic Association. J. Franklin Jameson, then Professor of History at Brown, made the arrangements. The fees were only twenty-eight dollars a lecture, but Wilson was richly paid in prestige since other participants were men of eminence, such as Seth Low, ex-mayor of New York, and Francis Wayland, dean of the Yale Law School. According to a contemporary newspaper the audiences consisted of many of the most important people in Providence—businessmen, educators, and public officials, including members of the City Council. The lectures were fully reported in the press. They show that in talking to an audience of practical men about actual problems of government, Wilson displayed a gift for clear, effective exposition and an easy mastery of detail that were quite different from his effusions on lyceum platforms. Apparently he was a success. After the first lecture he wrote his father: "I was extremely well received and I think I can say that I made a decided hit. After the lecture Colonel Goddard, who introduced me, and who is one of the richest men in an extremely rich town, as well as a man of sense and of cultivated tastes, took me to his house and entertained me most handsomely. He tried to make me believe, by almost every turn of the conversation, that I was quite a distinguished man! I came home so puffed up that I could hardly speak to my own family."[48]

On January 10, 1889, Wilson talked about "Systems of Municipal Organization," and a week later about "The Government of Berlin." In the first lecture he put the modern industrial city into historical perspective, asserting that ancient and medieval cities were political commonwealths, while the modern city was an economic center dominated from without by the national state, with national citizenship minimizing interest in municipal affairs. After reviewing systems of municipal administration in Germany, France, and England, Wilson turned to the United States and found much to criticize, including excessive interference by state legislatures and a lack of civic spirit that played into the hands of politicians.[49]

In the lecture on the government of Berlin, Wilson insisted that the subject was "not a foreign example, strictly speaking; it is just as truly an English example. It is a pan-Teutonic example of processes that seemed to inhere in the ancient polity of the people to which we belong." What he especially admired in Berlin was the effort to revive a sense of municipal citizenship by enforced public service. Ten thousand people, he said, served the city without pay under threat of losing their franchise and paying higher taxes. In courts of summary justice laymen were associated with the magistrates; about three thousand people, including women, helped in the distribution of poor relief; and a large city council effectively controlled the purse strings. Wilson's enthusiasm was tinged with caution. He apparently admired the three-class system in Prussia, which weighted the franchise heavily in favor of property owners; like his hero Mr. Gladstone, he saw the "better middle class" as the safest repository of self-government. Nevertheless, he held that a special advantage of the Berliners' wide participation in administration was that it helped to head off socialism: "Socialism is an infinitely easy thing for the voters and an infinitely difficult one for the administrator; and people who constantly handle affairs will see that Socialism is an extreme difficulty or an impossibility." Finally, Wilson reverted to a favorite theme, the effectiveness of aroused and directed public opinion: "If I have made a single impression . . . I have meant it to be this, that there are other ways of reforming a city than by changing the disposition of power. The imperious demand is to get citizens stirred up and interested. In the greatest centers of corruption one single day of public indignation sweeps all away and leaves the atmosphere purified for months or years afterwards."[50]

On November 11, 1889, Wilson gave the first address in another lecture series at Brown, devoted to "The State and Social Reform." The *Providence Journal* reported that "a large and cultured audience" received him with great applause. His topic was "What Ought Government to Do?" The talk was fully reported both by the *Providence Journal* and the *Boston Herald*. Again Wilson used the language of conservatism but proposed reform and the active intervention of government. He began by deriding cranks and faddists, especially the followers of Edward Bellamy, whose recently published novel *Looking Backward* had created more sympathy in the United States for socialism in two years than Marx had done in forty: "Was there ever a time when people followed more fads or notions, or were looking about for more novelties? Was there ever a time when a new novel started greater political agitation? Was there ever a time when imagination took the place of scientific fact, not that people have gone crazy, but they are ready to receive any and all new things?" But after this conservative start, the lecturer went on to condemn unrestrained free competition, saying, as in his classes at Wesleyan, "Business is business, which means that business is not Christianity."[51]

On June 27, 1890, during his last weeks at Wesleyan, Wilson delivered the commencement oration at the graduation day ceremonies at Worcester Polytechnical Institute in Massachusetts. His topic was "Modern Systems of City Government." The talk followed the lines of his addresses at Brown University, but at one point he struck out on an entirely new tack. He remarked that the dominant elements in a modern industrial city are the manufacturing and commercial classes, who think of profits rather than of the wants of their neighbors. They are not fitted to care for the needs of the great majority of the inhabitants. Instead, there must be more democratic control by the people of the tenements themselves, and men must think of the city not as an economic institution, semipublic and semiprivate, but as an organic whole. This is radical doctrine, and it is not surprising that someone in the audience wrote Wilson nearly a year later that he was sure the talk had "aroused some of the conservative citizens of that conservative old town to a vivid realization of present conditions."[52]

In his writing and public lecturing Wilson's purpose, aside from the obvious need to augment his income, was essentially political: to preach the gospel he had learned from Edmund Burke, the gospel of orderly change, of reform without revolution. His studies of municipal government pushed him even further from the unthinking laissez faire of his Princeton days toward acceptance of the state as a force for good in promoting economic and social well-being. He was also moving away from his earlier elitist concept of government and distrust of democracy in the direction of accepting as necessary the active participation of the lower classes in government. Thus, the essentials of Wilson's future brand of progressivism, "the New Freedom," were now made manifest, although later in his academic career his political philosophy swung back to the right.

It was no matter of chance that Wilson's career at Wesleyan was short. In 1886 his friends' campaign to get him back to Princeton had been abortive; but in the summer of 1888 Robert Bridges wrote Wilson that the "scheme in prospect" was already well advanced. The scheme was to found a new chair of political science, so that Princeton might give instruction "in the whole subject of practical legislation." "When the chair is founded," wrote Bridges, "of course you are the man for it. I believe you have enough friends in power, looking after you, to put you there." Bridges wrote frequent letters about efforts to induce the newly elected President Patton, Professor Sloane, and prominent trustees to favor Wilson's candidacy. In these endeavors several members of the class of '79 played an important part, especially four who were already prominent in the world of business: Cyrus McCormick, Edward Sheldon, Cornelius C. Cuyler, and Cleveland Dodge. All of them eventually became Princeton trustees; McCormick was one by 1889.[53]

Meanwhile, Wilson promoted his own candidacy. In 1887 he wrote Bridges about the possibility of his taking Professor Sloane's chair of history should Sloane be elected president of Princeton in place of McCosh, who had resigned. The next year he wrote the article entitled "An Old Master" for the *New Princeton Review*. Ostensibly in praise of Adam Smith—what could better please conservative trustees?—the essay found Smith admirable less as an economist than as an academic lecturer and writer. When Frederick Jackson Turner read it some years later, he called it "a plea for Woodrow Wilson in the professorial chair." Wilson, in fact, laid it on the line: "Some of the subtlest and most lasting effects of genuine oratory have gone forth from secluded lecture desks into the hearts of quiet groups of students; and it would be good policy to endure much indifferent lecturing—watchful trustees might reduce it to a minimum—for the sake of leaving places open for the men who have in them the inestimable force of chastened eloquence." Wilson described Smith, in terms he would surely have liked to apply to himself, as one who had "the artist's eye," broad understanding, and the gift of eloquence—in short, one who "must write *literature* or nothing . . . Such men will not, I am persuaded, always seek in vain invitations to those academic platforms which are their best coigns of vantage."[54]

This aspirant did not have long to wait. In the summer of 1889 a

sudden vacancy at Princeton was created by the death of Alexander
Johnson, Professor of History and Political Economy, and President
Patton offered Wilson the place. Bridges urged him to accept, but he
refused, in part because he wanted to teach politics, not economics,
above all because he could not leave Wesleyan in the lurch. He wrote
Bridges that although he was "under no *contract* obligation" to stay at
Wesleyan, he felt obligated to do so. If he were to leave, the department would collapse, since a small college has "by no means the same
chances for obtaining a good or even a tolerable man on short notice
that Princeton has." The Wesleyan authorities had treated him "not
only honourably but generously," so he must stay at least another year.[55]

In the fall of 1889 the movement to bring Wilson to Princeton was
renewed, but opposition appeared. One of the older trustees is reported
to have remarked, "He's a Southerner and will make trouble." Another
was opposed to allowing a free-trader to teach economics. In November, on the eve of a trustees' meeting, Bridges wrote Wilson:

> I have arrived at some of the arguments which certain of the Philistines
> have seen fit to whisper behind their hands: 1) Prof. Wilson is no doubt
> a fine scholar, but he comes from the South and we want to know more
> about his patriotism, and general views on national topics. 2) He is, we
> hear, a little heterodox (shades of Calvin and Witherspoon protect us).
> 3) He is too learned and deep to interest students. 4) We are fearful
> of his strong affection for English institutions.—These things are chaff
> which intelligent men laugh at, but we know there is an element in
> Princeton which is hardly reasonably intelligent.

The Philistines were apparently strong enough to defer action on Wilson's candidacy. Patton supported him, however, and his classmates
continued to campaign. In February 1890 he finally received word of
his election as Professor of Jurisprudence and Political Economy.[56]

Even though he had been maneuvering for it for four years, Wilson
did not at once accept the Princeton offer. Wesleyan, he was assured,
would do almost anything to keep him; he had also been approached
about a new chair of American History, Literature, and Eloquence at
Williams. He first asked for a salary of $3,500, more than any Princeton
professor was receiving, then came down to $3,400, its top salary, and
finally settled for $3,000, the usual remuneration for a full professor,
with the assurance that he would be required to teach economics for
no more than two years, that he could eventually devote himself solely
to politics, with a teaching load of four lectures a week, and that he
could continue to hold his lectureship at Johns Hopkins. In practical
matters Woodrow Wilson sometimes showed himself a true member of
"that unbending race," the Scots.[57]

Wilson's farewell to Wesleyan was a pleasant contrast to his unhappy separation from Bryn Mawr. He helped the authorities to find a successor, asking Albert Shaw to consider the position, and approaching Herbert B. Adams to suggest other names. The college newspaper reported the "cordial esteem" that Wilson had gained among the undergraduates on account of his teaching and interest in athletics. It noted that in addition to imparting knowledge, Wilson had gone out of his way to inculcate a sense of political duty and patriotism. Indeed, the Wesleyan students remembered him so favorably that when Wilson returned to give a talk at Middletown in the fall of 1891, they rose and gave the college cheer as he appeared on the platform.[58]

Wilson retained an admiration for Wesleyan and kept up his connections there for many years. In 1900 he wrote his friend A. W. Hazen, "I have an affection for Middletown and its people out of all proportion to the length of my residence there—in proportion to the extraordinary kindliness and attractiveness of the community. I could wish that I might seem really to belong to it." Wesleyan's admiration proved as lasting. When the university celebrated the two hundredth anniversary of John Wesley's birth in 1903, Wilson was asked back to give the principal address, and a report of the event commented on the host of friends he had made among the alumni of the college and the citizens of Middletown.[59]

Lecturer at Johns Hopkins

1888–1898

Dr. Wilson is here. Homely, solemn, young, glum, but with that fire in his eye that means that its possessor is not of the common crowd.

—Frederick Jackson Turner, 1889[1]

AFTER completing *The State* in the spring of 1889, Wilson put aside serious writing in favor of more popular and more lucrative authorship. Yet at the time he believed that this was only temporary, and that he would eventually complete "The Philosophy of Politics." To keep himself in a state of readiness for that *Meisterwork,* he stayed abreast of scholarly literature about government, in French and German as well as in English, and emancipated himself from all teaching that did not fall within the field of politics, broadly defined. He taught no more economics or history after the academic year 1891-1892.

A most important means whereby Wilson maintained his reputation as a political scientist was his stint as a lecturer at Johns Hopkins from 1888 to 1898. He usually gave a course under the general title "Administration," delivering twenty-five lectures over a five-week period. He did not like to be away from home, but the $500 stipend was an important supplement to his regular salary. As he wrote his father in January 1889, "It will be a sadly dreary business being separated so long from Ellie and the babies; but Ellie and the babies must be supported —so must the separation." [2]

One way in which President Gilman enriched the teaching at Johns Hopkins was to invite outside lecturers in great numbers. During the first twenty-five years some three hundred came to speak, sometimes in single talks, sometimes in courses for credit. Herbert B. Adams fully agreed with this method of preventing instruction from becoming arid or anemic. He especially liked to call back successful alumni of the historical seminary; it was part of his own method of spurring his

188

students toward professional achievement. Asked to return as lecturers in history, politics, and economics were Albert Shaw, H. C. Adams, J. Franklin Jameson, E. R. L. Gould, W. W. Willoughby, and others, but none so frequently nor for so many lectures at a time as Woodrow Wilson.[3]

At Bryn Mawr, Wesleyan, and Princeton Wilson's pupils were nearly all undergraduates, who he felt were capable of mastering only the rudiments of his field. But at Johns Hopkins he taught graduate students, who challenged him to do his best. They were on the whole a remarkably able and ambitious group of young men. The galaxy of historians who studied under him includes Charles M. Andrews, James S. Bassett, W. R. Commons, Charles H. Haskins, Charles D. Hazen, John H. Latané, and Frederick Jackson Turner. Others he taught were the noted sociologist Edward A. Ross; the municipal reformer Frederick C. Howe; Newton D. Baker, later Wilson's Secretary of War; and John II. Finley, who became Professor of Politics at Princeton at Wilson's instigation and eventually editor of the *New York Times*. Men such as these had high aspirations, dedicated to the service of society. Here was an audience worth reaching. Wilson's gratification on returning to Johns Hopkins was reflected in a letter from his father, written in 1889: "I can really sympathize with you in the satisfaction you experience in getting back to Johns Hopkins once more, where intellectual life rolls in its highest waves;—a satisfaction which is augmented by the fact that you are, yourself, a sort of magna pars where there is so much that is great . . . I do not doubt as touching the impression you are making—and as you perceive this it must be very pleasing to your thoughts everyway. You are preaching a Gospel of order, and thus of safety, in the department of political morals and conduct." [4]

Johns Hopkins showered other honors besides the lectureship on Wilson. He was elected president of the Alumni Association in 1889, awarded the John Marshall prize in 1893, and repeatedly urged to join the faculty. But the admiration was never fully reciprocated. The scientific approach to knowledge represented by Johns Hopkins remained antipathetic to Wilson. To his mind the painstaking garnering and arranging of facts might actually obscure more than it elucidated. It had become "scientific," Wilson wrote, "to disclose morbid moods, and the conditions that produce them; scientific to regard man, not as a centre or source of power, but as subject to power; a register of external forces instead of an originative soul, and character as a product of man's circumstances rather than of man's mastery over circumstance." [5]

What especially aroused Wilson's ire about Johns Hopkins was its attitude toward literature. It was not merely that H. B. Adams had too little regard for style, or that Richard T. Ely was a "dribbler" who had "an infallible nose for a weak phrase"; it went far deeper. During his annual stay at Johns Hopkins in 1891 he was told that J. W. Bright of the English department had said of some book that it was "mere literature." Wilson stormed into the Bluntschli Library snorting, "Mere literature—mere literature; I'll get even with him." He "got even" through an article, "Mere Literature," published in the *Atlantic Monthly* in 1893, and later the title of a collection of essays. It began: "A singular phrase this, 'mere literature,'—the irreverent invention of a scientific age. Literature we know, but 'mere literature'? We are not to read it as if it meant *sheer* literature, literature in the essence, stripped of all accidental or ephemeral elements, and left with nothing but its immortal charm and power. 'Mere literature' is a serious sneer, conceived in all honesty by the scientific mind; which despises things that do not fall within the categories of demonstrable knowledge." Then followed a frontal attack on the impersonal, dehumanized *Wissenschaft* that Johns Hopkins had imported from Germany. "There is indeed," wrote Wilson, "a natural antagonism, let it be frankly said, between the standards of scholarship and the standards of literature." Again: "Scholarship is material; it is not life . . . Scholars, therefore, do not reflect; they label, group kind with kind, set forth in schemes, expound with dispassionate method. Their minds are not stages, but museums; nothing is done there, but very curious and valuable collections are kept there." [6]

Thus, Wilson was not entirely happy with his lectures at Johns Hopkins. He felt obliged to hand out information that students could not easily obtain except from him, such as the details of a recent English local government act. He complained to his wife, "there's no chance for me to catch fire as I go." As time went on, Wilson's lectures became somewhat more hortatory and less factual, although they were always scholarly and made abundant reference to the contemporary scene. [7]

Wilson's lectures were deliberately varied from year to year. He received three-year appointments for 1888-1890, 1891-1893, and 1894-1896, on the assumption that he would give courses in a sequence within each period, with a logical progression of topics. Such symmetry proved impossible in practice. New students were constantly entering the seminary, so that there had to be some review and repetition. Wilson sometimes altered his own plans as he went along. Thus, in 1889 he intended to give fifteen or sixteen lectures on local government at the provincial or county level and eight or nine on municipal government, but he had so much to say on the first topic that he used up twenty-three lectures before he was through with it, and deferred municipal government to the next year. It is also possible that he failed to finish his preparation for the lectures on municipal government and therefore strung out the earlier material. Several sets of notes for his lecture courses are extant, none of which he quite completed; most of them peter out after half a dozen classes. He was constantly pressed for time, since he was usually doing other work in Baltimore in addition to preparing his formal lectures.[8]

Although labeled Administration, Wilson's courses sooner or later covered almost the entire field of government, at least in Western Europe and the United States. He did not neglect, however, the field of administration narrowly defined. A course prospectus for the year 1891 explained:

It is intended to make the lectures given in 1891 cover, in the first place, a discussion of the general questions of public law with which administration concerns itself; and in the second place, an examination of the establishment and training of a professional civil service. This plan will involve, as its first part, a tolerably wide survey of the history and general principles of public law; and, as its second part, a consideration of the history of foreign experience in the establishment of a trained, technical, public service, the feasibility and desirability of the introduction and enforcement of a similar training in our own administrative organization and the results to be expected.[9]

Wilson's lecture notes reveal that he was still wrestling with the problem propounded in his essay "The Study of Administration" in 1887: how to reconcile an efficient, professional civil service with self-government and individual liberty. He explicitly repudiated the idea that democracy must be sacrificed to efficiency: "the State is an instrumentality for quickening in every suitable way (there has been a long history of disastrous experiment) both collective and individual development. BUT you must take care that there is really an intimate organic connection between the Administration and the community as a whole, with its diverse and complex interests, that the Administration is in very truth an organ, and not an outside power (however benevolent), holding the people in tutelage." Wilson flatly contradicted Francis Lieber's dictum that liberty depended infinitely more on administration than on constitutions. On the contrary, liberty consisted in self-government: paternalism did not become liberty because it was gentle and considerate. The great problem, Wilson insisted again and again, was how to adapt the French and German science of administration, which had been created by and for a supreme central authority, to the needs of a decentralized, free society. Americans had been too busy to stop and speculate about this. Finally, Wilson introduced the scholarly student of affairs as a *deus ex machina* to straighten things out: "A theory of navigation is useful to sailors—but they haven't time to think about it in a high wind—much less to construct the like for themselves—that must be done on land." Wilson would have much preferred to be himself in command of a ship on the high seas of politics; but even as a landlubberly scholar, he intended to have some influence on the navigation of the ship of state by evolving right principles and persuading others to act on them.[10]

Members of the historical seminary later recalled Woodrow Wilson as one of the best, if not the very best, of their academic lecturers—his material well organized, his delivery precise and clear, his manner pleasing. His was "a combination of Presbyterian fervor and Virginia charm." "I have never," said one, "known a man with more respect for what he was trying to do." "In action," said another, "his mind reminded me of a smooth-working engine; every time the piston moved, it punched out an idea." Charles M. Andrews, in a letter to his mother, wrote concerning Wilson's course in Administration: "It is a live subject taught by a live man. I am trying to take full notes for they are very valuable. When completed I shall have them bound as I did those on Roman Law, for they are worth it." [11]

Fifty years afterward, Andrews vividly remembered Wilson's lectures:

Wilson stood at a small desk with a sloping top at one end of a long table. He did not read his lectures but kept notes on a series of little slips of paper perhaps 6″ x 4″ or less. He would glance at a card occasionally and as he went on shuffle the cards. He might use two or three dozen in the course of an hour's lecture . . .

Wilson's lectures were like a breath of fresh air compared with others we heard. We came into contact with a mind not only rich with knowledge of his subject but endowed with the gift of lucid, clear, emphatic presentation. No course we took gave us such a sense of the power of a single individual to shed light on the most difficult problems. We all felt it. He was not stiff or formal; he was almost conversational in tone. We enjoyed the lectures so much that we sometimes neglected to take notes. His manner was ingratiating and friendly; he seemed to take us all in. But he made no concessions; there was no play to the gallery whatever; he never sought to draw men to him. But he was eager to interpret his ideas. He used simple forms of speech—that was one reason for his lucidity; there was nothing he said we did not understand. After class he was friendly and very genial, always willing to answer questions. No one could touch him as a lecturer, although others may have furnished us with more information.[12]

Wilson's students and colleagues were aware that his lectures were in part a preparation for his projected work on the philosophy of politics. Like Max Beerbohm's Savanarola Brown, he got credit for producing a masterpiece before publication; the minutes of the historical seminary for February 12, 1897, quote a member's remark that there was more room for original work in social or economic history than in politics, "for after Professor Wilson's book there will be little left to be written."

Wilson was welcomed back at the boardinghouse where he had lived as a student. The fact that he was not living at home allowed him to see more of the students, which enhanced his influence among them. He continued his interest in the Johns Hopkins House of Commons and in the local chapter of his fraternity, and he occasionally attended meetings of the historical seminary, reading a paper or joining in the discussion. At one of these Turner read a paper on the Wisconsin fur trade and was immensely heartened when Wilson praised it, saying, "this is the kind of atmosphere in which we can breathe." The layout of the seminary room and the Bluntschli Library also promoted informal contacts. Lyman P. Powell, who acted as librarian of the seminary during his student days, remembered how Wilson would come into his office ten or fifteen minutes before the lecture, throw himself into a chair, put his feet on the desk, and talk—"he was always stimulating, frequently amusing." [13]

Some of Wilson's students kept in active touch with him for years after they left the seminary. Charles M. Andrews, who followed Wilson at Bryn Mawr, used to visit him in Princeton. Lyman P. Powell arranged for him to lecture before university extension groups. Charles H. Haskins in 1890 wrote him long letters about his own researches, his job opportunities, and the situation at Johns Hopkins. Later Wilson tried to get Haskins to come to Princeton.[14]

Frederick Jackson Turner afterwards testified that it would be hard to overstate the influence that Wilson exerted on him both at Johns Hopkins and later. For a number of years the two men remained in close communication. When in 1889 Reuben G. Thwaites, secretary of the Wisconsin State Historical Society, asked Wilson to recommend Turner for reappointment at the University of Wisconsin, Wilson wrote that he had formed a positive affection for Turner after six weeks of acquaintance at Johns Hopkins and that he hoped some day to get him on the same faculty as a colleague. He later approached Turner about taking the Hedding professorship at Wesleyan, which he had vacated when going to Princeton. In 1896 Wilson tried to persuade Turner to join him on the Princeton faculty. On his part Turner once recommended Wilson for a position to which he himself aspired, head of the history department at Wisconsin. "I truly believe," he wrote Wilson, "you have a great service to perform for this country by impressing your ideal of politics upon its young men." [15]

In 1889, four years before Turner published his famous essay "The Significance of the Frontier in American History," Wilson wrote him from Wesleyan: "You will remember, I suppose, our talks in Baltimore on the growth of the national idea, and of nationality, in our history, and our agreement that the role of the West in this development was very great, a leading role, although much neglected by historians." Although Wilson later repudiated any notion that he assisted Turner in formulating the famous frontier theory, Turner's own recollection was different. He testified that Wilson helped him in several ways. All his ideas and ambitions were broadened, he wrote, and his imagination was kindled by Wilson's conversations and lectures. Through Wilson he was introduced to Walter Bagehot, whose theory of the organic growth of institutions deeply impressed him. In talks with Wilson, Turner also gained new ideas about the South and sectionalism. [16]

While admiring him for his brilliance on the lecture platform, some other members of the historical seminary found Wilson aloof and distant. According to John Finley, "Wilson was always, figuratively if not literally, on the platform; one felt that he was not capable of sitting down in conference with his students." Edward A. Ross thought that he "did not seem to take a strong personal interest in the graduate students or advise them in their researches." Frederick C. Howe, one of Miss Ashton's boarders, said that Wilson "fraternized absently" with the men at table and told good stories, but he found him in general "austere, never inviting intimacies." [17]

Howe wrote that whereas Albert Shaw aroused his enthusiasm by giving him visions of a future in which grand new cities would arise, Wilson "dealt in abstractions about the Constitution," and "was interested in the fathers of the Republic, especially the Virginia statesmen, who were writers of great documents." According to Howe, Wilson looked backward: "Listening to him, I got hints of impressions received at home, when preachers lamented our lukewarmness to Christian ideals, our neglect of responsibility to the church . . . Great men had departed from Capitol Hill; the Senate no longer reverberated to the high morality of earlier days. Democracy was not concerned over issues of great constitutional import. Politics had become the struggle of vulgar interests, of ignoble motive, of untrained men." He preached "government by *noblesse oblige*" and "gave us no glimpse of the economic background of the British ruling class. There was always the assumption that these public men were not moved by private gain. It was never hinted in his lecture-room that the British landed gentry, bankers, and businessmen enacted laws to protect their own class and group . . . He was not interested in economics." [18]

Howe's estimate of Wilson as a political conservative during his academic years corresponds with a generally held opinion. Thus, Oswald Garrison Villard, who knew him well, thought that up to the time he ran for the governorship of New Jersey in 1910 "Wilson was what any fair-minded man would call a conservative if not a reactionary." Arthur Link, his most authoritative biographer, has written, "Perhaps the most striking feature of Wilson's thought during the period [1879-1902] was its conservatism, both with regard to the nature of government and the functions and duties of the state." Such a judgment, however, is not quite valid, for Wilson did not take a consistently conservative line. When faced with the special problems of the modern industrial city, for example, he expressed opinions at variance with laissez-faire economics and assumed a stance that corresponded more closely with his later progressivism. Such a point of view was strikingly displayed in the lectures he gave at Johns Hopkins in 1896.[19]

At the time Baltimore was gripped by intense political excitement. In November 1895 a coalition of Republicans, independent municipal reformers, and the American Federation of Labor had overthrown a corrupt and incompetent Democratic machine in an election in which a Johns Hopkins professor had his jaw broken and several persons were killed. A reform mayor, Alcaeus Hooper, and a Republican city council were put in office. It was not long before Hooper's intention to clean up the city ran head-on into the desire of the councilmen for the spoils of office. The city council refused to ratify Hooper's nonpartisan appointments, insisting that he select only regular Republicans. By February 1896 matters had come to a complete impasse, and it looked as though the bright hopes of the reformers would collapse.

Exactly at this juncture Wilson started giving his annual course at Johns Hopkins, his topic being "Municipal Organization." His lectures aroused so much interest that they were thrown open to the public. Soon stenographic reports of them were published in the *Baltimore News*, which supported the cause of Mayor Hooper and the reformers.

In the lectures Wilson compared British and American local government, again much to the advantage of the former. He found fault with municipal government in the United States for the same reasons that he had previously criticized the federal government: fractionalization of power with consequent lack of clear responsibility and paralysis of public opinion. Division of powers and checks and balances in municipal government were "ridiculous," and bipartisan boards "an invention of the devil." In place of the usual mayor-and-council organization he proposed a scheme not unlike the commission plan to municipal government first put into effect in Galveston, Texas, in 1901. The first three points of a seven-point program were as follows:

1. That one body should possess both adminitrative and ordinance-making power, with the mayor serving merely as chairman.

2. That a minority of this governing board should be trained officials, chosen by competitive examinations.

3. That the majority should be chosen on a single, city-wide ballot. From Prussian practice Wilson borrowed another point—"an enforcement of compulsory citizenship duties," including loss of franchise and higher taxes as punishments for those refusing to serve on unpaid committees formed to administer such things as poor relief, tax assessment, and mercantile arbitration.[20]

These recommendations, with the exception of compulsory office-holding, followed familiar channels of Wilson's thought, but there were significant departures. The headline of the first fully reported lecture ran: PROF. WILSON ADVOCATES MUNICIPAL OWNERSHIP OF GAS WORKS AND STREET RAILWAYS. Wilson here argued that city governments should be given "more important, more wide-reaching, and conspicuous functions." Private ownership of public utilities he called a "pernicious principle" because "water works and gas works are not something devised for the benefit of private companies, but for the whole city." [21]

A modern industrial city, said Wilson, should not be an economic corporation, with the property-holders as chief stockholders, but "a humane economic society." He proposed a radical extension of the powers and scope of minicipal government. Rapid transit should be operated by cities and "so managed that lines should be provided to relieve congested parts of the city, whether those lines paid financially or not." Public charity should be organized on such a thorough basis "as to be independent of private charity, and should be made the imperative legal duty of the whole." "The same arguments that are valid for the need of public safety are valid also for the need of public charity, and the latter even more than the former. For public charity and public education are a sort of moral sanitation." [22]

Even more at variance with the usual image of Wilson as a conservative who distrusted the masses and looked fondly to England, where men of leisure provided pure and efficient government, was his treatment of the idea that city government should be the concern of the upper classes:

We cannot look to the selfish interest of the leading classes alone to advance the interests of the city . . . They will insist upon a good police system, perhaps, but they will not be inclined to insist upon thoroughness of sanitation in those parts of the city which they do not occupy, nor will they urge the city to provide in general that higher education which they can provide for themselves. The upper classes often, likewise, make their wealth tell corruptly on the way in which the city makes its expenditures, so as to secure more than their share of advantages from the outlay for paving, lighting, locomotion, preparing of districts for occupation, etc. The wealthy classes cannot, therefore, be relied upon to promote the delicate and difficult tasks which arise from the masses of men being economically dependent upon the city.

Wilson condemned the New York City Board of Finance, elected only by those paying at least $250 per year in rent or possessing taxable property in excess of $500, because "the modern industrial city, with its wide social functions, must act in many things involving the heaviest expenditures, not for property owners, but for the working and economically dependent classes." He cited Princeton Borough in support of his contention that those who pay the most taxes are not the best judges of municipal need:

In Princeton . . . we have an illustration of the control of public improvements in accordance with the desire of the poorer classes. Streets in the poorer districts of town were improved first. Now that is not what a body of wealthy property-owners would arrange to do. Yet— unpalatable as the truth may be—the management of affairs by these poorer classes—mostly Irish and negroes—has resulted in a better condition than if it had been left to the educated classes. These poorer districts threatened the health of the town, and the improvement of the streets effected improvement also in the condition of sanitation and drainage.

This was surely a departure for the man who in the pages of the *Atlantic Monthly* in 1889 had feared European immigration as a threat to American democracy, and it is surely no plea for government by *noblesse oblige.*[23]

These Baltimore lectures show, then, that Wilson's early political and economic outlook was less consistent than has generally been realized. His later alleged "conversion" to progressivism did not mark an unprecedented shift to the left but continued a point of view he had earlier expressed. It may be difficult to reconcile the Brown University lectures of 1889, the Worcester Polytechnic address of 1890, and the Johns Hopkins lectures of 1896 with some of Wilson's conservative utterances, but this simply means that his ideas about economics and social democracy were not fixed. They shifted with changing circumstances and with the character of his audience. Wilson once told Professor Robert McElroy that he considered himself "a Christian anarchist who subscribed to no body of belief save that found in the New Testament." He attempted to view contemporary situations on their merits, following in the footsteps of Burke, "the apostle of the great English gospel of Expediency." [24]

At the close of his lecture series in 1896 Wilson was asked to be one of six speakers at a great civic mass meeting "composed of citizens, irrespective of party, who believe in good government." Its purpose was to support Mayor Hooper and "to tell the City Council what the people thought of their anarchistic tendencies." The principal attraction was Theodore Roosevelt, then a New York City police commissioner; another speaker was Charles J. Bonaparte, later a member of Roosevelt's cabinet.

The "Monster Non-Partisan Assemblage" met at the Baltimore Music Hall on March third; the crowd was estimated at from three to four thousand. An orchestra played beforehand. Roosevelt, addressing the crowd as "fellow Americans," made what one reporter called "a burning address," emphasizing the harm that the Baltimore city councilmen were doing to the Republican Party. He recommended that all appointive power be placed in the hands of the mayor; then the people would know whom to blame for poor administration.[25]

Wilson's speech was the shortest of the evening, but according to a stenographic report published in the *Baltimore Sun* it was more punctuated with "Laughter," "Cheers," and "Applause" than any other. He thanked the City Council for giving him such excellent advertising by making his lectures so timely. "I suddenly found," he said, "that I had become an authority on municipal government, simply because I got in the position of agreeing with the best people in town."

In this first important venture into the political arena Wilson gave the people of Baltimore sound advice:

What I want to know is whether you who are here to-night have come to this meeting "to stay"? By that I mean whether this will be a display of spasmodic strength on your part, or whether you will put your shoulder to the wheel of good government. All I say is that if you have come "to stay" the City Council has not (Cheers). Take up the sword before you take up the horn.

The motive of this meeting is to show that the last election meant something and that the next election will mean something (Applause). The next is more important from the politicians' standpoint than the last (Laughter). Before the last election there was a tacit understanding that the city government should be reformed as you intended it to be. The question of machineries and arrangements are not questions of this moment. If any of these spoilsmen says that he did not comprehend that understanding, he may not be a knave, but he is certainly a fool (Applause).

I am a believer in the long processes of reform. Everything will come as you mean it if only you will continue to mean it.[26]

Theodore Roosevelt and Woodrow Wilson share the same platform and employ the same gesture when addressing a municipal reform meeting in Baltimore in March 1896. This was undoubtedly the first political caricature of Wilson.

Wilson's success both in the Johns Hopkins lectures and on the stage of the Music Hall helped his later political fortunes. When the Democratic Convention met in Baltimore in 1912 to choose a presidential candidate, it was reported that Wilson enjoyed local support, partly because his speech about the fight between the mayor and the councilmen "had helped to predispose many Baltimoreans in his favor." Both Charles H. Grasty and Fabian Franklin, who in 1896 were editors of the *Baltimore News*, later actively promoted Wilson as candidate for the presidency, Grasty as editor of the *Baltimore Sun* and Franklin as editor of the *New York Evening Post*.[27]

In 1902 Johns Hopkins celebrated its twenty-fifth anniversary, and the occasion turned out to be a personal triumph for Woodrow Wilson. He received an honorary degree, and the citation revealed that he was being urged—unsuccessfully as it turned out—to succeed Herbert B. Adams as head of the historical seminary. The *Baltimore News* reported that when the names of the recipients of honorary degrees were read, the name most cheered was Wilson's.[28]

Since President Gilman was also retiring at this time, it fell to Wilson to present him with a testimonial on behalf of the faculty, alumni, and graduate students. The *Baltimore Sun* reported that Wilson's performance was the most notable event of the demonstrations. According to the reporter, "the perfection of manner, the impressive sincerity, and the winning sympathy of that man as he stood in the presence of that great assembly, and the fine, strong, vibrant voice, heightened immeasurably the effect of his admirably chosen words. One felt that he was listening to a man who possessed that rare personal quality to the sway of which men in all ages have delighted to bow."[29]

In his opening remarks Wilson said to Gilman, "America is not a child of books, she is a child of action,—and the sort of learning which you have fostered is learning in action, not in reminiscence." He went on:

If it be true that Thomas Jefferson first laid the broad foundation for American universities in his plans for the University of Virginia, it is no less true that you were the first to create and organize in America a university in which the discovery and dissemination of new truths were conceded a rank superior to mere instruction, and in which the efficiency and value of research as an educational instrument were exemplified in the training of many investigators. In this, your greatest achievement, you established in America a new and higher university ideal, whose essential feature was not stately edifices, nor yet the mere association of pupils with learned and eminent teachers, but rather the education of trained and vigorous young minds through the search for truth under the guidance and with the cooperation of master investigators—*societas magistrorum et disciplorum.* That your conception was intrinsically sound is attested not only by the fruitfulness of the institution in which it was embodied at Baltimore, but also by its influence upon the development of the university ideal throughout our country, and notably at our oldest and most distinguished seats of learning.[30]

Woodrow Wilson had reason indeed to praise Johns Hopkins University. The connections he formed and the reputation he established there were of the highest importance in furthering his professional career. The historical seminary had originally enabled him to become a respected professional in the field of political science. Through the university he had then gained positions at Bryn Mawr and Wesleyan. Finally, his lectureship, a badge of high academic distinction, had helped to advance his position at Princeton and in the academic world at large. His annual visits to Baltimore kept him in active touch with the world of scholarship in a way that would have been impossible had his teaching been entirely centered on the college hill at Middletown or in the village of Princeton. The caliber of students he taught at Johns Hopkins and the kind of courses he gave forced him into an annual bout of thorough study of the literature of his field that rescued him, at least in part, from a tendency to despise "mere knowledge." His ability to clarify and to illuminate what he learned gained him the respect and admiration of men who were to be among the foremost scholars and leaders of opinion of the next generation.

Although Wilson thought of himself more as a literary man than a scholar, his long and active connection with Johns Hopkins made him familiar with solid learning. He learned how to talk to scholars in their own language. He came to appreciate the importance of research in the life of a university, and the importance of its proper tools: libraries and laboratories. This understanding later made him more effective as President of Princeton, principally when recruiting faculty members. It also helped him to see Princeton in larger perspective and to know what was needed to turn a college into a university. From Johns Hopkins, as from Virginia, Wilson gained the idea of a university as a community, with no institutional barriers between faculty, graduate students, and undergraduates, so that older and younger scholars might communicate easily, to their mutual advantage.

XI

The Golden Nineties

1890–1902

I seem myself to have become in so many ways another fellow,—more confident, steady, serene, though not less susceptible to all sorts of influences which experience might have been expected to render me indifferent to: enjoying in a certain degree a sense of power,—as if I had gotten some way upon the road I used so to burn to travel,—and yet fairly restless and impatient with ambition, as of old—a boy and yet a man.

—Woodrow Wilson, 1895[1]

THE ELECTION of the Reverend Francis L. Patton to succeed James McCosh as President of Princeton in 1888 was an apparent victory for clerical control of Princeton's destinies. Patton was not merely a Presbyterian minister but a noted theologian and polemicist. He had been an active, almost vindictive, prosecutor in a heresy trial in Chicago in 1874 that drove David Swing, a liberal, out of the Presbyterian ministry. A Britisher, who habitually wore a white lawn tie and black frock coat, Patton fairly exuded scholasticism, and his appointment at first offended the alumni. But he made a point of placating his opponents, even to the extent of attending football practice. He won over one important group of alumni with an amusing talk to the Princeton Club of New York, in which he said that the president of an American college "must be able to live in a sleeping-car and partake with impunity of the regulation pastry of a railroad station," and that, severe as these conditions were, he was ready to meet them. What was more important, he apparently favored the progressives, who wanted to make Princeton a center of learning. "A university," he said in his inaugural address, "is meant to be a place of research. We are finding that the professor who has ceased to learn is unfit to teach, and that the man who sees nothing before him to kindle his own enthusiasm will chill the little enthusiasm the student may carry into the class room." [2]

As it turned out, Patton was too indolent to take sides in the developing struggle at Princeton between the Presbyterian church and the forces of conservatism, on the one hand, and a more liberal alumni faction, on the other. Yet under pressure from influential alumni he made appointments based more on scholarship than upon orthodoxy, as in Wilson's case, and thus augmented the so-called "young faculty," who were determined to change Princeton from a college into a university.[3]

Although the caliber of the faculty improved during Patton's fourteen years in office, academic standards did not keep pace. In his inaugural address he said, "College administration is a business in which trustees are partners, professors the salesmen and students the customers." He was prepared to please the customers by allowing them to stay in college with a minimum of exertion. Under his administration standards of academic achievement and of discipline were slack. He stated openly that it was a good thing for a young man to go to college "even if he did no more than rub his shoulders against the buildings." It was not likely that undergraduates could resist this point of view. For many, studies became a matter of enforced attendance at lectures in term time, followed by a few nights of hasty cramming for examinations, punctuated by the "poler's recess" at nine o'clock, with cheering, blowing horns, shooting firecrackers, and firing pistols out of windows. "We resisted culture," recalled an alumnus, "with a vigor, a resourcefulness, an invincible clan spirit that must have been the despair of the devoted and frequently scholarly men whose task it was to train our adolescent minds."[4]

When Wilson returned to Princeton in 1890, the number of undergraduates was 750, a striking increase from the 400-odd when he had graduated only eleven years before. By 1902 there were over 1200 undergraduates and 117 graduate students. No less striking was the change in the character of college life. In spite of the disorderliness in Wilson's time, the underlying tone was serious, as evidenced by the preponderance of the two literary societies, Whig and Clio, and by the high proportion of students preparing for the ministry. Daily dress was formal: Princeton undergraduates of the 1870's wore stiff collars, cravats, and waistcoats with gold chains; out-of-doors they added bowler hats and chesterfields. By 1890 the universal dress was dirty corduroy trousers, a black turtleneck sweater, and a soft cap. Whig and Clio were beginning a gradual decline in spite of efforts by faculty members and alumni to save them, and in their place arose a proliferation of less academic activities. Over half the space in the *Princetonian* for 1890-91 was devoted to accounts of athletic events. Whereas in the fall of 1878 the championship football team managed by Wilson had played six games, the 1890 team played thirteen games. There was a freshman team with a full schedule. Athletics had become a cult.[5]

Other extracurricular activities had burgeoned. The rather casually run *Princetonian* of the seventies, a fortnightly, now came out three times a week, and in 1892 it became a daily. In the 1870's a few daring undergraduates could put on a theatrical show only in the secrecy of Whig Hall. Now the Triangle Club openly staged plays and musicals. Aided by the talents of Booth Tarkington, it went on tour in 1892, as did the Glee, Banjo, and Mandolin Clubs. By 1893 a casino had been built for undergraduate performances, with a well-equipped stage, greenrooms, showers, and rehearsal rooms. The casino represented a radical, even shocking, break with the Calvinist tradition of the earlier College of New Jersey, which led to the following colloquy alleged to have taken place between a returning alumnus and an undergraduate:

Graduate: "What's that building?"
Student: "It's the casino, sir—the Triangle Club theatre."
Graduate: "And where are your dance halls? Where are your gambling halls?" [6]

The extraordinary efflorescence of what came to be known as "college life" was, of course, not peculiar to Princeton; it was a nationwide phenomenon. Formerly college had been principally a means of preparing for the professions, but now it became increasingly a four-year quasi-vacation. Its serious purpose, so far as there was one, became the acquisition of status and friends—especially friends who would be useful in later life. Princeton in the 1890's was unique only in the degree of its students' immersion in college life. Nowhere else was there such intense class spirit, nor so elaborate a system of hazing; nowhere else did the entire undergraduate body and a high proportion of the faculty attend not only every football game but even every practice; nowhere was the devotion of the alumni to the college more intense, nor was adolescence so prolonged. Jesse Lynch Williams, who wrote many stories about Princeton life, remarked that Princeton undergraduates were "altogether more cubbish and yawping than at much smaller colleges." He attributed this in part to the college's isolation. The village of Princeton was merely an appendage to the college, and at this time students did not leave it even on weekends. Living within shouting distance of each other, undergraduates were thrown upon their own resources for recreation and depended upon college tradition for guidance as to behavior. So it was that sophomores snowballed freshmen, that every class stole the bell clapper, and that Seniors sang on the steps on Nassau Hall, which no Junior would ever venture to do.[7]

The "horsing" in classes was even more highly organized than in the 1870's. For instance, when Professor Cameron gave a lecture once a year in his freshman Greek course instead of having the students recite, it had become a "tradition" for them to take their notes on toilet paper and to steal the professor's broad felt hat, which was later cut into pieces as souvenirs. Non-Princeton graduates on the faculty were special targets. A Yale alumnus in the Engineering School was harassed when he was suspected of stealing Princeton's football signals and sending them to New Haven; a Harvard man who taught German was hounded out of Princeton within a year. But teachers who had something to give were spared. Bliss Perry wrote that he grew "fond of those careless, warm-hearted undergraduates, in their black sweaters and corduroy trousers," and found that many of them had a latent interest in literature. There was no disorder in either Perry's classes or those of Andrew West, from whom students learned that Horace wrote poetry rather than grammatical exercises and that Latin comedy could be funny. But no member of the Princeton faculty had a greater following than Woodrow Wilson[8]

It was later related that when Wilson first arrived at Princeton he was suspected of effeminacy because he had taught at Bryn Mawr. The students soon tested his mettle by bringing a drunken Irishman into the classroom. Wilson noticed him and inquired, "Who asked you to come here, sir?" "The shtoodents invoited me in." "Well," said Wilson, "I'll invoite you out again." Taking him by his coat collar, he hustled the intruder downstairs, then returned to the classroom as though nothing had happened. From then on he had the class tamed. Whether or not this story is true, the contemporary records attest that Wilson was an immediate success. In a communication to the Princeton trustees in November 1890, President Patton wrote, "I have to report that Professor Wilson has entered upon his duties in the department of Jurisprudence and Political Economy, and that he is winning golden opinions from the students, and abundantly proving his eminent fitness for the position." At the start of Wilson's second year the *Princetonian* reported that the old chapel had to be fitted up as a lecture hall for him because there was not enough room in the classroom to which his elective course in jurisprudence had been assigned.[9]

Wilson taught political economy at Princeton for only two years. From then on his courses were confined to the field of public law and politics; all were electives for juniors and seniors. He gave only four lectures a week, on Mondays and Tuesdays at eleven in the morning and five o'clock in the afternoon. The classes were so large that there was no opportunity for recitation. It was Wilson's habit to dictate for ten or fifteen minutes at the beginning of each lecture—a time-wasting procedure since the material could have been printed and distributed in advance. Notes of previous years were, in fact, printed and sold as pamphlets because the material varied little from year to year. After the dictation Wilson had students close their notebooks while he discussed the topic of the day, often referring to contemporary affairs. It was made clear that nothing was to be reported to the press. These informal discourses were so beautifully expressed and so interesting that people not taking Wilson's courses dropped in as auditors. "It was never any trouble," recollected a former student, "to get someone else to sit in your seat if you wanted to cut." Sometimes there was standing room only. Princeton students, like those at Wesleyan and Johns Hopkins, remembered the earnestness of Wilson's delivery, the occasional gesture with the forefinger, and the way his face lighted up as he made a point or indulged in humor. There was no impression of condescension; he was talking as one man to others. As a former pupil expressed it, "you recognized right off that here was a man who was neither a hayseed nor a fossil, but a living human being."[10]

On his part Wilson was excited by the size and response of his audience. He wrote Heath Dabney in 1891, when some of his classes already numbered 160 men, "it stimulates me immensely to have to stimulate so many minds with the more abstract topics of jurisprudence." According to his colleague Winthrop Daniels, Wilson was more effective with the big introductory courses, open to all upperclassmen, than with the more advanced courses, open only to seniors. And aside from suggesting bibliographies and criticizing style in dissertations, Wilson showed little interest in the work of the few graduate students who came under his charge.[11]

Since the lectures were the core of Wilson's undergraduate courses, a student could get by, or even achieve an honor grade, simply by memorizing the dictated material, except for special tests on outside reading assigned in lieu of class work when Wilson was absent at Johns Hopkins. He no longer required the close reading that he had exacted from his students at Wesleyan. Although he used to tell the story of one of his students who wrote on an examination book, "This test is unfair. It requires thought," the examination papers for his Princeton courses reveal that he was seldom unfair in this way. For the most part students were asked merely to regurgitate what they had written in their notebooks. Apparently Wilson hated to correct exams; their crudeness of expression and muddiness of understanding cost him such pain that he claimed he could read no more than a dozen papers a day.[12]

At Princeton even more than at Johns Hopkins Wilson was not only giving academic instruction but preaching a gospel of service. According to Hardin Craig he justified popular government and defended universal suffrage "on the ground that all sane men, having merely lived and met the issues of living, are able to judge between right and wrong, wisdom and folly; in fact, that they judge these things extremely well." But democracy and political liberty under law had been a slow growth and a tender one; they could easily be subverted by folly or selfishness. Therefore, "educated men should be leaders in the kind of reform, at once conservative and progressive, that consists in the restoration to greatness of the tradition handed down by our forefathers."[13]

Ernest Poole's opinion of Wilson at Princeton was just this side of idolatry. He wrote that Wilson helped him and his companions to understand the world in which they lived. "Homely and plain, with a rugged style, there was magnetism in that man and often a gaunt humor too." Poole recollected that Wilson visited students' rooms and talked about America past and present. He recommended books, including Jacob Riis's *How the Other Half Lives*, which helped lead Poole toward work in a settlement house.[14]

Wilson sometimes preached to the students in a literal sense as well. He was asked repeatedly to the Philadelphian Society, the Princeton undergraduate religious organization. In May 1894 the *Princetonian* reported that he spoke before the society and "took as his theme the practical philosophy taught by the Bible; he said that the righteous man should not be long-faced or morose, but joyful, diligent, fervent in spirit. We are to-day living in the light and should do our whole duty." A year later he reversed his field. Choosing as his topic "meditation" and basing his remarks on the First Psalm, "he said the Bible is like a deep translucent pool, reflecting for a man what he chooses. It is deep enough or shallow enough for any man. In this age, when so much is made of Christian activity, we are apt to forget meditation." Occasionally Wilson preached to the most difficult congregation of all—the Princeton undergraduates assembled in compulsory chapel. That he succeeded even here is revealed by the following letter home from a student.

Woodrow Wilson preached yesterday afternoon at chapel and was fine. I have the greatest admiration for him, and it pleases me greatly to have found a man I really admire.

He is one of those rare men you meet at times with real personal magnetism. As a boy said to me after leaving chapel yesterday afternoon, "He had them right there" (extending his fingers and closing them over something tight and hard) "and never let go until he was through." It was true. There was no stretching or lounging in seats while he was talking.[15]

On the eve of Wilson's departure for Princeton his cousin Mary Hoyt made a prediction. "How the boys will adore you," she wrote, "and how they will face about to your point of view, and how they will argue in the House of Commons and call on you for speeches when Princeton comes out ahead in football and how your system of not-watching will turn them all into honorable gentlemen." Her prediction was fulfilled. Wilson could never resist a chance to exert leadership, and the Princeton students, like those at Johns Hopkins and Wesleyan, responded eagerly. No other member of the Princeton faculty had so much to do with extracurricular affairs. Wilson addressed one mass meeting to urge the incorporation of the Princeton Athletic Association and another to organize resistance to a proposal to build a trolley line from Trenton to Princeton. His signature appeared on a treaty between his debating society, Whig Hall, and its rival, Clio, concerning recruitment of members. Although he did not found another House of Commons, he, Bliss Perry, and Winthrop Daniels coached the Princeton debating team in the first intercollegiate contests with Yale and Harvard. According to Daniels, Wilson suffered such acute pain when listening to the debates that he could not attend them. "I have seen him," wrote Daniels, "pacing back and forth through the ambulatory of the Commencement Hall when a debate was in progress, unable to go away, and still less able to sustain the verbal affront which the crudeness and immaturity of his protégés was certain to inflict."[16]

Wilson sometimes became an intermediary between students and faculty. In 1895 the seniors introduced a "Faculty Song," in which unpopular teachers were treated with scant courtesy. The next year, when some faculty members favored forbidding the song, Wilson insisted that such an attempt would be impossible and would only make them ridiculous. Hence a new verse:

> Here's to Woodrow Wilson, oh,
> Our legal adviser, don't you know,
> He said they can't stop us, so let her go.
> Here's to Woodrow Wilson, oh.[17]

An anecdote of Booth Tarkington's testifies to Wilson's popularity. Apparently a man in the class of 1892 pretended that a cigarette-making machine was a press with which he was counterfeiting two-dollar bills, and his classmates swallowed the hoax. In consternation they called a class meeting. Someone suggested referring the matter to Woodrow Wilson; others demurred at approaching a member of the faculty; whereupon one man said, "I'd take any matter to Woodrow Wilson as soon as I would to my father." The memory of Wilson that Tarkington carried from his college years was wholly favorable:

I think we felt that Wilson understood us and understood us more favorably than any other man on the faculty. We had a feeling that we were being comprehended in a friendly way, that he'd be for us and that he'd be straight with us . . . We did not see any rigidity in him. I saw in him only an agreeable, supremely intelligent human being—wise—kind—but a fellow human being. He *looked happy*. His eyes were bright. As I picture him in the memory of undergraduate years, I see gaiety in his eyes. He seemed to be a person getting what he wanted out of life.[18]

A notable occasion on which Wilson fought on the side of the students occurred when the honor system in examinations was introduced at Princeton during the academic year 1892-93. Although he has been given credit for its introduction, the actual initiative seems to have come from leaders of the class of 1893, who first approached the Dean of the Faculty, James Murray, and found him sympathetic. Wilson, who had known the honor system at the University of Virginia and long favored it, defended it strongly when it came before the faculty. There was debate over the proposed wording of the pledge each student was to sign: "I pledge my honor as a gentleman that during this examination I have neither given nor received assistance." President Patton, dubious about the entire proposal, yielded the chair and attacked the pledge from the floor. He ridiculed the romantic notion of a "gentleman's honor" that would allow him to fight a duel or seduce a woman but not to cheat at cards. Bliss Perry remembered vividly Wilson's response:

Now Wilson, although he had not a drop of Southern blood in his veins, liked to think of himself as a Virginian born. He was fond of phrases and knew their power over the student mind, and he resented Patton's ridicule of "chivalry" as if it were directed against Virginia and himself. He grew white and very quiet, and it was then that he was most dangerous. In his reply, he was scrupulously courteous to the President, who had for personal reasons retained his British citizenship, but Wilson understood the sentimental side of American undergraduates far better than a foreigner, and he managed to convey that impression with unmistakable clearness and with a passion that swept the faculty off their feet. They voted to retain the phrase "my honor as a gentleman," and it has remained in force to this day.[19]

The honor system was not only a victory for the students but the first important victory of the "young faculty." It was introduced in the midyear examinations of January and February 1893. According to the *Princetonian* it was "an *unqualified* success" among the upperclassmen, but a few underclassmen deliberately broke the pledge. An honor committee of seniors persuaded three of the cheaters to go to their teachers, confess their fault, and accept a zero. One, however, remained defiant, and the honor committee recommended that he be expelled. When this proposal came before the faculty, some of the older men, with the support of the President, were disposed to exact a lighter penalty, but the "young faculty" supported the students and carried the day. Wilson was in Baltimore when this occurred; the strength of his feelings about it is shown in a letter to Winthrop Daniels: "You can imagine with what emotions your recital of the difficulties of carrying out the verdict of the student committee on cheating filled me; I dare not trust myself to say anything yet by way of comment. But my thankfulness that the vote of the younger men saved the college from irreparable disgrace is simply inexpressible!" Meanwhile the students had taken the matter in their own hands by packing the offender's bags and putting him on the train. A laconic notice in the *Princetonian* told of the event: "*P——, ex-95, has left college.*"[20]

Throughout Wilson's personal correspondence during the nineties there are frequent references to athletics. He followed Princeton's fortunes in intercollegiate contests as closely as any undergraduate. His cousin Mary Hoyt was amazed at the way he waved his umbrella and cheered when attending a baseball game. He was not above shouting to the referee to call a foul on an opponent. Once he became so preoccupied that he moved onto the field, and play had to be stopped until he was escorted back to the sidelines. How great was his concern is suggested by a letter to his classmate Robert Bridges in 1892:

Alas, no! There's no ghost of a chance of our beating Yale. If the 32-0 experience is not repeated, I shall be thankful. This is not because Penn., the despised Penn., beat us; but because (this is in confidence) incredibly stupid coaching, without invention or even a decent understanding of the possibilities of the game, has thrown admirable material—admirable in spite of hurts and mishaps—away. I would not say this to any one else. The boys may take a brace and *hold* Yale; but as for *doing* anything against her, or any other strong opponents, that is out of the question. I am going to see the game, but I shall know what to expect.[21]

The preponderance of evidence refutes the allegation that Wilson actually coached the Princeton football team. But he was active in putting the athletic affairs of the college on a more businesslike basis, first as a member of the Graduate Advisory Council, on which he served from 1891 to 1894, and then as a member of the Faculty Committee on Outdoor Sports from 1891 to 1902. Those who served with him on these committees found him faithful in attendance, fertile in suggestion, and much interested in promoting clean sport. One purpose of both the Graduate Advisory Council and the incorporation of the Princeton Athletic Association was to improve efficiency and honesty in handling money. By 1890 forty thousand dollars a year passed through the hands of the undergraduate treasurer; this was too large a sum for him to deal with efficiently, and it was a temptation to dishonesty. One treasurer pocketed $1800 before he was discovered, The Graduate Advisory Council met to consider the larceny, and according to Max Farrand, a member, "one of the men, a business man, said, 'By God, he's clever. Only last week he came to my office and borrowed $100, and I'm rather disposed to let him have it, if he's clever enough to hoodwink me as he has.' Other business men on the committee agreed in admiring the culprit's ingenuity. Wilson said nothing while they talked, but finally, when they had stopped, he said: 'I'm thinking of Bill —— and I'm sorry for him.' "[22]

By the 1890's American football had developed ills that have plagued it ever since. Professionalism was so common that it had even penetrated secondary schools. In 1889 Princeton and Harvard broke off relations because of a squabble over required personal affidavits of amateurism by the players on both teams. Pictures of the Princeton teams reveal the change in spirit: whereas in the late 1870's members were well groomed and neatly dressed, those in the early nineties affected a mucker pose—they let their hair grow in unruly mops (ostensibly to protect their skulls), wore sloppy uniforms, and sneered at the cameraman as presumably they sneered at their opponents. The game had become so dangerous, especially since a chess-playing member of the Harvard faculty invented the flying wedge, that serious injury was commonplace. The Yale-Princeton game, by now played in New York on Thanksgiving Day, attracted 15,000 spectators. For three or four hours a parade of carriages packed with college boys and alumni moved up Fifth Avenue past windows and store fronts draped with Yale blue and the Princeton orange and black. The enthusiasm of the spectators was matched by the quasi-religious attitude of the players. When the Princeton football team returned to the locker room after beating Yale in 1893, no one thought it sacrilegious for them to stand "naked and covered with mud and blood and perspiration and sing the doxology from beginning to end." Nor was it thought unmanly for the Yale team to be "crying like hysterical school-girls."[23]

A strong feeling developed that college football had gotten out of hand. In his annual report for 1892-93 President Eliot of Harvard protested the extravagant expenditures on sports: when it was necessary to practice "constant economy . . . in expenditure for intellectual objects; how repulsive, then, must be foolish and pernicious expenditures on sports!" In the winter of 1894 the Cornell faculty insisted that games be played on college grounds and that the players be bona fide students in good standing. The Harvard faculty attempted, unsuccessfully, to abolish football altogether. Meanwhile, there was public controversy, in which Wilson joined.[24]

On February 13, 1894, at the Contemporary Club in Philadelphia, Wilson debated the affirmative side of the question "Ought the Game of Football to Be Encouraged?" against Professor Bert G. Wilder of Cornell. The large audience included "most of the football lights of the city and many society men and women." In his defense Wilson played on two favorite themes—the role of the gentleman in society and the importance of leadership. Since football had become national in scope, he said, it was important that the leadership of gentlemen keep it manly and clean, like cricket in England. Opposition to football came from colleges where the sport was not well organized. Princeton had lost only in the years "when she had not sense enough to win—or, in other words, the men organizing didn't have the qualities of generalship." Wilson defended the game as building character: it developed not only the normal virtues of athletics—"precision, decision, presence of mind, and endurance"—but other qualities not common to all games—"co-operation with others, and self-subordination." He saw no evil in large gate receipts because the money did not go to the players but supported other sports. The newspapers reported that Wilder's rebuttal was received in silence. Apparently Wilson had already won the audience, which was probably predisposed to him in any case.[25]

Since Wilson later deplored the "sideshows" of college life that diverted attention from the performance in the main tent, one must wonder why he ardently defended the greatest distraction of them all— why it was that football so mesmerized him that he was blind to its faults and to its perversion of values. There was a strong streak of combativeness in his nature that may have sought this vicarious expression. Football may have been for him one of the emotional equivalents of righteous war. Football also may have fascinated Wilson because it represented in microcosm what most interested him in the larger world of politics: effective human action under leadership for clearly recognized goals.

Treating the Princeton undergraduates as friends and busying himself in their affairs, Wilson won their respect and affection. During the eight years from 1896 to 1903 the seniors seven times elected him "Favorite Professor."[26]

Wilson was as active and influential in the affairs of the Princeton faculty as in those of the students. Bliss Perry vividly remembered his first encounter with Wilson:

> The first faculty meeting struck me as very formal and conducted with the strictest parliamentary procedure. Its solemnity was a bit lightened at the start by a tall Princetonian who crossed the room and held out his hand. 'Are you the Perry who used to play on the Williams nine?' I admitted the fact. 'Well, I shall never forget that catch you made in left field when you played Princeton!' Those words sounded very loud in the hushed silence, for President Patton had already called us to order to listen to Dr. Duffield's opening prayer; and it was not until after the meeting that I could explain that the glory of that catch in left field belonged to my brother Walter and not to me. My seat that day and for the next seven years was next to the chair of a long-jawed, homely, fascinatingly alert man who was addressed by the President as 'Professor Wilson.'

Wilson became floor leader of the "young faculty." Perry found him an able debater against some of the older men, who were trained in Presbyterian assemblies and skilled as parliamentarians. Perry's one criticism was that Wilson was sometimes less than polite to the older men, whose resistance to change the "young faculty" resented. These younger men, most of whom had sat at the feet of James McCosh and caught his vision of Princeton as a university, were even more acutely aware of her shortcomings because they had earned higher degrees elsewhere. They were in close touch with the younger alumni among the Princeton trustees.[27]

Wilson's position of leadership in the Princeton faculty was by no means limited to formal debates. No other member, except perhaps Andrew West, was so active in committee work. He served eight years as secretary of the Discipline Committee, nine years as chairman of the Committee on Special and Delinquent Students, eleven years as Senior Class Officer. He also served terms on the committees on Outdoor Sports, on the Graduate School, and on the Library. The faculty chose him by ballot to represent them on a committee to communicate with the trustees at six different times—more frequently than anyone else. Such a record testifies that at this time Wilson did not have to mount a platform to exert leadership and that he could cooperate easily in conducting the practical business of the college.[28]

One of the subjects of controversy between the clerical and alumni factions on the Princeton Board of Trustees, as well as between the "old" and "young" segments of the faculty, was a proposal that, on the occasion of its 150th anniversary in 1896, the College of New Jersey change its official name to Princeton University. The liberal faction favored the change, if only as an expression of intent; the conservatives, who had once voted down McCosh on the issue, doubted whether Princeton was ready to assume the new status—was it wise, they asked, to change from "the best of colleges" to "the worst of universities"? One suspects that they feared a new freedom of scholarly investigation that would weaken the religious tone of the college. But the proponents of change proved stronger than the guardians of the status quo, and during the sesquicentennial anniversary Princeton declared itself a university.[29]

Woodrow Wilson was chosen to deliver the principal address on educational policy at the Sesquicentennial. The appointment was not merely an expression of esteem, for Wilson had already expounded a theory of university education. In 1893, representing the National Education Association, he had addressed a session of the International Congress on Education at the Chicago World's Fair on the topic, "Should an Antecedent Liberal Education Be Required of Students in Law, Medicine, and Theology?"; in 1894 he had spoken before the annual meeting of the American Bar Association at Saratoga Springs on "The Legal Education of Undergraduates" and had written an article for *The Forum* entitled "University Training and Citizenship." On all three occasions Wilson argued vigorously and effectively for what would now be called general education, as providing both the best preprofessional training and the most useful preparation for citizenship. He urged that college students be introduced to a broad spectrum of integrated knowledge and made to traverse "the region of general principles—where alone the true light of discovery burns." The budding lawyer should be exposed to jurisprudence, to the historical origins of law and its place in society (as in Wilson's own courses). The doctor should know man as more than a physical organism. The minister must "understand mankind if he is to lead them in better ways of living."[30]

Although on the progressive side at Princeton, Wilson's position relative to the country at large was conservative—Charles W. Eliot called it "a little archaic." He set himself squarely against the dominant trends of the time. For example, he was dubious about college education for women and totally opposed to coeducation. When in 1894 a friend wrote asking his opinion of a proposal to introduce coeducation at the University of Virginia, he replied:

It distresses me very deeply that the University of Virginia should think, even through a minority of its faculty, of admitting women to its courses. I have had just enough experience of co-education to know that, even under the most favorable circumstances, it is most demoralizing. It seems to me that in the South it would be fatal to the standards of delicacy as between men and women that we most value . . . I do not mean that it leads to vice; though occasionally it does; but it *vulgarizes* the whole relationship of men and women. To say more than that would be only to give particular instances. The generalization is a fact itself, and of my own observation.

Besides, where is the necessity? Women now have excellent colleges of their own; where their life can be such as is fit for women. What an age this is for going out of its way to seek change!

I wish I could write all that my heart contains in this matter. As it is, I can only pray that the University may be led away from such gratuitous folly!

Wilson rejected "the disease of specialization" and the vocationalism of the scientific schools and state universities as conducive to "a hard technicality and mean contraction of view." He opposed the elective system of studies that had been introduced at Harvard as leading to chaos and lack of discipline.[31]

Wilson's academic conservatism was never more clearly or more publicly displayed than in his address at Princeton's Sesquicentennial Celebration. The Sesquicentennial, held on October 20-22, 1896, was perhaps the most elaborately staged academic festival that the United States had ever seen. The organizing genius behind it was Andrew Fleming West, Giger Professor of Latin, whom the trustees had given a leave of a year and a half and an initial budget of fifteen to twenty thousand dollars. West made the occasion an international event. Invitations went to the Universities of Bologna, Paris, Heidelberg, Moscow, Oxford, and Cambridge and to the Royal Society, as well as to Harvard, Yale, Amherst, the University of Texas, and the American Academy of Arts and Sciences. The physical arrangements were elaborate. Vying with the autumn colors were hundreds of yards of orange and black bunting, festooned from the college buildings. Two triumphal arches bestrode Nassau Street: one was a gift from the town; the other said farewell to the college on one side—"AVE VALE COLLEGIUM NEOCAESARIENSE"—and hail to the university on the other—"AVE SALVE UNIVERSITAS PRINCETONIENSIS." To enhance the ceremonies, West asked the visiting dignitaries and Princeton faculty to wear academic dress. Many of the Princeton professors had never possessed such robes, but their wives and their wives' dressmakers produced garments of a style and magnificence never seen before. In addition to the major proceedings, there were scholarly lectures by foreign recipients of honorary degrees. To amuse the many distinguished guests and returning alumni, there was a football game, an orchestra concert under the direction of Walter Damrosch, and a torchlight parade reviewed by Grover Cleveland.[32]

One of the two principal events of the second day was the address by Woodrow Wilson, representing the American Whig Society. The audience was certainly the most important that Wilson had ever faced, containing men who would hold his destiny in their hands, as he may have suspected. The autumn of 1896 was a time when men of property and education were fearful: on election day a fortnight hence William Jennings Bryan, the "rattle-pated boy, posing in vapid vanity and mouthing resounding rottenness," might be elected President of the United States, which to them meant financial, moral, and political catastrophe. Wilson fell in with the mood of the gathering. His address, "Princeton in the Nation's Service," fairly breathed the spirit of Burkean conservatism. After sketching the history of Princeton, with emphasis on the public service of her graduates, he put forth a prescription for a college education that would produce new James Witherspoons and James Madisons. His emphasis was more than ever on the lessons of the past. "We are in danger," Wilson said, "to lose our memory and become infantile in every generation. That is the real menace under which we cower everywhere in this time of change. The Old World trembles to see its proletariat in the saddle; we are dismayed to find ourselves growing no older, always as young as the information of our most numerous voters." The remedy for present ills was to educate an elite of gentlemen schooled in the wisdom of the past through study of Greek and Latin, history and politics, and "the literature of your own race and country."[33]

Wilson maintained that he was much mistaken "if the scientific spirit of the age is not doing us a great disservice, working in us a certain great degeneracy." It was not the fault of the scientist, who had "done his work with an intelligence and success which cannot be too much admired." It was "the work of the noxious, intoxicating gas which has somehow got into the lungs of the rest of us, from out the crevices of his workshop . . . I should tremble to see social reform led by men who have breathed it; I should fear nothing better than utter destruction from a revolution conceived and led in the scientific spirit." "Do you wonder, then," Wilson went on, "that I ask for the old drill, the old memory of times gone by, the old schooling in precedent and tradition, the old keeping of faith with the past, as a preparation for leadership in the days of social change?"

Wilson closed his address by sketching his dream of a "perfect place of learning." He saw it as

the home of sagacious men, hard-headed and with a will to know, debaters of the world's questions every day and used to the rough ways of democracy: and yet a place removed,—calm Science seated there, recluse, ascetic, like a nun, not knowing that the world passes, not caring, if the truth but come in answer to her prayer; and Literature, walking within her open doors, in quiet chambers, with men of olden times, storied walls about her, and calm voices infinitely sweet; here "magic casements opening on the foam of perilous seas, in faery lands forlorn," to which you may withdraw and use your youth for pleasure; there windows open straight upon the street, where many stand and talk, intent upon the world of men and affairs. A place for men and all that concerns them; but unlike the world in its self-possession, its thorough way of talk, its care to know more than the moment brings to light; slow to take excitement; its air pure and wholesome with a breath of faith; every eye within it bright in the clear day and quick to look toward heaven for the confirmation of its hope. Who shall show us the way to that place?

Who indeed? George McLean Harper wrote that after the address he heard an aspirant for Patton's place as President of Princeton remark to a friend that he had given up hope. Throughout the address Wilson was interrupted by applause, especially "when he pleaded for sound and conservative government, and an education that shall draw much of its inspiration from the best and oldest literature." When he had finished, there was a torrent of clapping and cheering, led by a phalanx of members of the class of '79. Soon afterward Ellen Wilson wrote Mary Hoyt:

It was the most brilliant,—*dazzling*—success from first to last. And *such* an ovation as Woodrow received! I never imagined anything like it. And think of *so* delighting *such* an audience, the most distinguished, everyone says, that was ever assembled in America;—famous men from all parts of Europe . . . As for the Princeton men some of them simply fell on his neck and wept for joy. They say that those who coult not get at Woodrow were shaking each other's hands and congratulating each other in a perfect frenzy of delight that Princeton had so covered herself with glory before the visitors. And that of course is what makes it such a sweet triumph; it was not a selfish success, it all redounded to the honor of Princeton before the assembled academic world.[34]

Others, however, who heard or read Wilson's address were less enthusiastic. Some delegates, among them President Francis Amasa

Walker of M.I.T., were outraged by what they took to be an attack on science. The magazine *Popular Science* merely reprinted portions of the address relating to science without comment: apparently the editor, J. McKean Cattell, thought they were damning enough by themselves.[35]

Wilson did not always appear in such a conservative role in educational philosophy as he presented himself at the Sesquicentennial. For instance, in 1894 he had taken a stand that was radical for the day in his address before the American Bar Association on the training of lawyers. The President who was to appoint Louis Brandeis to the Supreme Court was foreshadowed by the professor who told the assembled lawyers that every teacher of law should be not only a political scientist but a sociologist and should "exhibit law as an instrument of society, and not as the subject-matter of a technical profession."[36]

Although Wilson's greatest pedagogical success came as a lecturer, he was also aware of the weaknesses of the lecture system and cast about for ways to encourage more active learning. In his article for *The Forum* in 1894 he had urged that colleges devise means of encouraging students to get "inside" of books. The scheme he proposed was the germ of the preceptorial system that he later introduced at Princeton:

> A considerable number of young tutors, serving their novitiate for full university appointments, might easily effect an organization of the men that would secure the reading. Taking them in groups of manageable numbers, suggesting the reading of each group, and by frequent interviews and quizzes seeing that it was actually done, explaining and stimulating as best they might by the way, they could not only get the required tasks performed, but relieve them of the hateful experience of being tasks, and cheer and enrich the whole life of the university.[37]

Although Wilson held that students could best prepare themselves for future service by study of the past, such study should be inquiring and critical. In a talk entitled "Spurious versus Real Patriotism in Education," delivered before the New England Association of Schools and Colleges in 1899, he warned against glorification of the American past and urged that pupils be encouraged to think for themselves:

> This nation originated in the sharpest criticism of public policy. We originated, to put it in the vernacular, in a kick, and if it be unpatriotic to kick, why, then, the grown man is unlike the child. We have forgotten the very principle of our origin if we have forgotten how to resist, how to agitate, how to pull down and build up, even to the extent of revolutionary practices if it be necessary, to readjust matters. I have forgotten my history if this be not true history. When I see schoolrooms full of children, going

through genuflections to the flag of the United States, I am willing to bend the knee if I be permitted to understand what history has written upon the folds of that flag. If you will teach the children what the flag stands for, I am willing that they should get down on both knees to it. But they will get up with opinions of their own; they will not get up with the opinions which happen to be the opinions of those who are instructing them. They will get up critical. They will get up determined to have opinions of their own. They will know that this is a flag of liberty of opinion, as well as of political liberty in questions of organization.

Just as Wilson's political conservatism allowed for growth and change and concealed a reformer, so the apparent conservatism of his pronouncements on education could not belie the fact that he wanted to promote a new kind of academic training—a training that would engage students' attention and prepare them for active service to society.[38]

An idyllic quality suffused academic life in Princeton during the 1890's. The invasion of wealth began only at the end of the decade, and the members of the Princeton faculty were the natural elite of the community. Everyone knew everyone else, and among many of them there were strong bonds of intimacy, affection, and respect. Wilson wrote Frederick Jackson Turner in 1896, "The intercourse in college circles is free, natural, and delightful." No one seemed to be affluent, but all were comfortably situated. Their houses were commodious; they were attended by servants; some of the men rode horseback, and the women rode in buggies. There was an active social life—formal calls, teas, dinner parties, and receptions—but at the same time an easy informality. If anyone was in trouble or even temporarily alone, the community gathered around. When Ellen Wilson went off for a visit in 1892, Woodrow could not accept half the dinner invitations he received, and Andrew West asked him to live at his house. When during another of Ellen's rare absences Stockton Axson was stricken with appendicitis, Wilson wrote his wife that literally dozens of people had offered help—some who had never before been in the house.[39]

Although Wilson's teaching, committee work, lecturing, and writing kept him under constant pressure, he rationed his time to keep part of every day free for recreation and social intercourse. He was regular in attendance at athletic events, plays, concerts, and college ceremonies; he bicycled, walked, played billiards, and started to play golf. According to Bliss Perry: "There is absolutely no question in my mind that in the latter years of his professorship Wilson was the most popular member of the Princeton faculty. I remember that people would almost crowd around him when of an afternoon he was playing pool

or billiards at the Nassau Club. He was the best man there to sit
around and chat with, because he was genuinely friendly and also
because of his inexhaustible fund of stories."[40]

With a handful of the younger faculty members—George McLean
Harper, Bliss Perry, John Howell Westcott, Winthrop Daniels, and
John Grier Hibben—Wilson was on terms of intimacy. They were constantly in and out of each other's homes. Wilson's closest friend was
John Grier Hibben, of the philosophy department. Even though Hibben lived at the other end of town, hardly a day went by that Wilson
did not see him, even if it only meant dropping in for fifteen minutes
between tea and supper. Hibben was a man of deep kindliness and
great probity. It was Hibben who helped make arrangements for Wilson to go abroad in 1896 and who saw him off at the boat; it was
Hibben who adjured him to take vacations and husband his strength.
When the Hibbens got a leave of absence and went off to Europe in
1900, Wilson could hardly bear the separation.

Beth Hibben was as much Wilson's friend as was her husband. She
was only one of a number of women with whom he formed close ties,
with the knowledge and approval of his wife Ellen. "My best friends
have all been women," he once said to a colleague. Certainly he never
appeared happier than when in the company of "clever and conversable" women, such as Henrietta Ricketts, who had something like a
salon at Princeton. With several women—among them Edith Gittings
Reid, Mrs. Crawford Toy, the Misses Lucy and Mary Smith, and later
Mrs. Mary Allen Peck—Wilson corresponded for many years, discussing
his affairs and his aspirations.[41]

According to Mrs. Reid, Wilson felt that real friendship was not
easy for him because he must give his whole heart and receive equal
affection, "measure for measure." "Once he had made a close friend
loyalty literally took possession of him and he would not let go." He
tended to endow friends with virtues they did not possess, fitting
them into his own model for men and women, created out of his
traditions and tastes. "We, his friends," Mrs. Reid wrote, "dearly as
we knew he loved us, were quite sure he would not have known
whether our eyes were blue or brown; but our ideas, our lives, he
knew—or thought he did; were they not a living part of his own?"[42]

Wilson's chief source of happiness was his family. When Ellen and
Woodrow were separated, they corresponded nearly every day, and
every letter was filled with protestations of affection and gratitude. To
his wife Wilson poured out his hopes and fears, his ambitions and
frustrations, his predilections and prejudices. In a typical passage he

detailed his feelings after going to "that terrible play of Oscar Wilde's" (*Lady Windermere's Fan*) in New York:

> I was *overwhelmed* with tenderness for you, my pure and perfect little wife. I am always on such occasions fairly *intoxicated* with the thought of the sweet simplicity of our lives; with your genuineness—with the quiet and love of our home—with the privilege of high thinking and plain living—with the delight of being simply your lover and husband and close companion, not a pretense or an artificiality or a breach of privacy in all our life. How unspeakably precious a thing it is, this life that is all our own in which we are sure that we love and trust and help one another.[43]

On her side Ellen repaid Woodrow's love with admiration and devotion that fell hardly short of idolatry—witness the passage:

> I would like to find the "great heart word" which would tell with what a *passion* of love and joy and pride in you my heart is swelling. Dearest, it is my deliberate conviction—nay, I do not *believe* it, I *know*—that the combination of qualities found in you is the rarest, finest, noblest, grandest of which human nature is capable. It is a combination which, if put into a book in all its truth, would be censured by every critic as impossible—an unwarranted idealism. What! such strength and nobility of character combined with such ineffable tenderness, such unselfishness and thoughtfulness in things great and small, a nature so exquisitely gifted in powers of sympathy—of understanding others . . . and the orator's gift—the "personal magnetism" and *all* those gifts that go to make a born leader of men, combined with powers of thought of such a kind that he must undoubtedly rank as a *genius*, no less than Burke himself; and added to all this a strength of will and powers of application which result in achievements so great that while yet in his early manhood his rank is among the foremost thinkers of his age! [44]

Woodrow and Ellen had many points of view in common. Both were Presbyterians of a liberal tinge. Both were southern, with southern attitudes toward family responsibility, the role of women, and Negroes. Both were consciously genteel and just as consciously not fashionable. They even shared their dislikes. Both were cool toward Carey Thomas of Bryn Mawr, for instance, as well as some of the "old faculty" at Princeton and some of its "moss-back" trustees.

Ellen's most obvious service to Woodrow was the efficient way in which she ran their home. She not only took entire charge of the household but kept most of the accounts, being more sensible and hard-headed than Wilson in money matters. She gave her daughters their early schooling because she thought the elementary schools in Princeton unsuitable for girls. Above all, she protected Woodrow from petty worries and disturbances, so that he could pursue his daily round of writing and preparing lectures without interruption.

But Ellen's services went beyond the household. For instance, besides learning German, she corrected proof for Wilson. One of the games at the dinner table was to carry on conversation in proof-reading style. Woodrow would say, "The soup comma my dear comma is delicious semicolon Maggie is an excellent cook period. No wonder exclamation You taught her period"; to which the reply would be, "Thank you comma Woodrow period." Ellen often gave sound advice. She restrained Wilson's impulsiveness and a tendency to make snap judgments.

On at least one occasion Ellen Wilson angled for a job for Woodrow without informing him. In June 1897 she wrote John Bates Clark suggesting that Columbia appoint her husband for a lecture course. Her letter reveals how much she knew about his career. It also shows her financial sense: at Johns Hopkins Wilson received $500, but here she raises that figure to "$1,000, or less":

Princeton, June 3, 1897

My Dear Mr. Clark,
I am about to do a very odd thing;—I am going to write you a confidential letter; not only without Mr. Wilson's knowledge, but with the flat assurance that if he *did* know he would veto it flatly! Naturally I am feeling dismayed at such an unprecedented procedure,—and yet I will "do the deed" . . . Of course a man,—or a woman,—of the world would think us a pair of silly children to make a tragedy of five weeks separation [at Johns Hopkins]. But his temperament;—his way of putting his *whole self* into every lecture, and every written page, really make it rather important for his physical and mental well-being that I should constantly be at hand, to "rest" him, as he says . . . It has occurred to me that "something might come of it" if one of his friends would just say to Mr. Low; "By the way Wilson of Princeton, who really is an uncommonly good lecturer, has a yearly furlough of five weeks in which he gives a course at the J.H.U.; wouldn't it be a good scheme if we tried to capture him ourselves for these five weeks?" Would you "mind" saying that to Mr. Low,—"only that and nothing more"?
By his practice of making his courses alternating,—open to juniors and seniors,—the lectures would really number fifty and cover more ground than a full college lecture course of an hour a week for the year. It is almost like adding another professor to the faculty for $1,000, or less, instead of $5,000 or $7,000. The Hopkins has shown her cleverness in securing a number of such courses. It is a cheap means of borrowing brains and reputations from other institutions! The course he gives there is for graduate students on "Administration." Personally, (of course I have no idea what he would think of it,) I should like him to give at Columbia some such course as his Princeton one on "Public Law"; because it is really to some extent a course in good citizenship, and I have seen what a stimulating and bracing effect it has had on our fellows. In that subject, more distinctly perhaps than some of the others, his strong, high character "tells"; no less than his capacity for clear thinking and forcible,

vivid expression. I should like to see him a "power for good" in that great city,—provided he did not have to *live* in it! But I must "stop this";—and I am surely tempted to let it end its career in the wastebasket, so much do I fear you will think me presumptuous. But no, I will not turn coward! . . .

> Yours most cordially,
> Ellen A. Wilson

Clark apparently replied favorably, but nothing came of the project.[45]

Wilson liked gaiety, play-acting, conversational fencing, and badinage, but these had little appeal for his wife. He liked to read Gilbert's *Bab Ballads* aloud; she got so tired of them that she finally hid the battered volume. "I am not gamesome," she said. It was partly because of her awareness of these differences, and of her absolute trust in Woodrow, that she encouraged his friendships with "conversable" women.[46]

Their daughters—Margaret, Jessie, and Nell—spent a large part of every day with their parents, who showered them with affection. With his daughters Woodrow could occasionally be firm, but never was he known to show anger within the home. "He was as charming to his family," recollected a girl who grew up with his daughters, "as though they had all been strangers." He was a continuing source of delight to his children because of his endless collection of songs sung in a light tenor voice, his stories, his gentle raillery, his occasional impersonations of a drunken Irishman or a heavy Englishman, and his ability to enter into their world. In fact, children in general liked Wilson. He treated them with an elaborate courtesy: if he met a child he knew on the street he would stop and have a word, or gravely doff his hat and smile.[47]

The Wilson girls occasionally quarreled or disobeyed their mother or Maggie, the cook, and were spanked; they never thought to disobey their father. They were brought up by their mother—and later by their grandfather—to regard him as a great man. The only criticism ever voiced about the Wilson family was that the adoration Wilson received at home was not good for him. If only, some thought, his offspring had been three obstreperous sons instead of three worshipful daughters, he might have learned to deal more effectively with opposition outside the home.[48]

Throughout the Princeton years the Wilsons filled their home with a crowd of relatives. Some were more or less permanent residents: Ellen's older brother, Stockton Axson (now on the Princeton faculty), and her younger brother, Edward; her sister, Margaret; George Howe, Jr., son of Wilson's sister Anne; and, during the last years of his life, Wilson's father. The permanent household averaged eight or ten, without counting the two servant girls. In addition, in-laws, cousins, and quasi-cousins came for visits that often lasted several weeks. Not only did Ellen and Woodrow feed all these people, but they sent the boys to school and college at their own expense. Wilson helped indigent relatives by trying to find them jobs and sometimes making outright gifts of money.

One reason Ellen was particularly solicitous of Wilson was that his health was precarious. He suffered from headaches, dyspepsia, repeated "gastric crises," and a facial tic. He was always seeking new remedies—quinine, calomel, bismuth, cascara, special diets, and fasting. His father and friends urged him to slow down. Thus, in 1890 Dr. Wilson wrote him, "Let me beg of you, my darling son, that you will so arrange your affairs as that overwork may not pull down your constitution and shake the foundations of your health."[49]

Wilson could not take his father's advice. His extended family was a constant drain on his purse, driving him to find means of supplementing his regular income—by writing, mostly for magazines, and by public lecturing. This hurt his progress as a scholar. It also meant that he was always in danger of exhausting his too slender store of energy. Even though he was methodical in work and kept regular hours—to bed at ten, up at eight, meals exactly on schedule, never more than four hours of writing a day—he was under unremitting pressure. He took no real vacation, save what was incidental to professional engagements—such as a lecture series in Boulder, Colorado, in 1894—until he went abroad in 1896.

In 1895-96 the Wilsons built a house of their own. Because of this additional burden of his finances, Wilson worked harder than ever and earned over $4000 by his pen in 1895. The result was an attack of neuritis so severe that he could no longer write with his right hand. His wife and father were genuinely alarmed. "Woodrow is going to die," said Dr. Wilson. Over Wilson's protests Ellen insisted that he accept the offer made by a wealthy neighbor to send him abroad to recuperate while she remained at home to get the new house ready for occupancy. When college closed in 1896, Wilson sailed from New York to Glasgow on a slow boat, the S.S. *Ethiopia*. At once he began to recover. He presided over the ship's concert and met some charming Southerners, with whom he traveled for a time in Scotland. For two months he bicycled through England and the Scottish lowlands. An indefatigable and systematic sightseer, he covered a great deal of territory. He returned to Princeton refreshed, although it was long before he could write normally, and he had to teach himself to write with his left hand.[50]

According to Stockton Axson, Wilson was a changed man after the crisis of 1896. Before that time he had found time to "loaf and invite his soul." He and Axson would go for long bicycle rides. Or he, Axson, and Dr. Wilson would enjoy leisurely, three-cornered chats. But after 1896 Axson and Dr. Wilson talked alone; Woodrow was up and away. The crisis, thought Axson, "freshened his sense of mission in the world"; it was as though he said, "I must be about my father's business." in 1899 Wilson had a recurrent bout of neuralgia. His friends worried more than ever. In 1900 Hibben wrote him from England, "As Bridges said of you in the last conversation I had with him just before leaving, 'If Tommy Wilson would only loaf for a while, and drink Scotch whisky, it would be all right.' " Wilson did begin to take vacations, but in his correspondence there is evidence that he still sought nostrums. A Dr. Pritchard sold him an electrical machine; one Alois V. B. Swaboda prescribed exercises night and morning and asked for a testimonial; Wilson wrote for information about a Dr. Quackenbos who wrought cures through hypnosis.[51]

Throughout Wilson's years as a teacher he hoped to obtain a post that would pay enough to meet his family obligations and yet leave time for his "literary studies." Thus, he was tempted in 1892 to accept the offer of the presidency of Indiana, which paid $6000—just twice his current salary. After long discussions with Ellen he turned down the position as being unlikely to yield much leisure, but at her urging he "stirred up" the Princeton Trustees, who granted him a $500 raise. It made him the highest-paid man on the Princeton faculty except President Patton.[52]

As time went on, not merely the lack of opportunity to pursue his own studies made Wilson willing to leave Princeton, but also his lack of sympathy with the President and the Board of Trustees. Patton was incredibly slack in administration, even to the extent of not answering important letters, and in the developing struggle between the old and new faculty he stood aloof. Although during the nineties the Board of Trustees became leavened with some of the young, wealthy alumni who wanted to raise Princeton's standing in the world of education, they were constantly frustrated by the clerical element, who were more interested in such questions as whether the college should provide billiard tables for undergraduates, whether the Princeton Inn should be licensed to serve wine and beer, how to prevent Princeton athletic teams from traveling on the Sabbath, and how to get faculty members to attend daily chapel.[53]

Wilson went to Princeton with the expectation—almost the assurance

—that President Patton would promote a project he had mentioned in his inaugural address, a graduate school of public law and jurisprudence. At the years passed, nothing came of it, although Wilson continued to ventilate the idea. Patton made no effort to push it. In a report to the Trustees on the eve of the Sesquicentennial he wrote that whereas he favored founding a graduate school of law, some of the faculty favored a graduate college of liberal arts. In determining which kind of graduate study to pursue, wrote Patton, "we shall be guided in all probability by the preferences of those who, it is hoped, will provide the necessary endowments."[54]

During the academic year 1896-97 Wilson came close to the breaking point with Princeton over the question of appointing Frederick Jackson Turner to the faculty. Apparently Patton put Wilson in charge of finding a successor to William M. Sloane, who had gone to Columbia, and influential trustees gave Wilson assurances that the man would teach American history only. Therefore, in the fall of 1896 Wilson approached Turner, then at Wisconsin, about the post. On Wilson's side most of the correspondence was written in Ellen's hand because Wilson still could not use a pen, and one letter—on the economics of a professor's life in Princeton—was written entirely by her. Wilson obviously tried to give Turner a perfectly honest picture of his situation. After retailing the obvious assets of Princeton, he frankly admitted that the library was poor, there were as yet few graduate students, rents were high, and schools were not good. Meat cost 18-20¢ a pound; milk 8¢ a quart; butter, 30-40¢ a pound; and servants (apparently considered a necessity), $12 to $16 a month. Yet Mrs. Wilson was able to provide for a household of ten—including food, light, servants, rent, heat, and water—at an average cost of $187 a month.[55]

Turner's name went before the Princeton Trustees in December 1896, but no action was taken. Wilson wrote Turner, "A plague on boards of Trustees! . . . Our president does not bother us by having a mistaken policy, he daunts us by having no will or policy at all." The matter was to be brought up again in March, but meanwhile it became known that Turner was a Unitarian, and Wilson's colleague West, undoubtedly echoing some clerical members of the board, "showed the most stubborn prejudice about introducing a Unitarian into the faculty." At their March meeting the Trustees refused to elect Turner, alleging lack of funds for a separate chair of American history. Wilson was furious. He attempted unsuccessfully to gain access to the Tustees' minutes and wrote Turner, "I am probably at this writing the most chagrined fellow on this continent! . . . it is no doubt just as well that I have not now a chance to go elsewhere."[56]

Within a year that opportunity came. Wilson was asked to be the

The Wesleyan University faculty in 1889. Standing on the right, sporting a bowler, sideburns, and a cane, is Caleb T. Winchester of the English Department, Wilson's close friend. Wilson admired the high level of competence among his colleagues at Wesleyan.

Woodrow Wilson as a professor at Princeton, 1890–1902. In addition to teaching popular courses in politics and jurisprudence, he coached debating, took an active interest in athletics, and served on important faculty committees. The undergraduates chose him as their favorite professor seven times.

Ellen Axson Wilson, circa 1895. When she and Wilson were parted, they wrote each other daily, and their marriage proved a continuing love affair.

The Reverend Francis Landey Patton (*upper left*), President of Princeton, 1888–1902. His inefficiency and indifference to academic standards led to his replacement by Wilson. Frederick J. Turner (*upper right*), Edward A. Ross, and Charles M. Andrews. These men, all destined to achieve high professional eminence, studied under Wilson at Johns Hopkins and much admired him. With Turner Wilson formed a warm friendship.

first president of the University of Virginia, which heretofore had no president but rather an annually elected chairman of the faculty. The pressure put on Wilson to accept the post was strong. Two former fraternity mates now on the Virginia faculty, Heath Dabney and Charles W. Kent, assured him that he was the faculty's only choice and was independently sought by both the alumni and the Board of Visitors. The Board itself was disposed to give Wilson "pretty much anything he asked for." He would be both professor of jurisprudence and president, with an ample salary and a house. The Governor of Virginia, J. Hoge Tyler, personally urged Wilson to accept.[57]

The offer was highly attractive. The University of Virginia was second only to Princeton in Wilson's esteem, and he idealized the Old Dominion. He wrote Charles Kent that the offer would probably be "the highest honor of my lifetime." But eventually he decided to decline.[58]

Wilson was dissuaded from leaving Princeton at the urging of a group of wealthy Princeton trustees, all but one of whom were members of the class of '79. They told him that although it was not practicable to make him a definite promise at the time, there was no honor too high for him at Princeton. They even offered to pay him to remain. The upshot of their endeavors was a formal contract in which "the party of the first part," Woodrow Wilson, agreed for a term of five years not to sever his connection with Princeton and not to give lectures at other institutions that would interfere with his duties at Princeton. In return "the party of the second part," five alumni, agreed for five years to pay Wilson $2500 a year over and above his salary.[59]

Wilson told C. C. Cuyler, the principal agent in arranging the contract, that it would release his thought "for quiet hours, continuous thought, uninterrupted labor." During his last years as a professor the pressures did indeed relax somewhat. He could at last afford to take regular vacations with his family, first in the Virginia mountains, later in the Muskoka Lakes in Canada. In 1899 he went to Britain again, with Stockton Axson for a companion. After corresponding with people as divers as Thomas Nelson Page, Frederick Jackson Turner, and Theodore Roosevelt, he found in John Finley, his former Johns Hopkins pupil, the kind of man with whom he could share the teaching of politics—"a gentleman and a scholar in the broad and genial meanings of those words," familiar with the practical details of government. His writings were earning more and more. Bliss Perry offered him twice the usual fee for an *Atlantic Monthly* article, and *Harper's Magazine* paid $12,000 for the serial rights to a popular history of the United States that would later be published in book form.[60]

Wilson had acquired a sense of power that revealed itself whenever he mounted a platform or pulpit. "In my own opinion," wrote Bliss Perry, who was devoted to him, "his 'tragic fault' lay in the excess of self-confidence which was one of the most fascinating of his virtues." He had made a habit of success, derived from inflexible purpose and self-discipline. He had come to trust his own logic and his own instincts. He could have been holding a mirror to himself when, in a talk to undergraduates, he described his idol Gladstone: "He stood for the type of what a man may make of himself when fired by high ambition and resolve. To some Gladstone appeared to possess a certain degree of arrogance, and yet it was only the self-confidence arising from long study and training—a sort of arrogance which any man may well have. In the presence of questions concerning man's relations to God, this self-confidence was entirely lacking, as though he recognized that he was but a child in the Presence of the Infinite." Wilson, too, had a humble sense of submission to the divine will, combined with the perhaps arrogant assumption that God would call him to a place where he could render signal service to his fellow men.[61]

At the close of the nineties Wilson still thought that his greatest achievement would be to write "The Philosophy of Politics." He applied to the Princeton Trustees for a sabbatical leave in either 1901-1902 or 1902-1903, depending on when his American history had been completed. The Trustees agreed to grant him leave, but before he was free to take it, they had elected him President of Princeton University.[62]

XII

Literary Historian

The historian needs an imagination quite as much as he needs scholarship, and consummate literary art as much as candor and common honesty. Histories are written in order that the bulk of men may read and realize; and it is as bad to bungle the telling of the story as to lack knowledge.

—Woodrow Wilson, 1896[1]

WILSON WAS in the habit of referring to himself as a "literary fellow," and he kept hoping for a job that would allow him to give most of his time to "literary studies." Such employment never came. Nevertheless, day after day, in both term-time and vacation, he sat down at his rolltop desk and wrote, working to the limit of his slender store of energy while Ellen guarded his study door.

During his years at Bryn Mawr, when stories under the pseudonym "Edward Copplestone" failed to find a publisher, Wilson discovered that he had no talent for fiction. The hope that he might be a poet died harder; as late as 1895 he sent his wife verses in her praise, beginning:

> You were the song I waited for.
> I found in you the vision sweet,
> The grace, the strain of noble sounds,
> The form, the mind, the mien, the heart,
> That I had lacked and thought to find
> Within some spring within my mind,
> Like one awakened from dreaming
> To the blessed confidence of sight.

Three days later he wrote her:

No, sweet, I am no poet . . . and those lines written the other day are no poem. The night I wrote them I thought they were. A hot fire was in my brain; my imagination was thronged with every sweet image of love; and, while I wrote, I thought I was writing poetry . . . That I am an idealist, with the heart of a poet, I do not hesitate to avow:

229

but the fact is not reassuring. On the contrary, it is tragical. My heart fairly breaks to utter itself like a poet,—and cannot.[2]

Wilson's greatest desire was to be a "literary politician," but during the 1890's he had to put this ambition aside to find more remunerative literary employment. He wrote popular history and essays for leading magazines—the *Atlantic Monthly, Century, Forum, Harper's*. Although he succeeded as the world counts success, in that editors and publishers clamored for the products of his pen and paid him well, this very success was a misfortune: most of what he wrote in the 1890's was journeyman stuff, written under pressure. He did not have sufficient time to study or reflect, and he was forced either to skimp preparation or to work over old materials. It is significant that from about 1890 on he no longer found the time for annotating books that had been his earlier practice.

While Wilson's principal writings during his years at Princeton were in the field of history, he also turned out essays on life and literature with such titles as "On Being Human," "When a Man Comes to Himself," and "Mere Literature." The prevailing tone was one of optimism and idealism. Wilson shunned whatever he considered morbid, sophisticated, or citified, and in his vocabulary "modern" was a symbol for all three. Better to look back. "Literature," he wrote, "grows rich, various, full-voiced largely through the rediscovery of truth, by thinking re-thought, by stories re-told, by songs re-sung." His essays provided both uplift and comfort; reading them was somewhat like going to church. The homiletic tone derived from the fact that Wilson was constantly engaged in public lecturing. Many of his published essays had done previous service on the platform, so that there was no hard and fast line between his career as an author and as a speaker.[3]

There is abundant evidence to support the assertion of Charles D. Atkins, former Secretary of the Society for the Extension of University Teaching, that Wilson became "one of the immortals of the American lecture platform," ranking with Charles W. Eliot and Phillips Brooks. In 1900 Atkins' predecessor, John Nolen, begged Wilson to repeat a course he had given in Philadelphia on "Great Leaders of Political Thought." "Your lectures," wrote Nolen, "represent so exactly what we want that we feel compelled to ask you again and again." He was "a man who could talk about potatoes," said John B. McMaster, "and make it sound like Holy Writ." Wilson was so much in demand that he often received two or three times the usual fees for academic lectures, and he was so often away from Princeton that President Patton once referred derisively to his "traveling fellowship." The following entry from his diary for January 1, 1898, entitled "Appointments for the year," reveals the number of appearances already contracted for, the fees he was to receive, and his habit of repeating topics:

"Democracy," Oberlin, Ohio, Jan. 4	$100
"Religion and Patriotism," Calvary Church, N.Y., Jan. 16	—
"Leaders of Men," Miller Church, Princeton, Jan. 20	—
"Burke," "Bagehot," and "Maine," Balto., Feby 23-25 $100 ea.	$300
"Democracy," Mt. Holyoke, March 9	$100
"Democracy," Stamford, Conn., March 17	$100
"Municipal Govt.," Brooklyn, Apr. 30, May 7, 14, 21, 28	$300
"Patriotic Citizenship," Princeton, May 30	—
"Const. Govt., in the U.S." [five lectures], Richmond, Va., Oct.	$400
"Political Liberty," Orange, N.J., 14 April	$100
"Walter Bagehot," Rosemont, April 19	$50
"Leaders of Men," Bridgeport, Ct., 24 May	$100
"Patriotism," Hodgensville, Ky., June	$60
"Education in Patriotism," Cooper Union, Nov. 19	$50
	$1,760[4]

As he freely and frequently confided to his wife, Wilson enjoyed his triumphs as a popular lecturer. In 1894, for instance, he wrote her from Boulder, Colorado: "I am rejoiced to say that I not only keep my audience here, but draw new people at every lecture, till now I have quite a 'following.' One man expressed his enthusiasm by exclaiming, 'Why, that fellow is a whole team *and the dog under the wagon.*'" He became adept at feeling the mood of an audience, as is corroborated by contemporary stenographic reports. In December 1900, for example, Wilson was one of six speakers at a dinner of the New England Society of New York City, the others being President Hadley of Yale, Senator Beveridge, St. Clair McKelway of the *Brooklyn Eagle*, and two military men. Wilson was the last speaker, and it was nearing midnight when he was called. Yet he was interrupted over twenty times—as much as the five previous speakers together—by "laughter," "applause," "laughter and applause," "great laughter."[5]

There was danger in this ability to establish rapport with an audience. According to his friend Bliss Perry, Wilson was sometimes carried away and said things he did not mean. On one occasion in Philadelphia he made the wholly uncharacteristic remark that the United States would never be a democracy until there was a Negro woman in the White House, and friends of his had a hard time keeping it out of the newspapers. Yet Wilson's long practice in winning strange audiences was later of immense benefit to him in politics, and his hundreds of appearances in places as remote as Denver, Chicago, and Plymouth, Massachusetts, vastly increased his circle of acquaintances, as well as giving him a greater understanding of the national scene.[6]

Wilson's most important task during his professorial years, and one that had lasting influences on him, was his study of American history. He is generally granted a minor place among American historians, principally because of a small textbook *Division and Reunion, 1829-1889,* and the more pretentious *History of the American People.* Yet he was not a professional historian. His formal training was limited to two thin courses at Princeton and a once-a-week seminar at Johns Hopkins. He taught history—along with economics and politics—to undergraduates at Bryn Mawr and Wesleyan, but never again after his appointment to the Princeton faculty in 1890.

It is possible for a historian to overcome both lack of previous instruction and lack of the day-to-day immersion in the materials afforded by teaching if he has a passion for investigation. Wilson had read widely but unsystematically in the field of history, especially biography, but he was not at all what the Germans call a *Forscher,* with a passion to seek out, to question, and to confirm his sources. His works were based entirely on published sources; there is no evidence that he ever did any original historical research.

Wilson's labors as a historian were further handicapped by the fact that his historical writing was auxiliary to two other purposes: to make money and to provide background for his projected "Philosophy of Politics." The first meant that he was always writing under pressure of publishers' deadlines, and that the form, the length, and to a degree the contents were dictated to him. And as a political philosopher it was his habit to look for the larger meaning, to generalize; he lacked sufficient feeling for the incidental, the unique, and the concrete. Thus, he did not write history, but about history.

Wilson was not content to inform but must also instruct and inspire. Historical writing, he said, should not merely "make complaisant record of deeds honorably done and plans nobly executed in the past." It must also "build high places whereon to plant the clear and flaming light of experience, that they may shine alike upon the roads already traveled and upon the paths not yet attempted. The historian is also a sort of prophet." On another occasion he wrote that the historian must not merely discover truth but "must make others see it just as he does . . . Their dullness, their ignorance, their prepossessions are to be overcome and driven in, like a routed troop, upon the truth." In writing history, as in teaching, Wilson lacked the quality of vicariousness, the willingness to be forgotten. Like an importunate guide from whom the traveler cannot escape, he was constantly at the reader's elbow.[7]

The persistent desire to edify partly accounts for a style that was often too rhetorical. Frequently the striking phrase or the colorful adjective either substituted for the facts or distorted them. But in spite of Wilson's handicaps and crotchets, his works on American history, found a wide and lucrative audience. He even gained a hearing among the historical fraternity. He was one of the first to see the importance of Turner's work on the influence of the West, and he formulated generalizations regarding the causes of the Civil War that affected later historiography.

In judging Wilson, one must remember that history as a profession was new in America. Not one of Wilson's contemporaries in the field of general American history had been trained as a historian. James Ford Rhodes pursued a business career until he was nearly forty; John Fiske was trained as a linguist and philosopher; James Schouler was a practicing lawyer for most of his life; and John B. McMaster taught English at the College of the City of New York and engineering at Princeton before publishing the first volume of his *History of the People of the United States*. By modern standards these men can all be found wanting in method, judgment, and rigor. All betrayed obvious bias. All had a Messianic urge to inspire their readers toward right views about their country, which warped their presentation. If Woodrow Wilson the historian is to be treated fairly, he must be judged in the light of his time.[8]

In April 1889, just as he was finishing *The State*, Wilson received a letter from Albert Bushnell Hart of Harvard, asking him to write the third in a series of three small books under the title "Epochs of American History." The first, on the Colonial period, was to be written by Reuben G. Thwaites, Secretary of the Wisconsin State Historical Society; the second, on *The Formation of the Union*, by Hart himself. The books were intended both to serve as college texts and to instruct the general reader. Copy was to be delivered to the publisher —Longmans, Green—within a year; each author was to receive $500 on completion of the manuscript.[9]

It may seem curious that Wilson, who had written no historical work whatever, should have received this offer. As it happened, Hart's first candidate had been J. Franklin Jameson, who refused. Jameson may have suggested Wilson's name. but Hart's memory of half a century later was that he had met Wilson at an American Historical Association meeting and was immediately impressed by his ability to make new generalizations and to induce others to see them.[10]

Wilson was attracted by the proposition at once, asking only that the time limit be extended to not less than twenty months; otherwise, with his nervous disposition he might injure his health by trying to fulfill an impossible contract. Longmans assented to the extension. Mistakenly, as it turned out, Wilson accepted the flat fee in spite of the advice of his friend Robert Bridges that he ask for royalties. He also essentially agreed to Hart's title, "Epoch of Division and Reunion." He set to work in the summer of 1889 and continued the task in 1890— by which time Thwaites's volume was off the press—but made little progress. In June 1891, already six months beyond the deadline, he closeted himself every morning in an empty student's room in Witherspoon Hall, but at the end of the summer the manuscript was still only half written. In the spring of 1892 the publishers wrote a needling letter that hurt Wilson's feelings. There followed a fourth summer of unremitting labor. Toward the end of it Wilson wrote Bridges: "I've carried out my programme for the 'vacation,' and am now nearing the end of the first draft of it. I trust it will need very little revision to be the final draft. I've put into it already almost everything I know—and some things I don't know but only believe."[11]

One reason Wilson found *Division and Reunion* such hard going was that he did not have a backlog of class lectures, which provides the basis for many texts. He came to most sources cold, having to read, digest, consider, and compress as he went along—and he was not a fast reader. Furthermore, he wanted to make the little book a work of literature, so he was not content merely to set the materials forth but must embellish them. Finally, he went far over the word limit and had to cut the manuscript by perhaps a quarter.[12]

Even after copy had been delivered, Wilson's difficulties were not over. Hart still thought the manuscript too long as well as unbalanced. He objected to Wilson's spelling and stylistic mannerisms, to omissions in his bibliographies, to lack of dates and other specifics, to bias in the treatment of Sherman's march to the sea, and to failure to observe certain textbook forms, such as subheadings in the body of the text.[13]

Wilson put up resistance. He had already cut so much, he wrote Hart, that to do more would mutilate the book; better to spend still another summer and rewrite the whole. He did not see why so much bibliography was necessary and had deliberately omitted such a work as Henry Wilson's *The Rise and Fall of the Slave Power in America* because of its "grossly partisan" bias against the South. He had conceived of the book as "a literary sketch" rather than strictly a textbook, and he disliked paragraph headings that interrupted the flow of narrative. As for Sherman, Wilson was convinced that the general's cruel policies were deliberate, whereas the sufferings of northern prisoners in southern prison camps were merely incidental to the economic prostration of the Confederacy. Above all, Wilson fought for his idiosyncrasies of style and spelling, even insisting on the English *-our* ending in such words as "labor" and "harbor." He wrote Hart:

"I have all my life been a close student of style,—appearances to the contrary notwithstanding!—and I beg you will believe that my choice in this matter is neither haphazard nor a result of weak fondness for what has come from my pen. "The style is the man," after all; and, in my opinion, (as I should like to tell Wilson's reader) punctuation is a part of style—and capitalization, too, for that matter."[14]

In these and other matters the author and the editor compromised. Wilson toned down his comments on Sherman, included *The Rise and Fall of the Slave Power in America* in his references, and supplied subheadings. Hart on his part allowed Wilson some of his cherished mannerisms and accepted bibliographies at the ends of the five sections of the book, although he and Thwaites had supplied them at the end of every chapter. Hart later remembered Wilson as a man who "would work in harness." "He was a first-rate co-worker," said Hart, ". . . always reasonable. He knew what he knew—no one could scare him out of a conclusion—he was markedly tenacious of his own opinions. But no one had to agree with him; there was no fault in disagreement." The correspondence between the two men bears out their mutual respect. Hart wrote Wilson, "Editorship is a light task when the writer so far perfects his work, and takes in good part the suggestions of one less experienced than himself." Wilson in turn wrote, "I regard it as nothing but a compliment to be credited with the sanity of submitting to criticism without irritation or misunderstanding"; and again, "I recognize the shortcomings of my style very keenly, and am unaffectedly obliged to you for your watchful criticism of it."[15]

Division and Reunion, 1829-1889 was published in the spring of 1893 as a pocket-sized volume in small type. It contained 326 pages including index, plus twenty pages of introductory material, with five colored fold-out maps illustrating topics in political geography such as the Oregon and Texas boundary controversies and the legal status of slavery in states and territories. The book ran to about 80,000 words—approximately the length that a short high school textbook of today devotes to the same period. Even so, *Division and Reunion* was longer than the companion volumes by Thwaites and Hart. There is clear evidence of Wilson's difficulties when forced to compress it so drastically. The first major section, on the Jacksonian period, 1829-1841, is longer than any of the others (88 pages), more original, and more elaborately written. The sections on "The Slavery Question, 1842-1856" and "Secession and Slavery, 1856-1865" number 77 and 76 pages respectively, are more conventional in interpretation, and contain passages of undigested information poured out huggermugger. The last section, "Rehabilitation of the Union, 1865-1889," although covering a time span nearly twice as long as any other, contains only 46 pages, and its three chapters are progressively shorter and more perfunctory. The book is unbalanced in other ways. The banking controversies of the Jacksonian era are given twenty-five pages, while the intellectual awakening and the social reform movements of the period receive less than four. In the section devoted to the post-Civil War period there is no specific mention whatever of intellectual movements or reform organizations.[16]

Yet *Division and Reunion* has real merit. It has pace and liveliness. While the text is occasionally marred by strained metaphor, as when Jackson's monetary policy designed to halt inflation is described as "a small pill against the earthquake," Wilson's idiosyncrasies are less apparent here than in his later historical writing, perhaps because of Hart's watchful editing. And although the book is sometimes weak in narrative, its characterizations of people and events are often striking, even brilliant. Witness this quick sketch of the formation of the Republican Party: "It got its programme from the Free Soilers, whom it bodily absorbed; its radical and aggressive spirit from the Abolitionists, whom it received without liking; its liberal views upon constitutional questions from the Whigs, who constituted both in numbers and in influence its commanding element; and its popular impulses from the Democrats, who did not leave behind them, when they joined it, their faith in their old party ideals."[17]

When he wrote *Division and Reunion,* Wilson had not been west of Ohio, but he had gained, especially through his friendship with Frederick Jackson Turner, a strong impression of the influence of the West on American history, which had thus far been neglected. In the course of gathering materials he wrote to Turner, seeking "that *self-expression* by the West touching it [*sic*] material and political ambitions, its attitudes of separation or cooperation, as the case might be, towards the rest of the country, its sentiment toward Congress and the national policy." Although Turner could not at once supply the documents, Wilson accepted the idea that American democracy and nationalism were hatched on the frontier. In *Division and Reunion* he portrayed the Jacksonian movement as bringing to the front of the stage "the men of daring sagacity, and resource, who were winning the western wilderness for civilization." Timid and conservative people might be afraid because the new men were "without sensibility or caution," but they were "forces of health, hasty because young, possessing the sound but unsensitive conscience which belongs to those who are always confident in action." From them came "a distinctively American order of politics, begotten of the crude forces of a new nationality."[18]

In *Division and Reunion* Wilson genuinely attempted to be impartial in his treatment of North and South. Before starting the task, he wrote Hart that ever since he had formed his own judgments, he had been a Federalist, and that he hoped that this fact, plus his nonsouthern blood, would make it possible to detach his historical judgment from his "affectionate, reminiscent sympathies" for the South. Later he wrote to his Virginia friend Heath Dabney in a somewhat different vein but to similar effect: "Perhaps you have seen one of the enclosed circulars and have already pitied me the necessity of doing justice to those abolition-ist rascals and the other characters of ante-bellum and post-bellum times. And I am afraid I *shall* do them justice! I am getting most unrea-sonably impartial in this latitude." Yet try as he would, he could not conceal his prosouthern bias. It appeared both in little ways—such as using southern names for battles ("Manassas" for Bull Run and "Pitts-burg Landing" for Shiloh)—and in large ones, as in his treatment of slavery. He privately told members of the Johns Hopkins historical seminary in 1890 that slavery "had done more for the negro in two hun-dred and fifty years than African freedom had done since the building of the pyramids." In *Division and Reunion* he did not go that far, but he was at pains to abate "the charges of moral guilt for the establish-ment and perpetuation of slavery which the more extreme leaders of the anti-slavery party made against the slaveholders of the southern States." He argued that the institution was forced on all the colonies against their wishes by the "selfish commercial policy of the mother country." The Southerners could not rid themselves of the institution because "the slaves were too numerous and too ignorant to be set free," and when the cotton gin made the South "the chief cotton field of the world . . . slavery seemed nothing less than the indispensable instru-ment of southern society."[19]

In treating the actual condition of the bondsmen, Wilson made the amazing assertion, "Slavery showed at its worst where it was most seen by observers from the North—at its edges, in the border States." There, he wrote, "slaves were constantly either escaping or attempting escape, and being pursued and recaptured, and a quite rigorous treatment of them seemed necessary." But in the heart of the South "conditions were different, were more normal." There domestic servants were indulgently treated, and "among the masters who had the sensibility and breeding of gentlemen, the dignity and responsibility of ownership were apt to to produce a noble and gracious type of manhood and relations really patriarchal." It was true that on the very big plantations, where Negroes were "massed in isolation," there might be harsh treatment, and that the domestic slave trade was an odious feature of the system, but cruelty was exceptional and most slaves were humanely treated. Wilson admitted slavery was wasteful of resources and hard on the "poor whites," but nowhere did he condemn the system as inherently wrong. The Abolitionists were portrayed as irresponsible extremists who helped to bring people "into the frame of mind to welcome even civil war for the sake of reform."[20]

In spite of these evidences of prosouthern bias, *Division and Reunion* was remarkable in that it represented a deliberate attempt at a dispassionate analysis of the background of secession and civil war. Up to this time the field had been held by partisans. To the northern historian James Schouler, as well as to the transplanted German, Hermann von Holst, slavery was a sin and secession a crime; southern leaders might have been sincere, but they were deluded. To apologists for the Confederacy slavery was an inescapable inheritance and an acceptable if unfortunate means of keeping an inferior race under tutelage, and secession was a constitutional right justified by northern invasion of southern constitutional guarantees.

Wilson argued that the South was right in law but wrong in history. He maintained that the southern theory of states' rights and a dissoluble federation was originally held by the founding fathers, and that Daniel Webster's view that the Constitution had created "a single federal state, complete in itself, enacting legislation which was the supreme law of the land, and dissoluble only by revolution," was something they had never dreamed of. But the later doctrine of the Union accorded with the march of events. "If we were not to possess the continent as a nation," wrote Wilson, "and as a nation build up the great fabric of free institutions upon which we had made so fair a beginning, we were to fail at all points. Upon any other plan we should have neither wealth nor peace sufficient for the completion of our great task, but only discord and wasted resources to show for the struggle. It may, nevertheless, be doubted whether this was the doctrine upon which the Union had been founded."[21]

The reason the South had not changed her ideas, Wilson argued, was that "she had not changed her condition. She had not experienced, except in a very slight degree, the economic forces which had created the great Northwest and nationalized the rest of the country; for they had been shut out of her life by slavery." Eventually she and her principles had been overwhelmed by "the mighty strength of the nation with which she had fallen out of sympathy."[22]

In the quarter century following the Civil War, however, the South had finally been brought into a new Union by the agencies of steam and electricity. "Freed from the incubus of slavery, she had sprung into new life; already she promised to become one of the chief industrial regions of the Union . . . Northern capital poured into the South; northern interests became identified with southern interests, and the days of inevitable strife and permanent difference came to seem strangely remote."[23]

The appearance of a new theory of secession was obviously regarded as an event. No textbook would today receive as much critical attention as did *Division and Reunion.* The *New York Sun* devoted three columns to it; the *Nation* and the *Atlantic Monthly* both gave it a full page; the review in the *Political Science Quarterly* was placed first among seventeen. Wilson's interpretation had great attractions. He received praise in one review because he refused "to engage in the old dispute upon the ground originally occupied by the disputants, but leads us away to another position, from which both sides of the shield can easily be seen." In politics a new generation was tired of the "bloody shirt," and ready to forget war hatreds. Similarly in history it was a relief to read an account of southern secession and the Civil War that did not assess blame and find culprits. How much more comforting to accept the idea that the great struggle had been the result of inexorable processes and that both sides were in a measure right![24]

In spite of the interest it aroused and the praise it received, Wilson's contention that the North evolved a new constitutional theory to fit its centralized industrial economy while an unchanging South held fast to the states' rights doctrines of the founding fathers drew heavy fire from the most knowledgeable reviewers. Frederick Bancroft, writing in the *Political Science Quarterly* thought that Wilson's contentions were "nothing less than amazing," since it was clear that the South had taken more and more extreme political views as northern economic superiority became more apparent. Frederick Jackson Turner, who called himself an "enthusiast" for *Division and Reunion,* nevertheless wrote Wilson that the South "did not remain preserved by the ice of slavery like a Siberian mammoth" but in fact changed greatly.[25]

There were also those for whom any defense of the Lost Cause was anathema. A group of Union veterans in Worcester, Massachusetts, took violent exception to Wilson's theory that the South truly joined the Union only after having been conquered in the Civil War. They wrote Wilson a letter in which they condemned his theories as "wrong in principle, dangerous in tendency and disparaging of the motives of the Union soldiers who fought not to form a 'New Union,' but to defend

and preserve a Union that they believed and proved to be indissoluble."
Hermann von Holst found that Wilson's southern bias "cast a film
over his eyes" and prevented him from seeing the moral element in
the irrepressible conflict.[26]

Wilson was unrepentant and returned the fire. In the *Atlantic
Monthly* for August 1893 he made a vigorous attack on northern historians of the anti-slavery struggle. In a review of the first two volumes
of James Ford Rhodes' *History of the United States from the Compromise of 1850* he wrote that the author completely lacked the virtues
needed for his task: "catholicity of sympathy, a most delicate and dis-
criminating appreciation of opposite points of view, and a rare literary
skill in nicely modulated statement." Wilson charged that Rhodes saw
the South as "a foreign country . . . a region from which many rumors
come to him . . . he has no authentic knowledge or realization of it
himself." He had read too much antislavery propaganda to see the
situation objectively.[27]

At a meeting of the American Historical Association in New York
in 1896, Wilson again attacked northern historians who based their
accounts of the South on travelers' tales. The result, he said, was "a
sort of phantasmagoria. I have lived in the South more than one half
of the years I have reached already, and I do not recognize it in these
pictures." Moreover, northern historians wanted the Southerner to regret his past, which Wilson refused to do—"There is nothing to apologize for in the past of the South, absolutely nothing to apologize for."
This talk later brought a fierce rebuttal from John W. Burgess, who
doubled as a political scientist and nationalist historian. In the introduction to a general history, *The Middle Period, 1817-1858*, which
partially overlapped *Division and Reunion*, Burgess threw down the
gauntlet to a certain "distinguished professor of history and politics . . .
The time has come when the men of the South should acknowledge
that they were in error in their attempt to destroy the Union, and it is
unmanly in them not to do so . . . not one scintilla of justification for
secession and rebellion must be accepted." Small wonder that Ellen
Wilson gave up hope of getting her husband a lectureship at Columbia
when she heard that Burgess would have to approve the appointment.[28]

Division and Reunion set Wilson to pondering the whole course of
United States history, and he soon began work on a book on the subject. In 1894 he wrote his friend Turner that he was halfway through
the Colonial period and asked if Turner would be willing to go over
the manuscript. Turner refused because he was afraid of absorbing
Wilson's ideas into his own work, especially since they were so close

to his own already. He nevertheless wrote that he thought Wilson capable of writing "*the* American history of our time." Wilson replied that he hoped to fulfill such high expectations, "But, oh, it goes hard! . . . I pray that it may go easier or it will kill me. And yet it would be a most pleasant death. The ardour of the struggle is inspiriting. There is pleasure in the very pain,—as when one bites on an aching tooth."[29]

Meanwhile Wilson wrote a number of articles revealing the directions of his thought. For the *Forum* he wrote a biting review of a popular history of the United States, by Goldwin Smith, in which he rebutted the "expansion of New England" view of American development. Indeed, the Middle States had more reason to be called the seat of American nationalism than either New England or the South. In the eighteenth century, wrote Wilson, the Middle Colonies were more "American" than the regions north or south of them in their mixture of population, their variety of governmental structures, their materialism, and their progressive way of doing things. In writing this, Wilson was indebted, as he freely admitted, to passages in Frederick Jackson Turner's essay, "The Influence of the Frontier on American History," which he had read before publication. The book review goes on to develop the theme that had been a topic of discussion between Wilson and Turner at Johns Hopkins: the importance of the West as the seat of American Nationalism and the home of the "typical American."[30]

Wilson played a variation on this theme in an essay entitled "A Calendar of Great Americans," published in the *Forum* in February 1894. To qualify for inclusion, a man had to be not only great but typically American. Hamilton and Madison were rejected as "Englishmen bred in America"; the Adamses and Calhoun as "great provincials"; Jefferson because of "the strain of French philosophy that weakened and permeated his thought"; and Benton because of his "shallow and irrelevant" classical learning that made him see the Roman Senate in the Capitol at Washington. Asa Gray (the only scientist mentioned) and Emerson were excluded because they were "the authors of such thought as might have been native to any clime." By attention to concrete cases Wilson arrived at "canons of Americanism," which he described as follows:

The American spirit is something more than the old, the immemorial Saxon spirit of liberty from which it sprung. It has been bred by the conditions attending the great task which we have all the century been carrying forward: the task, at once material and ideal, of subduing a wilderness and covering all the wide stretches of a vast continent with a single free and stable polity. It is, accordingly, above all things, a hopeful and confident spirit. It is progressive, optimistically progressive, and ambitious of objects of national scope and advantage. It is unpedantic, unprovincial, unspeculative, unfastidious, regardful of law, but as using it, not as being used by it or dominated by any formalism whatever; in a sense unrefined, because full of rude force, but prompted by large and generous motives, and often as tolerant as it is resolute.

The complete list of those who qualified as great Americans was: Franklin, Patrick Henry, Washington, Marshall, Clay, Webster, Jackson, Sam Houston, Lowell, Lincoln, Lee, Grant, and George Ticknor Curtis. The largest contingent—five of the thirteen—came from the West. Wilson admired Lincoln above all—"the supreme American of our history":

> The whole country is summed up in him: the rude Western strength, tempered with shrewdness and a broad and human wit; the Eastern conservatism, regardful of law and devoted to strict standards of duty. He even understood the South, as no other Northern man of his generation did. He respected, because he comprehended, although he could not hold, its view of the Constitution; he appreciated the inexorable compulsions of its past in relation to slavery; he would have secured it once more, and speedily if possible, in its right of self-government when the fight was fought out. To the Eastern politicians he seemed like an accident; but to history he must seem like a providence.[31]

For a time Wilson promoted Turner's theories so much, both in print and on the platform, that he was chosen as one of two commentators on a paper read by Turner before the American Historical Association in 1896, entitled "The West as a Field of Historical Study." It is curious that Wilson and Turner so unaffectedly admired each other even though their careers as scholars, teachers, and writers were antithetical. Wilson was content to let others do the digging, was careless of facts, and was ever ready to generalize from a modicum of knowledge; Turner, "a glutton for data," was never satisfied that he knew enough. In teaching, Wilson's great success was as a lecturer, especially to undergraduates; Turner's, as an inspiration and guide to graduate students. Wilson's method of work was to compose right along with his research, using only his own or borrowed books; Turner amassed thirty-four letter-sized file drawers of notes for a book he never completed. Wilson saw history in terms of politics, constitutional development, military affairs and "great men." Turner cast a wider net: he thought that historians needed to use the data and methods of not only political science and geography but of all social sciences. Wilson delighted publishers by producing three historical works plus two volumes of essays in the dozen years that spanned his career as a historian. The more than four decades of Turner's professional career were strewn with the wreckage of books contracted for and never written. But Turner had the last word. Whereas Wilson's historical writings would

now be completely forgotten were it not for his later eminence in politics, Turner's influence was "almost immeasurable . . . an influence
so great that American history has been reinterpreted and rewritten because of him." There is justice in the final judgment, for Turner made
history a vocation, while Wilson used it as a means to other ends.[32]

During this period Wilson was trying to assess the task of the historian. He wrote an essay, "On the Writing of History," published in the
Century Magazine in 1895, in which he argued that the historian
needed literary skill above all: "[Truth] is a thing ideal, displayed by
the just proportion of events, revealed in form and color, dumb till
facts be set in syllables, articulated into words, put together into sentences, swung with proper tone and cadence." Wilson weighed the merits
and demerits of various historians, all of whom, no matter what their
virtues, he found wanting. Macaulay could bring to focus an amazing
variety of knowledge, but was too obviously an advocate for the Whigs:
Carlyle could paint in vivid colors, but lacked "that pure radiance in
which things are seen steadily and seen whole"; Gibbon was "too remote from the ordinary levels of our human sympathy"; John Richard
Green wrote in "always the same key" and was handicapped by his
plan of organization. Having put these worthies in their place, Wilson
proceeded to explain how he thought history should be composed. The
historian should not plan the whole but let the materials carry him
along as he works from period to period. "A trifle too much knowledge
will undo him. It will break the spell for his imagination." He had better
read the materials as he writes to keep his vision fresh. Let him remember "that his task is radically different from the task of the investigator.
The investigator must display his materials, but the historian must
convey his impressions."[33]

In March 1896 the *Century Magazine* published another piece, "On
an Author's Choice of Company," in which Wilson maintained that if
a writer is to "write for immortality" he must steep himself in the great
literature of the past and develop a style that, while genuinely his own,
reflects a comradeship with earlier writers. "May an author not," asked
Wilson, "in some degree by choosing his literary company, choose also
his literary character, and so when he come to write, write himself back
to his masters?" He held up to admiration Charles Lamb, who, when a
new book came out, always read an old one, and whose style in its
"self-pleasing quaintness" reflected the Elizabethans. Wilson expressed
a taste for "old-fashioned romance" over "what is modern and analytic
and painful." He argued that history had ceased to be literature be-

cause critical examination of sources confused the reader, so that "the story, for the sake of which we would believe the whole thing was undertaken, is oftentimes fain to sink away into the footnotes."[34]

Wilson had opportunity to apply his literary theories in a popular biography of George Washington that appeared in serial form in *Harper's Magazine* in 1896 and was then published as a book. He was better paid than ever before, receiving $300 for each of the six installments, plus later book royalties, which went far toward making it possible to build the house on Library Place. But beyond its earnings, there is little that even Wilson's friends could find to say in the book's favor.[35]

Even if allowance is made for the fact that it was written in haste, *George Washington* is an astonishingly bad book. It is unbalanced: 180 pages out of 300-odd are devoted to the period before Washington took command of the Continental Army. There are eight pages on Braddock's defeat but only two on the Yorktown campaign, a paragraph on the Farewell Address, and no mention whatever of the Neutrality Proclamation of 1793. The first chapter, the longest, is devoted to a saccharine picture of Colonial Virginia, where the scattered plantations were directed "by strong, thinking, high bred men," where small holders, except on the frontier, were merely dutiful tenants, and where Negro slavery was a means whereby the rural aristocracy acquired patriarchal virtues.[36]

Wilson wrote a friend, "To make Washington real and thoroughly human is just what I am trying to do; in a certain sense it is all I am trying to do." When the hero finally reached the stage, however, he was as faultless and bloodless as the prig invented by Parson Weems. One reads the book in vain for any solid information about Washington's character, his abilities, or his political opinions. One is not even sure of his appearance: as a boy he had "steady, grey eyes," but later he met the sallies of lively women "with a look from his frank, blue eyes." The only thing certain is that he was an aristocrat who could bear no slight to his honor and who rode all the way to Boston to protest a diminution in rank. "He went," wrote Wilson, "very bravely dight in proper uniform of buff and blue, a white-and-scarlet cloak upon his shoulders, the sword at his side knotted with red and gold, his horse's fittings engraved with the Washington arms, and trimmed with the best style of the London saddlers." Even his hunters—Magnolia, Blueskin, Ajax, and Chinkling—were of the finest blood. Later, his "noble figure," his "mien as if it were a prince," his "sincere and open countenance," and his "ease of salute" helped to abash the rabble and to prevent the Revolution from degenerating into license.[37]

The most deplorable feature of the book is the style. Wilson's effort to achieve an approximation of Lamb's "self-pleasing quaintness" resulted in writing that was mannered, ornate, sentimental, and imprecise. It produced such grotesque sentences as:

Privateering, too, was cousin-germain to something still better; 'twas but a sort of formal apprenticeship to piracy.
For the rest, the old Dominion made shift to do without towns.
It was a country in which men kept their individuality very handsomely withal.
He had to build his character very carefully by the plumb to keep it at an equilibrium, though he might decorate it, if he were but upright, as freely, as whimsically even, as he chose, with chance traits and self-pleasing tastes, with the full consent and knowledge of the neighborhood.

Wilson used archaisms freely, such as "for the nonce," "was fain to," "waxed bold," "'twas," and "'twere," and affixed stock adjectives to many nouns—such as "thrifty burghers," "gallant courtiers," "dashing soldiers," or "frank Virginians."[38]

How could Wilson, who had written clean prose before and was to do so again, fall into this verbal morass? Partly he was the victim of his own devotion to the past. Partly, too, since *George Washington* was designed for a wide audience, he adopted the tone of many popular lecturers or preachers and talked down to his readers. "Readers," he wrote elsewhere, "are a poor jury. They need enlightenment as well as information; the matter must be interpreted to them as well as related. There are moral facts as well as material and the one sort must be as plainly told as the other." Wilson's sentimental, "uplifting" style accorded well with the Genteel Tradition and with the tastes of the people who thronged lyceums and put their children to reading *Little Lord Fauntleroy* and *Black Beauty*. His admiring classmates gave him an elaborate dinner after the publication of *George Washington* and presented him with a copy of a bust of the hero by Houdon. His mail was crammed with letters from other admirers. Even the historian Claude Van Tyne, who was critical of Wilson's scholarship, thought that the literary execution of *George Washington* was masterly and that the deliberately archaic language was eminently fitted for a book dealing with the Colonial period.[39]

Wilson was at times aware of the defects in his writing. In a letter to his friend Edith Gittings Reid in 1897 he observed of the style of his essays:

The phrasing is too elaborate: has not the easy pace of simplicity. The sentences are too obviously wrought out with a nice workmanship. They do not sound as if they had come spontaneously, but as if they had been waited for,—perhaps waited for anxiously. The fact is not so.

They come fast and hot enough usually, and seem natural moulds for my thought. But I am speaking of the impression they make when read—the impression they make upon *me* after they are cold,—when read in the proof for example. I write in sentences rather than in words: they are formed *whole* in my mind before they begin to be put upon the paper, usually,—and no doubt that is the reason they seem *cast*, rather than naturally poured forth, and have lines of artificiality in their make-up.

Later, when contemplating a text designed especially for southern schools, to be national in spirit yet fair to the southern point of view, he wrote Mrs. Reid again: "It must be a work of art or nothing,—and I must study the art. I must cultivate a new style for the new venture: a quick and pellucid narrative, as clear as the air and colored with nothing but the sun, stopped in its current here and there, and yet almost imperceptibly, for the setting in of small pictures of men and manners, coloured variously, as life is . . . Neither the style of the essays, nor the style of Washington will do,—and I have no other, except that of 'Division and Reunion,' which is equally unsuitable."[40]

Meanwhile publishers were competing for Wilson's services. In 1894 Dodd, Mead tried unsuccessfully to get him to collaborate with James Schouler in writing a history of the United States. In 1897 Walter Hines Page, then editor of the *Atlantic Monthly,* also failed to persuade Wilson to write "*the* history of the Civil War." Soon Harper induced Wilson to sign a contract for the southern school text; at Wilson's insistence he was to receive a ten percent royalty on the retail instead of the wholesale price. The project fell through when in 1899 Harper sold its textbook division, and with it Wilson's contract, to the American Book Company. Wilson was intensely annoyed, objecting that his services could not be sold like merchandise, but the American Book Company refused to relinquish the contract, and the school text died there. No sooner had word of this debacle reached the publishing world than three different houses—Century, Doubleday & McClure, and Harper & Brothers—began bidding against each other for a general history of the United States. Each one offered Wilson higher royalties than usual. In 1900 Harper got the contract by offering to run the history first as a serial in *Harper's Magazine* at $1000 for each of twelve installments, and later in book form with an expected sale of over 100,000 copies. Closing the deal took nearly four months because Wilson, having been paid too little for *Division and Reunion* and having been "sold" without his consent to the American Book Company, made sure of getting the best possible terms.[41]

Wilson delivered the first portion of his history in June 1900 and completed it in the summer of 1902. Installments appeared in *Harper's*

Magazine throughout 1901 and once in 1902, but Wilson wrote more than had been planned, and only about half appeared serially. The whole work was published late in 1902 under the title *A History of the American People*, in deliberate imitation of John Richard Green's *A History of the English People*, which was allegedly Wilson's model for his history. Harper, who had published Green's book in four volumes, used a similar format for Wilson's history. The manuscript totalled about 280,000 words, today a normal length for a one-volume school or college text. It was inflated to five volumes by using a large type face that allowed little more than 300 words a page, by including appendices containing documents, and by putting in nearly eight hundred illustrations, often chosen with little relevance to the text. The work was issued in various forms. There was a subscription edition in leather, a standard trade edition, later a "popular" edition, and even a special edition for Princeton alumni, bound in orange and black.[42]

For all the pretentiousness of its packaging, *A History of the American People* deserved the epithet later given it by a Princeton colleague of Wilson's—"a gilt-edged potboiler." It was all too clearly written in haste. Reviewers who knew the monographic materials doubted whether Wilson made much use of even those mentioned in his bibliographies, since the narrative contained little information not found in standard secondary sources. In much of the work Wilson simply paraphrased, or even repeated verbatim, portions of books and articles he had written earlier. On one occasion he repeated with a few slight verbal changes a passage from John Fiske's *Old Virginia and Her Neighbors*. How little he cared for detailed accuracy is revealed in a letter to R. W. Gilder, editor of the *Century Magazine*: "That was an amazing error in dates you caught me in, but it does not embarrass me. I am not a historian: I am only a writer of history, and these little faults must be overlooked in a fellow who tries to tell a story and is not infallible on dates."[43]

Evidence of carelessness can also be seen in the book's lack of proportion and its extraordinary omissions. Ten pages are devoted to the Ku Klux Klan and its suppression—more space than is given to the Populists, the Greenback Party, the Knights of Labor, and the American Federation of Labor all together. There is no reference to Paine's *Common Sense*, *Marbury vs. Madison*, the Yazoo land frauds, or the Erie Canal. Washington's Farewell Address receives a single sentence, and Marshall's great nationalist decisions have only a paragraph. The imbalance becomes even more striking when one compares Wilson's work with that of his alleged model. John Richard Green's great achievment in his *History of the English People* had been to subordinate the political narrative to the life of the people as a whole, so that priests, reformers, scientists, authors, and humble workers in the field appeared as often in his pages as warriors, ministers, and monarchs. Wilson's volumes, in contrast, are almost exclusively political. As in *Division and Reunion*, there is a detailed discussion of the banking controversy of the Jacksonian period—thirty pages—whereas the literature of the period is given a single paragraph. The only serious social history is a chapter on life in the Confederacy during the Civil War; for the rest, the author contents himself with rhetoric: "The boatman's song on the long western rivers, the crack of the teamster's whip in the mountain passes, the stroke of the woodman's axe ringing out in the stillness of the forest, the sharp report of the rifle of huntsman, pioneer, and scout on the fast advancing frontier, filled the air as if with the very voices of change, and were answered by events quick with the fulfilment of their prophecy."[44]

As this passage suggests, Wilson's history is written in much the same style as the biography of Washington. The same faults—overuse of adjectives, deliberate archaism, stilted expression, and clumsy metaphor—reappear. But in many ways the style of *A History of the American People* shows improvement. The self-criticism revealed in Wilson's letters to Mrs. Reid had worked benefit. The narrative has more pace; extreme mannerisms have been eliminated; adjectives are less relentlessly hitched to helpless nouns; there is more attention to specific detail. The improvement can be clearly seen in certain parallel passages. For instance, in *George Washington* Wilson introduced a section on the change in British policy after 1763 as follows:

'Twas hardly an opportune time for statesmen in London to make a new and larger place for England's authority in America, and yet that was what they immediately attempted.

In *A History of the American People* the sentence performing the same service is more specific and informative:

It was the worst possible time the home government could have chosen in which to change its policy of concession towards the colonies and begin to tax and govern them by act of Parliament; and yet that was exactly what the ministers determined to do.[45]

A History of the American People is better balanced than *Division and Reunion* and *George Washington*, and it does not grow increasingly sketchy and perfunctory, as do the earlier books. In the first half Wilson skillfully works in a good deal of relevant English history, so that American affairs appear not in isolation but in their proper perspective as part of the larger history of the Atlantic community. The American

Revolution is treated with commendable objectivity; Wilson clearly favored the American cause but understood the British imperial dilemma and sympathized with the plight of the American Loyalists. Throughout the five volumes appear characterizations of public men, such as Hamilton, Calhoun, Lincoln, and Cleveland, that are both picturesque and shrewd. The description of Jefferson Davis during the collapse of the Confederacy is uncanny in that it could so easily be applied to Wilson himself during his second term in the White House:

> Not a little of the dogged perseverance and undaunted action of those closing months of the struggle had been due to the masterful characteristics of Mr. Jefferson Davis, the President of the Confederacy . . . He had the pride, the spirit of initiative, the capacity in business that qualify men for leadership, and lacked nothing of indomitable will and imperious purpose to make his leadership effective. What he did lack was wisdom in dealing with men, willingness to take the judgment of others in critical matters of business, the instinct which recognizes ability in others and trusts it to the utmost to play its independent part. He too much loved to rule, had too overweening a confidence in himself . . . He sought to control too many things with too feminine a jealousy of any rivalry in authority. But his spirit was the life of the government. His too frequent mistakes were the result as much of the critical perplexities of an impossible task as of weakness of character. He moved direct, undaunted by any peril, and heartened a whole people to hold steadfast to the end.[46]

The fifth volume of the history, covering the period from 1865 to 1900, is strikingly conservative in approach. Wilson portrayed the railroad strike of 1877 and the Pullman boycott of 1894 as dangerous threats to law and order and commended the use of federal troops to suppress them. He accepted as necessary the removal of the "incubus" of the "ignorant and hostile" Negro vote in the South, even if some of the methods used to effect the disfranchisement were distasteful. Although granting the west coast Chinese the virtues of skill, intelligence, industry, and thrift, he excused the Caucasian laborers who demanded the exclusion of these "Orientals, who, with their yellow skin and strange, debasing, habits of life seemed to them hardly fellow men at all, but evil spirits rather." Wilson expressed fear of the recent hordes of immigrants, "multitudes of men of the lowest class from the south of Italy, and men of the meaner sort out of Hungary and Poland, men out of the ranks where there was neither skill nor energy nor any initiative of given intelligence." Many of these new immigrants "had left their homes dissatisfied not merely with the governments they lived under but with society itself, and . . . had come to America to speak treasons elsewhere forbidden." Wilson was aware of the genuine grievances underlying the Granger, Greenback, and Populist move-

ments, but he deplored their "errors of opinion," especially monetary
inflation, as the product of "crude and ignorant minds." He admired
Bryan's oratorical ability and conceded his sincerity, but regarded his
defeat in 1896 as a deliverance. Grover Cleveland was a hero for
having stood firm against all attempts to tamper with the gold standard.
Wilson had so far abandoned his Gladstonian liberalism as to approve
of the imperialism of 1898:

> A quick instinct apprised American statesmen that they had come to a
> turning point in the progress of the nation, which would have disclosed
> itself in some other way if not in this, had the war for Cuba not made
> it plain. It had turned from developing its own resources to make con-
> quest of the markets of the world. The great East was the market all
> the world coveted now, the market for which statesmen as well as mer-
> chants must plan and play their game of competition, the market to
> which diplomacy, and if need be power, must make an open way. The
> United States could not easily have dispensed with that foothold in the
> East which the possession of the Philippines so unexpectedly afforded them.

Only in the very last sentence of the history is there a suggestion of
the earlier, more progressive Woodrow Wilson who had argued for
state action as a means of improving the lot of the workingman and of
curbing corporate selfishness:

> Statesmen knew that it was to be their task to release the energies of
> the country for the great day of trade and manufacture which was to
> change the face of the world: to ease the processes of labor, govern
> capital in the interest of those who were its indispensable servants in
> pushing the great industries of the country to their final value and per-
> fection, and to make law the instrument, not of justice merely, but also
> of social progress.[47]

The critical reception accorded Wilson's history varied. Although
some general reviewers were ecstatic, the professional historians criticized its omissions, its lack of detail, and the thinness of its scholarship.
In a sardonic review in *The Critic*, George Louis Beer suggested that
Wilson's style derived from his southern background:

> In the South before the war, oratory was practically the sole medium
> of intellectual expression. The essence of successful oratory lies in appeal-
> ing to the emotions, to sentiment, rather than to cold reason. This is a
> fundamental characteristic of Wilson's writings . . . He suggests, rather
> than defines; we gather impressions, not clear-cut conceptions. He gives
> us the atmosphere rather than the sharply drawn general lines. What
> his style lacks is precision; he seems unable to formulate a concept
> concisely. It is a style ill adapted for the treatment of legal institutions
> or of economic questions, but these questions Wilson does not treat in his
> book. It will be apparent that such a style has distinct charm. Its very

vagueness, its tendency toward general rather than specific statements, and the consequent absence of detail make Wilson's work preeminently comprehensible and readable.

In later years Wilson was inclined to side with these critics. In 1909, for instance, he confessed to a southern audience: "I was guilty myself of the indiscretion of writing a history, but I will tell you frankly, if you will not let it go farther, that I wrote it not to instruct anybody else, but to instruct myself. I wrote the history of the United States in order to learn it. That may be an expensive process for other persons who bought the book, but I lived in the United States and my interest in learning their history was, not to remember what happened, but to find out which way we were going."[48]

However Wilson might deprecate his history, he was not in the least averse to having the American public buy it. Even though Harper promoted it by putting out a variety of editions, by extensive advertising, by house-to-house canvassing, and by tying it in with subscriptions to *Harper's Magazine*, Wilson repeatedly badgered the publishers about their performance and eventually attempted to buy back the copyright. Harper refused to sell, and in rebuttal to Wilson's charges wrote that "no history and no literary work of any kind (excluding fiction) of a similar number of words, has brought to the author as great a revenue as your American Nation [sic] has, in the same time." They claimed that no other publishing house could have sold more copies. The royalty reports have disappeared, but according to data in the Woodrow Wilson Papers in the Library of Congress *A History of the American People* earned its author over $40,000 by the time he entered politics in 1910.[49]

Wilson retired from the writing of history in 1902 with no great achievement behind him. None of his three books on American history is read today; in fact, his reputation as a historian would be higher if he had written only *Division and Reunion*. Yet his friends in the historical profession did not despair and kept urging him toward more scholarly work. At least four times J. Franklin Jameson asked Wilson to write for the *American Historical Review;* Wilson always turned him down, finally confessing, "I know you will deem me a churl, but really the thing is impossible, honourable as I should feel to find a place in the *Review* to be. The fact is, that the editors of the popular monthlies offer me such prices nowadays that I am corrupted." In 1902 Albert Bushnell Hart tried to persuade him to do a volume for the "American Nation" series, but Wilson refused on the ground that he must go back to writing about politics.[50]

Happily, Wilson did not leave the field of historical writing before producing one piece that showed how well he could do when he mastered the materials and abandoned the effort to achieve a distinctive literary style. In 1899 Lord Acton asked him to write a chapter on the period 1850-1861 for the volume on the United States in the *Cambridge Modern History*. Wilson accepted and produced a first manuscript in 1900, although the piece was not put into final form until 1902, the same year as his history, and the volume in which it appeared was not published until 1907. The editors of the *Cambridge Modern History* liked the work so much that they asked Wilson for three more chapters covering the period 1789-1850, but he refused and J. B. McMaster wrote them in his stead.[51]

"State Rights, 1850-1861," an essay of about 20,000 words, had none of the carelessness or the stylistic mannerism that marred *George Washington* and *A History of the American People*. Wilson still maintained the opinions advanced in *Division and Reunion* as to the mischievousness of the antislavery crusade, the legal correctness of the southern position on states' rights and secession, and the lot of the Negro, but his theories were now expressed with far more precision, with due qualification, and with adequate factual support. The essay closed with this just and eloquent passage about the Civil War:

> For the whole country it was to be the bitterest of all ordeals, an agony of struggle and decision by blood: but for one party it was to be a war of hope. Should the South win she must also lose—must lose her place in the great Union she had loved and fostered, and must in gaining independence destroy a nation. Should the North win, she would confirm a great hope and expectation, establish the Union, unify it in institutions, free it from interior contradictions of life and principle, set it in the way of consistent growth and unembarrassed greatness. The South fought for a principle as the North did: it was this that was to give the war dignity and supply the tragedy with a double motive. But the principle for which the South fought meant standstill in the midst of change; it was conservative, not creative; it was against drift and destiny; it protected an impossible institution and a belated order of society; it withstood a creative and imperial idea, the idea of a united people and a single law of freedom. Overwhelming material superiority, as it turned out, was with the North; but she had also a greater advantage; she was to fight for the Union and for the abiding peace, concord, and strength of a great nation.[52]

As this passage makes manifest, Wilson's study of history helped to make an American of one who in a sense had started life as an alien in his own country—half unrepentant Southerner and half transplanted Britisher. It completed a process of which the first explicit evidence appeared when he had the courage to tell an audience at the University of Virginia that he rejoiced that the South had lost the Civil War. He had substituted Lincoln for Gladstone as his hero and had accepted the principles of Lincoln as superior to those defended by the South. Furthermore, his historical studies, like his public lecturing, eventually helped to make Wilson a more effective politician, able to vary his approach in different parts of the country and at the same time communicate with the people as a whole.

In 1904 Wilson was asked to speak before the Historical Science section of the Congress of Arts and Science held at the great St. Louis Exposition. In an address entitled "The Variety and Unity of History" he attempted a synoptic view of the discipline. He now freely admitted that historians were immensely indebted to the specialists for the richness and complexity of the materials they had brought to light. The problem was how to produce a synthesis in which the labors of the specialist and the general historian would be combined.[53]

Wilson rejected one approach to this problem, represented by H. D. Traill's *Social England* and the *Cambridge Modern History*, in which monographs by a variety of authors were fitted into an over-all scheme. These were laudable, but there was "no whole cloth, no close texture," along with too many repetitions and omissions. The answer, according to Wilson was to train a new generation of historians, who in their higher studies should receive training in both generalization and specialization. Graduate students should first be put to studying the larger picture so that they might "become accustomed to view the life of man in society as a whole." Only after such training should they attempt "new collections of fact."

Wilson's essay "On the Writing of History," published only a decade before, had been shallow, partisan, and "literary" in a pejorative sense. But this St. Louis address was remarkable for its sophistication, moderation, and controlled eloquence. It is full of sound sense and might be published as a tract for the times today. It marked as much of an advance in Wilson's conception of history as his essay on "State Rights" for the *Cambridge Modern History* had marked progress in the discipline itself.

After writing a succession of potboilers, Wilson finally gave promise of becoming a worthy member of the historical guild. He had also achieved a new identity with America. And yet, one may ask, was it worth it? Was it not unfortunate that he poured out his slender store of energy on ephemeral tasks for which he was ill prepared and which he undertook principally because he needed money? The time spent

in producing sentimental essays and history books now unread and almost unreadable was time taken away from "The Philosophy of Politics," a work for which he was far better prepared by long familiarity
with the field, by scholarly training, and by inclination.

XIII

Unfinished Business:
"The Philosophy of Politics"

Long talk with Professor Woodrow Wilson about recent development in
"congressional government." Attractive-minded man—something like a young
John Morley—literary in language, with a peculiarly un-American insight
into the actual workings of institutions as distinguished from their nominal
constitution.

Beatrice Webb, 1898[1]

EVEN THOUGH most of his
published writings during the years of his professorship at Princeton
were in the field of history, Wilson never abandoned his intention to
write "The Philosophy of Politics," the book that was to make manifest
the dynamics of the modern state. Why he felt fitted for the task and
how high his ambition reached are shown by this passage in a private
journal, written in 1889:

If slow development is an intention and promise of long life, I may
certainly expect length of days sufficient for the accomplishment of all I
have planned to do. I have come slowly into possession of such powers as
I have, not only, but also into consciousness of them, into the ability to
estimate them with just insight. Now that I am getting well into the
thirties I begin to see my place in the general order of things . . .
The phrase that Bagehot uses to describe the successful constitutional
statesman I might appropriate to describe myself: "A man with common
opinions but uncommon ability." I *receive* the opinions *of others* of the
day, I do not *conceive* them. But I receive them with a vivid mind,
with a quick imagination, and a power to see as a whole the long genesis
of the opinions received. I have little impatience with existing conditions;
I comprehend too perfectly how they came to exist, how natural they
are. I have great confidence in progress and am conscious of a persistent
push behind the present order.
It was in keeping with my whole mental make-up, therefore, and in

255

obedience to a true instinct, that I chose to put forth my chief strength in the history and interpretation of institutions, and chose as my chief ambition the historical explanation of the modern democratic state as a basis for the discussion of political progress, political expediency, political morality, political prejudice, practical politics, &c. It is a task not of origination, but of interpretation. Interpret the age: i.e. interpret myself. Account for the creed I hold in politics. Institutions have their rootage in the common thought and only those who share the common thought can rightly interpret them. No man can appreciate a parliament who would not make a useful member of it (e.g. Carlyle). No one can give an account of anything of which he is not tolerant. I find myself exceedingly tolerant of all institutions, past and present, by reason of a keen appreciation of their reason for being—*most* tolerant, so to say, of the institutions of my own day which seem to me, in an historical sense, intensely and essentially reasonable, though of course in no sense *final*. Why may not the present age write, *through* me, its political *autobiography?*[2]

Having performed the drudgery of writing *The State* principally to prepare himself for the great work that would crown his professional career, Wilson then undertook to clear potential rivals from his path. In 1889, as we have seen, he found that James Bryce's *The American Commonwealth* fell short of the highest excellence. In 1891 he dealt harshly with two other competitors: Henry Sidgwick's *The Elements of Politics* and John W. Burgess' *Political Science and Comparative Constitutional Law*. Writing for *The Dial* Wilson found Sidgwick's book deficient in historical sense: it took little account of the individuality, prepossessions, enthusiasms, and antipathies that make a nation unique and alive. "The study of politics," he asserted, "should not be a study of comparative anatomy—the State is not a cadaver."

When asked by Horace Scudder to review Burgess' book for the *Atlantic Monthly*, Wilson at first demurred. "I shall open the book," he wrote Scudder, "expecting to find a great deal to disagree with and criticize, and I suppose that that is a frame of mind which would make my purpose to be impartial . . . rather awkward to carry out." Swallowing his qualms, he did write the review, in a way that may explain the bitterness of Burgess' subsequent attack on Wilson's interpretation of the Civil War. Although granting Burgess' work the negative virtues of clarity of organization and argument, Wilson questioned the author's qualifications for writing about politics at all. "He has strong powers of reasoning," Wilson wrote, "but he has not the gift of insight. This is why he is so good at logical analysis, and so poor at the interpretation of history. This is why what he says appears to have a certain stiff, mechanical character, lacking flexibility and vitality." Worst of all, Burgess wrote not "in the language of literature, but in the language of

science," using words as counters and constructing sentences "upon
the homeliest principles of grammatical joinery." Failing to write
literature, the makers of such books also failed to write truth. For
truth demanded awareness of human life in all its strange mixture of
opinion, prejudice, whim, ignorance, impulse, and circumstance.[3]

Through insight and literary skill, Wilson hoped to penetrate and reveal the life of politics. He therefore pleaded that the public give heed
to the literary politician, exemplified by such men as Bagehot: "The
literary politician . . . stands apart and looks on, with humorous
sympathetic smile at the play of policies. He will tell you for the asking
what the players are thinking about. He divines at once how the parts
are cast. He knows beforehand what each act is to discover. He might
readily guess what the dialogue is to contain. Were you short of
scene-shifters, he could serve you admirably in any emergency. And he
is a better critic of the play than the players."[4]

Yet after preparing the ground so carefully, Wilson was never able
to complete "The Philosophy of Politics." Throughout his years as a
professor he worked at the task intermittently. Among his papers in the
Library of Congress is evidence of one beginning after another. There
is, for instance, a copybook of 142 pages carefully numbered in pencil
but containing only chapter headings on the inside cover and two pages
of notes. Another notebook contains odd jottings, quotations, a worked-
over introduction, and several ideas for organization, along with possible titles and subtitles—"THE STATE, OBJECT LESSONS IN POLITICS";
"STATESMANSHIP, Studies in Politics"; "THE LIFE OF STATES, The Idea of
the State as affected by *Modern Political Conditions*"; "MODERN POLI-
TICS, Studies in Political Philosophy"; and "The Strings of Life—the
Law Within the Law." There are manila envelopes labeled with such
titles as "City Gov't" and "The Modern Democratic State: Its Ends and
Functions," which contain scraps of text, lecture notes, odd notes, and
queries, such as "What effect may railroads (all the instrumentalities
which make populations movable and detach from local connections
and attachments) be expected to have on local self-govt., and in producing nationality?" or "Must not a philosophy of politics, being a
philosophy of men in the masses, be a philosophy of the obvious?" The
envelopes also contain projected tables of contents, of which this is the
most complete:

 I. The Life of States:
    (1) History of States
    (2) Their nature
    (3) Their structure
    (4) Their ends and functions.

II. Political Stability: The Nature, Sources, and Functions of Law.
III. Political Liberty (Obedience to the laws of the social organism).
IV. Political Privilege (The selection of those prepared to rule).
V. Political Progress (Modification by experience. The function of authority).
VI. Political Prejudice (the statical [sic] force of opinion).
VII. Political Expedience (Political Therapeutics).
VIII. Political Morality (Obedience to the laws of political progress).
IX. Practical Politics (The use of political means).[5]

One gets the impression from this olla-podrida of false starts that Wilson was up against a task from which he instinctively drew back. He may have set his sights too high. In history he could excuse a failure by admitting that after all he was not a historian. But in political science—or "politics," as he preferred to call it—he was a professional. Whereas his background in history was sketchy, in politics he had mastered the scholarly literature of the day, in French and German as well as in English, and had kept up with it from year to year. It was in this area that he lectured, both to undergraduates at Princeton and to graduate students at Johns Hopkins, and was known at home and abroad. His ambition to write a great work on politics was of a higher order than his hope to write good history, but in this his chosen field his powers of self-criticism were also stronger.

Wilson left enough evidence so that a person familiar with his writings can gain an idea of some probable themes of the unfinished opus. They may be inferred not only from scattered memoranda but also from lecture notes and fugitive writings published during the dozen years that he was a professor at Princeton.*

Wilson's central preoccupation in the 1890's was what he called "the Modern Democratic State," which he regarded as the highest stage of human political evolution. In his essay "Character of Democracy in the United States," published in 1889, he had considered democracy in the United States as merely an offshoot of institutions developed by the English, a "specialized species of English government." But by 1901 he had come to view it as something both unique in itself and prophetic for the future of mankind:

This history of the United States is modern history in broad and open analysis, stripped of a thousand elements which, upon the European stage, confuse the eye and lead the judgment astray . . . There is here

---

* Just as this book was going to press, I heard that a first draft of "The Philosophy of Politics" had been found and will be published in a forthcoming volume of *The Papers of Woodrow Wilson*. It will be interesting to see how closely the actual text of "The Philosophy of Politics" parallels this modest attempt to hypothecate it.

the best possible point of departure, for the student who can keep his head and knows his European history as intimately as he knows his American, for a comparative study of politics which shall forever put out of school the thin and sentimental theories of the disciples of Rousseau.

It is an offshoot of European history and yet it is so much more than a mere offshoot. Its processes are so freshened and clarified, its resources are so abundant and accessible, it is spread upon so wide, so open, so visible, a field of observation, that it seems like a plain first chapter in the history of a new age. As a stage in the economic development of modern civilization, the history of America constitutes the natural, and invaluable, subject-matter and book of praxis of the political economist. Here is industrial development worked out with incomparable, logical swiftness, simplicity and precision—a swiftness, simplicity and precision impossible against the rigid social order of any ancient kingdom. It is a study, moreover, not merely of the make-up and setting forth of a new people, but also of its marvelous expansion of processes of growth, hurried forward from stage to stage as if under the experimental touch of some social philosopher, some political scientist making of a nation's history his laboratory and place of demonstration.[6]

A key phrase is "processes of growth." Wilson regarded political development as closely analogous to biological evolution, and political institutions as the product of economic and social necessities. Law, he told his students, "is a growth and the result of growth. It is the growth of society recorded in institutions and practices." One of the principal reasons Wilson now praised American democracy, where once he had feared it, was that he saw it as the completest development of an inexorable process.[7]

Wilson called democracy "unquestionably the most wholesome and livable kind of government the world has yet tried." In the United States it was no longer in danger of following the Aristotelian cycle and degenerating into tyranny because it was "not the rule of the many, but the rule of the *whole* . . . for the rule of the majority implies and is dependent upon the cooperation, be it active or passive, of the minority." In ancient democracies there was always "a substratic, non-citizen class which often proved a sleeping volcano," but there was no such threat in modern American democracy because of "its entire openness to criticism by all, and its possible conduct by all,—the absence of distance, exclusiveness or mystery about it." It gained strength because the press and other vehicles of public opinion were not in opposition to government but participated in it. The strongest justification for such a democracy was moral: "It is for this that we love democracy: for the emphasis it puts on character; for its tendency to exalt the purposes of the average man to some high level of endeavor; for its principle of common assent in matters in which all are interested; for its ideals of duty and its sense of brotherhood."[8]

However, viewing the world at large, Wilson feared that democracy would be a long time developing, even though he saw "tendencies toward a common governmental type, and that type the American." So few peoples were ready for them that democratic institutions were discredited as often as they were admired. "Their eccentric influence in France, their disastrous and revolutionary operation in South America, their power to intoxicate and powerlessness to reform . . . have generally been deemed to offset every triumph or success they can boast." Doubt of the capacity of most races to govern themselves without a long period of tutelage led Wilson to the apparently paradoxical position of accepting the new imperial position of the United States in the Philippines and Puerto Rico as a means of promoting democracy. "It is our peculiar duty," he wrote, "as it is also England's . . . to impart to the people thus driven out upon the road of change, so far as we have opportunity, or can make it, our own principles of self-help; teach them order and self-control in the midst of change; impart to them, if it be possible, by contact and sympathy, and example, the drill and habit of law and obedience which we long ago got out of the strenuous processes of English history."⁹

A former Princeton colleague once wrote of Wilson, "He was intellectually a devout disciple of democracy. But he learned by the tuitions of his mind and not of his heart." Too reserved and too conscious of his own intellectual superiority to be a democrat in spirit, Wilson had to come by slow stages to accept democracy as an inexorable fact of life in the modern world, and to see it as beneficent. He had strong doubts whether it could be successfully practiced outside of the English-speaking world, except in pockets like Switzerland. For years he taught his classes that a homogeneous population was a precondition of successful constitutional government. This was the reason he feared the influx into the United States of new immigrants from southern and eastern Europe, whom he considered inferior. By the same token he acquiesced in the disfranchisement of the Negro Southerner. But eventually he came to the conclusion that even with a mingling of races a democratic nation could be formed—with certain provisos:

It is noteworthy that a common national character can be imparted to a vast and heterogeneous population, drawn, like our own, from almost all the races of the civilized world, provided
(1) Differences of language be eliminated and conducting media for thought, principle, ideals be provided.
(2) A vital common life exist, which will untie classes by freeing individuals; by keeping economic channels open upon equitable conditions to all; and by organizing political action in the common interest and upon a true cooperative principle.

(3) Leadership be of the truly organizing and transforming sort, preserving and propagating and illustrating the best ideals and traditions.

(4) A system of education (pedagogic or other) lead the mind of each generation along substantially the same road of knowledge and memory and training.[10]

In the second proviso Wilson spoke of keeping "economic channels open upon equitable conditions to all." He did not think that equality of economic opportunity would happen automatically. It would require state action. Although his tone was conservative, although he derided "impractical reformers" and "sentimentalists" who seized on small ills and exaggerated them, although he cast scorn on the Populists and repudiated Socialism—he nevertheless explicitly argued that the state was a positive good and not a necessary evil. This point of view appears in his lecture notes and his notes for "The Philosophy of Politics" again and again. Here are a few examples:

The State is neither a mere necessity nor a mere convenience, but an abiding natural relationship; the invariable and normal embodiment and expression of a higher form of life than the individual: of that common life which gives leave to the individual life; and opportunity for completeness: makes it possible; makes it full and complete: makes it spiritual.

Misconception That government is a necessary evil, and that Liberty consists of having as little of it as possible. The State is a higher form of life than the individual.

Omnipotence of govt. is the first postulate of law. Socialistic measures: minute restrictions upon bequests, confiscation of land, &c., though revolutionary *as policy* would not be revolutionary as being governmental usurpation. The govt. can do all it will—if it dare. What else is eminent domain?[11]

The positive state by its very nature imposes limitations on personal liberty, as Wilson made explicit. He distrusted the notion of abstract liberty—it smacked too much of the French Revolution. It was, he thought, "a word of enthusiasm,—adventure,—heroism,—romance. A word also of license and folly, stained with bloodshed and crime." He wrote that it was "a fundamental error" to imagine liberty "to consist of as little government as possible, and [to conceive] of scientific anarchy as its ideal." Liberty can only exist where there is law and power to enforce it; it is tied to order and adjustment: "LIBERTY is to be found *only where there is the best order.* The *machine* free that runs with perfect adjustment; the *skein* free that is without tangle; the *man* free whose powers are without impediment to their best development."[12]

By what criteria is one to determine the limits of state and individual action? Wilson answered by reference to "the great English doctrine of Expediency." "Expediency" (or "expedience"), one of his favorite words, had more than one meaning. Occasionally he used it in the pejorative sense of short-sighted action taken to accomplish an immediate purpose, but much more often he described it as a positive good: "Expediency is the first, second, and last criterion of the excellence either of constitutional provision or of statute: and that nation, and that only, is capable of self-government which is capable of self-restraint to do nothing but that which is expedient. This is political wisdom, political balance, political self-direction." The concept was connected in his mind with the Burkean idea of orderly change. "Progress," said Wilson, "may perhaps be accepted as at any rate the ultimate object of all political action." Expediency was a technique of progress, the means whereby the state adapted to social and political change. It involved due regard for accidents of time, place, circumstance, and culture. It meant dealing with practical situations without stubborn adherence to principle. "Politics must follow the actual windings of the channel of the river: if it steers by the stars it will run aground." Expediency rejected revolution as destroying "the atmosphere of opinion and purpose which holds institutions to their form and equilibrium." It welcomed compromise, expecting no more than half a loaf. A characteristic definition appeared in Wilson's first inaugural address as President of the United States: "We shall deal with our economic system as it is and as it may be modified, not as it might be as if we had a clean sheet of paper to write upon." So defined, expediency became what Theodore Roosevelt called "the art of the possible," awareness of limitations. As Wilson put it, "It is the discovery of what they can *not* do . . . that transforms reformers into statesmen; and great should be the joy of the world over every reformer who comes to himself."[13]

Wilson taught his classes at Princeton that there were two moralities, one individual and one social, with quite different rules:

(1) Individual Ethics are not based upon *expediency*—they are based upon some absolute standard of right and wrong. Individual ethics are based upon the relationship between God and man. Principle of morals is the principle of self-abnegation, not that of the survival of the fittest.

(2) Social Ethics—Each individual must give up some point in his own view in order to make a compromise, in order that any body of men may agree. In bettering society, all of society including the great majority of ignorance, must be advanced. The *impracticable* man who will not compromise, may be right according to *individual ethics*, yet he is no use whatever to society. Practicality is the law of social amelioration.[14]

Personal sin was the violation of God's commandments, whereas "*Political Sin* is the transgression of the law of political progress."

Wilson was aware of, but undisturbed by, the fact that the two might conflict. In a lecture series in Philadelphia in 1895 he included Machiavelli as one of six "Leaders of Political Thought." Machiavelli, he told his audience, was "not so bad a man as he has been painted." The Florentine's great contribution to mankind was to erect statecraft into "a distinct science, unencumbered by ethical considerations." He erred in leaving morality out of his calculations and having regard only to craft and courage, but "his purpose and ideal were nevertheless exalted. His lifelong effort was to give Italy national freedom and an ordered and beneficent government." Here was the same Wilson who as a young man had admired that master of Machiavellian *Realpolitik,* Bismarck.[15]

Although Wilson accepted democracy, he thought that to be successful it must be indirect. The people may, and should, select, observe, and criticize their rulers, but they themselves could not carry on government. "Properly organized democracy," wrote Wilson, "is the best government of the few." It is not for the people to govern but to elect the governors, "and these governors should be elected for periods long enough to give time for policies not too heedful of the transient breezes of public opinion." Wilson strongly rejected both the initiative and the referendum as likely to encourage the "nuisance" of demagogues and "professional reformers" and to discourage and discredit the independent judgment of popular leaders. Even on the gravest questions, which touched every citizen, Wilson trusted the judgment of the leaders before that of the people themselves. In his "Philosophy of Politics" notes he observed:

It is asked . . . whether direct expressions of the will of the people be not the only just way of determining some of the graver questions of state policy, as, for instance, the question of peace and war. On the contrary is it not a pertinent suggestion that such questions may involve elements visible or appreciable only by the few—the selected leaders of public opinion and rulers of state policy. Only to them will it be apparent upon which side lies obedience to the highest, most permanent and just ends of the nation. Only to them may it be revealed what these ends are. The many might vote blindly or selfishly. Merchants will be opposed to the disturbance of trade; agriculturalists to the interruption of crops, some to the incurring of national danger, all to risk and expense. The popular vote would probably have drawn us into the vortex of the French revolution, would doubtless have held us back from the second assertion of our rights against Great Britain. And, as regards other questions, are not the straight lines—the projected course—of national progress more likely to be seen by the thinking few who stand upon the high places of the nation than by the toiling multitudes in the valleys who give no part of their day to so much as an endeavour to descry these things? Must not the nation have trained eyes?[16]

Because of his belief in the vital importance of leadership in a democracy, Wilson returned repeatedly to the problem of organizing government so that it would offer an attractive career for trained leaders, by focusing public attention upon them, by leaving them free to act, and by giving them scope to educate the public about issues. At the same time he was at pains, as his notes show, to allay fear of demagoguery:

It is common to charge democracy with creating demagogy. The charge is indiscriminating. If democracy is in opposition then demagogues have their golden chance. If there be a contest between the powers that be and the people demanding to be themselves instated in the seat of govt. then indeed the demagogue may sow and reap a very harvest of stormy power. The men who led the plebeians in ancient Rome, the Jacobite orators who harangued in the clubs of Paris, the men who fomented the Chartist disturbances in England furnished types of the true demagogue—the impudent, brawling fellow who is loud and indiscriminate in his denunciations of all who may be honoured for name or place, or violent in his attacks upon all established order, base in his interest to the sordid interest and low passion . . .

If democracy is 'in power' such fellows must look to themselves. The power of those who lead the people has only to be made the real power of responsible political rule, bringing upon them the centered trust, and therefore, the concentrated gaze of the nation, in the conduct of public affairs, to prove the demagogue's leaden weight to drown him.[17]

In much of what he wrote about leadership Wilson traversed familiar ground. For instance, in an address before the Virginia Bar Association in 1897 entitled "Leaderless Government" he brought up to date what he had written in *Congressional Government* about the fractionalization of power in the federal government and the irresponsibility, indirection, and inefficiency that resulted. He urged some way whereby the President, speaking for the nation, could be given authoritative power to initiate legislation so that Congress would not be at the mercy of local interests.[18]

The most important change in Wilson's attitude toward American politics was his discovery of the actual power of the presidency. In his earlier writings, notably *Congressional Government,* he had portrayed the President as a rather shadowy, ineffectual figure, distinctly subordinate to Congress. Then through his study of American history he came to realize that the presidency in the hands of a Jackson or a Lincoln was quite different from what it had been in his early manhood, during the administrations of Grant, Hayes, Garfield, and Arthur. The career of Grover Cleveland first induced him to revise his opinion. In an article in the *Atlantic Monthly* in March 1897, entitled "Mr. Cleveland as President," Wilson wrote that Cleveland had "refreshed our notion of the American chief magistrate." Cleveland had shown that "the President stands at the center of legislation as well as of administration in executing his great office" and that with a strong-minded President, willing to take the initiative, power might go the length of Pennsylvania Avenue and lodge in one man instead of in the many-headed Congress.[19]

Another political scientist to make note of the potential power of the presidential office was Henry Jones Ford, who in *The Rise and Growth of American Politics,* published in 1898, presented the thesis that an increase in presidential power was both an inevitable process and a return to the ancient Teutonic tradition of elective monarchs. Wilson admired Ford's work, introduced it as required reading in his course in politics, at Princeton, and in 1908 brought Ford to Princeton as a professor of politics.[20]

With the Spanish-American War and the great expansion of overseas commitments of the United States there came, as Wilson noted, a still further accretion of presidential power. The wheel had come full circle, back to the early days of the republic. "For the first twenty-six years that we lived under our federal constitution," wrote Wilson, "foreign affairs, the sentiment and policy of nations oversea, dominated our politics, and our Presidents were our leaders. And now the same thing has come about again. Once more it is our place among the nations that we think of; once more our Presidents are our leaders."[21]

In considering the need for leadership and the proper organization to improve its recruitment and operation, Wilson did not limit his attention to Washington. As his lectures at Johns Hopkins showed, he was a keen student of local government. He deplored archaic arrangements, such as the multiplicity of elective offices with short terms, that attracted only "petty men of no ambition, without hope or fitness for advancement." He discussed with his classes in constitutional government at Princeton how trained intelligence could be put to work in a permanent civil service for matters involving technical skill, while other matters could be left in the hands of untrained administrators chosen from the people at large. He never quite resolved the conflict between his long-time admiration for an unpaid civil service like the English justices of the peace, which meant that men of wealth must run the government, and the necessity in a democracy of admitting "individuals of every class . . . to the competition without regard to social standing or derivation," which meant that administrators must be paid. Here, as elsewhere, he was a hesitant democrat.[22]

For his courses in politics at Princeton Wilson attempted to define the qualities that the leader in a democracy should possess:

Common Elements [of leadership]: Ordinary ideas, extraordinary abilities (W. Bagehot) The habitual ideas of the governing group or class or of the existing task as performed in the past, and a power of effective presentation, progressive modification, a power to conceive and execute the next forward step, and to organize the force of the State for the movement.

This, upon analysis, presupposes
                    The sensitive,
                        the conceiving and interpreting,
                            the initiative mind
with the addition of will power or of such subtle persistency as will put strong wills at the disposal of the managing intellect.[23]

Wilson was soon to have the opportunity to discover whether he possessed these faculties. With his election as President of Princeton in 1902 he became at last a leader instead of a student of leadership. It may be regretted that he never finished "The Philosophy of Politics," since he was so obviously better fitted to write effectively in his chosen field than in history or belles lettres. His close, realistic, and continuous observation of the actualities of politics was not wasted, however; it went far to explain his later success after he was suddenly catapulted into the political arena with his nomination for the governorship of New Jersey in 1910. The years of study that were intended to fit a literary politician for authorship helped to prepare an active politician for office.

Part Three: College President

XIV

Call to Power

I find, now that I get a certain remove, that my election to the presidency has done a very helpful thing for me. It has settled the future for me and given me a sense of *position* and of definite, tangible tasks which takes the flutter of restlessness from my spirits.

—Woodrow Wilson, 1902[1]

IT HAD BEEN generally understood that Princeton's Sesquicentennial Celebration of 1896 was to be the prelude to higher standards, improvement in the faculty, and the creation of a graduate school of liberal arts and perhaps a law school and a medical school. But although the number of undergraduates increased and the physical plant continued to grow, with the building of a library, dormitories, and a gymnasium, all in Gothic style, there was little progress elsewhere. Five years later, over 90 percent of the students were undergraduates, and of the 117 graduate students the majority were part-time "Seminoles," whose principal occupation was studying for the Presbyterian ministry at the Princeton Theological Seminary. There were no professional schools except for an undergraduate school of engineering and a graduate school of electrical engineering attended by five students. Princeton remained an overgrown and ingrown country college, not seriously regarded in the academic world.[2]

President Patton was blamed for the stagnation, with ample reason. He was by all accounts "a wonderfully poor administrator," incompetent and dilatory in matters of detail, unwilling to take initiative in large matters of policy or to try to raise money for Princeton's obvious needs. He was too soft-hearted to ask for the retirement of superannuated professors. When new appointments were made, they were apt to be drawn from the narrow circle of Princeton alumni; there was sometimes "outrageous nepotism, with jobs given to the sons, relatives, or friends of the right people." In matters of discipline the Patton administration was indecisive, with the result that there was hazing and general rowdiness. Dr. Patton was frankly indifferent to raising academic standards, because he thought most undergraduates incapable of serious work. The slackness of the Patton regime helped to create two peculiar situations upon which Woodrow Wilson's administration later foundered: the special position of Dean West as head of the Graduate School, and the proliferation of undergraduate eating clubs of an unusual character.[3]

Since Patton had committed himself in 1896 to promoting an enlarged graduate school with a separate building to house it, the Trustees appointed a "Special Committee on the Graduate College" in 1897, but after two years of making no progress it became so discouraged with Patton's lack of support that it asked to be discharged. A different method of advancing the project was resorted to in 1900, when a separate graduate school was created under its own dean. Since little initiative was to be expected from the President of the University, the Dean of the Graduate School was made directly responsible to the Trustees and was granted extraordinary powers. He had charge of courses, admissions, and the award of fellowships and degrees. He chose his own Graduate School committee from the University faculty. Thus, the Graduate School became autonomous, an *imperium in imperio*.[4]

As Dean of the Graduate School the Trustees appointed Andrew Fleming West, Giger Professor of Latin. Son of a Presbyterian minister and a graduate of Princeton in 1874, West had joined the Princeton faculty in the closing years of the McCosh era. He was an effective teacher, who made his subject come alive. His special field was the Middle Ages, and he wrote a study of Alcuin as an educator that was well regarded. It was not because of his teaching or his scholarship, however, that West had become by 1900 one of the three most highly paid men on the Princeton faculty, but because of his abilities as a money-raiser and organizer. At the time of the Princeton Sesquicentennial he was excused from teaching to act as secretary of the Committee on Endowment and the Celebration Committee. In both capacities he was successful: Princeton's endowment was more than doubled, and the Sesquicentennial Celebration was probably the finest academic pageant that the United States had yet seen.[5]

In his various capacities West gained the admiration of men of wealth and power. It was he who persuaded Grover Cleveland to attend the Sesquicentennial, and Cleveland became so charmed with Princeton in general and West in particular that he settled in the village after retiring from the presidency and named his home "Westland." Another close friend was Junius S. Morgan of the banking family, a former student. At the time of the Sesquicentennial Morgan gave the University a Vergil collection valued at $50,000. In 1898 he built a mansion in Princeton and became an unpaid associate librarian in charge of the classical collections. Still another intimate was the powerful and wealthy trustee Moses Taylor Pyne, whose family gave the Pyne Library in 1896.

West was a big man, with a barrel chest and florid complexion. He had a genial manner and almost hypnotic charm: a characteristic gesture was to clap his arm around another man's shoulders. "Andy Three million West, sixty-three inches around the chest," as the faculty song described him, was generally popular with undergraduates, although a few thought he played favorites and cut too many classes.[6]

Early in his career West suffered a terrible blow when his wife went permanently insane after the birth of their only son. It may have been this affliction that made him unusually sympathetic to those in distress. He gave generously in time and effort to help people in trouble, as when he took into his home a critically ill colleague, along with his wife and child. Perhaps to compensate for his unhappy personal circumstances, he dined out a great deal and kept an excellent table. He was a delightful conversationalist, whose talent for light, sometimes slightly malicious verse was appreciated by his colleagues. Still other features that made him a pervasive influence in the Princeton community were that he spoke well in public, worked diligently, and was devoted to Princeton. He had the reputation of being a consummate academic politician, who could work behind the scenes and cover his tracks.

Although West's original contributions to scholarship ended with the Princeton Sesquicentennial, no one on the Princeton faculty was more desirous of raising standards for both undergraduates and graduate students. At his insistence the faculty passed a series of recommendations regarding graduate work that are as relevant today as when they were written. More industry and accumulation of knowledge was not enough: a graduate student was expected to display independent scholarly judgment and to distinguish between what was important and what was of less relevance. West was not content with attempting to train graduate students; he wanted to civilize them. Rejecting the Germanic tradition of impersonal *Wissenschaft* that dominated much American graduate work, he—like Wilson—turned to England for inspiration. His dream was to create a graduate college resembling those at Oxford and Cambridge, equipped with Gothic quadrangles, gardens, comfortable rooms with fireplaces, and a great dining hall. When West asked a faculty wife to characterize him in one word, she is reported to have said, "Dean West, I should say you are a very *monumental man*." He was determined that his monument should be a many-spired Gothic college with himself as master, presiding over the high table and intoning Latin graces before meals.[7]

The latter years of the Patton administration saw a rapid change in the atmosphere of Princeton, both on campus and in town. In the early nineties Princeton was still an isolated, self-contained village, with most of its houses near Nassau Street, the main thoroughfare. Fields of grain stretched outside the windows of the house that the Wilsons rented in 1890. Then the metropolitan invasion began. Very wealthy men, such as Moses Taylor Pyne, bought or built mansions on the outskirts of the village, and somewhat less affluent men bought dwellings in town. Of the house and stables that Junius Morgan was building in 1898 it was remarked, "That is not a house, but a civilization." More and more the old simplicity of life, in which the faculties of the College of New Jersey and the Princeton Theological Seminary had set the tone, gave way to suburbia.[8]

A corresponding change took place among the undergraduates. In the early nineties Princeton students boasted of the democracy of Old Nassau, where a man was judged by worth, not birth, where a miner's son might be elected captain of the football team, and where every member of a college class was ipso facto deemed the blood brother of every other. The standard undergraduate costume, a black jersey and corduroy trousers, minimized differences of wealth and background. Princeton was so closely identified with Presbyterianism that the outside world tended to confuse the college and the theological seminary. But around the turn of the century there came an increasing influx of boys of wealth from private preparatory schools, such as the Hill, Lawrenceville, Andover, Exeter, and St. Paul's. In less than a decade the proportion of Presbyterians among the undergraduates dropped from two-thirds to less than one-half; the number of Episcopalians doubled, and President Patton was heard to boast that he was head of the finest country club in America.[9]

These changes were accompanied by the development of a system of upperclass clubs that eventually dominated undergraduate social life. Formerly students "ate around" at boarding houses like Mrs. Wright's, where Wilson had taken meals during his freshman and sophomore years, or small, evanescent clubs like the Alligators, to which he had later belonged. But starting with the Ivy Club, founded in 1879, and then the University Cottage Club, founded in 1887, permanent eating clubs appeared. They were limited to the two upper classes, and they owned their own houses, which clustered along Prospect Street running east from the campus. As time went on, the clubs attracted strong alumni support; indeed, their houses were often designed to serve as dormitories for returning old grads.

Up to about 1895, when there were only five clubs taking in less than a third of any one class, the clubs had little effect on the general current of undergraduate life. Many prominent undergraduates did not join them, and the debating societies, Whig and Clio, still retained something of their former glory. But between 1895 and 1902 clubs proliferated, until by the close of Patton's administration there were eleven, taking in more than half of each class. To many students, joining a club —and not just any one but the right one—became all-important. In his autobiography, *The Bridge,* Ernest Poole told how he felt when he heard he had been blackballed by one of the four top clubs: "The news came like a thunderbolt. With a cold, sick feeling the bottom dropped out of my college life."[10]

In addition to the upper-class clubs, sophomore clubs appeared in the late nineties, formed for the purpose of getting their members into the higher clubs en bloc. Since faculty regulations prevented them from becoming permanent organizations, they changed their names every year but kept distinctive headgear, from which they came to be known as the "dark blue hats," the "red hats," the "green hats," and so forth. Further down the line were freshman clubs, whose members aspired to the right of succession to the sophomore clubs. These were known as "followings."

No longer were undergraduates indistinguishable from each other in their attire. The clubmen now wore distinctive insignia, so that at a glance one could tell whether a man was "clubable" or not and, if clubable, just where in the hierarchy he stood. No longer did seniors indicate in class polls, as they did until 1899, that they admired Princeton most because of its democratic spirit.[11]

These developments did not go unnoticed. Concern was expressed that the social clubs were killing interest in Whig and Clio. The *Princeton Alumni Weekly* voiced dismay at the system for promoting cliques and destroying spontaneity. Those who gained admission had merely shown foresight in choice of associates; those who failed to get in were branded as "queer, unlikable, and non-clubable." "It is a perplexing situation," opined the *Weekly,* "and some day it is going to cause us trouble." But it was hard to know what to do, and the Patton administration characteristically did nothing. Dean Samuel Ross Winans, whose reports to the Princeton Trustees were a continuing catalogue of disorders that the college authorities were unable to control, deplored the costliness of the clubs, their antidemocratic tendency, and the unhappy situation of those not elected, but he saw no solution.[12]

A wit of the time compared Harvard (because of its elective system) to a dinner *à la carte,* Yale to a *table d'hôte,* Columbia (because one could graduate in three years) to a quick lunch, and Princeton to a picnic. Although the faculty contained some first-rate scholars and devoted teachers, loafing was all too easy at Princeton. During the first two years of required courses the undergraduates had to work with a degree of regularity, but in the upper-class years there were several elective courses "of little substance, no system, and feeble standards." Less serious students "tended to exploit this situation and actually established a fashion according to which it was bad form to elect courses that required work." When a few bold professors attempted to enforce higher standards, "they found themselves confronted with empty benches."[13]

Princeton was especially weak in science. The John C. Green School of Science was regarded by the scientific fraternity as something between a joke and a scandal. The equipment was scanty and the curriculum archaic: undergraduate candidates for the B.S. degree were not permitted, for instance, to study physics until their junior year. The School of Science was supported almost entirely by tuition fees and offered no scholarships, yet its enrollment more than tripled during the Patton regime until it numbered 37 percent of the total enrollment of the University. This growth took place merely because its standards of admission and performance were lower than those in the Academic Department, so that the School of Science became a haven for the ill prepared and the idle.[14]

The situation was close to intolerable for the able, vigorous men of the "young faculty" who had been students under James McCosh and caught his vision of Princeton as a center of learning. In 1897 discontent became so general that the Trustees appointed a Committee on University Affairs to make an investigation. It heard testimony from various members of the faculty, including Woodrow Wilson, but in a subsequent report contented itself with recommending that Patton spend more time at his job, that discipline be better administered, and that there be greater coordination of studies. Then late in 1900 a cabal led by the newly appointed Dean West and William F. Magie, Professor of Physics, assumed the proportions of a rebellion. Over Patton's opposition they forced the appointment of a faculty committee to investigate the scholarship of the Academic Department and to make proposals for reform. They were especially anxious to improve the curriculum of the upper-class years by abolishing "pipe" courses and insisting on a coordinated series of courses in a single field for each student. The committee became known as the "Vice Committee" because it also made a thorough investigation of the slackness of certain faculty members. Its recommendations were debated in a series of meetings of the Academic Faculty in the spring of 1901, at which Patton vigorously opposed change with what one faculty member remembered as "a humorous diabolism that was irresistible."[15]

Woodrow Wilson shared the general dissatisfaction, and had it not been for the $2500 a year that a group of Princeton trustees was paying him to stay, he might well have moved on to the presidency of the University of Virginia. It was noted, and with some surprise, that he did not join in the "Vice Committee" debates. According to a later "inside" story in the *New York Sun*, "Dr. Wilson has been distinguished in the recent differences of opinion in the faculty by his consistent silence. The hotter the debates the tighter have his lips been held together." The most obvious explanation was that Wilson knew he was in line for the presidency and did not want to antagonize Dr. Patton. His brother-in-law Stockton Axson, however, a member of the Princeton faculty at the time, insisted that Wilson held off because he thought the reforms proposed by the committee were mere patchwork—better hold his fire until there was opportunity to propose more fundamental change.[16]

Patton was successful in preventing action on curriculum and standards in 1901, but his success cost him his job a year later. The reform group on the faculty managed to exert influence on the trustees through their allies among the alumni. For instance, Professor R. T. H. Halsey of Yale, a Princeton alumnus, asked a group of Princeton trustees to dinner at the Waldorf with men from Harvard, Johns Hopkins, and Columbia. Halsey asked the men from other universities to describe how Princeton was regarded in the academic community: the trustees "were told in no uncertain terms that Princeton was becoming the laughing stock of the academic world, that the President was neglecting his duty, the professors neglecting theirs, the students neglecting theirs, that Princeton was going to pieces."[17]

In addition, the "young faculty" turned for help to their counterpart among the trustees, the group of alumni from the McCosh era, all of whom were wealthy businessmen or lawyers and had scant patience with Patton's religious fundamentalism and inefficiency. The Sesquicentennial and the decision to change Princeton from a college to a university had been the result of a partnership between the two groups:

now they cooperated again to force Patton out of power. Early in 1902 an inner circle of "young trustees" informed Patton that he must either resign or allow the affairs of Princeton University to be run by an executive committee. They then asked Woodrow Wilson to draw up detailed plans for the latter arrangement. Wilson, in consultation with Professors Henry B. Fine and Cyrus Brackett, the other members of a committee representing the faculty before the Trustees, drew up the following extraordinary memorandum describing the duties of the proposed executive committee:

COMMITTEE consisting of three members of the Faculty and two members of the Board of Trustees, appointed by the Board of Trustees, and empowered
(1)   To formulate and recommend to the Faculty and Board of Trustees such changes in the curriculum and in the coordination of studies as may seem best for the University.
(2)   To formulate and recommend to the Faculty and Board of Trustees such measures as may seem best adapted to increase the efficiency of instruction in the studies of the curriculum, whether singly or as parts of a system; and to superintend the administration of such measures when adopted.
(3)   To formulate and recommend to the Faculty and Board of Trustees such regulations as may seem wise for maintaining a reasonably high standard of study among the students of the University and a reasonably strict system of discipline for failure in study; and to see to the enforcement of such regulations.
(4)   To propose to the Board of Trustees all changes in or additions to the *personnel* of the Faculty of the University. And to take such action in the matter as the Board may decide.
Item: Nothing to be said about the relationship of the Committee to the President of the University.
Item: Privilege of attendance and right of debate in the Board of Trustees to be accorded to the Faculty members of the Committee whenever matters lying within the field of the Committee's functions are under consideration. This to be provided for in the By-Laws of the Board.[18]

In a letter accompanying the memorandum Wilson wrote that he and his colleagues "thought it imperative for the subsequent peace of mind of the faculty that this plan be clearly understood on all hands to have originated wholly with the trustees and not with any member or members of the faculty ambitious of power. I say nothing of *our* peace of mind; it is out of the question that the men who put this plan into execution can have any until the work is done; and then perhaps all they can hope for is peace of *conscience*." A month of negotiation followed, during which Patton, against Wilson's advice, was given membership in the new Executive Committee, and Grover Cleveland, recently elected a Princeton Trustee, was made chairman. Wilson,

Fine, and Brackett were appointed the faculty members. It is apparent throughout the correspondence that the Trustees placed great reliance on Wilson's judgment; one of them, Cyrus McCormick, thanked him for his "cool, clear-visioned advice."[19]

President Patton's position was clearly untenable. By the end of May he was willing to concede that it might be better for the University if he stood aside to make way for reform, but there was the question of the salary of $10,000 that he had counted on for six more years, as well as the $4,000 salary as professor of theology that he had expected for an indefinite period. After receiving assurances that he would not suffer financially and that he might continue his professorship, Patton offered his resignation as President at a Trustees' meeting on the morning of June 9. The Trustees accepted. Patton immediately proposed Woodrow Wilson as his successor. Suspending the bylaws that required a day's interval between the resignation of one President and the election of another, the Trustees unanimously elected Wilson as the thirteenth President of Princeton and the first layman to hold the office.[20]

A committee of Trustees who had known Wilson as an undergraduate, plus Dr. Patton, was deputed to inform him of his election. The event could not have come as an entire surprise. More than a week earlier C. C. Cuyler, one of his classmates on the board, had said to him, "It looks now, Tommy, as though you were going to have a great deal of responsibility." It was Cuyler who had made arrangements whereby Wilson was paid an annual retainer to keep him at Princeton. He and most of the men who negotiated Patton's resignation were fellow members of the class of '79. A Trustee later wrote Wilson that the way the Board had instantly united and elected him appeared to be clearly "the act of Providence," but the evidence suggests that his friends had given Providence a good deal of advance assistance. It was rumored at the time that there were three other candidates for the Princeton presidency: Andrew F. West, the Reverend Simon J. McPherson, Headmaster of Lawrenceville; and Henry van Dyke, Murray Professor of English Literature, and that the quick action of the Trustees in electing Wilson was a means of averting "an undignified scramble for office." This account is corroborated by the program of the "coronation banquet" given Wilson by his '79 classmates: it contains a cartoon of the Princeton Tiger clasping Wilson, who is clad in a bathing suit, while in the water are top hats labeled with the initials of West, McPherson, and van Dyke. Thomas J. Wertenbaker wrote, without giving authority, that Wilson was chosen only after Patton had advised strongly against West.[21]

FLUMEN -SALIS

ME AND TOMMY

A cartoon on the menu of the "Coronation Banquet" given by Wilson's Princeton classmates to celebrate his election as President of the University. The Princeton Tiger clasps Tommy Wilson to its bosom, while floating away are hats labeled "H.V.D." (Henry van Dyke), "S.J.McP." (Simon J. McPherson), and "A.F.W." (Andrew Fleming West), who were rumored to be aspirants for the office.

Because he was the first layman to direct Princeton's destinies and because of the dramatic suddenness of his election, Wilson's elevation to the presidency made headlines and elicited editorial comment all over the country. The choice was generally acclaimed. Southern newspapers in particular were delighted at the choice, which they regarded as an accolade to a native son.[22]

More important than the public acclaim was the warm and instantaneous reaction of the Princeton faculty. A committee of the faculty, of which Dean West was a member, drew up a resolution proclaiming the "general approval" of the election "in which the faculty have special reason to join." Wilson's classmate Professor William F. Magie, a leader in the fight against Patton, wrote from Europe that he could hardly tell Wilson with what relief he now looked forward to the years ahead. "I feel," he wrote, "as if my fighting days were over—I hope not my working days—but that I can now pursue the glorious arts of peace and do my duty without irritation of mind." He added that he had seen Henry van Dyke's brother, Professor Paul van Dyke, who was "very cordial in his expressions of satisfaction at your election." Both Magie and van Dyke were later numbered among Wilson's opponents.[23]

Wilson regretted having to give up his plan to write "The Philosophy of Politics," and it was a wrench to leave the house that he and Ellen had built on Library Place and move to Prospect, the President's mansion. But on the whole he reveled in his new eminence. It was good to know, he wrote a friend, that the men who had been closest to him believed in his capacity to undertake the tasks that his new position demanded. He wrote his wife that he hated to leave Princeton even for a vacation, "now that everybody is so *durn* polite to me as a great personage."[24]

Wilson's lifelong friend Edith Gittings Reid thought that during the first months of his presidency of Princeton Wilson "was happier, gayer than he had ever been in his life, or than he was ever to be again." Work went more easily, and he found time for play. He finished the manuscript of *A History of the American People* in June; in July he wrote his inaugural address and cleared his desk. Ellen then insisted that he get out of town while she directed the move to Prospect, so he went off to New England for a round of visits to friends. His daily letters home tell that he was as happy as a child out of school, whether he was watching vaudeville for three and a half hours at Keith's Theatre in Boston, fishing for cod with friends at Northeast Harbor, or spending a week with his close friends the Hibbens in the White

Mountains. The one bit of formal business he recorded was an attempt to see an elderly, very wealthy Princeton alumnus, without heirs, to ask him to his inauguration. Wilson made a special trip to Boston to find this Isaac C. Wyman, but missed connections. Later Dean West found Wyman and persuaded him to leave his fortune to endow the Graduate College, with results that profoundly affected Wilson's career.[25]

Throughout this carefree month Wilson had been thinking about the needs of Princeton. "The right to *plan*," he wrote Ellen, "is so novel, the element of vexation, the sense of helplessness we had for so long is so entirely removed, that it is a pleasure to think out the work that is to be done. If it did not have the incalculable money element in it, there would be no touch of worry about any of it." By the end of his short vacation Wilson and formulated his plans. The directness and boldness of his approach can be seen in a longhand memorandum outlining a confidential report he was to give the Trustees in October. He proposed nothing less than to make Princeton over:

Memo.   Report to Board of Trustees, October, 1902
Essential soundness and splendid *esprit* of the present College.
But insufficiently capitalized

(1)	Too much work	⎫ Not attractive to ambitious men or to
	Research choked	⎪ men who desire gentle *status*. Men now
(2)	Too little pay	⎬ preparing for college positions. Our
(3)	Insufficient equipment	⎭ own part in preparing teachers.*

What is necessary (besides reorganization of studies)
New methods (the tutorial system)
Strengthening of Weak Departments, e.g., History, Economics, Biology
Equipment: Recitation Hall—Physical Laboratory—Biological Laboratory
Increase of Salaries.
School of Science: Re-endowed, reorganized. Equipment and Support.
    Remarks on depending on fees.
Schedule of minimum *Cost*.

Not to be classed with its immediate rivals as a *University* in either development or equipment. *Not* classed with them any longer, as a matter of fact, in academic circles. *Comparative Statistics.*
What is necessary:
    Graduate School. (What it would mean besides mere building and additional courses of instruction.) Our men in the schools.*
    School of Jurisprudence (explained)
    Electrical School (Reputation already gained)
    Schedule of Minimum *Cost*

---

*These two phrases were written in later in a different color of ink.

Housing and feeding of the students. (Reputation of Princeton for expensiveness and bad food, esp. in Freshman and Sophomore years.) Ways and means.

31 Aug. '02[26]

Wilson's first report to the Trustees took up the precarious financial situation of the University. The budget of over two hundred thousand dollars a year remained in balance only because of annual gifts totaling over twenty-seven thousand dollars. At 4 percent, this annual giving represented capital of nearly $700,000. "We are in effect, therefore," Wilson wrote, "using a capital of $700,000 which we do not own or control. This is evidently a very unsound, a very unsafe business situation."[27]

But Wilson did not propose merely to get enough money to support the existing budget. He informed the Trustees that the following expenditures would be required to put undergraduate instruction on a sound basis:

Increase of salaries	$ 250,000
Maintenance of present expenses	690,332
Fifty tutorships at $45,000 each	2,250,000
Two Professorships of History	200,000
Two Professorships of Economics	200,000
Library Endowment	500,000
Recitation Hall	150,000
Physical Laboratory	200,000
Biological Laboratory	150,000
Additional Biological Instruction	212,000
School of Science	1,000,000
Business offices of the University	200,000
	$6,002,832

Wilson warned the Trustees that if Princeton were to fulfill its moral obligations to is public, funds must be found at once. "Without these things we are not doing honestly what we advertise in our catalogue," Wilson wrote, and if the improvements could not be made, it would be more honorable to curtail the activities of the University.

Even after immediate needs were met, Wilson advised, there would be additional requirements to put Princeton on a level with other institutions. To make Princeton a real university, the first and most obvious need was a graduate college along the lines proposed by Dean West. This, with necessary endowments and additions to the faculty, would cost $3,000,000. Wilson did not think that Princeton should have a medical school because it was so far from a metropolitan center, but he proposed a school of jurisprudence, which he had been advocating for several years and which he defined as "a school in which law was taught only to university graduates and by men who could give it its full scholarly scope and meaning without rendering it merely theoretical or in any sense unpractical,—men who could, rather, render it more luminously practical by making it a thing built upon principle, not a thing constructed by rote out of miscellaneous precedents." Its cost was to be $2,400,000. Nor did he skimp science. In addition to the million and a half already proposed for scientific projects, Wilson urged the building of "a fully equipped electrical school" ($750,000) and "a museum of natural history" ($500,000). The additional funds needed "to create a real university" were estimated at $6,650,000.

These sums amounted to over four times the existing endowments. Even so, argued Wilson, they did not cover all Princeton's needs. He was worried, for instance, that Princeton was "in danger of becoming regarded, to her great detriment and discredit, as one of the most expensive places in the country at which a student can take up residence." New dormitories were needed, as well as better eating facilities, especially for sophomores and freshmen. Wilson closed his first presidential report by expressing the confident expectation that the many projects he proposed might "prove easier in the accomplishment than we can now foresee, and with the full assurance that we shall find genuine and deepening satisfaction and reward in mastering the difficult task because of the spirit of love and devotion in which we shall undertake and prosecute it."

Wilson's inauguration as President of Princeton University took place on October 25, 1902. It was a perfect autumn day, and the pretty village of Princeton was alive with banners and bunting. The Pennsylvania Railroad had run a special train to Princeton for the event; the streets were thronged with well-dressed people. The academic procession that preceded the ceremonies included delegates from over a hundred institutions of learning. In a gesture of liberalism women's colleges were invited, four of which were represented. Booker T. Washington, the Negro leader, whom Wilson admired, was present as representative of Hampton Institute, much to the dismay of one of Wilson's southern relatives. Literary men among the guests included Mark Twain, William Dean Howells, and Walter Hines Page, whom Wilson later appointed as ambassador to the Court of St. James. There was a solid phalanx of men representing wealth and power, including the steel magnate H. C. Frick; J. Pierpont Morgan, who came in a special train; Robert T. Lincoln, son of the former President; and Thomas B. Reed, Speaker of the House of Representatives. Accompanying Morgan were George Harvey, head of Harper's publishing

PENNSYLVANIA R. R.

INAUGURATION OF

PRESIDENT WOODROW WILSON

ALSO

FOOT BALL

COLUMBIA vs. PRINCETON

AT

Princeton, N.J.

October 25, 1902

SPECIAL TRAIN

Will leave TRENTON at 12.10 P. M., arriving at PRINCETON at 12.40 P. M.

RETURNING, Leave Princeton at close of Game.

J. B. HUTCHINSON,	J. R. WOOD,	GEO. W. BOYD,	D. C. WALSH,
General Manager.	Gen'l Pass. Agent.	Asst. Gen'l Pass. Agent.	Div. Ticket Agt.

10-20-1902. 100. Allen, Lane & Scott, Printers, 1211-13 Clover Street, Phila

Pennsylvania Railroad poster.

house, who was later to play a decisive part in launching Wilson's political career.

Grover Cleveland and Dr. Patton addressed the audience before Wilson. Both talked the language of conservatism. Cleveland hoped that Princeton would never act in sympathy with importunate restlessness and doubtful innovation." He urged that the Trustees apply business principles to the administration of the University and demand of both instructors and students "the same assiduity as are necessary in the world of business." Patton urged the faculty to support Wilson even when their judgments did not agree with his. At the same time he assured the audience that the new President could be trusted to keep faithfully to the traditions of the past and predicted that there would be "nothing revolutionary in his policy.[28]

One who saw Wilson for the first time at his inaugural vividly remembered the occasion:

Woodrow Wilson arose. I had never seen him, but something about the man held my attention, even before he spoke. He was faultlessly dressed and gave the impression of immaculate cleanliness. His figure was erect but supple; and he seemed very tall because of his slenderness. His long, thin face wore a smile of joy and pride free of arrogance or conceit. He spoke without the slightest effort in a voice as clear as any bell. Both his enunciation and pronunciation were perfection. He did not strut about the stage; he made a few movements of his hands and resorted to no trick of the professional orator. Though I have forgotten his words, I recall that I was delighted with the man and the speech, but felt that the wild ovation which followed it was somewhat over-done. When the crowd passed to shake the hand of the speaker, I smiled and bowed, without extending my hand. Wilson flashed an understanding glance of gratitude. I learned later that he detested hand-shaking with a multitude of strangers.

During the ceremonies Bliss Perry was sitting behind a bull-necked, unimaginative, very wealthy trustee. Someone next to Perry remarked, "Wilson will be all right if he can make fellows like H—— see what he's driving at." Wilson's Johns Hopkins friend Franklin Jameson was also in the audience; he wrote another friend that Wilson's speech was beautiful but that Princeton had less need of his doctrines than of participation in the wider world of scholarship, "lest Princeton, surrounded by the plutocracy, become a sleepy Oxford on a much inferior basis of acquirements."[29]

Wilson's Sesquicentennial address, "Princeton in the Nation's Service," had celebrated Princeton's past; now that he was charting her future, he spoke on "Princeton for the Nation's Service." The earlier oration had been marred by that overelaboration of phrase that makes most of his essays and *George Washington* unreadable today. The inaugural address was written with clarity and directness. Its style was designed to carry meaning rather than to create effect; it reflected Wilson's new self-confidence and sense of purpose.

Both in tone and substance the address was conservative. In matters pertaining to the curriculum it followed almost exactly the prescription proposed by James McCosh when he was inaugurated as President of Princeton in 1868. Wilson declared, "the classical languages of antiquity offer a better discipline and are a more indispensable means of culture" than any modern language except our own. Men must be drilled in mathematics that they may "get the lifelong accepted discipline of the race." They must know the lessons of the past through the study of history, literature, and philosophy. Wilson's principal theme, one that he had belabored before, was the importance of general education as a basis for both effective citizenship and specialized studies. He used the adjective "general"—"general learning," "general training," "general education," "general studies"—over twenty times. This emphasis echoed President McCosh's insistence that the principal purpose of a college education was not to impart knowledge nor to give professional preparation but "to draw out and improve the faculties that God has given."[30]

The inaugural departed most noticeably from the Sesquicentennial address in that Wilson tried to make peace with the scientists. Science had a place in general education, he said, "not less distinguished than that accorded literature, philosophy, or politics." It "has had its credentials accepted as of the true patriciate of learning." How little Wilson really grasped the point of view of the scientist, however, was apparent when he said that those areas of science "which lie in controversy, the parts of which are as yet but half built up by experiment and hypothesis, do not constitute the proper subject matter of general education."

Wilson saw the task of a university as twofold: "the production of a great body of informed and thoughtful men and the production of a small body of trained scholars and thoughtful investigators." He was clearly more interested in the former than in the latter. He considered it essential that "the merchant and the financier should have traveled minds, the engineer a knowledge of books and men, the lawyer a wide view of affairs, the physician a familiar acquaintance with the abstract data of science." Above all, a university must develop the social understanding of its sons, quicken their consciences, and make them eager to serve their fellow men. "What we seek in education is a full liberation of the faculties, and the man who has not some surplus of thought and energy to expend outside the narrow circle of his own task and interest is a dwarfed, uneducated man."

His undergraduate orientation appeared in Wilson's comments about graduate study. "I should dread to see," he said, "those who guide special study and research altogether excused from undergraduate instruction, should dread to see them withdraw themselves altogether from the broad and general survey of the subjects of which they have thought to make themselves masters." Of the many projects Wilson had proposed to the Trustees the only one he mentioned specifically in the inaugural address was the building of a Graduate College, which he made clear should be so organized and situated that it would enrich the life of the undergraduates: "We mean to build a notable graduate college . . . We shall build it, not apart, but as nearly as may be at the very heart, the geographical heart, of the university; and its comradeship shall be for young men and old, for the novice as well as for the graduate. It will constitute but a single term in the scheme of coordination which is our ideal. The windows of the graduate college must open straight upon the walks and quadrangles and lecture halls of the studium generale."

Wilson's election marked the triumph of the alumni over the Presbyterian Church as the ultimate arbiters of Princeton's destiny. He was thoroughly aware that he must cultivate his new constituency. Late in the afternoon of inaugural day a crowd of alumni gathered to cheer him outside Nassau Hall. He answered in what the *Princeton Alumni Weekly* described as "a sort of heart-to-heart talk from one Princeton man to another." He asked for support in a curiously elliptical way: "I ask that you will look upon me not as a man to do something apart, but as a man who asks the privilege of leading you and being believed in by you while he does the things in which he knows you believe." Here Wilson unwittingly posed the central problem of his presidency of Princeton: to convince the alumni that they did in fact share his vision.[31]

XV

Conservative Reformer

1902–1906

Why not be satisfied with the happy life at Princeton? Why not congratulate ourselves upon the comradeship of a scene like this and say, "This is enough, what could the heart desire more?" Because, gentlemen, what this country needs is not more good fellowship; what this country needs now more than it ever did before, what it shall need in the years following, is knowledge and enlightenment. Civilization grows infinitely complex about us; the tasks of this country are no longer simple; men are not doing their duty who have a chance to know and do not equip themselves with knowledge in the midst of the tasks that surround us.

—Woodrow Wilson, 1902[1]

NO SOONER was Woodrow Wilson inaugurated as President of Princeton than he set out to woo his constituency, the alumni. On November 8, 1902, he spoke at the Princeton Club of Chicago, and on December 11 to a dinner at the Waldorf-Astoria that was said to be the largest alumni gathering yet held in the United States outside a college campus. On both occasions he presented his dreams for the University. The old campus, he said, would be ringed with buildings in Tudor Gothic style. They would include a natural history museum, open quadrangles housing new professional schools, and an especially beautiful quadrangle containing the little community of graduate students whose presence on campus would be an inspiration to the undergraduates. He described the corps of tutors who would "transform thoughtless boys performing tasks into thinking men." When he said that the tutorial system alone would cost two and a quarter million dollars, there were whistles from his auditors. Wilson remarked that he hoped they would get over their whistling because they could thank their stars he did not ask for four million.[2]

During the academic year 1902-03 Wilson barnstormed from the Atlantic coast as far west as Minneapolis and St. Louis, trying to persuade Princeton men that his vision of a university was also theirs.

They applauded, cheered, laughed at his jokes, and sang a song with this chorus:

> For Woodrow Wilson, Woodrow Wilson,
> He's one of us, a son of Nassau Hall,
> It's Woodrow Wilson, Woodrow Wilson,
> It's Wilson, Wilson, Wilson, that is all!

But songs and cheers were not immediately convertible into dollars, so that at the same time Wilson rode the circuit he was also begging from individuals. By direct, personal letters to affluent alumni, asking each one to give $5,000 a year for three years, he built up a contingency and reserve fund that amounted to over $100,000 a year. As no larger sums for endowment were forthcoming, in the spring of 1903 Wilson wrote a long letter to Andrew Carnegie claiming that Princeton was both American and "thoroughly Scottish." He rang every change on Princeton's needs, from the graduate college to the fifty tutors (here described as "reference librarians"). The steel magnate visited Princeton and gave $150,000 to dam a meandering stream southeast of the Princeton campus to make the present Carnegie Lake, but he gave nothing for the serious needs of Princeton University. Wilson is reported to have told Carnegie later, "We asked for bread and you gave us cake."[3]

Whatever progress Wilson could make without money, he did. Within two years of his election all the reforms that the faculty had demanded during the latter years of the Patton administration were accomplished: academic standards were raised; qualifications for admission were stiffened; discipline was tightened; the administrative system was made more efficient; and the undergraduate curriculum was thoroughly overhauled.

According to Professor William B. Scott, one of the top paleontologists of the world and a leader of the "young faculty," Wilson's election as President of Princeton brought "a wonderful revivification and clearing of the air." Professors threw away old lecture notes and wrote new ones. Easy markers were persuaded to jack up their standards. In a song the seniors memorialized the case of one professor who had been notoriously "gentle, easy to drive, and kind":

> He had to make his courses hard,
> Or he couldn't play in Woodie's yard.[4]

The faculty had announced in October of Wilson's first year in office that students must pass over half their courses or be dropped, and the alumni were informed, "When a student is dropped nowadays, he is likely to stay dropped." "Forty-six Mid-year Flunks: and What It Means" was the headline on the cover of the *Princeton Alumni Weekly* after midyear examinations in 1903. A year later there was a similar report, after which the number of failures declined: the undergraduates were convinced that the faculty meant business. Later a toastmaster introducing Wilson at an academic dinner said that if ever Princeton had been an easy place to get into, "that time was succeeded by a period when it is one of the easiest places to get out of in all the collegiate institutions in America." Nor was it any longer easy to get in. Wilson told the alumni to stop "miscellaneous endeavors to turn every boy's footsteps toward Princeton" and "send only the choice spirits, the most useful, all-around Christian gentleman, who has the stuff to make the place." More than a quarter of those who applied for admission in 1903 were refused. From an undergraduate enrollment of 1307 in 1903-04, the first year in which the new rules of admission and performance were in full force, the enrollment of the college dropped steadily to a low of 1187 in 1907-08, and then slowly rose again.[5]

The attempt to raise standards inevitably caused an outcry. A trustee threatened to resign because he was so crazed by the letters mothers wrote on behalf of their sons. "I want to help you all I can, my dear Dr. Wilson," he wrote, "but I submit, 'Do you think the game is worth the candle?'" With fine inconsistency the headmaster of Lawrenceville charged that Princeton was debasing her standards by dropping history from the admission requirements and making them too stiff by demanding physics instead of chemistry for S.B. candidates. At an alumni dinner Wilson described a letter received by an older Princeton man from his undergraduate son complaining how much harder the work had become: "Princeton," observed the young man, "is becoming nothing but a damned educational institution."[6]

Nevertheless, the new standards were generally well received. They had the strong support of the faculty, the most active trustees, and the more thoughtful alumni and parents. Wilson and Henry B. Fine, the new Dean of the Faculty, were reasonable in applying them and in allowing time to make adjustments. They were also at pains to communicate with the students. Thus, in a letter to the *Daily Princetonian* in February 1903 Wilson explained that two or three delinquent students were not dropped because their failures had been incurred before the new rules were promulgated. In 1905, when there were loud complaints about midyear failures, Dean Fine furnished the *Princetonian* with figures revealing that the number of delinquencies was no greater than the previous year and that most of the victims were freshmen. The outcry then died down, and Wilson wrote the editor of the *Princetonian* thanking him for publishing the facts.[7]

Higher academic standards were matched by improved behavior. In

1910
That's All!

A cartoon in a 1903 issue of the Princeton undergraduate humorous magazine, which suggested that Wilson's attempt to raise academic standards would empty the college.

June 1903 Dean Winans reported to the Princeton Trustees that Wilson's first year in office had been more quiet and free from disorder than any in the four years he had been in office. In his opinion the gain was due in no small measure "to the temper of the student body itself and the quickened, expectant interest they are taking in the expansion and prosperity of the university." It was also a result of firmness. Whereas the number of petty regulations was reduced, those retained were strictly yet reasonably enforced. Beer drinking was allowed, for instance, and the use of wine at annual dinners of student organizations, but drunkenness was punished. Although there were occasional eruptions, the endemic, systematic disorder for which Princeton had been noted gradually became a thing of the past.[8]

Up to this time there was no regular departmental organization at Princeton. Each man on the faculty was directly accountable to the President alone, although in practice men in particular fields of study cooperated informally. Furthermore, the faculties of the Academic Department and the John C. Green School of Science were independent of each other, even to the degree that the academic faculty had its own professors of physics and astronomy and the scientific faculty had its own instructors in languages. In June 1903 the Trustees voted that the President be authorized "to organize the work of the faculty under Departments at his discretion, and that he be empowered to do this even when it may prove necessary to create departments which shall include instruction in both the Academic and Scientific sides of the University." Wilson thereupon created departments cutting across the boundaries of the two faculties and appointed department heads to whom he turned over many of the details of administration. He kept the reins of power, however, firmly in his own hands.[9]

The organization of departments gave Wilson the close and active assistance of the men who headed them, but Wilson's closest allies on the faculty were John G. Hibben, Stuart Professor of Logic, and Henry B. Fine, Dod Professor of Mathematics. Jack Hibben was the only man with whom Wilson was on terms of affectionate, day-to-day intimacy. During Wilson's first five years as President of Princeton Hibben not only served as confidant but helped in numberless ways with the details of administration. He served on important committees, helped to recruit faculty members, acted as a vehicle of communication, and when Wilson fell seriously ill in 1906, was appointed acting president.[10]

Henry B. Fine was one of the few people in Princeton who called Wilson "Tommy." He had been one class behind him in college and

succeeded him as Managing Editor of the *Princetonian*. As an undergraduate Fine was interested in athletics, played in the college orchestra, and graduated first-ranking scholar and valedictorian of his class.
His intellectual interests were varied, but he finally settled on mathematics, studied in Germany, and earned a Ph.D. at Leipzig. He was
one of the founders of the American Mathematical Society and eventually became its president. He wrote college texts on algebra and
calculus that were said to be unexcelled in accuracy of statement and
comprehensiveness. As a teacher Fine was noted for clarity of presentation and impatience with dullness. He was greatly respected by the
undergraduates for his integrity, fairness, and interest in their affairs,
especially athletics. In person he was impressive, almost Olympian—
tall, lean, handsome, and dignified. Wilson appointed Fine as Dean
of the Faculty in 1903, to take direct charge of academic standards
and discipline. The outspoken Faculty Song, that barometer of student
opinion, paid him this accolade at the end of his first year in office:

> Here's to Harry, our brand-new dean,
> His bones are big and his legs are lean.
> Gives the students all fair play,
> He's doing well, so let him stay.[11]

Under President Patton the weakest part of Princeton had been the
School of Science. By the end of the Wilson administration the University was well on its way toward becoming one of the principal
centers of pure science and mathematics in the world. Laboratories
were constructed, standards were raised, and men of the highest
eminence joined the faculty. Most of this was Fine's doing, but Wilson
cannot be denied credit. Whatever his previously expressed opinions
about scientific method, he was determined from the first to do as
much for science and mathematics as for the humanities. He forced
himself to learn as much about science as was necessary to assess the
needs of the University; for the rest he trusted Fine. It was a case in
which Wilson compensated for his deficiencies by appointing the best
possible deputy and giving him full confidence and support.[12]

The most powerful man on the faculty next to Wilson was undoubtedly Dean West, both because of his autonomous position as Dean of
the Graduate School and because of the support he could command
from powerful trustees and alumni. Wilson distrusted West; shortly
after his inauguration he told Bliss Perry, "If West begins to intrigue
against me as he did against Patton, *we must see who is master.*" But
at first the two men cooperated. During the academic year 1902-03,
while West was on a trip investigating graduate study in European
universities, he wrote Wilson friendly letters, full of detail, incident,

and humor, and pledging full support. Wilson was pleasantly surprised with West's generous words and apparent lack of jealousy.[13]

The first major reform of Wilson's administration at Princeton was a thorough revision of the undergraduate curriculum during his second year in office. It is an academic truism that changing a curriculum is harder than moving a graveyard, although in this case the groundwork had been laid by the University Committee on Scholarship that Patton had circumvented three years earlier. Wilson now appointed a Committee on the Course of Study, with himself as chairman and Dean West, head of the former committee, as secretary. It held dozens of meetings, some sessions being six hours long, and completed its recommendations in April 1904. Putting Dean Fine in the chair, Wilson took the floor and steered the report through four meetings of the faculty, who voted upon it item by item. Eventually it was adopted unanimously.[14]

In the course of the discussions over the curriculum Wilson occasionally demonstrated impatience with those who disagreed with him. After he had given a long, fine-spun explanation one day in faculty meeting, his friend George M. Harper accused him of quibbling. Wilson's color changed and he gave Harper a verbal scorching. When walking home feeling depressed about the incident, Harper felt a hand on his shoulder. It was Wilson, who said, "Don't let this little spat spoil our friendship." The two men made up there and then. "If he had done that later," said Harper, "he would have made fewer enemies."[15]

In spite of Wilson's occasional lapses of temper, the way in which the new curriculum was put through was eminently democratic. On this occasion Wilson practiced the "common counsel" he often preached. When it was all over, he wrote his wife that the final report was not exactly the scheme he had originally proposed but was in fact much better. The arrangements were as agreeable to everyone as possible because they truly embodied the collective judgment of the Princeton faculty.[16]

The new curriculum provided for both general education and moderate specialization. For freshmen the course of study was prescribed; men with different schooling, said Wilson, "have to be licked into shape, and the same shape." Sophomore year included a mixture of required subjects and electives chosen with a view to later concentration. During the upper-class years a student had to take three of his five courses in a special field and one outside it, with one elective. The emphasis throughout was on bringing different courses into organic relationship with each other. To provide more depth, the course load was reduced from seven to five, and class hours were increased from two to three. During senior year honors candidates were offered pro-seminaries, in which students presented and discussed their own work.[17]

These arrangements were validly criticized as over-rigid for the first two years, reflecting Wilson's opinion, "I know better than any sophomore what sophomores should study." Moreover, they were accompanied by rigid admission requirements, demanding Latin, Greek, and either French or German from candidates for the A.B. degree. Latin was a prerequisite for both the Litt. B. and B.S. degrees. Although it was certainly not their intent, the entrance requirements were alleged to favor boys in private preparatory schools over those in high schools. Nevertheless, the new Princeton curriculum marked an important turning point in American University education. It was a declaration of war on what Wilson called "the loose and showy elective system" that Harvard had introduced under Charles W. Eliot. The *New York Times* prophesied accurately that Princeton's "comprehensive attempt to reduce chaos to order" might become a type for institutions desiring to concentrate on general training at first, with a system of carefully controlled election later. Eventually Harvard itself followed a similar path when it introduced "concentration and distribution" under A. Lawrence Lowell and required courses in "General Education" under James B. Conant.[18]

In his first swing around the alumni circuit Wilson told the Chicago alumni, "I want to make Princeton a place where the most brilliant teachers will feel they have got to teach. I want to give it a distinction that will admit of no competitor." He made it a matter of first concern to raise the caliber of the faculty. For instance, when John Finley resigned as Professor of Politics in June 1903, Wilson approached Harry A. Garfield, who had made a reputation as a municipal reformer in Ohio. He informed Garfield that he very much distrusted "symmetrical theories" derived from books and that politics was so much a matter of life and experience that he would hesitate to trust its instruction to a mere academician. Garfield thereupon visited Wilson at Princeton and in the course of a wide-ranging conversation of an hour and a half was swept off his feet. He at once agreed to join the Princeton faculty, even though it meant financial sacrifices.[19]

Wilson scored another coup when Frank Thilly was persuaded to leave the University of Missouri to accept a professorship of psychology at Princeton. Apparently at Hibben's suggestion, Thilly went to Princeton to discuss the position in January 1904; Wilson recorded his impressions in his diary: "Ellen and I took dinner at Jack's to meet Prof. Thilly, whom we found most ingenuous and interesting,—a man after our own hearts in simplicity and genuineness,—and withal of singular penetration and charm in his talk, a highly trained native American of the Abraham Lincoln type, with his faculties released by education of unusual range and thoroughness." In the ensuing two days Wilson had more conversations with Thilly, and in the next fortnight wrote him three cordial letters saying that other members of the Princeton faculty were enthusiastic at the prospect of his coming, that he need have no worries about any conflict between science and revealed religion, and that funds could be found to pay for his move to Princeton. Thilly accepted, even though Princeton could not match his present salary; he closed his letter of acceptance as follows: "In conclusion let me thank you—and that most sincerely—for the frank and openhearted manner in which you have treated me in the whole matter. I have felt all along that I was dealing with human beings, with men of heart and soul, and not with dead things, and the introduction of the personal, human element has made everything so delightfully pleasant and warm for me."[20]

Wilson turned over to Dean Fine the principal responsibility for recruiting men in science and mathematics, and Fine performed brilliantly. While abroad in 1905, he persuaded James Jeans, one of the two or three ablest young mathematical physicists in England, to leave Cambridge and join the Princeton faculty in September. A year later Owen Richardson followed Jeans from Cambridge to accept a chair of physics; during his eight years at Princeton he did the work on electron emission that later won him the Nobel prize.[21]

Regenerating the faculty promised to be a slow process because much deadwood remained from the Patton regime, and of incompetent teachers it may be said—as Jefferson remarked of Federalist officeholders—that few die and none resign. Wilson did not wait for natural attrition. At his first meeting with the Board of Trustees it was voted, on a motion by Grover Cleveland, that "the President of the University be fully authorized by the Board of Trustees in reorganizing the teaching force to create such vacancies as he may deem for the best interests of the University."[22]

Below the professorial level Wilson used his power of removal at once. In April 1903, for instance, after consultation with senior professors, he relieved a Latin instructor of his position because, he frankly told him, he was unable to handle "the very skittish colts in our classes." He wished the circumstances at Princeton were "less peculiar and less exacting" and promised him assistance in getting a position elsewhere. Later Wilson removed three full professors—a procedure that today would certainly call down the condemnation of the American Association of University Professors and make it difficult to enlist men of eminence and integrity. Two of the men were removed for failure in the classroom: one was unable to keep order and gave ridiculously high grades; the other was lazy and had the habit of letting his classes out half an hour early. The third was a brilliant but erratic language professor, very popular with the students but unable to work with the new departmental organization. He was also highly critical of Wilson personally and—which was especially abhorrent to Wilson—made mildly off-color remarks in class, such as that women were good for raising bread, babies, and Hell. After a bitter confrontation in the President's office the man was told he had to go. But as he was a Princeton graduate with powerful connections, and his classmates rallied strongly in his favor, Wilson was forced to relent to the extent of allowing a year of grace before the man's departure.[23]

With the support of those who had put him in office, Wilson determined to regenerate the Board of Trustees as well as the faculty. In December 1903 the Trustees took note of the repeated absences of two of their number and empowered the President to take action. In 1906 Wilson, Grover Cleveland, and W. J. Magie, Chancellor of New Jersey, demanded the resignation of two trustees who had been involved in the Equitable Life Insurance scandal. Wilson and a small nominating committee effectively controlled new appointments to the Board of Trustees until after the quarrel over the Quad Plan in 1907.[24]

In 1903 Raymond Fosdick transferred to Princeton after two years as an undergraduate at Colgate. Soon after he arrived, he met Wilson walking across the Princeton campus and recognized him by his picture. At Colgate it was customary for undergraduates to doff their hats to the president of the college, which Fosdick now did. Wilson smiled, raised his hat in return, then stopped, and this conversation ensued:

"You're new here, aren't you?"
"Yes, sir," I replied.
"And I see you are not a Freshman," he continued, because I was not wearing the prescribed Freshman cap.
I told him I was entering as a Junior, and I answered two or three of his questions about Colgate. He chatted in a friendly manner for a minute or two, and then, as we parted, he said: "I wish you would drop in to see me."

Fosdick did as he was asked, which was the start of a friendship that lasted until Wilson's death. As Fosdick remembered him at this time, Wilson was a fascinating person:

Wilson on first appearance was not what would be called a handsome man. Indeed he was curiously homely. He had what he himself described as a "horse face"—a long, thin, and generally unsmiling visage with strong jaws. He had also an extraordinarily keen gaze, which could sometimes be disconcerting. But his eyes were nevertheless his best feature; they could light up with humor and kindliness, and his whole face would soften as it reflected his thoughts. His figure was tall and lithe, and he held himself erect and walked with a brisk pace. When I first met him he was forty-seven years old, and the mark of leadership was on his face and bearing.[25]

Although few came to know him as well as Fosdick, Wilson kept in close touch with the undergraduates. He made a point of learning their names and had an uncanny ability to remember students long after they had graduated. He and Dean Fine consulted with the elected Senior Council about the affairs of the University. "The University authorities," Wilson wrote, "feel the counsel of these men to be indispensable. They know that it will be seriously given and that its chief motive will be a love for the University, a care for its best interests, a desire to see its life bettered in every possible way for which opinion is ripe or can be ripened." Such an attitude helps to explain why higher standards of academic performance and of personal behavior could be imposed with relatively slight resistance.[26]

Continuing to hold his chair of politics, Wilson lectured on jurisprudence and constitutional government to two or three hundred juniors. Extant lecture notes reveal that he dictated much the same material as when he had first started lecturing at Princeton, but the dictated portions were now embedded in an extempore connected discourse that was sometimes so eloquent that it held students spellbound. Occasionally they burst into applause or stamped their feet at the end of his lectures. Fifty years later Raymond Fosdick declared: "For me Woodrow Wilson lit a lamp which has never been put out. All my life I have remembered him as the inspiring teacher who introduced us to the kingdom of the mind, and held up before our eyes what Whitehead later called an habitual vision of greatness."[27]

In an undergraduate notebook now in the Princeton University Library there is this notation: "May 9, 1904—Woodrow much peeved and gave permission for students to leave class. No one left." The author later recalled what had happened:

At that time it was the unwritten law of the campus that if a professor or instructor was not in the classroom by the time the bell on Nassau Hall had stopped ringing, the class or lecture was called off and no cuts were taken. On the date stated in the above quoted memorandum, most of the students attending this lecture were standing or sitting around on the ground at the Dickinson Hall entrance to the narrow stairway leading to the third floor lecture room, waiting for the bell on Nassau Hall to start ringing before going up to their seats. As we sat there we saw President Wilson walking slowly down the walk from Prospect to Dickinson Hall. Suddenly, he stopped, turned around and walked rapidly back in the direction of Prospect again, and we realized that he had forgotten the notes of his lecture. We waited there to see if he would be able to return in time to reach the lecture room before the bell stopped ringing. In less than a minute we saw him leave Prospect again and come hurriedly along the walk towards Dickinson Hall with his lecture notes in his hand. It was evident that he would reach the lecture room before the bell stopped ringing and the students who were sitting outside of Dickinson Hall got up quickly and entered the building; they went part way up the stairway to the lecture hall and stopped, packing the stairway so closely that President Wilson was unable to get to the lecture room before the bell had stopped. Then we entered the lecture room and took our seats, waiting to see how President Wilson would handle the situation. Without making any comment, President Wilson instructed the spotters to take the numbers of the vacant seats. This resulted in such coughing and shuffling of feet throughout the entire lecture hall that President Wilson stopped the spotters and announced that no cuts would be taken, that any student who desired to do so could leave the lecture room at once and that three or four questions on the next examination would be from the day's lecture. The lecture room was absolutely quiet, not a student left his seat, and, after waiting for about a minute, President Wilson proceeded with his lecture as if nothing had happened.

I was deeply impressed by President Wilson's ability to handle over 200 unruly students so quickly and so successfully and I believe that this is one of the reasons why, some years later, I became an Alternate Delegate to the Baltimore Convention and campaigned throughout this area [Norristown, Pa.] for the election of Woodrow Wilson as President of the United States.[28]

As President of Princeton Wilson continued his interest in the extra-curricular affairs of the undergraduates. He went to football practice, sometimes walking behind the team with the coaches and making suggestions. According to Donald Herring, who played on the Princeton team for three years, Wilson had "an intelligent, analytical knowledge of football." He regularly attended undergraduate musical or dramatic performances and annual dinners of student organizations. His greatest interest, however, was debating.[29]

Debating was in a state of decline when Wilson became head of Princeton. Fewer men were attending college with the idea of going into the law or the ministry. Freshmen joined Whig and Clio only to drop out when elected to upper-class clubs. Increasingly the Halls became the resort of the "non-clubable." Wilson did what he could to stem the tide. He gave strong support to the efforts of Hardin Craig, a young English professor, to restore debating to its former glory. It was clear to Craig that Wilson's interest "rested on his faith in self-directed, spontaneous intellectual activity on the part of the students themselves."[30]

The undergraduates hoped that Wilson, as the first layman to head Princeton, would abandon compulsory chapel, and he did abolish a previously required Sunday afternoon service. But for other services attendance requirements were stiffened. When a group of undergraduates asked the President to make chapel services optional, he replied with mock gravity, "Why, gentlemen, it *is* optional. If you wish to go to chapel you may."[31]

Although Wilson considered religious services to be as much a part of Princeton life as daily classes, he was not a sectarian. As his principal biographer has remarked, he was "first a Christian and secondarily a Presbyterian." Early in his administration he publicly disagreed with Dr. Patton, who had called Princeton "a Presbyterian college." No, said Wilson, Princeton "is a Presbyterian college only because the Presbyterians of New Jersey were wise and progressive enough to found it." He explicitly rejected dogmatism: "It is a very awkward thing to be certain that you are right and the other man wrong. When we see how much other denominations have accomplished and how much spirituality they contain it is awkward to regard ourselves as the only elect people of God . . . Believe me, you engender the spirit of doubt by stating a thing dogmatically. Between the ages of eighteen and twenty-two you create doubt by ramming dogma down the throat."[32]

Wilson led daily chapel exercises once or twice a week and occasionally preached. He departed from custom by replacing much extempore prayer with passages from the Book of Common Prayer, such as the Prayer of St. Chrysostom or the General Confession. When reading Scripture he turned again and again to a few favorite passages, such as the First Psalm—"Blessed is the man that walketh not in the counsel of the ungodly"—or the thirteenth chapter of First Corinthians —"And now abideth faith, hope, charity, these three, but the greatest of these is charity." "When these old words came ringing through, carried by the magnetism of Wilson's voice," wrote Raymond Fosdick, "I do not say that the students were spellbound, but they were significantly silent."[33]

Wilson's religious outlook was marked by a wholehearted but un-

reflective faith. "He seemed to regard religious character very much
as he did physical health," wrote a friend, "something all-important but
naturally springing from the laws of right living and not overen-
hanced by theological discussion." He went to church to seek refreshment, not to wrestle with doubt or to speculate on the nature of the
Deity."[34]

In "The Young People and the Church," an address delivered before the Pennsylvania Sabbath School Organization in 1904, Wilson
insisted, "the truths which are not translated into lives are dead truths
and not living truths." "We call a man noble," he said on another occasion, "only when he has spent his power, not upon himself; when he
has used his surplus energy for other men." He preached a gospel of
action. The following notes for a sermon delivered in the Princeton
University Chapel epitomize his recurrent message that men should
serve God and their fellow men with zeal, sincerity, common sense,
and love:

II Corinthians, III., 8. "For the letter killeth, but the spirit giveth life."
Parallel passage, John, VI, 63. "It is the spirit that quickeneth; the flesh
profiteth nothing: the words that I speak unto you, they are spirit and
they are life."

We are too apt to think of duty, not as an enterprise or an expression
    of our faculties, but as a routine, not heeding the warning of the text,
    "we are unprofitable servants: we have done that which was our duty
    to do."
There is life only where there is growth: and there is no growth so long
    as we stick in the letter of our instructions or our examples.
    The unhappy formality of morals.
    The mistaken emphasis of one virtue. A ribbon for each virtue?
    Spiritual initiative.
    The adaptation of duty to environment and opportunity.
        The wisdom and duty of each case consist in the circumstances of
        that case.
The "spirit" spoken of in the text undoubtedly the spirit of love, which
    is the spirit of Christ. The spirit which translates all law into privilege.
    How does Love give Life?
        By satisfaction of inborn instincts.
        By release of faculties otherwise pent up or dwarfed.
        By revelation of opportunity.
            Character, not an original, but a by-product.
        By enlargement of view.[35]

A diary that Wilson kept briefly in January and February 1904
records the inevitable irritations that attended the job of directing
Princeton's destinies. The day after New Year's, while in bed with a
cold and neuralgia, he had a long talk with Henry W. Green, a trustee,

concerning a professor's complaints about his salary. Green "quite agreed that B——'s conduct in the matter had been extraordinary and altogether inexcusable." On January 4 he discussed a vacant professorship of psychology with Professor Ormond: "He has taken a fancy to Moore of Chicago and has to be talked to at length to be restored to an overview of the whole field." On the same day he had to go to the powerhouse to find out why the steam heat had been turned off, and he was told there was a broken connection. On January 5 he and Ellen "had a long talk beside the study fire on means of giving me sufficient relaxation and mental stimulus amidst my miscellaneous and distracting administrative duties." January 6 was a day of routine business, at the close of which he went to bed with a distressing headache. On the seventh and eighth the death of Grover Cleveland's daughter Ruth cast a cloud over his spirits. On the ninth, another day of routine, he was breaking in a new part-time secretary, a sophomore—"a capital fellow, but weak in spelling." On January 12 he complained, "Kept in my office until quarter of 5 on business that might have been finished before three if academic men were only prompt in movement and brief in statement." Later entries tell of interminable committee meetings; a professor who was "disagreeable, as usual, because classes likely to be popular are put at the same hour with his"; an evening with class secretaries "to discuss ways and means of controlling the serious evil of drinking at class reunions at Commencement"; another evening spent investigating a report that two men were selling freshman examination papers; a conversation with the father of a student who had died in the infirmary; an occasion when Wilson had three young faculty members to dinner but "talked too much—finally engrossing the conversation"; and two more days of ill health.[36]

The diary reveals that his life was not all routine and vexatious interruption. On January 10 his friend Mrs. Toy of Cambridge, Massachusetts, arrived for a visit. She was, Wilson wrote, "as alert and full of (half artful) charms as ever. Always draws me on to talk my best." The next evening there was a dinner party at which the Hibbens and a Dr. Littleman were guests. "A very bright, interesting circle and our pleasure much added to by songs, chiefly Scottish, very naturally and sweetly sung by Mrs. Toy, after dinner, just before we broke up." Later entries mentioned a class of '79 dinner in New York, dinner parties in Montclair and Philadelphia—all three described as "delightful"—and a concert by the Kneisel quartet. "The first part," wrote Wilson, "was modern and disturbing, but the concluding part, fr. Beethoven, gave the mind tone again, and sent us home happy. I walked home with the Hibbens and sat with them until nearly eleven."

The diary makes clear that the greatest pleasure in Wilson's life, outside his family, was his intimacy with the Hibbens. He noted not only their daily conversations but even the days when Mrs. Hibben could not see him because of a toothache or when Jack was out of town. Jack continually lifted burdens from his shoulders, whether by investigating candidates for professorships or by comforting the parents of the boy who had died. Above all, the diary confirms that Wilson could talk to Jack with freedom. This was the more important since one result of his election to the presidency of Princeton was personal isolation. He no longer dropped in to play billiards and tell stories at the Nassau Club. People did not call at Prospect with the same freedom as they had at Library Place. Even when they did call, a card on the door told them that people having business with the President should see him at his office in '79 Hall.[37]

Wilson depended more than ever on his family for companionship. At home he was invariably cheerful and considerate. On festive occasions, such as Christmas, he often completely abandoned his usual dignity and behaved in a fashion that people who saw him in public might have thought quite out of character. There might be charades, with Wilson dressed in his wife's hat, a feather boa, and a velvet curtain trailing behind, imitating a society woman's affected handshake; or he might make a mock serious oration, gesturing with his feet instead of his hands. On one New Year's Eve he gathered the family around the dining room table, each with one foot on the table, and then all went to the front door to let the old year out and the new year in. This, he said, was an old Scottish custom.[38]

Wilson's wife had not been happy to leave their own home on Library Place for the President's mansion, nor to shift from the obscurity of a professor's wife to the prominence of the first lady of Princeton. Nevertheless, she graciously did all that her new position required. She redecorated the interior of Prospect and planted a new garden. She helped to improve the care given the patients in the college infirmary. Wilson respected her judgment in affairs of the University and on occasion deferred to it. In 1903, for instance, he intended to appoint a nephew, George Howe, to an instructorship in Latin. The young man was fully qualified, but Mrs. Wilson argued that the appointment would be unwise since it would destroy a reputation for "almost romantic disinterestedness." Wilson was at first unwilling to sacrifice his nephew to his reputation but eventually gave in, and Howe was not appointed.[39]

Wilson's isolation at Prospect was the more serious because he was now, in his own phrase, "submerged in petticoats." The household consisted of his wife, his three daughters, and Margaret Axson, his sister-in-law, who later married a member of the Princeton faculty. Stockton Axson now lived elsewhere, and there were no more nephews to live with them while going through Lawrenceville and Princeton. A grievous loss was the death of Wilson's father. Dr. Joseph Wilson lived long enough to see his son elected President of Princeton, after which he told his grandaughters, "Never forget what I tell you. Your father is the greatest man I have ever known." But within months he was dead after a painful illness, and Wilson wrote a friend, "it has quite taken the life out of me to lose my lifelong friend and companion. I have told you what he was to me. And now he is gone and a great loneliness is in my heart." Margaret Axson thought that the wholly feminine atmosphere now surrounding Wilson "must have prevented a beneficial hardening of his already thin skin," and that "he missed the toughening that tough-hided sons would have given him." Apparently Ellen appreciated the lack because she had a billiard table installed at Prospect and invited men to play with Woodrow; "He needs to talk more with men," she explained to Professor Capps.[40]

It was difficult to preserve privacy at Prospect, set in the midst of the Princeton campus. Undergraduates cut through the grounds on their way to the athletic fields, and excursionists, brought in by the new trolley line from Trenton, picnicked there. In the summer of 1904 Wilson had a handsome iron fence, firmly set in concrete, built around the Prospect grounds, enclosing five acres of the campus. When the undergraduates returned in September, many of them were furious, maintaining that Wilson had no right to keep part of the campus to himself. The *Nassau Literary Magazine* ran a defiant editorial, asserting that "when fifteen hundred men are agreed that a certain fence should disappear it would seem that its doom is sealed." A prominent trustee tried without success to persuade Wilson to remove the fence before the alumni returned for the Yale game. The editor-in-chief of the *Princetonian,* Edward H. Hilliard, who understood why the fence was necessary, went to Wilson to urge him to make a public explanation. He was taken aback when Wilson flatly refused, saying that when a man was right, he need not make explanations.[41]

One dark night a group of undergraduates took action. Upperclassmen dragged freshmen out of bed, furnished them with picks and shovels, and had them dig out a section of the fence and sink it so deep in the ground that the next morning only the tops of the spikes showed. Wilson promptly repaired the fence but took no other action. The incident was apparently closed until the seniors put on their annual costume parade. Ten very tall seniors, wearing tight-fitting black gowns, black masks, and peaked black hats, represented the fence. They carried placards such as "Peek-a-boo" and "Don't feed the animals." In their midst they dragged a pig in an express cart, with the implication that the President was "hogging the campus." Wilson was clearly hurt and protested to prominent members of the class, although he eschewed formal disciplinary action. Twenty years later his daughter Jessie (Mrs. Francis B. Sayre) displayed coldness toward Norman Thomas simply because he had been a member of "the class that was so cruel to father." "Imagine how he must have impressed his daughters," Thomas commented, "that this memory should linger after the crowded years with their glory and their tragedy in the Wilson family."[42]

Ensuing classes forgot about the fence around Prospect, and it remains to this day. But the incident revealed how fragile was Wilson's popularity with the undergraduates if he appeared to violate custom, even though in general he was very much liked and respected by them. It showed too how easily he could be hurt and how difficult it was for him to shrug off a slight.

No sooner had the new curriculum gone into operation than Wilson embarked on the project he had advocated for more than a decade—the enlistment of a corps of tutors to guide and stimulate undergraduates. Their function was not to be to cram knowledge into students, nor to impart it systematically, but to inspire men "to willing daily use of their own faculties." They must be young enough to understand the difficulties of beginners and should therefore be hired for only five years. After that time, Wilson thought, men would go to seed or find the job intolerable.[43]

Even though he failed to persuade Andrew Carnegie or anyone else to give the more than two million dollars needed to endow the scheme, Wilson proposed that Princeton go ahead with the plan anyway, paying for it by annual pledges until endowment could be found. Those who suggested a more cautious approach were overborne when Wilson's wealthy classmate Cleveland Dodge agreed to underwrite any deficit. The haste with which the preceptorial system was introduced is shown by the fact that most of the preceptors had been hired before the Princeton Trustees formally accepted the plan on June 12, 1905.[44]

In Princeton's past the word "tutor" had acquired an unpleasant connotation, a combination of drillmaster and spy, so Wilson adopted the word "preceptor" instead. The preceptors were to be equivalent in rank to assistant professors and were usually to be hired for from three to five years. Salaries ran from $1,500 to $2,000—adequate but not generous compensation by the standards of the time.[45]

Wilson performed the extraordinary feat of recruiting forty-five men in March, April, and May, 1905. Although he enlisted the aid of department chairmen, he did an amazing amount of letter writing and interviewing himself. He interviewed every candidate whom he did not know personally, and this interview was sometimes, as it had been with Harry A. Garfield, the deciding factor. Robert K. Root, for instance, was well situated at Yale, was dubious about the new method of instruction, and questioned whether a Yale man could be happy at Princeton, but he did consent to go and see Wilson. This is his recollection of the meeting: "My interview lasted some forty minutes. Mr. Wilson asked me no questions about myself, but spoke with winning eloquence about his plans for Princeton. Before five minutes had passed I knew I was in the presence of a very great man . . . Before the talk was over my loyalties were entirely committed to him. Had Woodrow Wilson asked me to go with him and work under him while he inaugurated a new university in Kamchatka or Senegambia I would have said 'yes' without further question." Wilson was so successful in luring young men from other universities that twenty candidates were said to be seeking four preceptorships in the English department.[46]

In recruiting for the new system, Wilson and his colleagues sought far and wide. Thirty-seven of the original preceptors were hired away from twenty-five other institutions; only twelve were recruited from the Princeton faculty. It was gratifying to lure men from Columbia, Harvard, and Johns Hopkins, where till then Princeton had been regarded as second-rate.

In selecting preceptors, Wilson's instinct was to put personality and teaching ability ahead of scholarly qualifications. Explaining the new program in April 1905, he said:

> The importance of the whole system lies in the character of the men who are being obtained. in the first place they are being selected along very careful lines, and only those are taken who will feel a certain love for the place, and who are in entire sympathy with its spirit, and understand the scope of the plan that is being developed. They are to be selected primarily upon their stand as gentlemen, men who are companionable, clubable, whose personal qualities of association give them influence over the minds of younger men. If their characters as gentlemen and as scholars conflict, the former will give them the place.

At one point Wilson offered a preceptorship in any department he chose to John J. Moment, a teacher at Lawrenceville School with a fine record in undergraduate studies at Princeton but no graduate training whatever. After Moment refused the offer, Dean Fine persuaded Wilson that it was unfair to offer positions to schoolmasters or to any others unqualified for later academic advancement. Evidence of serious scholarly interest was therefore considered an essential: thirty-seven of the forty-nine original appointees had already received their doctorates—seven from Harvard, five from German universities, five from Johns Hopkins, four from Chicago, and only three from Princeton.[47]

The preceptorial method of instruction was designed for "reading subjects," such as literature, philosophy, political science, economics, history, and foreign languages, and was not adapted to science and mathematics. Yet it seemed unfair to give additional instructors to one side of the University and not the other. Dean Fine was therefore allowed to recruit mathematicians and offer them the title "preceptor," even though the instruction they gave might be traditional in form. The extraordinary group of young men he hired, just at the time when recognition meant most to them, helped to make Princeton a mecca for mathematical study. The physical sciences were allowed to hire extra assistant professors in lieu of preceptors; in selecting these men, William F. Magie quite frankly put capacity for research ahead of promise as a teacher.[48]

Wilson took care to prepare the undergraduates for the preceptorial system. He explained that the new scheme was meant to stimulate them to "a greater feeling of independence." He expressd hope that the system would "make the studies of the University both vital and delightful." He did not even like to use the word "system" because he expected the utmost variety and imagination in the way preceptors worked. He encouraged meetings in the preceptors' rooms or undergraduate clubs, and during the evening, so that place and time would create an atmosphere "free from all formality or restraint."[49]

The first preceptors threw themselves into their work, in part because they were devoted to Woodrow Wilson. "When you met the man in conference or in conversation, you at once felt a compulsion to be your best, not in self-consciousness nor to accredit yourself, but because something in him called for it, and anything but your best seemed unfitting." They had to work exceptionally hard because they were expected to keep abreast of all the courses given in a department, yet it was so exciting that many of them later looked back on the early days of the preceptorial system as the happiest time of their academic lives. Three who wrote reminiscences of their experience quoted Wordsworth's lines:

> Bliss was it in that dawn to be alive,
> But to be young was very Heaven![50]

Methods varied. Students were generally divided into groups of four or five. They might be found sitting around the fire in a preceptor's living room reading a play, listening to German *Lieder* on a phonograph, analyzing a student's report of an historical incident, or discussing poetry and drinking beer at an inn in Kingston, a nearby hamlet. According to Charles G. Osgood, the most successful preceptors drew men out by Socratic questioning, and a session often ended with the question still in midair, "running to ground outside, in another corner of the campus or at a club." The former barriers between students and faculty disintegrated, and lifelong friendships were forged between undergraduates and the only slightly older men who guided their studies.[51]

Preceptors did not give day-to-day grades, but at the end of a semester they were expected to make estimates of a student's performance. This judgment counted for a large if variable part of the final grade. A man whose performance in preceptorials had been unsatisfactory might be barred from final examinations, although such a coercive measure was seldom necessary.[52]

The preceptorial system was hailed as an immediate success. The *Nassau Literary Magazine* declared that it was "generally even universally popular," that it had given "an enormous impetus to general reading," and that the undergraduates were more interested in their studies than at any time within the memory of the senior class—all as a result of "more intimate personal contact with men of learning, culture, and keen intelligence." Students felt a sense of personal responsibility toward a preceptor that they did not feel toward a lecturer: "Many a fellow who would shirk his work day after day in the class room, and read, sleep, or dream all through a lecture, feels it in a measure discourteous to treat his preceptor in his own room in so cavalier a fashion."[53]

Near the close of its first year Wilson reported on the preceptorial system to a gathering of applauding Princeton alumni in Cleveland, Ohio. He said that the new spirit of study at Princeton would surprise some of his auditors, among whom he recognized men who in college had been "ingenious in resisting the processes of learning." He had recently heard an undergraduate say in a tone of condemnation that men were actually talking about studies in the clubs. "He evidently regretted that," said Wilson, "as an invasion of the privileges of undergraduate life." In the past there had been too much of the schoolboy spirit; now under the influence of the preceptors Princeton students were becoming "what every university student ought to be, namely, reading men."[54]

The future would show that Wilson was oversanguine about the preceptorial system, but at first the only worry was financial. When Wilson took office in 1902, the annual budget of Princeton University was $225,000; by 1906 it had grown to $556,000. The deficit, which had to be made up by annual donations or by borrowing, increased in four years from $27,000 to $113,000. Wilson in 1902 had called dependence upon annual giving "a very unsound, a very unsafe business situation," yet by his own impetuous insistence that the preceptorial system be introduced before it was endowed he had made the financial situation far more precarious. The University was now dependent upon the continuing support of a few wealthy alumni, which meant that these men had a potential veto on educational policy.[55]

There can be no doubt that Wilson's first four years as President of Princeton were extraordinarily successful. The institution advanced so rapidly under the influence of higher standards, more efficient administration, a coherent curriculum, better faculty morale, and the preceptorial system that Princeton men boasted that their alma mater was "doing more for the average undergraduate than any other college or university in America." Princeton was attracting admiration from other colleges. Oren Root of Hamilton College, father of Elihu Root, wrote that Wilson had his "hearty endorsement" and that no educational proposition in his lifetime had so carried him away as Wilson's plans for the preceptorial system. Wilson was in constant demand to speak at other universities and at meetings of schoolteachers.[56]

Although he achieved quick fame as an educational reformer, Wilson remained, as President Patton predicted, a conservative. "The educator," Wilson insisted, "has no business trying new things. It is his business to gather the best out of the past and present it in forms which have the sanction of time, instead of running after new fads and theories." There was nothing new in demanding Greek and Latin as a prerequisite for the B.A. or in forcing students to choose courses according to a prearranged plan, and the preceptorial system was obviously an adaptation of practices already established at Oxford and Cambridge. Moreover, Wilson explicitly set himself against some of the most important and characteristically American developments in higher education. Early in his presidency he irritated those connected with city universities like Columbia by saying that a university which was robbed of a community atmosphere by its urban location could not provide the best education. "If the students, after they leave the lectures and classrooms of the university, can at once dive out into the street of a great city . . . they are not getting the benefit of a university. They are going to a day school." He said that the difference between the state universities and private institutions like Princeton was the difference between "imitation" and "individuality." He insisted that before entering on vocational studies, men should have a four-year undergraduate course devoted to teaching "the disinterested truths of pure science . . . the truths of pure philosophy, and that literature which is the permanent voice and song of the human spirit." Even at the graduate level he hoped that Princeton would have a school of "jurisprudence," devoted to the principles of the law, rather than a "law school," devoted to its practice, and he told Cyrus Mc-Cormick that he did not think anything like the Harvard Business School was consistent with Princeton's system and purpose.[57]

Princeton's education was reserved for an elite who could afford four or more years in general studies while paying expensive board and lodging in an isolated academic community. Wilson was not a snob. He had sympathy for the urchin in the slums "who knows more of the prudences of life when he is five than most of us knew when we were five-and-twenty," and he expressed the opinion that if he could fill a whole college with former slum children, there might be extraordinary progress in scholarship. He pitied the idle rich. "Some young men," he said, "brought up in the lap of luxury . . . seem to know as little about the world as it is possible for a person to live nineteen years and know." He went out of his way to befriend Raymond Fosdick, the "non-clubable" transfer student from Colgate. But it did not seem to bother him during his first years as President of Princeton that by defining university education as he did he was also reserving it for the relatively affluent.[58]

Wilson's educational philosophy at this time became even more conservative than it had been earlier. Formerly, for instance, he had insisted that a teacher of law to undergraduates must be a sociologist. Now he repudiated sociology before an audience of Chicago business-men because it seemed to deal only with the abnormal. "Whenever anyone teaches anything queer nowadays he calls it sociology." There was no professor of sociology at Princeton and no course so labeled when he became President in 1902, and none when he left eight years later.[59]

Wilson's views on higher education during his first years as President of Princeton reveal him as to some degree a prisoner of the academic environment in which he had spent most of his adult life. When he

defended so-called liberal studies, insisted on the primary importance
of undergraduate instruction, and extolled the virtues of an isolated
academic community, he was simply pointing to characteristic features
of Princeton. The curricular changes introduced during his presidency
were originally inspired by James McCosh. The preceptorial system,
although an innovation, was especially tailored to the needs of the
Princeton undergraduates, many of whom had gone to college for
reasons other than study, and who were now to be seduced into using
their minds. When Wilson criticized other colleges and universities,
he was displaying the same partisanship that made him care so intensely about Princeton's success in intercollegiate competition,
whether in athletics or debating. In short, his prescription for university education in America was essentially a celebration of the peculiar virtues of Princeton University as it might be reformed and
regenerated under his leadership.

During the first years of his presidency of Princeton Wilson's health
appears to have been better than usual. In the summer of 1904, however, he overstrained while portaging a canoe on vacation with his
family on the Muskoka Lakes in Ontario, and early in 1905 he had
to be operated on for hernia. After the operation he was stricken with
phlebitis and spent five weeks in the hospital, followed by a con-
valescence in Florida. At about the same time his old enemy, neuritis,
reappeared and was so painful that at times he could not sign his
name and had to use a rubber stamp. In April 1905 the family suffered
a terrible bereavement with the death by drowning of Edward Axson,
Ellen's much younger brother, along with his wife and baby son. He
had joined the household when the Wilsons were at Wesleyan and
had lived with them for eight years while attending Lawrenceville
and Princeton, so that he was almost as much a son as a brother. Both
the Wilsons were profoundly cast down by the tragedy. Even a year
later the mere mention of Ed Axson was enough to make Wilson's
voice choke and his eyes fill with tears.[60]

Wilson had nevertheless learned to compartmentalize ill health and
sorrow and go about his business. Then one morning in late May 1906
he awoke to find that he could not see out of his left eye. He was taken
to specialists in Philadelphia, who gave an alarming report. Ellen Wilson wrote a friend that Woodrow had been told he was suffering from
hardening of the arteries "due to prolonged high pressure on brain and
nerves. He has lived too tensely . . . Of course, it is an awful thing—dying by inches—and incurable." At first the doctors prescribed complete
bed rest and implied that Wilson's active career was at an end. Later

they modified their stand in favor of a three months' vacation, after which the patient might resume work but must avoid excess. Hibben took over Wilson's duties as President. When the Trustees met on June 11, 1906, they voted a resolution, proposed by Grover Cleveland and seconded by Moses Taylor Pyne, expressing solicitude for Wilson's condition and, "in recognition of the fact that this condition is a direct result of close application and unremitting devotion to his labors on behalf of the University," enjoining him to prolong his vacation until completely restored to health and vigor. Wilson and his family then sailed for England, to spend a quiet summer at Rydal in the Lake Country. He was not allowed to read, nor could he write much because of neuralgic pains in his right hand. It was an open question whether he would resume his duties as President of Princeton in the fall—or ever again.[61]

The Quad Plan Fight

1906–1908

Our new methods of study require as their soil and indispensable environment a new social coordination,—a coordination which will not only make sure of a constant and natural intercourse between teacher and pupil, but also knit the student body itself together in some truly organic way which will insure vital intellectual and academic contacts, the comradeship of a common life with common ends.

—Woodrow Wilson, 1907[1]

WILSON'S enforced vacation in the Lake Country in 1906 was a success in every way. He strolled with his wife along the shores of Grasmere and hiked over upland pastures with his daughters. He formed a lifelong friendship with Fred Yates, a portrait painter who delighted Wilson at their first introduction by remarking that he and his family were "poor, but, thank God, not respectable." Yates brought out all the fun and companionship in Wilson's nature. On rainy days Wilson and his wife sometimes played whist; more often he slept.[2]

There was a strong vein of fatalism in Wilson, even superstition. He was fascinated by the Ouija board, apparently believing it had occult qualities. He considered thirteen his lucky number: it delighted him that there were thirteen letters in his name, that he was the thirteenth President of Princeton, and that he was inaugurated into office during his thirteenth year on the faculty. On a higher plane a Calvinistic sense of predestination helped to sustain him in his great conflicts because he believed that he would not be allowed to fail. The same feeling carried him through spells of exhaustion and ill health. When the time came to give in, he resigned himself to the inevitable so completely that the natural powers of healing came into full play.[3]

Late in August Wilson went to see two physicians in Edinburgh, one an oculist and the other a cardiovascular specialist. Both reported an almost spectacular recovery. The eye was healed, although the vision was never fully restored, and Wilson was given permission to read. What was more important, he was told that with proper moderation he could go back to work—that for a man of his temperament it was better, in fact, to return to his job than to spend an idle, anxious year abroad.[4]

Wilson sailed back to America early in October, but from this time on he so ordered his days as to conserve his energies and reduce tension. He at last got a full-time professional secretary instead of relying on part-time undergraduate assistants. He started taking month-long midwinter vacations in Bermuda. He had always exercised by bicycling or walking, but now that the increase of motor traffic made these more difficult, he took up golf. On medical advice he followed the prescription friends had urged long ago—to drink Scotch whisky in moderation. He somehow learned to go to sleep at once at any time of day; he called it pulling down the curtains of his mind. This regimen was so successful that the man who had been told, in his fiftieth year, that his active career was at an end managed to weather thirteen more crowded and strenuous years as President of Princeton, Governor of New Jersey, and President of the United States until he collapsed while campaigning for ratification of the League of Nations in September 1919.

Except during vacations, when he could be approachable and friendly, Wilson deliberately cut down on casual human contacts, which were a drain on his energy. More than ever he depended for personal refreshment on his family and a few intimates. He now tended to meet members of the Princeton community only in his official capacity, which made it more difficult to prepare the ground for change or to find out when proposals should be tempered with caution. At the same time he was more in a hurry. If, as seemed likely, his days were numbered, he felt he must complete his plans for regenerating Princeton immediately.

On Wilson's return to Princeton he was met by a rush of work. There was a meeting of the Board of Trustees, four months of arrears in correspondence, and increasing pressure to take an active part in politics. The most immediate problem, however, was what to do about Dean West, who had been offered the presidency of the Massachusetts Institute of Technology.

In spite of his distrust of West, Wilson during the early years of his presidency had little or no cause to complain. The Dean gave him loyal support both in the faculty and at large. West was secretary of the committee that promoted the new curriculum; it was on his motion that the Academic Faculty ceased to meet by itself. He lauded the preceptorial system, even though it deferred the establishment of the Graduate College. In a speech to Princeton alumni in Orange, New Jersey, in November 1904 West paid a tribute to Wilson that was reported to have brought the audience to its feet. "Princeton is going ahead," said the Dean, "and knows where she is going under the inspiring leadership of one of her sons. Dr. McCosh founded the modern Princeton, and his pupil and successor has taken what he founded, has developed it, and carried it along, and the ideas he represents are the full expression of what Princeton ought to be."[5]

As time went on, however, West's patience began to wear thin. Although Wilson had made the Graduate College a first order of business in his inaugural address, he afterwards did little to advance the project beyond contributing a perfunctory preface to an elaborate brochure that West put out in 1903 to attract potential donors. The President made no serious effort to raise money for the project, and according to West's later recollection, he deterred the Dean from trying to raise money on his own.[6]*

But West had support in high places. In 1904 Grover Cleveland had been appointed chairman of the Trustees' Committee on the Graduate School, of which Moses Taylor Pyne was also a member. In June 1905, at the same meeting that approved the preceptorial system, Cleveland told the Princeton Trustees that it was time to fish or cut bait in regard to the Graduate School. Although nine years ago Princeton had declared itself a university, it as yet had no school of law or medicine nor any prospect of either. The one way to prove Princeton's right to high standing, as well as to forestall the humiliating charge that Princeton had begun what it could not finish, was to create a Graduate School, with provision for a first-class faculty, fellowships to attract able students, and a residential hall. Cleveland, as mouthpiece for his friend West, insisted that the next major drive for funds after the preceptorial system had been endowed should be to support the Graduate School, and especially the Graduate College to house its students.[7]

In spite of lack of encouragement from Wilson, West collected money enough to rent and furnish "Merwick," an estate with a house that could lodge twelve men and board twenty, surrounded by ten acres of grounds. It was opened as a residence for graduate students

---

* It is important to distinguish between the Graduate School and the Graduate College. The Graduate School was a semi-autonomous department of the University—including faculty, students, a dean, and a faculty advisory committee. West and his supporters wanted to enlarge and improve the Graduate School by providing additional faculty and fellowships. They also wanted to build a residential Graduate College, where students and faculty would live together.

in September 1905, with Howard Crosby Butler, Professor of Art and Archaeology, as master. It was intended as a pilot study for the full-fledged Graduate College. The graduate students wore gowns at dinner, which was preceded by a Latin grace. Every Wednesday evening Dean West presided, bringing with him a distinguished guest; on these occasions the men wore evening dress.[8]

Then in the autumn of 1906 West was offered the presidency of the Massachusetts Institute of Technology. As a classicist with no knowledge of or taste for science and a positive aversion to vocational education, he was a strange choice, and it is open to question whether he seriously considered taking the position. In any case, he made the offer public, and it strengthened his hand. Both the *Princeton Alumni Weekly* and the *Daily Princetonian* expressed alarm at the prospect of his leaving the University. At a meeting of the Trustees' Graduate School Committee, held at Grover Cleveland's house, West was asked to state his position. He said that he was attracted by the M.I.T. offer because he was discouraged by the long delay in endowing the Graduate School and he did not want to be identified indefinitely with an unsuccessful enterprise. According to his later recollection, when he was asked whether this was all he had in mind, he answered, "no, but I think it is sufficient and is all I should say now." Wilson, who was present, joined in a request that he tell the whole truth. West then said that the trouble was that he had not hit it off with Wilson, even though he had given loyal support. For half an hour he recalled instance after instance in which Wilson had, he felt, been unfair to him, but closed by saying, "President Wilson, if I have said anything untrue or unfair to you, I ask you to point it out now. Whether I go or stay I would like it to be on an unmistakable basis, and I hope on a basis of friendship too." Wilson sat for a time silent, his head bowed, according to West's account, and then said, "I am bound to say you have a remarkable memory."[9]

Some of Wilson's friends among both the Princeton Trustees and the faculty wanted him to use this opportunity to let West go and thus remove a potentially divisive influence. But Wilson, according to Ray Stannard Baker, felt that he should not be moved by his personal feelings and that as a matter of principle West should be asked to remain. He himself, therefore, wrote the following resolution, which was voted unanimously by the Board of Trustees:

RESOLVED: That the Board learns with the utmost concern of the possibility that Professor Andrew F. West may accept a call which would take him away from Princeton. The Board would consider his loss quite irreparable. By his scholarship, by his ideals, by his fertility in constructive ideas, he has made himself one of the chief ornaments and one of the indispensable counsellors of the place. The Board has particularly counted upon him to put into operation the Graduate College which it has planned. It begs to assure him that he cannot be spared and that the Board trusts that should he remain, its hopes and his may be sooner realized, because of this additional proof of his devotion.[10]

West decided to remain. On the same day that he sent his formal declination to M.I.T. he wrote Wilson a friendly note, hoping for "team work." Nevertheless Wilson's friend the Reverend Melanchthon W. Jacobus, a trustee and a member of the Graduate School Committee, was worried: he feared, as did Wilson, that West would not willingly subordinate his purposes to those of the University as a whole.[11]

A few days after the announcement of West's decision there was a dinner in his honor at Merwick, attended by graduate students and faculty members. After it the Dean was escorted home by torchbearers wearing academic robes. There was reason enough for celebration— Wilson and the Trustees were apparently committed to making the Graduate College their next important project.[12]

During the long summer in England Wilson had been maturing a plan that was a natural corollary of the preceptorial system: the establishment of a number of residential quadrangles, somewhat on the lines of the Oxford and Cambridge colleges. This was not a new idea. President Eliot of Harvard had proposed it twice, as had Charles Francis Adams at an address at Columbia in 1906. Closer to home, George M. Harper had suggested it in 1898 as a means of bringing Princeton faculty and students into closer relationship. Wilson himself had mentioned the idea in a talk to a group of alumni in 1905.[13]

Wilson first presented the scheme in a confidential "Supplementary Report" to the Princeton Trustees in December 1906. He explained that the existing club system at Princeton had resulted in a disintegration of undergraduate morale and impaired democratic spirit, both by dividing classes into competing cliques and by promoting luxury. He expressed the hope that the clubs could be turned into quadrangles by adding dormitories to their existing buildings, although still allowing them some right to choose their members. As Wilson envisaged the Quadrangle (or simply Quad) Plan, all four classes would be combined into new social units; some younger faculty would be in residence, and older ones would be nonresident members. After discussion, a Committee on the Supplementary Report of the President was appointed, with Wilson as Chairman, to examine the plan further and report to the trustees at a later meeting. The other members of the committee were Cleveland Dodge, Robert Garrett, Bayard Henry, Melanchthon W. Jacobus, David B. Jones, and Moses Taylor Pyne.[14]

Grover Cleveland at once saw a threat to the Graduate College and thus informed Wilson's close friend Cleveland Dodge. Dodge assured him that Wilson would do nothing to injure that project and, since the plan to build resident undergraduate colleges would take a great deal of money, there was no way of carrying it out immediately. But in January 1907 Princeton received a bequest of $250,000 from Mrs. Josephine Thomson Swann to build a Graduate College, and in Wilson's eyes this apparently took care of the commitment made to Dean West. Wilson proposed to go ahead with the Quad Plan immediately. He was also moved to do so because the club situation had reached a state of crisis.[15]

During Wilson's first year as President of Princeton a committee of trustees under the chairmanship of Moses Taylor Pyne had investigated the club system and concluded that it was on the whole beneficial: the clubs were orderly and solvent, they promoted good manners, and they encouraged alumni to return to the college. Granting the misfortune that some deserving men were left out, the committee nevertheless recommended the founding of new clubs, since "the formation of each new club gives thirty students each year the comfort of a pleasant club house with its good food, comfortable surroundings, library and fellowship," at little more cost than an ordinary boarding-house. With this encouragement the number of clubs increased from eleven to thirteen, and the proportion of upperclassmen in them grew from about two-thirds to over three-quarters.[16]

But dissatisfaction with the system mounted. Bicker Week, the period when club elections took place, was described as an "annual frenzy" and "a blight, destroying sleep and friendships." As the membership in upperclass clubs increased, the plight of those left out became more deplorable: men often left college after failing election. The clubs, ranged alongside each other on Prospect Street, entered a period of "competitive armament" with the erection of more and more luxurious buildings. The houses belonging to the Ivy and Cottage Clubs were each reputed to cost over $100,000—yet they each catered to only sixty men. By 1907 matters had reached a point where the *Daily Princetonian* solemnly asserted that the college was "face to face with a social crisis which is at any time likely to throw our whole social system into chaos." The trouble did not center so much on the upper-class clubs themselves as upon a complex situation that had developed among the underclassmen.[17]

The system of lower-level clubs that had sprung up as "feeders" to the Prospect Street clubs tended increasingly to dominate the social life of freshmen and sophomores. The sophomore clubs—called "hat lines" because of distinctive headgear—began to control elections to upper-class clubs by banding together to accept or refuse election as a block. Thus, for instance, in 1907 all but one of the men taken into Ivy Club came from a single sophomore club, the Vieni. The sophomore clubs in turn chose certain freshman clubs as "followings." The choice of those who entered the most desirable upper-class clubs was therefore in practice made early in freshman year by self-appointed campus politicians, drawn from large preparatory schools. Furthermore, arrangements for freshman club memberships were often made during the senior year in schools sending large contingents to Princeton, such as Lawrenceville and St. Paul's, so that each entering class was sorted out into a social hierarchy at matriculation—a procedure that the *Daily Princetonian* termed "the most pernicious and evil influence in the University."[18]

These developments were in gross violation of an inter-club treaty that had been drawn up to regulate elections to upper-class clubs, especially to prevent clandestine pre-pledging before Bicker Week. According to this agreement, which was printed in full two or three times a year in the *Daily Princetonian,* each sophomore on entering a club signed an elaborate pledge stating upon his word of honor as a gentleman that he had made no prior agreement to join. Upperclassmen, similarly, were obliged to pledge their word that they had engaged in no illegal soliciting. The penalty, assessed by an Inter-Club Treaty Committee, was expulsion or suspension from a club. This proved unenforceable. The temptation of weaker clubs to offer election to desirable sophomores, and of underclassmen to gain advance assurance of election to a club, was stronger than solemn pledges. This situation was especially humiliating for men who had prided themselves on their self-policing at examinations under the honor system.[19]

The Inter-Club Treaty also created a social barrier between upperclassmen and underclassmen. Sophomores seen consorting with upperclassmen were accused of "bootlicking," and upperclassmen seeking the company of younger men were suspected of proselytizing. It reached a point where the *Daily Princetonian* argued that for the present it was essential "that absolutely no intercourse exist between upperclassmen and underclassmen."[20]

The Inter-Club Treaty Committee, representing all the upper-class clubs, met frequently during the first four months of 1907. Wilson and Dean Fine, along with Professors Harry A. Garfield and Paul van

Dyke, attended the meetings by invitation of the undergraduates, primarily as observers but occasionally making observations when their opinions were asked. The Board of Governors of the Cottage Club was so distressed by the violations of the Inter-Club Treaty and by the treaty's effect in cutting off normal social intercourse that it formally requested these men to suggest remedies. Some undergraduates, even in preferred clubs, were ready to abandon the whole system.[21]

In striking contrast to his tactics with regard to initiating revision of the Princeton curriculum and appointing preceptors, Wilson engaged in little advance consultation with the faculty about the Quad Plan. The only formal discussion of which there is record took place on April 15, 1907, when he met by appointment with the other three men who had been called in to consult on the club situation—Henry B. Fine, Harry A. Garfield, and Paul van Dyke. The meeting was held in Wilson's study at Prospect in the evening. Even with this small group of friends Wilson rose to speak. Before launching into a description of the Quad Plan, he explained that he had not intended to introduce it for several years but that the clubs had created a situation demanding immediate action. He showed blueprints for combining existing club buildings into quads and asked for opinions. Fine and Garfield strongly favored the scheme, but Paul van Dyke, a member of the Ivy Club, was dubious. He said he hesitated to approve action that meant the end of Ivy.[22]

Meanwhile the ad hoc committee of trustees appointed in December had held meetings. At the March meeting of the Board, Wilson reported verbally on its progress. One member of the committee, David B. Jones of Chicago, was even more convinced than Wilson that drastic action was necessary. Unless something was done immediately to reform the social situation, he wrote Wilson, all hope of getting money for Princeton would end, because no large donors would want merely "to fill in the background of the club life as it now exists"; the clubs would strangle the university.[23]

When the Trustees met on the morning of January 10, 1907, Wilson, as chairman, presented the report of the Committee on the Supplementary Report; it was written by him but unanimously accepted by the other members. The report argued that the only adequate means of promoting Princeton's intellectual and academic revitalization was to group the undergraduates in "residential quadrangles, each with its common dining hall, its common room for intercourse and diversion, and its resident master and preceptors; where members of all four of the classes shall be associated in a sort of family life, not merely as neighbors in the dormitories but also as comrades at meals and in many daily activities,—the upper classes ruling and forming the lower, and all in constant association with members of the Faculty fitted to act in sympathetic cooperation with them in the management of their common life." The report of the committee differed from Wilson's report of the previous December in putting more stress on the academic benefits to be derived from the Quad Plan, but it again adverted to the evils of the club system. The effect of the Quad Plan, it stated flatly, must be "either their abolition or their absorption." The hope was expressed that they might be expanded into small residential quads if they would be public-spirited enough to cooperate. The report closed by recommending that the President of the University be authorized to take such steps as might seem wisest for maturing "this general plan," for seeking counsel of interested parties, and for working out details.[24]

After the formal presentation of the report Wilson spoke further, emphasizing that the purpose of the plan was primarily academic and that the clubs dominated the picture simply because they happened to stand in the way. The Trustees then agreed to postpone discussion until after lunch and voted that the report and the President's remarks on it be reprinted in the *Princeton Alumni Weekly*.

The afternoon of June 10 was devoted entirely to discussion of the Quad Plan. In the course of it M. Taylor Pyne, a charter member of Ivy and author of the earlier report exonerating the club system, rose and briefly explained why he had changed his mind. Finally the Trustees voted to adopt the recommendations of the Committee on the Supplementary Report. On the face of it, this was an extraordinary procedure. The Quad Plan was certain to cost money, and the University was running a large deficit. The scheme was at least a partial violation of the formal commitment to Dean West in regard to the Graduate College. Strong opposition should have been foreseen. The one trustee who voted in the negative did so not because he was inherently against the plan but because he thought the board was being stampeded. "I looked around at the Board," he later reported, "at 'Momo' Pyne and 'Cleve' Dodge and Cyrus McCormick and Mr. Cleveland and the rest of them, and wondered if I had gone crazy or if all the rest of them were crazy. It seemed to me that the thing to do was to hear President Wilson's ideas, table the motions, go away and think it over, and at the next meeting ask him to restate it all to us." Nicholas Murray Butler, no friend of Wilson's recollected that in committee meetings Wilson spoke with such clarity and persuasiveness that he wrought suspension of one's own judgment, and the immediate reaction was, "Yes, yes—why not?" Now this power of persuasion had mesmerized the Princeton Trustees into embarking on a project that they were to repudiate only four months later.[25]

In the Trustees' defense it may be observed that a precedent for liquidating the upper-class clubs had been established by President McCosh's abolition of the Princeton fraternities forty-odd years earlier. The reason for McCosh's action was similar to Wilson's: the fraternities were a divisive and anti-intellectual influence. Furthermore, the great burgeoning of the club system had taken place very recently—only five of the thirteen clubs were more than a dozen years old and only two were more than twenty—so that the Trustees had no notion of their strength.[26]

First reactions to the Quad Plan were favorable. During the month of June Wilson received a dozen letters from faculty members, alumni, and parents agreeing with his diagnosis of the evils of the club system and praising him for taking action. At Commencement time Wilson had sent a memorandum to the clubs urging that "by an act of supreme self-sacrifice" they allow themselves to be absorbed into the University. Debate in the clubhouses followed, during which objections were voiced but in temperate tones. A member of the Board of Governors of Cap and Gown, one of the strongest clubs, wrote Wilson that the club would hold up construction of a new clubhouse already started until they consulted with him. He said that all regretted bitterly that the club situation had reached such an acute stage and they were ready to adopt any plan that would be for the good of the University. A story in the *New York Evening Post* on June 25 reported that Princeton alumni generally agreed with Wilson as to the clubs' abuses and would support him in his scheme to correct them. Wilson spoke at the Jamestown Exposition on July 4 and then took his family off for two months to the Ausable Club, deep in the Adirondacks, apparently persuaded that Princeton would follow his leadership now as in the past.[27]

Two days after the *Evening Post* account the *New York Sun* had told quite a different story. It reported that there was dissatisfaction in the Princeton community. One faculty member, according to the *Sun*, said that Wilson was a fool to think he could decide who should or should not be a man's friends, and that there would be trouble persuading the clubs, all of which were incorporated under the laws of the State of New Jersey, to give up their property. No sooner had Wilson reached the Adirondacks than he began to receive intimations of serious opposition. Henry van Dyke wrote him regretting that there had been no consultation with the faculty; he thought the Quad Plan "full of the gravest perils to the life and unity of Princeton." Andrew West in a bitter letter of July 10 said that the sweeping and unexpected action of the Trustees had so disheartened him that he was unable to think of anything else or to shake off a feeling of dismay at the trouble that lay ahead. He felt bound to say that both the plan and the method of putting it across, without discussion by the faculty, were "not merely inexpedient, but morally wrong." "If the spirit of Princeton is to be killed," West concluded, "I have little interest in the details of the funeral." West, Henry van Dyke, Paul van Dyke, and Jesse Lynch Williams, editor of the *Princeton Alumni Weekly*, fomented resistance to the Quad Plan by buttonholing or writing letters to prominent alumni and trustees, insisting that Wilson's methods were dictatorial and his plans were Utopian, un-Princetonian, and confiscatory. Grover Cleveland was convinced that the Quad Plan was a violation of a pledge to Dean West to build the Graduate School. These opponents soon found willing allies among the Philadelphia and New York club-men, who had at first assumed, as had the fraternities a generation earlier, that they were powerless to resist the Princeton authorities, but who now organized in opposition.[28]

Under a barrage of protest Wilson's supporters began to fall away. By mid-July Moses Taylor Pyne was no longer sure that the Quad Plan was the best remedy for the ills of the club system; by September he was violently against it and approached individual faculty members urging them to join his opposition. Bayard Henry, another member of the committee that had presented the Report on Social Coordi-nation, underwent a similar change of heart and arrived at the opinion that Wilson's idea of serving all students the same food was "socialistic and not natural." Even Wilson's faithful classmate Cleveland Dodge, who had underwritten the preceptorial system, suggested that it might be well to go slow. Andrew C. Imbrie, one of five term trustees elected by the alumni, who privately held the opinion that any benevolent bandit who would put a stick of dynamite under each clubhouse should receive an honorary degree, contented himself with acting as a means of communication between the alumni and the President.[29]

To the various correspondents who protested or asked for further information Wilson wrote placatory letters, explaining that there would be ample opportunity for discussion, but to his friend Cleveland Dodge he wrote, "The fight is on, and I regard it, not as a fight for the develop-ment, but as a fight for the restoration of Princeton. My heart is in it more than it has been in anything else, because it is a scheme of salva-tion." Stockton Axson told Winthrop Daniels that he had never seen Wilson "more stiffly bent and insistent on a project; he thought he

The University Cottage Club (above) and the Ivy Club, built during the early years of Wilson's presidency of Princeton. Each was reputed to have cost over $100,000, merely to provide an eating place for fewer than sixty upperclassmen.

Henry Burchard Fine, John Grier Hibben (*above*), Andrew Fleming West, and Moses Taylor Pyne. These four associates were most deeply involved with Wilson's administration at Princeton. At first all gave him strong support, and Hibben was his closest friend. But during the later controversies West, Pyne, and Hibben moved into opposition.

The Princeton Graduate College in 1913 (complex of gothic buildings at lower right). Wilson had wanted the college placed at "the geographical heart of the University" (tower of Nassau Hall at extreme upper left), but Dean West's views prevailed.

"Colonel" George Harvey and Senator James Smith, Jr. These two engineered Wilson's entrance into politics in 1910. Smith was the most powerful Democratic politician in New Jersey; Harvey was editor of the *North American Review* and *Harper's Weekly*.

THE SACK RACE

Which Is the Better Able to Overcome His Handicap?

"The Sack Race." In their campaigns for the governorship of New Jersey in 1910 both Wilson and his Republican opponent, Vivian M. Lewis, were handicapped by charges that they were controlled by the bosses of their parties.

might resign if it were not put through, with perhaps minor concessions in detail, within two or three years."[30]

Wilson returned to Princeton in September as to a battlefield, and one in which the enemy already occupied commanding positions. By prearrangement the *Princeton Alumni Weekly* ran letters against the plan in its first four issues, starting with a long diatribe by Henry van Dyke. Although the magazine offered to open its pages to both sides, its weight was thrown against Wilson. A most damaging opponent was H. G. Murray, Secretary of the Committee of Fifty, Princeton's fund-raising organization, who let it be known that opposition to the Quad Plan among the alumni in the New York area and elsewhere was so overwhelming as to put the University into financial jeopardy. He had been unable, he wrote a trustee, to collect more than $300 since Wilson's announcement of the "quad scheme"; his cancellations ran into thousands.[31]

Although when Wilson first proposed the Quad Plan he mentioned restoration of Princeton's democratic spirit as one of its aims, his major emphasis was definitely not in that direction. Again and again he insisted that the plan's purpose was not primarily social. He was not attacking the Prospect Street clubs as clubs; he wished to liquidate them only because they inhibited scholarly endeavor. It was, in fact, Wilson's opponents who emphasized the democratizing features of his Quad Plan. They sometimes did so by frankly defending an aristocratic position. For instance, Henry Fairfield Osborn wrote Wilson that he preferred to see Princeton attract a class of men "who have the good fortune to be born with some means and with natural advantages of home culture and refinement." Adrian H. Joline in a bitter letter to the *Princeton Alumni Weekly* wrote that he wanted to see men come out of Princeton who had shown their ability to survive in a competitive social life. Princeton's purpose was "to send forth men qualified to deal with the problems of life and not purely closeted students, tamed by preceptors, or perhaps matrons, launched into the world from the cloisters of a 'Quad.' " An alumni committee of the Ivy Club presented a quaintly Darwinian defense of social exclusiveness, pointing out that many freshmen now came from the great preparatory schools, where groups of boys were formed "by natural selection." "The work that Princeton should do for our country," said the Ivy Club report, "cannot be fully accomplished unless she attracts all grades of boys including the wealthier and more socially desirable boys into her halls." But because these "desirable" boys had enjoyed greater liberty, they would be impatient of restrictions on their social habits, and any compulsory eating plan would send them elsewhere. The attitude was put in a nutshell in a remark attributed to a Philadelphia matron: "No one is going to make my boy eat with muckers."[32]

Although Wilson had not consulted the faculty while hatching the Quad Plan, he now asked for a formal expression of opinion in order to strengthen his hand with the alumni and Trustees. At a faculty meeting in late September his friend Winthrop Daniels presented a motion written by Wilson:

RESOLVED: that in the plan recently sanctioned by the Board of Trustees for the social coordination of the University this Faculty do concur; and that a committee of seven from this body be appointed to cooperate with the President of the University, the Dean of the Faculty, and the Committee of the Board of Trustees already constituted to elaborate the plan in question.

The opposition countered with a substitute resolution by Henry van Dyke, presented in the form of an amendment, proposing a joint trustee-faculty committee to cooperate with the President and Dean of the Faculty in investigating the social conditions of the University and finding means of curing evils in order to promote "the unity, democracy, and scholarly life of the undergraduates." Wilson, in the chair, asked if this motion had a seconder. He was seen to turn pale when his closest friend Jack Hibben rose and seconded van Dyke's motion. Wilson was incredulous. "Do I understand," he asked, "that Professor Hibben seconds the motion?" "I do, Mr. President," came the grave reply. It had been known that Hibben was skeptical about the Quad Plan, but no one thought that he would become a leader of the opposition.[33]

Four days later, on October 1, there came a test of strength in the form of a roll-call vote on van Dyke's motion. A vote against it was understood to be a vote in support of the Prseident and the Quad Plan. The motion was rejected by a vote of 80 to 23. This large majority was somewhat misleading, however, because 49 of 50 preceptors had voted on the administration side; the President had gained the suffrage of the older faculty, men with tenure, by the narrow margin of 31 to 22. It was charged that the overwhelming support of the preceptors was a "bread-and-butter vote" since they were dependent upon the President for renewal of their contracts. This was probably unfair: all the evidence shows that most of the preceptors felt an admiration for Wilson approaching reverence. Most of them were from other universities and were therefore without attachment to the existing social system at Princeton. To Oswald Veblen, a preceptor who had gone to Princeton from the University of Chicago, the division in the faculty—quite aside from the particular issue—was between those who wanted to keep Princeton a college and those who wanted to make her a university.[34]

After the vote on the Henry van Dyke amendment Paul van Dyke called upon Wilson to deal frankly with the faculty and tell them what he had in mind. One of the preceptors recorded in his diary how Wilson appeared on this occasion:

I shall never forget him standing there erect behind the desk, the gavel (mallet head) grasped in his right hand, with the end of the handle occasionally placed firm against the top of the desk as he leaned slightly forward in the earnestness of his plea, and his voice occasionally thrilling with an unusual amount of *visible* emotion (for him)—while he stated his dignified position that the faculty must express its opinion without publicly "investigating" before he could go before the students and alumni in advocacy and explanation of the idea. The whole thing in superb language and diction. A truly wonderful man.

Wilson devoted the entire sesson to an elucidation of the Quad Plan. Some of those present thought it one of the great addresses of his career. He said that too much emphasis had been placed upon the Quad Plan as a remedy for existing evils, whereas in fact its purpose was intellectual: it was "a necessary sequel to the preceptorial plan, and based upon a definite conception of education, as a process by which educational influences form mind and habit." Viewed from the inside, he said, the clubs were not vicious, but by their nature they kept everyone else outside: the faculty was outside, the honormen were outside, the lower classes were outside, the University was outside. In other universities fraternities performed the same function of separating the social life from the intellectual life. Now was the time for Princeton to take the lead in forming a university organization where intellectual influences could dominate. He closed with the words, "I beg of you to follow me in this hazardous but splended adventure."[35]

Further faculty action on the Quad Plan was deferred to a later meeting. As it turned out, the faculty never did have a chance to vote directly on its merits because the Trustees killed it at a meeting on October 17. Their action took the form of three resolutions: first, to reconsider their action of the previous June in accepting the recommendations of the Committee on the Supplementary Report of the President; second, to ask the President to withdraw the recommendations made in that report; third, to disband the committee. Undoubtedly the principal reason for this extraordinary reversal of judgment was the storm of opposition that the Quad Plan had stirred among the alumni. Their action was also closely tied to the financial situation.

The University was already running a deficit of about $100,000 per year because of the preceptorial system. The Quad Plan was certain to cost a great deal more money, and it threatened to reduce income by alienating alumni donors. To cap it all, 1907 was a panic year on Wall Street, and the wealthy men who dominated the Board of Trustees were genuinely alarmed.[36]

Wilson's first thought was to resign, and he went so far as to write out in shorthand a strong protest against the action of the Board in killing his scheme before it had been adequately debated. But he changed his mind because, as he wrote his friend Dr. Jacobus, although he had gained nothing from the experience but mortification and defeat, he felt he had no right to jeopardize the University, especially when the very men who forced him to surrender had made financially possible all that he had accomplished hitherto.[37]

The Quad Plan debacle was partly the result of serious mistakes in leadership. Wilson took few people into his confidence in the matter, and as a result of this failure to prepare the ground, he had few effective allies. In his formal presentation of the proposal his unabashed use of the first person singular is striking: "The questions I am about to approach and their proper solution have been taking form in my mind for many years"; "I have long foreseen the necessity of thus drawing the undergraduates together into genuinely residential groups"; "The details of the adjustments which would be necessary I have in large part thought out." He talked repeatedly of working the business out by "common counsel," but in practice he was only willing to discuss ways of working out the details, not the essential idea.[38]

Wilson was a victim of his own success. For five years he had carried all before him. Some of the men who now opposed him had formerly been singing his praises. On the very eve of the presentation of the Quad Plan Henry van Dyke told Wilson that he was "of more value to the University than any other man, than any ten men," and Grover Cleveland wrote him in terms of affection and admiration. He could not foresee that these men would turn against him or that, if they did, they could sway the alumni, whose devotion to him had been repeatedly attested. Wilson was also unable to anticipate defeat because he was so certain that he was right. His conviction of rightness was in some cases a source of strength, but in the Quad Plan episode it proved a handicap. Opposition, he felt, was based either on ignorance or on unworthy motives. He was unwilling to discuss half measures or alternative solutions: he came to believe that the Quad Plan, and the Quad Plan alone, was necessary to the salvation of Princeton.[39]

The Quad Plan dispute continued to poison the air even after the matter was apparently closed. At the time they voted down the plan, the Trustees passed a resolution proposed by Cleveland Dodge and seconded by M. Taylor Pyne to the effect that the Board recognized that Wilson's convictions had not changed and that he was at liberty to try to convince the Princeton community that the Quad Plan was "the real solution of the problem of coordinating the social and intellectual life of the University." This appeared to give Wilson a clear license to continue to agitate his scheme, but it was passed only after a substitute motion proposed by Mr. Cleveland had been voted down, to the effect that the Board would cooperate with the President in "correcting the evils existing in the social and academic co-ordination of the University." Apparently Mr. Cleveland's motion was intended to silence further discussion of the Quad Plan, and men opposed to Wilson behaved as though it had been passed. Mr. Pyne himself soon took this tack, in spite of his action in the trustees' meeting. Writing a fellow trustee only six days later, he said that the Trustees had voted down the Quad Plan because it was "absolutely Utopian and could not be carried out under any consideration." It was distinctly understood, wrote Pyne, that the President's withdrawal of the plan was final, and the only reason it was not turned down harder was to spare the President's feelings. The *Princeton Alumni Weekly* did not report the Dodge-Pyne resolution, but instead reported the claim of several trustees that the Board intended to quash the plan indefinitely. Wilson was so much disturbed by what he took to be an attempt to muzzle him that he again contemplated resignation, but friends on the Board of Trustees assured him that the resolution giving him a green light to agitate for the Quad Plan meant exactly what it said and told him to ignore Pyne. The way had been opened for a breach between the two men.[40]

There was no one whom Wilson could less afford to antagonize than Pyne, who had dedicated himself to being a Princeton trustee. He had been elected to the Board in 1885, and for thirty-six years thereafter he never missed a meeting. In order to be near the University, he moved to a beautiful estate on the edge of Princeton, "Drumthwacket," in 1895. Pyne had inherited great wealth, which he and his family lavished on Princeton. His gifts were beyond numbering because so many were anonymous. And his services went far beyond money. He was responsible for the forming of Princeton alumni associations, for the institution of the office of Alumni Trustee, and for the founding of the *Princeton Alumni Weekly*. The words of an English observer were often repeated: "No one has done for any college what Pyne has done for Princeton." A few people thought that he had little conception of the function of a university and that, as the Sir Roger de Coverley of Princeton, he was somewhat proprietary, but such critics were few. A strikingly handsome man of singular modesty and charm, "Momo" Pyne was the most beloved Princeton alumnus. He was also the most powerful.[41]

The Quad Plan fight cast a permanent shadow over Wilson's relations with other members of the Princeton community. He and West were forever alienated. Grover Cleveland, coached by West, came to regard Wilson as dishonorable. Former President Patton, who continued on the Princeton faculty as professor of theology, joined the opposition, along with Henry and Paul van Dyke, and William F. Magie, head of the physics department, who was an influential figure among the faculty.[42]

By far the worst blow for Wilson was the end of his friendship with Jack Hibben. Hibben had been one of the first to doubt the wisdom of the Quad Plan and had written Wilson a forthright letter to this effect. Wilson wrote a warm reply, in which he declared, "You have done your duty and I love and honour you for it; I shall try to do mine, and so win your love and respect. You would not wish me to do otherwise. And your friendship, by which I have lived, in which I have drawn some of the most refreshing, most renewing breath of my life, is to be as little affected by our difference of opinion as is everything permanent and of the law of our hearts." Yet when Hibben not only opposed the Quad Plan but became a leader of the opposition, Wilson was hurt. The day the plan was killed, Beth and Jack Hibben paid a friendly call at Prospect to try to cheer up Wilson. He treated them so discourteously that the next day he wrote a letter of apology for the ungentlemanly way he could behave when a "black mood" was on him. The amenities were preserved for a time, but the old intimacy could not be restored. The friendship finally ended once and for all when Hibben again opposed Wilson in the later Graduate College controversy. According to Stockton Axson, the breach left a permanent scar on Wilson's spirit. From this time on he was afraid of such close friendship. His daughter Margaret was of the opinion that the two major tragedies in Wilson's life were his failure to put across the League of Nations and the break with Hibben.[43]

Wilson's experience in the Quad Plan fight hardened him, and it was principally after this time that people often found him personally cold. He reserved his energies for the platform and for official occasions, fending off casual human contacts. He treated Albert Shaw, his close friend of the Johns Hopkins days, so distantly on one occasion that Shaw asked a Princeton friend if he could unwittingly have caused offense. "Not at all," was the reply, "I am sure that he counts you as a friend, but he has been so worn down by this friction that it seems to have changed his manner." Davis R. Dewey, another Johns Hopkins acquaintance, had a similar experience. Ellery Sedgwick discovered how great the contrast could be between Wilson's public and private manner when, somewhat against his will, he attended a Groton School dinner where Wilson was the principal speaker. Most of the guests were hostile to this slayer of the dragons of privilege on the Princeton campus, but Sedgwick was carried away:

The Woodrow Wilson of that night I cannot forget. The ascetic figure, the uncompromising features, the scrupulous courtesy, the perfection of utterance, the cogency of argument, the passion behind the word. He spoke as I had never heard a man speak before. Isaiah might have been at his elbow—and was for aught I know. Anyway, my heart and mind seemed tuned to his discourse, and that night I went home a burning disciple. Rushing up the stairs of my house and opening the door, I shouted upstairs to my wife, "I have been listening to a great man! I know it! Wilson will be famous."

The next morning, still glowing, Sedgwick took the train for Princeton and called on Wilson to tell him of his enthusiasm. Wilson gave him a chilling reception: "never was blanket so cold, so clammy, so all extinguishing," wrote Sedgwick, "as that with which he promptly enveloped me." Yet even after this experience Sedgwick remained a follower.[44]

Wilson himself began to make a virtue of belligerence. He told a Chicago audience that he was a good fighter, that on the whole he would rather fight than not. In an address celebrating the one hundredth birthday of Robert E. Lee he maintained that no leader is made up entirely of gentle qualities. "When you come into the presence of a leader of men you know that you have come into the presence of fire, —that it is best not incautiously to touch that man,—that there is something that makes it dangerous to cross him, that if you grapple his mind you will find that you have grappled with flame and fire."[45]

Wilson's change of behavior in the direction of greater haste, less tolerance of disagreement, and less willingness to bear fools gladly may have been the result simply of the bitterness of the defeat and broken friendships he suffered as a result of the Quad Plan affair. It may also have been a natural result of the breakdown in health in 1906 that made him husband his slender surplus of energy. It is also possible that the severe retinal hemorrhage Wilson suffered at that time was accompanied by slight cerebral arteriosclerosis, which in turn may have caused—as it commonly does—changes of character in the direction of greater egocentricity, withdrawal, suspicion, and aggressiveness.[46]

Whatever the unhappy effects of the Quad Plan struggle on Wilson personally or on his position at Princeton, it enhanced his reputation in the country at large. Newspaper comment on the scheme was generally favorable, and magazines with national circulation took note of it. In July 1907 *Life* devoted the entire editorial page in one issue and a lead editorial in another to discussion of the project. The *Review of Reviews* published an article describing the plan and praising it as "a fundamental and courageous move in the direction of vitality and wholesomeness in academic life." Even after the scheme was withdrawn, an editorial in the *Chicago Evening Post* took issue with the *Princeton Alumni Weekly's* statement that it was dead: "The 'quad' plan has been given intellectual existence and it must continue to live in the making of our universities almost as vitally as if it were embodied in stone on the Princeton campus." The plan was being discussed at Michigan and Wisconsin, stated the editorial, and would certainly catch the attention of some dynamic educator.[47]

In dealing with the Quad Plan, the press focused on the issue of "college democracy" against social privilege. This emphasis mirrored the mood of the time: the country was well into the progressive period, and the Muckrakers had schooled the public in the idea that the interests of the plain people were endangered by wealth and privilege. Whereas Wilson's role had formerly been that of an academic conservative, now he was clad in the mantle of a progressive. To the country at large his dispute with the Princeton clubs was analogous to Theodore Roosevelt's struggles with the trusts, the meat packers, and the railroads.

This change in Wilson's public image accorded with a shift in his own thinking. He began to see his defeat at the hands of the Trustees as one in which University policy had become the victim of entrenched wealth. In this belief he was encouraged by two of his strongest supporters on the Board, David B. Jones and Melanchthon W. Jacobus. Jones wrote Wilson on November 12, 1907, that he would be sorry if Moses Taylor Pyne withdrew financial support from the University— as he briefly threatened to do when Wilson insisted on continuing to promote the Quad Plan—but that he would be "infinitely more sorry to see the University dominated by the club men of New York, Philadelphia, and Pittsburgh." Jacobus urged Wilson to speak to as many alumni meetings as possible and in all his addresses to "make clear not only the issue which is joined, but the money spirit of the opposition. The present day is not propitious for the tyranny of wealth, and if the plain people of our alumni are at one with you on the Quads as against the clubs, they will be a hundred fold more so on freedom against the dictation of dollars."[48]

In January and February 1908 Wilson spent a month in Bermuda, attempting to restore his health and spirits. He found it an ideal place to forget the Princeton troubles. He met Mark Twain, who appeared to enjoy his company, as well as various island dignitaries, and he was lionized by Mrs. Mary Allen Peck, a divorcee whom he had met the previous year and with whom he formed a close friendship. He was even able to joke about his defeat, saying that he didn't get the quads, but he got the wrangles. But he returned to Princeton as determined as ever to have his way.[49]

Wilson now decided—as Jacobus had urged—to go over the heads of the Princeton Trustees and appeal to the alumni for support. His first address, to the Baltimore alumni on March 10, 1908, was conciliatory. He still thought that his method of promoting the intellectual life of the undergraduates was the best, he said, but with its withdrawal a special responsibility now rested upon the alumni and other counselors of the University to find other solutions that would accomplish the same purpose, and he would willingly cooperate with them. But two days later he talked to the Princeton Club of Chicago before a friendly audience that applauded his every word, and here his tone was quite different. It was ironical, he said, that a fundamental change in the course of study at Princeton caused hardly a ripple of excitement among the alumni, but when it came to altering the social life, there was a storm. He inveighed against the club system that favored private school boys and athletes and forced men to do the very thing that a university ought to discourage—to standardize themselves, to conform at all costs. Although still insisting that his purpose was intellectual, Wilson now stressed academic democracy, expressing "absolute sympathy" with the American ideals of a classless society and complete equality of opportunity. More than ever he believed that the systematic changes he had proposed were necessary, and not only for Princeton: every university, he said, must reorganize "so that some sort of natural and agreeable life will be provided for men whether or not they struggle for social preferment."[50]

Wilson also campaigned for the Quad Plan among the undergraduates. In the spring of 1908, for instance, the junior class gave him a dinner, at which Wilson told them what he thought a university was for and why the quads were needed. At the end of it most of the students were standing on their chairs and cheering; only a few club-men kept their seats. The later opinion of some undergraduates of this period was that Wilson had won the support of a majority of the under-graduates for the Quad Plan. There is no way of knowing with certainty, but it is striking to find that the senior members of the Cot-tage Club wrote Wilson a joint letter in June 1908 expressing their sincere appreciation of his earnest and effective efforts on Princeton's behalf and pledging "sympathetic support" for the future. In the social hierarchy Cottage ranked next to Ivy.[51]

Wilson's continuing campaign for the Quad Plan failed to bear fruit. From time to time an alumnus wrote that he had been won over, but a few commendatory letters and the applause from undergraduates were no substitute for the two million dollars that it was estimated the scheme would cost. When a wealthy Princeton trustee offered to build a single experimental quadrangle, Wilson turned the offer down, since he thought the unit would merely become a haven for the non-clubmen and might defer complete realization of his plans to re-organize undergraduate social life.[52]

Yet the agitation was not entirely barren of beneficial results. Over the opposition of Wilson and his supporters on the Board of Trustees a three-man committee of trustees was authorized in January 1908 to confer with a committee of alumni about remedying the evils of the club system. The Trustees' committee delivered a report in April 1908, which exonerated the clubs of many of the charges levied against them and found them generally "creditable academic organizations, and conducive to the maintenance among their members of a cleanly, manly, and fairly studious life." Most of the abuses, the committee found, flourished outside the clubhouses rather than within: the de-moralizing struggle to secure election, the barrier between classes owing to the Inter-Club Treaty, and the unfavorable influence that competition for membership had on scholarship in favor of frenetic pursuit of extracurricular activities. As a result of recommendations by this committee and of action by the undergraduates themselves the freshman and sophomore clubs were abolished. The University estab-lished required commons for underclassmen and voluntary commons for upperclassmen not in clubs. The Inter-Club Treaty, was abandoned. Nevertheless, the very existence of the new committee on social con-ditions was a rebuff to Wilson's leadership, as was its whitewash of the upper-class clubs; the reforms were calculated to make the clubs' continued existence acceptable. Wilson acquiesced, but not happily.[53]

In June 1908 Wilson's former classmate Cleveland Dodge asked Wilson to join him on a yachting trip, but Wilson refused, saying that he wanted to forget Princeton. The last year with its frustrations had gone hard with him. He was exhausted and suffering acutely from neuritis. His wife insisted that he go abroad to rest and get Princeton out of his system. When sympathetic trustees offered to pay his way, he refused, telling his wife, "I may have to oppose some of these men upon the vital educational policies of Princeton, and I should be trussed up if I accepted such favors from them." He sailed alone on the S.S. "California." Jack Hibben saw him off, evidence that even though their intimate friendship had ended, their estrangement was not yet complete.[54]

On shipboard Wilson took systematic exercise by jog-trotting in a secluded corner of the deck; he slept twelve to fourteen hours a day. After his arrival in Scotland he bicycled from Edinburgh south to the Lake District, stopping at the village of Ecclefechan to see Carlyle's grave and at Carlisle to try to find the house in which his mother had been born. He wore shorts, a blue shirt and tie, and an old tweed coat, the pockets stuffed with a few necessities and the *Oxford Book of English Verse*. When it rained, as it often did, he wore a black woolen cape he had bought in Edinburgh for the extravagant price of three guineas. In mid-July he reached Grasmere, where he was affectionately received by the Fred Yateses. He remained in the Lake District for the rest of the summer, except for a four-day visit to Skibo, Andrew Carnegie's vast estate in the Highlands.[55]

At the start of the vacation Wilson was unable to get the Princeton discouragements out of his mind. He wrote Ellen that he had actually turned to some unfamiliar poetry in the *Oxford Book of English Verse* and dug into a heavy tome on English constitutional history to prevent himself from examining wounds scarcely healed. In Grasmere he unburdened himself to the Yates's, telling them of the pain he felt because of the disloyalty of the friend he had trusted. As the summer wore on, his spirits rose. He made new friends, both British and American, and greatly enjoyed their company. One of them, Theodore Marburg, recollected that Wilson "was most companionable, never monopolizing the conversation but always chatty, interesting, and ready with amusing anecdotes to fill the turn of the talk." The frequent letters his family received, in spite of the neuralgia that made writing painful, were full of incident and humor. They revealed Wilson's natural affinity for Scotsmen of every sort and condition as well as his ambivalence toward the English, whom he sometimes found cold and rude.

He wrote to his daughter Jessie about the English attitude toward Americans:

It is not exactly an attitude of condescension, but it is an attitude of tolerant curiosity: as if they would *like* to know what Americans are like and what they think and how they talk and act and feel about the ordinary things of existence, but are not very *keen* about it,—do not regard it as *very* interesting, and would, on the whole, rather talk to their own kind and about their own things. It is as if their normal intense self-concentration were, through an impulse partly of kindliness, partly of curiosity, adjourned that they may for a moment notice the stranger who, orbitless, has swum into their ken. I do not like it, for it makes talking to them seem too little like genuine human intercourse to be thoroughly worthwhile. With an American I can really grapple:—which, perhaps, proves nothing except that I am as provincial as they are.[56]

At the end of the summer Fred Yates wrote Ellen Wilson about her husband's departure from Grasmere. "He goes away to-day," wrote Yates, "and there will be a mighty vacuum in Rydal—he has been a part of our summer . . . He was like a boy last night in his light-heartedness. You wouldn't think he ever had a care—it has done him good to come over . . . he has gone back home with renewed vigor and love of a whole neighborhood."[57]

The long, healing summer restored Wilson in body and spirit and gave him time for reflection, but it did not change his opinions or allay his resentments. In fact, he was more sure than ever that his pedagogical theories were right, more determined than ever that they should be put into practice.

He now attempted to revive the Quad Plan by persuading the Carnegie Foundation to give $3,500,000 to Princeton to put it into operation. "The whole college world is waking to it," he wrote Andrew Carnegie, "slowly but very definitely, turning vaguely toward the very solution I have thought out for Princeton. If I could carry it out here, it would be of universal and revolutionary influence, but I cannot without money, and some one must give me the money." Things had come to a turning point in his life, he wrote a friend of Carnegie's, and if he could not get funds for his plan he must give up "mere college administration" since his convictions made it impossible to continue with things in which he did not believe. Cleveland Dodge, a member of the governing board of the Carnegie Foundation, tried to convince fellow members of the soundness and importance of Wilson's plans; in March 1909 he reported that some of them were enthusiastic. Carnegie himself turned out to be the insurmountable obstacle; he vetoed the project. It proved impossible, one of his associates wrote Wilson, to convince the great philanthropist of the difference between Princeton and "some ambitious high school that wants to turn itself into a college."[58]

At Princeton controversy initiated by the Quad Plan continued. At a *Princetonian* dinner in the spring of 1909 Dean West made a clever speech seeking to undermine Wilson and his policies, very subtly done with an apparent air of candor and geniality. The President of the University was the last speaker, and when he rose, his face was grim, his lower jaw clenched. His talk opened, "It is my lonely privilege, in gatherings of educated men, to be the only person who speaks for education." He asked the young men before him whether they wanted to take a high road or an easy one, and then described his vision of what Princeton might be if it put away childish things. It was a dangerous heresy, he said, to think of college as an interlude or a time of diversion. In words that revealed how his sympathy for the victims of the club system was being transmuted into a broader democratic sympathy, Wilson charged that it was a poor preparation for life to live in a community where artificial social barriers cut you off from people who were different. "One of the things that makes us unserviceable citizens is that there are certain classes of men with whom we have never been able to associate, and whom we have, therefore, never been able to understand. I believe that the process of a university should be a process of unchosen contacts with modern thought and life and particularly with the life of our own country." When Wilson had finished, the students stood up and cheered while he sat silent and unsmiling. On the way home with Stockton Axson he muttered, "Damn their eyes—damn their eyes."[59]

He scored a similar triumph at a Cottage Club dinner, at which ex-President Patton was the other principal speaker. Patton launched a witty and apparently devastating attack on his successor's plans to reform undergraduate life; he spoke entirely in parables and elicited gales of laughter, in which Wilson joined. In answer Wilson spoke extemporaneously for thirty or forty minutes, using parables in the same way, and demolished Patton. When he sat down, he received an ovation. In the opinion of an officer of the club there was hardly a man in the room who would have refused if Wilson had at that moment asked for the keys to the club.[60]

Wilson's refusal to abandon his scheme for reorganizing Princeton's social life continued to cause perturbations among metropolitan alumni, with threats to stop contributing to the University unless the Quad Plan were renounced once and for all. Moses Taylor Pyne felt especially strongly about this, and he took it upon himself to announce at a dinner of the Princeton Club of New York that the scheme was dead. Even some of Wilson's most loyal supporters now urged him to keep silent.[61]

Wilson refused to give up. He urged the Quad Plan or something similar for other universities. In October 1908 he appeared before a distinguished convocation at the seventy-fifth anniversary of Haverford College. In introducing him, President Sharpless of Haverford said that people were becoming accustomed "to look to Princeton for the newest and best things in thought and collegiate management." Wilson proceeded to give a comprehensive review of American college education. Its primary need was a coherent, required curriculum, but the most difficult problem was to capture the interest of the students, who were engaged in the multifarious trivialities together known as "college life." Extracurricular organizations absorbed the energies of many of the best men. Wilson drew laughter by telling the story of an able Princeton undergraduate who refused a fellowship in psychology because "he had to run the college." The only way to make the life of the mind foremost and to relegate diversions to their proper place was to establish a true academic community in which faculty and students were thrown together in their daily lives.[62]

In an address at St. Paul's School in June 1909 Wilson blamed the fact that the sideshows were swallowing up the main circus on people of wealth and said that he did not know whether he wanted to continue as ringmaster. "There are more honest occupations than teaching," he said, "if you can't teach." His social sympathies were clearly turning against the constituency that Princeton represented. In a Phi Beta Kappa address at Harvard in July 1909 he claimed that the proliferation of campus activities occurred because the businessmen's sons now crowding colleges had no interest in books. In an article entitled "What Is a College For?" published in *Scribner's Magazine* in November 1909, he wrote that wealth was a positive handicap to young men, dulling their effort and purpose. This was a far cry from his inaugural address of seven years before with its aristocratic overtones.[63]

The struggle over the Quad Plan must be regarded as one of the climacterics of Wilson's life. It made his situation at Princeton so difficult that he began to think of another position or another profession. It embittered him and brought out a harsh side of his character not before revealed, but at the same time it toughened him so that he was later able to deal with politicians on their own terms. It made him more distrustful of wealth and enlarged his social sympathies. Finally, it initiated a radical change in his political outlook.

Toward Progressivism

It would be deeply unjust to say that our great corporations are "predatory" in their intentions or in their methods.

—Woodrow Wilson, 1907

I need not remind you of the various abuses in the business world which recent legislation has been more or less unsuccessfully attempting to correct . . . of the thousand and one ways in which what were thought to be the business interests of the country were pushed forward without regard to anything but the profit of those immediately concerned.

—Woodrow Wilson, 1909[1]

D U R I N G most of his term as President of Princeton Wilson's academic traditionalism was matched by his stance in politics. He had been swinging to the right even before he was elected, and afterwards his political opinions became for a time even more explicitly conservative. He may have been influenced in part by the fact that he was thrown into daily contact with corporation lawyers and men of great wealth, upon whose good will the present solvency and future growth of the University depended.

Wilson's political opinions along with his abilities as a public speaker began to attract the attention of conservatives who wished to rid the Democratic party of Bryan. In May 1902, a month before he was chosen President of Princeton, an anonymous letter appeared in the *Indianapolis News* recommending him as Democratic nominee for the presidency. Two years later Wilson swayed an important and politically sophisticated audience when, on November 29, 1904, he gave an address on "The Political Future of the South" to the Society of Virginians in New York City. The Democrats were still smarting from defeat: Theodore Roosevelt had recently carried every state outside the solid South in gaining the presidency over Alton B. Parker, the conservative New Yorker whose nomination had been a repudiation of Bryan's leadership in the Democratic party. In this speech Wilson proposed to rid the party of Bryan once and for all. Attributing defeat to the "populists and theorists" who ought never to have been allowed into Democratic counsels, he urged that the South lead the nation in thrusting such men from the party and returning to moderation and time-tested principles. "The country as it moves forward in its great material progress," he said, "needs and will tolerate no party of discontent or radical experiment; but it does need a party of conservative reform, acting in the spirit of law and of ancient institutions." The *New York Times* reported that Wilson's address was received with "wild applause" and the *New York Sun* stated that it "was greeted with one of the most remarkable demonstrations of approval that has been manifested at a public dinner in this city for a long time."[2]

Among those who observed Wilson's ability to win an audience and who approved his stand in national politics was George Brinton McClellan Harvey, editor of *Harper's Weekly* and president of Harper & Brothers, the firm that had published *George Washington* and *A History of the American People*. Harvey was one of the most brilliant journalists of his time. At the age of twenty-eight, only thirteen years after starting in as a cub reporter in a small Vermont town, he had been appointed by Joseph Pulitzer as managing editor of the *New York World*. A few years on Wall Street enabled him to make a fortune and to become the associate of leading financiers and promoters. He had a flair for politics, and during a brief sojourn in New Jersey he was instrumental in securing the support of the Democrats of that state for Grover Cleveland in 1892.[3]

Colonel Harvey attended Wilson's inaugural at Princeton, where it is alleged that he conceived the idea that Wilson should be President of the United States. In any case, he bided his time until the Lotos Club of New York City gave a dinner in Wilson's honor on February 3, 1906, and he was one of the speakers. Harvey told the club members that the Princetonian possessed ideal qualities for the presidency and that it was with "a sense of almost rapture" that he hoped to be able to vote for him some day.[4]

Before retiring that night, Wilson wrote Harvey a warm letter expressing gratitude for his remarks. He did not profess, however, to take Harvey's "nomination" seriously. When St. Clair McKelway, editor of the *Brooklyn Eagle*, proposed to interview him in order to launch his campaign for the Democratic nomination in 1908, Wilson asked him to desist, saying that he had no ambition for high political office. But Harvey was not to be dissuaded. *Harper's Weekly* promoted Wilson's candidacy in March, April, and May 1906, quoting favorable comment from newspapers all over the country. *The North American Review,* which Harvey also controlled, ran a lead editorial in its April issue urging that the country needed relief "from the strenuous and histrionic methods of Federal administration now exemplified in the White House" and expressing the conviction that Wilson met "all the exigencies of the situation."[5]

The *Literary Digest* of April 11, 1906, ran a story of Harvey's efforts to boom Wilson, starting with the Lotos Club dinner, about which it commented wryly: "The name, needless to say, was wildly applauded. All names for the presidency are wildly applauded. Newspapers, furthermore, always make mention of candidates thus nominated." It seemed unlikely that an academic figure with no political experience whatever would be seriously considered for the presidency. Yet at this time another event occurred which suggested that Harvey was not the only influential Democrat who had an eye on Wilson, and that the latter was perhaps not unwilling to be considered for high office. It was Wilson's appearance before the annual Jefferson Day dinner of the National Democratic Club at the Waldorf-Astoria in New York City on April 16, 1906.[6]

From a political viewpoint, this was a far more important gathering than the Lotos Club dinner. The four hundred-odd guests included Tammany sachems, national committeemen, Congressmen, Senators, former cabinet officers, and men of affairs such as Thomas Fortune Ryan, Harry Payne Whitney, August P. Belmont, and William Mc-Adoo, who was later to serve in Wilson's cabinet and marry his daughter Nell. Here sat the right wing of the Democratic party. In addition to Wilson the speakers were George B. McClellan, Mayor of New York City; Judson Harmon of Ohio, formerly Attorney General under Grover Cleveland; and John M. Gearin, United States Senator from Oregon.[7]

Mayor McClellan spoke first. He set the tone by affirming that if the Democratic party was to follow the ideals of its founder it should be "individualistic and conservative" and resist the "spirit of unrest and hopelessness sweeping around the world, a spirit which masks under the name of socialism, collectivism, communism, but which has for its object the subversion of existing law and order, and ultimately manifests itself by the flaming torch and the red flag of anarchy."

Wilson followed. His assignment was to speak on Jefferson the man, and he had prepared this talk with unusual care. Formerly Jefferson had not been one of Wilson's heroes. He had been supremely indifferent to the sage of nearby Monticello while at the University of Virginia. Later he had left Jefferson out of his "Calendar of Great

Americans" because of "the strain of French philosophy that permeated and weakened all his thought." But now he found that Jefferson was a child of the frontier who lived among "the plainest people of his time and drank directly at the sources of Democratic feeling." The apparent contradiction of the man was that although "he preached the abstract tenets of a speculative political philosophy, he nevertheless took leave to act like a wise American politician." When he had to choose between adhering to his theory of the Constitution or violating it in order to purchase Louisiana, he chose the latter course.[8]

Turning to the contemporary scene, Wilson suggested that the maladies in the body politic could be cured by a resort to the prescriptions of Jefferson. These spelled a return to laissez faire. Americans must emphatically reject, announced Wilson, the nostrums of socialism. It would be the utmost folly to attempt to curb the power of corporations, which were a natural form of business organization. Instead, the law must find ways of rooting out the dishonest individual in the corporation. "It is persons who do wrong, not corporations, and when persons do wrong they should suffer the penalty of the law." Wilson found nothing especially alarming in the contest between capital and labor and suggested that it was better to let the parties fight it out than to have the government intervene. "Capital will not discover its responsibilities if you aid it. Labor will not discover its limitations if you coddle it." Here, as elsewhere, the law should act only as umpire. Neither Andrew Carnegie nor William Graham Sumner ever denounced government intervention in the economy more fervently than did Wilson now: "It was a principle of Thomas Jefferson's that there should be as little government as possible,—which did not mean that there must not be any government at all, but only that men must be taught to take care of themselves. I heartily subscribe . . . because moral muscle depends upon your showing men that there is nothing to take care of them except God and themselves."

The stenographer's report of the Jefferson Day dinner makes it manifest that Wilson captured his audience. His hearers started to applaud when he remarked that the difficulty with believing in the people is that you know so many of them; from then on his address was punctuated by fifteen outbursts of "applause" and one of "laughter"; at the end there was "prolonged applause." For none of the other three speakers, all men of political prominence, did the stenographer note reaction from the audience. Two conclusions are obvious: that Wilson was on the way to winning support from the practical and powerful men who were among his hearers, and that he was appealing for their suffrage when he told them exactly what they wanted to hear.

During the entire period when he was agitating for the Quad Plan Wilson was flirting with politics. No sooner had he returned from England in October 1906 than he discovered that James Smith, Jr., Democratic boss of Essex County, New Jersey, egged on by George B. Harvey, was promoting him for United States Senator. He quashed the movement at once, saying that his first duty was to Princeton. But later, after the Republicans had captured solid control of the state legislature in the November elections, Harvey tried to persuade Wilson to accept the empty honor of nomination for Senator by the minority Democrats when the legislature convened in January 1907. Wilson was finally convinced, however, by his friend and Princeton classmate Edwin A. Stevens, also a candidate, that he was being used by the bosses as a stalking horse against the progressive element among the New Jersey Democrats, so he withdrew his name. It was an embarrassing incident and it made him aware of his political inexperience.[9]

The indefatigable Harvey did not give up: he continued to insist that Wilson should be nominated as Democratic candidate for the presidency in 1908 or, failing that, in 1912. He set one of his ablest writers, William O. Inglis, to promoting the candidacy before the public. He meanwhile lined up support among such conservative Democrats as Adolph Ochs, owner of the *New York Times;* Col. Henry Watterson, editor of the *Louisville Courier-Journal;* Major James C. Hemphill of the *Charleston News and Chronicle;* and August Belmont, financier. At Harvey's instigation Dr. John A. Wyeth, a friend of Wilson's, arranged a dinner at Delmonico's where Wilson met William F. Laffan, editor of the ultraconservative *New York Sun,* and Thomas Fortune Ryan, who enjoyed rather dubious fame as a traction magnate and Wall Street operator. Wyeth later wrote Wilson that these men were in a panic because they saw businessmen brought close to slavery by government regulation, and they were "beating the bushes for some Moses to lead them out of the wilderness."[10]

Laffan and Ryan were eager to determine the economic and political views of this putative Moses. Wilson obliged by writing a carefully composed "Credo," which avowed all that his new friends could desire. It was an uncompromising statement of extreme legal conservatism. The Credo opened by explaining that Wilson's early training had been in the law and that he regarded the Constitution and the ancient common law as adequate to correct the vices of modern business. Since the object of constitutional government was the freedom of the individual, statutes were needed to single out guilty individuals in the intricacies of modern business transactions. Wilson repudiated "the direct regulation of business through governmental commissions." He defended freedom of contract and, by inference, repudiated social legislation. "Under the constitution of the United States," he wrote, "there is secured to us that most precious of all the possessions of a free people, the right of freedom of contract. Destroy that right, and we cease to be a free people . . . The men who would abridge or abrogate this right have neither the ideas nor the sentiments needed for the maintenance or for the enjoyment of liberty." Wilson closed by condemning any assumption by the President of powers not rightfully his as well as any attempts to diminish the power of the courts.[11]

In 1906, 1907, and the early months of 1908, Wilson delivered himself of a series of speeches and magazine articles that showed what the generalities of the Credo would mean in practice. While not blind to the evils in the economic organization of the country, he believed that they were negligible at the operating level, where actual commodities were exchanged or manufactured. The real "predatory wealth," he maintained, was in the stock markets, where by secret processes so-called "financiers" manipulated securities so as to bilk the public of millions; in effect, these men were engaging in sheer theft. Wilson's frequently repeated cure for such practices was to seek out the individual in the corporate maze. "One really responsible man in jail, one real originator of the schemes and transactions which are contrary to public interest legally lodged in the penitentiary, would be worth more than one thousand corporations mulcted in fines, if reform is to be genuine and permanent." "There is no such thing," he told the Cleveland Chamber of Commerce, "as corporate morality or corporate integrity or corporate responsibility." When a corporation was fined, the public paid. The true solution was to pass statutes requiring corporations to reveal their doings to public officials and making certain specific abuses—such as stock-watering—illegal. Then the guilty individual could be found and punished without disturbing the corporation in its legitimate functions. Where regulation was necessary, offenses should be defined by law and punishments imposed by the judiciary, not the executive department.[12]

Wilson's Calvinistic insistence on punishing the guilty individual was accompanied by criticism of the Sherman Anti-Trust Law as clumsy and ineffectual, and by repeated attacks on regulatory commissions, whether at the state or federal level. While admitting that some regulation was permissible in the sphere of public utilities, Wilson expressed fear that current efforts to remove abuses were fully as dangerous as the abuses themselves. He attributed the panic of 1907, for instance, principally to "rate legislation against railroads . . . which made it impossible for the railroads to borrow money." "Government supervision will not free us or moralize us," he declared, "it will in the long run enslave and demoralize us." It represented the high road to socialism and the extinction of American liberties.[13]

Much else that Wilson said at this period displayed a conservative bias. He called a graduated income tax a means of penalizing wealth, and he insisted that a national child labor law was the first step to federal control of "every particular of the industrial organization and action of the country." He condemned labor union leaders as a class representing a minority interest who were "as formidable an enemy to equality and freedom of opportunity" as the "so-called capitalist class."[14]

Whatever the implications of some of his actions, by no explicit statement, public or private, did Wilson at this time admit that he was seriously contemplating an active career in politics. In fact, he repudiated that he would like to be one of a corps of "practical thinkers, of practical talkers, who don't have to win—just as practical as the politicians, but with a longer time to wait." He wished to achieve a position analagous to that of his mentor Walter Bagehot, the "literary politician." He was encouraged in this ambition when in November 1907 a *New York Times* reporter went to Princeton and spent an evening with him in his lamplit study at Prospect. The resulting interview was published with pictures and a banner headline as the lead article covering the entire front page of the Sunday magazine section on November 24. The reporter was obviously taken with Wilson, whom he described as "sitting in his office chair, erect, alert, alive in every degree of a man's best conception of republican ideals." Wilson opened the conversation by saying that he objected to having his name mentioned for political office because he had "the interest of constitutional ideals too much at heart to become entangled in the embarrassment of political promises." Political promises must be kept and must not interfere with long-time ideals. He then spoke pungently on public matters, such as the causes of the panic of 1907, and the imprudence of Theodore Roosevelt. He suggested that the country might benefit from a "common council" of men who combined practical knowledge of affairs and the long view. Such a man, in his opinion, was J. P. Morgan, who had helped Wall Street weather the recent financial storm; another such man, implicitly, was Woodrow Wilson.[15]

Wilson's official assumption of a role aloof from the political arena weakened in 1908, when apparently he entertained a faint hope that he might achieve his boyhood ambition of entering public service. Early in that year George Harvey persuaded Joseph Pulitzer of the *New York World,* one of the two or three outstanding Democratic newspapers in the country, to publish an editorial written by Harvey himself favoring Wilson for the presidency. In June 1908 the *North American Review,* with Wilson's full knowledge and consent, published in a series of essays entitled "Claims of the Candidates" an article favoring him for the Democratic nomination. Henry James Forman, editor of the magazine, had previously written to Wilson, "I do believe that you are a possible recipient of the nomination at Denver, and my only anxiety is to have your claims properly presented."[16]

To achieve the presidency in 1908, Wilson would have to beat out William Jennings Bryan for the Democratic nomination and then face Theodore Roosevelt if the latter ran for a third term, as it was freely predicted he would. Further presumptive evidence that Wilson was making himself available for the presidency is found in the way in which he carefully differentiated himself from both men. At one time Wilson and Roosevelt had been cordial acquaintances. Wilson had praised Theodore Roosevelt as the kind of man America needed in politics. He had visited Roosevelt at Oyster Bay and been charmed by his home life. Roosevelt in turn had praised Wilson's speeches and writings and asked him to spend a night at the White House so they could talk. It is impossible to say exactly when Wilson cooled toward Roosevelt, but in the years 1906-1908 he attacked him—usually by obvious implication rather than directly—for overextension of the executive power and imprudence in promoting regulatory legislation. This pleased the conservative Democrats. At the same time Wilson kept a foot in the camp of the reformers by criticizing the Roosevelt administration for failure to promote reduction of the tariff or federal regulation of banking and credit.[17]

Privately expressing the wish that Bryan could be "knocked into a cocked hat," Wilson maintained publicly that Bryan was "the most charming and lovable of men personally, but foolish and dangerous in his political beliefs." He tried to withdraw from an agreement to speak at the National Democratic Club dinner in 1908 when he heard that Bryan was to be there, and made an appearance only when assured that Bryan would not attend after all. He said he did not wish to embarrass the Great Commoner by attacking his "foolish notions" in public. When asked by a *New York Times* reporter just what these foolish notions were, Wilson refused to say: "There are specific objections that I could point out in Bryan, political propositions in his platform that I consider absurd and could never endorse, but what use would it serve any one if I named them? No matter how humble my prospects, I should still be accused of political intention if I went into these matters." Wilson was in fact making himself more available as a Democratic candidate by setting himself up as a clear alternative to Bryan without crossing swords with the Nebraskan on specific issues.[18]

There was some talk of nominating Wilson for Vice-President as Bryan's running mate in 1908, but before sailing for Britain in June, he told Stockton Axson that under no circumstances would he consent to this. The faint possibility that he might yet receive the presidential nomination led him to stay in Edinburgh during the Democratic convention so that he could be reached by cable. He wrote his wife that he felt silly "waiting on the possibility of the impossible happening." There was evidently not a ghost of a chance of stopping Bryan, but since Colonel Harvey was at the convention, he had best not be incommunicado. But when the Democrats met in Denver in July, Bryan was firmly in control and was easily nominated on the first ballot. Wilson's name was never mentioned.[19]

Colonel Harvey's efforts to propel him into politics apparently helped to renew Wilson's old interest in the practical working of the federal government. The result was his last scholarly work, *Constitutional Government*, published in 1908. For some years he had been of the opinion that *Congressional Government* was becoming hopelessly out of date. In the spring of 1907 he was given an opportunity to take a new look at the federal government when he was invited to present a series of lectures under the auspices of the George Blumenthal Foundation at Columbia University. Although a condition of his appointment was that the lectures be afterwards published, they were originally delivered from notes. Not until nearly a year later, while vacationing in Bermuda in the winter of 1908, did he produce the manuscript published by the Columbia University Press under the title *Constitutional Government in the United States.*[20]

In a prefatory note Wilson made clear that *Constitutional Government*, like its predecessor, was intended not merely to describe but to instruct. The work was presented in the hope that it might be "serviceable in the clarification of our views as to policy and practice." He again insisted that the government was not a static Newtonian system but a political organism with a constantly changing life of its own. He once more pleaded for arrangements that would promote effective leadership, party responsibility, and legislation for the general welfare rather than for selfish and particular ends.[21]

Constitutional Government is a much sounder book than its more famous forerunner. In *Congressional Government* Wilson's vision of the United States had been distorted by the opinions of Walter Bagehot as well as by his hope of adapting British political practices to the American scene. Now, after twenty years of mature observation, he looked at the political system of the United States with cool realism and an informed historical sense. He still disapproved the way the House of Representatives did business in committee, where legislative processes were hidden from the public eye and the lack of public debate prevented decisions based on "common counsel," but he admitted that in such a large body the committee system might be the only efficient way to operate. He deplored the bosses but considered them necessary to the maintenance of party organization, since reformers were unwilling to work sufficiently hard and long. Where *Congressional Government* had been characterized by extraordinary economic naïveté, Wilson now revealed awareness of economic realities, as when he doubted the value of newspaper opinion because of the special interests that controlled the principal newspapers, or when he expressed concern that the poor man fared badly in the courts because he could not afford the costs of litigation.

The most remarkable difference between Wilson's earlier and later studies of American political practice was his treatment of the office of the President, for which he had gained a new respect. In *Congressional Government* one short, perfunctory chapter entitled "The Executive" was slipped in toward the end of the book; in it the President appeared as a rather shadowy figure, dominated by Congress, limited in function to administration, and sharing his power with the cabinet. In *Constitutional Government* the chapter on the presidency preceded those on all other organs of government. Wilson now saw the chief executive as occupying "the vital place of action" in the American constitutional system. He poured scorn on those who, through constitutional scruple, had held back from using the full power of the office, believing mistakenly in the "strict literary theory of the Constitution, the Whig theory, the Newtonian theory," and acting as though "Pennsylvania Avenue should be even longer than it is." "The President," Wilson maintained, "is at liberty, both in law and in conscience, to be as big a man as he can. His capacity will set the limit; and if Congress be overborne by him, it will be no fault of the makers of the Constitution,—it will be from no lack of powers on his part, but only because the President has the nation behind him and Congress has not."[22]

In explaining the chief executive's originative power in the federal government, Wilson outlined the methods he himself was later to employ in prodding Congress into constructive action. His central premise was the fact that the President alone represented the nation as a whole and thus could command far more attention than any other political figure. He could sway the House of Representatives, exerting a power greater than the Speaker, because he could speak directly to the nation. Indeed, wrote Wilson, "The Constitution bids him speak, and times of stress and change must more and more thrust upon him the attitude of originator of policies." Because of this attitude Wilson was later to revive—and with great effect—the personal message to Congress, a practice that had been abandoned for over a century. He recognized that the technique of enlisting public opinion was likely to be more effective with the members of the House, who were elected every two years, than with the Senate, who enjoyed six-year terms and who, in 1907, were not accountable to the people directly but were elected by state legislatures. Wilson recommended that the President enlist the support of the Senate by confidential correspondence with its leaders. This again accorded with his later practice.[23]

Constitutional Government gives an insight into Wilson's ultimate failure in foreign affairs. Even though he recognized that the Senate held tenaciously to its right of independent judgment in this area, he thought that in a showdown the President could win. His defense of this opinion suggests the overconfidence in the power of the presidential office that later led him to disaster:

One of the greatest of the President's powers I have not spoken of at all: his control, which is very absolute, of the foreign relations of the nation. The initiative in foreign affairs, which the President possesses without any restriction whatever, is virtually the power to control them absolutely. The President cannot conclude a treaty with a foreign power without the consent of the Senate, but he may guide every step of diplomacy, and to guide diplomacy is to determine what treaties must be made, if the faith and prestige of the government are to be maintained. He need disclose no step of negotiation until it is complete, and when in any crucial matter it is completed the government is virtually committed. Whatever its disinclination, the Senate may feel itself committed also.

Moreover, Wilson's final personal tragedy—his breakdown in health while crusading for the League of Nations—is also foreshadowed by this passage on the crushing burden of the presidential office:

No other man's day is so full as his, so full of the responsibilities which tax mind and conscience alike and demand an inexhaustible vitality. The mere task of making appointments to office, which the Constitution imposes upon the President, has come near to breaking some of our Presidents . . . And in proportion as the President ventures to use his opportunity to lead opinion and act as spokesman of the people in affairs the people stand ready to overwhelm him by running to him with every question great and small . . . Men of ordinary physique and discretion cannot be Presidents and live, if the strain be not somehow relieved. We shall be obliged always to be picking our chief magistrates from among wise and prudent athletes—a small class.[24]

Both in tone and in substance *Constitutional Government*, like Wilson's other writings and addresses of the time, was conservative. He opposed the initiative and referendum, inveighed against federal paternalism, and took the view that federal regulation of labor conditions was a ridiculous overextension of the power to regulate interstate commerce. One of the best chapters in the book attempts a defense of the states against federal encroachments of power. Wilson also defended the Senate from the charge that it was a "rich man's club," dominated by the railroads and trusts. Although he admitted that this might be so in places where wealth exerted most political power, he did not think it true of rural and recently settled states, where Senators were apt to be "quiet gentlemen" who had not made fortunes but had grown rich in the esteem of their fellow citizens. That the Senate contained proportionately more members from rural constituencies than from urban did not bother Wilson because that body "represents the population of the country, not in its numbers, but in its variety; and it is of the utmost consequence that the country's variety should be represented as well as its masses."[25]

In the course of defending the unequal representation of population in the Senate, Wilson excoriated urban life and celebrated rural and small town America. Into the eastern states, he wrote, "a miscellaneous immigration has poured social chaos." "In those hot centres of trade and industry, where a man's business grips him like an unrelaxing hand of iron from morning to night, and lies heavily upon him even when he sleeps, few men can be said to have any opinions at all." Instead, men acquire "a miscellany of mental reactions, never assorted, never digested," from the metropolitan press. Contrast the happy situation elsewhere:

In small towns, in rural countrysides, around comfortable stoves in crossroads stores, where business shows as many intervals as transactions, where seasons of leisure alternate with seasons of activity, where large undertakings wait on slow, unhastening nature, where men are neighbors and know each other's quality, where politics is dwelt upon in slow talk with all the leisure and fond elaboration usually bestowed on gossip, where discussion is as constant a pastime as checkers, opinion is made up with an individual flavor and wears all the variety of individual points of view.

This passage shows that whatever their differences in particular policies, Wilson was far closer to William Jennings Bryan in his social sympathies than to such metropolitan types as George Harvey, William F. Laffan, and Thomas Fortune Ryan. It is hardly a coincidence that at the same time he was preparing *Constitutional Government* for the press, while on vacation in Bermuda in January and February 1908, he also reached the decision to appeal to "the plain people of our alumni" against the metropolitan clubmen who had defeated the Quad Plan.[26]

A definite shift to the left in Wilson's political outlook first became apparent in April 1908, when he again spoke before the Jefferson Day dinner of the National Democratic Club in New York City. While the tone of his address was suited to the conservatism of the audience, and he reiterated much he had said before about the dangers of unrestricted executive power and the need for a return to government by law, he also made a volte-face in regard to state regulation of business enterprise. He warned that corporations controlled by a few men had become so large that they threatened to rival the government itself; they must be curbed. "No one now advocates the old *laisser faire*," declared Wilson, "or questions the necessity for a firm and comprehensive regulation of business operations in the interest of fair dealing, and of a responsible exercise of power." He sounded a grave warning that unless there was sensible reform, there might be revolution: "I want to say to all corporation lawyers, 'If you would save the corporation, you will come out from cover and tell the legislators what is needed. You know what is needed, they don't. By telling them you will save the corporation. If you don't you will have the mob at its door in a decade.' "[27]

It is worthy of note that this second Jefferson Day address followed closely on his speech to the Princeton alumni in Chicago, in which he had first publicly turned the Quad Plan fight into one for social democracy against social privilege. The Princeton Trustees had by then also repudiated his leadership by proposing reforms in the club system, against Wilson's will. The struggle with what he had come to regard as entrenched wealth and privilege at Princeton apparently affected his political outlook.

After Wilson's return from his summer abroad in 1908, more convinced than ever that the Quad Plan was a cure for the social and academic ills endemic in American colleges, he soon revealed his new political attitude as well. On September 30 he appeared before the American Bankers' Association at Denver, Colorado, and told that the

United States was threatened for the first time with class warfare, that issue might soon be joined "between the power of accumulated capital and the opportunities of the masses of the people." The increasing attraction of socialism, however impractical its program, was a natural protest against corporate selfishness. Whereas recently Wilson had expressed fear of the expansion of government at the expense of private enterprise, he now observed that the most striking fact about the organization of modern society was "not the power of government, but the power of capital."[28]

Having assumed for the first time an unmistakably progressive stance, Wilson proceeded to tell the bankers that they were the most criticized interest in the capitalist community because the most isolated. They were "singularly remote from the laborer and from the body of the people" and equally remote "from the farmer and the small trader of our extensive countryside." They ignored the social and political functions of banking in their search for quick profits in speculative enterprises of dubious value. They should end the capital famine in rural districts by establishing branch banks. They should find a way to develop a safe and flexible currency. Bankers, in short, should become statesmen and learn to serve the general public. This remarkable address, containing ideas that later found legislative form in the Federal Reserve Banks and Federal Farm Loan Banks, was read into the Congressional Record.[29]

Wilson's conversion to progressivism was not yet complete. During the presidential campaign of 1908, Roland Morris, a former student active in the Democratic party in Pennsylvania, tried to persuade him to allow Bryan to speak on the Princeton campus and to ask him to lunch at Prospect, but Wilson flatly refused; the Great Commoner spoke at Princeton Junction. In an address on Robert E. Lee in January 1909 Wilson reverted to the theme that the country was in danger from excessive governmental regulation and that the only thing needed to cure corporate ills was to chastise the guilty individuals. But less than a month later, in an address on "Abraham Lincoln: A Man of the People," Wilson displayed the new note of sympathy with the mass of the people that had characterized his talk to the American Bankers' Association. He claimed that the most important trait of a popular leader was "a universal sympathy for those who struggle, a universal understanding of the unutterable burdens that were upon their backs." In his Princeton Baccalaureate Address of June 1909 he seemed in part to have slipped back into conservatism again when he condemned trade unions as breeders of "unprofitable servants"—a denunciation that was widely published and later hurt Wilson politically.

But his ill opinion of trade unions was balanced by an equally severe arraignment of corporate malpractices, in which he took a position exactly contrary to his former one. No longer were the misdeeds of corporations considered the responsibility of a few dishonest men who should be ferreted out; instead, they were the product of a system, in which honest men were trapped. An inevitable corollary of this new point of view was to favor an increase in state regulation of private enterprise.[30]

After the Denver convention of 1908 Wilson again defined his role in the political scene as that of a talker, not a doer. There was, however, a new urgency, a more explicit desire to act as a prophet. He closed the address on Lee with the words:

> I wish there were some great orator who could go about and make men drunk with the spirit of self-sacrifice. I wish there were some man whose tongue might every day carry abroad the golden accents of the golden age when we were born a nation; accents that would ring like tones of reassurance around the whole circle of the globe, so that America might again have the distinction of showing men the way, the certain way, of achievement and of confident hope.[31]

Wilson's most notable public pronouncement during the years 1908 and 1909 was a long article in the *North American Review* attacking the Payne-Aldrich tariff law, which had been passed by a Republican Congress and signed by President Taft in August 1909. He was persuaded to write the piece by George Harvey, who informed him that the country was "red-hot over this tariff atrocity" and he should therefore "sound a bugle blast" and assume leadership. Wilson readily agreed. He had been interested in the tariff question since he was a young man; attacking the system of protection was a familiar and congenial task. The article that he sent to Harvey, entitled "The Tariff Make-Believe," was readable and knowledgeable. It described the various "jokers" and special favors written into the new tariff act and castigated the furtive processes by which it had been put through Congress. It demanded that tariff rates be gradually lowered until their purpose was principally revenue, not protection. Wilson now clearly aligned himself with the Democrats, maintaining that the tariff law was a result of the fact that the Republican party had established a business constituency demanding and receiving special favors. Wilson also now wrote as a progressive, denouncing the great business combinations that the tariff had fostered; he claimed that the recent scandals of American business came from "their power to crush, their power to monopolize."[32]

Wilson's turn toward progressivism made him more politically available. Given the mood of the country in 1909, with the Muckrakers in full cry and the general public demanding reform of every sort, there was no future in politics for anyone who expounded a philosophy acceptable to traction magnate Thomas Fortune Ryan or to William F. Laffan of the *New York Sun.* If Wilson was to fulfill George Harvey's prediction and rise to the highest political office in the land, it must be as a progressive. His shift to the left in 1908 was apparently triggered by the Quad Plan controversy, but it is also probable that he was astute enough to know that this move might improve his chances in the political arena.

XVIII

Defeat

1909–1910

The fight at Princeton was one of incredible bitterness. One could get such bitterness only in a school, a church, a town library committee, or a benevolent society.

—Booth Tarkington, 1940[1]

T H E wounds left by the Quad Plan dispute did not readily heal. The Princeton Trustees were so divided either for or against Wilson that it proved difficult even to agree on filling vacancies in the Board. The factionalism extended to the alumni. In March 1909 anti Wilsonians put up Wilson Farrand, an articulate member of the opposition, for Alumni Trustee, an officer selected by a postal ballot of Princeton graduates, whereupon Wilson's friends tried unsuccessfully to find someone to run against Farrand. How clear cut the division in the alumni had grown, and how bitter the feeling, is suggested by a letter of August 21, 1909, to Wilson from John W. Barr, Jr., who was later to run for Alumni Trustee in support of the administration: "The men who are not in sympathy with you make a great deal of noise, but do not carry much weight, as they are largely recruited from those who enjoy life to the full on gratuities or an allowance given them by their indulgent parents. It seems to me that if I were endeavoring to accomplish a great work such as you have undertaken, I would regard it as a compliment for the men of this type to be lined up in opposition to me."[2]

There was dispute over the projected Graduate College to house graduate students and over Dean West's status as Dean of the Graduate School. Wilson had often argued that the proposed Graduate College should be at the heart of the University. Remembering his own experiences as a graduate student at Virginia and Johns Hopkins, where he had enjoyed close friendships and had exerted influence among the undergraduates, he wanted to create a similar situation in Princeton,

353

so that older and younger men might mingle. West had originally gone along with this idea, and the brochure he published on the Graduate College in 1903 implied that it would be at the heart of the University. But the experimental residence for graduate students that West had established at Merwick was at least half a mile to the northeast of the college campus, and its social life was entirely apart from that of the undergraduates. In 1907 West told the Trustees that to place the permanent Graduate College in or next to the central campus, with its distracting diversions, would make the task of developing its true life almost impossible. The Dean appeared to be attempting to pull the college away from intimate connection with the University.[3]

In 1908 the question of the Graduate College site seemed to have reached a conclusion satisfactory to Wilson. The $250,000 bequest of Mrs. Swann's to build Thomson College, a residence for graduate students, stipulated that the building should be placed on the Princeton campus. According to a legal opinion written by William J. Magie, ex-Chancellor of New Jersey, the terms of the Swann bequest clearly ruled out Merwick. After prolonged discussion and examination of half a dozen locations it was decided to place Thomson College on the grounds of Prospect, the President's residence. Grover Cleveland and M. Taylor Pyne had supported West in favoring a more distant site, but when the decision to build at Prospect was finally made, they gave in with good grace.[4]

Closely tied to the question of the site of the Graduate College was that of West's status and powers as Dean of the Graduate School. The Princeton Trustees had granted the Dean extraordinary powers during the slack Patton regime. Subject only to the provisos that he consult the President of the University and report annually to the Board of Trustees, the Dean was in entire charge of all the affairs of the Graduate School—arranging the curriculum, admitting students, awarding fellowships, and granting degrees. To be sure, there was a faculty committee, but it was selected by West himself.[5]

For six years Wilson did not disturb these arrangements. But in 1906 Professor Edward Capps went to Princeton from Yale, with the assurance that his particular function was to strengthen the faculty of the Graduate School. On his arrival he was appointed to the faculty committee on the Graduate School, but he was puzzled as to his function because Dean West made decisions without consulting the committee members, even on important matters such as the granting of degrees. Finally Capps went to Wilson and asked him just what his relationship to West and the Graduate School should be. Wilson said that although he realized the situation was difficult, he did not want

Comm. March 2, 1908

Graduate College

Permanent nature of the decision

Its radical nature
  a) As regards all Princeton precedents.
  b) Its ultimate results as illustrated in the experience
     of other institutions.
     What 50 yrs. hence?
     Natural tendency toward separation, hitherto over-
     come at Princeton, to her great distinction

A new conception of the Graduate College, not supported
  by the judgment of those upon whose approval the conception
  originally rested and upon whose approval its success
  depends.
  Coolness already apparent.

{ Idea of solidarity and reciprocal influence
                    vs.
  Aesthetic considerations and temporary advantage }

The legal obstacle

The Sites: West's
           My own
           A new one

Wilson's notes for a meeting of the Princeton Trustees' Committee on the Graduate School, summarizing his reasons for opposing Dean West's plan to locate the proposed Graduate College off campus. Wilson often spoke from such notes when making presentations or public addresses.

to interfere if he could help it and hoped the situation would right itself. When two other new professors of high distinction, Frank Frost Abbott and Edwin Grant Conklin, joined the faculty in 1908, they soon joined Capps in urging that the Graduate School be reorganized so as to put the Dean under control. In the fall of 1908 Dean Fine, in consultation with Capps and Conklin, drew up a new bylaw vesting control in a Faculty Graduate School Committee, appointed by the President of the University. West protested that this was a violation of Wilson's pledge of support given when the Dean refused the M.I.T. offer in 1906. He received the answer: "I wish to remind the Dean somewhat grimly that he must be digested into the processes of the University." Since these arrangements were concurred in by the two most powerful men in the Princeton Community, Wilson and Pyne, an uneasy peace prevailed. Men like Conklin and Capps, whose principal interest was the academic training of graduate students, were cool, however, toward Dean West's emphasis on the amenities. They thought it a waste of time, for instance, for young men to sit around in academic gowns or dinner jackets attempting, as West put it, to "recover the lost art of conversation." Even more threatening to the peace were rumors that Dean West was on the way to securing large sums to build a bigger and better Graduate College and that the site question would therefore be reopened.[6]

The dramatic controversies over the Quad Plan and the Graduate College have diverted attention from much else that went on during Wilson's second four years as President of Princeton. Progress did not cease because the Trustees and Faculty were divided over two particular issues. Although it proved impossible to secure funds for the Quad Plan, and although the Graduate School was as yet meagerly endowed, money came in for other important purposes. In 1907 Wilson wrote in a memorandum that Princeton's greatest need was a "museum of instruction" in biology, which would cost not less than $600,000. "The growth and salvation of the university," he wrote, "seem to depend on it." Gifts totaling nearly a million and a half dollars soon made possible the construction of two huge multi-purpose laboratories. In October 1908 the Palmer Physical Laboratory was opened for classroom use and experimental work in physics and chemistry. A year later the geological and biological sciences moved into Guyot Hall, a building almost as long as a football field. No longer could scientific study be considered a stepchild at Princeton.[7]

The conventional physical growth of the University continued as well. McCosh Hall, a classroom building, was completed in 1907. Wilson took special interest in the construction of new dormitories because of his ambition to house all undergraduates on campus, especially the freshmen, who had hitherto been obliged to lodge in boardinghouses throughout the town. His purpose was to provide better, cheaper housing and to mix the four classes. During his administration four new dormitories were completed and another was begun, so that by the time he resigned in 1910 all three upper classes and about a third of the freshmen were housed on campus.[8]

With strong encouragement and support from the Board of Trustees, Wilson insisted that only the best architects be hired and that the physical growth of Princeton should not be haphazard. When Henry B. Thompson, a new member of the Trustees' Committee on Grounds and Buildings, made his first official call on Wilson in 1906, he happened to express an opinion about where a new building should be placed; he was somewhat taken aback by the reply, "Thompson, as long as I am President of Princeton I propose to dictate the architectural policy of the University." Thompson later found that Wilson was much more amenable than this first encounter suggested. Although he disagreed with the President on the location of the new laboratories and helped to outvote him in the matter, he and Wilson became close friends and spent many hours going over drawings and specifications. In matters of detail, where principle did not seem to be involved or where a question was still fluid, Wilson could accept disagreement and even outright defeat gracefully.[9]

In 1907 Ralph Adams Cram, the outstanding expert on Gothic architecture in America, was appointed Supervising Architect of the University. He found Wilson to be one of the pleasantest men he had ever worked for—understanding, appreciative, and considerate. "I have never had a better client," he said, "and few as good." Cram discovered that Wilson could read plans with great facility and knew almost spontaneously the designer's intention. He wanted to see and understand everything. In the summer of 1907 alone, the architect wrote him over twenty letters concerning construction of the new laboratories, dealing with everything from the style of stone for a coping to the proper material for sheathing the roof. Cram was associated with Princeton for over a quarter of a century; under his direction the campus acquired uniformity of architectural style, with buildings logically placed in relation to two main axes, so that today it is one of the most attractive academic communities in the country.[10]

During the eight years of Wilson's presidency the annual budget of the university more than tripled, disbursements rising from something over $200,000 in 1902-1903 to over $700,000 in 1909-1910. Such a large operation obviously needed a competent financial director. On Wilson's initiative, therefore, the day-to-day expenditures of the University were placed under a single head, entitled the Financial Secretary to the Board of Trustees. Andrew C. Imbrie, who continued to serve as Alumni Trustee, was appointed to the position in April 1909. It was his duty to coordinate the day-to-day work of the University and to keep the President informed. Imbrie found Wilson always cordial and reasonable, although with people he did not like he was sometimes aloof and untactful. The Imbrie Papers reveal that Wilson kept in constant touch with details of administration, especially those that directly affected undergraduate social life, such as allotment of rooms in dormitories and efforts to prevent upperclassmen from selling second-hand furniture to freshmen at outrageous prices.[11]

Wilson's dreamed of an academic community in which undergraduates would rapidly mature, would learn to love the things of the mind, and would submit willingly to the discipline of study. Until that millennium arrived, however, he was quite willing to force undergraduates to behave themselves. In 1907 and 1908 he and Dean Fine conducted a campaign against the organized rowdiness for which Princeton had become noted. One of the most picturesque of these manifestations was the "Keg Hollow party," an amiable custom whereby a group of undergraduates would secretly buy a keg of beer, roll it downhill to Keg Hollow—a swampy dell at the head of what is now Carnegie Lake—and drink themselves prostrate. The Keg Hollow party became institutionalized as a sophomore affair held after Bicker Week, designed to heal the hard feelings that the club elections had caused. In 1907 Wilson personally forbade it. When some sophomores defied him and held it anyway, twenty-seven men were apprehended and suspended for three weeks, over the protest of the *Daily Princetonian* that some of those punished had only been onlookers. The undergraduates were told that in the future mere attendance at a Keg Hollow party would be reason for suspension. In reporting the incident to the Trustees, Dean Fine remarked, "We have every reason to believe that our action has put an end to organized affairs of this kind." In similar fashion the Senior Parades—in one of which Wilson had been lampooned about the Prospect fence—were abolished, along with excessive drinking at other affairs.[12]

Although there was glooming about his severity and his lack of reverence for "old customs," Wilson retained the respect and affection of the students, who commonly referred to him as "Woodrow" or "Woody." He was always willing to meet with groups of undergraduates, and the students of his day felt freer than they would today to go to the President of the University with their problems. The class of 1909 seems to have been especially close to him. It enjoyed four full years of his preceptorial system before the first flush of enthusiasm had passed and, like Wilson's own class of '79, it turned out far more than its quota of men who took a prominent part in Princeton's affairs. The only guest the members of "oughty-nine" asked to their class dinner at graduation was Wilson. His talk on this occasion, on the meaning of a liberal education, was apparently one in which Elijah seemed to be standing at his elbow; the mother of a member of the class, who was listening from outside, was in tears at the end of it.[13]

In his annual report for the year 1909 Wilson reviewed the first four years of the preceptorial system. It had not been found suitable, he wrote, for certain areas of study, such as mathematics, the sciences, and economics, nor for certain levels, such as elementary Greek. Its proper place was in areas demanding extended reading, where it had weaned undergraduates away from the feeling that they were performing meaningless tasks. "The men read subjects, they do not get up courses."[14]

An article in the *Daily Princetonian* also judged the preceptorial system a success. Its greatest virtue, in the opinion of the student paper, had been to break down the traditional barrier between students and faculty. "No longer is the function of the faculty entirely that of Greek tragedy—to inspire pity and fear,—fear at examination time, pity at all other times, in the mind of the undergraduate." Permanent friendships between teachers and students had been formed, whereby students had learned that the intellectual life was not a desiccated life. Other virtues were amelioration of the drudgery of required courses and fair marking.[15]

In spite of this favorable verdict, the system was in trouble. Its cost posed such a threat to the solvency of the University that even Wilson's friends among the Princeton trustees suggested that the number of preceptors be reduced; his enemies muttered against the system itself. When in June 1909 the contracts of eleven preceptors were renewed, the appointment in every case was made for only a single year. Preceptors themselves were beginning to resign before their terms of appointment were complete. The trouble was partly that they did not enjoy tenure. But more important, Wilson's insistence that a preceptor assist students with every course given by his department imposed a heavy burden. Edward S. Corwin said that in his first year at Princeton he read twelve thousand pages in preparation for his sessions with undergraduates. Thomas J. Wertenbaker found he was expected to assist in teaching American History, Money and Banking, Jurisprudence, Constitutional History, City Government, and Finance; it nearly broke his back. Such a burden was unfair to young scholars: it hurt their careers by leaving them no time or energy for their own scholarly work. Wilson's idea that Princeton could buy the services of these men for three to five years, squeeze them dry, and then hire another crop, was ultimately bound to fail. He had not thought through the human equation.[16]

Furthermore, Wilson was over-sanguine about the virtues of the preceptorial system. He had borrowed the Oxford and Cambridge tutorial system but not their general examinations, which promoted a general synthesis at the end of the college course. A. Lawrence Lowell, who later introduced tutors and general examinations at Harvard, remarked that to provide tutorial instruction without also instituting general examinations was like playing football without goal posts. The result of the lack of systematic arrangements to induce general study was that the preceptorial system in its early years was simply a pleasant means of inducing students to do required course work. The hope that there would be a great increase in independent reading was not fulfilled. More students went to the library, to be sure, because books were kept on reserve there for assignments, but the librarian reported to the Trustees in 1908 that the general circulation of books had actually declined during the three years the preceptorial system had been in operation. In the ten-year period from 1900 to 1910 circulation of the Princeton University Library rose from eighteen books per student per year to twenty-two, which hardly suggests the sudden inculcation of a passion for independent study.[17]

The faults in the original conception of the preceptorial system, coupled with Wilson's willingness to make unjustifiable claims for its success, revealed a tendency to generalize on insufficient evidence as well as a kind of self-hypnosis. He was led by his own ambitions, perhaps too by his own eloquence, into claiming as achievements what were still hopes for the future. Nevertheless, there can be no doubt of the system's immense benefit to Princeton, not only in vitalizing teaching but in bringing able young scholars to Princeton from all over the country. A high proportion were promoted to full professorships. Nine became chairmen of departments; four, deans; one, a charter trustee.[18]

The hiring of the preceptors was accompanied by successful efforts to attract older men of established reputation. When Professor Thilly resigned his chair of philosophy in 1906, Princeton reached all the way to Scotland to hire Norman Kemp Smith, then at the University of Glasgow. Smith told George M. Harper that he had gone to Princeton because he thought Wilson and Fine, both of whom had interviewed him, were "kingly men." In 1907, when it became necessary to fill two professorships in classics, Wilson got money from the Trustees to send Professor Westcott on a prospecting expedition to seventeen universities. He found the men he wanted at the University of Chicago: Edward Capps and Frank Frost Abbot. In the same year the biologist Edwin G. Conklin, then at the University of Pennsylvania, was pondering a call to Yale when he received a visit from two Princeton professors, who asked if he would consider joining the faculty. Conklin had never been to Princeton and was not much attracted, but he agreed to visit and have lunch with Wilson. At the meal Wilson broached his plans for the new laboratory of biological sciences and described his dream of setting up schools of study in fundamental fields—biology, law, mathematics. He captured Conklin's imagination. Taylor Pyne offered to build him a university house that he would be allowed to occupy for as long as he remained in Princeton. Conklin capitulated. When he first met Professor Capps the next fall, Capps asked, "What brought you to Princeton?" Conklin replied, "Woodrow Wilson, and what brought you here?" "The same," was the reply.[19]

When Wilson took office in 1902, the Princeton faculty was dangerously ingrown. Of the 108 men on the roster, 73 had Princeton degrees. Scholars from other colleges were not attracted to the University, nor was effort made to get them. Wilson changed all this. During his eight years as President the faculty increased to 172, and the percentage of Princeton men dropped from 68 to 41 per cent. In the positions below professorial rank, where there were no holdovers from the Patton regime to affect the proportion, only 29 per cent held Princeton degrees in 1910-11, whereas in 1902 their percentage had been 78. The striking decline in parochialism was accompanied by an immense increase in the quality of the men appointed. This infusion of new blood did more than anything else to fulfill James McCosh's dream of Princeton as a seat of learning to rival the great universities of Europe. Wilson's determination and ability to attract the best teachers and scholars spelled his greatest service to Princeton.[20]

In later years Wilson's solid achievements were all but forgotten, by friends as well as enemies, because his closing years at Princeton were marked by a bitter controversy that obscured everything else. It began when Dean West found the best possible means for reopening the campaign for a Graduate College along the lines he favored. In May 1909 he took Wilson a letter he had received from William Cooper Procter, the Cleveland soap magnate, offering $500,000 to Princeton to further the building of such a graduate college as West had described in his earlier brochure. Procter made two conditions: that Princeton should raise another $500,000 by May 1, 1910, and that the site chosen should be satisfactory to him. He added that he had examined Prospect and thought it unsuitable.[21]

The Procter offer was perfectly calculated to reopen warfare between the existing factions at Princeton. The circumstances surrounding the gift seemed like a deliberate affront to Wilson. Procter had never called on him while surveying the ground, and in sending the offer through West instead of directly, he seemed to be strengthening the Dean's hand. In barring the Prospect site and insisting on a location of his own choosing, he tried to reverse a decision of the Trustees reached after long discussion. His letter also hinted that he would designate in further respects how the money was to be spent; thus, he assumed a right to intervene in decisions that properly belonged to the Princeton administration.

An ad hoc committee, composed of three trustees, West, and Wilson, was immediately formed to communicate with Procter about the site. For a brief period it looked as though negotiations might break down entirely because Procter insisted on Merwick. On May 18, M. Taylor Pyne, chairman of the Graduate School Committee, wrote Ralph Adams Cram that he considered the Procter offer "a very doubtful quantity." Since Mr. Procter seemed inclined to force the Princeton authorities to put the Graduate College on the Merwick property, Princeton would lose the Swann money (now estimated at $320,000). "What he practically offers us," Pyne wrote Cram, "is $180,000 provided we can raise $500,000 more which, in itself, is not a good proposition." But Mr. Procter went to Princeton and, after trudging over several possible sites with Pyne, West, and Wilson, agreed to allow his money to be used to build on the golf links. The links were owned by the University, which was thought to satisfy the stipulation that Thomson College should be built on the Princeton campus. Pyne immediately became an enthusiastic advocate of the new location. It was, however, nearly as far from the actual campus of Princeton as Merwick and fully as isolated. Wilson opposed it for reasons he had held consistently and strongly: that the Graduate College should be at the center of the University so that graduate students and undergraduates would mingle.[22]

When the Trustees met on June 14, 1909, the lines were already drawn between those who favored the golf links site and those who followed Wilson in hoping that Procter could be persuaded to agree to a more central location. The Wilson faction won a temporary victory when a motion to rescind the previous action of the Board in placing Thomson College at Prospect was voted down. The discussion went on all summer and into the fall, as Wilson and his supporters suggested one place after another. Procter made no less than five more visits to Princeton, but did not change his mind. Nowhere but on the golf links, he informed Wilson through Pyne, was there "a satisfactory site for the Graduate College as he wished and expected to see it developed." Pyne himself became wholly committed to the golf links site and was bitter against trustees who opposed him. Another important convert was Ralph Adams Cram; Dean West won him around by pointing out how the new location, on a rise of ground beyond a greensward, gave opportunity for the architect to design a really striking building.[23]

As the autumn meeting of the Board of Trustees approached, Wilson realized he was losing ground. Therefore, as he had done with the Quad Plan, he sought faculty support, asking the recently appointed Graduate School Committee for an expression of opinion on the proposal to build the Graduate College on the golf links. On October 19 the committee split four to two on the issue; both the majority and minority submitted reports. The majority members—Fine, Capps, Conklin, and Daniels—argued that the distant site would produce disunity; would prevent desirable mingling of graduates, undergraduates, and faculty; would cause inconvenience because of the distance from libraries and laboratories; and would exclude from the common life of the Graduate School those students who could not afford to live at the Graduate College, which would create a division analogous to that between clubmen and non-clubmen among the undergraduates. It would also mean using large funds for an untested experiment. The minority members, West and Hibben—Wilson's former best friend again in opposition—maintained that the four-year experiment with graduate students at Merwick revealed that removing them somewhat from undergraduates promoted their best intellectual life and well-being, and that the Graduate College should be big enough to house all graduate students, with fees low enough so that poor men could afford them.[24]

Wilson now asked for a personal conference with Procter, and the latter obliged by coming east to meet him the day before the Trustees were to vote. Meanwhile, however, West had been to visit Procter in Cleveland to "advise" him. Pyne had also undercut the force of any last plea by informing Procter that Wilson's ideas about the interpenetration of the life of graduates and undergraduates seemed to him valueless, and that a majority of the Trustees' Committee on the Graduate

School was against Wilson on the site issue—which was not true. Procter remained adamant.[25]

On October 20, the evening before the Board of Trustees was to convene, its Committee on the Graduate School met to decide on a recommendation. After an extended discussion the committee by a vote of five to three passed the following resolution in support of Wilson:

Resolved: that, taking into consideration the administration of graduate students and the intellectual flavor of the University, we favor placing the new graduate building upon a location as central as possible, upon the University campus.

But the next day the full board overrode its committee, and Procter's offer was accepted, along with the golf links site, subject to provisos that the legal right to use Mrs. Swann's money for such a building be assured and that Procter further explain how he intended to use his gift. This resolution was carried by a vote of fourteen to ten.[26]

After this second serious defeat Wilson again considered resigning as President of Princeton. He had an additional reason to do so because at this juncture he was approached about becoming President of the University of Minnesota. There was little in his previous tastes or training to fit him for the post of head of a great state university. The University of Minnesota was over twice the size of Princeton and far more complex in organization. With its colleges of dairying, metallurgy, mechanic arts, and pharmacy, it represented the antithesis of the general education and devotion to pure learning that Wilson had been preaching. Nevertheless, Wilson's first reply to the Minnesota offer was so encouraging that three members of the Board of Regents took the long journey to Princeton to confer with him. For a short period Wilson apparently felt that he would rather take his chances with a state legislature than with the Princeton Board of Trustees, and was ready to throw in his lot with the plain people of a prairie state rather than continue dealing with young gentlemen from Lawrenceville and St. Paul's.[27]

In the meantime Pyne became uneasy about his own situation and his relation to Wilson. He had once called Wilson "Princeton's greatest asset," and he was aware that the University he so greatly loved would be hurt if the President resigned. He wrote Wilson's close friend Cyrus McCormick on November 3 that his purpose in supporting the Procter offer had been to protect Wilson and avert financial disaster: "Once we put it out that Princeton was rich enough to refuse half a million dollars because the giver wishes to put a building a few hundred yards one way or another, it would become almost impossible to collect money in any direction and the Alumni subscriptions would have fallen off woefully." A little later Pyne wrote Wilson a warm letter pointing out that he had given him strong support in the past and would do so in the future. The fact that he had opposed him on two issues had wrought no change in his feelings of admiration and affection. Some of Wilson's friends on the Board of Trustees also urged him to take no rash action because things would come out all right in the end. They were apparently working with Pyne to arrange to remove West as Dean of the Graduate School. Some of Wilson's supporters, including Dr. Jacobus, Cyrus McCormick, and Henry B. Thompson, had been arguing all along that the real issue was not the Graduate College but West's avidity for power, which the Procter gift enhanced.[28]

Wilson resisted efforts to turn the struggle into a personal confrontation between him and West. When Winthrop Daniels sent him a letter from West which he thought demanded action by the President of the University, Wilson asked Daniels to inform the Dean privately that his proposed plan (something involving teaching fellows) was "entirely illegal." He wanted, he said, to avoid the embarrassment of saying what he would have to say in faculty meeting if West continued on his course. He later wrote a trustee that he knew the Procter gift put West in the saddle, but that to disapprove it on this ground would make it appear a personal matter and would be wrongly interpreted by friends of the University.[29]

For a brief time it looked as though peace might be restored. Cram drew up preliminary plans for the new Graduate College, and throughout the month of December there was extended and apparently amicable correspondence about them among West, Wilson, Cram, and Capps. Wilson's only expressed objection was that the proposed Cleveland Tower looked too much like one to be erected at the Nassau Street entrance of Holder Hall, a new dormitory. Mr. Procter visited Princeton in December, and West asked the faculty to a reception for him at Merwick. About forty men attended, representing all shades of opinion, and the meeting was friendly. "It seemed like a real harmony meeting," reported Professor Howard Crosby Butler, resident master of Merwick, "to see Dr. Patton and West, Fine and Hibben, Daniels and Magie, Prest. Wilson and everybody else gathering about the beer and sandwiches and all having a good word to say for Procter."[30]

The truce proved fleeting. Wilson was being pushed from behind by members of the faculty who were fully as opposed as he to the decision to build the Graduate College off campus. When Pyne in November asked Dean Fine to try to persuade Wilson to accept the Trustees' decision, he received the reply, "I cannot urge the President to accept any of the parts of an arrangement except those in which I myself believe." West's opponents on the Faculty Committee on the Graduate School took occasion to renew criticism of what they thought was the undue luxury with which the Dean wanted to surround graduate students; their charges centered on such details as a private bath for every man and a separate breakfast room in addition to the regular dining hall. Dispute also continued over Mrs. Swann's bequest. Her executors had obtained legal opinions to the effect that the golf links fulfilled the stipulations of the will as to site, but Wilson felt that to call them part of the Princeton campus on the technicality that they happened to be owned by the University was a manifest violation of the intention of the testator; he was supported in this view by ex-Chancellor William J. Magie.[31]

As a compromise proposal Wilson conceived of using the Swann bequest to build Thomson College on the actual campus as a kind of "quad" where graduates and undergraduates would live together, while the Procter money might be used toward building a graduate college on the golf links. On December 22 he broached this idea to Procter in a long personal conference, but the latter refused to consider separation of the two gifts.[32]

Immediately after the meeting with Procter, Wilson penciled a note to Pyne saying, "The acceptance of this gift has taken the guidance of the University out of my hands entirely,—and I seem to have come to the end." Pyne replied that he hoped Wilson would reconsider what was obviously a hasty decision. But Wilson did not reconsider. On Christmas Day 1909 he wrote Pyne a long letter. He expressed admiration for Mr. Procter, but asserted that the faculty did not believe that a Graduate College on the golf links site could succeed: they had lost confidence in Dean West and disapproved of a departure from the original policy—in which West had formerly concurred—of placing the Graduate College at the heart of the University. If the Procter gift was to be accepted for a building on the golf links site, it must be separated from the Swann bequest and the latter used for its original purpose— to build Thomson College on the actual campus. "I am not willing to be drawn further into the toils," he wrote. "I cannot accede to the acceptance of gifts upon terms that take the educational policy of the University out of the hands of the Trustees and Faculty and permit it to be determined by those who give money." Neither his conscience nor his self-respect, Wilson wrote Pyne, would permit him to make any other decision, although he took the step with real grief that it should be necessary.[33]

Wilson knew that this letter meant war, and he sent copies to friends on the Board of Trustees. Yet he had no qualms about the rightness of his action. Early in November he had foreshadowed his ultimate rejection of the Trustees' decision in an address at the McCormick Theological Seminary in Chicago, in which he praised the "indomitable individual" who at some turning point says: "I go this way. Let any man go another way who pleases." Three days after delivering his ultimatum to Pyne he told a New Jersey State Teachers Convention that political liberty was kept alive by men who kicked over the traces. "The crying need of modern society," he said, "is the man who will fight for what is right without stopping to count the cost and consequence to loved ones." By his insistence on playing the role of the indomitable individual who champions the right despite the cost, Wilson touched off one of the most bitter and complex rows in all academic history.[34]

Some loyal friends on the Board of Trustees applauded Wilson's letter to Pyne. One wrote that he was glad Wilson had at last taken the bull by the horns; another that he had saved Princeton from an intolerable position; still a third that when Procter's plans were fully revealed, even Pyne would see that they were impossible, the close alliance between him and West would be broken, and the Dean would be easily eliminated. The Wilson faction devised a plan whereby a resolution refusing Procter's gift with strings attached was to be presented at a meeting of the Board of Trustees scheduled for January 13, 1910.[35]

Wilson's ultimatum tended, however, to lose him support from the uncommitted. One trustee wrote him a letter friendly in tone but making the pointed observation, "There is one thing that I cannot understand, and that is how it comes that West, who has been encouraged & endorsed, & prevented from accepting desirable offices in other institutions, is now regarded as unfit to administer anything." Another man, who two months before had expressed the opinion that Wilson was Princeton's best asset and that the Procter matter ought to be adjusted on terms satisfactory to him, now wrote Pyne that Wilson's recent action revealed his incapacity to work in a team or to carry on a full exchange of opinion.[36]

Everything depended on Moses Taylor Pyne. For a time he hesitated, unwilling to take up the gage of battle. Cleveland Dodge, Edward W. Sheldon, and Henry B. Thompson, in Wilson's camp, attempted to persuade him to accept Wilson's new contentions that West's ideas were unworkable because of strong faculty opposition and that to go along with the October decision to accept Procter's conditions was to rivet West to Princeton. Pyne fell ill, and Wilson wrote him a friendly note saying that he regretted if his action was the cause; he was sure they could all work out something that would be in the best interests of the University, whether he remained President or not. Pyne responded in a note signed "Affectionately yours" that he wanted to meet Wilson's wishes but was so convinced of the unwisdom of refusing the Procter gift that he was torn almost in two.[37]

Tension mounted as the mid-January meeting of the Trustees approached. Even Dean Fine, whose judgment was usually cool and detached, lost his bearings. Without consulting West and Hibben, the two minority members of the Faculty Committee on the Graduate School, Fine called together the other majority members—Capps, Conklin, and Daniels—and the four men drew up a memorial designed to strengthen Wilson's hand against West. They opposed segregation of graduate students and suggested that men would be repelled from Princeton by schemes of life that put emphasis upon considerations other than scholarship. "We cannot," the report concluded, "have a great graduate school without a great graduate faculty; and we cannot have a great graduate faculty unless the conditions here are of such a character as to attract strong men. And we cannot attract strong men by adherence to dilettante ideals."[38]

This report was unfair, both because West and Hibben had a right to be consulted and because it misrepresented their side of the argument. The two men later maintained that they would be willing to subscribe to everything in the "majority report" except the phrase "dilettante ideals." When taxed with unfairness in acting as he did, Fine was said to have excused himself by saying that he was afraid Wilson would resign.[39]

When the Trustees met on January 13, 1910, the Wilsonians went armed with the "majority report" of the faculty committee and a resolution rejecting Procter's offer because of the conditions concerning the site. But Pyne forestalled them by reading a letter from Mr. Procter in which he agreed to accept the President's demand that the Procter gift and the Swann bequest be separated, with one used to build a Graduate College on the golf links and the other a residence hall on the campus. Procter unfortunately added the remark that of course this would mean more money for bricks and mortar, less for endowing professorships and fellowships. This bombshell caused Wilson to lose his head. He burst out that the faculty did not care where the Graduate College was placed; the question was not one of location but principles. "If the Graduate School is based on proper ideals," he said, "our faculty can make it a success anywhere in Mercer County." By this offhand remark Wilson tossed away half his case. He undercut his supporters on the faculty who felt strongly that the location was indeed an issue, and he abandoned a position he had held consistently ever since his inauguration as President. From this time on the site issue was practically dead: the one phrase, "anywhere in Mercer County," had maimed it beyond cure.[40]

Worse followed. Pulling out West's earlier brochure on the proposed Graduate College, Wilson held it up before the gathering and said that the real reason the Procter bequest must be declined was that the ideals expressed in West's pamphlet were wrong, that a graduate school based on these ideas could not succeed. But, asked Pyne, who was sitting next to Wilson and had picked up the brochure when Wilson put it down, if the President was so opposed to West's ideas, why had he written a commendatory preface? At the time he wrote the preface, replied Wilson, he had not read the contents of the brochure. One of the clerical members of the Board then asked Wilson why he first proposed the idea of two colleges and then opposed it. Because, he answered, friends on the faculty had induced him to change his mind. But then why had he written Pyne in his letter of December 25 that the two-college scheme had the "hearty concurrence" of members of the faculty? Wilson was now mired in contradictions. To make matters still worse, another cleric remarked that the President's explanations did not seem "to comport with standards of strict honor," an observation that Wilson hotly denied.[41]

The only action taken at the Trustees' meeting of January 13 was the appointment of what came to be known as the "Committee of Five," to consult further with Mr. Procter and attempt to arrange a settlement. In the course of the proceedings Wilson managed to present the "majority report" of the Faculty Committee on the Graduate School, which served to muddy the waters still more.[42]

The January 13 meeting ended all hope of peace. Wilson's friends were shocked at the way the new Procter offer had been sprung, as if in a deliberate attempt to trick him into hasty utterance, and even more at the obvious attempt to catch him in falsehood. On the other side were ranged men who no longer had any faith in Wilson's judgment or in his word, and M. Taylor Pyne was their leader. He urged Procter to withdraw his gift and West to resign as Dean of the Graduate School—actions which would whip up such a whirlwind of criticism that Wilson would be blown out of office. He hoped at the same time to get assurances from Procter to renew his offer after a change of administration. But Procter refused to fall in with this, for fear the resulting controversy would harm Princeton.[43]

Pyne had no difficulty in finding allies in his sub rosa campaign to unseat Wilson. One trustee told him that there was now just one issue, Pyne versus Wilson, and that Pyne was more useful to the University than its President. Henry van Dyke had already declared his allegiance to Pyne. When Paul van Dyke returned from a trip to Europe in February, he sent word to Pyne that he stood by him as a matter of fundamental conviction: "if you want any one here to 'bell the cat,'" he wrote, "I beg you consider this letter an application for that honour." The van Dyke brothers had a large following among the alumni, but they did not play as important a part in the efforts to discredit Wilson as did two men less in the public eye—Wilson Farrand, headmaster of Newark Academy, and Jesse Lynch Williams, editor of the *Princeton Alumni Weekly*. It will be remembered that Farrand had been elected Alumni Trustee the previous year over protests from alumni who resented his patent opposition to the President of the University. According to his brother Max Farrand, he was pushed forward by Pyne in Trustees' meetings as the one man who could stand up to Wilson in public debate. Wilson Farrand now distributed among prominent alumni a private memorandum containing paired quotations designed to show that Wilson was a liar and a breaker of promises. He also promoted the candidacy for Alumni Trustee of Adrian H. Joline, who had been a vituperative opponent of the Quad Plan.[44]

As editor of the *Alumni Weekly*, Jesse Lynch Williams had been an active member of the van Dyke-West group that organized opposition to the Quad Plan. The issues of January 26 and February 2, 1910, reveal that he was again using his editorial position to turn his magazine into an anti-Wilson forum. They contained, for instance, the opinion of seven lawyers disagreeing with ex-Chancellor Magie and maintaining that the golf links site legally fulfilled the terms of Mrs. Swann's will; a letter from Howard Crosby Butler, resident master of Merwick, defending the record of graduate students who had lived there; the report of a lecture by Henry van Dyke on "Self-Development in Education," which was a slightly concealed attack on Wilson; and a resolution from members of the class of 1892, who at their midwinter dinner in New York demanded immediate acceptance of the Procter gift.[45]

The fight reached public notice. Again it was Wilson's foes who took the initiative. A report in the *New York Herald* of January 29 opened with the heading, "DR. WILSON FACES TURNING POINT IN PRINCETON'S LIFE —Sensational Developments Expected." The story explained that the Quad Plan had caused internal dissension at Princeton and that it had been supported by the faculty only because Wilson cracked the whip over the preceptors. It suggested that Wilson faced a fight with the alumni, who were lining up behind West, "an ardent supporter of Princeton traditions."[46]

At this particular time—while the Committee of Five was attempting to arrange a settlement with Procter—Wilson could not publicly retaliate. But a letter from Henry B. Brougham of the *New York Times* offered him a chance for an anonymous reply. Brougham wrote him that after talking with members of the Yale faculty who were cognizant of the situation, he had formed the opinion that the settlement of affairs at Princeton would profoundly affect the life of American colleges in general. Would Wilson supply guidance?[47]

Wilson answered Brougham the very day he received the letter. As in the previous dispute over the Quad Plan, he now generalized the Graduate College controversy into one between the forces of privilege and those of democracy. He portrayed West's ideas for a Graduate College as leading to "social exclusiveness." The issue was joined between "a college life in which all the bad elements of social ambition and unrest intruded themselves, and a life ordered upon a simpler plan under the domination of real university influence and upon a basis of real democracy."[48]

An editorial based on this extraordinary letter appeared in the *New York Times* on February 3, 1910. Brougham broadened the canvas still farther and defined the Princeton controversy as part of the larger struggle going on between special privilege and the people:

> The nation is aroused against special privilege. Sheltered by a great political party, it has obtained control of our commerce and our industries. Now its exclusive and benumbing touch is upon those institutions which should stand pre-eminently for life, earnest endeavor and broad enlightenment. The question at Princeton is not simply of locating a new building for the Graduate College. Involved with this project is the decisive settlement whether Princeton University, and with that institution Yale, Harvard, Columbia, Cornell, Chicago, and all other endowed universities are to direct their energies away from the production of men trained to hard, accurate thought, masters in their professions, intellectually well rounded, of wide sympathies and unfettered judgment, and to bend and degrade them into fostering mutually exclusive social cliques, stolid groups of wealth and fashion, devoted to non-essentials and the smatterings of culture.[49]

This portrayal of the Graduate College controversy as a struggle to preserve college democracy caught the attention of the country and made Wilson seem more than ever an exemplar of progressivism. The *Times* editorial did him harm at Princeton, however, since it was so patently unfair to West and so obviously came from the Wilson camp. The *New York Herald* reported that New York alumni were demanding that Wilson either repudiate the editorial or tender his resignation. Wilson Farrand suspected that Wilson himself was the author, as did Paul van Dyke, and there was a bitter confrontation between the latter and the President a month later, with Wilson admitting that the editorial was overdrawn but saying that it was essentially true, and van Dyke insisting that Wilson publicly repudiate it. If it had ever become known that Wilson personally supplied, in his letter, the material on which Brougham based his editorial, there can be hardly a doubt that he would have been forced to resign.[50]

Meanwhile the Committee of Five had interrogated Procter about his intentions. Thomas D. Jones, the chairman, sent the would-be donor a letter that had something of the tone of a district attorney grilling a witness. Not unnaturally, the long-suffering Procter finally withdrew his gift, just three days after the *Times* editorial. Wilson professed to be delighted. "At last we are free," he wrote Cleveland Dodge, "to govern the University as our judgments and consciences dictate! I have an unspeakable sense of relief. I most cheerfully give you the solemn promise you ask me to give: that I will not allow anything that is said to unseat me." In the press Wilson was praised as the "college president who turned down a million dollars." A typical reaction was that of the *Springfield Republican:* "The college president who serenely and deliberately lets half a million dollars slip through his fingers for the sake of certain educational or administrative principles should command general admiration. It is evident that Dr. Woodrow Wilson, the president of Princeton University, is the hero of such an episode."[51]

Wilson thereupon went off to Bermuda for a badly needed rest. "I did not realize until I got here," he wrote Ellen, "how hard hit my nerves had been by the past month. Almost at once the *days* began to afford me relief, but the nights distressed me. The trouble latent in my mind came out in my dreams. Not until last night did the distress —the struggle all night with college foes, the sessions of hostile trustees, the confused war of argument and insinuation—cease. But now the calm has come and I am very peaceful,—very, very lonely without my love to sustain me with her sympathy and understanding, but myself again."[52]

Yet in Princeton the battle raged with almost unimaginable ferocity. Lifelong friendships among faculty members were severed. Dean West, for instance, never again spoke to Dean Fine except on matters of business. The wives were, by common report, worse than the professors, who at least had to preserve enough of the amenities to carry on the business of the University. As a beleaguered and aggrieved minority on the faculty, the pro-West faction was more bitter than the Wilsonians, and for a time some of them talked of little else but their woes and their antipathy to the President of the University. Feuding even extended to the children. It was a period so unhappy that men and women on both sides attempted later to drive it out of their minds.[53]

Because of the approaching election for Alumni Trustee, there was controversy among the Princeton alumni as well as within the institution. When Farrand had been unopposed the previous year, a tacit understanding had been reached that there would be no opposition to John W. Barr of Louisville, Kentucky, in 1910. But with the nomination of Adrian Joline by the anti-Wilson faction, the balloting for Alumni Trustee took on the character of a vote of confidence or of censure. Barr and Joline each received endorsements from different alumni clubs, which were duly recorded in the *Princeton Alumni Weekly,* and their location shows clearly the geographical division of the sides between the metropolitan Princeton graduates who had previously opposed the Quad Plan and what one of Wilson's supporters called the "rural alumni." All but one of the seven alumni groups supporting Joline's candidacy came from the New York-New Jersey-Philadelphia area. The eighteen groups supporting Barr included twelve west of the Alleghenies. For four months a battle of arguments, charges, and countercharges raged in the alumni magazine. The anti-administration literature rang changes on the same few themes, which suggests that the agitation was organized. Jesse Lynch Williams later recollected that he gave up so much time to the fight that he neglected his profession of writing and suffered financially. The pro-Wilson communications appeared to be more spontaneous and were more varied in their approach, although one theme was stronger than any other: distrust of the metropolitan alumni.[54]

The dispute flourished in the newspapers. It reached a point where David B. Jones, a pro-Wilson trustee, attacked Pyne in an anonymous letter to the *New York Evening Post* for trying to muzzle the faculty and dragoon the Trustees with the purpose of turning Princeton into a "proprietary institution." Jones later disclosed his identity and was answered by another trustee, the Reverend John De Witt, who both defended Pyne and argued plausibly that Wilson made too much of where a "boarding house" should be placed. In addition to the newspaper debate, there was a pamphlet war, in the course of which Princeton alumni were bombarded with missives written by members of both sides. Several of these deal not with the Graduate College dispute but with the Quad Plan, which one of them called "The Phantom Ship."[55]

Before going to Bermuda in early February Wilson had intended to remove West as Dean of the Graduate School and had called together the majority members of the Faculty Committee to urge that they ask him to resign. They demurred on the ground that since the Dean was an officer appointed by the Board of Trustees, such an action would have the character of a mutiny. Wilson persuaded them that some form of faculty action might nevertheless be devised. Later, however, they returned to their original position, and Mrs. Wilson was intensely vexed because Fine was "so inconsiderate—so *cruel*" as to disturb her Woodrow's holiday by writing him in Bermuda that the committee would not support a move to get rid of West. Fine also persuaded some of Wilson's closest friends on the Board of Trustees to urge Wilson to drop his demand for West's resignation on the premise that it would only increase hard feelings and open him to the charge of vindictiveness. Wilson's friends were of the further opinion that he should drop any mention of the Quad Plan for a time and concentrate on projects that everyone could agree on, such as making an appeal for Graduate School professorships and fellowships.[56]

Another difficulty of which Wilson's supporters were aware was that he often acted without prior consultation with either faculty members or trustees. To obviate this, his long-time friend and benefactor Cyrus McCormick proposed an unofficial advisory committee. He suggested that Wilson should act on all important matters for a few months only after consulting a committee of advisors. Such a committee might include Robert Bridges, E. W. Sheldon, T. D. Jones, H. B. Fine, and perhaps Professor Capps. McCormick feared that Wilson would suffer shipwreck if he continued to navigate alone. Eight years earlier McCormick had been one of those who tried to put President Patton's presidency into committee because Patton would not act; now he proposed a similar course because Wilson acted precipitately.[57]

While Wilson was in Bermuda, his opponents had been attempting to organize the alumni against him. A Princeton dinner at Philadelphia on March 4 was dominated by the anti-administration faction. Henry B. Thompson, a pro-Wilson trustee, gave a reasonable defense of his administration, but on the program he was sandwiched between Henry van Dyke and Jesse Lynch Williams, both of whom gave highly emotional addresses on the other side. When Wilson returned to Princeton on March 9, he again gained the initiative because alumni of every stripe were anxious to hear his views. He made a "swing around the circle" in defense of his administration, talking to alumni in Baltimore, Brooklyn, Jersey City, and St. Louis. Rested by his trip to Bermuda and perhaps chastened by the advice of friends, he gave addresses that were temperate in tone and specific in content. The one at Baltimore set the pattern. In it Wilson reviewed the achievements of his administration, laying stress on the increase of opportunities for graduate study in the shape of new laboratories and the appointment of distinguished scholars to the faculty. The only reference to Dean West—an oblique one—was a statement that no one should use Princeton for any private purpose.[58]

Wilson told Dr. Jacobus on the eve of facing the New York alumni early in April that he was not looking forward to the event with enthusiasm but that he would give them "a very explicit and direct exposition," so that they would at least have no excuse if they did not comprehend the issues "stripped of all personalities." At the Princeton Club the next night the members were jammed in so tightly that Wilson had to get to the stage by going through the kitchens and up a back stairway, which led to the story that he had been brought in through "a secret passageway" to avert physical harm. Later testimony that Wilson confronted a cold and hostile audience is corroborated by a front-page story in the *New York Times*, written by a reporter who was not present but interviewed members of the audience immediately after the gathering. But Philip Rollins, who introduced Wilson from the platform, remembered the crowd as respectful if not noticeably friendly, and the stenographic record published in the *Princeton Alumni Weekly* noted "prolonged applause" when Wilson entered the room, "applause" again when he was introduced, "applause" and "laughter" during the speech, "applause" again at the end. Whatever the President's reception, the tension was great. It was heightened by the fact that an amusing anti-Wilson pamphlet had been distributed in the audience before he spoke.[59]

Wilson talked for nearly an hour, setting the controversy over the Procter gift in broad perspective and making a strong case for his belief in an integrated university. He frankly admitted that he had changed his mind about the Graduate College and that there had been much he did not understand about graduate instruction until new men with more experience than he had joined the faculty. Further evidence of a general change of attitude was a passage in which Wilson paid high praise to President Eliot of Harvard because he had pushed "the great body of scientific study which now lies at the basis of our life and thought into the curriculum" and had forced universities to give "unlimited hospitality to all the subjects of modern study." This was in sharp contrast to Wilson's former rather grudging acceptance of science and defense of the classics. It showed how explicitly, in pedagogy as in politics, he had moved from a conservative to a progressive position.

In none of these addresses to alumni had Wilson so much as mentioned the Quad Plan—evidence that he had taken the advice of friends on this topic. Nor did he make any suggestion that he was fighting for democracy against privilege and dilettantism. The opposition had at the same time been hurting its case by personal attacks on him. A strong groundswell of support began to appear in letters and resolutions sent to the *Princeton Alumni Weekly*. Wilson was heartened by his reception at alumni dinners and by letters of support. For instance, a New York alumnus who had opposed the Quad Plan wrote that he had now been won over and thought Wilson's courteous attitude during the recent controversy was highly creditable. A. Lawrence Lowell, recently elected President of Harvard, asked Wilson if there were any way of helping his cause by talking to trustees or prominent alumni; if he were to resign, it would not merely be a catastrophe for Princeton but a misfortune for the whole cause of college education in America.[60]

The moderate tone of Wilson's talks to alumni meant no willingness to abandon the fight. Although he had been persuaded not to demand West's resignation, as a substitute he urged the Trustees to consult the faculty for an opinion on how graduate studies should be administered. Even some of his most devoted followers argued against the move, but Wilson was insistent. On April 14, 1910, the following motion was presented to the Trustees:

RESOLVED: That the Faculty of the University be requested to express in such definite and explicit form as it may deem best its opinions as to the character, methods, and administration it regards as most suitable and desirable for the Graduate School.

After discussion, the motion was defeated by a vote of 14 to 11.[61]

Two days after the Trustees had refused his request for an appeal to the faculty, Wilson was to speak before a gathering of Princeton alumni in Pittsburgh. At the first mention of his name, he received a standing ovation. The very friendliness of the gathering seemed suddenly to release the bitterness of his disappointment over his recent defeat, and he lost his head, as he had lost it when he told the Princeton Trustees that the Graduate College might be built "anywhere in Mercer County," or when he supplied Brougham of the *New York Times* with inflammatory material for an editorial. Responding to a toast to "The University," he began by saying that he no longer knew who but himself he represented. Since the Trustees had denied him the opportunity of knowing what the faculty stood for, he occupied a place of "splendid isolation," and if isolation were necessary to make a man conspicuous, he was one of the most conspicuous men in America. He then proceeded to give a stump speech against the power of wealth and privilege. Perhaps nettled by the fact that he had been consistently opposed by the four men on the faculty who were members of the Presbyterian ministry and by five of the six clerics on the Board of Trustees, he also inveighed against the Protestant churches, which had "dissociated themselves from the lives of the country . . . They are serving the classes and they are not serving the masses. They serve certain strata, certain uplifted strata, but they are not serving the men whose need is dire. The churches have more regard to their pew-rents than to the souls of men, and in proportion as they look to the respectability of their congregations to lift them in esteem, they are depressing the whole level of Christian endeavor."[62]

In words that might have come from the tongue of Bryan or Debs, Wilson declared that the strength of the nation came not from the "conspicuous classes" but "from the great masses of the unknown, of the unrecognized men, whose powers are developed by struggle"; that the "masters of endeavor" did not come from the colleges "but from the great rough-and-ready workers of the world." It would have been a disservice to Abraham Lincoln to send him to college because he would have been cut off from common men. "The great voice of America," cried Wilson, "does not come from seats of learning. It comes in a murmur from the hills and woods and the farms and factories and the mills, rolling on and gaining volume until it comes to us from the homes of the common men. Do these murmurs echo in the corridors of the universities? I have not heard them."

Wilson defined his own role as that of a crusader for democracy: "I have dedicated every power there is in me to bring the colleges that I have anything to do with to an absolutely democratic regeneration in spirit, and I shall not be satisfied—and I hope you will not be— until America shall know that the men in the colleges are saturated with the same thought, the same sympathy that pulses through the whole great body politic." He concluded this extraordinary address with a melodramatic prediction: "If she loses her self-possession, America will stagger like France through fields of blood before she again finds peace and prosperity under the leadership of men who know her needs."[63]

What motivated this outburst? It may have been simply a concatenation of circumstance and mood. But the conclusion is unavoidable that it was also a bid for political favor. When in February Mrs. Wilson had learned that her husband's followers might not support him in demanding West's removal from office, she wrote him that this left him free to accept the nomination for Governor of New Jersey and to go into politics. She furthermore wrote of the Princeton controversy: "This thing has strengthened you *immensely* throughout the whole country, it is said there have been hundreds upon hundreds of editorials and all *wholly* on your side." If otherworldly Ellen Wilson could see the possible political advantage resulting from the Princeton controversy, Wilson himself must have been aware of it. He may have lost his head in Pittsburgh, and he may have been carried away, but what carried him away seems to have been the vision of high political office.[64]

Wilson's performance on this occasion did him no good in the Princeton community. His enemies published and distributed widely a pamphlet entitled *That Pittsburgh Speech,* giving excerpts of newspaper reports and editorials suggesting that Wilson was promoting his candidacy for Governor of New Jersey. Even faithful friends told him that the speech was overdone. He regretted his intemperance and explained in answer to a correspondent, "I spoke too soon after a meeting of the Trustees at which the majority vote seemed to me to create an impossible situation; but that is only an explanation of my stupid blunder, not an excuse for it. I shall try to remedy the situation when I can,—not by way of explanation, but by more just exposition of the matter." He was as good as his word. Nothing could have been in greater contrast to the Pittsburgh speech than his talk to the Chicago alumni on May 12. He lauded alumni gatherings and "the spirit of comradeship and solidarity bred in our colleges." He expressed high praise for Moses Taylor Pyne. Although he mentioned his hope that Princeton could be made "a school of pure democracy," where men could be taught to serve their country "without regard to class or private interest," he stated that this happy end should be achieved by common counsel.[65]

Wilson's praise of Pyne and his conciliatory tone probably reflected the fact that backstage efforts were being made to end the factional warfare. A group of Princeton trustees, in consultation with Mr. Procter, were seeking support for a compromise solution of the Graduate College controversy. To win over Wilson and his followers, West was to be persuaded or forced to retire as Dean of the Graduate School and become merely head of the residential Graduate College (with some such title as "Provost" or "Warden"), while matters of curriculum and studies were to be turned over to a new dean. In return for this concession the golf links site was to be accepted, and the money from the Swann bequest was also to be used for building there, if that were ruled legally possible. Such an arrangement could only be successful if endorsed by both Wilson and Pyne. Edward W. Sheldon put strong pressure on Wilson to accept, and although the latter did not commit himself, he at least agreed to entertain the proposition. Pyne had been hoping Wilson could be induced to resign, although he continued to deny it when challenged. But he had been warned by Henry B. Thompson in a strongly worded letter that Wilson's resignation would be followed by that of several influential and wealthy trustees as well as some of the distinguished professors who had recently joined the faculty; the University might also lose gifts totaling more than the Procter money. Pyne somewhat reluctantly agreed to the new plan and undertook to break the news to West.[66]

West later related how Pyne and Stephen S. Palmer, another trustee and Princeton benefactor, came to his house and told of a plan to bring peace. They then outlined the compromise that reduced West to a boardinghouse keeper and asked him to let them know his answer later. After they had gone, the Dean pondered the question for some time. Should he accept personal humiliation for the sake of Princeton, or should he fight? He decided to fight.[67]

Just at this time the wealthy octogenarian Isaac C. Wyman lay on his deathbed in Salem, Massachusetts. A member of the Princeton class of 1848, he was the one whom Patton and Wilson had unsuccessfully approached in the hope that he would give largely to Princeton. It was "Andy three millions West" who finally persuaded the old man to bequeath almost his entire estate to build the Princeton Graduate College, with West as one of the two trustees. A week after the conference with Pyne and Thompson, West heard that Wyman had died, and on May 21 the will was filed for probate. The newspapers reported that the estate amounted to ten million dollars; one report suggested that it might even reach thirty millions. West himself in a letter to Pyne estimated that Princeton would receive "*at least*" (italics his) two and a half million, and probably more. Much of the money, he said, would be available at once.[68]

When Wilson heard of the Wyman bequest, he remarked to his wife, "We've beaten the living, but we can't fight the dead. The game's up." His behavior was similar to that after he had suffered the retinal hemorrhage in 1906 and was told his active career was over. He accepted defeat with good grace. After consultation with the majority members of the Faculty Committee on the Graduate School, he decided that the size of the Wyman bequest altered the perspective. So much money could now go into professorships and fellowships that graduate students would flock to Princeton, no matter what the living arrangements. Obviously, too, West must remain as Dean. As he should have done long before, Wilson had a personal conference with West and sought an accommodation, saying that West had a great work to do and he would back him up. Edward Sheldon, one of the most level-headed of Wilson's friends among the Trustees, wrote Cyrus McCormick, "Indeed, the President has acted in a most admirable way, and his loyalty to the University, his self-sacrifice, and his breadth of mind have won the praise of all of us."[69]

His opponents did not behave with magnanimity. West privately circulated light verse making fun of Wilson and his followers—an action hardly calculated to soothe sore feelings. During a meeting of the Grounds and Buildings Committee at which Wilson was present, Pyne and two other pro-West trustees behaved in a way that made Henry B. Thompson, the chairman, feel disgusted and ashamed because it was so obviously their intention to humiliate the President. John L. Cadwalader, who had sided with Pyne in the previous controversy, wrote that he thought this action unpardonable. Wilson was greatly discouraged, but he played the game through to the end. Procter renewed his pledge for a Graduate College on the golf links site on June 6, and it was promptly accepted at a special meeting of the Board of Trustees three days later. At Commencement on June 14 Wilson made the presentation of a solid gold cup, eighteen inches high, from the alumni to Mr. Pyne in recognition of his twenty-five years of service on the Princeton Board of Trustees. He spoke of Pyne as though nothing had happened to mar their former friendship, describing Pyne's devotion and generosity to the University as being beyond all praise. In his reply Pyne made no mention of Wilson but said that he took the cup to be an expression of confidence in himself and approval of his course as trustee.[70]

There were, however, rays of comfort. Wilson still kept his hold on the undergraduates, who paid him tribute in their annual Faculty Song:

> Here's to Woodrow, king divine,
> Who rules this place along with Fine.
> We have no fear he'll leave this town
> To try for anybody's crown.

At commencement he received immense ovations from both the seniors and the alumni. Even more gratifying was the result of the Alumni Trustee election. In spite of the strenuous campaigning in his favor,

Adrian H. Joline, the candidate of the Pyne faction, received less than 40 per cent of the ballots against John W. Barr, Jr., the pro-Wilson candidate. Wilson himself wrote Harry A. Garfield the day after commencement that the settlement seemed to be a real one, although certain "disaffected spirits" were trying to make trouble. He felt that there was at least a fighting chance that things could be guided as they should be.[71]

Wilson's defeat over the Graduate College was ostensibly the result of a chance event, the death of Wyman, but even if that had not happened and Wilson had won his purpose of having West removed from the deanship, he would have brought his administration dangerously close to shipwreck. Wilson's foes were not free of guilt: Dean West was an intriguer and not easily amenable to control; William F. Procter attached overly stiff conditions to his gift to the Graduate College; Henry and Paul van Dyke in their zeal for the "old Princeton spirit" evinced little understanding of Princeton as a center of scholarship; M. Taylor Pyne, Bayard Henry, Wilson Farrand, Jesse Lynch Williams, and other opponents on occasion displayed pettiness and vindictiveness. Some of the opposition to Wilson was the inevitable reaction of those who feared any change as a threat to the established order, and the Quad Plan was enough in itself to cause constant apprehension and irritation among conservative Princetonians. Other bitterness stemmed from the fact that Princeton was a Presbyterian institution; in good Calvinist fashion neither side was disposed to forgive the sins of the other but preferred to consign opponents to perdition.

After all allowances are made, Wilson must still be held primarily responsible for creating the difficult situation in which he found himself. As one trustee observed, the question, "Where shall we build a boardinghouse for graduates?" was not so important that it should have been allowed to tear the University apart. Wilson not only exaggerated issues, but he obscured them by shifting his ground, often without warning, which mystified and hamstrung his followers and hardened the opposition. He talked of "common counsel" but failed to take even his most loyal supporters into his confidence. He professed to be motivated by "principles," but an important factor in the Graduate College dispute was his personal antipathy to West, which he did not like to admit. Finally, he beclouded the issues and infuriated his opponents by introducing the largely spurious issue of "democracy" versus "social exclusiveness."[72]

Wilson's behavior during this period of tension again suggests that he may have been suffering from an early mild attack of the cerebral arterial sclerosis that laid him low at the height of his fight for ratification of the League of Nations in 1919. It is said to be characteristic of a person in the early stages of this disorder that his temper varies. At one moment he may be agreeable and eager to please; at another, highly irritable. "The mood of the moment tends to govern conduct," according to an authority, "although the emotional state may change quickly, either spontaneously or when other thoughts are suggested." Such alternation of mood was highly characteristic of Wilson during the six months when the Graduate College controversy was at its height.[73]

Wilson's mistakes in leadership during his last year in academic life caused men to forget the notable service he had performed for Princeton. He could justifiably assert that he had found Princeton a college and made it a university. Yet friends as well as foes forgot this essential fact in petty squabbles over whether West held "dilettante ideals" or whether Wilson broke a commitment to the Dean.

As has often been remarked, Wilson's eight years as President of Princeton provided a forecast of his later eight years as President of the United States. In both cases his first years in office were remarkable for their constructive achievement, arrived at in cooperation with others. In putting through the new curriculum, in hiring preceptors, and in erecting new laboratories, Wilson cooperated with his colleagues on the faculty and fellow members of the Board of Trustees as he later cooperated with congressional leaders and others in forcing through Congress the first honest revision of the tariff since the Civil War, the Federal Reserve Act, and the Clayton Anti-Trust Act. His first reforms at Princeton—higher academic standards and an improved curriculum—were the culmination of an agitation that had begun during the Patton administration. Similarly, the tariff, banking, and anti-trust legislation of his first two years as President of the United States were the climax of many years of discussion. In both cases there was a demand for leadership in predetermined directions, and he supplied it.

Both at Princeton and in Washington a final catastrophe made men forget his earlier achievement, and in both cases it was partly of Wilson's own making. He became less disposed to seek advice, broke with supporters who presumed to disagree with him, and damned the opposition. At the same time his one-track mind tended to focus on a single issue and to elevate it into supreme importance. At Princeton the integration of graduate and undergraduate dormitories was unduly exalted into a matter of principle, while other aspects of graduate education were temporarily neglected; later he exalted the League of Nations as a panacea for the ills of the world, ignoring other elements of a just and stable peace settlement. In both cases it seemed as though he was driven by some fatal Icarus complex, flying higher and higher and more and more alone until his downfall acquired a quality of tragic inevitability.[74]

Departure

I'll confide in you—and I have already confided to others—that, as compared with the campus politician, the real article seems like an amateur.

—Woodrow Wilson, 1911[1]

THE GRADUATE COLLEGE
controversy helped in several ways to launch Woodrow Wilson's career
in active politics. His situation at Princeton had become so distasteful
that he was ready to contemplate a change; he told Stockton Axson
that although he would regret resigning because it would give his
enemies so much satisfaction, he had no interest in administering a
gentlemen's club. The conviction that his foes represented the forces
of privilege continued to drive him toward sympathy with progressivism, which in the prevailing mood of the country was an asset
politically. Whatever the real issues at Princeton, the public saw Wilson
only as the college president who had turned down a million dollars,
and, as one magazine editor put it, "When a university takes action
that causes it to forfeit a million dollars, some principle must be at
stake." That principle, so Wilson had persuaded the world at large,
was democracy. A later campaign biography described the division in
Princeton over the Quad Plan and the Graduate College as follows:
"It was the chasm that divides democracy and aristocracy, respect for
the rights of manhood and submission to the rights of property. It was
an ineradicable instinct in President Wilson and the men who supported him that the life of the students must be made democratic; the
opposition felt no indignation at the existence in college of those social
distinctions which they believe must always prevail in the world."[2]

The controversies at Princeton had an unhappy effect on Wilson's
character. He became more harsh, more ruthless in dealing with opposition, more skilled in promoting his interests. Yet this toughening
process may have been a necessary prelude to success in the world of

practical politics. Wilson often remarked later that professional politicians were far easier to deal with than those in academic life. The Princeton presidency, furthermore, had schooled him in administration, in conceiving and implementing policies, in advocacy, and in the technique of appealing to a wider constituency over the heads of immediate opponents.[3]

During the two years after the abortive attempt to advance him for the Democratic presidential nomination in 1908, Wilson helped to promote his eventual entry into politics by playing an active role as a literary politician, holding forth on public questions, both from the platform and in print. It is significant that, at the height of the progressive period, he renewed his earlier interest in municipal government. In dealing with the problems of the industrial city, he had previously defended active intervention of the government into the economy, even to the degree of state socialism, and had argued that cities should be organized to improve the lot of the laboring classes, not to keep down the taxes of the wealthy. Now, as formerly in his lectures at Johns Hopkins, Wilson proposed to simplify the structure of municipal government by drastically reducing the number of elective officials and concentrating power in their hands. This was exactly what municipal reformers wished to accomplish through the commission plan of city government first introduced at Galveston, Texas, after the disastrous flood of 1901. Wilson became especially interested in a particular concomitant of the commission plan, the short ballot. When a Short Ballot Association was formed in New York in 1909, he was chosen for the advisory board and was later elected president of the organization. The two vice-presidents were William U'Ren, a well-known reformer from Oregon, and Winston Churchill, a popular novelist who had been active in New Hampshire politics. The basic ideas of the association were that "only those offices should be elective which are *important* enough to attract (and deserve) public examination" and that "very few offices should be filled by election at one time, so as to permit adequate and unconfused public examination of the candidates."[4]

The short ballot was designed to do what Wilson had been preaching since his undergraduate days: to make government clearly visible to the people so that they could understand and therefore control it, and at the same time to make officials feel primarily responsible to the electorate. No sooner had Wilson espoused the reform, however, than he began to portray it as a miraculous means of eliminating corrupt political machines. So long as voters had to choose between candidates for scores of petty offices, he said, political machines and bosses were necessary, because to avert chaos there must be some agency for pre-screening candidates and ensuring the selection of nominees for all positions. Once introduce the short ballot, however, and voters could nominate and assess candidates for office without the help of machines; officials would then obey the voters rather than the bosses, and the happy result would be "the destruction of all machines by the simple process of making the business of politics so simple that there is nothing that necessitates the existence of a machine." Wilson even went so far as to insist that it was "the high duty of every lover of political liberty" to support this reform. "Another great age of American politics will have dawned," he wrote, "when men seek once more the means to establish the rights of the people and forget parties and private interests to serve a nation."[5]

Of course, this was a ridiculous overstatement. No particular item of electoral procedure was going to destroy party machinery that had been elaborated over scores of years and that was a necessity to democratic government, whether there were five or five hundred names on a ballot. As in his former proposal that cabinet members have seats on the floor of Congress, or in his recent insistence that graduate students be housed with undergraduates, Wilson immensely exaggerated the importance of the reform he happened to favor. His one-track mind seized a particular aspect of a problem and inflated it beyond its true significance.

As Wilson moved further toward identification with progressivism, he inveighed against the sins of business. On January 17, 1910, he addressed the bankers of New York City at the Waldorf-Astoria, facing an audience that included J. Pierpont Morgan and Franklin MacVeagh, Secretary of the Treasury. In a speech that offended Morgan, he charged—as he had at Denver in September 1908—that bankers were not interested in the small borrower or small enterpriser but gave all their attention to the big borrower and the large corporation. On May 6, 1910, he addressed a convention of the New Jersey Bankers' Association at Atlantic City. It was late when he took the dais, but Wilson captured the audience at once by telling the story of a Virginia gentleman who came home the worse for wear very late one night and inadvertently woke his wife, who asked him the time. He replied it was about midnight. Just then the clock struck three. "What do you make of that?" she exclaimed. "My dear," he responded, "would you believe that damn Yankee invention against the word of a southern gentleman?" Wilson gave his auditors the word of a southern gentleman that it was early in the evening and then proceeded to tell them how to run their business in the public interest. The most revealing aspect of his talk was that he again departed from his earlier insistence that to end corporate malpractice one need only find the guilty individual and punish him. Now he maintained that even men of unimpeachable honesty had done great harm because they ran their businesses for private rather than public purposes. It was necessary that they be held to a new standard: the interest of the people as a whole. If bankers ignored the general welfare of the nation, they would start "those processes of danger and decay" that would ultimately result in bringing their own enterprises "to a quick and disastrous end." Wilson hinted that he favored a central bank of issue organized under the control of the federal government. In closing, he told his hearers that the age had come when, if they were not statesmen, they had no right to be bankers. Even though it was long after midnight when he finished, the stenographer recorded that he received "great applause."[6]

The response of the New Jersey bankers suggested that Wilson was, as he later described himself, "a progressive with the brakes on." His tone was one of moderation, and he deprecated "convulsive, agitated, almost revolutionary means" of overcoming the ills of society. He was careful to dissociate himself from Bryan, and he balanced denunciation of corporate malpractices with criticism of labor unions. He also appeared to be something less than a thoroughgoing progressive in his attitude toward the initiative, referendum, and recall—mechanisms whereby reformers hoped to achieve "direct democracy." As a devotee of Edmund Burke, Wilson disliked anything that weakened the exercise of independent, individual judgment on the part of elected representatives. Furthermore, the initiative, referendum, and recall would still further clutter up the voting machinery that he hoped to simplify through the use of the short ballot.[7]

In short, Wilson's speeches and writings during the last years of his presidency of Princeton revealed him as enough of a progressive to win support from voters who desired reform, especially in the direction of restraining the power of corporate wealth, but at the same time temperate enough not to alienate conservatives. Among the latter was George B. Harvey, who continued to promote Wilson's political fortunes. In May 1909 Harvey predicted in *Harper's Weekly*, "We now expect to see WOODROW WILSON elected Governor of the State of New Jersey in 1910 and nominated for President in 1912 upon a platform demanding tariff reform downward." The most important immediate step was to gain support for Wilson among New Jersey Democrats.

Early in 1910, therefore, Harvey sought out James Smith, Jr., the most powerful Democratic boss in the state, and urged him to get behind Wilson.[8]

"Jim" Smith was an Irish Catholic boss of the old school. After starting out as a grocery clerk and then entering municipal politics, he had quickly risen to the top. From 1893 to 1899 he served in the United States Senate, where he achieved a certain notoriety as one of the "sugar senators" who balked Grover Cleveland's efforts at tariff reform. He had not held political office since then, but he still controlled the Democratic political machine in Essex County, the most populous county in the state. He was also involved in a variety of business interests—banking, manufacturing, real estate, newspapers, shipping, and public utilities. A tall, powerful man with a smooth, childlike face and considerable charm, Smith was an impressive figure. He acted his part to perfection. His usual daytime garb was a cutaway with a white waistcoat and a pleated silk shirt. He was always accessible, whether at his desk near the front window of the Federal Trust Company in Newark or at his home in the evening. He selected candidates, mapped campaign strategy, and distributed party funds, sometimes from his own pocket. He had come to know and to admire Wilson when his sons were students at Princeton, and he used to call on the President occasionally at Prospect.[9]

Harvey had no great difficulty in persuading Smith to agree to support Wilson, but Smith alone could not carry New Jersey. The chairman of the Democratic state committee was James R. Nugent, Smith's nephew, who favored Frank S. Katzenbach of Trenton, a former candidate for the governorship. Nugent did, however, issue a statement on January 19, 1910, that Woodrow Wilson was "without doubt, the most popular Democrat in the East," and that the New Jersey delegation to the Democratic convention in 1912 would be pledged to him. Rank-and-file machine Democrats were less enthusiastic. Wilson was thought to be antilabor, and he had not won his spurs in local politics.[10]

In the meantime, Wilson had to be induced to run, and this was not easy. The Graduate College controversy was now in full swing, and he was not one to back out of it, especially since friends were begging him not to resign as President of Princeton. If he publicly entertained the prospect of accepting the gubernatorial nomination, his position at Princeton would be weakened. At a conference in late January Harvey asked Wilson point-blank what he would do if he were definitely offered the nomination "on a silver platter," with no effort on his part, and no pledges. Wilson went no further than to agree to give the matter serious consideration. Shortly afterward Harvey went off to

England, with assurances of support for Wilson from Smith but no positive assurance that his candidate would agree to run.[11]

From January until late June 1910, Wilson gave no formal indication that he was interested in entering politics; during most of this time he was immersed in the Graduate College dispute. Yet his covert memorandum to Brougham of the *New York Times,* creating the public impression that in his battle at Princeton he was actually fighting for the forces of democracy against social exclusiveness, was certainly calculated to advance him politically. In "that Pittsburgh speech," with its extreme attack on the forces of privilege, its prediction of impending disaster, and its suggestion that America needed new leadership, Wilson clearly hinted at his availability. The attack on Protestant churches surely did not harm him among the predominately Roman Catholic Democrats of New Jersey, some of whom were suspicious of Wilson as a "Presbyterian priest." The *Brooklyn Times* remarked editorially of the Pittsburgh speech, "No one will deny that there is very much of truth in Dr. Wilson's statement, but it is not easy to repress the suspicion that there is between the lines a suggestion that Woodrow Wilson is the man the people are crying for."[12]

Wilson did not content himself with making political capital out of the Princeton controversy. In mid-March 1910 he appeared among an impressive array of speakers at a dinner of the National Democratic Club in New York City in memory of Grover Cleveland. A political reporter for the *Brooklyn Citizen,* signing himself "Mul," reported that Wilson easily carried off the honors of the evening. He observed: "President Wilson is one of the ablest Democrats that it has been 'Mul's' good fortune to hear within the last twenty-five years. He . . . has a wit as keen as the edge of a Saladin's scimitar, and yet he is a broadminded man, a man with statesmanlike views, and a capacity for lucid, logical statement, that but few of our national orators possess . . . I have devoted considerable space to President Wilson for the reason that he is what the politicians call a 'coming man.' "[13]

Wilson "came" still further when he addressed a "dollar dinner" of the state executive committee at Elizabeth, New Jersey, on March 29, 1910. Therefore he had spoken only to the elite of the Democratic party; for the first time he faced the rank and file. He apparently scored his usual success. The *Trenton True American* used nearly half the front page to report his words and to describe how he was cheered by over six hundred enthusiastic Democrats. His talk was later published in *Harper's Weekly* under the title, "Living Principles of Democracy." It centered on the role that the Democratic party might assume in dedicating itself to the service of the country. It attacked monopoly and

TRUE AMERICAN

NEWSPAPER FOR NEW JERSEY PEOPLE.

The Weather

Cloudy—Warmer.

NEW JERSEY, WEDNESDAY, MARCH 30, 1910.

PRICE—TWO CENTS.

Woodrow Wilson in Remarkable Address Outlines Principles and Program of Present=Day Democracy

Sound Democratic Doctrine Preached by Woodrow Wilson

(THE HIGH LIGHTS OF A SPEECH DELIVERED BY WOODROW WILSON AT ELIZABETH LAST NIGHT, AND HERE SUBMITTED AS CONTAINING NOT ONLY THE FUNDAMENTALS OF DEMOCRACY, BUT A SAFE AND SENSIBLE PROGRAM UPON WHICH TO APPEAL TO THE PEOPLE.)

Not the success of party, but the service of the country, should be of first consideration.

The drift toward Democracy should make us eager not for office, but for an opportunity to put Democratic principles into action. Governments do not exist for those who desire to hold office.

If the young men come to us, we may be sure that the future is ours and that the Democratic party is the real choice of the Nation.

The Democratic party has profound and abiding confidence in the people themselves. The Republican party rests its confidence in those who are the most conspicuous leaders of the country's business.

Democracy is meant to serve the people as a whole rather than particular vested interests.

The interests must be accommodated to the general welfare, whether that be pleasing to the interests or not.

The individual, the single living person, not the corporation, is the only rightful possessor alike of rights and privileges.

Government must be for the convenience of the individual, not for his suppression.

The Democratic party is a party.

WOODROW WILSON.

Cheered by Hundreds of Enthusiastic Democrats at "Dollar Dinner" in Elizabeth.

NOT SHOUTING OLD SLOGANS, NOT LOOKING BACKWARD, BUT FORWARD

The Party of Profound and Abiding Confidence in the People, Not a Party That Looks to Corporate Influences As the Hope of the Nation.

One of the Most Significant Utterances of the Day.

Elizabeth, New Jersey, March 29.—Woodrow Wilson, president of Princeton University, was cheered by more than 600 Democrats at the Dollar Dinner of the Democratic Executive Committee tonight when he declared that the time had come for the Democratic party to give the country the kind of tariff regulation that would reduce high prices on commodities, and to remedy existing conditions in State and Nation, as it was certainly evident on all sides that the people are weary of the sort of government the Republican party is handing out. A new era was at hand, he said, and it was up to the Democratic party to take advantage of its opportunities. United States Senator Thomas P. Gore, of Oklahoma, also spoke.

President Wilson spoke as follows:

The signs and portents of the time are all certainly most encouraging to those who believe that the Democratic party can be serviceable to the country at this juncture of its affairs. It would seem that everywhere the thought of men who are anxious for the welfare of the country is turning

hand makes our duty the thing that we should principally consider. The great governments of this country, State and Nation, do not exist for the purpose of affording opportunities to those Democrats or those Republicans who desire to hold office, but the Democratic and Republican parties alike are intended for the service of the Nation. It would be very uncomfortable to look forward towards the responsibilities of success, if we did not know what we were to do with it when it came.

In order to determine this all-important question, we must remind ourselves that our duty is of the present and the future. We are not old men looking over our shoulders, recalling past difficulties, shouting old slogans, fretting over old jealousies and divisions, but men of our own day, looking forward, looking about us, studying the needs and circumstances of the Nation as a whole and seeking an opportunity to make our counsels heard in the affairs of the country we love.

YOUNG MEN SHALL PROVE PARTY'S WORTH

Report of an address by Wilson to rank-and-file Democrats in March 1910. Although he was not yet an avowed candidate for Governor of New Jersey, he made himself available by keeping in the public eye and by assuming the stance of a moderate progressive.

the Republican party. It eloquently forecast a coming political renaissance. In substance, however, it was relatively conservative; it condemned excessive use of the power of government.[14]

The other main speaker at the dollar dinner was Senator Thomas P. Gore of Oklahoma, who was cheered when he urged Wilson to make the sacrifice and run for governor with an eye to the presidency in 1912. The Wilson boom was now on, and it was reported to be the principal topic of conversation when New Jersey Democratic leaders met at Atlantic City in mid-April.[15]

In early June, James Smith received assurances from powerful Midwestern politicians that if he got Wilson elected Governor of New Jersey by a big margin, they would support him for the presidency. But Smith was worried about his own opposition in New Jersey politics. He therefore arranged for a friend to write Wilson a letter sounding out his attitude toward the existing Democratic organization. If elected Governor, would he accept the organization, or would he break it down and build up one of his own? Wilson replied that the last thing on his mind was to erect a personal machine; as long as the Smith machine supported policies aimed at restoring the state's reputation, it would be "inexcusable" to antagonize it. But this attitude would last only as long as he was left "absolutely free in the matter of measures and men." Smith accepted these terms.[16]

Meanwhile Smith faced a revolt from within the Democratic state committee, most of whom favored Frank S. Katzenbach. Smith telephoned Harvey after his return from abroad in late June and told him that unless Wilson would definitely agree to accept the nomination if offered, he could not hold back the tide of Katzenbach sentiment. Harvey quickly arranged a meeting for June 26 of Wilson, Smith, himself, and "Colonel" Henry Watterson, editor of the *Louisville Courier-Journal* and a power in the Democratic party. Wilson, who was on vacation in Old Lyme, Connecticut, wired that he could not attend because there was no local train, but Harvey sent an aide on a desperate journey by train and automobile, and he managed to bring Wilson to Harvey's home in New Jersey in time for the dinner and a memorable evening. Smith and Harvey told Wilson that he could have the New Jersey governorship "by acclamation" and would later have a fair chance of gaining the presidency. Watterson agreed to "take off his coat" and support him for the 1912 nomination.[17]

Even so, Wilson hesitated. He was a relatively poor man: his independent income was only about $2000 a year, plus whatever he could make by lectures and articles. He had three unmarried daughters still to provide for, plus continuing demands from penurious relatives. He quoted "Mr. Dooley's" advice, "If anny Dimmicrat has a stiddy job he'd better shtick to it." Furthermore, he felt an obligation to Princeton. Friends continued to urge him not to resign. Thomas D. Jones, a highly respected Trustee who had always stood by him, wrote early in June that if he resigned then, it would look like petulance over the Wyman bequest. Jones begged him not to allow feelings of irritation or depression, however justifiable or inevitable, to deter him from accomplishing his long-time purposes for the University. Moreover, the election of John Barr as Alumni Trustee and the ovations for Wilson at Commencement time showed that he still retained the affection and trust of the great majority of Princeton men.[18]

Before committting himself, Wilson wrote letters to his intimates among the Princeton Trustees, explaining the situation and saying that he could only leave the University with their free consent. After consultation, his friends all agreed that he need have no moral qualms about going into politics. Finally, nearly three weeks after the dinner with Harvey, Watterson, and Smith, he decided he would accept the nomination, if offered. He wrote Cleveland Dodge that, in view of what he had taught his students about public duty, he did not see how he could avoid this opportunity for service. After a conference arranged by Harvey with important Democratic leaders of New Jersey on July 12 Wilson made public his decision. In an open letter to the *Newark Evening News* and the *Trenton True American,* published on July 15 and 16 respectively, he wrote that there had been so much interest in his possible nomination for governor that it would be "an affectation and a discourtesy" for him to remain silent any longer. He was not a candidate, and if he consulted his own wishes, he would stay in Princeton, but if it should be the desire of "a decided majority of the thoughtful Democrats of the State" that he accept the nomination, then it would be his duty, "as well as an honor and a privilege, to do so."[19]

This announcement was received with a burst of enthusiasm by New Jersey and metropolitan newspapers. With few exceptions Wilson's entrance into politics was hailed. The *Newark Evening News* was of the opinion that his nomination would rehabilitate the Democratic party and elevate the character of the coming campaign. The *New York World* expressed similar sentiments. The *New York Evening Post* looked beyond New Jersey, charging New Jersey Democrats to "use every effort toward the securing of a candidacy which would help both the party and the cause of good government not only in their own state but throughout the country."[20]

Nevertheless, it did not prove easy for James Smith to deliver Wilson the nomination. Sentiment for Katzenbach among party workers remained strong, and there was little grass-roots enthusiasm for Wilson. It was the judgment of several insiders that if Katzenbach had not refused to agree to run until late July, he might well have received the nomination. At this juncture Smith made an alliance with Robert Davis, his principal rival for leadership of the New Jersey Democrats. Davis was boss of Hudson County, which was almost as populous as Smith's own bailiwick. Having started as a plumber and, like Smith, worked his way up the political ladder, he was faced with revolt by a progressive Jersey City Mayor, M. Otto Wittpen, who was also a gubernatorial candidate. By allying himself with Smith in support of Wilson, Davis hoped both to snuff out Wittpen's chances and to gain a share of state patronage.[21]

The Democratic party of New Jersey was divided, as was the Republican, into conservative and progressive factions. With the announcement of Smith's and Davis' support of Wilson, this division came into the open. Progressives charged that Wilson's candidacy was being promoted by the very forces they had been fighting for years— the big city bosses, and behind them the New York City financial and corporate interests that had made New Jersey "the mother of trusts," a synonym for corruption and for what Elihu Root later called "invisible government." The fact was not lost upon progressive editors such as James Kerney of the *Trenton Evening Times* and Matthew C. Ely of the *Hudson Observer* that George Harvey was closely connected with J. Pierpont Morgan; the *Observer* charged that Wilson was letting himself "be used as a catspaw, to serve the purposes of the bosses" in heading off reform.[22]

The Wilson candidacy suffered a further blow when on August 16 the New Jersey Federation of Labor passed a resolution denouncing him as a foe of labor on the basis of his remarks in the Baccalaureate address of 1909 about "unprofitable servants." The charge was so damaging that Wilson for once broke his silence and wrote Edgar R. Williamson, editor of the *American Labor Standard,* that he had been misrepresented, that in the address he had not been attacking trade unions but merely trade union abuses, that in fact he had always been "a warm friend of organized labor." Labor, he declared, had as much right to organize as capital. Just as he regarded the business corporation as indispensable, even though it was guilty of offenses against the common interest, so he regarded labor unions. But this letter looked too much like a deathbed conversion, and Wilson did not win over the labor union leaders.[23]

Even before the row over his candidacy broke into the open, Wilson himself wondered why the bosses were so anxious to nominate him, because he had made it perfectly clear that he was an independent person whom they would not be able to control. One answer he came to was that a reformation had taken place in American politics and the bosses had realized they must conduct themselves more honorably. More realistic was his other conclusion: that the bosses saw the obvious practical advantages of a Democratic victory, whether or not they could control the governor. The Republicans had controlled the state government of New Jersey for seventeen years. A Democratic victory at the polls would make it possible for the bosses to reward their hungry followers.[24]

That Wilson would ever turn on the bosses and break their power, as in fact he later did, was inconceivable to them. The first commandment of practical politics is loyalty, and Wilson, owing his election to Smith and Davis, would never, they believed, bite the hands that fed him. And even if he should attempt defiance, they were convinced that a complete novice would have little chance of success against men whose entire adult lives had been devoted to the complex and difficult art of practical politics. Undoubtedly the opinion of Smith and Davis concurred with that of a Princeton Trustee who wrote a friend that Wilson had lost his head because he thought applause at dinner tables meant support, and that he would be "a child, a dear delightful infant, left to the tender care of James Smith."[25]

Although their seclusion was more than usually interrupted, Wilson and his family were able to spend nearly three quiet months at Old Lyme in the summer of 1910; he had a last chance to rest and build up his energy before plunging into a new career. In the evenings he sat on the porch of the boarding house and read poetry aloud to his wife and girls. For exercise he explored country roads on foot and played golf on a sheep pasture, where the hazards were bayberry bushes and rocks. When politics called him back to New Jersey in mid-September, his face was tanned and his step had a spring in it.[26]

The event that brought him back from his seaside retreat was the New Jersey Democratic convention, which met in the Taylor Opera House at Trenton on September 15, 1910. Smith and Davis thought they controlled a majority, and there were confident predictions that Wilson would receive support from over 1000 of the 1400-odd delegates, but still they were uneasy. Although the opposition had weakened its effectiveness by dividing its support among three "favorite sons," they controlled nearly as many delegates among them as the Hudson and Essex County bosses. Then there was the undercurrent of support for

Katzenbach among Smith's and Davis' followers. The division between
the bosses and the progressives was less clearcut than has sometimes
been portrayed. Factional, local, and personal differences also played
perhaps a predominate part. Nevertheless the progressive elements
in the convention were generally cool toward Wilson. If he were to
be sure of nomination, he must win on the first ballot.[27]

The convention was tumultuous. There were challenges of delegates'
credentials, shouting and booing from the spectators (including a group
of Princeton students in a pro-Wilson cheering section led by one of
Smith's sons), and a fight in which one delegate broke a cane over
another's head. A Katzenbach seconder threw the gathering into an
uproar by charging that Wilson was the tool of the "financial interests"
who were attempting to foist him on the convention by "bargain and
sale and the double cross." The processes of seating delegates and
making nominations took so long that it was not until 4:30 P.M. that
balloting began. Wilson won a first-ballot nomination by a narrow
margin, gaining 749½ votes out of a total of 1416.

The convention was ready to break up when John R. Hardin, the
chairman, announced, "We have just received word that Mr. Wilson,
the candidate for the governorship, *and the next President of the
United States,* has received word of his nomination; has left Princeton,
and is now on his way to the Convention." Hardin asked the band to
play, and five minutes later Wilson appeared on the platform. Two
of Harvey's aides had fetched him from Princeton, where he was playing golf, and he was still wearing a knitted golf jacket under his coat
when he appeared before the restive, curious delegates, some still
sullen from defeat.

Wilson opened his acceptance speech, which he had written out in
advance, by thanking the delegates for the honor done him, and then
he caught the attention of his auditors by declaring his total political
independence: "As you know, I did not seek the nomination. It has
come to me absolutely unsolicited, with the consequences that I shall
enter upon the duties of the office of Governor, if elected, with absolutely no pledges of any kind to prevent me from serving the people of
this state with singleness of purpose. Not only have no pledges of any
kind been given, but none has been proposed or desired." This statement was greeted with cheers, which mounted as Wilson went on to
declare in unequivocal terms his support of the "sound, businesslike,
and explicit platform" the convention had adopted earlier. He closed
with a stirring peroration:

The future is not for parties "playing politics," but for measures conceived in the largest spirit, pushed by parties whose leaders are statesmen

not demagogues, who love, not their offices but their duty and their opportunity for service. We are witnessing a renaissance of public spirit, a reawakening of sober public opinion, a revival of the power of the people, the beginning of an age of thoughtful reconstruction that makes our thoughts hark back to the great age in which democracy was set up in America. With the new age we shall show a new spirit. We shall serve justice and candour and all things that make for right. Is not our ancient party the party disciplined and made ready for this great task? Shall we not forget ourselves in making it the instrument of righteousness for the State and for the Nation?[28]

The next day the *New York Times* reported that Wilson's speech had the effect of "stirring in his hearers a hope and confidence in the outcome of his candidacy which obliterated all delegate lines." The *New York World* reported that New Jersey Democrats had not displayed such enthusiasm for a generation. According to the *Newark Evening News,* many of Wilson's late foes were won over then and there. Delegates rushed to the platform to carry the new leader in triumph. He had to be protected by a cordon of police as he left the hall and was borne away in an automobile.[29]

The party platform, which the Democrats had endorsed before the balloting, had been composed the day before, with Harvey present during the deliberations. The text revealed Wilson's hand. It contained a plank dealing with control of corporations that must have been written by him, demanding legislation against corporate actions or methods of organization that destroyed free competition or hurt the public interest, with penalties visited upon guilty individuals. The rest of the platform was mostly a straightforward declaration of progressivism. It called for reorganization and economy in the state government, equalization of the tax burden, a public service commission with ample power to fix public utility rates, an employers' liability act, conservation of natural resources, a corrupt practices law, and civil service reform. It denounced the Payne-Aldrich law and demanded that Congress revise tariff schedules downward. This liberal platform, supported outright by Wilson, supplied him with ready-made campaign material and helped to win the backing of progressive Democrats, independents, and insurgent Republicans.[30]

At only one point did the platform fall short of pure progressive doctrine. Wilson was still opposed to the direct primary as a means of nominating candidates for office and apparently used his influence to prevent an outright endorsement of such reform. The platform merely contained a muddily phrased statement calling for the simplification of nominating machinery so as to give voters the right to make nominations; this might or might not mean primary elections. Apparently Wilson at this time did not take seriously a Democratic preferential primary for United States Senator that had been held on August 20, at the time delegates were chosen for the Trenton convention. The primary was not legally binding, nor was it considered of much importance because until the Seventeenth Amendment in 1913 Senators were chosen by state legislatures, and the New Jersey legislature was so districted that the chance of the Democrats' electing a majority seemed remote.[31]

Shortly after the Democratic convention the New Jersey Republicans met and nominated for Governor Vivian M. Lewis, state commissioner of banking and insurance, an able lawyer long active in state politics. In the Republican convention there had been a fight between the conservative wing, directed by an oligarchy commonly known as the "Board of Guardians" and the so-called "New Idea" progressive faction. The latter had lost out narrowly in several key votes. Even though the Republican platform was on the whole a progressive one, partly at Lewis's own insistence, he was handicapped during the ensuing campaign by the obvious conservatism of the dominant elements in his party.[32]

Four days after his nomination Wilson met with Democratic leaders in Princeton. The Mercer County delegation had voted solidly for Katzenbach in the recent convention, and as a gesture of reconciliation some of them were asked to the conference in Wilson's study in Prospect. During discussion of various details of the coming campaign, the professional politicians were amazed at Wilson's grasp of detail. He discussed local political affairs "as if they were the one thing in the world in which he had been taking an interest." He remembered the names of the men and made them feel very much at home. The meeting lasted three hours, and those attending were charmed by their reception.[33]

At first Wilson displayed political naïveté when it came to dealing with campaign funds. When his friend Thomas D. Jones sent him a check, he returned it, saying that he hoped to pay for his personal expenses during the campaign out of his own pocket; fees from lecture engagements could make up the few hundred dollars he would lose. Later he came to realize that campaigns cost money beyond the extent of a professor's savings, and he was glad to accept "sinews of war" from Cleveland Dodge and other wealthy friends. According to a credible estimate, the cost of his gubernatorial campaign ran over one hundred thousand dollars, and the funds came from the following sources: Princeton friends, $3500; wealthy acquaintances of George B. Harvey $10,000; James D. Smith, Jr., $50,000; Democratic state committee, the rest.[34]

Wilson spent the first two or three days of every week attending to his duties as President of Princeton, but for the rest he was entirely at the disposal of the campaign managers, who arranged a strenuous schedule so that he thoroughly canvassed the state. His campaign opened with an appearance before a working-class audience in St. Peter's Hall, Jersey City. Wilson began by talking over the heads of his audience in terms of service and principles, and he brought in a Negro story that was not particularly apposite. His effort seemed a failure until the end, when he acknowledged that this was his first political speech and left his case in the hands of the jury that would try him. This simple, direct appeal gained a response that his formal talk had not evoked, and the audience cheered him for several minutes.[35]

Wilson quickly learned to communicate with the audiences he met at fair grounds, on street corners, in auditoriums, and in smoke-filled political clubs. Joseph S. Hoff, Chairman of the Mercer County Democratic Committee and Wilson's family butcher of many years, was afraid that Wilson would be too "classic" to appeal to ordinary voters, but he found that his fears were groundless. "He worked audiences up," said Hoff, "so that they'd begin to think he was one of them." An Irish cabman put it more picturesquely, "You ought to hear him speak. You would think he was going to put his finger on your nose."[36]

Wilson's ability to reach the common run of voters was achieved without loss of dignity or taste. He did not rant or shout; he did not call his opponents names; he constantly talked of principles and policies. An editorial in the New York Times remarked that he puzzled opposition politicians because he had a sense of humor and because he displayed "amazing fairness and courtesy to the opposition party." His weakness at the very first was that he talked in generalities, so that even Democratic newspapers chided him for avoiding live state issues. Stung by such criticism, he said in an address at Newark on September 30, with Smith and his lieutenants in the audience, that he not only stood by every plank in the Democratic platform but went beyond it. He wanted even more stringent laws controlling corporations than the platform called for and more extensive rate-making powers for the Public Service Commission. He wanted more opportunity for the people to participate directly in politics and urged a constitutional amendment providing for direct election of United States Senators. He declared his faith in democracy—in the judgment of "that great voiceless multitude of men who constitute the great body and the saving force of the nation."[37]

The Newark speech marked a turning point in the gubernatorial campaign. Wilson had broken clean from his conservative past. Having long preached the doctrine of political expediency, he now practiced it with a vengeance. He had moved toward an uncompromisingly progressive position in which he could say, "I am and always have been an insurgent." Lewis responded by this shift to the left by following along in the same direction. Wilson was quick to exploit the development. To an overflow crowd at Atlantic City he said that his opponent was a man for whom he had great respect, but that as he added item after item to his personal platform, it resembled Wilson's own more than the official one by the Republican party.[38]

The Republicans circulated pamphlets indicating that Wilson was an enemy of labor unions, of the Catholic Church, and of immigrants from central and eastern Europe—the last supported by damning quotations from *A History of the American People*. The most dangerous of these charges was probably that relating to labor unions, since the New Jersey Federation of Labor was formally opposed to his candidacy. Wilson fought back by claiming that the Republicans were "false friends" and that his former criticisms had merely reflected a fear that labor would develop such strong class feeling that popular government in the common interet would be impossible. The warm response Wilson received from working-class audiences suggested that he may have won over some of the rank and file, although union leaders continued to oppose him.[39]

Speaking to an audience in Trenton on October 3, Wilson made the extraordinary assertion that he was unaware that any particular person was responsible for his nomination. Therefore, he was not likely to be influenced by subtle pressures from corrupt interests. Even the *Newark Evening News*, which had supported him strongly from the first, attacked this statement, maintaining Wilson ought to know that if he were elected, he would have to face demands from Senator Smith, Robert Davis, and George Harvey, who claimed responsibility for his nomination as gubernatorial candidate. However eloquently Wilson might preach democracy and a regeneration of political life, the fact was that he had been forced on a reluctant Democratic convention by the power of two notorious bosses. The opportunity to erase this stigma came when George L. Record, leader of the New Idea Republicans and a candidate for Congress, accepted an offhand challenge that Wilson had issued to Republican spokesmen to debate issues with him. Wilson's campaign managers urged him to ignore Record, but he finally decided that he would lose more by silence than by meeting Record head-on. It was too late to rearrange his speaking engagements for a debate, he announced on October 11, but he would be glad to answer in writing any questions put to him, and Record was at full liberty to publish the answers. Record sent Wilson nineteen questions designed to search out the difficult and potentially embarrassing topic of Wilson's relationship to the Democratic bosses and the financial interests behind them. In answer, Wilson for the most part reiterated earlier statements or pointed to the Democratic platform, but Record also asked whether Wilson agreed that direct primary laws should be extended to cover candidates for governor, Congress, and national conventions. Wilson had previously opposed such measures, and had seen to it that the Democratic platform hedged on them, but now he came out unequivocally in their favor. This turnabout on the issue of primaries was of great importance because shortly after the gubernatorial election Wilson would have to decide whether to support James Martine, the perennial also-ran whom a desultory preferential primary election had chosen as the Democratic candidate for Senator, or James Smith, who had done more than any other man to make him Governor. If Record had not pushed him into an uncompromising declaration in favor of the primary, it is conceivable that he would not later have supported Martine against Smith.[40]

The cutting edge of Record's questionnaire concerned the boss system. Did Wilson admit it existed? Did he admit that it was bipartisan? Did he admit that it was tied to corruption and to dominance of the state of New Jersey by corporations seeking privileges? Wilson freely answered yes to these questions. Coming closer to home, Record said that he had been fighting the Republican "Board of Guardians" for years; would Wilson fight the Democratic "Overlords," who represented the same system of boss control? Wilson answered, "Certainly; I will join you or anyone else in denouncing and fighting any and every one, of either party, who attempts such outrages against the government and public morality." Record asked how Wilson could say that the Democratic party had been reorganized and the Republican party had not, unless he could show that the party had changed its leaders or the leaders had changed their opinions. Wilson answered that the party was seeking to change its leaders, and would obviously do so if it won the election. "If I am elected," he wrote, "I shall understand that I am chosen leader of my party and the direct representative of the whole people in the conduct of government." Record's next query was whether there was a progressive movement in the Democratic party corresponding to that in the Republican party. Wilson not only answered in the affirmative but went beyond the question to make it crystal-clear that he considered himself entirely free of commitments to the Democratic bosses:

Before I pass to my next question, will you not permit me to frame one which you have not asked, but which I am sure lies implied in those I have answered? You wish to know what my relations would be with the Democrats whose power and influence you fear, should I be elected Governor, particularly in such important matters as appointments and the signing of bills, and I am very glad to tell you. If elected, I shall not, either in the matter of appointments to office or assent to legislation, or in shaping any part of the policy of my administration, submit to the dictation of any person or persons, special interest or organization. I will always welcome advice and suggestions from any citizen, whether boss, leader, organization man, or plain citizen, and I shall constantly seek the advice of influential and disinterested men, representative of their communities and disconnected from political "organizations" entirely; but all suggestions will be considered on their merits, and no additional weight will be given to any man's advice or suggestion because of his exercising, or supposing that he exercises, some sort of political influence or control. I should deem myself forever disgraced should I even in the slightest degree cooperate in any such system or any such transactions as you describe in your characterization of the "boss" system. I regard myself as pledged to the regeneration of the Democratic party which I have forseen above.

This was, on the face of it at least, a repudiation of the assurance Wilson had made to Smith in June that he would not interfere with the existing Democratic organization, as the Essex County boss must have realized. But he probably could not bring himself to believe that this man, whom he genuinely admired, would turn on him. And even if Wilson should challenge the bosses, how could a rank amateur be expected to wrest control of the Democratic party from men who made politics their business? In any case, for the present Smith and his allies were helpless. They had no choice but to continue to give Wilson full support.[41]

Even before he agreed to run for Governor, Wilson had told a man with long experience in New Jersey politics that he felt confident he could manage the political machine. He abundantly demonstrated his political skill in the gubernatorial campaign of 1910. Smith probably expected to use Wilson, but Wilson used him. Without making a single pledge except not to interfere with the party machine—and even this was qualified—Wilson gained the support of the bosses, who saw to it that he was nominated. He then turned around and wooed the progressives, even though this meant repudiating the men who had done most to advance him politically. Oswald Garrison Villard, editor of the *New York Evening Post,* one of his strongest supporters at this time, was of the opinion that Wilson knew exactly what he was about. The particular tactics he used were probably not premeditated since his moves had to be made on short notice, to meet immediate demands of the campaign. This only made those moves the more remarkable. It took extraordinary awareness of public sentiment as well as nerve on Wilson's part to shift his ground in the heat of battle and redeploy in a stronger position.[42]

Wilson's answer to Record's questionnaire brought the last doubting Democrats to his banner, along with many New Idea Republicans and independents. The New Jersey press was now almost unanimously in his favor. He campaigned strenuously to the end. He sought to attract the labor vote by detailing plans for workmen's compensation, and he frankly attacked Republican misrule in the state. He made even more explicit his independence of the bosses and suggested that if they thought they could control him, they had "picked out the wrong man after all."[43]

Immediately after his nomination for the governorship Wilson announced that he intended to resign as President of Princeton University at the regular meeting of the Board of Trustees on October 20, 1910. Meanwhile, he so arranged his political engagements that he could attend to Princeton affairs and even give his regular Monday and Tuesday lectures on jurisprudence to undergraduates. Some of his friends apparently hoped he would not give up his office but would rather await the result of the November election. His foes among the trustees, however, thought he should have called a special meeting in September to present his resignation; they were determined that he should remove himself in October. If he did not, they threatened to present to the Board the following resolution:

Resolved that, in the judgment of the members of this Board, the position of the President of the University as a candidate for office before the public, and the impossibility of the performance of his duties are so inconsistent with the retention of the office as to work to the injury of the University.

If Wilson would resign, however, his enemies were willing to be generous about financial arrangements and about how the event should be reported to the public.[44]

It was customary for the President to ask one of the clerical members of the Board of Trustees to open meetings with prayer, but the minutes for October 20, 1910, begin as follows: "The President of the University occupied the chair and opened the meeting with prayer." On looking around the gathering, Wilson had noticed that his friend Dr. Jacobus, his one clerical supporter on the Board, was not present; he chose to give the prayer himself rather than allow the opposing faction to pray over his demise. He then asked for a motion that regular business be suspended "in order that he might bring before the Board a matter of some importance." When this motion passed, he presented a formal note of resignation, which he had previously written out. He then left the room. The Trustees immediately accepted the resignation, with an expression of regret, and a committee was appointed to draw up a suitable resolution and present it to the Board at the next meeting.[45]

At a meeting on November 13 the Princeton Trustees adopted unanimously a resolution, written by Dr. Jacobus and toned down by Pyne and others, praising in almost extravagant terms Wilson's administration of his office as President of Princeton. They voted him the honorary degree of Doctor of Laws, and they offered to pay his salary and allow him to occupy Prospect until February. The resolution, beautifully hand written and illuminated on parchment, was sent Wilson in an orange and black leather folder reposing in a silk-lined mahogany box; it is among his papers in the Library of Congress today. He accepted the honorary degree, but refused to take any salary after October 20. As soon as it was possible to clear up the detritus of twenty years in Princeton, he moved with his family into cramped quarters in the Princeton Inn.[46]

On November 5 Wilson closed his campaign for the governorship in James Smith's Essex County, with talks to large crowds in East Orange in the afternoon and Newark in the evening. He traversed ground long familiar—the "unspeakably selfish Payne-Aldrich tariff," the need for legislation that would cast light into corporate business—and closed with characteristic observations about the interconnection between public opinion and political leadership:

> If I were to sum up all the criticism that has been uttered against the honorable and distinguished gentleman who is now President of the United States, it would be summed up in this: That the people are disappointed that he has not led them . . . I don't know why he refrains. The disappointment of the people is perfectly evident because he refrains, and they long to see somebody go in there and put on Congress the pressure of opinion of the whole United States. Now that is the only thing that will disentangle the complicated affairs of New Jersey: to put somebody in the Governorship who will bring to bear on legislation the pressure of opinion of the whole of New Jersey.[47]

Throughout nearly two months of strenuous campaigning—making two, three, and four speeches a day, undergoing the constant jostling of indiscriminate human contacts and the indignities of irregular meals and of travel by automobile at a time when roads were dusty and rough, Wilson's energy and spirits had never flagged. He was obviously invigorated by awareness that at last he was on the way to fulfilling his boyhood dream of becoming a statesman.

It was generally conceded that Wilson would win the election; the only dispute was over the probable size of his margin. The *New York Times* predicted that he would carry New Jersey by 7,000 votes; Jim Smith predicted 25,000 and the ever-ebullient George Harvey, 40,000. Wilson outdid all predictions: he was election Governor of New Jersey by a margin of over 49,000 votes—in a state that Taft had carried by 83,000 votes only two years before. It was apparent that he had also put himself on the path to the White House. The *Literary Digest,* which summarized nationwide newspaper opinion, said that he and Governor Judson Harmon were the most likely candidates for the Democratic nomination in 1912; it quoted the *New York Globe*: "All over the country Democratic thought will turn to Dr. Wilson as the appointed one for 1912. A progressive Democrat who is able to escape the anger of conservative Democrats, and a Southern man who has lifted himself out of sectional strife, Dr. Wilson is plainly being chosen by destiny."[48]

Shortly after his election as Governor, the Princeton seniors asked Wilson to dinner, at which he gave them a short talk. Booth Tarkington, who was present, vividly remembered two points he made on this occasion: first, that in any decision a man has to make, it may seem that there are several courses open to him, but this is not true—there is only one right course of action; and second, that in their lives men are in the grip of forces beyond their control. He felt, he said, as though he had stepped into a boat bound for an unknown destination, but he was happy to be in it and glad to trust the decision of the pilot.[49]

Wilson had been preparing for this voyage for forty years, ever since he decided to emulate Gladstone. He trained himself for statesmanship by exerting leadership in the campus microcosm, by constant study of the actualities of politics, by assuming the role of literary politician, by acting as "Prime Minister" of the Princeton faculty, by adapting his political beliefs to the exigencies of the moment, and—above all—by learning how to sway men to his purposes from the rostrum. Like the Calvinist he was, he believed in predestination, but also—and this too was in the Calvinist pattern—he gave destiny a helping hand.

The day after Wilson's talk to the seniors Tarkington saw him start out on a walk. He was well dressed in a gray sack suit and a black fedora hat. "His bearing," said Tarkington, "seemed to carry out what he had said the night before; he seemed happy and confident, just walking where his feet would take him."[50]

Epilogue

IT PROVED difficult to choose a successor to Woodrow Wilson at Princeton. The bitter division within the Board of Trustees that had developed at the time of the Graduate College controversy did not disappear with Wilson's departure. M. Taylor Pyne was resolved that the next President should be submissive to the will of the Trustees, whereas Wilson's friends feared that this would mean dictation by Pyne. An ad hoc Committee on the Selection of a President considered over fifty names, including that of Theodore Roosevelt, without reaching agreement. Three times it reported that it was unable to find a candidate who could command strong support among the Trustees and faculty. At a meeting in January 1912 a majority of the Trustees decided that the interregnum had lasted long enough. They voted to discharge the selection committee and at once elected John G. Hibben as President of Princeton by a vote of seventeen to nine, with four trustees not present.[1]

Hibben's election was ostensibly a victory for Wilson's foes. As a result, two of his friends resigned from the Board of Trustees and withdrew all financial support from Princeton; a few faculty members also found positions elsewhere. When Hibben was inaugurated on May 11, 1912, Wilson, although invited, did not attend. The *New York Times* reported the ceremony as a triumph of conservatism. President Taft and Chief Justice White spoke against radicalism in politics; Hibben promised to follow a conservative course in education. As for Wilson, it was almost as though he had never existed: "Not once was the name of Woodrow Wilson so much as mentioned. From the speeches and ceremonies a stranger could not have guessed that such a person ever ruled the destinies of that campus. Once when Dr. Hibben paid his tribute to his 'great predecessor, that great teacher, and man of learning, that wonderful man,' a stir of deep interest ran through the listening assemblage that subsided with faint sounds of stifled laughter, when he went on to make clear that he was speaking of Dr. McCosh." It remained for President A. Lawrence Lowell of Harvard to speak the one word in praise of Wilson's accomplishments, when he said that every college and university in the country owed Princeton a debt for the institution of the preceptorial system.[2]

The official policy of silence continued for a generation. In 1939, when I first went to Princeton to gather materials for this book, a dormitory had been erected in memory of M. Taylor Pyne and a hall of mathematics in memory of Henry B. Fine; there were twenty John Grier Hibben memorial scholarships; and a massive bronze statue of Dean West had been placed in the central court of the Graduate College. The only sign of Wilson's affiliation, however, was his portrait in the faculty room in Nassau Hall, along with those of earlier presidents of the university. The division of sentiment among older men on the faculty and the Board of Trustees still persisted, although many preferred to forget the whole thing.[3]

The deliberate avoidance of any memorial to Wilson was a reflection of the fact that some trustees continued to cherish antipathy toward him. Wilson for his part continued bitter about his defeat at Princeton. When he asked members of his class of seventy-nine to dinner at the White House in 1914, he did not send invitations to a trustee and a faculty member who had opposed him. In 1923, shortly before he died, he said to Raymond Fosdick, "Princeton was bought once with Ivory Soap money, and I suppose it is for sale again." Wilson "rescued" Winthrop Daniels, one of his former supporters on the faculty, by appointing him to the Interstate Commerce Commission. He hoped to do something similar for Henry B. Fine: he first promoted Fine for the presidency of Johns Hopkins and later offered him the ambassadorship to Germany. Mrs. Wilson wrote the Dean's sister, Miss May Fine, urging her to use her influence to persuade him to accept. She and Mr. Wilson had always felt, she remarked, that they could not bear to have Woodrow get out of the Princeton situation so splendidly while Harry remained at the university under Hibben.[4]

Fine refused Wilson's offer, even though Cleveland Dodge offered to put up $25,000 a year to make it financially possible. It was not merely that he had no desire for such eminence but also that he did not wish to interrupt his professional career. Furthermore, he was not in the least unhappy under the new administration. According to Fine's later testimony, Hibben proved himself a "singularly happy choice" as Wilson's successor. His first act after appointment was to seek out the leaders of the pro-Wilson faction and beg them to join him in furthering the work Wilson had begun. At the first faculty meeting after his inauguration he announced that he was giving up the President's former prerogative of appointing committees and turning the power of appointment over to the faculty itself. Thus, the faculty became for the first time a truly democratic body. Under Hibben no former Wilsonian had cause to complain that he was in any way discriminated against. When in 1922 the charge was made in the *New York Evening Post* that Hibben had used his position as president to the detriment of Wilson's former supporters on the faculty, a number of the latter wrote him an open letter utterly repudiating the charge and stating their absolute faith in his innate fairness, as shown in all his relations with them and with their colleagues.[5]

Had Hibben not acted as he did, there might have been an exodus from Princeton of many of its best men. Instead, many of the strongest men that Wilson had brought to Princeton remained, and a high proportion of them ascended to positions of power. Thus, the damage to the university caused by the bitter squabbles of Wilson's last years there was far less than might have been expected. None of the gains made during his administration were lost.

In fact, much of what Wilson had initiated reached full fruition only after he left. The kinks in the preceptorial system were ironed out, such as the overloading of the preceptors and their arbitrary shortness of tenure. Under the Hibben administration the title "preceptor" as an academic rank was gradually abandoned; instead, faculty members of all ranks gave tutorial instruction, from full professors down to the most recently appointed instructor. It was manifestly more fair and more efficient to have the burden so shared. The preceptorial method of instruction still flourishes at Princeton. It has been refined and elaborated over the years so that it is more effective today than ever in achieving Wilson's purpose of introducing undergraduates to the companionship of learning.[6]

The undergraduate curriculum went through further changes during the Hibben administration. In 1925 the so-called "four-course plan" was introduced, whereby juniors and seniors did independent work in lieu of a fifth course. Today Princeton students engage in a variety of independent studies and also take general examinations in their junior and senior years, so that they gain both a synoptic view of their field and a feeling for detailed research. These changes represent a further evolution of the essential philosophy laid down in the curricular report of the committee that Wilson headed in 1903.[7]

On October 22, 1913, the Princeton Graduate College was formally opened with ceremonies planned by Dean West. Again William Howard Taft was the principal speaker, and again Wilson declined an invitation to attend. Taft gave an address praising Grover Cleveland, and West explained his belief that graduate students should become civilized, personable human beings as well as scholars. It was a great triumph. Yet in the same year the Dean suffered a significant defeat. He had hoped to regain the autonomous status he had held during the Patton regime, but instead the Trustees wrote new bylaws making the Graduate School in every aspect of its administration subject to the President of the University and the standing committees of the Board of Trustees and the faculty, so that in theory and practice it became a constituent part of the University. Thus, one of the original causes of the difficulties between West and Wilson was erased.[8]

The issue of the site of the Graduate College was settled once and for all when the splendid Gothic complex of buildings was constructed on the golf links. Graduate students sometimes complained of being far from the main campus, but the distance has since been reduced by a road cut across a former portion of the links, so that the "graduate palace," as it is called, is little over half a mile from libraries and laboratories. The Princeton graduate students still have almost nothing to do with undergraduates, but even in universities where the contacts are closer, this aloofness holds true. Wilson's hope that undergraduates and graduate students would fraternize to their mutual benefit, as they had done at Virginia and Johns Hopkins in his youth, was not likely to be realized no matter what the living arrangements.[9]

The system of upper-class clubs has continued, although about once in every college generation there has been some sort of protest or effort to reform a system that artificially sorts men into a social hierarchy. In 1903, during Wilson's first year as President of the University, the *Princeton Alumni Weekly* deplored the annual frenzy of club elections, spreading over the campus like a blight, destroying sleep and friendships; but the editor could see no help for it. In 1964 the author of a column in the *Alumni Weekly* wrote in similar terms: the election struggle was "that thing nobody really likes, but which everybody nevertheless must accept and carry out again." In 1967, sixty years after Wilson presented the Quad Plan to the Princeton Trustees, a subcommittee of the faculty maintained that the upper-class clubs isolated the students' social life from their intellectual life, contrary to the true purposes of the University. As a cure, the subcommittee suggested the establishment of a "quadrangle" or "college" residential system.[10]

Until recently the university administration dealt gingerly with the club situation. In 1955, however, President Dodds and the Board of Trustees assured upperclassmen not joining clubs that separate facilities would be provided for them, "offering meals, service, and amenities comparable with those enjoyed at Prospect Street" but at moderate rates. Wilcox Hall was built, offering not only these advantages but a library of ten thousand volumes. Connected with it are dormitories housing some six hundred men from the three upper classes, the whole composing a "quadrangle." The new center is run by the Woodrow Wilson Society, an organization of undergraduates. Thus has been created something very like the solution Wilson scorned in 1908—a "quad" for the "non-clubable." Under this new arrangement Princeton appears to be moving toward the situation of the 1890's when fewer men joined upper-class clubs and there was little stigma to staying out. Already weaker clubs are closing down, since some undergraduates prefer the Woodrow Wilson Society and Wilcox Hall.[11]

In 1930 Harvard started dividing its undergraduate body into "houses," much like Wilson's projected "quads," and Yale soon followed with the institution of "colleges." Both universities were enabled to do so by magnificent gifts from Edward A. Harkness, a Yale graduate. In each case the authorities were careful to secure the full support of their faculties before acting and to avoid any such head-on clash with undergraduate clubs as had taken place at Princeton in 1907. The benefits wrought by the Harvard houses and Yale colleges were much as Wilson had predicted: they reduced social distinctions and promoted more spontaneous intellectual activity and closer contact between teacher and student. There are those who regret that Princeton has not followed Wilson's lead and made a similar division of the undergraduates. It may be argued, however, that the need at Harvard and Yale was greater than at Princeton, where because the undergraduates are fewer and more homogeneous, there is a greater corporate sense among them, and where the preceptorial system already encourages easy, friendly contact with the faculty.[12]

From the time he arrived at Princeton in 1890, Wilson hoped to see the establishment of a school of jurisprudence to train men in the philosophy of law and so fit them for service to society. It was one of the disappointments of his presidency that this personal goal was never realized. In 1947, however, the Trustees named an existing School of Public and International Affairs after Wilson, secured it an endowment of $2,000,000, and provided it with suitable housing. In 1961 the Woodrow Wilson School received an anonymous gift of $35,000,000. With this lavish support the university announced that it hoped to do as much to improve training for government service as Johns Hopkins had done for graduate instruction and as Teachers College, Columbia, had done to raise the level of elementary and secondary education. There could be no more fitting memorial to the man who had hoped to dedicate Princeton to the nation's service.[13]

Notes · Index

ABBREVIATIONS USED IN NOTES

Baker, *WW*	Ray Stannard Baker, *Woodrow Wilson: Life and Letters;* Vol. I, *Youth, 1856-1890* (New York, 1927); Vol. II, *Princeton, 1890-1910* (New York, 1931); Vol. III, *Governor, 1910-1913* (New York, 1931).
Baker Papers, LC	Ray Stannard Baker Papers, Library of Congress.
EAW	Ellen Axon Wilson.
Public Papers	*The Public Papers of Woodrow Wilson,* ed. Ray Stannard Baker and William E. Dodds, Vols. I and II, *College and State* (New York, 1925).
PUL	Princeton University Library.
PWW	*The Papers of Woodrow Wilson,* ed. Arthur S. Link, Vol. I (Princeton, N.J., 1966).
WW	Woodrow Wilson.
WW Papers, LC	Woodrow Wilson Papers, Library of Congress.

Notes

CHAPTER I. Family Background and Youth, 1856-1875

1. WW, "Robert E. Lee: An Interpretation," in William Allen White, *Woodrow Wilson: The Man, His Times, and His Task* (Boston, 1924), p. 55. The principal source for this chapter is Ray Stannard Baker, *Woodrow Wilson: Life and Letters* (New York, 1927), I, i-iii, hereafter referred to as Baker, WW, I.

2. In 1907 Wilson wrote of Rev. James Woodrow's death: "It takes away . . . one of the noblest men I have ever known. A man of many small failings, I am glad, for my own comfort, to remember, but a man made to love in the quiet Scottish fashion . . . and to be loved, and gifted to an extraordinary degree with the powers that make a great thinker and a great man of science. He followed duty to obscure places and kept himself in mere faithfulness from the eye of fame; but his friends and intimates knew him for a man who might have placed his name among the great names of our men of learning. It pleases me to think of the gracious and helpful influences he has brought into the life of a nephew who never told him how much he owed to him." WW to John G. Hibben, Jan. 26, 1907, WW Papers, LC.

3. Mrs. Isabella Jordan to Ray Stannard Baker, n.d., Baker Papers, LC.

4. E. S. Craighill Handy is of the opinion that Wilson's bent toward politics originated in observing his father's activities in the general assembly of the Southern Presbyterians: "His father's outstanding organizational role as permanent secretary of the Southern Presbyterians was an important factor in Woodrow Wilson's education by reason of the fact the boy Tommy attended the meetings and aided in recording the proceedings. Undoubtedly this experience did much to implant in him a desire to emulate his father as a leader and organizer." Handy to Bragdon, May 27, 1960.

5. J. H. McNeilly, "The Rev. Joseph R. Wilson, D.D.," *The Southern Presbyterian*, 47:4 (May 18, 1899); J. R. Wilson to WW, March 27, 1877. This and all ensuing letters to WW from his parents are in WW Papers, LC.

6. Interview with George M. Harper, July 1, 1939. This portrayal of Dr. Wilson draws on the following sources: George C. Osborn, "The Influence of Joseph Ruggles Wilson on His Son," *North Carolina Historical Review*, 32:2 (October 1955); Stockton Axon, "Woodrow Wilson as Man

of Letters," *Rice Institute Pamphlets*, 22:216 (October 1935); J. H. McNeilly, "The Rev. Joseph R. Wilson, D.D.," p. 4; White, *Woodrow Wilson*, pp. 12-18 and *passim;* Arthur Walworth, *Woodrow Wilson: American Prophet* (New York, 1958), ch. i; and many letters from Joseph Wilson to his son in the WW Papers, LC. There are several photographs of Dr. Wilson in the Thackwell Collection in the Princeton University Library.

7. Baker, *WW*, I, 38.

8. *Ibid.*, p. 5.

9. WW to Edith Gittings Reid, Feb. 3, 1902, Baker Papers, LC; Josephus Daniels to Bragdon, Feb. 28, 1945. My hypothesis that Wilson's father gave him confidence is contrary to the view presented by Alexander L. and Juliette George in *Woodrow Wilson and Colonel House: A Personality Study* (New York, 1956). They suggest that Wilson was intimidated by his father, was envious of and secretly hostile toward him, but that he hid these feelings even from himself by lifelong protestations of admiration and affection. I am in essential agreement with them on one point: that Wilson's compulsive desire for political power was a "compensatory value, a means of restoring the self-esteem damaged in youth" (p. 320).

The attempt to plumb Wilson's subconscious reaches extraordinary lengths in *Thomas Woodrow Wilson: A Psychological Study*, by Sigmund Freud and William C. Bullitt (Boston, 1966). They conjecture that Wilson gave in wholly to his father's domination and that in repressing the natural masculine father-hostility he transferred it to any dominant characters that crossed his path, such as Andrew F. West, Henry Cabot Lodge, and Raymond Poincaré.

10. Wilson's mother was christened Janet Woodrow but was later known as Jessie or Jeanie. This sketch of her character is drawn from Baker, *WW*, I, 32-35; White, *Woodrow Wilson*, pp. 53, 58-61; and the many letters to her son in the WW Papers, LC.

11. WW to Ellen Axson Wilson, April 19, 1888, in Eleanor Wilson McAdoo, ed., *The Priceless Gift* (New York, 1962) pp. 163-164; David Bryant, in White, *Woodrow Wilson*, p. 59.

12. WW, "The Young People and the Church," Oct. 13, 1904, *Public Papers*, I, 474-475.

13. Raymond B. Fosdick, "Personal Recollections of Woodrow Wilson," in Earl Latham, ed., *The Philosophy and Politics of Woodrow Wilson* (Chicago, 1958), p. 30; notebook of 1874-1875, labeled "T. W. Wilson, Private," PUL.

14. Entry dated Dec. 28, 1889, in notebook labeled "Journal, October 1887 to," WW Papers, LC; Rev. Alexander J. Kerr, ms. notes on WW, PUL; WW to Cary Grayson, n.d., in Baker, *WW*, I, 68; Eleanor Wilson McAdoo, *The Woodrow Wilsons* (New York, 1937), pp. 41-42; Winthrop Daniels, memorandum on WW, Baker Papers, LC. An authoritative discussion of Wilson's religious beliefs appears in Arthur Link, "Woodrow Wilson: Presbyterian in Government," in George L. Hunt, ed., *Calvinism and the Political Order* (Philadelphia, 1965), pp. 157-174.

15. "The Bible and Progress," May 7, 1911, *Public Papers*, II, 292-294.

16. WW, *A History of the American People* (New York, 1902), II, 60.

17. Reid, *Woodrow Wilson,* p. 19.

18. Mrs. Isabella Jordan to R. S. Baker, n.d., Baker Papers, LC.

19. Reid, *Woodrow Wilson,* p. 39; WW, "John Bright," *University of Virginia Magazine,* March 1880, in *Public Papers,* I, 56-58.

20. Janet W. Wilson to WW, May 20, 1874, WW Papers, LC; William Barnwell, in Baker, *WW,* I, 59; David Bryant to R. S. Baker, n.d., Baker, *WW,* I, 78.

21. Rev. Dr. A. M. Fraser to R. S. Baker, n.d., in Baker, *WW,* I, 74.

22. For an authoritative account of Wilson's world of fantasy, see "Wilson's Imaginary World," editorial note, PWW, pp. 20-22; for specific examples, see *ibid.,* pp. 22, 24-25, 28, 43-46, 54-56, and *passim.* A typical order was as follows: "General Orders—No. 1,000. Sergeant Thomas to Williams, Sergeant Major, Royal Lance Guards, having retired from the service on account of ill health, resulting from old age, I hereby by right of Parliament granted me on the 1st of January 1872 Promote Alexander T. J. Evans to the rank of Sergeant-Major, Royal Lance Guards. January 5, 1875. Thomas W. Wilson, Lieutenant-General, Duke of Eagleton, Commander-in-Chief Royal Lance Guard." *PWW,* p. 22.

23. The most detailed account of Theodore Roosevelt's boyhood is in Carleton Putnam, *Theodore Roosevelt* (New York, 1958).

CHAPTER II. Campus Leader, 1875-1879

1. WW, Introduction to John Rogers Williams, *The Handbook of Princeton* (New York, 1905), p. 5.

2. *Princetonian,* June 13, 1878.

3. *Nassau Literary Magazine,* 34:204 (December 1878); William B. Scott, *Some Memories of a Palaeontologist* (Princeton, 1939), pp. 35-36.

4. *Laws of the College of New Jersey* (Princeton, n.d.), leaflet in undergraduate scrapbook of Edward J. Van Lennep '78, Princeton Collection, PUL; Trustees' Minutes, June 18, 1879; Oct. 27, 1875; Dec. 22, 1875.

5. Anonymous letter in *Princetonian,* March 21, 1878; Harold Godwin, *History of the Class of '79* (Princeton, 1879).

6. Scrapbooks of Rev. Alexander J. Kerr '79, Theodore McNair '79, and Edward J. Van Lennep '78, Princeton Collection, PUL; Trustees' Minutes, June 18, 1878, and Faculty Minutes, Feb. 19 and 21, 1878.

7. *Nassau Herald* (yearbook), 1879; *Nassau Literary Magazine,* 32:348-349 (March 1876); Trustees' Minutes, June 26, 1876. Rev. A. J. Kerr '79 used to tell of a student who during the great revival at Princeton put a notice on his door, "Keep out. I am a Christian but studying for exams." E. S. Wells Kerr to Bragdon, Aug. 6, 1962.

8. *Princeton Bric-à-Brac,* 1876, p. 5; Faculty Minutes, March 31, 1876; Thomas Jefferson Wertenbaker, *Princeton, 1746-1896* (Princeton, 1946), p. 331.

9. For McCosh's career, see M. A. DeWolfe Howe, "Princeton and James McCosh," in *Classic Shades* (Boston, 1928), pp. 123-162; Frederick Rudolph, *The American College and University* (New York, 1962), esp. pp. 297-300; Wertenbaker, *Princeton, 1746-1896,* pp. 290-343; John Grier

Hibben, "James McCosh," in *Dictionary of American Biography* (New York, 1933), XI, 615-617; Lawrence R. Vesey, *The Emergence of the American University* (Chicago, 1965), pp. 22-28, 41-43, 48-52, and *passim;* William M. Sloane, ed., *The Life of James McCosh: A Record Chiefly Autobiographical* (New York, 1896). For a detailed exposition of McCosh's views regarding Darwin's *Origin of Species,* see James McCosh, *Christianity and Positivism* (New York, 1874), Appendix, Article II, pp. 346-362.

10. Nicholas Murray Butler, *Across the Busy Years* (New York, 1939), p. 90.

11. Wertenbaker, *Princeton, 1746-1896,* pp. 280-281, 317-323; Faculty Minutes, Sept. 17, Nov. 15, 17, and 29, Dec. 1, 1875; Trustees' Minutes, Dec. 22, 1875.

12. WW, address at Nott memorial celebration, Union College, Sept. 29, 1904, in *Union University Quarterly,* 1:185 (November 1904); interview with William A. Magie, Aug. 6, 1940. In the process of getting permission to quote letters from and interviews with Princeton alumni who had known Wilson, I received invaluable assistance from Dr. T. Jefferson Webb of Princeton, N.J. Dr. Webb ferreted out the names and addresses of descendants of nearly forty men.

McCosh and his wife regularly visited students who were ill. One Princeton alumnus remembered vividly the cheer the two of them shed when they called on a group of students down with mumps. McCosh was gay and full of jokes, although as he left, he said, "I must be going now, but before going I'll have a word of prayer with ye . . . We beseech Thee, Dear Lord, to forgive the sins of these Thy young servants, which they have committed in time past, for which Thou hast temporarily laid them aside." John M. T. Finney, *A Surgeon's Life* (New York, 1940), pp. 40-41.

13. The "bright young men" included Henry B. Fine (mathematics), Theodore W. Hunt (English), William F. Magie (physics), Alexander T. Ormond (philosophy), William B. Scott (paleontology), William M. Sloane (history), and Andrew F. West (classics).

14. In a study of Wilson's career as President of Princeton, Hardin Craig maintains that he was influenced by the epistemology of McCosh. He admits, however, that Wilson had little interest in methodology and formal logic, so that he may have been unconscious of the bearing of McCosh's philosophy on his own thought. That Wilson was aware of no special intellectual debt to McCosh, outside of the field of education, is suggested by the fact that although he often spoke and wrote of him, he never, so far as I am aware, mentioned his philosophical views. See Hardin Craig, *Woodrow Wilson at Princeton* (Norman, Oklahoma, 1960), pp. 42-61.

15. Interview with Robert H. McCarter, July 15, 1940.

16. William Delpuech to Bragdon, Jan. 21, 1940; Harold Godwin, *History of the Class of '79,* p. 5; David C. Reid to Bragdon, Jan. 21, 1942; Edwin Anderson Alderman, *Woodrow Wilson,* memorial address delivered before a joint session of Congress, Dec. 15, 1924 (Washington, 1924), p. 4.

17. WW, "My Journal," June 3, 1876, *PWW*, p. 132. The journal covers pp. 132-229 in *PWW*, with other material interspersed.

18. WW, "My Journal," June 11, 1876, *PWW*, p. 138; July 3, 1876, *PWW*, p. 148; Aug. 5, 1876, *PWW*, p. 167; Oct. 27, 1876, *PWW*, p. 217.

19. WW, "My Journal," July 4, 1876, *PWW*, pp. 148-149; Nov. 6, 1876, *PWW*, p. 221; Nov. 8, 1876, *PWW*, p. 222; Nov. 10, 1876, *PWW*, p. 223.

20. WW, "My Journal," Sept. 5, 1876, *PWW*, p. 189.

21. Janet W. Wilson to WW, Nov. 15, 1876, WW Papers, LC.

22. Janet W. Wilson to WW, Jan. 20, 1879.

23. J. R. Wilson to WW, Jan. 25, 1878, WW Papers, LC.

24. J. R. Wilson to WW, March 27, 1877; March 20, 1879; Jan. 10, 1878.

25. J. R. Wilson to WW, July 26, 1877.

26. WW to J. R. Wilson, May 23, 1877, *PWW*, 265-266.

27. Baker, *WW*, I, 81-82; D. C. Reid to Bragdon; Janet W. Wilson to WW, Dec. 2 and 10, 1878; interview with Rev. Alexander J. Kerr, June 21, 1940 ($30 for books). Reid's memories of Wilson were based principally on acquaintance as a freshman, since he dropped out of college after that for a period and then graduated with a later class. Kerr ran a book agency.

28. Philippus W. Miller to Bragdon, Nov. 15, 1939; Charles C. Black to Bragdon, Nov. 14, 1941; Kerr interview; scrapbook of A. J. Kerr, Princeton Collection, PUL.

29. Robert Bridges, "Woodrow Wilson," *Fifty Years of the Class of 'Seventy-nine* (Princeton, 1931), pp. 2-4; WW, typewritten ms. of speech at University Club, Chicago, March 12, 1908, R. S. Baker Papers, PUL.

30. WW to Francis Champion Garmany, April 22, 1897, scrapbook of F. C. Garmany, Princeton Collection, PUL; WW to Charles Talcott, July 7, 1879, in Baker, *WW*, I, 110.

31. The account of Whig Hall and Wilson's part in it is based, except where noted, on Jacob N. Beam, *The American Whig Society of Princeton University* (Princeton, 1933), pp. 177-197, supplemented by examination of the following records of the society in the Princeton archives: "Record Book," 1875-1878, 1878-1884; "Constitution and By-Laws," 1876-1883; "The Book of the Library, A.W.S.," Nov. 16, 1877—Dec. 12, 1878; *Annual Histories of Whig Hall, 1870-1909* (Princeton, 1909); "Roll Book," 1874-1894.

32. Henry W. Frost to Bragdon, Jan. 21, 1942; Charles W. Scribner to Bragdon, Jan. 19, 1942; Henry S. Scribner to Bragdon, Feb. 3, 1942; Edward E. Worl to Bragdon, Jan. 20, 1942; A. J. Kerr and McCarter interviews.

33. Edward E. Worl to Bragdon, Jan. 20, 1942.

34. George Santayana, *Persons and Places* (New York, 1841), p. 58; WW, *Princetonian*, Feb. 27, 1879.

35. Baker, *WW*, I, 87-88.

36. Constitution of the Liberal Debating Club, ms. in Wilson's handwriting, Johns Hopkins University Library; *Princetonian*, Feb. 6, 1879.

The Constitution of the Liberal Debating Society, with amendments, is in *PWW*, pp. 245-249.

37. "Who's Who in '79," *Fifty Years of '79* (Princeton, 1931), pp. 237-304 *passim*, summaries of careers of W. T. Elsing, M. G. Emery, H. Godwin, R. H. McCarter, E. W. Sheldon, C. A. Talcott, J. E. Webster, and H. Woods; C. A. Talcott to WW, June 1, 1879, WW Papers, LC. Letters to Wilson from Godwin, McCarter, Sheldon, Talcott, and Woods are in the WW Papers, LC. In addition to Talcott, McCarter and Sheldon wrote Wilson that they expected him to achieve prominence in politics. McCarter to WW, Aug. 5, 1879; Sheldon to WW, March 5, 1881.

38. McCarter interview; WW, "My Journal," June 3, 1877, *PWW*, 272. The minutes of the Liberal Debating Club for over forty meetings between March 31, 1877, and April 2, 1879, are reprinted in *PWW*. At the time of graduation each member of the Liberal Debating Society received a copy of one of Shakespeare's plays signed by all the members. Wilson's copy of *Hamlet* is among his papers in the Library of Congress.

39. A spirited account of the balloting for editors from '79 is found in a letter from Robert Bridges to his father, John Bridges, February 15, 1878; Dickinson College Library; a penciled copy of the balloting is in the scrapbook of T. M. McNair, president of the class, Princeton Collection, PUL.

40. McCarter interview. Two other editors, William F. Magie and G. S. John, had similar recollections. The method used to decide which portions of the *Princetonian* came from Wilson's pen was, briefly, as follows. I started with the assumption that the Managing Editor would write lead editorials, especially for his first number (May 2, 1878) and the two numbers prepared for the press at the end of the academic year after most students had gone home (June 25, 1878) and at the start of the next year before they arrived (Sept. 26, 1878). From a reading of these editorials and then of all the editorials during Wilson's tenure of office, it soon became obvious that Wilson wrote the entire editorial page except during the latter months of his tenure of office—after mid-February 1879—when Henry B. Fine, his successor as Managing Editor, also made contributions. Wilson's emphasis differed from that of his predecessor, C. J. Williams, and of his successor. Wilson had also developed a characteristic style—somewhat overelaborate, sometimes caustic, with a lavish use of commas and something of the cadence of speech. Familiarity with this style led me to other attributions, which cannot be documented here, but of which I am confident.

41. *Princetonian*, May 2, 1878; Dec. 5, 1878; Sept. 26, 1878.

42. *Princetonian*, Nov. 7, 1878.

43. *Princetonian*, May 2, 1878; June 25, 1878; March 27, 1879; Jan. 30, 1879.

44. *Princetonian*, May 2, 1878; Dec. 5, 1878; March 27, 1879.

45. *Princetonian*, May 2, 1878; May 16, 1878; Oct. 10, 1878; Oct. 24, 1878.

46. *Princetonian*, Sept. 26, 1878.

47. WW, "My Journal," Sept. 28, 1878, *PWW*, pp. 400-401; *Princetonian*, Oct. 24, 1878. A letter to Wilson from his mother indicates that he had consulted his parents about the presidency of the Baseball Club.

She advised him to resign in order to pursue studies connected with his future interests. Janet W. Wilson to WW, Nov. 20, 1878.

48. Parke H. Davis, "What Woodrow Wilson Did for American Football," *St. Nicholas Magazine*, 20:113 (November 1912).

49. The rules before and after the shift to rugby are found in the *Nassau Literary Magazine*, 31:205 (December 1875), and the *Princetonian*, Nov. 16, 1876.

50. Parke H. Davis to W. W. Watt, June 28, 1932, furnished me by Watt.

51. McCarter interview.

52. *Princetonian*, Oct. 24, 1878; Nov. 7, 1878.

53. *Princetonian*, Nov. 7, 1878; Oct. 10, 1878; April 10, 1879.

54. *Princetonian*, Dec. 5, 1878. For an account of the 1878 season, see *Athletics in Princeton: A History*, ed. Frank Presbrey and James Hugh Moffet (New York, 1901), pp. 287-292.

55. *Savannah News*, July 29, 1902.

56. McCarter and Magie interviews; Fletcher Durell to Bragdon, Dec. 5, 1940.

57. There was considerable overlap in the membership of these three groups; only two of the nine members of the Liberal Debating Club, for instance were not members of the Witherspoon Gang.

58. A. J. Kerr interview; Hiram Woods to R. S. Baker, Dec. 9, 1925, Baker Papers, LC; William R. Wilder, "Presentation Oration," *Nassau Herald*, 1879, pp. 30-31.

59. Magie interview; *Princetonian*, Feb. 13 and 27, 1879.

60. Ruth Cranston, *The Story of Woodrow Wilson* (New York, 1945), p. 24.

61. White, *Woodrow Wilson*, pp. 74-75; Baker, *WW*, I, 106.

62. Beam, *The American Whig Society*, p. 192.

63. J. R. Wilson to WW, March 20 and April 17, 1879; WW, "My Journal," June 19, 1876, *PWW*, p. 143; WW, "Cabinet Government in the United States," *Public Papers*, I, 20; Talcott to WW, May 21, 1879, *PWW*, p. 484.

64. WW to Charles Talcott, July 7, 1879, in Baker, *WW*, I, 110.

65. *Program of Sexennial Reunion, Class of 1879*, June 15, 1885, PUL; McCarter Interview; Edward J. Van Lennep '78 to Bragdon, Nov. 28, 1941; Henry W. Frost '80 to Bragdon. The class of 1909 had seven Princeton trustees, but the number includes alumni trustees, who are elected for only five years, in addition to charter trustees, who hold office indefinitely. All of the '79 members of the Board of Trustees were charter trustees.

CHAPTER III. The Study of Politics

1. WW, "The Interpreter of English Liberty," *Mere Literature and Other Essays* (Boston and New York, 1900), p. 113.

2. J. R. Wilson to WW, March 27 and Dec. 22, 1877, Jan. 23 and 25, 1878, WW Papers, LC; Registrar's Records, Princeton University (consulted with permission of Mrs. Woodrow Wilson).

3. Baker, *WW*, I, 85; Registrar's Records.

4. To arrive at a fair judgment of Wilson's academic performance, it was not enough merely to examine the grades kept in the registrar's office. Sometimes marking was ridiculously high: grades of 97, 98, and 99 were commonplace, and in Dr. McCosh's course in psychology Wilson once stood second with a mark of 99.8. Instructors varied so greatly in their scales of grading that a 75 in one course might in fact be better than a 90 in another. I therefore went to the original records that gave the grades of all students, found out how many stood above and below Wilson in each course, and from this information derived a percentile rank, which is more revealing than the grade since it shows his relative standing. There was naturally some oscillation of Wilson's rank, even in a particular subject, but averaging together the percentiles in all courses in different fields of study, I obtained the following academic record for his four years at the College of New Jersey:

Field of Study	*Average Percentile Rank*
History	91
Philosophy (including courses in logic, psychology, science and religion, ethics)	84
Latin	76
Greek	75
Mathematics	70
Political science (including political geography, political science, political economy)	67
English (including rhetoric, elocution, English literature)	61
Bible (freshman year only)	46
French (sophomore year only)	37
Physical sciences (including anatomy, chemistry, physics, astronomy)	37

His respectable standing in Greek, Latin, and mathematics suggests that Wilson was fairly well prepared in these required subjects before going to Princeton, and the low standing in science is in accord with his indifference and even antipathy toward science and the scientific method. The low average in political science may seem surprising, given Wilson's special interests, but the average was pulled down by a low rank (48th percentile) in political economy. That this marked a distaste for the subject is suggested by the fact that when he took logic with the same teacher, Dr. Atwater, he once stood third in the class with a percentile rank of 98. Later at Johns Hopkins, Wilson found economics distasteful. The relatively low grade in English courses may be explained by the fact that he disliked speaking or writing on set subjects alien to his interests, as shown when he paid fines rather than submit essays in the American Whig Society. The low grade in Bible corroborates other evidence that, although he was a professing Christian, Wilson's interests were secular rather than theological. The poor record in French may mean little, because the former Polish revolutionary who taught the course was irascible and incompetent and Wilson deliberately defied him in class. And yet Wilson's writings reveal an animus toward French politics and culture that may have reflected the views of his idol Edmund Burke.

Some slight injustice may be done Wilson by presenting his record in this way. For instance, he was 38th of 105 men *ranked* at graduation, but 122 men received diplomas, and the 17 unranked men may have been below him. Furthermore, 47 members of the class had gone by the wayside: three had died, some had withdrawn because of poverty or ill health or to transfer to other institutions, but an undeterminable number had been academic casualties, who might fairly be ranked below Wilson. At best, though, his rank is somewhere near the bottom of the fourth quartile.

5. WW, "My Journal," June 15 and Nov. 18, 1876, *PWW*, pp. 141, 229.
6. WW, "The Ideal Statesman," Jan. 30, 1877, *PWW*, pp. 241-244.
7. WW to Ellen Axson, April 22, 1884, in Baker, *WW*, I, 87.
8. WW, *"My Reading* (Principal Works)," longhand list in notebook, labeled "Private," WW Papers, LC; McMillan Lewis, *Woodrow Wilson of Princeton* (Narberth, Pa., 1952), p. 38. Many of Wilson's annotations are reprinted in *PWW*; see, e.g., those on John Richard Green's *A History of the English People* on pp. 387-393. The catalog of books entitled *"My Reading* (Principal Works)" is as follows:

1876

Addison's Works, Vol. III	
Woodfall's Junius, Vol. I	
Lecturers on Shakspere, Vol. II	Hudson
Milton's Political Works, Vol. I	Macson
Shakspere's Works, Vol. I	White
Macaulay's Essays, Vol. II	
Jeffrey—Modern British Essayists	
Boswell's Johnson, Vol. I	
Life of Goldsmith, Vol. I	Foster
Addison's Works, Vol. II	
Dante's Inferno	
Shakspere's Works, Vol. XI	White

1877

Works of Dan'l Webster, Vol. I	
Life of Dan'l Webster	Curtis
Wilkes, Sheridan, and Fox	Rae
Shakspere's Works, Vol. VI	White
Words, Their Use and Abuse	Mathews
Hours with Men and Books	Mathews
Ticknor's Life and Letters, Vol. I	
Success and Its Conditions	Whipple
French Revolution, Vol. I	Carlyle
French Revolution, Vol. II	Carlyle
Manual of the Constitution	Farrar
Edmund Burke, An Historical Study	Morley
Short Studies on Great Subjects	Froude

1878

Variorum Shakspere—Hamlet	Furness
Practical Political Economy	Price
Richard Cobden	McGilchrist
Cobden and Political Opinion	Rogers
History of the Constitution of the U.S., Vol. I	Curtis
History of the Constitution of the U.S., Vol. II	Curtis
Comparative Politics	Freeman
Critical Miscellanies (First Series)	Morley
Huskisson's Speeches, Vols. I and II	
Recollections and Suggestions	Earl Russell
Greville's Memoirs, Geo. IV and Wm. IV, Vol. I	
Brougham's Works, Vol. III	
History of the English People, Vols, I and II	Green
Webster's Works, Vol. III	
Reminiscences of Dan'l Webster	Harvey
The Federal Government	Gillet
Life and Speeches of Henry Clay	
Life of Dan'l Webster, Vol. II	Curtis
The Great Conversers	Mathews
The English Constitution	Bagehot
Life of Alex Hamilton, Vol. I	Morse

1879

Critical Miscellanies (Second Series)	Morley
Sartor Resarts	Carlyle
Oratory and Orators	Mathews
Beauties of Ruskin	
Growth of the English Constitution	Freeman
Brief Biographies of English Statesmen	Higginson
History of the Constitution of the U.S., Vol. III	Curtis
Samuel Johnson	Stephen, Leslie
Speeches of John Bright, Vol. III	
Lieber's Political Ethics, Vol. I	
Lieber's Civil Liberty and Self-Government	
History of English Literature, Vol. I	Taine

This list is of course incomplete. For instance, Wilson's diary shows that he had read Macaulay's *History of England* in 1876, and the text of his essay "Cabinet Government" shows that he had read Theodore Dwight Woolsey's *Political Science*.

9. *Princetonian,* Feb. 27, 1879.

10. "Class Biographies," *The Class of 1879: Princeton College, Quin-decennial Record, 1879-1894* (New York, 1894), p. 118. Wilson's very first published writings appear to have been the following seven little homilies in the *North Carolina Presbyterian,* of which his father was briefly editor in 1876-1877: "Work-day Religion," Aug. 6, 1876; "Christ's Army," Aug. 17; "The Bible," Aug. 30; "A Christian Statesman," Sept. 1; "One Duty of a Son to His Parents," Oct. 8; "The Positive in Religion," Oct. 8; and "Christian Progress," Dec. 20. All are marked by straight-forward piety: Christianity is a matter of day-to-day effort; overcome

evil desires; read the Bible; statesmen should follow Christian principles, not expediency; sons should respect their parents; and so forth. All but one are signed by the pseudonym "Twiwood." The author is indebted to T. H. Spence, Executive Director of the Historical Foundation of the Presbyterian and Reformed Churches, Montreat, North Carolina, for furnishing him copies of them. All are reprinted in *PWW*.

11. WW to Ellen Axson, Oct. 30, 1883, in Baker, *WW*, i, 104.

12. *Princetonian*, Feb. 27, 1879; Oct. 10 and Sept. 27, 1878.

13. A set of notes on Atwater's course are in "Lecture Notes Taken in Princeton by the Edison Electric Pen," compiled by William R. Barricklo, Princeton Collection, PUL.

14. *Princetonian*, Feb. 7, 1878.

15. *Princetonian*, May 2, 1878.

16. *Princetonian*, May 2, 1878.

17. *Princetonian*, April 26, 1877.

18. WW, "Prince Bismarck" and "William Earl Chatham," *Public Papers*, I, 1-18. The essay on Chatham was awarded a prize of twenty dollars.

19. WW, "Cabinet Government in the United States," *International Review*, 7:146-163 (August 1879), reprinted in *Public Papers*, I, 19-42.

20. WW, longhand draft of letter to Sloane, n.d. (answered Dec. 9, 1883); Janet W. Wilson to WW, Nov. 20, 1878; WW Papers, LC; J. R. Wilson to WW, Feb. 25 and April 10, 1879.

21. Theodore Dwight Woolsey, *Political Science* (New York, 1877), I, 299-303.

22. WW to A. B. Hart, June 3, 1889, Baker Papers, LC. In his speech "The Ideal Statesman" Wilson stated that Daniel Webster "may be said to have been the greatest statesman this country has produced," *PWW*, 242.

23. Walter Bagehot, *The English Constitution*, in Mrs. Russell Barrington, ed., *The Life and Works of Walter Bagehot* (London, 1915), V, 116-366.

24. *Ibid.*, pp. 318, 205, 166, 178; *Public Papers*, I, 28, 40-41, 35-36.

25. Wilson's admiration for Bagehot persisted. William Starr Myers, who knew Wilson first when a graduate student at Johns Hopkins and who served under him as a member of the Princeton faculty, wrote: "Although I heard Wilson speak literally hundreds of times on all sorts of occasions, he seldom, except in political 'stump' speaking, failed to refer to or quote Bagehot, that 'acute observer,' as he called him." W. S. Myers, "Wilson in My Diary," in Myers, ed., *Woodrow Wilson: Some Princeton Memories* (Princeton, 1946), p. 36.

26. See Arthur S. Link, *Wilson: Road to the White House* (Princeton, 1947), pp. 17-19, including footnotes, and the following articles in *The Nation:* "The Way Congress Does Business," 16:145-146 (Feb. 27, 1873); "Political Responsibility," 16:176 (March 13, 1873); "Shall the Cabinet Have Seats in Congress?" 16:233-234 (April 3, 1873); "The Causes of Congressional Failure," 26:414 (Jund 27, 1878); "Cabinet Officers in Congress," 28:243-244 (April 10, 1879).

27. An unpublished article by Wilson entitled "Some Thoughts on the Present State of Public Affairs" makes explicit Wilson's desire to change

the composition of Congress so that it would include young men who had trained themselves for leadership by acquiring skill in debate. Long-hand ms., signed "Junius," n.d., WW Papers, LC.

28. WW, "Self-Government in France," *PWW*, pp. 515-538; minutes of the Liberal Debating Society, April 5, 1877, *PWW*, p. 256.

CHAPTER IV. The Study of Law, 1879-1881

1. WW to Ellen Axson, Oct. 30, 1883, in Baker, *WW*, I, 109.

2. Baker, *WW*, I, 104. One of these cards is in the Baker Papers, LC.

3. *Catalogue of the Officers and Students of the University of Virginia: Fifty-fifth Session, 1878-1879* (Richmond, 1879), p. 25. For descriptions of student life at Virginia at this time, see Philip A. Bruce, *History of the University of Virginia* (New York, 1920), IV and *A Sketch of the University of Virginia* (Richmond, 1885); Hugh Young, *A Surgeon's Autobiography* (New York, 1940), pp. 40-47; Paul B. Barringer, James M. Garnett, Powell Page, eds., *University of Virginia*, 2 vols. (New York, 1904).

4. *Virginia University Magazine*, December 1880, p. 129; interview with R. Heath Dabney, March 22, 1941 (honor system).

5. "We Study Too Much," *Virginia University Magazine*, October 1880, pp. 5-9. A copy of the magazine in the Alderman Library, University of Virginia, has a penciled inscription attributing this article to Wilson's friend R. H. Dabney.

6. *Virginia University Magazine*, January 1881, p. 233.

7. *Sketch of the University of Virginia*, p. 23.

8. Dabney interview; WW, address at University Club, Chicago, March 12, 1908, typewritten ms., R. S. Baker Papers, PUL.

9. John Bassett Moore to Bragdon, July 8, 1941.

10. *Catalogue, 1878-1879*, p. 6; Samuel B. Woods to Bragdon, Jan. 15, 1942.

11. John P. Blair to Bragdon, Dec. 6, 1941. There is a sketch of Minor's career in Barringer et al., eds., *University of Virginia*, I, 358-368.

The Olympian figure of Minor overshadowed the reputation of his colleague Stephen O. Southall, who taught equity as well as mercantile, constitutional, and international law. Yet Southall was better than competent—a tireless worker, a fluent speaker, and a man of broad culture.

12. WW to Charles Talcott, Dec. 31, 1879, WW Papers, LC.

13. WW to Charles Talcott, May 20, 1880, WW Papers, LC.

14. Faculty Minutes, June 1 and July 1, 1880, Alderman Library, University of Virginia.

15. Janet W. Wilson to WW, Nov. 18, and J.R. Wilson to WW, Nov. 19, 1879, WW Papers, LC; WW to Charles Talcott, Dec. 31, 1879, and WW to Robert Bridges, Feb. 25, 1880, *PWW*, p. 606; J. P. Blair to Bragdon, Dec. 6, 1941; S. B. Woods to Bragdon, Jan. 15, 1942; Rev. Edward Earle Bomar to Bragdon, Dec. 12, 1942; Braxton D. Gibson to Bragdon, Jan. 3, 1942.

16. *Virginia University Magazine*, January 1880, pp. 193-194.

17. Charles W. Kent, "Woodrow Wilson of Virginia Alpha," typewritten ms., Alderman Library, University of Virginia; S. B. Woods to Bragdon; J. P. Blair to Bragdon. Phi Kappa Psi was founded in order to counteract the tendency of college men to avoid the struggle of life and to inculcate in its members the idea that their talents should be used for the benefit of their fellow men. Guy Morison Walker, *The Record of Phi Kappa Psi* (New York, 1906), p. 9.

18. Dabney interview.

19. *Virginia University Magazine,* January 1880, pp. 194-195; WW to Harriet Woodrow, April 1880 (exact date not given), Thackwell Collection, PUL; A. W. Patterson, *Personal Recollections of Woodrow Wilson* (Richmond, 1929), pp. 10-11.

20. WW to R. H. Dabney, May 31, 1881, Alderman Library, University of Virginia.

21. Dabney interview; WW to Harriet Woodrow, April 1880, Thackwell Collection, PUL (Jefferson's birthday celebration); Arthur Walworth, *Woodrow Wilson: American Prophet* (New York, 1958), p. 26.

22. James Bones to Janet Woodrow Wilson, Jan. 13, 1880, in Baker, *WW,* I, 130. See WW's letters to Harriet Woodrow, Thackwell Collection, PUL, and Helen Welles Thackwell, "Woodrow Wilson and My Mother," *Princeton University Library Chronicle,* 12:6-18 (Autumn 1950). The Thackwell Collection contains two girlhood photographs of Harriet Woodrow.

23. J. R. Wilson to WW, May 6, June 5, 1880; Janet W. Wilson to WW, June 6, 1880; Mrs. Thomas Wilson ("Auntie") to WW, June 14, 1880, WW Papers, LC.

24. Janet W. Wilson to WW, June 6, 1880.

25. J. R. Wilson to WW, June 5 and 7, 1880.

26. WW to Charles Talcott, Dec. 31, 1879, WW Papers, LC; "Students' Record, University Library, 1878-1888," Alderman Library, University of Virginia.

27. WW to Charles Talcott, May 20, Oct. 11, 1880, WW Papers, LC.

28. WW, "Congressional Government," *PWW,* pp. 548-574. The article is not dated, but a letter from Wilson to Robert Bridges suggests that it was completed in the summer of 1880. WW to Bridges, Sept. 18, 1880, *PWW,* p. 677. Like the essay on French politics, it failed to find a publisher and remained in manuscript until published in the first volume of *PWW.*

29. Except where noted, the description of WW's activities in the society is based on the "Minutes of the Jefferson Society of the University of Virginia, 1875-1895," ms., Alderman Library. The minutes are sometimes incomplete; there are none, for instance, for April, May, and June 1880.

Wilson at this time had so little interest in Jefferson that he did not visit Monticello during his student years at the University of Virginia. He first went to Jefferson's home in 1897. WW, diary, Sept. 20, 1897, WW Papers, LC.

30. Judge Kenneth A. Baine to Bragdon, Dec. 20, 1941.

31. *Virginia University Magazine,* March 1880, pp. 342-343; Patterson, *Personal Recollections,* p. 28.

32. WW, "John Bright," *Virginia University Magazine*, March 1880, pp. 354-370, in *Public Papers*, I, 43-59.

33. WW, "Mr. Gladstone: A Character Sketch," *Virginia University Magazine*, April 1880, pp. 401-420, in *Public Papers*, I, 63-88. Compare specifically *Public Papers*, I, 81-87, with *Gentleman's Magazine*, 58:469-475 (March 1873).

34. W. C. Bruce, *Recollections*, (Baltimore, 1936), pp. 5-37.

35. "Students' Record, University Library, 1878-1888." This record reveals that Bruce, like Wilson, was experimenting with his signature. Sometimes he signed himself "W. C. Bruce" or "Wm. C. Bruce," but by the end of the year he generally brought in his distinguished middle name, so: "Cabell Bruce," "Wm. Cabell Bruce," or "W. Cabell Bruce." He used the latter form from then on.

36. Minutes of the Jefferson Society; Dabney interview; Janet W. Wilson to WW, Oct. 28, 1879.

37. *Virginia University Magazine*, May 1880, p. 447. For the debate as a whole, the best single source is Bruce, *Recollections*, pp. 71-79. Other sources used here are Patterson, *Personal Recollections*, pp. 14-18; Baker, *WW*, I, 121-123; *Virginia University Magazine*, May 1880, pp. 445-453; Dabney interview; letters to Bragdon from K. A. Baine, E. E. Bomar, B. D. Gibson, Virginia Tidball (Jan. 8, 1942), and S. B. Woods. The *Virginia University Magazine* report of Wilson's address is reprinted in *Public Papers*, I, 60-62.

38. B. D. Gibson to Bragdon.

39. *Public Papers*, I, 60-62.

40. S. B. Woods to Bragdon.

41. WW to Charles Talcott, May 20, 1880, WW Papers, LC.

42. *Virginia University Magazine*, October 1880, p. 51.

43. W. C. Bruce, "John Randolph of Roanoke: A Sketch," *Virginia University Magazine*, October 1879, pp. 7-42.

44. WW to Harriet Woodrow, Sept. [Oct.] 5, 1880, Thackwell Collection, PUL.

45. Charles W. Kent to WW, March 1890 (no day given), WW Papers, LC.

46. Except where noted, the account of Wilson's presidency of the Jefferson Society and the revision of its constitution is based on the minutes of the society from October 9, 1880, through January 15, 1881, supplemented by the Dabney interview.

47. Constitution and By-laws of the Jefferson Society of the University of Virginia (Charlottesville, 1881); Dabney interview. The fraternity interference with the Jefferson Society is described in detail in R. H. Dabney, "Secret Fraternities," *Virginia University Magazine*, April 1881, pp. 390-392. Other evidence is scattered throughout the magazine. See also P. A. Bruce, *History of the University of Virginia*, IV, 88, 97.

48. Baker, *WW*, I, 128, quoting a letter from S. J. Shepherd to WW, Nov. 6, 1914.

49. Dabney interview.

50. E. E. Bomar to Bragdon.

51. J. R. Wilson to WW, April 2, 1880; Janet W. Wilson and J. R.

Wilson to WW, Dec. 14, 1880; Janet W. Wilson to WW, n.d. (after December 14, 1880).

52. WW to R. H. Dabney, Feb. 1, 1881, Alderman Library, University of Virginia (sudden departure); J. P. Blair to Bragdon.

53. See Edith Gittings Reid, *Woodrow Wilson: The Caricature, the Myth, and the Man* (New York, 1934), pp. 7-8.

54. WW to J. B. Minor, Dec. 2, 1886, Alderman Library, University of Virginia; Stockton Axson to R. S. Baker, n.d., Baker Papers, LC.

55. WW to Charles W. Kent, May 29, 1894, and WW to R. H. Dabney, Nov. 10, 1902, Alderman Library, University of Virginia; WW to McLean Tilton, Alumni Secretary, Dec. 25, 1921, in *University of Virginia Alumni News*, Feb. 28, 1922.

56. WW to C. W. Kent, March 26, 1890, Alderman Library, University of Virginia; *University of Virginia Alumni Bulletin*, 2:53-55 (June 12, 1895; WW, "Leaderless Government," address to Virginia State Bar Association, Aug. 4, 1897, *Public Papers*, I, 336-359.

57. Correspondence between WW and R. H. Dabney, 1911-1913, Alderman Library, University of Virginia; Patterson, *Personal Recollections*, pp. 35-36; W. C. Bruce, *Recollections*, p. 76; E. M. Hugh-Jones, *Woodrow Wilson and American Liberalism* (New York, 1949), pp. 5-6.

CHAPTER V. Unhappy Interlude, 1881-1883

1. WW to Ellen Axson, Oct. 30, 1883, in Baker, *WW*, I, 158.

2. This chapter is based primarily upon Baker, *WW*, I, 130-167, supplemented by materials in the WW Papers and Ray Stannard Baker Papers, LC, and collections of letters in the Alderman Library, University of Virginia, and the PUL.

3. WW to R. H. Dabney, March 22, 1881, Alderman Library, University of Virginia.

4. Louis D. Bannon, memorandum of a conversation with Henry Wilson Woodrow during 1912 presidential campaign, transcribed by Francis R. Berkeley, Curator of Manuscripts, Alderman Library, University of Virginia, Feb. 21, 1947.

5. WW to Harriet Woodrow, n.d. (Sept. 25?) and Sept. 26, 1881, Thackwell Collection, PUL. See also Helen Wells Thackwell, "Woodrow Wilson and My Mother," *Princeton University Library Chronicle*, 12:6-18 (Autumn 1950).

6. WW to Harriet Woodrow, April 22 and May 10, 1881, in Baker, *WW*, I, 136. The WW Papers, LC, contain a longhand list of books Wilson owned about this time. Approximately half of them are political works. The literary works, except for one volume by Mark Twain, are all English—Matthew Arnold, Bacon, Boswell, Byron, Carlyle, Chaucer, etc.

7. E. I. Renick to WW, Jan. 15, April 25, and April 29, 1882, WW Papers, LC: *Record of the Class of '79 of Princeton College: 1879-1882* (New York, 1882), p. 45; WW to Charles Talcott, Sept. 22, 1881, in Baker, *WW*, I, 139-140.

8. "Handbook of Georgia Courts and Georgia Practice," longhand ms. notebook, WW Papers, LC.

9. Judge George B. Hillyer to R. S. Baker, n.d., in Baker, *WW*, I, 148-149.

10. J. R. Wilson to WW, Aug. 20, Oct. 21, and Dec. 15, 1881, WW Papers, LC.

11. Power of attorney was granted Wilson by his parents on June 13, 1882, and extended on May 9, 1883. The lands in Burt County, Nebraska, were sold between 1885 and 1891. Documents and correspondence in WW Papers, LC.

I have found no specific contemporary record of the earnings of the firm of Renick & Wilson. In January 1883 Wilson wrote his friends Bridges and Dabney that they had collected only a few minute fees but hoped to do better. In a letter to William M. Sloane late in 1883 Wilson implied that the firm was getting an increasing amount of business. WW to Robert Bridges, Jan. 4, 1883, and WW to Robert Bridges, Jan. 11, 1883, in Baker, *WW*, I, 152; longhand draft of letter from WW to W. M. Sloane, n.d. (answered Dec. 9), 1883, WW Papers, LC.

The second volume of *The Papers of Woodrow Wilson*, edited by Arthur S. Link (Princeton, N.J., 1967), covering the years 1881 to 1884, appeared after this book had gone to press. It contains material on Wilson's legal career in Atlanta that was not available to me when this chapter was written. The new evidence shows that Wilson's legal practice was not wholly unsuccessful and that toward its close he was beginning to attract clients, although he continued to be dependent on his father for financial support.

12. "Letters from a Southern Young Man to Southern Young Men," longhand ms., WW Papers, LC. The WW Papers also contain a penciled draft of the constitution of the Georgia House of Commons.

13. WW to Robert Bridges, Jan. 10, 1883, PUL; "Some Legal Needs," longhand ms., WW Papers, LC.

14. WW to R. H. Dabney, Jan. 11, 1883, in Baker, *WW*, I, 140-147.

15. *Public Papers*, I, 89-94.

16. WW to R. H. Dabney, in Baker, *WW*, I, 153-154; WW to Robert Bridges, Jan. 4, 1883, in Baker, *WW*, I, 152; "New Southern Industries," *New York Evening Post*, April 28, 1882; WW, "Committee or Cabinet Government?" *Overland Monthly*, Series A-3:17-33 (January 1884), in *Public Papers*, I, 95-129. In March 1883 Bridges attempted to place Wilson's ms. "Government by Debate" with G. P. Putnam's. The firm was unwilling to bring it out as a trade book but offered to publish it at the expense of the author. In June *Scribner's Magazine* turned it down. G. P. Putnam to R. Bridges, March 12, 1883, WW Papers, LC; Charles Scribner's Sons to WW, June 11, 1883, among letters to R. Bridges, PUL.

The final revision of the article in the *Overland Monthly* was not completed until Wilson went to Johns Hopkins in September 1883. It is treated here rather than in a later chapter because nearly all the work was done while Wilson was in Atlanta or shortly thereafter.

An excellent article by Wilson that denounced the system of leasing out convicts to private contractors in Georgia was published in the *New York Evening Post* on March 7, 1883. *PWW*, II, 306-311.

17. WW to W. M. Sloan, longhand draft, n.d. (answered Dec. 9, 1883), WW Papers, LC.

18. WW to R. H. Dabney, Alderman Library, University of Virginia.

19. The courtship is described in Baker, *WW*, I, 159-167; Eleanor Wilson McAdoo, ed., *The Priceless Gift* (New York, 1962), pp. 3-12; and Arthur Walworth, *Woodrow Wilson: American Prophet* (New York, 1958), pp. 35-38. The quotation describing Ellen Axson is from WW to her, Oct. 11, 1885, in McAdoo, ed., *Priceless Gift*, p. 4.

CHAPTER VI. The Historical Seminary at Johns Hopkins, 1883-1885

1. WW to Ellen Axson, Oct. 30, 1883, in Eleanor Wilson McAdoo, ed., *The Priceless Gift* (New York, 1962), p. 34.

2. Max Eastman, *Heroes I Have Known* (New York, 1942), p. 285; John Davies, "The Lost World of Andrew Fleming West '74," *Princeton Alumni Weekly*, Jan. 15, 1960, p. 11n; Charles N. Eliot, speech printed in *Johns Hopkins University, Celebration of the Twenty-fifth Year of the Founding of the University and the Inauguration of Ira Remsen, LL.D., as President of the University, February Twenty-first and Twenty-second, 1902* (Baltimore, 1902), p. 105.

3. W. Carson Ryan, *Studies in Early Graduate Education: The Johns Hopkins, Clark University, University of Chicago*, Carnegie Foundation for the Advancement of Teaching, Bulletin No. 30 (New York, 1939), p. 27; Hugh Hawkins, *Pioneer: A History of the Johns Hopkins University, 1874-1889* (Ithaca, N.Y., 1960), pp. 69-71. These two books were the principal sources for my description of the Johns Hopkins University (hereafter referred to as JHU). See also Frederick Rudolph, *The American College and University* (New York, 1962), esp. pp. 269-275. Only half of the Hopkins bequest was devoted to the university as here described; the other half went to the hospital and the medical school, which was founded later. For a synoptic view of the change from the "discipline and piety" that had formerly characterized American colleges to the concept of a university, see Lawrence R. Vesey, *The Emergence of the American University* (Chicago, 1965).

4. Ryan, *Early Graduate Education*, p. 30. See also Hawkins, *Pioneer*, pp. 38-62 and *passim*.

5. For the origin of the graduate fellowships and the later careers of early fellows at Johns Hopkins, see Hawkins, *Pioneer*, pp. 81-90.

6. Josiah Royce, "Present Ideals of American University Life," *Scribner's Magazine*, 10:38 (September 1891).

7. Daniel C. Gilman, Inaugural Address, Sept. 12, 1876, in Ryan, *Early Graduate Education*, p. 30.

8. Baker, *WW*, I, 179; H. B. Adams, *The College of William and Mary: A Contribution to the History of Higher Education, with Suggestions for Its National Promotion* (Washington, 1887), p. 68; interview with Charles M. Andrews, May 30, 1941. Sources used for this sketch

of Adams and for the general work of the historical seminary include W. Stoll Holt, ed., *Historical Scholarship in the United States, 1876-1901, as Revealed in the Correspondence of Herbert B. Adams* (Baltimore, 1938); John Spencer Bassett, "Herbert Baxter Adams," *Dictionary of American Biography*, I (New York, 1927), 68-69; Hawkins, *Pioneer*, pp. 172-176 and *passim;* John Dewey to Bragdon, July 14, 1940; interviews with: Davis R. Dewey, Dec. 11, 1940; John H. Finley, Feb. 3, 1940; Lyman P. Powell, March 26, 1940; Albert Shaw, July 17, 1940; and William A. Wetzel, July 4, 1940.

9. Hawkins, *Pioneer*, pp. 177-186; interviews with Dewey, Finley, Powell, and Shaw.

10. See Elizabeth Donnan and Leo F. Stock, eds., *An Historian's World: Selections from the Correspondence of John Franklin Jameson* (Philadelphia, 1956), pp. 18-43.

11. H. B. Adams, *The Study of History in American Colleges and Universities* (Washington, 1877), pp. 173-199. This book contains a picture of the library and a diagram of the complex of rooms used by the historical seminary.

12. "Records of the Historical and Political Science Association and of the Seminary of History and Politics," 2 vols., ms. in the JHU Library (Adams' comment on the seminary is in the entry for May 8, 1884); Wetzel interview; (on Adams' treatment of students). My description of the seminary is based on the "Records"; Vol. I covers 1877-1892, with a gap from November 21, 1879, to January 4, 1884, and Vol. II covers 1892-1901. H. Hale Bellot wrote in *American History and Historians* (Norman, Okla., 1939), pp. 176-177, that Johns Hopkins had the first "true seminary" in this country and its part in promoting higher studies in history and the social sciences was "astonishing."

13. JHU Records, in JHU Library; Baker, WW, I, 173-178; *Johns Hopkins University Register, 1883-84*, p. 85.

14. WW to Ellen Axson, Nov. 27 and Dec. 22, 1883, in Baker, WW, I, 182.

15. *D.A.B.*, s.v. Herbert Baxter Adams; J. F. Jameson to Albert Shaw, Nov. 5, 1882, in Donnan and Stock, eds., *An Historian's World*, p. 22; WW to Ellen Axson, Oct. 16, 1883, in Baker, WW, I, 174-175.

16. WW to Ellen Axson, in Baker, WW, I, 179-180.

17. WW to R. Heath Dabney, Feb. 17, 1884, Alderman Library, University of Virginia; WW to Ellen Axson, Oct. 30, 1883, in Baker, WW, I, 184, 186-187; Stockton Axson to R. S. Baker, February 1925, Baker Papers, LC.

18. R. T. Ely, *Ground under Our Feet* (New York, 1938), p. 105; Reid, *Woodrow Wilson*, p. 38.

19. Charles H. Shinn to WW, Jan. 22, 1884, WW Papers, LC: Henry Crew to Bragdon, Nov. 5, 1941; interview with Albert Shaw, July 17, 1940, and letters from Shaw to WW, 1884-1885, WW Papers, LC.

20. Joseph Ames to R. S. Baker, June 4, 1927, Baker Papers, LC; WW to Ellen Axson, Feb. 2, 1884, in McAdoo, ed., *Priceless Gift*, p. 49; penciled, interlineated verses among jottings in small notebook containing 1885 calendar, WW Papers, LC.

21. WW to Ellen Axson, April 5, 1885, in Baker, *WW*, I, 193; Ely, *Ground under Our Feet*, p. 114.

22. Reid, *Woodrow Wilson*, pp. 33-34.

23. Landon Williams to Bragdon, Aug. 11, 1942; C. H. Shinn to WW, n.d., WW Papers, LC; Reid, *Woodrow Wilson*, p. 34.

24. Ely, *Ground under Our Feet*, p. 114; Augustus W. Long, *A Segment of the American Scene: A Son of North Carolina* (Durham, N.C., 1939), pp. 183-184; WW to Ellen Axson, Dec. 18 and Nov. 25, 1884, in McAdoo, ed., *Priceless Gift*, pp. 103-104, 94-95.

25. Ely, *Ground under Our Feet*, p. 109.

26. Seminary Records, Jan. 18, 1884; interview with Albert Shaw, July 17, 1940. For summaries of Von Holst's views, see Michael Kraus, *A History of American History* (New York, 1937), pp. 337-349, and the essay on Von Holst in William T. Hutchinson, ed., *The Marcus W. Jernegan Essays in American Historiography* (New York, 1937), pp. 60-83.

27. Seminary Records, Jan. 18, 1884; Donnan and Stock, eds., *An Historian's World*, p. 38n.

28. Seminary Records, April 18, 1884. For evidence of H. B. Adams' attitude toward federal aid to education, see his plea for a federal subsidy to the College of William and Mary and for the establishment of a federal school of administration in Adams, *College of William and Mary*.

29. WW to Robert Bridges, Feb. 29, 1886, PUL; WW, *Congressional Government* (Boston, 1885), pp. 28-30.

30. John Dewey to Bragdon, July 14, 1940; Seminary Records, April 18, 1884.

31. Seminary Records, April 25, 1884.

32. WW to Ellen Axson, Jan. 4, 1884, in Baker, *WW*, I, 189.

33. J. F. Jameson, diary, May 9, 1884, quoted in Donnan and Stock, eds., *An Historian's World*, p. 38n; Seminary Records, May 9, 1884.

34. WW to Ellen Axson, Aug. 31, 1884, in Baker, *WW*, I, 217.

35. WW to Ellen Axson, Nov. 11 and 28, 1884, in Baker, *WW*, I, 219.

36. Gamaliel Bradford, "Wilson's Congressional Government," *The Nation*, 40:142-143 (Feb. 12, 1885).

37. *Johns Hopkins University Register, 1884-1885*, pp. 47, 53.

38. WW to R. Heath Dabney, Feb. 14, 1885, Alderman Library, University of Virginia.

39. J. R. Wilson to WW, Oct. 29, 1884, WW Papers, LC; WW to Ellen Axson, Nov. 8, 1884, and Feb. 20, 1885, in Baker, *WW*, I, 235-236.

40. WW to Ellen Axson, Dec. 18, 1884, in Baker, *WW*, I, 199. See *The Debutante* (Johns Hopkins University, Baltimore, 1889), pp. 55-56, for an account of the origins and organization of the Johns Hopkins House of Commons.

41. Memorial to WW, signed by officers of Johns Hopkins House of Commons, May 30, 1884, WW Papers, LC; *Debutante*, p. 55; *Hopkins Medley* (Baltimore, 1890), p. 71; interview with John C. French, July 18, 1941.

42. WW to Ellen Axson, Oct. 17, 1884, in Baker, *WW*, I, 218; Seminary Records, October 1884 to May 1885.

43. Ely, *Ground under Our Feet*, pp. 112-113. Herbert B. Adams

sent out a printed notice announcing the venture and asking scholars to send materials. WW Papers, LC.

44. Ely, *Ground under Our Feet*, p. 113. In addition to the manuscript itself, in the Baker Papers, LC, there is in the WW Papers, LC, a notebook entitled "A History of Political Economy in America," containing Wilson's notes, some in shorthand, some in longhand. See William Diamond, *The Economic Thought of Woodrow Wilson* (Baltimore, 1943), pp. 26-32, for various influences that appear to have altered Wilson's economic philosophy while he was at Johns Hopkins.

45. Alastair Buchan, *Spare Chancellor: The Life of Walter Bagehot* (London, 1959), pp. 246-253; Baker, *WW*, I, 180-181; Seminary Records, Oct. 11, 1884; Hawkins, *Pioneer*, pp. 181-184.

46. WW, paper on eight American economists (1885), Baker Papers, LC.

47. WW to Ellen Axson, Dec. 2, 1884, in Baker, *WW*, I, 220; WW to H. E. Scudder, March 3 and April 8, 1885, Houghton Library, Harvard University.

48. WW to Ellen Axson, Feb. 24, 1885, in Baker, *WW*, I, 228-230.

49. Henry Crew to Bragdon, Nov. 5, 1941.

50. H. B. Adams, *College of William and Mary*, pp. 76-81; Ely, *Ground under Our Feet*, p. 114; Seminary Records, Feb. 27, 1885.

51. Janet W. Wilson to WW, n.d. (autumn 1883), WW Papers, LC.

52. Over fourteen hundred letters between Ellen Axson Wilson and Woodrow Wilson have been preserved. A well-edited selection of the correspondence, with a running narrative and arranged chronologically, has been published in McAdoo, ed., *Priceless Gift*. Not much of importance to the biographer has been omitted from this selection, and many of the omissions are found in Baker, *WW*, I and II. All will eventually appear in *The Papers of Woodrow Wilson*.

53. Stockton Axson to R. S. Baker, n.d., Baker Papers, LC; WW to Ellen Axson, Nov. 9, Dec. 7 and 18, 1884, in Baker, *WW*, I, 167, 242, 243.

54. Mrs. Arthur Tedcastle to R. S. Baker, Baker Papers, LC; WW to Ellen Axson, Feb. 17, 1885, in Baker, *WW*, I, 204.

55. WW to Ellen Axson, Dec. 18, 1883, in McAdoo, ed., *Priceless Gift*, p. 39.

56. WW to Ellen Axson, June 1, 1884, in McAdoo, ed., *Priceless Gift*, p. 70.

57. WW to Ellen Axson, Dec. 28, 1883, in Baker, *WW*, I, 207; Nov. 13, 1883, in McAdoo, ed., *Priceless Gift*, pp. 36-37.

58. WW to Ellen Axson, Jan. 29, 1885, in Baker, *WW*, I, 241.

59. WW to Ellen Axson, Feb. 5, 1884, in McAdoo, ed., *Priceless Gift*, p. 50, and Jan. 14, 1885, in Baker, *WW*, I, 197-198.

60. WW, "American Universities," *New York Evening Post*, June 27, 1884.

61. Edwin Grant Conklin, whose field was biology, reported that when he entered Johns Hopkins in 1888, Wilson was "a shining ideal for students in all departments of the University," and his picture already adorned the walls of the historical seminary. E. G. Conklin, "As a Scientist Saw Him," in *Woodrow Wilson: Some Princeton Memories*, ed. William Starr Myers (Princeton, 1946), p. 52.

62. H. B. Adams to the President and Executive Committee of the Johns Hopkins University, "A Plea for the Organization of the Department of Historical and Political Science," May 29, 1886, in Holt, ed., *Historical Scholarship*, p. 87; WW to H. B. Adams, March 29, 1887, in Holt, ed., *Historical Scholarship*, p. 97; interview with W. A. Wetzel, July 4, 1940 (Gilman's standing invitation to WW to join the faculty).

CHAPTER VII. Congressional Government

1. WW to Ellen Axson, Oct. 30, 1883, in Eleanor Wilson McAdoo, ed., *The Priceless Gift* (New York, 1962), p. 32.
2. These eight books of Wilson's academic years were published as follows: *Congressional Government: A Study in American Politics* (Boston, Houghton Mifflin, 1885); *The State: Elements of Historical and Practical Politics* (Boston, D. C. Heath, 1889); *Division and Reunion, 1829-1889* (New York, Longmans, Green, 1893); *An Old Master and Other Political Essays* (New York, Charles Scribner's Sons, 1893); *Mere Literature and Other Essays* (Boston, Houghton Mifflin, 1896); *George Washington* (New York, Harper and Brothers, 1896); *A History of the American People* (New York, Harper and Brothers, 1902); *Constitutional Government in the United States* (New York, Columbia University Press, 1908).
3. WW to Houghton Mifflin Co., April 4, 1884, in Baker, *WW*, I, 216.
4. WW to Ellen Axson, Jan. 8, 1884, in McAdoo, ed., *Priceless Gift*, p. 46.
5. WW, *Congressional Government*, Meridian ed. (New York, 1956), pp. 167-168, 162, 48, 63, 48. This edition is cited hereafter as *CG*.
6. *CG*, pp. 154, 176, 26.
7. *CG*, p. 100.
8. Lucy Salmon to R. S. Baker, Jan. 6, 1926, Baker Papers, LC.
9. *CG*, pp. 25-54.
10. *CG*, pp. 54-56.
11. *CG*, pp. 57-134.
12. *CG*, p. 139.
13. *CG*, p. 141.
14. *CG*, pp. 142-143.
15. *CG*, p. 144.
16. *CG*, pp. 148-150.
17. *CG*, pp. 153-156.
18. *CG*, p. 153.
19. *CG*, pp. 157-158.
20. *CG*, pp. 159-161.
21. *CG*, pp. 164-170.
22. *CG*, pp. 170-171.
23. *CG*, pp. 179-184.
24. *CG*, pp. 184-187.
25. *CG*, pp. 187-192.
26. *CG*, pp. 196-200.
27. *CG*, pp. 206, 215.
28. Walter Lippmann, Introduction to *CG*, pp. 13-15.

29. WW to R. Heath Dabney, Oct. 28, 1885, Alderman Library, University of Virginia.

30. J. R. Wilson to WW, Jan. 30, 1885, WW Papers, LC.

31. Undated clippings in WW Papers, LC; *Atlantic Monthly*, 65:144 (February 1885).

32. *The Nation*, 40:142-143 (Feb. 12, 1885).

33. Undated clippings, WW Papers, LC; Baker, *WW*, I, 224.

34. *New England and Yale Review*, n.s. 9:284-286 (March 1886).

35. *Atlantic Monthly*, 57:180-193 (February 1886).

36. *Atlantic Monthly*, 57:452-553 (April 1886).

37. Interview with A. Lawrence Lowell, May 23, 1939.

38. H. B. Adams to WW, Nov. 10, 1889, WW Papers, LC; Freeman Snow, "A Defense of Party Government," *Papers of the American Historical Association*, 4:309-328 (July 1890).

39. A. B. Hart, "The Speaker as Premier," *Atlantic Monthly*, 67:380-386 (March 1891); F. V. Fisher, "Party Government," *Westminster Review*, 140:425-432 (October, 1893).

40. *Middletown Constitution*, June 22, 1889. This incident is treated in more detail in Chapter IX.

41. James Bryce, *The American Commonwealth* (London and New York, 1888), I, 157 and n, 158, 168-169, 177; Bryce to WW, Dec. 2, 1891, WW Papers, LC.

42. J. F. Jameson, "The Origin of the Standing Committee System in American Legislative Bodies," *Annual Report of the American Historical Association* (Washington, 1893), pp. 393-399; L. G. McConachie, *Congressional Committees* (New York, 1898), pp. vii-viii, 58-67, 208-209.

43. *CG*, pp. 19-23.

44. The Columbia University lectures, delivered under the Blumenthal Foundation, were published in 1908 as *Constitutional Government in the United States;* chap. iii, one of the most prescient pieces of analysis Wilson ever wrote, is devoted to the presidency.

45. Arthur S. Link, *Wilson: Road to the White House* (Princeton, 1947), p. 15; Roland Young, "Woodrow Wilson's *Congressional Government* Reconsidered," in Earl Latham, ed., *The Philosophy and Politics of Woodrow Wilson* (Chicago, 1958), pp. 201-213.

46. George B. Galloway, "*Congressional Government:* Unfinished Business," in Latham, ed., *Woodrow Wilson*, pp. 214-217; Walter Lippmann, Introduction to *CG*, p. 8.

CHAPTER VIII. Bryn Mawr, 1885-1888

1. WW, diary, Oct. 20, 1887, WW Papers, LC.

2. Margaret Taylor McIntosh, *Joseph Wright Taylor* (Haverford, Pa., 1936), pp. 184-210.

3. Edith Finch, *Carey Thomas of Bryn Mawr* (New York, 1947), p. 1. The account of Miss Thomas is drawn principally from this source, supplemented by a memoir by her youngest sister, Helen Thomas Flexner, *A Quaker Childhood* (New Haven, 1940), an interview with Charles M. Andrews, May 30, 1941, and a conversation with L. M. Donnelly and

Edith Finch, July 18, 1941. A most unfavorable picture of Carey Thomas is found in Margaret Farrand Thorp, *Neilson of Smith* (New York, 1957), pp. 77-83.

4. WW to Ellen Axson, Nov. 27, 1884, in Eleanor Wilson McAdoo, ed., *The Priceless Gift* (New York, 1962), pp. 95-96; James E. Rhoads to WW, Dec. 1, 1884, WW Papers, LC.

5. Ellen Axson to WW, Nov. 28, 1884, WW to Ellen Axson, Nov. 30, 1884, in McAdoo, ed., *Priceless Gift* pp. 96-97, 99; J. R. Wilson to WW, Jan. 15, 1885, WW Papers, LC; "Agreement between the Trustees of Bryn Mawr College and Woodrow Wilson," dated Jan. 10, 1885, but signed by Wilson later, WW Papers, LC; WW to R. Heath Dabney, Feb. 14, 1885, Alderman Library, University of Virginia.

Prevailing starting salaries for men in Wilson's situation appear to have run from about $800 to $1000. See the correspondence of H. B. Adams in W. Stull Holt, ed., *Historical Scholarship in the United States* (Baltimore, 1938).

Wilson had been job hunting before the Bryn Mawr offer. No sooner had he settled in at Johns Hopkins than he wrote Professor William M. Sloane about the possibility of getting a position at Princeton that would allow him to restrict himself to his special studies in "constitutional and administrative systems." Sloane replied that there was no opening at the time but encouraged Wilson to try again in the future. Longhand draft of letter from WW to Sloane, n.d., and Sloane to WW, Dec. 9, 1883, WW Papers, LC.

In May and June 1884 Wilson, spurred by the desire to earn enough to marry Ellen Axson, seriously considered taking a position at the University of Arkansas, before he settled for the less remunerative but more honorific appointment as Fellow in History at Johns Hopkins.

6. Finch, *Carey Thomas*, p. 164.

7. WW to R. H. Dabney, Oct. 28, 1885, Alderman Library, University of Virginia.

8. Mrs. F. A. Leslie to R. S. Baker, n.d., Baker Papers, LC; Alys Smith Russell to Bragdon, Jan. 20, 1943.

9. WW to EAW, May 30, 1886, in Baker, WW, I, 278-279; WW to R. H. Dabney, May 31, 1888, Alderman Library, University of Virginia.

10. Arthur J. Hopkins to R. S. Baker, Jan. 1, 1926, Baker Papers, LC; Paul Shorey to R. S. Baker, n.d., Baker Papers, LC; WW to W. H. Page, Sept. 30, 1885, WW Papers, LC; Finch, *Carey Thomas*, p. 164; WW to Robert Bridges, Nov. 18, 1886, PUL.

11. Mary Hoyt to R. S. Baker, n.d., Baker Papers, LC. Stockton Axson, Mrs. Wilson's brother, also furnished Baker with reminiscences of life in the parsonage on Gulph Road.

12. Wilson's own descriptions of his courses appear in the *Bryn Mawr College Program, 1885-1886, 1886-1887, 1887-1888* (Philadelphia, 1886), and in Herbert B. Adams, *The Study of History in American Colleges and Universities* (Washington, 1877), pp. 225-228.

13. WW, lecture notes, autumn 1885, WW Papers, LC. In this defense of the value of discussion Wilson took the general idea and some of the arguments from Bagehot's *Physics and Politics,* Chap. V; see Bagehot, *Life and Works,* ed. Barrington (London, 1915), VIII, 101-132.

14. Mrs. Arthur H. Scribner and Mary Tremain to R. S. Baker, in Baker, *WW*, I, 262, 290-291, corroborated by letters to Bragdon from Elizabeth Blanchard Beade, n.d. (1942), and Mrs. Alba Johnson, Nov. 11, 1942.

15. Mrs. Alba Johnson to Bragdon, Nov. 11, 1942; Mary Tremain to R. S. Baker, in Baker, *WW*, I, 290-291; *Bryn Mawr College, President's Report to the Board of Trustees, for the Year 1886-1887* (Philadelphia, 1887), p. 18. In answer to a specific question, none of the eight former Bryn Mawr students with whom I correspondended remembered that Wilson had anything to do with the Bryn Mawr House of Commons. The conclusion that he did is based on the following undated notes for a prospectus to England in President Rhoad's handwritig: "There are, of course, societies. Chief among them is a House of Commons modelled on the English one because the American House of Representatives does not lend itself to debate, and has too complicated a system of committees with too much uninteresting work to be done outside the sessions. The House meets fortnightly. It has a Prime Minister, Home and Foreign Secretaries, a Speaker, a Clerk, and a Sergeant at Arms—the tallest of the students. The bills under discussion for this year have been for the abolishment of capital punishment, the restriction of foreign immigration, and the prohibition of the sale of alcoholic liquors. A bill for international copyright according to a scheme lately set forth by the Nineteenth Century has just been passed." Copy furnished me by Edith Finch. Everything in these notes—the purposes of the society, the criticism of the House of Representatives, and the motions in the form of bills—is wholly characteristic of Wilson.

16. Alys Smith Russell to Bragdon, Jan. 20, 1943; Mrs. John MacArthur Harris to Bragdon, Oct. 20, 1942, and March 14, 1943; Susan B. Franklin to Bragdon, Oct. 16, 1942.

17. Interview with C. M. Andrews, March 30, 1941.

18. Mrs. Alba Johnson to Bragdon, Nov. 11, 1942; Mary Tremain to R. S. Baker, n.d., in Baker, *WW*, I, 291; WW to Robert Bridges, Dec. 30, 1887, PUL. Wilson also remarked that teaching women relaxed his mental muscle in a letter to James B. Angell, Nov. 7, 1887, Baker Papers, LC.

19. WW to Carey Thomas, Aug. 29, 1885, President's File, Bryn Mawr College.

20. Jane Bancroft Robinson to R. S. Baker, Jan. 6, 1926, Baker Papers, LC.

21. Lucy Salmon to R. S. Baker, Jan. 15 and Feb. 1, 1926, Baker Papers, LC. The account of her fellowship is drawn from these letters. For the life of Miss Salmon, see Louise Fargo Brown, *Apostle of Democracy: The Life of Miss Lucy Maynard Salmon* (New York, 1943).

22. "Woodrow Wilson, The President's Policies Analysed in the Light of His Natural Inhibitions and His Past Record," by A. Neutral, *The Nation*, 103:258 (September 14, 1916).

23. WW to EAW, Oct. 4, 1887, in Baker, *WW*, I, 291-292.

24. WW to H. B. Adams, April 1886, in Arthur Walworth, *Woodrow Wilson: American Prophet* (New York, 1958), p. 41.

25. WW to H. B. Adams, Nov. 27, 1886, in Walworth, *Woodrow Wilson*, pp. 88-89.

26. WW to Edwin Seligman (editor, *Political Science Quarterly*), Nov. 11, 1886, in *Political Science Quarterly*, 56:401 (September 1941); Lindsay Rogers. "A Professor with a Style," *Political Science Quarterly*, 56:507-514; WW, "The Study of Administration," *Political Science Quarterly*, 2:197-222 (June 1887), and 56:481-506. WW's article on administration attracted the attention of Almont Barnes, who wrote him a letter praising it and apparently suggesting that an important principle of administration was clear differentiation of functions among different departments and clear lines of authority. Wilson agreed but thought that of even more fundamental importance was over-all coordination of functions from above—especially by such bodies as the European Councils of State, composed of both experts and ministers. WW to Almont Barnes, June 28, 1887, Baker Papers, LC.

27. WW to Robert Bridges, March 3, April 4, May 29, and Nov. 29, 1887, PUL; "A Vicious Way of Legislating," *New York Evening Post*, March 9, 1887; WW, "Taxation and Appropriation," in Albert Shaw, ed., *The National Revenues: A Collection of Papers by American Economists* (Chicago, 1888), pp. 106-111.

In a notebook in the WW Papers, LC, is a penciled ms. of an unfinished story by Wilson. Entitled "Margaret," it concerns a lovely girl, "a fair bloom hidden away in the seclusion of a far Southern forest." Her father, Dr. Pierce, was a man of large fortune, high breeding, and cultured tastes, and his wife was "a lovely woman who had at once as cultivated tastes and as blue blood as his own." But the mother died giving birth to the daughter, and Doctor Pierce took to drink. He had a distinguished record during the Civil War, showing "coolness and daring in the face of the hurtling and whistling dangers of the battle-field." After the war he retired with his beloved daughter to a rural retreat, and there the story breaks off.

28. The incident is described in Baker, *WW*, I, 264-266; references to it appear in letters from WW to Bridges, March 14, March 17, and April 6, 1886, PUL.

29. Shaw, ed., *National Revenues*, pp. 26-27; WW to Robert Bridges, April 6, 1886, PUL; R. Ewing, Chairman of the Board of Public Works and Affairs, Nashville, to WW, May 28, 1887, WW Papers, LC. Wilson was informed that the Wake Forest degree came because Johns Hopkins men on the faculty swore by him. T. Dixon, Jr., to WW, June 7, 1887, WW Papers, LC.

30. WW to Horace Scudder, May 12, 1886, Houghton Library, Harvard University.

31. Henry Sumner Maine, *Popular Government* (London, 1885).

32. Maine, *Popular Government*, pp. 238-239, 145, 247.

33. WW to Horace Scudder, May 12, 1886, Houghton Library, Harvard University.

34. WW to Horace Scudder, July 10, 1886, in Baker, *WW*, I, 272-273.

35. WW, "Of the Study of Politics," *New Princeton Review*, 3:188-199 (March 1887), in *An Old Master and Other Political Essays* (New York, 1893), pp. 31-57.

36. WW to R. H. Dabney, Nov. 11, 1887, Alderman Library, University of Virginia; WW to Robert Bridges, Dec. 30, 1887, PUL.

37. WW to J. B. Angell, Nov. 7, 1887, Baker Papers, LC.

38. WW, diary, Oct. 20, 1887, WW Papers, LC.

39. Mrs. Leah Goff Johnson to Bragdon, Nov. 10, 1942; Mrs. Sylvia Wagenet Harris to Bragdon, Oct. 20, 1942; Finch, *Carey Thomas*, p. 175.

40. Finch, *Carey Thomas*, p. 150; WW to EAW, April 27, 1885, in Baker, *WW*, I, 256.

41. *The Bryn Mawr Program, 1886-1887* (Philadelphia, 1886), p. 30; Bryn Mawr College files, 1887 contract with WW, rough copy furnished me by Miss Edith Finch.

42. WW to R. H. Dabney, Jan. 25, 1887, Alderman Library, University of Virginia. The account of Wilson's dealings with President Rhoads follows that in Finch, *Carey Thomas*, pp. 176-178.

43. WW to Robert Bridges, Dec. 30, 1887, PUL.

44. Paul Shorey to R. S. Baker, n.d., Baker Papers, L.C.

45. Arthur J. Hopkins to R. S. Baker, Jan. 16, 1926, Baker Papers, LC; Alys Smith Russell to Bragdon, Jan. 20, 1943; interview with C. M. Andrews, March 30, 1941 (on change in contract policy). Wilson was not alone in finding Carey Thomas difficult to deal with. Although she helped to launch many promising scholars, including W. E. Hocking, Paul Elmer More and Paul Shorey, in addition to Woodrow Wilson, men often thought her high-handed and sometimes devious. "It was said in the profession that at Bryn Mawr you did not occupy a chair; you sat on your suitcase." Thorp, *Nelson of Smith*, p. 77, and passim.

CHAPTER IX. Wesleyan, 1888-1890

1. WW to Robert Bridges, Aug. 28, 1888, PUL.

2. WW to EAW, March 9, 1889, in Baker, *WW*, I, 315.

3. Frank W. Nicholson, ed., *Alumni Record of Wesleyan University* (Middletown, 1931); Albert Shaw to J. Franklin Jameson, Oct. 22, 1888, in Elizabeth Donnan and Leo F. Stock, eds., *An Historian's World: Selections from the Correspondence of J. Franklin Jameson* (Philadelphia, 1956), p. 45n; J. F. Jameson, diary, May 23, 24, and 26, 1888, *ibid.*, p. 44n.

4. WW to Robert Bridges, Jan. 27, 1880, in Baker, *WW*, II, 6.

5. *Wesleyan University Catalogue, 1888-89* (Middletown, 1888); Carl F. Price, *Wesleyan's First Century* (Middletown, 1931).

6. *Wesleyan University Catalogue, 1888-1889*, pp. 62-65.

7. Stockton Axson to R. S. Baker, n.d., Baker Papers, LC; Stockton Axson, "Memorial Address," in *A Memorial to Caleb T. Winchester, 1847-1920* (Middletown, 1921). Wilson's correspondence gives abundant evidence of his great and continuing admiration for Winchester.

8. The house is now torn down and the site occupied by the Phi Nu Theta fraternity; the present number is 200 High Street.

9. *Wesleyan University Bulletin*, No. 2 (April 1888), pp. 6-7; Baker, *WW*, I, 299-300; Stockton Axson to R. S. Baker, n.d., Baker Papers, L.C.

10. Eleanor Wilson McAdoo, ed., *The Priceless Gift* (New York, 1962), p. 171; Stockton Axson to WW, May 10, 1889, WW Papers, LC; Stockton

Axson, "Woodrow Wilson as Man of Letters," *Rice Institute Pamphlet*, 22:225 (October 1935).

11. J. R. Wilson to WW, March 6, 1889, WW Papers, LC; WW to J. R. Wilson, Dec. 16, 1888, in the *New York Times*, May 17, 1931.

12. J. F. Jameson, diary, November 1888, in Donnan and Stock, eds., *An Historian's World*, pp. 45n, 46n; J. F. Jameson to WW, Nov. 20, 1888; *ibid.*, p. 46; J. F. Jameson to WW, May 28, 1890, WW Papers, LC.

13. *Wesleyan Argus*, Sept. 29 and Oct. 12, 1888, Jan. 18 and March 12, 1889; *Middletown Constitution*, March 16, 1889; *Olla Podrida '91* (Middletown, 1890), p. 136; interview with Frederick M. Davenport, July 28, 1941.

14. *Wesleyan University Catalogue, 1888-89, 1889-90;* examinations given by WW at Wesleyan, WW Papers, LC.

15. WW, *An Old Master and Other Political Essays* (New York, 1893), pp. 20-21.

16. H. Monmouth Smith to Bragdon, 1941; Josephine Westgate to Bragdon, Feb. 15, 1942.

17. Arthur N. Burke to Bragdon, Jan. 24, 1942; unnamed student quoted in Carl F. Price, "Woodrow Wilson at Wesleyan," *Wesleyan University Alumnus*, 8:5 (March 1924); Josephine Westgate to Bragdon. The first part of this paragraph is a distillate of recollections from letters received by me.

18. *Wesleyan Argus*, Feb. 15, 1889; H. M. Smith to Bragdon, 1941; George N. Gardiner to Bragdon, March 21, 1941; examination for juniors on the Constitution, with six of ten questions on text of *The Federalist*, WW Papers, LC; *Wesleyan Argus*, Feb. 15, 1890; A. N. Burke to Bragdon, Jan. 24, 1942; George H. Opdyke to Bragdon, March 18, 1941; interview with W. W. Thompson, Feb. 14, 1941; Josephine Westgate to Bragdon.

19. G. H. Opdyke to Bragdon, March 18, 1941; J. S. Pullman to Bragdon, April 21, 1941.

20. WW to Moses S. Slaughter, Aug 2, 1888, WW Papers, LC; "Preparatory Work in Roman History," *Wesleyan University Bulletin*, No. 5 (Oct. 15, 1889), signed "W. W."

21. Seward V. Coffin to Bragdon, March 3, 1941, F. S. Goodrich to Bragdon, 1941, and interview with F. M. Davenport, July 28, 1941 (examination incident); interview with W. W. Thompson, Feb. 14, 1941; G. H. Opdyke to Bragdon, March 18, 1941.

22. *Wesleyan Argus*, Jan. 18, 1889.

23. Price, *Wesleyan's First Century*, pp. 163-164, and interview with F. M. Davenport, July 28, 1941; *Wesleyan Argus*, March 19, April 13, May 25, 1889; *Middletown Constitution*, June 1, 1889.

24. *Middletown Constitution*, June 22, 1889.

25. This account of Wilson's part in football at Wesleyan is based on the *Wesleyan Argus; Springfield Daily Republican; Hartford Daily Courant; Olla Podrida '90* (Middletown, 1889); *Olla Podrida '91; Middletown Constitution;* correspondence with the following Wesleyan alumni during 1940-1942 (former football players starred): Rev. Edward A. Bawden, *Seward V. Coffin (the most important source), Frank D. Dains, Rev. F. S. Goodrich, *P. L. Johnson, Frank B. Littell, *George E. Man-

chester, Eugene A. Noble, *George H. Opdyke, *A. W. Partch, *John
S. Pullman, Rev. Charles P. Tinker, and Mrs. Lewis G. Westgate; inter-
views with Mrs. Oscar H. Kuhns and Mr. and Mrs. Wilson W. Thompson;
Nelson C. Hubbard to Carl F. Price, Aug. 13, 1931, Wesleyan University
Library; Rev. James H. MacDonald to Seward V. Coffin, Dec. 7, 1935;
S. V. Coffin to fellow members of the "Mystical Seven" of the Wesleyan
class of 1889, Dec. 26, 1889 (last two sent me by S. V. Coffin); Stockton
Axson to R. S. Baker, n.d., Baker Papers, LC.

It was difficult to discover the truth about Wilson's connection with
Wesleyan football. Parke H. Davis, a former Princeton player, in an article
in St. Nicholas in 1912 claimed that Wilson as coach of the Wesleyan
team was "one of the founders of the modern game." But former members
of the Wesleyan teams denied and even ridiculed the notion that Wilson
had coached them. Wilson's name does not appear in two histories of
Wesleyan football, one published only two years after he had left Middletown. Carl F. Price's picturesque and circumstantial account of Wilson
exhorting the Wesleyan stands to cheer for their team in a Thanksgiving
Day game with Lehigh in 1889 appeared in the *Wesleyan Alumni Magazine* in 1924 and has gained wide currency. Price described a dismal
situation, with Wesleyan two touchdowns behind, rain pelting, the Wesleyan stands silent and disconsolate, at which point Wilson appeared, clad
in a raincoat, upbraided the Wesleyan rooters, and led cheers with his
umbrella, which so inspired the Wesleyan team that they twice swept
down the field and tied the score. But contemporary accounts of the
game show this story to be so inaccurate in detail that it cannot be used
as evidence. The Wesleyan-Lehigh game was indeed a tie, but it was
played on a dry field, it did not take place on Thanksgiving Day, and
Wesleyan tied the score not by sustained marches down the field but
by a 40-yard field goal and a lucky break.

26. At that time the rules were such that the team kicking off invariably gained possession of the ball. The advantages of Wilson's "rotation"
system were that plays went off very rapidly, giving the opponents no
time to get ready, and that each play set up the next one.

27. *Wesleyan Argus*, Dec. 9, 1889.

28. WW to EAW, Aug. 28, 29, 30, and 31, 1889, in Baker, WW, I,
321-322.

29. WW to R. Heath Dabney, Nov. 7, 1886, in Baker, WW, I, 276-
278; interview with C. H. McIlwain, Jan. 2, 1940; WW to Ellen Axson,
April 27, 1885, in McAdoo, ed., *Priceless Gift*, pp. 137-138; WW to
EAW, March 9, 1899, *ibid.*, p. 169. The extraordinary degree to which
serious students of government then relied on German sources can be
seen in a bibliography that Wilson prepared for a course at Johns Hopkins: 22 German titles, 15 French, and 12 English. He filled a little
japanned box labeled "Jurisprudence" with titles of articles, monographs,
and books, each on a separate card: over two hundred refer to German
sources; only five each refer to French and English ones. WW Papers, LC.

30. Arthur Link, *Wilson: The Road to the White House* (Princeton, 1947),
p. 21. *The State* was published by D. C. Heath, Boston, in the fall of
1889. In the preface Wilson thanked H. B. Adams, J. M. Vincent, J. F.
Jameson, and Munroe Smith for reading portions of the manuscript.

Jameson had confided to his diary on January 16 and 17, 1889, that Wilson's material was "very clear and well-presented" but that his chapters on Greece and Rome were insufficient, lacking perception and grasp; a later unspecified portion was better, "though still inadequate in many points of detail." Donnan and Stock, eds., *An Historian's World*, p. 48n.

31. *The State*, pp. 211, 566.

32. *The State*, pp. 2, 1, 575.

33. See esp. Bagehot, *Physics and Politics*, chap. v. All the other works are included among the "representative authorities" cited in *The State*. For an exposition of how Darwinian theory and Spencerian philosophy led to racist interpretations of English and American institutions as evolving from primitive Aryan or Teutonic society, see Edward North Savath, "Race and Nationalism in American Historiography: The Late Nineteenth Century," *Political Science Quarterly*, 54:421-441 (September 1939).

34. *The State*, pp. 658, 637-668 *passim*. For the connection between social Darwinism and conservative laissez faire in the United States in the seventies and eighties, see Richard Hofstadter, *Social Darwinism in American Thought* (Boston, 1955), esp. the intro., pp. 3-12, and chap. ii, on William Graham Sumner.

35. *The State*, pp. 659-660.

36. *The State*, pp. 661-668.

37. *The State*, p. 651. Wilson strongly advocated public schools as "necessary for the preservation of those conceptions of freedom, political and social, which are indispensable to free individual development." "No free government," he wrote, "can last in health if it loses hold of the traditions of its history, and in the public schools these traditions may be and should be sedulously preserved, carefully replanted in the thought and consciousness of each succeeding generation." *The State*, p. 667.

38. John B. Clark, *The Philosophy of Wealth: Economic Principles Newly Formulated* (Boston, 1885); WW to John B. Clark, n.d. (1887) in *John Bates Clark: A Memorial* (privately printed, 1938), p. 20. WW's letter to Clark was the start of a warm friendship, involving not only the two men but their families. Clark's influence on Wilson is described in William Diamond, *The Economic Thought of Woodrow Wilson* (Baltimore, 1943), pp. 32-34.

39. "Wilson's 'The State'," *The Nation*, 49:522-523 (Dec. 26, 1889); *Atlantic Monthly*, 65:114 (January 1890); *Overland Monthly*, n.s. 15:222 (February 1890); A. B. Hart to WW, Nov. 23, 1889; F. J. Turner to WW, Jan. 23, 1890; J. W. Jenks to WW, Sept. 10, 1889; H. B. Adams to WW, Nov. 14, 1889; WW Papers, LC. There is a sheaf of undated newspaper reviews, all favorable, in WW Papers, LC.

40. There are scattered royalty reports from D. C. Heath in WW Papers, LC; Laura Shearer Turnbull, *Woodrow Wilson: A Selected Bibliography* (Princeton, 1948), p. 3; WW, *Der Staat* (Berlin-Leipzig, 1913). Around 1906 or 1907 Wilson advised William Starr Myers, who was "precepting" a course in government at Princeton, "Use one part *The State* to nine parts water. I no longer believe what I wrote in the first part of that book." He was referring particularly to the portions based on Sir Henry Maine's theories of primitive government. W. S. Myers,

"Wilson in My Diary," in W. S. Myers, ed., *Woodrow Wilson: Some Princeton Memories* (Princeton, 1946), p. 37.

41. WW, "Bryce's 'American Commonwealth,'" *Political Science Quarterly*, 4:153-169 (March 1889), reprinted in *Public Papers*, I, 159-178.

42. *Atlantic Monthly*, 64:577-588 (November 1889), reprinted with slight changes in WW, *An Old Master*, pp, 99-138.

43. For the development of the Lyceum movement and allied self-improvement societies, see Victoria and Robert Ormond Case, *We Called It Culture: The Story of Chautauqua* (New York, 1948), pp. 22-26. Wilson's outside speaking engagements in the single year 1889 included: Jan. 10, "Systems of City Organization," and Jan. 17, "The Government of Berlin," Brown University Historical and Economic Association; Feb. 11—March 23, twenty-five lectures on "Administration," Johns Hopkins University; March 15, "The Development of Law," Johns Hopkins Historical Seminary; April 30, "George Washington," joint church service, North Church, Middletown, Conn.; May 17, "Comparative Politics," Owl Club, Hartford, Conn.; July 20, "A Literary Politician," New England Assembly (Chautauqua), Northampton, Mass.; Oct. 15, "A Literary Politician," Methodist Church, Middletown; Nov. 11, "What Ought the Government to Do?" Brown University Historical and Economic Association; Nov. 14, (topic unknown), Social Fraternity, Middletown; Dec. 3, "Leaders of Men," Y.M.C.A., Middletown.

44. "Make Haste Slowly" (title given by editors), *Public Papers*, I, 179-186. The lecture was reported in the *Hartford Courant*, May 1, 1889.

45. Program for "Third Season," Connecticut Valley Sunday School and Chautauqua Assembly, Laurel Park, Northampton, Mass., July 17-24, 1889, from bound volumes of "Prospectuses and Programs, July 26, 1887, to July 6, 1933, of the Connecticut Valley Sunday School and Chautauqua Assembly," Forbes Library, Northampton. The *Springfield Daily Republican*, July 22, 1889, published a full summary of the lecture, which so closely approximates the exact phraseology and order of topics in the essay "A Literary Politician" in *Mere Literature and Other Essays* (Boston, 1896), pp. 69-103, that the reporter must have been exceptionally accurate or else borrowed Wilson's manuscript. The *Springfield Daily Republican*, July 21, 1889, reported that Wilson's talk had "a value which many lectures have not," since the speaker was "in full harmony with his subject"; the *Northampton Daily Herald* of July 21 singled out Wilson's talk in a headline as an "Eloquent Address."

46. *Wesleyan Argus*, Oct. 27, 1889; *Atlantic Monthly*, 76:668-680 (November 1895); WW, *Mere Literature and Other Essays*, pp. 69-103; *Hartford Courant*, Dec. 5, 1889. The manuscript of "Leaders of Men," now in WW Papers, LC, has been edited with notes and an excellent introduction by T. H. Vail Motter, *Leaders of Men* (Princeton, 1952).

47. W. M. Daniels to R. S. Baker, n.d., Baker Papers, LC.

48. Donnan and Stock, eds., *An Historian's World*, pp. 47-48; "Report of the Professor of History, J. F. Jameson," in *Annual Report of the President to the Corporation of Brown University*, June 20, 1889 (Providence, 1889), pp. 44-45; *Providence Journal*, Jan. 11, 1889; WW to J. R. Wilson, Jan. 13, 1889, in the *New York Times*, May 17, 1931.

49. *Providence Journal*, Jan. 11, 1889.

50. *Providence Journal*, Jan. 18, 1889.

51. Summary drawn from both the *Providence Journal* and the *Boston Herald*, Nov. 12, 1889.

52. Graduation Day at Tech," *Worcester Telegram*, June 27, 1890; *Worcester Spy*, June 27, 1890; Fred W. Speirs to WW, Feb. 18, 1891, WW Papers, LC.

53. Robert Bridges to WW, Dec. 7, 1887, n.d. (summer 1888), and Sept. 8, 1888, PUL; Edward W. Sheldon, "Talk to U.S. Trust Co. Club," Dec. 8, 1927, Edward W. Sheldon Papers, PUL.

54. WW to Robert Bridges, Jan. 30 and Nov. 30, 1887, PUL; WW, *An Old Master and Other Political Essays*, pp. 3-28; J. F. Turner to WW, Oct. 20, 1893, WW Papers, LC. A careful reading of the essay shows that Wilson did not commit himself to the concept of the "economic man" whose blind selfishness works for economic good. Instead, he tried to excuse Smith for leaving out of account "the operation of love, of benevolence, of sympathy, and of charity in filling life with kindly influences" on the ground that he had dealt with these in his *Theory of Moral Sentiments.*

55. Robert Bridges to WW, July 23 and July 30, 1889, PUL; WW to Bridges, Aug. 9, 1889, in Baker, *WW*, I, 323-324.

56. Bridges to WW, Nov. 5, Nov. 20, and Nov. 29, 1889, Jan. 24, 1890, PUL; R. R. Craven (Clerk of Board of Trustees) to WW, Feb. 17, 1890, WW Papers, LC.

57. A. W. Hazen to WW, April 4, 1889, WW Papers, LC; Horace Scudder to WW, Dec. 20, 1889, Houghton Library, Harvard University (the Williams offer); Francis L. Patton to WW, n.d. (February or March 1890), and WW to J. R. Wilson, March 20, 1890, in the *New York Times*, May 17, 1931; WW, *An Old Master*, p. 8.

58. Albert Shaw to WW, May 2 and June 6, 1890, Charles H. Haskins to WW, July 2, 1890, WW Papers, LC; *Wesleyan Argus*, June 28, 1890; Stockton Axson to EAW, Nov. 17, 1891, WW Papers, LC.

59. WW to A. W. Hazen, July 18, 1900, in Baker, *WW*, I, 423; *Wesley Bicentennial, Wesleyan University* (Middletown, 1904). The WW Papers, LC, corroborate Wilson's continuing admiration and affection for Wesleyan. He corresponded with Rev. A. W. Hazen for many years, and there is a scattering of other letters from former colleagues and students. For two or three years he was also asked to give advice on football.

CHAPTER X. Lecturer at Johns Hopkins, 1888-1898

1. Frederick Jackson Turner to Caroline Mae Sherwood, Feb. 13, 1889, Huntington Library, San Marino, California.

2. WW to Joseph R. Wilson, Jan. 13, 1889, in the *New York Times*, May 17, 1931. Although Wilson's formal appointment as Lecturer in Administration came to an end in 1897, he returned to Johns Hopkins in 1898 to give three public lectures on Burke, Bagehot, and Sir Henry Maine.

3. Sources for information about Johns Hopkins during Wilson's years

as lecturer include *Johns Hopkins University Register*, 1887-88 through 1896-97; *Johns Hopkins University Circular*, 1888-1897; *Annual Report of the President of Johns Hopkins University*, Nos. 13-22, 1888-1897. On Gilman's use of visiting lecturers, see W. Carson Ryan, *Studies in Early Graduate Education* (New York, 1939), pp. 40-43, and Hugh Hawkins, *Pioneer: A History of the Johns Hopkins University, 1874-1889* (Ithaca, N.Y., 1960), pp. 106-107. Adams' tendency to hold up successful alumni as exemplars was mentioned in interviews with Charles M. Andrews, March 30, 1941, Davis R. Dewey, Dec. 11, 1940, Lyman P. Powell, March 26, 1940, and William A. Wetzel, July 4, 1940. See also Frederick C. Howe, *Confessions of a Reformer* (New York, 1926), p. 35.

4. For the impact of the historical seminary on two graduates of country colleges, see Edward A. Ross, *Seventy Years of It* (New York, 1936), pp. 40-51, and Howe, *Confessions of a Reformer*, pp. 1-35. J. R. Wilson to WW, March 6, 1889, WW Papers, LC.

5. WW, *Mere Literature and Other Essays* (New York, 1896), p. 12

6. Stockton Axson to R. S. Baker, n.d., Baker Papers, LC; Powell interview; WW, *Mere Literature*, pp. 3, 19-21. Wilson urged Stockton Axson to go to Johns Hopkins following his graduation from Wesleyan, but after an unhappy year he returned, with Wilson's blessing, to study under Caleb T. Winchester.

7. WW to EAW, March 1, 1889, in Eleanor Wilson McAdoo, ed., *The Priceless Gift* (New York, 1962), pp. 167-168.

8. Some overlapping and repetition from year to year is found in Wilson's notes for his lectures in administration in the WW Papers, LC. The discrepancies between what he planned and what he actually presented show up when comparing the course announcements in the *Johns Hopkins University Register* with the descriptions in President Gilman's annual reports. Wilson's letters home from Baltimore contain frequent mention of other work in progress; he liked to make the most of the superior library facilities there. According to the recollections of Frederick C. Howe, Wilson spent most of his time in his room by himself, preparing lectures and writing. *Confessions of a Reformer*, p. 35.

9. *Johns Hopkins University Register*, 1890-91 (Baltimore, 1890), p. 68.

10. WW, "First Year Course, ADMINISTRATION," undated lecture notes, WW Papers, LC. The Wilson Papers also contain a longhand draft of an article on the problem of creating an effective civil service that would not be separate from the people. In it he explicitly rejected the idea that foreign methods could be imported: "It is *impossible*, and any one in his senses knows it is." He dealt more directly with the relationship between popular opinion and administration. Universal suffrage exercised in the immediate conduct of government was "nothing but a clumsy nuisance, a rustic amidst delicate machinery. But indirectly exercised, as voicing the general convictions of justice and expediency, as supervising the greater forces of formative policy, it is altogether safe and beneficent —altogether indispensable." There was therefore need for a new theory of administration as adapted to a democracy, so that democratic governments could carry "those enormous burdens of administration which the needs of this industrial and trading age are so fast accumulating."

11. Edward A. Ross to Bragdon, May 2, 1941; Rockwell D. Hunt to Bragdon, Aug. 6, 1957; Howe, *Confessions of a Reformer,* p. 35; Wetzel interview; Powell interview; Charles M. Andrews to Elizabeth Byrne Andrews, May 7, 1888, copy furnished me by Andrews.

12. Andrews interview. Whereas Adams and Ely discussed sources a good deal, Wilson merely posted a carefully prepared bibliography that students might copy. R. D. Hunt to Bragdon, Aug. 6, 1957. Manuscript copies of such bibliographies are in the Johns Hopkins University Library and the WW Papers, LC.

13. F. J. Turner to Caroline Mae Sherwood, March 2-3, 1889, Henry Huntington Library (consulted by permission of the Director); Turner to William E. Dodd, Oct. 7, 1919, in Wendell H. Stephenson, ed., "The Influence of Woodrow Wilson on Frederick Jackson Turner," *Agricultural History,* 19:252 (October 1945); Historical Seminary Records, 1886-1897, *passim;* Powell interview. In 1891 Mrs. Wilson, the three daughters, and a nurse accompanied Wilson to Miss Ashton's. In other years Wilson left his family behind.

14. Andrews and Powell interviews; C. H. Haskins to WW, May 25 and 29, July 2, 1890, WW Papers, LC.

15. WW to R. G. Thwaites, May 26, 1889, WW Papers, LC; F. J. Turner to WW, Jan. 20, 1890, WW Papers, LC.

16. WW to F. J. Turner, Oct. 23, 1889, Houghton Library, Harvard University; WW, quoted in W. E. Dodd to F. J. Turner, Oct. 3, 1919, and F. J. Turner to W. E. Dodd, Oct. 7, 1919, in Stephenson, ed., "The Influence of Woodrow Wilson on Frederick Jackson Turner," p. 252.

17. Interview with J. H. Finley, Feb. 2, 1940; E. A. Ross to Bragdon, May 2, 1941; Howe, *Confessions of a Reformer,* p. 35.

18. Howe, *Confessions of a Reformer,* pp. 6-7, 38.

19. O. G. Villard, *Fighting Years: Memoirs of a Liberal Editor* (New York, 1939), p. 219; Arthur Link, *Wilson: The Road to the White House* (Princeton, 1947), pp. 34, 24.

20. *Baltimore News,* Feb. 7 and 26, March 3, 1896.

21. *Baltimore News,* Feb. 26, 1896.

22. *Baltimore News,* Feb. 26, March 3, 1896.

23. *Baltimore News,* Feb. 26, Feb. 28, 1896; WW, "Character of Democracy in the United States," *Atlantic Monthly,* 64:584 (November 1889).

24. Interview with Robert N. McElroy, Nov. 20, 1940; WW, "The Interpreter of English Liberty [Burke]," *Mere Literature,* p. 158.

25. *Baltimore News* and *Baltimore Sun,* March 4, 1896. The four principal Baltimore newspapers—the *American,* the *Morning Herald,* the *News,* and the *Sun*—all reported the Music Hall gathering at length, devoting from three to five columns to it; all but the *Morning Herald* gave it editorial comment.

26. *Baltimore Sun,* March 4, 1896.

27. W. Calvin Chesnut, "Mr. Baker Supports Mr. Wilson," *Johns Hopkins Alumni Magazine,* 18:81-82 (March 1940). Wilson's lectures at Johns Hopkins were opened to the public again in 1897, and about sixty "persons from the city" attended. Wilson did not like this arrangement. He wrote his friend Edith Gittings Reid, "By admitting a general mixed

audience to my lectures, they made it impossible to preserve their original character as class lectures; and by allowing them to *count* as class lectures they made it impossible for me to make them really popular." June 18, 1897, Baker Papers, LC. This was one reason he did not continue at Johns Hopkins after 1897, although he appeared there for occasional lectures. Other reasons were that he hated to be away from home, that Johns Hopkins was in financial straits, that he had less need of the $500 stipend, and that his long absences in Baltimore subjected him to criticism at Princeton.

28. *Johns Hopkins University Celebration of the Twenty-fifth Anniversary of the Founding of the University and Inauguration of Ira Remsen, LL.D., as President of the University, February 21 and 22, 1902* (Baltimore, 1902), p. 101; *Baltimore News,* Feb. 22, 1902. For an account of Gilman's offer to Wilson to succeed Herbert B. Adams and Wilson's refusal, see Holt, ed., *Historical Scholarship in the United States,* p. 91n.

29. *Baltimore Sun,* Feb. 22, 1902.

30. *Johns Hopkins University Celebration,* pp. 38, 39-40.

CHAPTER XI. The Golden Nineties, 1890-1902

1. WW to EAW, Jan. 24, 1895, in Eleanor Wilson McAdoo, ed., *The Priceless Gift* (New York, 1962), p. 193.

2. Thomas Jefferson Wertenbaker, *Princeton, 1746-1896* (Princeton, 1946), pp. 344-346; *Speech of Prof. Francis L. Patton, D.D., LL.D., President-Elect of Princeton College, at the Annual Dinner of The Princeton Club of New York, March 15, 1888,* pamphlet in PUL, p. 2; *The Inauguration of Francis Landey Patton, June 20, 1888* (Princeton, 1888), pp. 19-20.

3. Wertenbaker, *Princeton, 1746-1896,* pp. 365-367 and *passim.*

4. William B. Scott, *Some Memories of a Palaeontologist* (Princeton, 1942), p. 218; Wertenbaker, *Princeton, 1746-1896,* pp. 347, 365. *Poler* was Princeton slang for a "grind." Hence the verb *to pole,* meaning "to cram."

5. This picture of student life at Princeton in the nineties is drawn from Andrew C. Imbrie, "There Was Gold in the Golden '90's," *Daily Princetonian,* Jan. 12, 1933; Ernest Poole, *The Bridge: My Own Story* (New York, 1940), pp. 54-70; Jesse Lynch Williams, *Princeton Stories* (New York, 1895), *The Adventures of a Freshman* (New York, 1899), and "Student Life" in Joshua L. Chamberlin, ed., *Universities and Their Sons* (Boston, 1898), I, 554-567; interviews with Wallace D. McLean, Feb. 2, 1940, Ralph Barton Perry, May 29, 1945, Booth Tarkington, Nov. 27, 1940, Frederick R. Whitman, May 24, 1940; files of *Princetonian* (*Daily Princetonian* after April 15, 1892), September 1890–June 1902.

6. *Daily Princetonian,* 17 (1892-93), 18 (1893-94); interview with George C. Wintringer, July 12, 1941.

7. Williams, "Student Life," *Universities and Their Sons,* p. 537.

8. Interview with Louis I. Reichner, July 15, 1941, and R. B. Perry;

Bliss Perry, *And Gladly Teach* (Boston, 1935), p. 134; Wertenbaker, *Princeton, 1746-1896*, p. 366.

9. *New York Tribune,* June 15, 1902; Trustees' Minutes, Nov. 13, 1890, PUL; *Princetonian,* Oct. 14, 1891.

10. Catalogues, College of New Jersey, 1890-91 through 1895-96, Princeton University, 1896-97 through 1901-02; Whitman interview, May 24, 1940; William G. Spicer to Bragdon, Nov. 22, 1941. I also draw on interviews with Robert N. McElroy, Nov. 20, 1940, Andrew C. Imbrie, June 10, 1939, H. Gordon Pierce, Dec. 22, 1943, McLean, and Reichner; George L. Denny to Bragdon, Dec. 22, 1943.

11. WW to R. Heath Dabney, July 1, 1891, Alderman Library, University of Virginia; Winthrop M. Daniels to R. S. Baker, n.d., Baker Papers, LC; McElroy interview; interview with Max Farrand, May 1, 1942.

12. Interview with Williamson U. Vreeland, March 25, 1940; examination papers in WW Papers, LC, and in PUL; interview with W. M. Daniels, March 30, 1940. Daniels' recollection that Wilson hated to correct papers is corroborated by Wilson's correspondence; although in most matters he was scrupulously punctual, he sometimes took a month to report examination results.

13. Hardin Craig, *Woodrow Wilson at Princeton* (Norman, Okla., 1960), pp. 13-14.

14. Poole, *The Bridge,* p. 65. Another Princeton alumnus recollected that Wilson penetrated the defenses of the undergraduates and aroused in them some real intellectual interest: "He started us reading, and showed glimpses of the world so attractive and worth while that we went in a little way in spite of ourselves." McCready Sykes, *Princeton Alumni Weekly,* Feb. 13, 1931, in Wertenbaker, *Princeton, 1746-1896,* p. 366.

15. *Daily Princetonian,* May 6, 1894, April 5, 1895; anonymous letter dated March 10, 1902, in *Pittsburgh Leader,* Sept. 22, 1902, Charles W. MacAlpin Scrapbook, PUL.

16. Mary W. Hoyt to WW, April 6, 1890, WW Papers, LC; *Princetonian,* Nov. 13, 1891; *Daily Princetonian,* April 9, 1895, April 11, 1893; Perry, *And Gladly Teach,* p. 135; W. M. Daniels to R. S. Baker, n.d., Baker Papers, LC.

17. A. C. Imbrie and W. D. McLean interviews.

18. Booth Tarkington interview.

19. H. G. Murray to Bragdon, Dec. 4, 1940; *Daily Princetonian,* Jan. 13, 1893; Perry, *And Gladly Teach,* pp. 130-131.

20. Wertenbaker, *Princeton, 1746-1896,* p. 364; *Daily Princetonian,* Feb. 9, 1893; WW to W. M. Daniels, Feb. 27, 1893, Yale University Library; *Daily Princetonian,* Feb. 22, 1893.

21. Mary W. Hoyt to R. S. Baker, n.d., Baker Papers, LC; interviews with Jesse B. Riggs, July 17, 1941, and Charles H. McIlwain, Jan. 2, 1940; WW to Robert Bridges, Nov. 18, 1892, PUL.

22. Reichner and Farrand interviews. Parke H. Davis wrote in the *Princeton Alumni Weekly,* Nov. 4, 1925, that Wilson took a major part in coaching the 1890 Princeton team (quoted in Baker, *WW,* II, 14-15), but Edgar A. Poe, captain of the team—who according to the custom of the day would have asked Wilson to coach—had no such recollection,

nor did two other members of the team, Jesse B. Riggs and William G. Spicer (joint interview with E. A. Poe and J. B. Riggs, July 17, 1941; W. G. Spicer to Bragdon, Nov. 22, 1941). For Wilson's service on athletic committees, see Frank Presbrey, ed., *Athletics at Princeton: A History* (New York, 1901), pp. 56-57.

23. Presbrey, ed., *Athletics at Princeton,* pp. 338, 340, 357-361, and *passim.*

24. Frederick Rudolph, *The American College and University* (New York, 1962), p. 390; *Daily Princetonian,* Dec. 12, 1894, Feb. 8 and March 7, 1895.

25. The debate was reported in the February 14 editions of the Philadelphia *Press, Times, North American,* and *Public Ledger;* quotations are from the last two.

26. *Nassau Herald* (yearbook), 1896-1903. Twice he shared the honor with Bliss Perry and John Grier Hibben.

27. Perry, *And Gladly Teach,* p. 129.

28. Faculty and Trustees' Minutes and Princeton catalogues, 1890-1902, PUL.

29. Wertenbaker, *Princeton, 1746-1896,* pp. 368-369.

30. The two speeches and the article are reprinted in *Public Papers,* I, 222-258; quotations are from pp. 224, 226, and 253.

31. C. W. Eliot to Daniel C. Gilman, Jan. 17, 1901, in Laurence R. Vesey, "The Academic Mind of Woodrow Wilson," *Mississippi Valley Historical Review,* 49:614 (March 1963); WW to Charles W. Kent, May 29, 1894, Alderman Library, University of Virginia; *Public Papers,* I, 229, 250-251. I derived many suggestions and much information from Vesey's article.

Like his mentor James McCosh, Wilson never tired of taking pot shots at the elective system. In the football debate at Philadelphia, for instance, he said, "Why is it that Harvard doesn't win at football? President Eliot says that they don't play it well because of the elective system of studies, and I think he's probably right. The elective man is never subject to discipline." *Philadelphia Public Ledger,* Feb. 14, 1894.

In opposing coeducation, Wilson was apparently generalizing from his experience at Wesleyan, where there were fifteen women and two hundred men. In 1892 J. Franklin Jameson, writing from Brown to ask Wilson's views of coeducation, remarked, "Your opinion, based upon Middletown experience, was if I remember decidedly adverse" (Feb. 12, 1892, WW Papers, LC).

32. Trustees' Minutes, Feb. 14, 1895, PUL; *Memorial Book of the Sesquicentennial Celebration of the Founding of the College of New Jersey and of the Ceremonies Inaugurating Princeton University* (New York, 1898), pp. 20-21 and *passim.* For impressions of the Princeton Sesquicentennial through the eyes of a transatlantic visitor, see J. J. Thompson, *Recollections and Reflections* (London, 1936), pp. 178-180. Woodrow Wilson was a member of the ad hoc faculty committee to draw up plans for the Sesquicentennial, of the Committee on the Sesquicentennial Celebration, and of the subcommittee on honorary degrees. His influence in the latter was probably responsible for the award of an honorary doctorate to three men who figured prominently in his profes-

sional career: John Bates Clark, Professor of Political Economy at Columbia; Daniel Coit Gilman, President of Johns Hopkins; and Horace Scudder, formerly of Houghton Mifflin Company and now editor of the *Atlantic Monthly.*

33. *Memorial Book,* pp. 120-121 and *passim.* The address is reprinted in *Public Papers,* I, 259-285.

34. George McLean Harper, "A Happy Family," in William Starr Myers, ed., *Woodrow Wilson: Some Princeton Memories* (Princeton, 1946); p. 3; *Memorial Book,* p. 102; EAW to Mary W. Hoyt, Oct. 27, 1896, in McAdoo, ed., *Priceless Gift,* p. 207.

35. Scott, *Some Memories of a Palaeontologist,* p. 226; *Popular Science,* n.s. 4:908-910 (Dec. 18, 1896); interview with Edwin G. Conklin, March 24, 1943. Both Scott, a paleontologist, and Conklin, a biologist, thought that Wilson was not in fact unfriendly to science but that he expressed himself ineptly. Conklin attributed Wilson's slight understanding of science to his lack of laboratory experience. He suspected that the odd metaphor, "calm science seated there, recluse, ascetic, like a nun," had been inspired by the stained glass windows in the old School of Science building on the Princeton campus.

36. *Public Papers,* I, 236, 240.

37. *Public Papers,* I, 258.

38. WW, "Spurious versus Real Patriotism in Education," address before the New England Association of Colleges and Secondary Schools, Oct. 13, 1889, in *The School Review,* 7:602-603 (December 1889).

39. WW to F. J. Turner, Nov. 13, 1896, Houghton Library, Harvard University; WW to EAW, April 2, 1892, in Baker, *WW,* II, 52; WW to EAW, Feb. 22, 1900, in McAdoo, ed., *Priceless Gift,* p. 220. See also Perry, *And Gladly Teach,* pp. 126-159. After a visit to Princeton in the nineties Mark Twain wrote in a letter to his host: "Princeton would suit me as well as heaven; better in fact, for I shouldn't care for the society up there." Twain to Laurence Hutton, in Charles G. Osgood, *The Lights in Nassau Hall* (Princeton, 1951), p. 36n.

40. Interview with Bliss Perry, Jan. 27, 1940. Wilson's personal library contains a well-thumbed handbook *Modern Billiards: A Complete Textbook of the Game.*

41. Interview with William A. Magie, June 12, 1939; interview with Henrietta G. Ricketts, July 31, 1943; Perry, *And Gladly Teach,* pp. 154-155.

42. Edith Gittings Reid, *Woodrow Wilson: The Caricature, the Myth, and the Man* (New York, 1934), pp. 64-66.

43. WW to EAW, Feb. 4, 1894, in McAdoo, ed., *Priceless Gift,* p. 185. The Wilsons were frequently separated because of his many lecture engagements and because they refused to leave the children alone for even a single night until the youngest was nearly fifteen years old.

44. EAW to WW, April 3, 1892, in McAdoo, ed., *Priceless Gift,* pp. 175-176.

45. EAW to John Bates Clark, June 3 and 9, 1897, lent me by Rev. Alden H. Clark.

46. Interview with Margaret Axson Elliott, June 14, 1939; Baker, *WW,* II, 57.

47. The best account of Wilson's home life appears in Eleanor Wilson

McAdoo, *The Woodrow Wilsons* (New York, 1937), pp. 17-70. See also George McLean Harper, "A Happy Family," in Myers, ed., *Woodrow Wilson: Some Princeton Memories,* pp. 1-18. Other sources: interviews with Mrs. Herbert Agar, July 20, 1940; Mrs. Carl C. Brigham, April 14, 1939; Lewis and Richard Cuyler, July 5, 1939; Mrs. Bradford Locke, July 13, 1939; Margaret Perry, May 15, 1940; Mrs. James D. Quackenbush, June 18, 1960; Margaret Axson Elliott.

48. The opinion that Wilson should have had sons was expressed by Jacob N. Beam (interview, Dec. 19, 1939), Rev. Samuel A. Harlow (letter to Bragdon), George M. Harper (interview, July 1, 1939), Andrew F. West (interview, July 1, 1939).

49. Joseph R. Wilson to WW, Sept. 15, 1890, WW Papers, LC. References to his health in Wilson's correspondence are too numerous to catalogue.

50. Baker, *WW,* II, 43-44, 75-85.

51. Stockton Axson to R. S. Baker, n.d., Baker Papers, LC; J. G. Hibben to WW, Aug. 13, 1900; W. B. Pritchard to WW, April 30, 1900; Alois V. Swaboda to WW, April 2, 1902; H. M. Alden to WW, Oct. 8, 1900; all in WW Papers, LC.

52. McAdoo, ed., *Priceless Gift,* pp. 176-178. Wilson received $3,000 his first two years at Princeton, 1890-1892. For the next four years his salary was $3,500, one hundred dollars more than any other full professor. In 1896-97 it dropped to $3,000 perhaps because the $500 raise in 1892 had been technically a living allowance and the Wilson's had now built a house of their own. In 1897-1901 Wilson's income from the endowed McCormick professorship of jurisprudence and politics was $4,410. In 1901-02 the income of his professorship dropped to $4,025 because of a reconversion of certain bonds, and meanwhile Andrew F. West's salary had been raised to $4,500 when he became Dean of the Graduate School. Trustees' Minutes, 1890-1902, PUL.

53. Magie interview; Scott, *Some Memories of a Palaeontologist,* pp. 218, 233; Wertenbaker, *Princeton, 1746-1896,* chap. x; Trustees' Minutes, 1890-1902 *passim,* PUL.

54. WW to Robert Bridges, July 23, 1889, PUL; *Daily Princetonian,* March 22, 1893; Trustees' Minutes, June 8, 1896, PUL.

55. WW to F. J. Turner, Nov. 5 and 15, 1896, and EAW to Turner, Dec. 15, 1896, Houghton Library, Harvard University.

56. WW to F. J. Turner, Dec. 15, 1896, and March 31, 1897, Houghton Library, Harvard University; WW, diary, Jan. 21, 1897, WW Papers, LC (on West's opposition to Turner); Charles E. Green (secretary of Board of Trustees) to WW, March 27 and April 2, 1896, WW Papers, LC.

57. WW, diary, Aug. 20, 1897, WW Papers, LC (on Dabney's assurances); C. W. Kent to WW, April 1, 1897; W. H. Perkinson to WW, March 20, 1897; George W. Miles to WW, March 30, April 7, and May 25, 1897; A. W. Patterson to WW, April 11, 1898; J. Hoge Tyler to WW, April 9, 1898; all in WW Papers, LC.

58. WW to C. W. Kent, April 22, 1898, Alderman Library, University of Virginia. According to Stockton Axson, Wilson had three principal reasons for refusing the Virginia offer: his deep devotion to Princeton,

his dream of developing a new kind of law school at Princeton, and a deepening satisfaction with literature as a profession. Transcript of a conversation between Axson and R. S. Baker, Jan. 12, 1925, Baker Papers, LC.

59. C. C. Cuyler to WW, March 25, April 8 and 20, May 16, June 23, 1898; Cyrus McCormick to WW, March 31, April 2, 3, and 18, 1898; contract between WW and five alumni; all in WW Papers, LC.

60. WW to C. C. Cuyler, June 23, 1898, WW Papers, LC; WW to Thomas Nelson Page, June 7, 1889, Baker Papers, LC; WW to F. J. Turner, March 10, 1900, Houghton Library, Harvard University; Theodore Roosevelt to WW, March 13, 1900, WW Papers, LC; Bliss Perry to WW, March 13, 1900, WW Papers, LC; Baker, *WW*, II, 126n.

61. Perry, *And Gladly Teach*, p. 157; WW, talk on Gladstone to Philadelphian Society, *Daily Princetonian*, May 3, 1901.

62. Trustees' Minutes, Oct. 19, 1900, PUL.

CHAPTER XII. Literary Historian

1. WW, "The Truth of the Matter," *Mere Literature and Other Essays* (New York, 1896), pp. 185-186.

2. WW to EAW, Feb. 16 and 19, 1895, in Eleanor Wilson McAdoo, ed., *The Precious Gift* (New York, 1962), pp. 197-199.

3. WW, "On an Author's Choice of Company," *Mere Literature*, pp. 57-58. Once he had earned a reputation, Wilson took care to be well paid for his writing. In 1898, for instance, when sending an article to R. W. Gilder, editor of the *Century Magazine*, he wrote, "Please do not think it indelicate to say a word about remuneration. I have of late received always at least one hundred and fifty dollars for an essay and I should not like to fall *below par*." March 18, 1898, WW Papers, LC.

4. Charles D. Atkins to Bragdon, April 11, 1941; John Nolen to WW, June 12, 1900 (copy supplied me by Charles D. Atkins); Eric F. Goldman, *John Bach McMaster, American Historian* (Philadelphia, 1943), p. 68; interview with Lyman P. Powell, March 26, 1940 (Powell preceded Nolen as Secretary of the University Extension in Philadelphia); WW, diary, Jan. 1, 1898, WW Papers, LC. By the end of the year the list of twenty-five engagements had increased to thirty-seven. The total amount to be received should have been $1,660; Wilson frequently made such errors.

5. WW to EAW, Aug. 2, 1894, in Baker, *WW*, II, 72-73; stenographic report of speech before the New England Society of New York City, Dec. 22, 1900, reprinted as "The Puritan" in *Public Papers*, I, 360-367.

6. Bliss Perry, *And Gladly Teach* (Boston, 1935), p. 156; interview with Perry, Jan. 27, 1940.

7. WW, "The Course of American History" (address at the semicentennial anniversary of the New Jersey Historical Society, May 16, 1895), *Mere Literature*, p. 213; WW, "The Truth of the Matter," *Mere Literature*, p. 162.

8. See Goldman, *John Bach McMaster*, pp. 14-27, 45-49, 108-121, and *passim;* Michael Kraus, *A History of American History* (New York,

1937), pp. 349-395 and *passim*; William T. Hutchinson, ed., *The Marcus W. Jernegan Essays in American Historiography* (Chicago, 1937): Lewis Ethan Ellis, "James Schouler," pp. 84-101; William T. Hutchinson, "John Bach McMaster," pp. 122-143; Jennings B. Sanders, "John Fiske," pp. 144-170; Raymond Curtis Miller, "James Ford Rhodes," pp. 171-190. The author is indebted to the last two volumes for their discussion of Wilson as a historian (Kraus, pp. 453-461; Hutchinson, essay by Louis Martin Sears, pp. 102-121), and also to Marjorie C. Daniels, "Woodrow Wilson —Historian," *Mississippi Valley Historical Review*, 21:361-374 (December 1934).

9. Albert Bushnell Hart to WW, April 23, 1889, WW Papers, LC.

10. Elizabeth Donnan and Leo F. Stock, eds., *An Historian's World* (Philadelphia, 1956), p. 5 on; interview with A. B. Hart, May 14, 1941.

11. WW to A. B. Hart, May 13, 1889, Baker Papers, LC; Hart to WW, June 5, 1889, WW Papers, LC; Robert Bridges to WW, May 8, 1889, WW Papers, LC; WW to Horace Scudder, Aug. 11, 1892, Baker, *WW*, II, 123; WW to Hart, April 9, Oct. 25, 1892, Baker Papers, LC; WW to Bridges, Aug. 18, 1892, PUL. I wish to express my gratitude to Mr. Edward E. Mills of David McKay Company for furnishing me with a photostatic copy of the contract Wilson signed with Longmans, Green & Co. on June 24, 1889, and with royalty reports of *Division and Reunion* from 1913 to 1939, when it went out of print. During those years (20 to 46 years after initial publication) 43,706 copies were sold.

12. WW to A. B. Hart, Jan. 20, Aug. 24, Oct. 25, 1892, Baker Papers, LC.

13. A. B. Hart to WW, Nov. 12, 1892, WW Papers, LC.

14. WW to A. B. Hart, Oct. 25, Nov. 2, 3, 5, 28, 30, Dec. 3, 5, 7, 9, 13, 20, 1892, Baker Papers, LC. "Wilson's reader" was the proof-reader of John Wilson and Son, Cambridge, Mass., the firm that printed the book.

15. Hart interview; Hart to WW, Nov. 12, 1892, WW Papers, LC; WW to Hart, Nov. 15, 28, 1892, Baker Papers, LC.

16. WW, *Division and Reunion, 1829-1889* (New York and London, 1893).

17. WW, *Division and Reunion*, pp. 90, 188.

18. WW to F. J. Turner, Oct. 23, 1889, Baker Papers, LC; Turner to WW, Oct. 31, 1889, Jan. 1, 1890, WW Papers, LC; WW, *Division and Reunion*, pp. 25, 11.

19. WW to A. B. Hart, June 3, 1889, Baker Papers, LC; WW to R. Heath Dabney, Oct. 31, 1889, Alderman Library, University of Virginia; Seminary minutes, Feb. 28, 1890, "Records of the Historical and Political Science Association and of the Seminary of History and Politics," I, 1877-1892, Johns Hopkins University Library; WW, *Division and Reunion*, pp. 123-129 and *passim*.

20. WW, *Division and Reunion*, pp. 125-127, 164, 166-167.

21. *Ibid.*, pp. 44-45. Hermann von Holst in a review of *Division and Reunion* (in the June 1893 *Educational Review*) noted that Wilson's theory of a changing view of the Constitution, crystallized by Daniel Webster in his *Second Reply to Hayne*, was apparently drawn from

Henry Cabot Lodge's life of Webster. See Lodge, *Daniel Webster*, American Statesman Series (Boston, 1883), pp. 169-176.

22. WW, *Division and Reunion*, p. 212.

23. *Ibid.*, p. 298.

24. *New York Sun*, undated clipping signed W.H.H., in WW Papers, LC; "A Historian's Facts" (unsigned), *The Nation*, 56:279 (April 13, 1893), written, according to Oswald Garrison Villard, by A. J. Nelling (Villard to Bragdon, Nov. 12, 1940); *Atlantic Monthly*, 72:274 (August 1893), unsigned review; *Political Science Quarterly*, 8:533-534 (September, 1893). Other reviews included—with authors where given: *Annals of the American Academy of Political and Social Science*, 4:125-127 (April 1893), E. R. Johnson; *Educational Review*, 6:87-90 (June 1893), Hermann von Holst; *Atheneum* (London), No. 3469 (April 21, 1894), p. 507; *Chatauquan*, 8:248 (March 1893); *Yale Review*, 2:213 (August 1893).

25. Frederick Bancroft, *Political Science Quarterly*, 8:533-534 (September 1893); F. J. Turner to WW, July 17, 1893, WW Papers, LC.

26. Commander, Post No. 10, G.A.R., Worcester, Mass., to WW, April 29, 1893, WW Papers, LC; *Educational Review*, 6:84 (June 1893).

27. "Anti-Slavery History and Biography," *Atlantic Monthly*, 72:268-277 (August 1893), unsigned reviews by WW of John T. Morse, *Abraham Lincoln* (Boston and New York, 1893), Edward L. Pierce, *Memoirs and Letters of Charles Sumner*, III and IV (Boston, 1893), and James Ford Rhodes, *History of the United States from the Compromise of 1850*, I and II (New York, 1893).

28. Remarks by WW on F. J. Turner's paper, "The West as a Field for Historical Study," *Annual Report of the American Historical Association for the Year 1896* (Washington, 1897), I, 295; John W. Burgess, *The Middle Period, 1817-1858* (New York, 1897), pp. x-xi. Burgess had been previously attacked by Wilson in a review in the *Atlantic Monthly* (see Chapter XIII); he himself had been a Unionist in Tennessee, fled the secessionists' "reign of terror," and served in the Union Army at the risk of being shot as a deserter if captured. See his *Recollections of an American Scholar* (New York, 1934), p. 41 and *passim*.

29. WW to F. J. Turner, Dec. 10, 27, 1894, Houghton Library, Harvard University; Turner to WW, Dec. 24, 1894, WW Papers, LC. Max Farrand testified: "Wilson used to talk a good deal about history. One of his favorite themes was that each generation must rewrite history for its own purposes. He talked again and again—I was going to say a hundred times—about his dream of writing a short history of the United States which should fill the same place as Green's *History of the English People*." Interview, May 1, 1942.

30. WW, "Mr. Goldwin Smith's View of Our Political History" (unsigned), *Forum*, 16:489-499 (December 1893); F. J. Turner, "The Influence of the Frontier on American History," *Annual Report of the American Historical Association for 1893* (Washington, 1894), p. 220. Turner had read the essay from manuscript to Wilson before it was printed, and Wilson had suggested a phrase that Turner used, "the hither edge of free land." F. J. Turner to Wm. E. Dodd, Oct. 7, 1919, quoted in

Wendell H. Stephenson, ed., "The Influence of Woodrow Wilson on Frederick Jackson Turner," *Agricultural History*, 19:253 (October, 1945).

31. WW, "A Calendar of Great Americans," *Mere Literature and Other Essays*, pp. 199-200, 208, and *passim*.

32. See WW, "The Course of American History," *Mere Literature*, pp. 213-247; *Annual Report of the American Historical Association for 1896* (Washington, 1897), I, 292; Ulrich B. Phillips to Carl Becker, Oct. 13, 1925 (Turner's passion for facts), quoted in Ray Allen Billington, "Why Some Historians Rarely Write History: A Case Study of Frederick Jackson Turner," *Mississippi Valley Historical Review*, 50:15 (June, 1936); Lee Nathaniel Newcomer, "Frederick Jackson Turner and His Meaning for Today," *Social Education*, 27-244 (May 1963), (the breadth of Turner's conception of history); Merle Curti (Turner's influence), quoted in Max Farrand, *Frederick Jackson Turner: A Memoir* (privately printed, n.p., n.d.), p. 8.

33. WW, "On the Writing of History," reprinted as "The Truth of the Matter," *Mere Literature*, pp. 167-169, 175-178, 182-183, and *passim*.

34. WW, "On an Author's Choice of Company," *Mere Literature*, pp. 50-51, 54, 60-61, and *passim*.

35. *Harper's Magazine*, January, March, May, July, September, November, 1896; WW, *George Washington* (New York and London, 1896); H. M. Alden, of Harper & Bros., to WW, June 28, 1895, WW Papers, LC. Even Wilson's devoted brother-in-law Stockton Axson found fault with the "over-styled manner of writing" ("Woodrow Wilson as Man of Letters," p. 260).

36. WW, *George Washington*, p. 39 and *passim*.

37. WW to John D. Adams, Dec. 10, 1896, Baker Papers, LC; WW, *George Washington*, pp. 54, 101, 92-93, 110, 175, and *passim*. In the passage about the horses Wilson paraphrased Henry Cabot Lodge's life of Washington. See Lodge, *George Washington*, American Statesman Series (Boston, 1888), I, p. 110.

38. WW, *George Washington*, pp. 21, 6, 28, 29, and *passim*. Wilson's style was the subject of a savage attack in a little book, *The Story of a Style*, by William Harlan Hale (New York, 1920). Hale, a disillusioned former supporter, weakened his case by manifest ill temper, contradictions, misstatements of fact, and a pseudo-Freudian approach. Nevertheless, his verbal autopsy of *George Washington* (which he wrongly asserted to be Wilson's most important work) is thorough, perceptive, and funny.

39. WW, "The Truth of the Matter," *Mere Literature*, pp. 169-170; Claude H. Van Tyne, review of *History of the American People*, *Annals of the American Academy of Political and Social Science*, 21:134 (May 1903).

40. WW to Edith Gittings Reid, June 18, Sept. 3, 1897, in Edith Gittings Reid, *Woodrow Wilson: The Caricature, the Myth, and the Man* (New York, 1934), pp. 68-71. Wilson used to tell Stockton Axson that a writer was like a boxer; he must consciously practice every blow and feint through unremitting training, so that when it comes to the real fight, his moves will be second nature. Axson to R. S. Baker, memoranda of talks in February 1925, Baker Papers, LC.

41. Dodd, Mead to WW, March 20, 1894; Walter Hines Page to WW,

July 25, 1897; contract between WW and Harper & Brothers, Jan. 31, 1898 ("retail price" written in instead of "wholesale"); WW to American Book Co., Dec. 11, 1889; Henry H. Vail, of American Book Co., to WW, Dec. 16, 1899, Jan. 13, 1900; R. W. Gilder, of Century Co., to WW, Jan. 1, Jan. 13, Dec. 13, 1900; Walter H. Page, of Doubleday & McClure, to WW, Dec. 23, 1899; H. M. Alden, of Harper & Brothers, to WW, Jan. 9 and 27, Feb. 16, March 13 and 26, April 3, 1900; all in WW Papers, LC.

42. WW, *A History of the American People,* 5 vols. (New York, 1902); correspondence between WW and Harper & Bros., 1900-1909, *passim,* WW Papers, LC; Laura Shearer Turnbull, *Woodrow Wilson: A Selected Bibliography* (Princeton, 1948), p. 8.

43. Interview with Edward S. Corwin, June 9, 1939; reviews by George Louis Beer, *The Critic,* 42:173-176 (February 1903), and C. H. Van Tyne, *Annals of the American Academy of Political and Social Science,* 21:131-134 (May 1903); Marjorie L. Daniell, "Woodrow Wilson—Historian," *Mississippi Valley Historical Review,* 21:363-374 (December 1934); WW to R. W. Gilder, Jan. 26, 1901, Baker Papers, LC. Critiques of *A History of the American People* also appear in Bliss Perry, "Woodrow Wilson as Man of Letters," *Century Magazine,* 35:753-757 (March 1913); Stockton Axson, "Woodrow Wilson as Man of Letters," pp. 263-270; Michael Kraus, *A History of American History* (New York, 1937), 457-461; L. M. Sears, "Woodrow Wilson," in Hutchinson, ed., *Jernegan Essays,* pp. 112-113; William E. Dodd, *Woodrow Wilson and His Work* (New York, 1920), p. 29.

For the passage paraphrased from Fiske, see *Old Virginia and Her Neighbors* (Boston, 1899), II, 281, and WW, *History,* I, 253.

44. See James Bryce, "John Richard Green," *Studies in Contemporary Biography* (New York, 1903), pp. 131-169; WW, *History,* III, 246.

45. WW, *George Washington,* p. 117, *History,* II, 124.

46. WW, *History,* IV, 310-311; Philip Rollins first called the description of Jefferson Davis to my attention (interview, June 25, 1940).

47. WW, *History,* V, 185, 212, 186, 127, 296, 300. The passages in which he castigated radical movements and recent immigrants were later used effectively by those attempting to head off Wilson's nomination for the presidency in 1912. See Arthur S. Link, *Wilson: The Road to the White House* (Princeton, 1947), pp. 381-382.

48. Signed reviews: C. H. Van Tyne, *Annals of the American Academy of Political and Social Science,* 21:131-134 (May 1903); G. L. Beer, *The Critic,* 72:173-176 (February 1903). Unsigned reviews: *American Monthly and Review of Reviews,* 25:746 (November 1902); *Athenaeum* (London), No. 3948 (June 7, 1903), 806-807; *Brooklyn Eagle,* (Nov. 15, 1902); *Independent,* 54:2957-2959 (Dec. 11, 1902), by Charles M. Andrews; *Nation,* 76:117-118 (Feb. 5, 1903), by William MacDonald; *Outlook,* 73:882-884 (April 11, 1903); WW, "Robert E. Lee, An Interpretation," *Public Papers,* II, 73.

49. Harper & Bros. to WW, Nov. 23, 1903, Feb. 2, May 12, 1904, May 11, 1905, May 7 and 11, 1906, Jan. 27, 1900, WW Papers, LC. The exact figure seems to have been $41,153.23, which includes the $12,000 Wilson received for the six installments in *Harper's Magazine.*

It is based on semiannual royalty reports June 1905–June 1910, plus a memorandum in Wilson's handwriting giving receipts for 1902, 1903, and 1904. WW Papers, LC.

50. WW to J. F. Jameson, Nov. 11, 1895, April 24, 1896, Feb. 2, 1898, Feb. 21, 1899, Baker Papers, LC; A. B. Hart to WW, Jan. 3, 1902, WW Papers, LC.

51. Lord Acton to WW, May 10, June 4, 1899; A. W. Ward to WW, Aug. 12, 1899, Jan. 13, 1900; G. W. Prothero to WW, April 2, 1902; all in WW Papers, LC.

52. WW, "State Rights," *Cambridge Modern History*, VII (New York, 1907), chap. xiii, pp. 405-442.

53. WW, "The Variety and Unity of History," in Howard J. Rogers, ed., *Congress of Arts and Science: Universal Exposition, St. Louis, 1904*, II (History of Politics and Economics, History of Law, History of Religion, Boston, 1906), pp. 3-20.

CHAPTER XIII. Unfinished Business: "The Philosophy of Politics"

1. David A. Shannon, ed., *Beatrice Webb's American Diary* (Madison, Wisconsin, 1963), pp. 48-49 (reprinted by permission of the Regents of the University of Wisconsin).

2. WW, entry of Oct. 29, 1889, in notebook entitled "Journal/1887 to," WW Papers, LC.

3. WW, "Bryce's American Commonwealth," *Political Science Quarterly*, 4:153-169, *Public Papers*, I, 159-178; WW, review of Henry Sidgwick, *The Elements of Politics*, in *The Dial*, 12:215-216 (November 1891); WW to Horace Scudder, Feb. 7, 1891, in Baker, *WW*, II, 106; WW, review of John W. Burgess, *Political Science and Constitutional Law*, in *Atlantic Monthly*, 67:112-117 (May 1891), unsigned, *Public Papers*, I, 187-197.

4. WW, "A Literary Politician," *Mere Literature and Other Essays* (Boston, 1896), pp. 101-102, first published in the *Atlantic Monthly* (November 1895).

5. Undated notebook, labeled "VII"; hardbound notebook, with title "The State" superimposed on subtitle "Object Lessons in Politics," containing two dates, "Aug. '92" and "5 June, 1899"; labeled manila envelopes; all in WW Papers, LC.

6. WW, "Character of Democracy in the United States," *Atlantic Monthly*, 64:581 and *passim* (November 1889); WW, "The Significance of American History," *Harper's Encyclopedia of American History* (New York, 1902), I, xxvi, xxxi (Preface). Under the heading "Democracy" in *Harper's Encyclopedia*, of which Wilson was an editor, was reprinted the earlier article in slightly altered form (Vol. III, pp. 68-78), so that Wilson in the Preface refuted Wilson in the body of the text.

7. Notes for course in Public Law, 1896-1897, WW Papers, LC. Wilson's essentially sociological approach to the study of law is emphasized in a most suggestive article by Kazimierz Grzybowski, "Woodrow Wilson on Law, State, and Society," *George Washington Law Review*, 30:808-852 (June 1962). Dr. Grzybowski is of the opinion that Wilson's main

contribution to legal science was "his systematic rejection of formal interpretation of the rule of law. For Wilson, jurisprudence ceased to be an autonomous discipline, and juristic interpretation had to employ additional data from the study of social life in order to arrive at a correct construction of law." According to Grzybowski, Wilson arrived at this conception by his own observation of the American scene, independently of European jurists who were pursuing a parallel course.

8. WW, "Democracy and Efficiency," *Public Papers*, I, 410 (wholesomeness of democracy); WW, notes, "The Nature of the Modern Democratic State," WW Papers, LC; WW, "The Ends and Functions of the Modern Democratic State," WW Papers, LC (role of press); WW, "Democracy and Efficiency," *Public Papers*, I, 398.

9. WW, notes for course in Jurisprudence, WW Papers, LC (tendencies); WW, "Democracy and Efficiency," *Public Papers*, I, 396, 412.

10. John H. Finley, "Obituary Notices of Members Deceased: Woodrow Wilson," *Proceedings of the American Philosophical Society*, LXIII, No. 3 (1924), vi; WW, Elements of Politics notes, Garfield transcription. The change of attitude toward the new immigration appears to have occurred shortly after the turn of the century. Wilson expressed uneasiness about the new immigrants in *A History of the American People,* published in 1902; in 1903 Harry A. Garfield transcribed Wilson's course lecture notes, from which the passage in this paragraph is quoted.

11. WW, "Philosophy of Politics" notes under heading "Political Liberty"; lecture notes entitled "Administration, Year Two"; lectures notes on Constitutional Law; all in WW Papers, LC.

12. WW, "Philosophy of Politics" notes under headings "Political Liberty" and "Introduction," WW Papers, LC. Wilson repeatedly presented to his classes the idea of freedom as a perfect adjustment of forces to carry out a purpose, using such similes as a train running on tracks and a kite held in the air on a string.

13. From a box of random notes for "Philosophy of Politics," WW Papers, LC; WW, "The Interpreter of English Liberty," *Mere Literature* (Boston, 1896), p. 158; WW, Elements of Politics notes, Garfield transcription (progress); WW, quoted in T. Vail Motter, ed., *Leaders of Men* (Princeton, 1952), p. 48; WW, "Philosophy of Politics" notes under heading "Expedience," WW Papers, LC; WW, Inaugural Address, March 4, 1913, *Public Papers*, III, 5; WW, "When a Man Comes to Himself," *Century Magazine*, 62:271 (June 1901).

14. Notes on WW's course in Jurisprudence, taken by Andrew C. Imbrie, PUL.

15. WW, notebook labeled "VII," WW Papers, LC; WW, lecture notes entitled "Leaders Pol. Thought," WW Papers, LC; WW, *Great Leaders of Political Thought, Syllabus of a Course of Six Lectures under the Auspices of the American Society for the Extension of University Teaching* (Philadelphia, 1895), p. 5. The six leaders were Aristotle, Machiavelli, Montesquieu, Burke, de Tocqueville, and Bagehot.

16. WW, hardbound notebook, "The State," WW Papers, LC (government of the few); Elements of Politics notes, Garfield transcription (initiative and referendum); "Philosophy of Politics" notes under heading "Organization," WW Papers, LC.

17. WW, "Philosophy of Politics" notes under heading "Organization," WW Papers, LC.

18. WW, "Leaderless Government," *Public Papers*, I, 336-359.

19. WW, "Mr. Cleveland as President," *Public Papers*, I, 287, 296, and *passim*.

20. Henry Jones Ford, *The Rise and Growth of American Politics* (New York, 1898), pp. 174-196.

21. WW, "The Ideals of America," *Public Papers*, I, 441.

22. WW, "Democracy and Efficiency," *Public Papers*, I, 409; Constitutional Government notes, Garfield transcription.

23. WW, Elements of Politics notes, Garfield transcription.

CHAPTER XIV. Call to Power

1. Eleanor Wilson McAdoo, ed., *The Priceless Gift* (New York, 1962), p. 228.

2. *Catalogue of Princeton University, 1901-02.*

3. Interview with Williamson U. Vreeland, March 24, 1940; interview with Ralph Barton Perry, May 29, 1945; William B. Scott, *Some Memories of a Palaeontologist* (Princeton, 1939), p. 218 (nepotism and indifference to academic standards). See also T. J. Wertenbaker, *Princeton, 1746-1896* (Princeton, 1946), pp. 344-390.

4. Trustees' Minutes, Oct. 1896–Oct. 1900 *passim*, Dec. 13, 1900; Andrew Fleming West, "A Narrative of the Graduate College of Princeton University from Its Proposal in 1896 until Its Dedication in 1915," confidential memorandum (typescript), prepared in 1920, revised in 1929, PUL.

5. Andrew Fleming West, *Alcuin and the Rise of the Christian Schools* (New York, 1892); *Memorial Book of the Founding of the College of New Jersey and of the Ceremonies Inaugurating Princeton University* (New York, 1898), pp. 182-185 and *passim;* Wertenbaker, *Princeton, 1746-1896,* pp. 368-369.

6. Sources for the portrayal of West include: Bliss Perry, *And Gladly Teach* (New York, 1935), pp. 155-156; John D. Davies, "The Lost World of Andrew Fleming West, '74" (unsigned), *Princeton Alumni Weekly*, Jan. 15, 1960, pp. 10-14; interviews with colleagues of West's on the Princeton faculty during Patton's administration, including Jacob N. Beam (March 29, 1941), Winthrop M. Daniels (March 30, 1940), George M. Harper (July 1, 1939), David Magie, Jr. (June 6, 1939), Bliss Perry (Jan. 27, 1940), and John H. Westcott (July 4, 1939).

7. "Standards of Graduate Work: Recommendations Adopted by the University Faculty, February, 1902," appended to report of the Dean of the Graduate School, Trustees' Minutes, March 13, 1902; A. F. West, *The Proposed Graduate College of Princeton University* (unsigned, privately printed, 1903); J. D. Davies, "The Lost World of Andrew Fleming West, '74," *Princeton Alumni Weekly*, Jan. 15, 1960, p. 16.

8. George M. Harper to Francis MacDonald, March 20, 1898, PUL.

9. *Nassau Herald*, Princeton, 1894 (two-thirds Presbyterian); Trustees'

Minutes, Oct. 21, 1902 (drop in Presbyterians); interview with Robert McNutt McElroy, Nov. 20, 1940 (Patton's boast).

10. Poole, *The Bridge*, p. 61. The account of the development of the upper-class clubs is drawn from the *Daily Princetonian*, XV-XXVII, 1890-1902; *Princeton Alumni Weekly*, I-II, 1900-1902; interviews with Princeton alumni; two fictional accounts of Princeton life by Jesse Lynch Williams (first editor of the *Princeton Alumni Weekly*), *Princeton Stories* (New York, 1895) and *The Adventures of a Freshman* (New York, 1899).

11. *The Nassau Herald*, a yearbook, annually reported senior class polls on reasons for preferring Princeton and on what each class prided itself on. Up to 1899 "democratic spirit" was the most common virtue in both categories. It did not appear again until 1911.

12. Jacob N. Beam, *The American Whig Society* (Princeton, 1933), p. 200; *Princeton Alumni Weekly*, Oct. 13, 1900, p. 216, April 19, 1902, p. 460; Trustees' Minutes, June 9, 1902.

13. *Bon mot* quoted in Edith Gittings Reid, *Woodrow Wilson: The Caricature, the Myth, and the Man* (New York, 1934), pp. 97-98; Craig, *Woodrow Wilson at Princeton*, p. 37; Wertenbaker, *Princeton, 1746-1896*, p. 384.

14. J. McKean Cattell, editor of *Popular Science Monthly*, who had scored Wilson's remarks on science at the Sesquicentennial and was later to deplore his election as President of Princeton, attempted to persuade the Association of Colleges and Preparatory Schools of the Middle States and Maryland to demand that the Trustees of Princeton put more science into the curriculum. Edwin Grant Conklin, "As a Scientist Saw Him," in William Starr Myers, ed., *Woodrow Wilson: Some Princeton Memories* (Princeton, 1946), p. 54.

15. Trustees' Minutes, June 14, 1897; interview with W. F. Magie, June 12, 1939 (origin and purposes of the "Vice Committee"); Minutes of the Academic Faculty of Princeton University, Nov. 21, 1900, March 20, April 3, 17, May 1, 5, 1901; Stockton Axson, "The Princeton Controversy," Baker Papers, LC. See also Wertenbaker, *Princeton, 1746-1946*, pp. 385-388. Magie used the term "cabal" in speaking of the origin of the "Vice Committee."

16. "Patton Out to Foil Clique," *New York Sun*, June 12, 1902; S. Axson, "The Princeton Controversy." Wilson's friend and colleague Winthrop Daniels was one of those who thought he had kept out of the debate because he had "inside notice" of his possible election to the presidency of Princeton (interview).

17. Interview with R. T. H. Halsey, March 30, 1941.

18. David B. Jones to WW, March 17, 1902; Cyrus McCormick to WW, March 19, 1902; WW, typewritten memorandum with corrections in his hand in ink; all in WW Papers, LC.

19. WW to David B. Jones, March 19, 1902, Cyrus McCormick to WW, March 29, 1902, WW Papers, LC. Rest of paragraph is based on correspondence between WW and David B. Jones, Cyrus McCormick, and C. C. Cuyler, WW Papers, LC; as well as F. L. Patton to James W. Alexander, April 5, and to Cyrus McCormick, April 12, 1902, Patton letter books, PUL.

20 F. L. Patton to David B. Jones, May 31, 1902, WW Papers, LC; Patton letter books, PUL; Trustees' Minutes, June 9, 1902; *The Charter*

and By-Laws of Princeton University (Princeton, 1899), p. 65. I thank John D. Davies for sharing his researches with me and sending me to consult the Patton letter books.

21. Trustees' Minutes, June 9, 1902; WW to EAW, June 1, 1902, in McAdoo, ed., *The Priceless Gift,* p. 224; S. Bayard Dod to WW, June 25, 1902, in Baker, *WW,* II, 130; "Patton Out to Foil Clique," "That Patton Resignation," "The Game that Dr. Patton Beat," *New York Sun,* June 11, 12, and 13, 1902; cartoon "Me and Tommy," in banquet program, Jan. 13, 1903, scrapbook of William B. Isham, Jr., '79, PUL; Wertenbaker, *Princeton, 1746-1896,* p. 388.

22. A scrapbook kept by C. W. McAlpin, who was Secretary to the University, contains over one hundred newspaper clippings dealing with Wilson's election (PUL). Southern newspapers represented include: *Atlanta Constitution,* June 11, 1902; *Savannah News,* June 12, 1902; *Birmingham Herald,* June 16, 1902; *Lexington* (Ky.) *Herald,* June 17, 1902; and *New Orleans States,* June 13, 1902.

23. Baker, *WW,* II, 149; W. F. Magie to WW, Aug. 13, 1902, WW Papers, LC.

24. WW to E. Washburn Hopkins, June 17, 1902, in Baker, *WW,* II, 135; WW to EAW, July 24, 1902, in McAdoo, ed., *The Priceless Gift,* p. 227.

25. Reid, *Woodrow Wilson,* p. 87; WW to EAW, July and August 1902, in McAdoo, ed., *The Priceless Gift,* pp. 226-230.

26. WW to EAW, Aug. 6, 1902, in McAdoo, ed., *The Priceless Gift,* p. 227; WW, handwritten memorandum, Aug. 31, 1902, WW Papers, LC.

27. WW, private report from the President to the Trustees, Oct. 21, 1902, PUL.

28. Contemporary accounts of the proceedings appear in *Princeton Alumni Weekly,* Nov. 1, 1902, pp. 53-63, and *Daily Princetonian,* special edition, Oct. 25, 1902.

29. George W. Watt, "Is the Liar In?" unpublished ms. lent me by the author; Perry interview; J. F. Jameson to Francis A. Christie, Oct. 31, 1902, in Elizabeth Donovan and Leo F. Stock, eds., *An Historian's World* (Philadelphia, 1956), p. 85.

30. McCosh, "Inaugural Address: Academic Teaching in Europe," *Inauguration of James McCosh, D.D., LL.D., as President of the College of New Jersey, Princeton, October 27, 1868* (New York, 1868), p. 42; WW, "Princeton for the Nation's Service," *Public Papers,* I, 443-461.

31. *Princeton Alumni Weekly,* Nov. 1, 1902, p. 61.

CHAPTER XV.   Conservative Reformer, 1902-1906

1. WW, address at Princeton alumni dinner at the Waldorf-Astoria, New York City, Dec. 13, 1902, in *Public Papers,* I, 472.

2. *Public Papers,* I, 467 and 462-473 *passim.* A scrapbook kept by Charles W. McAlpin, PUL, contains reports of the Chicago speech from the *Chicago Chronicle, Chicago Inter-Ocean,* and *Chicago Tribune,* Nov. 28, 1902.

3. WW, shorthand drafts and copies of typed letters to 27 alumni, with other names listed as possible donors, Jan.-April, 1903, WW Papers, LC; WW to Andrew Carnegie, April 17, 1903, Baker Papers, LC; Baker, *WW*, II, 156. Wilson's talks to alumni groups were reported in both the *Princeton Alumni Weekly* and the *Daily Princetonian;* in addition to the Chicago and New York dinners they included speeches at Harrisburg, Pa. (February 19), Pittsburgh, Pa. (March 7), Philadelphia, Pa. (April 14), Minneapolis, Minn. (April 23), St. Louis, Mo. (April 29), and Newark, N.J. (May 15).

4. William B. Scott, *Some Memories of a Palaeontologist* (Princeton, 1939), p. 256; interview with George M. Harper, July 1, 1939; "Faculty Song," Class of 1904 Song Book, PUL.

5. *Princeton Alumni Weekly*, March 7, 1903, cover and p. 356; March 3, 1904, p. 353; Ernest Martin Hopkins, ed., *Inauguration of Ernest Fox Nichols, D.Sc., LL.D., as President of Dartmouth College, October 14, 1909* (Hanover, 1909), p. 143; WW to Princeton Club of Newark, May 15, 1903, *Princeton Alumni Weekly*, May 23, 1903, p. 552; "General Summary," *Princeton University Catalogue*, 1902-03 through 1910-11.

6. Rev. David H. Frazer to WW, May 19, 1904, and Rev. Simon J. McPherson to WW, May 20, 1904, WW Papers, LC; McMillan Lewis, *Woodrow Wilson of Princeton* (Narberth, Pa., 1953), p. 36.

7. *Daily Princetonian*, Feb. 28, 1903, Feb. 27, 1905; Edward H. Hilliard, "Woodrow Wilson and the Fence," *Princeton Alumni Weekly*, Feb. 17, 1956, p. 6.

8. Trustees' Minutes, June 8, 1903, and *passim*.

9. Trustees' Minutes, June 8, 1903. Separate meetings of the Scientific Faculty ended in November 1904 with a resolution that it should moot only when the President convened it, which he never again did. Separate meetings of the Academic Faculty ceased a year later with a similar motion proposed by Dean West. Minutes of the Scientific Faculty, Nov. 28, 1904, and Minutes of the Academic Faculty, Dec. 12, 1905, Princeton University Archives, PUL.

10. The evidence of Wilson's continuing intimacy with Hibben is abundant, including dozens of affectionate letters from Hibben to WW (WW Papers, LC), a diary Wilson kept January-February 1904 (WW Papers, LC), and the personal testimony of members of the family and close friends (for instance, Margaret Axson Elliott, *My Aunt Louisa and Woodrow Wilson* (Chapel Hill, 1944), pp. 139-140; Edith Gittings Reid, *Woodrow Wilson: The Caricature, the Myth, and the Man* (New York, 1934), pp. 64-65. Stockton Axson was no longer living with the Wilsons and because of his familial relationship, deliberately avoided discussions with Wilson about university affairs. Stockton Axson, "The Princeton Controversy" (memorandum), February 1925, Baker Papers, LC.

11. See Oswald Veblen, "Henry Burchard Fine—In Memoriam," *Bulletin of the American Mathematical Society*, Sept.-Oct. 1929, pp. 726-730; William F. Magie, "Henry Burchard Fine," *Science*, 59:150-151 (February 8, 1929); L. P. Eisenhart, "Henry Burchard Fine and the Fine Memorial Hall," *Scientific Monthly*, 33:656-668 (Dec. 1931); communications to *Princeton Alumni Weekly* after Fine's death from John Grier

Hibben, George McLean Harper, Charles W. Kennedy, Ray Stannard Baker, Winthrop M. Daniels, B. S. Comstock, and Francis L. Patton, January 11, 1929, pp. 411-415; Class of 1904 Songbook, PUL.

12. George McLean Harper, "A Happy Family," in William Starr Myers, ed., *Woodrow Wilson: Some Princeton Memories* (Princeton, 1946), p. 11; interview with Edwin G. Conklin, March 24, 1943. Harper wrote that Wilson insisted on understanding everything brought to him for approval; if he did not understand it, he would defer action, which caused him an uneasiness that was painful to witness. Conklin was much impressed by Wilson's ability to pick up enough of the essentials of any topic to present it more effectively than those who knew the subject intimately. Shortly after he became President of Princeton, Wilson wrote Henry Fairfield Osborn, then Professor of Zoology at Columbia, for suggestions as to the needs of the Department of Biology, and he received 33 typewritten pages in reply. H. F. Osborn to WW, Sept. 10, 1902, WW Papers, LC.

13. Bliss Perry, *And Gladly Teach* (Boston, 1939), p. 159; for West's support of Wilson see Report of the Dean of the Graduate School, Trustees' Minutes, Dec. 3, 1903, and reports of West's talks to alumni in St. Louis (April, 1903), Orange, N.J. (November, 1905), and Cleveland (May, 1906), in *Princeton Alumni Weekly,* May 9, 1903, p. 519; Nov. 18, 1905, p. 130; June 2, 1906, p. 655; Stockton Axson, "The Princeton Controversy," Baker Papers, LC.

14. In a diary covering Jan. 1-Feb. 13, 1904, Wilson noted seven sessions of the Committee on Course of Study, WW Papers, LC; WW to EAW, April 14, 17, 26, 1904, in Baker, *WW*, II, 160.

15. George McLean Harper, "A Happy Family," p. 4 and Harper interview. William B. Scott, another friend, had similar recollections. When opposed or annoyed, Wilson grew arrogant and sarcastic, occasionally speaking in a way that Scott would have tolerated from no one else. Scott nevertheless found that Wilson was "always open to conviction and would change his mind when good reason was shown him." *Some Memories of a Palaeontologist*, p. 256.

16. WW to EAW, April 26, 1904, Baker, *WW*, II, 160; interviews with George M. Priest, Dec. 19, 1939, and Thomas Marc Parrott, Sept. 15, 1942.

17. WW, "The Revision of the Courses of Study," *Princeton Alumni Weekly,* June 18, 1904, p. 104; Report of the Committee on the Course of Study, Trustees' Minutes, June 13, 1904.

18. Hardin Craig, *Woodrow Wilson at Princeton* (Norman, Oklahoma, 1960), p. 46; William A. Wetzel to WW, May 3, 1907, WW Papers, LC (favoritism to private schools). WW, "A More Excellent Way," address to Brown University Teachers' Association, March 4, 1904, *Princeton Alumni Weekly,* March 19, 1904, p. 391; editorial, *New York Times,* Oct. 23, 1904. On October 22, 1904, the *New York Evening Post* ran a long article describing the revised Princeton curriculum. Wilson's characterization of the elective system echoed that of James McCosh, who in a famous debate with Charles W. Eliot in 1885 had called the Harvard President's defense of the elective system "large, loose, vague, showy, and plausible." William M. Sloane, ed., *The Life of James McCosh* (New York, 1896), p. 200n.

19. *Chicago Chronicle*, Nov. 29, 1902; WW to Harry A. Garfield, June 11, 1903 (lent me by Garfield); interview with Garfield, Feb. 14, 1940.

20. WW diary, Jan. 16-18, 1904, WW Papers, LC; WW to Thilly, Jan. 31, Feb. 1, Feb. 8, 1902, Baker Papers, LC; Thilly to WW, Feb. 2, 1904, WW Papers, LC.

21. H. B. Fine to WW, July 15 and 18, 1905, WW Papers, LC; Hugh S. Taylor, "Science Serves: Princeton's Scientific Departments—Their Growth and Reputation, Their Aid to Princeton and America," *Princeton Alumni Weekly*, March 17, 1941, p. 8.

22. Trustees' Minutes, Oct. 21, 1902.

23. WW to Charles W. L. Johnson, April 7, 1903 (lent me by Johnson); interviews with Jacob N. Beam, March 29, 1941, Wilson Farrand, Dec. 20, 1939, William A. Magie, June 12, 1939, Williamson U. Vreeland, March 24, 1940, and Harper; R. T. H. Halsey to WW, June 16, 1904, Wilson Farrand to WW, June 9 and 17, 1904, and James W. Alexander to WW, Oct. 18, 1904, WW Papers, LC; Wilson Farrand Papers, PUL.

24. David B. Jones to WW, March 15, 1904, WW Papers, LC; Trustees' Minutes, Dec. 10, 1903; WW, typewritten draft of letter to two trustees, December 1905, WW Papers, LC; Henry W. Green to Moses Taylor Pyne, Jan. 26, 1906, Bayard Henry to Pyne, Feb. 2, 1906, and Pyne to WW, Feb. 5, 1906, WW Papers, LC; Trustees' Minutes, March 8, 1906; scattered references in Moses Taylor Pyne Papers, PUL.

25. Raymond B. Fosdick, "Personal Recollections of Woodrow Wilson," in Earl Latham, ed., *The Philosophy and Politics of Woodrow Wilson* (Chicago, 1958), pp. 28-29.

26. Lewis, *Woodrow Wilson of Princeton*, pp. 52-54; WW, Introduction to John Rogers Williams, *The Handbook of Princeton* (New York, 1905), pp. xv-xvi.

27. Raymond Fosdick, *Chronicle of a Generation: An Autobiography* (New York, 1958), p. 50.

28. John Knox Fornance, "The Elements of Politics," longhand lecture notes, PUL; Fornance to Julian P. Boyd, Aug. 2, 1944, sent me by Boyd.

29. Interviews with Donald Herring, July 13, 1941, and Philip Rollins, June 25, 1943. Rollins thought that Wilson could have made his living as a football coach. Once on the train from New York to Princeton, Wilson became so interested in telling him about variations of mass plays and Rollins was so absorbed that they missed Princeton Junction and had to go on to Trenton.

30. Jacob N. Beam, *The American Whig Society* (Princeton, 1933), pp. 200-201; Hardin Craig, *Woodrow Wilson at Princeton*, pp. 7-8. The decline of debating was frequently noted in the *Daily Princetonian*. On January 10, 1905, an editorial urging clubmen to show Princeton spirit and be active in the Halls, even though "debating is not or cannot be as generally interesting as athletics," initiated a flurry of letters and editorials discussing the effect of the upper-class clubs on the Halls.

31. Report of the Dean of the Faculty, Trustees' Minutes, Dec. 12, 1903; Lewis, *Woodrow Wilson of Princeton*, p. 54.

32. Arthur S. Link, "Woodrow Wilson: Presbyterian in Government," address at the National Presbyterian Church, Washington, D.C., November

21, 1963, reprinted in George L. Hunt, ed., *Calvinism and the Political Order*, (Philadelphia, n.d.), p. 157; *New York Tribune*, Dec. 2, 1902.

33. Harold R. Medina, "The Influence of Woodrow Wilson on the Princeton Undergraduate, 1902-1910," *Princeton Alumni Weekly*, June 2, 1956, p. 6; Fosdick, "Personal Recollections of Woodrow Wilson," p. 30.

34. Winthrop Daniels to R. S. Baker, Baker Papers, LC. See Reid, *Woodrow Wilson*, pp. 91-92, for similar observations on Wilson's religious faith.

35. WW, "The Young People and the Church," address to Pennsylvania Sabbath School Association, Pittsburgh, Oct. 13, 1904, *Public Papers*, I, 479; report of Forefather's Day Address by WW at Lafayette Avenue Presbyterian Church, Brooklyn, in *Brooklyn Citizen*, Dec. 22, 1902; WW, longhand notes for sermon at Paget Presbyterian Church, Bermuda, Feb. 2, 1907, and at Princeton University Chapel, Feb. 17, 1907; Baker Papers, LC.

36. WW, diary, Jan. 1-Feb. 13, 1904, WW Papers, LC.

37. *Ibid.;* Elliott, *My Aunt Louisa and Woodrow Wilson*, pp. 193-195.

38. Interview with Mrs. F. Scott Agar, July 20, 1940; McAdoo, *The Woodrow Wilsons*, p. 75; interview with Margaret Axson Elliott, June 14, 1939.

39. McAdoo, *The Woodrow Wilsons*, p. 65 and *passim;* EAW to WW April 26, 1903, and WW to EAW, April 29, 1903, in Margaret Wilson McAdoo, ed., *The Priceless Gift* (New York, 1962), p. 231.

40. McAdoo, *The Woodrow Wilsons*, p. 59; WW to Edith Gittings Reid, Feb. 3, 1902, WW Papers, LC; Elliott, *My Aunt Louisa and Woodrow Wilson*, pp. 195-196; interview with Edward Capps, March 23, 1943.

41. S. Axson, "The Princeton Controversy"; Hilliard, "Woodrow Wilson and the Fence," pp. 3-6; *Nassau Literary Magazine*, 40:171-172 (Nov. 1904); C. C. Cuyler to WW, Oct. 11, 1904. Another account of this incident appears in Lewis, *Woodrow Wilson of Princeton*, p. 78. My account is based on the Hilliard article, contemporary evidence in *The Daily Princetonian* and the *Nassau Literary Magazine*, and a letter to me from Norman Thomas, July 18, 1960.

42. Thomas to Bragdon, July 18, 1960.

43. WW, talk to second annual dinner of Orange (N.J.) Alumni Association, *Princeton Alumni Weekly*, Nov. 18, 1905, p. 131; WW, address to Princeton Club dinner, New York City, Dec. 13, 1902, *Public Papers*, I, 470-471.

44. Robert Edwards Annin, *Woodrow Wilson: A Character Study* (New York, 1924), p. 13; M. T. Pyne to Henry B. Thompson, April 7, 1910, M. T. Pyne Papers, PUL; Trustees' Minutes, June 12, 1905.

45. Report of the Committee on Curriculum, Trustees' Minutes, June 12, 1905.

46. Robert K. Root, "Wilson and the Preceptors," in Myers, ed., *Woodrow Wilson: Some Princeton Memories*, pp. 13-14; G. M. Harper to Francis MacDonald, March 15, 1905, PUL. In the WW Papers, LC, there are thirty-one letters of acceptance and one refusal. Harper's letter to MacDonald shows that in the English Department candidates were voted on by the whole department, in consultation with Wilson. Nine letters written by Wilson to Winthrop M. Daniels, head of the Depart-

ment of History, Politics, and Economics, March 3-June 7, 1905 (Yale University Library), reveal that in this department decisions about the hiring of preceptors were made by Daniels and Wilson alone; they also show that Wilson was willing on occasion to defer to Daniels' judgment about particular men. Professor Williamson U. Vreeland, head of the Department of Modern Languages, asked a college textbook salesman for the names of the best young men in other institutions. He went to see them and asked those he liked best to Princeton to interview Wilson. "I remember on one occasion," said Vreeland, "I brought two over to see him the same day. One of them was very attractive socially, the other a little crude. Wilson had grave doubts about the latter man, wondering how he might fit in. I, however, had come to prefer him and insisted to Wilson that he was the better man. Wilson gave in and he joined the faculty." Interview, March 24, 1940. Edward S. Corwin's description of his first interview with Wilson is similar to Root's. Corwin, "Departmental Colleague," in Myers, ed., *Woodrow Wilson: Some Princeton Memories,* p. 19.

47. WW, talk at Princeton Press Club dinner, *Daily Princetonian,* April 17, 1905; John J. Moment to Bragdon, April 3, May 8, 1941; interview with Jacob N. Beam, March 28, 1941, and Beam to Bragdon, May 3, 1941.

48. Interview with Luther P. Eisenhart, June 9, 1939; Veblen, "Henry B. Fine—In Memoriam," p. 729; Eisenhart, "Henry Burchard Fine and the Fine Memorial Hall," *Scientific Monthly,* 33:567 (Dec. 1931); Magie interview, June 12, 1940. The first mathematics preceptors included Gilbert A. Bliss, Luther P. Eisenhart, William Gillespie, Oswald Veblen, and John Wesley Young; George D. Birkhoff was appointed in 1909. A list of the original preceptors, with their academic *curricula vitae,* appears in the *Report of the President for 1905* (Princeton, 1906), pp. 5-15. The institutions with which they had been previously connected and the number from each were: Princeton—twelve; Columbia and Yale—three each; College of the City of New York, Cornell, Dartmouth, Miami, Michigan, Williams, and Wisconsin—two each; Adelbert, Baylor, Bryn Mawr, University of California, Colgate, Hampden-Sidney, Harvard, Johns Hopkins, Lake Forest, Lehigh, Marine Biological Laboratory (Woods Hole), Missouri, Museum of Fine Arts (Boston), Oberlin, Pennsylvania, Philadelphia Central High School, Texas, Ursinus, and Washington University (St. Louis)—one each.

49. *Daily Princetonian,* April 28, 1905; WW, "The Princeton Preceptorial System," *The Independent,* 49:239-240 (Aug. 3, 1905), *Public Papers,* I, 487-490; Charles Grosvenor Osgood, "Woodrow Wilson," in Willard Thorp, ed., *The Lives of Eighteen from Princeton* (Princeton, 1946), p. 294. Osgood's essay and Myers, ed., *Woodrow Wilson: Some Princeton Memories,* written by seven Princeton faculty members, are invaluable sources. My account also draws on interviews and correspondence with the following men who served on the Princeton faculty under Wilson (preceptors starred): Jacob N. Beam*, Edward Capps, Harry C. Clemons, Edward G. Conklin, Edward S. Corwin*, Winthrop M. Daniels, Luther P. Eisenhart*, Edward G. Elliott*, Harry A. Garfield, William Gillespie*, Clifton R. Hall, George M. Harper, Radcliffe Heermance, Don-

ald G. Herring, Francis MacDonald*, David Magie*, William F. Magie, Robert M. McElroy, Herbert S. Murch, W. S. Myers*, C. G. Osgood*, George M. Priest*, W. K. Prentice, T. M. Parrott, W. U. Vreeland, Oswald Veblen*, T. J. Wertenbaker*, Andrew F. West, and John H. Westcott.

50. Osgood, "Woodrow Wilson," pp. 295-296; Root, "Wilson and the Preceptors," p. 15; J. Duncan Spaeth, "As I Knew Him and View Him Now," in Myers, ed., *Woodrow Wilson: Some Princeton Memories,* p. 87.

51. Osgood, "Woodrow Wilson," p. 294.

52. Only sixteen men were excluded from midyear examinations in 1906 for neglect of preceptorial assignments. Andrew F. West, "The Tutorial System in College," *Educational Review,* 32:511 (Dec. 1906).

53. *Nassau Literary Magazine,* 51:217-218 (Dec. 1905); *Daily Princetonian,* Feb. 27, 1906; Francis MacDonald, "Ten Years After," in F. P. McBreen, ed., *Ten Years of Princeton University* (New York, 1906), p. 43.

54. WW, "The Preceptorial System," address before the Western Association of Princeton Clubs, Cleveland, Ohio, May 1906, *Public Papers,* I, 491-492.

55. The figures are from the estimated budgets for 1902-03 (Trustees' Minutes, Oct. 11, 1902) and 1906-07 (Trustees' Minutes, Oct. 20, 1906). Of the $120,538 collected by the Committee of Fifty in 1906, $99,500 was given by 24 donors, and over $60,000 came from 3 sources. Treasurer's Report, in *Report of the President for 1906* (Princeton, 1907), pp. 25-27.

56. Committee of Fifty, *Princeton University: Some Characteristic Features* (Princeton, 1906), p. 33; Oren Root to WW, April 3, 1905, WW Papers, LC.

57. Osgood, "Woodrow Wilson," p. 285; *Rome Tribune* (N.Y.), Dec. 28, 1902, quoting a talk by Wilson at the Brooklyn Institute, Dec. 12, 1902; WW, notes for a talk to Princeton alumni in Minneapolis, April 24, 1902, in Lawrence R. Vesey, "The Academic Mind of Woodrow Wilson," *Mississippi Valley Historical Review,* 49:630 (March 1963): WW, "The Preceptorial System," *Public Papers,* I, 496; WW to Cyrus McCormick, March 3, 1909, Baker Papers, LC. Vesey's article is valuable because it relates his ideas to the contemporary scene, as does his important study *The Emergence of the American University* (Chicago, 1965). Wilson continued to oppose coeducation. When the mother of a student urged him to open Princeton's doors to girls in order to "remove the false glamor with which the two sexes see each other," Wilson retorted, "My dear madam, that is the very thing we want to preserve at all costs." Fosdick, *Chronicle of a Generation,* p. 49.

58. WW, "The Young People and the Church," *Public Papers,* I, 476-477.

59. WW, "Legal Education of Undergraduates," Aug. 23, 1894, *Public Papers,* I, 236; WW, talk before Commercial Club, Nov. 29, 1902, *Chicago Tribune,* Nov. 30. 1902.

60. Arthur Walworth, *Woodrow Wilson: American Prophet* (New York, 1958), pp. 96-97; in letters to prospective preceptors (WW Papers, LC) and to Winthrop Daniels in March 1905 (Yale University Library), Wilson used a rubber-stamp signature; McAdoo, *The Woodrow Wilsons,* p. 87; Elliott, *My Aunt Louisa and Woodrow Wilson,* pp. 209-210; Hardin Craig to R. S. Baker, July 5, 1927, Baker Papers, LC.

61. McAdoo, *The Woodrow Wilsons*, p. 93; EAW to Florence Hoyt, May 27, 1906, Baker Papers, LC; Baker, *WW*, II, 201-204; Trustees' Minutes, June 11, 1906.

CHAPTER XVI. The Quad Plan Fight, 1906–1908

1. WW, "Report of the Committee on the Supplementary Report of the President," *Public Papers*, I, 502.

2. Baker, *WW*, II, 204-205. See also Eleanor Wilson McAdoo, *The Woodrow Wilsons* (New York, 1937), pp. 93-96, and Eleanor Wilson McAdoo, ed., *The Priceless Gift* (New York, 1962), pp. 241-243.

3. Stockton Axson to R. S. Baker, Baker Papers, LC; Margaret Axson Elliott, *My Aunt Louisa and Woodrow Wilson* (Chapel Hill, N.C., 1944), pp. 228-231 (Ouija board); WW, talk to Chicago alumni, *Chicago Chronicle*, Nov. 29, 1902; interview with Wallace D. McLean, Feb. 2, 1940. McLean said that Wilson's partiality for the number 13 was so well known that, when he was staying in the Shoreham Hotel on the eve of his inauguration as President of the United States, the floor on which he had his headquarters was numbered 13 for the occasion and a silver 13 was attached to his bedroom door.

4. WW to EAW, Sept. 2, 1906, in McAdoo, ed., *The Priceless Gift*, pp. 242-243.

5. *Princeton Alumni Weekly*, Nov. 26, 1904, pp. 143-144. See also West's article describing and praising the preceptorial system, "The Tutorial System in College," *Educational Review*, 32:500-514 (Dec. 1908).

6. WW, Introduction to *The Proposed Graduate College of Princeton University* (Princeton, 1903); Andrew F. West, "A Narrative of the Graduate College of Princeton University from its Proposal in 1896 until its Dedication in 1915," typed memorandum prepared in 1920, revised in 1928, PUL. I am inclined to credit West's later recollection that Wilson discouraged his efforts to raise money on his own for the Graduate College. Throughout his presidency Wilson was consistent in attempting to centralize fund-raising efforts and to discourage solicitation for particular causes.

7. Trustees' Minutes, June 15, 1905. Later reports of the Graduate School Committee reiterated these points.

8. Report of the Dean of the Graduate School, Trustees' Minutes, Oct. 21, 1905; *Princeton University: Some Characteristic Features*, published by the Committee of Fifty (Princeton, 1906), pp. 39-40. The latter pamphlet, put out by the fund-raising organization that Wilson and Moses Taylor Pyne had set up in 1904, was a reprint of articles by graduates that had originally appeared in the *Newark Evening News*.

The funds to maintain the Merwick experiment came from Moses Taylor Pyne, Grover Cleveland, and seven or eight others. "Princeton: The Proposed Graduate College," record of the project compiled for Trustees' Committee on the Graduate School, Jan. 29, 1910, PUL.

Raymond Fosdick, a resident of Merwick in the academic year 1905-06, appreciated its urbanity, admired the "Master," Howard Crosby Butler, enjoyed meeting faculty members at dinner, and found it a "stimulating environment." Raymond Fosdick, *Chronicle of a Generation* (New York, 1958), pp. 61-62.

9. *Princeton Alumni Weekly,* Oct. 20, 1906, p. 56; *Daily Princetonian,* Oct. 18, 1906; West, "A Narrative of the Graduate College."

10. Baker, *WW,* II, 210; Trustees' Minutes, Oct. 20, 1906. Stockton Axson, a generally trustworthy witness, remembered Hibben as being among those who hoped very much that Wilson would let West go to M.I.T. Stockton Axson, "The Princeton Controversy," memorandum, Feb. 1925, Baker Papers, LC.

11. West to WW, Oct. 30, 1906; N. W. Jacobus to WW, Nov. 4, 9, 1906, WW Papers, LC.

12. *Daily Princetonian,* Nov. 9, 1906. No sooner had West turned down the presidency of M.I.T. than it was offered to Henry B. Fine—a much more logical choice. Moses Taylor Pyne wrote Wilson that Fine was "probably the most important and valuable man we have" and that the situation was much more serious than with West because Fine was obviously competent to do the job. Fine declined; he was quoted as saying that he felt he must stay at Wilson's side to keep him from making mistakes. The fact that the offer had been made to him was not generally known, and he enjoined his family to reveal it to no one. M. T. Pyne to WW, Nov. 7, 1906, WW Papers, LC; interviews with Jacob N. Beam, May 3, 1941, and with Mrs. Bradford (Phelina Fine) Locke, July 9, 1940.

13. Interview with A. Lawrence Lowell, May 23, 1939; G. M. Harper to Francis MacDonald, Jan. 27, 1898, Harper Papers, PUL; WW, talk to Orange Alumni Association, *Princeton Alumni Weekly,* Nov. 18, 1905, p. 131. Lowell argued for the collegiate idea in a Phi Beta Kappa Address at Yale in April 1907. He became President of Harvard in 1909 and eventually put the scheme into practice with the establishment of the House Plan.

14. Trustees' Minutes, Dec. 13, 1906.

15. Cleveland Dodge to WW, Dec. 19, 1906, WW Papers, LC; Trustees' Minutes, Dec. 13, 1906.

16. Report of Committee on Conference with Upperclass Clubs, Trustees' Minutes, June 8, 1903.

17. *Princeton Alumni Weekly,* May 2, 1903, p. 490; *Daily Princetonian,* Feb. 15, 1907.

18. *Daily Princetonian,* Feb. 28, 1907; *Nassau Herald,* 1907; Walter A. Wyckoff to Henry van Dyke, July 27, 1907, Henry van Dyke Papers, PUL; *Daily Princetonian,* Dec. 14, 1905. Wilson's supplementary report to the Princeton Trustees of December 13, 1906, contains a detailed description of the club system at this time. A picturesque account in fictional form appears in a novel, *Tolbecken,* by Samuel Shellabarger (Boston, 1956), pp. 103-106 and *passim.* Shellabarger observed: "Far more pervasive and indelible than the curriculum of arts or sciences was the training in social nuances expressed by the colors of hats the students wore. Red, indigo, light blue, dark blue, white, green—each symbol had meaning expressing distinction or the lack of it, one's place in the social hierarchy" (p. 106). See also Edwin M. Norris, *The Story of Princeton* (Boston, 1917), pp. 242-243.

19. The inter-club treaty in effect when Wilson first presented his Quad Plan may be found in the *Daily Princetonian*, Jan. 19, 1907. For expressions of dismay at the breakdown of the honor system with respect to club elections, see a letter from C. B. Newton and an editorial in the *Princeton Alumni Weekly*, May 28, 1904, pp. 545-547.

20. *Daily Princetonian*, Feb. 15, 1907. A revised inter-club treaty drawn up in March 1907 provided that the only intercourse between upper-class and sophomore clubs should be through designated representatives. This created a situation in which the representatives of the sophomore clubs, called "quays," held the most important voice in elections to the upper-class clubs. *Daily Princetonian*, March 11, 1907; Benjamin B. Chamber to WW, WW Papers, LC; "Report and Recommendations Affecting Undergraduate Social Conditions at Princeton University," by a committee of Princeton alumni acting with authorization of the Princeton Trustees, March 3, 1908, Andrew C. Imbrie Papers, PUL.

21. G. C. Fraser (representing Cottage Club) to H. B. Fine, March 18, 1907, WW Papers, LC; interview with Donald G. Herring, April 12, 1939. Herring, a member of Cap and Gown, thought that at least 40 percent of the members of the Inter-Club Treaty Committee favored abolishing the clubs.

22. Interview with Harry A. Garfield, Feb. 14, 1940. Letters from WW to Garfield, April 13, 1907, lent me by Garfield, and to G. C. Fraser, April 16, 1907, Baker Papers, LC, establish the date of this meeting and corroborate Garfield's memory of those present.

Ralph Adams Cram remembered looking over the Prospect Street club-houses with Wilson to see whether they could be combined into quads. Cram judged that they were of such diverse architectural styles that it would be better to start over than to try to combine a dozen disparate buildings into a harmonious whole. Interview with Cram, May 8, 1940.

23. D. B. Jones to WW, May 15, 1907, WW Papers, LC. J. Franklin Murphy, a member of the Governing Board of Tiger Inn, one of the most sought-after clubs, wrote Wilson that he was much concerned about the future of the Princeton clubs, that their tendency was to worsen rather than improve, that radical action was required, and that he would be very glad to do anything in the best interest of the University, even if it meant the abolition of the present club system. Murphy to WW, June 7, 1907, WW Papers, LC.

24. WW, "Report on the Social Coordination of the University," submitted to the Trustees of Princeton University, June 10, 1907; WW, "Address to the Board of Trustees," *Public Papers*, I, 502, 510, 514-515. The official title, "Committee on the Supplementary Report of the President," was generally abandoned after this report in the *Princeton Alumni Weekly* for the more descriptive title, "Committee on the Social Coordination of the University."

25. David B. Jones to WW, June 12, 1907, WW Papers, LC; Joseph B. Shea, in Stockton Axson, "Memorandum of the Princeton Controversy," Baker Papers, LC; interview with N. M. Butler, Feb. 4, 1940.

Robert Edwards Annin, in an unfavorable "character study" of Wilson, and Wilson Farrand, in an interview with me, insisted that the Princeton Trustees did not adopt the Quad Plan at their meeting in June 1907 but merely "received" the President's report on social coordination of the University as a basis for further discussion. Annin maintains that the Trustees were careful not to authorize Wilson to "implement" the plan but merely voted him power to take steps for "maturing" it. The Trustees' Minutes contradict these recollections. The Trustees received the Supplementary Report of the President on December 13, 1906, at which time there was preliminary discussion and a committee was appointed to consider and report later. At the meeting of March 14, 1907, the President reported verbally on progress. What happened at the meeting of June 10, 1907, is related above. The Trustees' action was reported in the minutes as follows: "After a full discussion on the Report of the Committee on the Supplementary Report of the President on Motion duly seconded the recommendation of the Committee was adopted." To be sure, the report of the committee authorizes the President to "mature the general plan" and to "mature detailed plans," but it is perfectly clear that when the Trustees accepted the report they had, as the *Princetonian Alumni Weekly* reported, "adopted the essential idea and purpose of the plan." Robert Edwards Annin, *Woodrow Wilson: A Character Study* (New York, 1924), p. 25; interview with Wilson Farrand, Dec. 20, 1939; Trustees' Minutes, Dec. 13, 1906, March 14, 1907, June 10, 1907: *Princeton Alumni Weekly*, June 12, 1907, pp. 613-614.

26. Thomas Jefferson Wertenbaker, *Princeton, 1746-1896* (Princeton, 1946), pp. 322-323. The clubs in existence in 1907 were founded in the following years: Ivy, 1879; Cottage, 1886; Colonial, 1891; Cap and Gown, Tiger Inn, 1892; Elm, 1895; Cannon, 1898; Campus, 1900; Quadrangle, Charter, 1901; Tower, 1902; Terrace, Key and Seal, 1904.

27. Favorable letters to WW from Edward A. Woods, Mrs. F. A. Story, Robert J. Walker, John W. Craven, Nelson B. Gaskell, Theodore H. Hunt, William B. Scott, John Ten Eyck, Linsly R. Williams, Edward A. Lovett, and George P. Norris, June 12-29, 1907, WW Papers, LC; WW, "Memorandum Concerning Residential Quads," *Public Papers*, I, 518-521; interview with Edward Elliott, June 11, 1939 (reception of plan at Cap and Gown Club); Franklin W. Murphy, Jr., to WW, June 18, 1907, WW papers, LC (reception of plan at Tiger Inn); William W. Phillips to WW, June 20, 1907, WW Papers, LC (representing Board of Governors of Cap and Gown); *New York Evening Post*, June 25, 1907.

28. *New York Sun*, June 27, 1907; Henry van Dyke to WW, July 3, 1907, Baker Papers, LC; A. F. West to WW, July 10, 1907, WW Papers, LC. In July and August Wilson received communications from the Princeton Club of Philadelphia, from a twelve-man Advisory Council appointed to represent the Ivy Club, from the President of the Quadrangle Club, from a representative of the Elm Club, and from Andrew C. Imbrie, Alumni Trustee, who transmitted a set of questions about the Quad Plan and the clubs on behalf of a number of alumni. Evidence of how West, the van Dyke brothers, and Jesse Lynch Williams organized opposition is found in letters in the Henry van Dyke Papers (PUL), especially from Paul van Dyke to his brother. They were extraordinarily bitter about "the incredible haste and almost levity of judgment by which we have been rushed into this radical revolution" and about the Board's being "stampeded into revolution by a single speech"; they resented that some-

one must now have courage to undertake the unpleasant task of "belling the cat."

29. M. T. Pyne to Bayard Henry, July 15, 1907, WW Papers, LC; interview with Jacob D. Beam, Dec. 17, 1939 (Pyne influencing faculty members); Bayard Henry to Henry B. Thompson, n.d. (before July 29, 1907), WW Papers, LC; Cleveland Dodge to WW, WW Papers, LC; Imbrie to Henry J. Cochran, July 2, 1908, Imbrie Papers, PUL (opinion of clubs); *Princeton Alumni Weekly*, Sept. 25, 1907, pp. 7-9 (Imbrie as emissary).

30. WW to Dodge, July 1, 1907, Baker Papers, LC; W. M. Daniels to J. G. Hibben, Aug. 9, 1907, Vernon S. Collins Collection, PUL.

31. *Princeton Alumni Weekly*, Sept. 25, 1907, pp. 4-7; H. G. Murray to Andrew C. Imbrie, Sept. 12, 1907, Imbrie Papers, PUL.

32. Osborne to WW, Sept. 18, 1907, WW Papers, LC; *Princeton Alumni Weekly*, Oct. 9, 1907, p. 38; "Report to the Board of Governors and Members of the Ivy Club, by the Special Council Appointed in the Matter of the Proposed Quad System," Oct. 10, 1907, pp. 4, 7-8, PUL.

Wilson's secretary, Gilbert F. Close, made a study of honors won by men in and out of clubs in the junior and senior classes from 1903-1904 until 1906-1907. Close reported that 9.2 percent of the clubmen received honors and 41.8 percent of the nonclubmen. He also found that, among clubmen, the lowest proportion of honors was received by those in the oldest clubs (Ivy, Cottage, Tiger Inn, Cap and Gown), the next lowest proportion in a middle group (Colonial, Elm, Cannon, Campus), and the highest proportion in the youngest clubs (Quadrangle, Charter, Tower, Terrace, Key and Seal). These figures were later disputed by John G. Hibben. Gilbert F. Close, "Statistics Showing the Relative Numbers of Clubmen and Non-clubmen Who Have Taken Honors," n.d. (apparently summer 1907), WW Papers, LC; J. G. Hibben to WW, March 25, 1908, WW Papers, LC.

33. Faculty Minutes, Sept. 26, 1907; Stockton Axson, "The Princeton Controversy."

34. Faculty Minutes, Oct. 1, 1907; interview with Oswald Veblen, June 9, 1939. Discussion of the charge that the preceptors voted for their "bread and butter" appears in William Starr Myers, ed., *Woodrow Wilson: Some Princeton Memories* (Princeton, 1946), pp. 28-29 ("Departmental Colleague," by Edward S. Corwin), p. 49 ("Woodrow Wilson in My Diary," by William Starr Myers), p. 82 ("As I Knew Him and View Him Now," by J. Duncan Spaeth).

35. William Starr Myers, "Woodrow Wilson in My Diary," p. 48; interviews with Edward S. Corwin, June 9, 1939, Thomas Marc Parrott, Sept. 15, 1942, and George Madison Priest, Dec. 19, 1939; WW, "Faculty Debate—THE QUADS," undated typed notes with interlineations in ink, Baker Papers, LC.

36. Trustees' Minutes, Oct. 17, 1907; Baker, *WW*, II, 260-261.

In their "psychological study" of Woodrow Wilson, Sigmund Freud and William C. Bullitt state that at this meeting Wilson distorted fact and deluded himself into insisting that the Princeton Trustees had adopted the Quad Plan at the previous meeting in June. This reveals, allege Freud and Bullitt, the beginning of a process of "mental degeneration." It is obvious that they accepted uncritically the slanted recollections of anti-Wilson members of the university community who maintained that the Quad Plan had never been adopted. The Trustees' minutes make it clear that the Board had adopted the plan and then thought better of it. Their first resolution reads: "RESOLVED, That the action taken by the Board last June on the recommendation of the Committee on the Supplementary Report of the President be reconsidered." Sigmund Freud and William C. Bullitt, *Thomas Woodrow Wilson: A Psychological Study* (Boston, 1966), pp. 124-126; Annin, *Woodrow Wilson: A Character Study*, pp. 27-30; Trustees' Minutes, June 10, Oct. 17, 1907.

37. WW, transcription of shorthand memorandum, Baker Papers, LC; Stockton Axson, "The Princeton Controversy"; WW to M. W. Jacobus, Oct. 23, 1907, Baker Papers, LC.

38. WW, "Supplementary Report of the President," Trustees' Minutes, Dec. 13, 1906; WW, "Address to the Board of Trustees," June 10, 1907, *Public Papers*, I, 511; WW, "Memorandum Concerning Residential Quads," *Public Papers*, I, 519. The phrase "common counsel" is found in WW, "Report on the Social Coordination of the University," "Address to the Board of Trustees," and "Memorandum Concerning the Residential Quads," *Public Papers*, I, 511, 517, 520.

39. Van Dyke to WW, March 5, 1907; Cleveland to WW, March 24, 1907; WW Papers, LC. See also Link, *Woodrow Wilson*, pp. 53-55.

40. Trustees' Minutes, Oct. 17, 1907; M. T. Pyne to Andrew C. Imbrie, Oct. 23, 1907, M. T. Pyne Papers, PUL; *Princeton Alumni Weekly*, Oct. 30, 1907; WW to M. W. Jacobus, Oct. 23, 1907, Baker Papers, PUL; M. W. Jacobus to WW, Oct. 25, Nov. 5, 1907, WW Papers, LC.

41. Editorials, biography, and tributes on occasion of Pyne's death, *Princeton Alumni Weekly*, April 27, 1921, pp. 661-666; "Moses Taylor Pyne," unsigned article, *Princeton Alumni Weekly*, Oct. 28, 1955, pp. 8-10; interviews with Max Farrand, May 1, 1942, and Jacob N. Beam, Dec. 18, 1939 (criticism of Pyne).

42. Interview with Robert McNutt McElroy, Nov. 20, 1940; Annin, *Woodrow Wilson: A Character Study*, pp. 22-23, 26-37 (Cleveland's and Patton's opposition to Wilson); interview with W. F. Magie, June 12, 1939. During the presidential campaign of 1912 it was rumored that a letter by Grover Cleveland attacking Wilson's actions as President of Princeton might be published by his opponents. In the face of such an eventuality, Wilson wrote out a careful statement of his attitude toward Cleveland during the last years of the former President's life. Wilson took the attitude that as Cleveland's health and vigor were failing and he was under West's control, he did not understand how Princeton's democracy was threatened by the forces of special privilege. The Cleveland letter was not published, and therefore Wilson's rebuttal remained in his files. It is printed as an appendix in Baker, *WW*, II, 358-360.

43. Hibben to WW, July 8, 1907, WW Papers, LC; WW to Hibben, July 10, 1907, in Arthur S. Link, "The Case for Woodrow Wilson," *Harper's Magazine*, 234:92 (April 1967); Arthur Walworth, *Woodrow Wilson: American Prophet* (New York, 1958), p. 112 (black mood);

Edith Gittings Reid, *Woodrow Wilson: The Caricature, the Myth, and the Man* (New York, 1934), pp. 108-109.

44. Interviews with Albert Shaw, July 17, 1940, and Davis R. Dewey, Dec. 11, 1940; Ellery Sedgwick, *The Happy Profession* (Boston, 1946), pp. 179-180. Sedgwick dated this event 1905, which must be a mistake since it clearly took place after Wilson had attacked the Princeton clubs.

45. WW, talk to University Club, Chicago, March 12, 1908, type-written ms., R. S. Baker Collection, PUL; WW, "Robert E. Lee: An Interpretation," address at University of North Carolina, Jan. 19, 1909, *Public Papers*, II, 68.

46. See Armando Farraro, "Psychoses with Cerebral Arteriosclerosis," Sylvano Areti, ed., *American Handbook of Psychiatry*, II, 1083-1084.

47. Editorials in *New York Evening Post*, June 25, 1907, *Hartford Courant*, June 26, 1907, *Boston Herald*, June 27, 1907, and *St. Louis Post-Dispatch*, June 30, 1907; *Life*, 50:54 (June 11, 1907), 50:80 (June 18, 1907); *American Review of Reviews*, 31:145 (Aug. 1907); *Chicago Evening Post*, Nov. 11, 1907. See also "To Nurture College Democracy," *Literary Digest*, 35:60 (July 13, 1907).

48. WW to M. W. Jacobus, Nov. 6, 1907, and D. B. Jones to WW, Nov. 12, 1907, in Baker, *WW*, II, 264-265; M. W. Jacobus to WW, Jan. 1, 1908, WW Papers, LC.

49. WW to EAW, Feb. 4, 1908, in McAdoo, ed., *The Priceless Gift*, pp. 245-246.

50. *Princeton Alumni Weekly*, March 11, 1908, pp. 370-371; WW, talk to Princeton Club of Chicago, at the University Club, March 12, 1908, typewritten ms., Baker Papers, PUL.

51. Interviews with Norman S. Mackie, Feb. 21, 1940, Jackie and Donald Herring, April 12, 1939, E. S. W. Kerr, May 24, 1940, Charles Savage, Jr., Feb. 27, 1942, and Theodore Leslie Shear, Aug. 5, 1945; Senior Section, Cottage Club, to WW, June 11, 1908, WW Papers, LC.

52. WW to M. W. Jacobus, June 1, 1908, Baker Papers, LC.

53. Trustees' Minutes, Jan. 1908; "Report of Henry B. Thompson, Edward W. Sheldon, and Andrew C. Imbrie to the Board of Trustees, April 8, 1908," *Princeton Alumni Weekly*, April 15, 1908, pp. 585-589; Alfred S. Dashiell, "The Princeton Clubs Today: A Survey," *Princeton Alumni Weekly*, June 8, 1928, 1076-1077. The committee of trustees presented figures on the scholarly achievement of clubmen and nonclubmen that differed markedly from those that Gilbert F. Close had furnished Wilson the previous year (see note 32).

The alumni committee brought in a separate report, which differed from the Trustees' principally in recommending that sophomores be admitted to the upper-class clubs and that a University Club, with membership open to the three upper classes, be founded. "Report of the Graduates' Committee," Junius S. Morgan, George C. Fraser, Franklin Murphy, William W. Phillips, C. B. Bostwick, Andrew C. Imbrie Papers, PUL. Freshman commons had been established earlier, but with separate dining rooms and sitting rooms for freshman clubs.

54. WW to Cleveland Dodge, June 18, 1908, WW Papers, LC; WW to EAW, n.d., in Baker, *WW*, II, 276.

55. McAdoo, ed., *The Priceless Gift*, pp. 249-254; Baker, *WW*, II, 278-282.

56. WW to EAW, June 26, 1908, partly in Baker, *WW*, II, 278, partly in McAdoo, ed., *The Priceless Gift*, p. 248; Fred Yates to EAW, Sept. 2, 1908, WW Papers, LC; Theodore Marburg to R. S. Baker, March 3, 1926, Baker Papers, LC; WW to Jessie Wilson, Aug. 4, 1908, WW Papers, LC.

57. Fred Yates to EAW, Sept. 2, 1908, WW Papers, LC.

58. WW to Andrew Carnegie, Jan. 13, 1908, Baker Papers, LC; WW to Frank A. Vanderlip, n.d., transcription of shorthand notes; Cleveland Dodge to WW, March 16, 1909; Henry S. Pritchett to WW, May 5, 1909; WW Papers, LC. Wilson unsuccessfully attempted to reach the ear of John D. Rockefeller through his daughter; see Edith Rockefeller Mc-Cormick to WW, Feb. 20, 1909, WW Papers, LC.

59. The *Princetonian* dinner was described in an undated memorandum from Stockton Axson to R. S. Baker, Baker Papers, LC; in McAdoo, *The Woodrow Wilsons*, pp. 99-100; and in an interview with Edward Elliott, June 11, 1939. The *Princetonian* report of the dinner, from which WW's quotation is taken, was apparently prepared from an abstract of the talk, furnished ahead of time (*Daily Princetonian*, May 1, 1909); the paper featured Wilson's address under a separate heading, "The Ideals of Princeton University." Axson and Elliott were present at the dinner, and Wilson's daughter was on a verandah outside; their accounts agree closely.

John G. Buchanan, a former member of the *Princetonian* board, recollects that at its close the undergraduates voted in favor of the Quad Plan. Buchanan thought that Wilson's address was the finest he had ever heard. "I timed the speaker," he wrote, "and found that he had spoken one hour and twenty-one minutes. He held us spellbound. I asked classmates how long they thought he had spoken, and the usual guess was twenty minutes." J. G. Buchanan to E. S. W. Kerr, April 24, 1964, copy sent me by Buchanan.

60. Col. Brown Rolston to Bragdon, Jan. 22, 1945. Rolston was Assistant Secretary of the Cottage Club at the time of the incident related here. After the meeting, according to Rolston's account, Wilson sat around the fire talking with twenty or thirty undergraduates and a few graduates, telling amusing stories. "We were completely enthralled by the charm of the man," wrote Rolston, "and although many of us, on more mature consideration, reverted to our old opinions on the club question, Wilson won us completely as friends."

61. C. W. Halsey to George M. Harper, Aug. 11, 1909, Andrew C. Imbrie Papers, PUL (alumni threat and Pyne's response); John C. Davis to WW, Jan. 6, 1906, and Cleveland Dodge to WW, Jan. 27, 1909, WW Papers, LC (Pyne's threat to resign); *ibid.* and Lawrence G. Woods to WW, May 3, 1909 (urging abandonment of Quad Plan).

62. *Address by Woodrow Wilson, President of Princeton University, at the Celebration of the 75th Anniversary of the Founding of Haverford College on October 16, 1908, at Haverford, Pa.*, pamphlet based on stenographic report, Haverford College Library. The abstract prepared beforehand is in the Close Collection, PUL; Baker quotes from it in *WW*, II, 283. The actual address is full of humor, which is not present in the abstract.

63. WW, address at St. Paul's School, Concord, N.H., June 3, 1909, in Baker, *WW*, II, 302-303; WW, "The Spirit of Learning," Phi Beta Kappa Address, Cambridge, Mass., July 1, 1909, *Harvard Graduates' Magazine*, 18:1-14 (Sept. 1909), *Public Papers*, II, 102-119; WW, "What Is a College For?", *Scribner's Magazine*, 46:570-577 (Nov. 1909), *Public Papers*, II, 160-177.

CHAPTER XVII. Toward Progressivism

1. "Woodrow Wilson Pleads for Light," interview, *New York Times*, Nov. 27, 1907; Baccalaureate Address, June 13, 1909, Gilbert F. Close Collection, PUL.

2. *Indianapolis News*, May 5, 1902; *New York Sun* and *New York Times*, Nov. 30, 1904. See also Arthur S. Link, *Wilson: The Road to the White House* (Princeton, 1947), pp. 96-97.

3. The account of Harvey and his promotion of Wilson for President is principally based on Link, *Wilson*, pp. 97-102, Robert Edwards Annin, *Woodrow Wilson: A Character Study* (New York, 1924), pp. 103-106, and Baker, *WW*, II, 196-198.

4. Ruth Cranston, *The Story of Woodrow Wilson* (New York, 1945), p. 70; Baker, *WW*, II, 196-197. Harvey received the honorary title of Colonel from a New Jersey governor.

5. WW to George Harvey, Feb. 3, 1906, in William O. Inglis, "Helping to Make a President," *Collier's Magazine*, 58:15 (Oct. 7, 1916), WW to St. Clair McKelway in Baker, *WW*, III, 12-13; *Harper's Weekly*, March 3, March 31, April 14, April 21, April 28, May 19, May 26, and June 2, 1906, *North American Review*, 83:491 (April 1906).

6. *Literary Digest*, 32:537 (April 11, 1906).

7. *National Democratic Club: Annual Dinner on Jefferson Day, April 16, 1906* (New York, 1906). This pamphlet contains a list of officers and guests and a stenographic report of the proceedings, from which my account of the speeches is taken. Wilson, who often gave important addresses from notes and rarely rewrote, worked out no less than four versions of this talk (Baker, *WW*, II, 199). The stenographic version differs markedly from previous drafts, which bears out Wilson's comment in a letter of December 17, 1902, to St. Clair McKelway about his habits of speaking: "I am afraid I am so constituted that I am obliged to be very unserviceable to newspaper men. I do not speak from manuscript, and whenever I have tried before an address to write out or dictate a brief summary of what I intended to say, or a long summary either for that matter, it has turned out that I actually said something very differently both in structure and expression, so that what appeared in the news was an independent article and not a correct report of my address." Baker Papers, LC.

8. Wilson had apparently changed his mind about Jefferson some time between writing "A Calendar of Great Americans," first published in February 1894, and writing the chapter on Jefferson's presidency for *A History of the American People*, published in 1902. In the former he ruled out Jefferson; in the latter he gave him high praise. See WW, "A Calendar of Great Americans," in *Mere Literature and Other Essays* (Boston, 1896),

pp. 196-198, and *A History of the American People* (New York, 1902), III, 168-170, 182-184.

9. Link, *Wilson*, pp. 104-107. In 1906 Wilson was appointed to his first public office, membership on the New Jersey Committee on Uniform State Laws.

10. Link, *Wilson*, pp. 110-111; George Harvey to WW, Dec. 17, 1906, WW Papers, LC; John A. Wyeth to WW, March 26, 1907, in William A. Diamond, *The Economic Thought of Woodrow Wilson* (Baltimore, 1943), p. 85.

11. WW, "Credo," Aug. 6, 1907, first written in shorthand, then typed with interlineations in ink, WW Papers, LC.

12. WW, "The Authors and Signers of the Declaration of Independence," July 4, 1907, in Baker, *WW*, III, 32-33; WW, "Ideals of Public Life," Cleveland Chamber of Commerce, Nov. 17, 1907. Close Collection, PUL.

The summary of Wilson's beliefs in 1906-1908 is based on the following sources: (1) "Patriotism," Southern Society, New York, Dec. 14, 1906, typed ms. from "Addresses, 1906-1910," collection of abstracts for addresses, plus a few printed transcripts, given to the Princeton University Library by Wilson's Secretary, Gilbert F. Close (hereafter cited as Close Collection); (2) "Grover Cleveland," place unspecified, March 17, 1907, celebrating Cleveland's seventieth birthday, typed ms., Close Collection; (3) Address to South Carolina Society of New York, March 18, 1907, transcript of shorthand notes, Baker Papers, LC, and an additional quotation from it in *Charleston News and Courier* (S.C.), Nov. 21, 1907; (4) "The Authors and Signers of the Declaration of Independence," Jamestown Exposition, Norfolk, Va., July 4, 1907, in *North American Review*, 186:22-33 (Sept. 1907), quoted in Baker, *WW*, III, 32-33; (5) "Ideals of Public Life," Cleveland Chamber of Commerce, Nov. 16, 1907, typed ms. in Close Collection and stenographic report in *The Cleveland Chamber of Commerce: Sixtieth Year* (Cleveland, 1908), pp. 219-230; (6) "Dr. Woodrow Wilson Defines Material Issues," interview with WW, lead article, *New York Times Magazine*, Sunday, Nov. 24, 1907; (7) "Woodrow Wilson Pleads for Light," interview with WW, *New York Times*, Nov. 27, 1924, apparently published because he felt the Nov. 24 article "hardly represented his views with sufficient accuracy and clearness"; (8) "Politics," *Atlantic Monthly*, 100: 635-646 (Nov. 1907), in *Public Papers*, II, 1-23; (9) "Government and Business," Commercial Club of Chicago, March 14, 1908, typed ms., Close Collection; (10) "Government and Business," Traffic Club of Pittsburgh, April 3, 1908, typed ms., Close Collection; (11) "Law or Personal Power," National Democratic Club, New York City, April 13, 1908, in *Public Papers*, II, 24-31, from typed ms., Close Collection, and in *New York Times*, April 14, 1908, containing extempore remarks not in former; (12) "The States and the Nation," *North American Review*, 187:684-701 (May 1908), in *Public Papers*, II, 32-53. This material is usefully summarized, with critical commentary, in Link, *Wilson*, pp. 107-119, and—with less sense of chronological nuance—in Diamond, *The Economic Thought of Woodrow Wilson*, pp. 64-86. Cleveland Chamber of Commerce, Nov. 16, 1907, Close Collection.

13. WW, "Law or Personal Power," April 13, 1908, *Public Papers*, II, 26; *New York Times*, Nov. 27, 1907; *New York Times*, Nov. 24, 1907;

WW, "Ideals of Public Life," Cleveland Chamber of Commerce, Nov. 16, 1907, Close Collection; WW, "Politics," *Public Papers*, II, 21.

14. WW, "Patriotism," Dec. 14, 1906, Close Collection; WW, "The States and the Nation," *North American Review*, 187:684-701 (May 1908); *Charleston News and Courier*, Nov. 21, 1907.

15. WW, "Ideals of Public Life," Nov. 16, 1907, *The Cleveland Chamber of Commerce* (Cleveland, 1908), p. 222; "Dr. Woodrow Wilson Defines Material Issues," *New York Times Magazine*, Nov. 24, 1907.

16. Link, *Wilson*, pp. 116-117; WW to Henry James Forman, April 10, 1908, WW Papers, LC; Mayo W. Haseltine, "Woodrow Wilson," *North American Review*, 187:844-850; H. J. Forman to WW, April 14, 1909, WW Papers, LC.

17. WW, "Spurious versus Real Patriotism in Education," *School Review*, 7:610 (Dec. 1899) (WW's praise of Roosevelt); Roosevelt to WW, Dec. 6, 1902, WW Papers, LC. Stockton Axson, who had an accurate memory, told R. S. Baker that Wilson broke with Roosevelt over the Panamanian intervention of 1903 (Axson to Baker, Baker Papers, LC). Yet in no case that I have discovered did Wilson publicly attack Roosevelt on foreign affairs; the criticism in 1906-1908 was entirely on domestic issues. The most explicit attack, by name, was in WW's *New York Times* interview, Nov. 24, 1907.

18. WW to Adrian H. Joline, April 29, 1907, in Baker, *WW*, III, 23; *Jersey City Journal*, March 10, 1908, and WW to J. R. Dunlap, April 1, 1908, in Link, *Wilson*, pp. 117-118; *New York Times*, Nov. 24, 1907.

19. Stockton Axson to R. S. Baker, Baker Papers, LC; WW to EAW, July 6, 1908, in Baker, *WW*, II, 277.

20. WW, *Constitutional Government in the United States* (New York, 1908), reprinted 1911, 1913, 1961. Wilson received $2,000 for the eight Blumenthal lectures. Other Blumenthal lecturers were his friend Albert Shaw and Henry Jones Ford, whom he brought to Princeton as Professor of Politics in 1908.

21. WW, *Constitutional Government*, p. v.

22. WW, *Constitutional Government*, pp. 73, 70.

23. WW, *Constitutional Government*, pp. 68, 72-74, 139-141. See Arthur Link, *Woodrow Wilson and the Progressive Era* (New York, 1954), pp. 40, 49, for instances in which Wilson as President made direct contact with Senators to induce them to support his legislative program. The Seventeenth Amendment, providing for direct election of Senators and ratified in 1913, strengthened the President's hand in that the Senate became more responsive to public opinion.

24. WW, *Constitutional Government*, pp. 77-80.

25. WW, *Constitutional Government*, pp. 124, 127-129, 120.

26. WW, *Constitutional Government*, pp. 116, 120.

27. WW, "Law or Personal Power," April 13, 1908, *Public Papers*, II, 25 and *passim; New York Times*, April 14, 1908; Trustees' Minutes, April 9, 1908. The text of this address in the *Public Papers* is that of the typed ms. in the Close Collection; the *New York Times* report repeats some of that text but also includes extempore remarks, such as the appeal to corporation lawyers quoted here.

28. WW, "The Banker and the Nation," *Public Papers*, II, 55-57.

29. *Ibid.,* pp. 59-63; *Congressional Record,* 62nd Congress, second session, 48, appendix: 502-503 (1908). There is no implication here that the ideas as to extension of credit to rural districts were original with Wilson.

30. Interview with Roland S. Morris, Feb. 27, 1942; WW, "Robert E. Lee: An Interpretation," Jan. 19, 1909, *Public Papers,* II, 77; WW, "Abraham Lincoln: A Man of the People," February 12, 1909, *Public Papers,* II, 95; WW, Princeton Baccalaureate Address, June 13, 1909, Close Collection, reprinted in *Daily State Gazette,* Trenton, N.J., June 14, 1909.

31. WW, "Robert E. Lee: An Interpretation," *Public Papers,* II, 81-82.

32. George Harvey to WW, May 10, 1909, Wilson Papers, LC; WW, "The Tariff Make-Believe," *North American Review,* 190:535-556 (Oct. 1909), in *Public Papers,* II, 120-146.

CHAPTER XVIII. Defeat, 1909–1910

1. Interview with Booth Tarkington, Nov. 27, 1940.

2. Correspondence in WW Papers, LC, and Pyne Papers, PUL; G. W. Barr to WW, Aug. 21, 1909, WW Papers, LC. Up to this time Wilson had in effect chosen new Trustees through the mechanism of ad hoc nominating committees appointed by himself. But when a vacancy occurred in June 1908, the Board voted down the formation of such a committee. Correspondence relating to the Farrand candidacy is in the WW Papers, LC.

3. "Communication from Andrew F. West to the Standing Committee of the Board of Trustees on the Graduate School, May 13, 1907," Vernon L. Collins Collection, PUL. A memorandum of Jan. 9, 1908, by Wilson to the Trustees on this subject, also in the Collins Collection, shows how explicitly the site issue was joined. Wilson wrote that the geographical separation of Merwick had already created in the Graduate College "a sense of administrative as well as social seclusion which has already been felt by the teaching body of the University and which, slight as it is and probably unconscious, is of course undesirable." The faculty, he wrote, could not achieve its intention of making the Graduate College a means of stimulating the undergraduates unless it were placed "in constant, visible, conscious contact with the stirring life of the place." Wilson finally reminded the Trustees that this conception was the one originally presented by West and accepted by the Board.

4. *Princeton University: The Proposed Graduate College, Record of the Project from 1896 to 1910,* prepared by Andrew F. West for the Trustees' Committee on the Graduate School, Jan. 29, 1910, pp. 26-31; Trustees' Minutes, April 9, 1908, which include a telegram from Cleveland congratulating the Trustees on finding a happy solution for a long-perplexing problem.

5. Trustees' Minutes, Dec. 13, 1900.

6. Interview with Edward Capps, March 23, 1943; Capps to Bragdon, June 28, 1943; Henry B. Fine, "Narrative of Woodrow Wilson's Presidency of Princeton," Baker Papers, LC; Andrew F. West, "Narrative of the Graduate College of Princeton University," PUL; interview with Edwin Grant Conklin; March 24, 1943; WW to M. W. Jacobus, March 27, 1909.

7. WW, transcription of shorthand memorandum, Jan. 7, 1907, WW Papers, LC. After seeing the plans for Guyot Hall, Henry Fairfield Osborn, curator of the Museum of Natural History in New York, wrote Wilson, "It will give Princeton a model building of its kind which biologists from all over America will come to see . . . It will meet the *unanimous* approval of the biologists of this and every other country." July 1, 1907, WW Papers, LC.

8. *Catalogue of Princeton University, 1910-1911* (Princeton, 1910). This contains both a map of the campus with dates of all buildings (frontispiece) and the rules governing the allotment of dormitory rooms (pp. 339-345). Rooms were reserved for 150 freshmen, scattered throughout the dormitories. Holder Hall, completed in 1910 during Wilson's last year as President, was in the shape of a quadrangle and contained a dining hall and common rooms so that it could be converted, if opportunity came, into a "quad."

9. Henry B. Thompson to R. S. Baker, undated, Baker, *WW*, II, 175.

10. R. A. Cram to WW, March 28, 1907, WW Papers, LC; interview with R. A. Cram, May 8, 1940; over twenty letters to WW from R. A. Cram, July–Aug. 1907, WW Papers, LC; R. A. Cram, *My Life in Architecture* (Boston, 1936), pp. 118-121.

11. Henry B. Thompson to R. S. Baker, undated, Baker Papers, LC; correspondence between Thompson and A. C. Imbrie, Feb.–March 1909; WW to Imbrie, March 25, 1909, Imbrie, "Report of the Financial Secretary of the Board of Trustees," confidential report to the Committee on Grounds and Buildings, May 25, 1912, Imbrie Papers, PUL; interview with Imbrie, June 10, 1939; Imbrie to WW, Dec. 13, 1909, WW to Imbrie, Dec. 17, 1909, Imbrie Papers, PUL.

12. Henry V. Julier, '04, to Bragdon, Dec. 20, 1963, interview with E. S. W. Kerr, '09, May 24, 1940; *Daily Princetonian*, May 20, 1907; Trustees' Minutes, Oct. 17, 1907, and Oct. 15, 1908.

13. Interview with Theodore L. Shear, '09, Aug. 3, 1943 (class dinner). Norman S. Mackie, E. S. W. Kerr, Farrington Carpenter, and John Buchanan, all of 1909, had similar recollections of the affair.

14. WW, *President's Report*, 1909, p. 6-7.

15. *Daily Princetonian*, May 1, 1909.

16. M. W. Jacobus to WW, Nov. 15, 1908, E. W. Sheldon to WW, Oct. 4, 1909, Jacobus to WW, April 12, 1909 (reporting attack on preceptorial system in Curriculum Committee of the Trustees), WW Papers, LC; Trustees' Minutes, June 14, 1909; interviews with E. S. Corwin, June 9, 1939, T. J. Wertenbaker, Dec. 18, 1939, Jacob N. Beam, Dec. 17, 1939, Clifton R. Hall, April 13, 1939, and Robert N. McElroy, Nov. 20, 1939.

17. A. Lawrence Lowell to Bragdon, Jan. 22, 1939; Report of Committee on Library and Apparatus, Trustees' Minutes, Oct. 15, 1908; "Library Circulation Increased Tenfold Since 1900," *Daily Princetonian*, May 20, 1939. The per capita use of the Princeton University Library quadrupled 1910-1939.

18. Robert K. Root, "Wilson and the Preceptors," in William Starr Myers, ed., *Woodrow Wilson: Some Princeton Memories* (Princeton, 1946), p. 16.

19. Interview with G. M. Harper, July 1, 1939; Trustees' Minutes, March 14, 1907; interview with J. H. Westcott, July 13, 1940; Edwin Grant Conklin, "As A Scientist Saw Him," in Myers, ed., *Woodrow Wilson,* pp. 58-69.

20. The figures in detail are as follows:

1902-1903—total on faculty, 108; men with first degree from Princeton, 68; men with higher degree from Princeton, 5; total Princetonians, 73 (68 per cent); total below professorial rank, 68; men with first degree from Princeton, 49; men with higher degree from Princeton, 4; total Princetonians, 53 (78 per cent).

1910-1911—total faculty, 172; men with first degree from Princeton, 65; men with higher degree from Princeton, 6; total Princetonians, 71 (41 per cent); total below professorial rank, 109; men with first degree from Princeton, 27; men with higher degree from Princeton, 5; total Princetonians, 32 (29 per cent). *Princeton University Catalogue, 1902-1903* and *1910-1911; Directory of Living Alumni, 1903* and *1911.* (Professors emeriti are not included in these reckonings.)

21. W. C. Procter to West, May 8, 1909, in *Princeton Alumni Weekly,* Feb. 16, 1910, p. 303.

22. Trustees' Minutes, June 14, 1909; M. T. Pyne to R. A. Cram, May 18, 1909, Pyne Papers, PUL; W. C. Procter to WW, June 7, 1909, in *Princeton Alumni Weekly,* Feb. 16, 1910, p. 303; Pyne to Cram, May 23. 1909, Pyne Papers, PUL.

23. Trustees' Minutes, June 14, 1909; M. T. Pyne to WW, July 6, 1909; E. W. Sheldon to Pyne, June 24, 1909, John B. Shea to Pyne, Oct. 12, 1909, Pyne Papers, PUL; Cram interview.

24. "Report of the Faculty Committee on the Graduate School on the Site of the Proposed Graduate College, Oct. 19, 1909," *Princeton Alumni Weekly,* Feb. 16, 1910, pp. 304-305.

25. W. C. Procter to M. T. Pyne, Oct. 13, 1909, Pyne to Procter, Oct. 5, 1909, Pyne Papers, PUL.

26. Trustees' Minutes, Oct. 21, 1909.

27. Pierce Butler, member of the Board of Regents of the University of Minnesota, to WW, Nov. 6, 1909, Butler to WW, Nov. 12, 1909, Dr. William Mayo to WW, Nov. 23, 1909, B. F. Nelson to WW, Dec. 15, 1909, WW Papers, LC; Butler to R. S. Baker, n.d., in Baker, *WW,* II, 313.

28. M. T. Pyne to WW, Oct. 25, 1908, WW Papers, LC; Pyne to Cyrus McCormick, Nov. 3, 1909, and to WW, Dec. 9, 1909, Pyne Papers, PUL; David B. Jones to WW, Nov. 9, 1909, Jacobus to Thompson, Dec. 23, 1909. Thomas D. Jones to WW, Dec. 30, 1909, WW Papers, LC; Thompson to R. S. Baker, Baker Papers, LC.

29. WW to W. M. Daniels, Dec. 14, 1909, in Baker, *WW,* II, 312; WW to Thomas D. Jones, Jan. 1, 1910; in Baker, *WW,* II, 320-321.

30. H. C. Butler to M. T. Pyne, Dec. 22, 1909, Pyne Papers, PUL. The extensive correspondence over the preliminary plans is in this collection.

31. Capps and Conklin interviews; Henry B. Fine to M. T. Pyne, Nov. 25, 1909, A. F. West to Pyne, n.d. [Dec. 1909] (faculty criticism), West to Pyne, n.d. [probably December] (legal opinions), Pyne Papers, PUL; WW to Pyne, Dec. 25, 1909, in Baker *WW,* II, 316 (illegality of golf links site).

32. M. T. Pyne to John B. Shea, Dec. 18, 1909, WW to Pyne, Dec. 25, 1909, W. C. Procter to Pyne, Dec. 28, 1909, Pyne Papers, PUL.

33. WW to M. T. Pyne, Dec. 22, 1909, Pyne to WW, Dec. 24, 1909, WW to Pyne, Dec. 25, 1909, in Baker, *WW*, II, 314-317.

34. WW, "The Ministry and the Individual," address at McCormick Theological Seminary, Chicago, Nov. 2, 1909, *Public Papers*, II, 181; "Wilson Talks to Teachers: The State and the Citizens' Duty to It," unidentified newspaper clipping, Dec. 29, 1909, WW Papers, LC.

35. Cleveland Dodge to WW, Dec. 28, 1909, David B. Jones to WW, Dec. 29, 1909, M. W. Jacobus to WW, Dec. 31, 1909, Henry B. Thompson to Jacobus, Jan. 6, 1910, Jacobus to WW, Jan. 7, 1910, WW Papers, LC. Further correspondence among Wilson's friends during the interim between Wilson's ultimatum on December 25 and the meeting of the Trustees on January 13, involving E. W. Sheldon, Cyrus McCormick, Jacobus, Henry B. Fine, and W. J. Magie, is in the Sheldon Papers, PUL.

It is doubtful if any academic dispute in history is better documented than the Graduate College controversy. There are hundreds of letters relating to it, along with other miscellaneous materials in the Baker Papers and the WW Papers, LC. The Baker Papers also contain memoranda about the struggle written by Stockton Axson, Henry B. Fine, and Henry B. Thompson. The controversy was well aired in the newspapers, by both news stories and communications to the editors, especially in the *New York Evening Post, New York Herald, New York Sun, New York Times, Newark News, Trenton True American, Philadelphia Press*, and *Philadelphia Public Ledger*. The richest materials are in the Princeton University Library. They include:

(1) Trustees' Minutes. These contain not only the minutes of the formal sessions of the whole board but reports of the Graduate School Committee and sometimes copies of correspondence.

(2) *Princeton Alumni Weekly*, Vols. IX and X (Sept. 1908–June 1910). Jesse Lynch Williams, the editor, who was deeply involved on the anti-Wilson side, published in the magazine important documents, speeches, editorial comment, and numerous letters from alumni and faculty members.

(3) Moses Taylor Pyne Papers. Pyne kept what appears to be a complete file of his immense correspondence about the controversy. It is particularly interesting after January 13, 1910, because it reveals that Pyne was working covertly to unseat Wilson.

(4) Edward W. Sheldon Papers. These perfectly complement the Pyne Papers since they contain scores of letters between Wilson's supporters, showing how they attempted both to assist and to control him.

(5) Wilson Farrand Papers. Farrand was one of the spearheads of the opposition to Wilson. His papers are especially useful in revealing efforts to get alumni support for Adrian H. Joline, the anti-administration candidate for Alumni Trustee in 1910. They also contain a typewritten account of the Graduate College controversy (cited as Farrand, "Narrative"), composed in 1912 and placed in the PUL with instructions that it should not be opened for thirty years. It was written in vitriol.

(6) Andrew F. West, "Narrative of the Graduate College of Princeton University from its Proposal in 1896 until its Dedication in 1915," typed

ms. prepared in 1920, revised in 1929. This is a useful compendium of all major events and documents in the birth of the Graduate College. It also gives West's side of the relations between him and Wilson, often in dramatic detail.

(7) Andrew F. West, "Record of the Graduate College." A rich and varied collection of official records, publications, correspondence, and *personalia,* originally kept by West in six large scrapbooks, much of it annotated by him.

(8) Vernon L. Collins Collection. This includes half a dozen folders containing some important letters about the site issue, with other miscellaneous materials.

(9) Pamphlets. The Graduate College controversy occasioned a pamphlet war among the Princeton alumni. The titles, with description, were (in approximate chronological order):

Coleman Peace Brown, *The Princeton Ideal: A Permanent Plan to Secure Social and Intellectual Coordination* (Philadelphia, Jan. 1910). A detailed proposal for dining halls, a University Club, and adaptation of existing upper-class clubs to achieve Wilson's purpose of combining intellectual and social life.

Princeton University: The Proposed Graduate College, Record of the Project from 1896 to 1910, compiled by Andrew F. West on request of M. Taylor Pyne, Jan. 29, 1910. A compilation of documents, objectively presented, even though certainly published to discredit Wilson, that was printed and sent to the alumni.

The Phantom Ship, or The Quad System: Some discussion of Its Merits; Also of the Effect of Its Continual Agitation Upon Princeton University, by "Alumnus" (later revealed as Robert Edwards Annin), n.d. [Feb. 1910]. Annin, who later wrote an unfavorable biography of Wilson (*Woodrow Wilson: A Character Study* [New York, 1924], attacked the wisdom of the Quad Plan and blamed Princeton's troubles on the continued agitation over it.

The Procter Gift: A History, "Printed at the Request of many of the Alumni of Princeton," March 22, 1910. An anti-Wilson compilation of excerpts from Trustees' Minutes, correspondence, and other documents.

In Re Princeton University: Correspondence in New York Evening Post between an "Alumnus" and a Trustee," March 4-18, 1910. An anonymous attack on Moses Taylor Pyne by David B. Jones, a Princeton trustee, answered by another trustee, the Rev. John De Witt. Published by anti-Wilsonians.

Cheer Up! "printed for the family only," April 1, 1910. An anti-Wilsonian collection of quotations, with antique woodcut illustrations.

The Graduate College and the Quads, by Fulton MacMahon, n.d. (perhaps April 1910, because it may reflect the swing of alumni opinion in Wilson's favor at that time). A defense of Wilson and his ideas.

That Pittsburgh Speech: and Some Comment, anonymous, n.d. Newspaper report of Wilson's speech to the Pittsburgh alumni, April 17, 1910, with hostile commentary from *Princeton Alumni Weekly* and various newspapers.

A Chronicle of Princeton (Being the First Book), by "Alexander Minimus," n.d. (internal evidence suggests it was written after the Princeton

Trustees' meeting of April 14, 1910). In form facetious, this is in fact
a quiet serious discussion of the Graduate College controversy, which the
author blamed on West's enjoying an *imperium in imperio.* He suggested
that the faculty be given complete control over the Graduate College.

The Graduate Colleges, Quads, Clubs and Fraternities in Princeton,
by Orville S. Brumback, Toledo, Ohio, May 30, 1910. An appeal to
bring back fraternities.

(10) Henry W. Bragdon Collection. Transcriptions of personal inter-
views with people who knew Wilson. About forty of these interviews
involve the Graduate College controversy, including those with Edward
Capps, Edwin G. Conklin, Ralph Adams Cram, Wilson Farrand, Andrew
C. Imbrie, William F. Magie, Booth Tarkington, Andrew F. West, and
John H. Westcott.

36. James W. Alexander to WW, n.d., John L. Cadwalader to Thomas
D. Jones, Nov. 9, 1909, WW Papers, LC; Cadwalader to M. T. Pyne,
Jan. 31, 1909, Pyne Papers, PUL.

37. Cleveland Dodge to WW, Dec. 31, 1909, Henry B. Thompson to
M. W. Jacobus, Jan. 6, 1910, WW to M. T. Pyne, Jan. 8, 1910, Pyne
to WW, Jan. 10, 1910, WW Papers, LC.

38. *Princeton Alumni Weekly,* Feb. 16, 1910, pp. 307-308. The report
was dated January 10.

39. Address by Hibben to Princeton Alumni Association in Montclair,
N.J., March 8, 1910, in *Princeton Alumni Weekly,* March 16, 1910, pp.
374-377; West, "Narrative."

40. W. C. Procter to M. T. Pyne, Jan. 12, 1910, Pyne Papers, PUL;
Trustees' Minutes, Jan. 13, 1910; Farrand, "Narrative." Farrand's account
of this meeting is highly colored and displays a Thucydidean ability to
put speeches in the characters' mouths, but in all essential details it is
corroborated by a letter from M. T. Pyne to W. C. Procter, Jan. 15,
1910, Pyne Papers, PUL.

41. Farrand, "Narrative." Wilson's supporters argued that his denial of
having seen the West brochure was a lapse of memory and that, in any
case, the preface was a perfunctory gesture, a mere act of "offhand good
will." West, however, insisted that Wilson not only had read the brochure
but had carefully revised the original manuscript from beginning to end;
this story became part of the official anti-Wilson canon. See Baker, *WW,*
II, 185; William Bayard Hale, "What Happened at Princeton," fourth
article in "Woodrow Wilson—A Biography," *World's Work,* 23:301 (Jan.
1912); Arthur Walworth, *Woodrow Wilson* (New York, 1958), I, 126;
A. F. West to Matthew C. Fleming, March 21, 1910, copies in Pyne
Papers, PUL, and in West, "Record"; Editor (Jesse Lynch Williams) to
Charles Yeomans, March 8, 1910, *Princeton Alumni Weekly,* April 6,
1910, p. 432.

Internal evidence supports the Wilson version of the story. His preface
to West's brochure was simply a passage from his first Report to the
Trustees in October 1902, with a few unimportant verbal changes and
no particular references to the contents of the brochure. The volume itself
contained passages so at variance with Wilson's policies that it is difficult
to see how he could have approved it in detail. For instance, in recruiting faculty members Wilson made a deliberate policy of drawing

men from other universities, whereas West in his brochure claimed that one of the virtues of the Graduate College would be to enable Princeton to recruit its faculty from within, to ensure "that the character of the Faculty would be such that the true Princeton tradition will be perpetuated with as much purity and strength as has been attained even in the old universities of Oxford and Cambridge." Wilson feared that Princeton was getting a reputation as an expensive place to live; West's brochure proposed that each student should have a suite of his own, consisting of a study with an open fireplace, a bedroom, and private bath. Trustees' Minutes, Oct. 21, 1902; West, *The Proposed Graduate College of Princeton University,* Princeton, 1903, Preface and pp. 9, 19.

Although it is more probable that Wilson treated the West brochure in a cursory fashion than that he carefully corrected it, this does not acquit him of making a serious mistake in administration. If the Graduate College was to be built—as he had promised—and if he distrusted West —as he asserted—it was surely his duty as President to see that the Dean's brochure did not express purposes in conflict with his own.

42. Trustees' Minutes, Jan. 13, 1910.

43. Henry B. Thompson to WW, Jan. 14, 1910, WW Papers, LC; WW to Thompson, Jan. 17, 1910, in Baker, *WW,* II, 322; M. T. Pyne to Cyrus McCormick, Nov. 9, 1909, Pyne to W. C. Proctor, Jan. 25, 1910, Pyne to Wilson Farrand, Jan. 15, 1910, Procter to Pyne, Jan. 30, 1910, Pyne Papers, PUL.

44. Henry B. Thompson to Cleveland Dodge, Jan. 14, 1900, Sheldon Papers, PUL; Henry van Dyke to M. T. Pyne, Jan. 6, 1910, Paul van Dyke to Pyne, Feb. 17, 1910, Pyne Papers, PUL; interview with Max Farrand, May 1, 1942; Wilson Farrand, "Woodrow Wilson Parallels— Private," carbon copies in Farrand Papers, also in Collins Collection, Pyne Papers, and West, "Record," PUL; Wilson Farrand to Lawrence C. Woods, March 7, 1910, Jarron Fisher to Wilson Farrand, April 1, 1910, Farrand Papers, PUL. Wilson Farrand wrote W. S. Elder on February 18, 1910 (Farrand Papers, PUL), that Wilson was motivated by "low considerations" and that a physician had told him that Wilson was suffering from a pathological condition.

45. *Princeton Alumni Weekly,* Jan. 26, 1910, pp. 244-251; Feb. 2, 1910, pp. 262-264.

46. *New York Herald,* Jan. 29, 1910.

47. H. B. Brougham to WW, Jan. 31, 1910, WW Papers, LC.

48. WW to H. B. Brougham, Feb, 1, 1910, Baker Papers, LC.

49. *New York Times,* Feb. 3, 1910.

50. *New York Herald,* Feb. 10, 1910; Farrand "Narrative"; stenographic report of conversation between Wilson and Paul van Dyke, March 16, 1910, Baker Papers, LC. See Annin, *Woodrow Wilson,* pp. 58-61, and Link, *Wilson: The Road to the White House* (Princeton, 1947), pp. 54-77, for discussions of the imbroglio over the *New York Times* editorial. On February 14, 1910, Edwin E. Slosson, Literary Editor of *The Independent,* wrote Dean West asking for alumni pamphlets and official statements. There is no specific evidence to show that West complied with the request, but a month later the magazine published an article entitled "The Differences at Princeton" by "A Friend of Princeton," which contained

both a defense of West's point of view and a criticism of Wilson's actions, based on information that could only have come from an insider. Slosson to West, Feb. 14, 1910, in West, "Record"; *Independent,* 58:574-576 (March 17, 1910), copy in West, "Record."

51. Thomas D. Jones to W. C. Procter, Jan. 26, 1910, Procter to Jones, Feb. 6, 1910, in *Princeton Alumni Weekly,* Feb. 16, 1910, pp. 299-301; WW to Cleveland Dodge, Feb. 7, 1910, in Baker, *WW,* II, 326. *New York Herald, New York Sun, New York Tribune, New York Times, New York World, Trenton True American,* Feb. 11, 1910; *Springfield Republican,* Feb. 8, 1910.

52. WW to EAW, Feb. 17, 1910, in Eleanor Wilson McAdoo, ed., *The Priceless Gift* (New York, 1962), p. 256.

53. Based on interviews with some thirty men who were members of the faculty at this time, plus half a dozen others who lived in Princeton. Starting with Wilson Farrand's "parallels," the anti-Wilson faction distributed private memoranda and lampoons. One of these, placed by Dean West in his scrapbook in February 1910, was entitled "Mr. Dooley on the Quad System, with Apologies to Mr. Dunne" (typewritten ms., n.d.). It was in form an attack on the Quad Plan and revealed bitterness toward Wilson. For instance, when "Mr. Hennessy" asked "Mr. Dooley" what it meant that "Wudrow" was an "idaylist," the latter replied, "I dinnaw exactly . . . but I think 'tis a man who says t'hell with all notions but mine." Other "Mr. Dooley" parodies, apparently by the same hand, are in the *Princeton Alumni Weekly,* Oct. 16, 1907, pp. 52-54 ("The Quo Vadis System" by "An Observer"), and in the Collins Collection ("The Battle of Princeton," typewritten ms., written after the Wyman bequest, May 1910). On the basis of their literary skill and complete familiarity with the anti-Wilson canon, one may hazard a guess that these were written by Jesse Lynch Williams.

54. *Princeton Alumni Weekly,* X, Nos. 16-33 (Jan. 26-May 23, 1910); Jesse Lynch Williams, "Twenty Years After," *Princeton Alumni Weekly,* April 5, 1929, p. 783.

55. Letters to the *New York Evening Post* from "An Alumnus" [David B. Jones], March 4, 1910, and from John De Witt, March 15, 1910, reprinted in *Princeton Alumni Weekly,* March 23, 1910, pp. 396-401. For a description of the pamphlets that appeared during these months, see n35 above.

56. WW to E. W. Sheldon, Feb. 11, 1910, Thomas D. Jones to Cleveland Dodge, Feb. 18, 1911, M. W. Jacobus to Dodge, Feb. 15, 1910, Sheldon Papers, PUL; EAW to WW, Feb. 28, 1910, in McAdoo, ed., *The Priceless Gift,* p. 261; Henry B. Fine to Sheldon, Feb. 26, 1910, Fine to Dodge, March 1, 1910, Sheldon Papers, PUL. Fine's letters mention the difficulty of getting Wilson to change his mind.

57. Cyrus McCormick to E. W. Sheldon, March 4, 1910, Sheldon Papers, PUL. McCormick complained in this letter that Wilson lacked tact in dealing with undergraduates and faculty and that he was willing to let the club situation get worse because, the worse it got, the more need there would be for the Quad Plan.

58. *Philadelphia Record,* March 5, 1910, *Princeton Alumni Weekly,* March 9, 1910, pp. 349-357; *Princeton Alumni Weekly,* March 16, 1910,

pp. 371-374 (Baltimore speech), March 23, 1910, pp. 394-396 (Brooklyn speech); March 30, 1910, pp. 412-415 (St. Louis speech). The Jersey City address was not published in the *Princeton Alumni Weekly*, but Wilson wrote a friend that it was "pieced together" from the others. WW to M. W. Jacobus, April 2, 1910, Baker Papers, LC.

59. WW to M. W. Jacobus, April 6, 1910, Baker Papers, LC; William F. McCombs, *Making Woodrow Wilson President* (New York, 1921), p. 28; David Lawrence, *The True Story of Woodrow Wilson* (New York, 1924), p. 29; Annin, *Woodrow Wilson*, pp. 62-63; *New York Times*, April 8, 1910; interview with Philip Rollins, June 25, 1943; *Princeton Alumni Weekly*, April 13, 1910, pp. 447-463.

60. A. C. Smith, Jr., to WW, April 28, 1910, A. Lawrence Lowell to WW, March 21, 1910, WW Papers, LC, For an explicit example of the way attacks on Wilson and the Joline candidacy for Alumni Trustee boomeranged, see the correspondence between Charles Yeomans and the editor of the *Alumni Weekly* in the *Princeton Alumni Weekly*, April 6, 1910, pp. 432-434. On April 4, D. R. Porter Bradford, an alumnus, wrote Wilson that the literature of the opposition had convinced him that Princeton owed Wilson gratitude for his stand. Bradford to WW, April 4, 1910, WW Papers, LC.

61. E. W. Sheldon to WW, March 22, 1910, Sheldon Papers, PUL; Trustees' Minutes, April 14, 1910. At the same meeting a vote for Dr. John T. M. Finney as candidate for Charter Trustee was carried by a vote of 14 to 13. Finney was thought to be on Wilson's side in the Graduate College controversy. The difference between the votes on his candidacy and on the resolution to submit the Graduate School question to the faculty suggests that two or three men who generally supported Wilson abandoned him on the resolution, presumably because they thought it would stir up the controversy.

A full-page article on Princeton in the *New York Tribune* entitled "Shall Princeton Give Her Students Training in Gentility of High Degree?" discussed the faculty attitude toward Dean West's interest in civilizing undergraduates and estimated that 10 per cent of the faculty supported West's ideas for the Graduate College, 80 per cent were opposed, and 10 per cent were neutral. According to Professor George McLean Harper, too—a generally fair-minded person although clearly on Wilson's side— the faculty was four to one in favor of Wilson as against West. This accords with the faculty vote at the time of the Quad Plan, and there is no reason to suppose that the alignment had changed significantly since then. But some of those who, if forced to choose, would have voted with the President, preferred that the issue not be presented. Both Fine and Capps told Wilson that they could get along with West as Dean because the majority members of the Faculty Committee were now able to control him. *New York Tribune*, April 17, 1910; George M. Harper to Wilson Farrand, Feb. 3, 1910, Farrand Papers, PUL; Henry B. Fine to WW, Feb. 24, 1910, Sheldon Papers, PUL.

62. "Princeton Day in Pittsburgh," *Princeton Alumni Weekly*, April 20, 1910, pp. 467-471. The four ordained Presbyterian ministers on the Princeton faculty were Dr. Patton, Henry and Paul van Dyke, and John Hibben.

63. *Princeton Alumni Weekly*, April 20, 1910, p. 471; *Public Papers*, II, 203. See Link, *Wilson*, p. 84n, for argument that the closing passage, which did not appear in the supposedly verbatim account in the *Princeton Alumni Weekly* but did appear in newspaper reports, was actually uttered by Wilson.

64. EAW to WW, Feb. 28, 1910, in McAdoo, ed., *The Priceless Gift*, p. 261.

65. *That Pittsburgh Speech: And Some Comment*, n.d.; WW to Isaac H. Lionberger, April 28, 1910, WW Papers, LC; "The Annual Dinner in Chicago," *Princeton Alumni Weekly*, May 18, 1910, pp. 533-535. Wilson was criticized even by journals generally friendly to him for the intemperance of his Pittsburgh address and for ignoring the function of a university in preserving and instilling culture. In a letter to the *New York Evening Post* Wilson acknowledged the justice of the latter charge but excused himself on the grounds that his talk had not been accurately nor fully recorded and that his mind was "a one-track affair," on which he could run only one train at a time. *New York Evening Post*, April 18, 1910; *Nation*, 40:395-396 (April 21, 1910); Link, *Wilson*, p. 85; WW to *New York Evening Post*, April 23, 1910.

66. Correspondence on the proposed compromise involving E. W. Sheldon, Cyrus McCormick, W. C. Procter, M. W. Jacobus, Thomas D. Jones, M. T. Pyne, E. C. Richardson, and John B. Shea, April 26–May 16, 1910, Sheldon Papers and Pyne Papers, PUL, and WW Papers, LC; Sheldon to WW, May 14, 1910, Sheldon Papers, PUL; Henry B. Thompson to Pyne, April 5, 1910, Pyne to Procter, May 10, 1910, Pyne Papers, PUL.

67. West, "Narrative."

68. F. L. Patton to Isaac C. Wyman, March 6, 1896, in West, "Record"; WW to EAW, Aug. 9 and 10, 1902, in McAdoo, ed., *The Priceless Gift*, pp. 227-228; "The Will of Isaac C. Wyman '48," *Princeton Alumni Weekly*, May 25, 1910, pp. 548-550; newspapers in West, "Record"; West to M. T. Pyne, May 22, 1910, Pyne Papers, PUL. Eleven of fifteen newspapers accounts gave the amount of the bequest as ten million dollars, as did *The Literary Digest*, 40:1126 (June 4, 1910). The total amount Princeton actually realized from the Wyman estate was about $660,000; during the first four years it produced only $84,500, of which $63,500 was used to build a house and garden for the Dean. Annual Reports of the Treasurer, Princeton University, 1911-1921. There is no implication here that West deliberately exaggerated the amount of the bequest; indeed, he warned Pyne that the newspaper accounts giving the amount as $10,000,000 were exaggerated. He merely took the figures he had been given by the other executor, John M. Raymond, who had been Wyman's lawyer.

69. Eleanor Wilson McAdoo, *The Woodrow Wilsons* (New York, 1937), p. 101; WW to Thomas D. Jones, May 30, 1910, Baker Papers, LC; West, "Narrative"; E. W. Sheldon to Cyrus McCormick, May 27, 1910, Sheldon Papers, PUL.

70. "The Last Game Won for Princeton," and "When Wyman Died," verses in West's handwriting, Pyne Papers, PUL; Henry B. Thompson to J. L. Cadwalader, May 31, 1910, Cadwalader to Thompson, June 6, 1910,

Pyne Papers, PUL; WW to Thomas D. Jones, May 30, 1910, in Baker, *WW*, II, 349; Trustees' Minutes, June 9, 1910; *Princeton Alumni Weekly*, June 15, 1910, pp. 601-602.

71. Baker, *WW*, II, 351; congratulatory telegram from Henry B. Thompson to WW, June 15, 1910, WW Papers, LC; *Princeton Alumni Weekly*, June 15, 1910, p. 597; Trustees' Minutes, Oct. 20, 1910; WW to Harry A. Garfield, June 15, 1910 (copy furnished me by Garfield).

72. Interview with John De Witt, *Philadelphia Record*, March 21, 1910 (boardinghouse site).

73. Armando Ferraro, "Psychoses with Cerebral Arteriosclerosis," *American Handbook of Psychiatry* (New York, 1959), II, 1085.

74. See Link, *Wilson*, pp. 90-91, for observations on the same theme, as well as on how the presidency of Princeton prepared Wilson for politics.

CHAPTER XIX. Departure

1. Henry Beach Needham, "Woodrow Wilson's Views," interview, *Outlook*, 98:940 (Aug. 26, 1911).

2. Stockton Axson to R. S. Baker, n.d., Baker Papers, LC; "Princeton and the Procter Gift," *Outlook*, 96:47 (Feb. 19, 1910); William Bayard Hale, "What Happened at Princeton," fourth article in "Woodrow Wilson —A Biography"; *World's Work*, 23:304 (Jan. 1912).

3. In an acid appraisal of Woodrow Wilson's career Harry Elmer Barnes wrote about academic politics: "It has frequently been stated that the most remarkable circumstance connected with Mr. Wilson's career is the fact that, with no experience in political life until 1910, he was able at once to exhibit rare power as a public leader and practical politician. Those who express wonder over this situation are obviously innocent both of the general nature of the conduct of college faculties and of the policies and technique of Mr. Wilson as president of Princeton. As any one who has had any experience with political life and college faculties knows all too well, the methods are identical . . . Wire-pulling and manipulation are as rife in any normal college faculty as they ever were in Tammany Hall or the Quay system in Pennsylvania. Moreover, the participants in the game of politics in the colleges are in general more intelligent than those in the public arena, and hence to that degree more subtle, invidious and ruthless." *History and Social Intelligence* (New York, 1926), p. 531.

4. Richard S. Childs to WW, Oct. 25, 1909, WW Papers, LC (notice of election as president of Short Ballot Association); "Woodrow Wilson Calls for Conference on 'Short Ballot,'" press release, Short Ballot Association, June 6, 1910, WW Papers, LC. For Wilson's advocacy of simplification of the machinery of municipal government, see "Civic Problems," address to Civic League of St. Louis, March 9, 1909, *Congressional Record*, 62nd Congress, first session, 47, part 5:4202-4205 (Aug. 19, 1911). The discussion of Wilson's interest in the short ballot is partly derived from Arthur S. Link, *Wilson: The Road to the White House* (Princeton, 1947), pp. 124-126.

5. WW, "Political Reform," address at City Club of Philadelphia, Nov.

18, 1909, *Public Papers,* II, 188-198; WW, "Hide and Seek Politics," *North American Review,* 191:585-601 (May 1910), in *Public Papers,* II, 204-224.

6. *New York World,* Jan. 18, 1910; WW, "Bankers and Statesmanship," May 6, 1910, *Public Papers,* II, 225-233.

7. "Elements of Politics," notes on WW's lectures by Joseph K. Fornance, 1904, PUL; WW, "Political Reform," speech at City Club, Philadelphia, Nov. 18, 1909, *Public Papers,* II, 189.

8. *Harper's Weekly,* 53:4 (May 15, 1909); Link, *Wilson,* p. 127. My account of Wilson's active involvement in New Jersey politics and his election as Governor of New Jersey is drawn in large part from Link's volume, which is based on meticulous and thorough study of both Wilson's papers and the contemporary scene. The third volume of Ray Stannard Baker, *Woodrow Wilson* (New York, 1931), deals with the New Jersey governorship. It is especially valuable in tracing Wilson's decision to run for office and his first campaign because it quotes generously from correspondence, contemporary accounts, and speeches. Other useful accounts, written by men who were active in New Jersey politics, are James Kerney, *The Political Education of Woodrow Wilson* (New York, 1926), and Joseph Patrick Tumulty, *Woodrow Wilson As I Knew Him* (New York, 1921).

9. The portrait of Smith is based on: Link, *Wilson,* pp. 140-141; Baker, WW, III, 43-45; Kerney, *The Political Education of Woodrow Wilson,* pp. 18-26; John Moody, *The Long Road Home* (New York, 1933), pp. 106-107; William O. Inglis, "Helping to Make a President," *Collier's,* 58:162 (Oct. 14, 1916); interview with George D. Smith, June 21, 1943.

10. *New York Tribune,* Jan. 19, 1910.

11. Link, *Wilson,* p. 142.

12. WW to H. B. Brougham, Feb. 1, 1910, WW Papers, LC; *Brooklyn Times,* April 18, 1910.

13. *New York Times,* March 18, 1910; "Mul's Letter," *Brooklyn Citizen,* March 20, 1910.

14. *Trenton True American,* March 30, 1910; *Harper's Weekly,* 59:9-10 (April 9, 1910), in *Public Papers,* II, 193-201.

15. *Trenton True American,* March 30, 1910; Associated Press dispatch, April 16, in *That Pittsburgh Speech: And Some Comment,* n.d., Princeton Collection, PUL.

16. George D. Smith interview; Link, *Wilson,* p. 143; John M. Harlan to WW, June 11, 1910, WW to Harlan, June 23, 1910, in Baker, WW, III, 53-54.

17. Link, *Wilson,* pp. 144-146; Baker, WW, III, 54-56.

18. Baker, WW, III, 62, 84; Thomas D. Jones to WW, June 1, 1910, WW Papers, LC; Baker, WW, III, 56-66; Link, *Wilson,* pp. 146-152.

19. WW to Cleveland Dodge, July 1, 1910, Baker Papers, LC; Baker, WW, III, 65-66.

20. Link, *Wilson,* pp. 152-153; *Harper's Weekly,* 54:4 (July 23, 1910) (quotations from editorials).

21. Link, *Wilson,* pp. 153-154; interview with Joseph S. Hoff, June 11, 1939; John R. Hardin to Bragdon, Oct. 23, 1942.

22. Link, *Wilson,* pp. 155-156.

23. Baker, *WW*, III, 70-72; Link, *Wilson*, pp. 159-160.

24. William Bayard Hale, *Woodrow Wilson: The Story of His Life* (New York, 1913), pp. 166-167, quoted in Baker, *WW*, III, 61-62.

25. J. L. Cadwalader to E. W. Sheldon, June 26, 1910, Sheldon Papers, PUL.

26. Baker, *WW*, III, 60-61, 77; interview with Williamson U. Vreeland, March 24, 1940; Rev. Edward M. Chapman to R. S. Baker, Dec. 25, 1925, Baker Papers, LC. Professor Vreeland and Rev. Chapman, who played golf with Wilson at Old Lyme, both reported that he was handicapped by poor eyesight and was therefore not an especially good player although he derived genuine pleasure from the game. Vreeland recollected that he once kept an appointment to play even though it was raining hard; Chapman wrote that he played the game "with patience, sense of control, and sense of enjoyment that made him a good companion."

27. The account of the Trenton convention is based principally on Link, *Wilson*, pp. 162-168, supplemented by Baker, *WW*, III, 73-81; Tumulty, *Woodrow Wilson As I Knew Him*, pp. 18-22; John R. Hardin to Bragdon, Oct. 23, 1942; Inglis, "Helping to Make a President," pp. 12-14, 41; *Newark Evening News*, Sept. 15, 1910; *New York Times*, Sept. 16, 1910. Hardin, who was chairman of the convention, contended that the boss-vs.-progressive aspect of the convention has been exaggerated.

28. Baker, *WW*, III, 79.

29. *New York Times, New York World, Newark Evening News*, Sept. 16, 1910.

30. Link, *Wilson*, pp. 63; *New York Times*, Sept. 16, 1910.

31. *New York Times*, Sept. 16, 1910; Link, *Wilson*, pp. 207-209.

32. *New York Times*, Sept. 21, 1910.

33. Kerney, *The Political Education of Woodrow Wilson*, pp. 62-64.

34. WW to Thomas D. Jones, in Baker, *WW*, III, 84-85; Link, *Wilson*, pp. 187-188.

35. Link, *Wilson*, pp. 176-177; *New York Times*, Sept. 29, 1910.

36. Hoff interview; Hardin S. Craig to R. S. Baker, July 5, 1927, Baker Papers, LC.

37. *New York Times*, Oct. 5, 1910; Link, *Wilson*, pp. 178-179.

38. Link, *Wilson*, pp. 179-186; *New York Times*, Oct. 14, 1910.

39. Link, *Wilson*, pp. 186-187, 183-184; *New York Times*, Oct. 3 and 31, 1910. The *Times* reports concern two meetings of the Essex County Trades Council at which resolutions were passed condemning Wilson. At both meetings efforts were made to discipline or censure men who publicly supported Wilson, but no action was taken.

40. *Newark Evening News*, Oct. 5, 1910; Link, *Wilson*, pp. 188-192.

41. Link, *Wilson*, pp. 192-195. See George C. Rapport, *The Statesman and the Boss: A Study of American Political Leadership Exemplified by Woodrow Wilson and Frank Hague* (New York, 1961), pp. 55-59, for a convincing argument that the New Jersey bosses were interested solely in patronage and did not see how Wilson could possibly prevent their getting it. There was no personal break between Wilson and Smith until after the election, when the Essex County boss insisted on putting his name before the New Jersey legislature as a candidate for the United

States Senate instead of James E. Martine, the choice of the Democratic primary. After his election as governor Wilson answered Smith's telegram of congratulation with a note in which he said that he felt deeply the confidence Smith had displayed in him and hoped to play his part so as to bring no disappointment to those who had trusted him. It was signed, "With much regard and deep appreciation." WW to James Smith, Nov. 9, 1910, furnished me by George D. Smith.

42. Charles C. Black to Bragdon, Nov. 25, 1941; interview with Oswald Garrison Villard, Jan. 18, 1940.

43. Link, *Wilson*, pp. 197-198.

44. *New York Times*, Sept. 16, 1910; M. T. Pyne to Cyrus McCormick, longhand draft of letter, n.d., Pyne Papers, PUL (pressing for WW's resignation); interview with Wilson Farrand, Dec. 20, 1939, and Farrand, "Narrative"; "Resolution proposed by J. L. Cadwalader in case resignation not forthcoming," longhand, Oct. 20, 1910, Pyne Papers.

45. Trustees' Minutes, Oct. 20, 1910; Wilson Farrand interview (why Wilson prayed); WW, "Letter of Resignation from Princeton University," Oct. 20, 1910, *Public Papers*, II, 269. The *New York Times* of Oct. 20, 1910, reported that Wilson's letter of resignation had been in the hands of the Secretary of the University for several days and that, although the Trustees would have been glad to give him a leave of absence during the gubernatorial campaign, he insisted on resigning. Pyne wrote W. C. Procter on Oct. 25, 1910: "As you have of course seen from the papers, and heard from West, Wilson is no longer President of Princeton. The thing was done, I think, in a very satisfactory and diplomatic way. According to the newspapers he forced his resignation on a reluctant board, although actually he was most reluctant to put it in and had to be told pretty positively that it had to be done." Pyne Papers, PUL.

46. Trustees' Minutes, Nov. 13, 1910; copy of M. W. Jacobus' original draft with excisions in pencil by Pyne and someone else, Pyne Papers; E. W. Sheldon to R. S. Baker, Oct. 25, 1927, Baker Papers, LC (refusal of salary); Eleanor Wilson McAdoo, ed., *The Woodrow Wilsons* (New York, 1937), pp. 116-117.

47. *New York Times*, Nov. 6, 1910.

48. *New York Times*, Nov. 6, 1910; Inglis, "Helping to Make a President," p. 41 (Smith's prediction); *Harper's Weekly*, 54:4 (Nov. 5, 1910) (Harvey's prediction); "States That Saw a New Light," *Literary Digest*, 41:906-907 (Nov. 19, 1910).

49. Interview with Booth Tarkington, Nov. 27, 1940.

50. Tarkington interview.

EPILOGUE

1. J. M. T. Finney, *A Surgeon's Life* (New York, 1940), pp. 236-237; interview with Dr. Finney, March 26, 1941 (Trustees' division); M. T. Pyne to Rev. John DeWitt, March 7, 1911, Pyne Papers, PUL; "Princeton University Faces Crisis in Search for President," *New York Herald*, June 4, 1911; Theodore Roosevelt to Finney, Oct. 20, 1911, lent me by

Finney; Trustees' Minutes, June 12, Oct. 26, 1911, and Jan. 11, 1912; interview with Wilson Farrand, Dec. 20, 1939 (sudden choice of Hibben). According to his letter to Finney, cited above, Roosevelt regarded the presidency of a great university as next in importance to the office of Chief Justice or President of the United States, but he did not think he was the right man for the job.

2. *New York Times*, May 12, 1912; interview with A. Lawrence Lowell, May 23, 1939. The trustees who resigned were Thomas D. Jones, who judged Hibben not strong enough to resist the ruling forces on the board, and Robert Garrett, who charged that Hibben's election had been ruthlessly engineered. Cleveland Dodge had already resigned. Faculty members who went elsewhere included Stockton Axson, Wilson's brother-in-law, and Edward Elliott, who had married his sister-in-law Margaret Axson. T. D. Jones to Parker Handy, Jan. 26, 1912, Vernon L. Collins Collection, PUL; Robert Garrett to Handy, Oct. 26, 1912, Pyne Papers, PUL.

3. *Official Register of Princeton University: Catalogue Issue, 1938-1939* (Princeton, 1939). The bitterness of feeling against Wilson is evidenced by folders of anti-Wilson material, much of it anonymous and scurrilous, collected by M. Taylor Pyne and Wilson Farrand. Pyne and Wilson Farrand Papers, PUL.

4. Interview with William A. Magie, July 13, 1939 (White House dinner); Raymond Fosdick to R. S. Baker, undated, Baker Papers, LC; EAW to May Fine, March 18, 1913, lent me by Mrs. Bradford B. (Phelina Fine) Locke. Mrs. Wilson wrote Miss Fine that because there were no outstanding problems with Germany at the time and most of the work of the embassy was carried on by subordinates, Dean Fine would have time to study and renew his scholarly contacts in German universities.

5. EAW to May Fine, March 18, 1913 (Dodge's offer); H. B. Fine to May Fine, April 22, 1913, lent me by Mrs. Bradford B. Locke (reasons for his refusal); H. B. Fine to R. S. Baker, undated memorandum, Baker Papers, LC; open letter from former Wilson supporters on Princeton faculty to J. G. Hibben, May 15, 1922, Vernon L. Collins Collection, PUL.

6. "Method of Undergraduate Instruction," *Catalogue of Princeton University, 1920-1921* (Princeton, 1920), pp. 67-69. See also *The Preceptorial Method of Instruction* (Princeton, 1914). As a member of the Advisory Committee to the History Department, I have firsthand knowledge of the way the preceptorial system flourishes at Princeton today.

7. See Donald A. Stauffer, *The Idea of a Princeton Education* (Princeton, 1946), pp. 12-17.

8. "The Lost World of Andrew Fleming West '74," unsigned [John D. Davies], *Princeton Alumni Weekly*, Jan. 15, 1960, pp. 12-13; *New York Times*, Oct. 23, 1913; Henry B. Thompson, "Review of the Controversies in the Administration of President Wilson at Princeton," undated memorandum to R. S. Baker, Baker Papers, LC. Scattered references to Dean West's desire for autonomy appear in M. Taylor Pyne's correspondence with other trustees on such details as whether graduate students should pay their fees at the office of the Dean of the Graduate School or directly to the Treasurer of the University. Pyne Papers, PUL.

9. At Harvard, where graduate students and undergraduates take many

of the same courses, there is very little personal intercourse between the two groups. The same holds true at Oxford and Cambridge, where they live in the same courts and quadrangles and eat in the same halls.

10. *Princeton Alumni Weekly,* May 2, 1903, p. 476; A. Franklin Burgess, Jr., "On the Campus," *Princeton Alumni Weekly,* Feb. 11, 1964, p. 4; *Princeton Alumni Weekly,* April 18, 1967, p. 8. For the history of the clubs under Hibben, see *Princeton and the Club System* (Princeton, 1924), a report of a committee to investigate the clubs appointed by President Hibben at the request of leading undergraduates; and Alfred S. Dashiell, "The Princeton Clubs Today: A Survey," *Princeton Alumni Weekly,* 28:1075-1091 (June 8, 1928). The most serious revolt against the system occurred in 1917 when ninety leading sophomores—among them a son of Grover Cleveland—refused to join any club and demanded that the existing system be abolished. "Sophomores Launch Plan for a University Center," signed by a committee: D. K. E. Bruce, R. F. Cleveland, S. Lloyd, Jr., J. S. Schmalz, and H. H. Strater, *Princeton Alumni Weekly,* 17:306-307 (Jan. 10, 1917).

In 1940 a poll answered by 1000 of the 1200 Princeton sophomores and juniors revealed that "only a small fraction" of them approved the club system: the principal complaints were that the method of selection did not allow a natural choice of companions and that the clubs were too expensive. *Daily Princetonian,* April 30, 1940.

11. President Harold W. Dodds and Clark Hungerford, Chairman, Trustees' Committee on Undergraduate Life, to the graduate boards of the upper-class clubs, Sept. 26, 1955, *Princeton Alumni Weekly,* Oct. 12, 1955, p. 3; *Undergraduate Education at Princeton: Official Register of Princeton University,* 54:58-60 (Oct. 1, 1962); conversations with A. Franklin Burgess, Jr., and others, April 17-19, 1964.

12. Interviews with A. Lawrence Lowell; Roger B. Merriman, Master of Eliot House, Harvard, May 29, 1940; John Potter, Head Tutor of Eliot House, June 6, 1940; A. C. Hanford, Dean of Harvard College, March 18, 1940; Beekman Cannon, Instructor at Yale, March 19, 1940; and Carl Albert Lohman, Secretary of Yale University, March 20, 1940; *Reports of the President of Harvard College,* 1928-29, 1930-31, 1931-32, 1938-39; "A Report on the House Plan by the Student Council," June 19, 1933, typed memorandum, and records and files in the office of the Dean of Harvard College; fugitive materials published by the Jonathan Edwards College press at Yale, 1938-39. When studying the Harvard houses and Yale colleges in 1939-1940, I was most impressed by the proliferation of cultural and intellectual organizations. In Jonathan Edwards College in 1938-1939, for instance, there was a newspaper, a literary magazine, a Gilbert and Sullivan Society, and a concert program. In Eliot House at the same time there was an orchestra, a classical club, and a group that put on an Elizabethan play. An unforeseen result of the house and college plans has been a great increase in participation in organized athletics.

It used to be said that the Harvard house plan was "a Princeton idea made possible by Yale money." The evidence refutes this assertion. A. Lawrence Lowell had proposed something similar before Wilson promulgated the quad plan, and Mr. Harkness denied that his support of the plans at either Harvard or Yale was inspired by Wilson. Edward S. Harkness to Bragdon, April 26, 1939. See also H. W. Bragdon, "Woodrow Wilson and Mr. Lowell," *Harvard Alumni Bulletin,* 45:597 (May 22, 1943).

13. "A Lasting Memorial to Woodrow Wilson," *Princeton Alumni Weekly,* May 9, 1947, pp. 4-6; "Plans for the $35,000,000: A Talk with Gardner Patterson," *Princeton Alumni Weekly,* Sept. 22, 1961, pp. 3-5.

Index

Asterisk (*) preceding title denotes Wilson's authorship.

161-173, 184-187, 189, 200, 208, 232; described, 167-168, 206; family life, 164-166, 169, 310, 438(8); friends, 164; method of teaching, 149; salary, 164; success, 162, 166-170, 187

Wesleyan Alumni Magazine, 440(25)
Wesleyan Argus, 166, 168, 170-172
Wesleyan University Bulletin, 169
West, Andrew Fleming, 205, 213, 226, 279, 293, 416(13), 461(9), 466(49); described, 271; and preceptorial system, 314, 467(5, 6); and presidency of M.I.T., 315-316, 356, 468(12); and presidency of Princeton, 277-278; Princeton's regard for, 406; in Princeton's Sesquicentennial, 215-216, 270-271; and Quad Plan, 321-322, 328, 370, 472(42); in rebellion against Patton, 274-275, 277-278, 292; relations with Wilson, 219, 292-293, 313-316, 328, 335, 365, 381, 414 (9), 482-485(35, 41, 50); and Wilson's new curriculum, 293, 313
  and Graduate College: in fight over site, 316-317, 320, 354-356, 361-363, 365-369, 372-373, 375, 379, 470(28), 478 (3, 4), 481-486(35, 41, 50, 53, 61); his dreams for, and Merwick, 271-272, 281, 314-315, 356, 363, 371; opens, 407-408; and Wyman, 280, 379
  as Graduate School Dean, 270-272, 292, 315, 353, 365, 369, 374, 376, 378-382, 486(61), 492(8); powers, 354-356; salary, 450(49)
West, American, Turner's works on, 233, 236
"West as a Field of Historical Study, The" (Turner), 242
Westcott, John Howell, 220, 361, 466 (49), 483(35)
Westminster Review, 138
Wetzel, William A., 444(3)
"What Is a College For?" 336
"What Ought Government to Do?" 184
"When a Man Comes to Himself," 230
Whig Hall. *See* American Whig Society
Whigs, 236

Whistler, James McNeill, 120
White, Edward Douglass, 405
White, William Allen, 43
Whitehead, A. N., 297
Whitney, Harry Payne, 339
Wilcox Hall, 408-409
Wilde, Oscar, 221
Wilder, William R., 35
Wilder, Bert G., 212
"William Earl Chatham," 50, 54-56, 61, 423(18)
Williams, C. J., 36, 418(40)
Williams, Jesse Lynch, 204, 322, 370, 373-376, 381, 459(10), 470(28), 481(35), 485(53)
Williams, Talcott, 105
Williams College, 172, 186, 213
Williamson, Edgar R., 393
Willoughby, W. W., 189
Wilson, Ann (Wilson's sister), 4, 11, 223
Wilson, E. B., 150
Wilson, Eleanor (Wilson's third daughter), 165, 223, 339, 449-450 (47)
Wilson, Ellen Axson (Wilson's wife), 164, 166, 169, 173-174, 188, 219-220, 224-225, 229, 240, 295, 303, 312, 333-334, 374, 406, 492(4); children, 188, 221, 445(13); correspondence from Wilson, 162, 174, 220-221, 229-230, 231, 279, 280, 293, 345, 372, 432(52); early married life, 146-148; letter on Wilson's health, 310; letter to John Bates Clark, 222-223; letters to Wilson, 221, 378; poem from Wilson, 229; relations with Wilson, 221-223, 302; on Wilson's sesquicentennial address, 217. *See also* Axson, Ellen Louise
Wilson, Henry, 234
Wilson, James (Wilson's grandfather), 3-4
Wilson, Jessie (Wilson's second daughter), 146, 223, 304, 334
Wilson, Jessie Woodrow (Wilson's mother), 5, 7, 9-10, 74, 90, 112, 333; christened, 414(10); letters to Wilson, 12, 25-26, 57, 81, 86-87, 119, 418-419(47); property, 93, 428(11)
Wilson, John, and Son, 452(14)
Wilson, Rev. Joseph Ruggles (Wilson's father), 4, 5-8, 10-11, 24, 44, 57, 65, 73-74, 112-113, 121, 145,